Re-Formed Catholic Anglicanism

Re-Formed Catholic Anglicanism

Editors

Charles F. Camlin

Charles D. Erlandson

Joshua L. Harper

Published by
Anglican Way Institute
Church of the Holy Communion Cathedral
17405 Muirfield Dr
Dallas, TX 75287 USA

Contents

Part I: Re-Formed Catholic Anglicanism

Part II: Luminaries of the Tradition

Contributors

Dr. David Anderson
Associate Professor in the Department of Classics and Letters
at the University of Oklahoma

The Very Rev. Cn. Lawrence Bausch
Rector of Holy Trinity Parish (Retired)
and former President of Forward in Faith North America (2015-21)

The Rev. Dr. Hans Boersma
St. Benedict Servants of Christ Chair in Ascetical Theology
at Nashotah House Theological Seminary

The Rt. Rev. Dr. Charles Camlin
Suffragan Bishop of the (REC) Diocese of Mid America,
Dean of Church of the Holy Communion Cathedral (REC)
and Dean of Cranmer Theological House

Mr. Clinton P. Collister
Research Associate, The Center for Theology, Law, and Culture,
Pusey House, Oxford

The Rev. Dr. Charles Erlandson
Assistant Rector of Good Shepherd Church (REC) and
Head of the Department of Church History
at Cranmer Theological House

Dr. Alex Fogleman
Assistant Research Professor of Theology
at the Baylor University Institute for Studies of Religion and
Founding Director of the Catechesis Institute in Waco, TX

Dr. Barbara Gauthier
Graduate of Duke University
obtaining her PhD (French) from Vanderbilt University
and has taught French, Latin, and Greek

The Rev. Barton J. Gingerich
Rector of St. Jude's Anglican Church (REC) in Richmond, VA

The Rev. Dr. Joshua L. Harper
Assistant Professor of Applied Linguistics
and Associate Academic Dean at Dallas International University
and Assisting Clergy at Church of the Holy Communion Cathedral (REC)

The Rev. Jarrod Hill
Associate Rector of Anglican Church of the Redeemer in Chattanooga, TN

The Rev. Ben Jefferies
Rector of The Good Shepherd Anglican Church in Opelika, AL

The Rev. Blake Johnson
Rector of Church of the Holy Cross in Crozet, VA

The Rev. Dr. Peter Johnston
Rector of Trinity Anglican Church in Lafayette, LA
Dean of Louisiana in the Diocese of the Western Gulf Coast,
and the Ministry President of Anglican Compass

The Rev. Tyler Kerley
Rector of Resurrection Anglican Church in Woodstock, GA

The Rev. Daniel H. Logan
Formerly Assisting Clergy at Christ the King Anglican Church in Birmingham, AL

The Rev. Dr. Gerald McDermott
Distinguished Professor of Anglican Theology at Reformed Episcopal Seminary
and Distinguished Professor of Theology at Jerusalem Seminary

The Rev. Dr. Greg Peters
Professor of Medieval and Spiritual Theology
in the Torrey Honors College of Biola University and
the Servants of Christ Research Professor of Monastic Studies and Ascetical
Theology at Nashotah House Theological Seminary

The Rev. Calvin Robinson
Priest in the Nordic Catholic Church
Minister-in-Charge, Christ Church Harlesden

The Rev. Dr. Steven Rutt
Vicar of St. Andrews (REC) and
Dean of the Western Convocation the Diocese of Mid-America
Founder of Covenant Renewal Ministries;
Professor at Cranmer Theological House and
Associate Professor of Biblical and Theological Studies
at Arizona Christian University

The Most Rev. Dr. Ray R. Sutton
Presiding Bishop of the Reformed Episcopal Church and
Ecumenical Dean of the Anglican Church in North America

Mr. James Syrow
Founder of Media Dei, web-design agency for churches, schools, & nonprofits, and
graduate of Binghamton University with a master's in computer science
(With thanks for the earthly life of Mr. Syrow, who passed away on June 13, 2024)

The Rev. Richard Tarsitano
Vicar of Trinity Anglican Church (REC) in Connersville, IN

The Rev. Michael Templin
Assistant Priest at Church of the Holy Communion Cathedral (REC)

The Rev. Hunter Van Wagenen
Assisting Priest at Christ Church (ACNA) in Vero Beach, FL

The Rev. Michael Vinson
Rector of St. Benedict's Anglican Church (REC) in Rockwall, TX

Dr. Joel W. West
Faculty Fellow at Hildegard College and
Managing Editor of *Cranmer Theological Journal*

The Rev. Ben Williams
Vicar of Saint James Church (ACNA) in Jackson, TN

The Rev. Nicholas Ziegenhagen
Associate Rector of Good Shepherd Church (REC) and
Headmaster of Good Shepherd School in Tyler, TX

Part I
Re-Formed Catholic Anglican Foundations

Chapter 1

Introduction

The Most Rev. Dr. Ray R. Sutton

Preachers shall ... teach nothing ... save what is agreeable to the teaching of the Old or New Testament, and what the Catholic fathers and ancient bishops have collected from this selfsame doctrine. And since those [Thirty-Nine] Articles of the Christian religion to which assent was given by the bishops in lawful and holy synod convened and celebrated by command and authority of our most serene princess, Elizabeth, were without doubt collected from the holy books of Old and New Testament, and in all respects agree with the heavenly doctrine which is contained in them; since, too, the book of public prayers [*The Book of Common Prayer*], and book of the consecration (*inauguratio*) of archbishops, bishops, priests, and deacons [The Ordinal] contain nothing contrary to this same doctrine, whoever shall be sent to teach the people shall confirm the authority and faith of those Articles not only in their sermons but also by subscription. Whoever does otherwise, and perplexes the people with contrary doctrine, shall be excommunicated.... They shall not teach vain and old wives' opinions and heresies, and papal errors, abhorrent to the teaching and faith of Christ, nor anything at all whereby the unlearned multitude be inflamed to love of novelty or contention.

1571 *Canons* (No. 6) of the Church of England[1]

---

[1] Henry Gee and William John Hardy, eds., *Documents Illustrative of English History* (New York: MacMillan, 1896), 476–477. Brackets mine. Complete reference to Canon 6 of the 1571 Canons of the Church of England: "No one without the bishop's permission shall publicly preach in his parish, nor shall he venture hereafter to preach (*concionari*) outside his cure and church, unless he has received permission so to preach, either from the queen through all the parts of the realm, or the archbishop through his province, or from the bishop through his diocese. And no power to preach shall be hereafter valid or have any authority save only such as shall be obtained after the last day of April of the year 1571. Preachers shall behave themselves modestly and soberly in every department of their life. But especially shall they see to it that they teach nothing in the way of a sermon, which they would have religiously held and believed by the people, save what is agreeable to the teaching of the Old or New Testament, and what the Catholic fathers and ancient bishops have collected from this selfsame doctrine. And since those Articles of the Christian religion to which assent was given by the bishops in lawful and holy synod convened and celebrated by command and authority of our most serene princess, Elizabeth, were without doubt collected from the holy books of Old and New Testament, and in all respects agree with the heavenly doctrine which is contained in them; since, too, the book of public prayers, and book of the consecration (*inauguratio*) of archbishops, bishops, priests, and deacons, contain nothing contrary to this same doctrine, whoever shall be sent to teach the people shall confirm the authority and faith of those Articles not only in their sermons but also by subscription. Whoever does otherwise, and perplexes the people with contrary doctrine, shall be excommunicated. In preaching they shall use such modest and grave apparel (*veste*) as may befit and adorn the minister of God, and such as was described in the book of the Admonitions. And they shall not demand money or any fee for a sermon, but shall be content with merely food and equipment (*apparatu*), and one night's hospitality. They shall not teach vain and old wives' opinions and heresies, and papal errors, abhorrent to the teaching and faith of Christ, nor anything at all whereby the unlearned multitude be inflamed to love of novelty or contention. Moreover, they shall always put forward such things as make to edification, and reconcile the hearers by Christian concord and love." Emphasis and brackets mine.

Try explaining the meaning of *Anglicanism* to the local baker. That's what once happened to a lady of the Hospitality Committee in my parish. She had ordered a cake for a reception to follow an upcoming service on Confirmation Sunday. On it was to be written in scrolled icing the name of the parish with "Anglican Church" after it, followed by "Congratulations to our Confirmands." On the Saturday before the service, the dear lady dutifully picked up the cake and brought it back to the kitchen of the parish hall. She opened the box and screamed. Instead of "Anglican Church," it said, "Angelican Church," as in "angels." She frantically returned the cake in time for the baker to make a last-minute correction in the script. He apologized for the mistake, qualifying that he thought we were a "Church of Angels." The lady explained that "we love angels but we're mere mortals." He explained that he didn't know what the Anglican Church is. She responded, "Well, a lot of Anglicans don't know either!" He then asked, "So what's the meaning of Anglican anyway?" She told him, "It's a common question," as she offered a brief explanation.

In one sense, the entire Anglican world is asking the same question. The Anglican Communion is in the midst of a massive realignment. The faithful are regrouping around the orthodox, Biblical epicenter of Global South Anglicanism. It has become a time of Reformation. It's no secret that reformations occur about every five hundred years in the history of the Church. The last one for Anglicans occurred nearly that length of time ago in the sixteenth century. Its *Formularies* produced at the time of the *Book of Common Prayer* and the *Thirty-Nine Articles of Religion* express an understanding of Anglicanism. The question is, "What is that definition?"

This book answers the question with the phrase *Re-formed Catholic Anglicanism*.* The premise of this book is that these words explain what in fact was the model by which the English Reformers were reforming the Church of England. The thesis is that they were not attempting to create a new church, theology, or even liturgy. They were endeavoring to reform the late Medieval Western Church that had become Roman Catholic with an ancient model of Catholic based on the Scriptures and the early church fathers. Unfortunately, this historic approach to Anglicanism has been mostly lost through more recent definitions of Anglicanism. Hence, the authors in this volume have contributed the following chapters.

At such a critical time and opportunity as this in Anglicanism, it is essential at least to understand the model used by God to convert, catechize, and expand a national church into an entire worldwide communion that is the third-largest church in the world. To set the table for the following consideration, however, I need to lay some foundation in this introductory chapter. I begin by summarizing three major ways Anglicanism has been defined.

Via Media Anglicanism

The most common way of defining Anglicanism for the last two hundred years has been as a *via media* or "Middle Way." This is the view that the sixteenth-century English Reformation was attempting to be the midpoint between two opposites, Roman

---

* In the following pages you will see several different phrases such *as reformed catholic, re-formed catholic, re-formed catholicism, re-formed catholic anglicanism*, etc. which all reflect the English Reformation project known as *Reformed Catholicism* that continues to this day.

Catholic and Protestant. Though some historians mistakenly like to claim that the Anglican Church began with the Protestant Reformation, it in fact did not. The word *Anglican* simply means "English." As such, the Anglican or English Church had existed long before the sixteenth century, going all the way back to the early Christians in Britain within the first two centuries of Christianity.[2] It had even been called the Church *in* England throughout the Middle Ages. Nevertheless, when the church separated from Rome to be referred to as the Church *of* England, the country moved back and forth under successive monarchs from being apart from Rome to back under Rome and eventually away from Rome again to being an indigenous church. Reform continued all during these periods, but the theological definition should not be confused with political solutions and other meanings of the Middle Way by English Reformers.

More and Cross, in their classic anthology of English Reformation writings, present an altogether different definition of Anglicanism. In doing so, they explain four ways that the English Reformers used the language of Middle Way, none of which was a definition of *Anglicanism*. Rather, they are various uses of the phrase to describe the context of a state church and various emphases of the English Reformation.

One was the political, which they describe as a moderating point between the late Medieval Roman view of the Pope as head of state and the "Genevan theories of state."[3] The phrase was applied in this manner in the cultural context of the Queen's Elizabethan Settlement of 1559–1663 to unify Roman Catholics and Protestants in her realm. Her sister Queen Mary had returned England to the papal authority of Rome, after her father Henry VIII and brother Edward VI had removed the nation from and maintained it as no longer part of the Roman Catholic Church. Following Mary's short-lived reign, Elizabeth came to the throne. She restored the nation and church as once again separate from the Roman Church. The nation, however, was left divided between Protestants and Catholics. Many of the Protestants had fled to protestant centers on the Continent where they had been influenced by Calvin's republic model, in which neither Pope nor Monarch was head of the Christian State. Elizabeth, according to More, proposed a Middle Way between these opposing political views. It was not an attempt, however, precisely to define Anglicanism.

More notes a second usage of *Middle Way* in the leading sixteenth-century Anglican theologian Richard Hooker. Hooker, at the beginning of his historic *Of the Laws of Ecclesiastical Polity*, develops a golden chain of moderation found in God. The English Reformer refers to the restraint of God's wisdom on "the effects of His power." He applies God's moderation of His wisdom and power to the polity of Church and State in the political context of the English Reformation. He speaks of the moderation of such virtues

---

[2] When a ninth-century king named Alfred the Great unified all of Britain into England, the ecclesial identity became the Church in England. It was called by that designation all through the Middle Ages. It was part of the Roman Catholic Church at that time, but it had not always been under the authority of the Bishop of Rome. For the first seven centuries of Christianity, the church in Britain had been an indigenous church within what is called the Undivided Church of the first millennium but not under the Bishop of Rome. However, all during the first fifteen hundred years of Christianity in Britain and then in England there had been a church of the English, the *Ecclesia Anglicana* (Anglican Church). In this sense Anglicanism didn't originate in the sixteenth century.

[3] Paul Elmer More and Frank Leslie Cross, *Anglicanism: The Thought and Practice of the Church of England* (Milwaukee, WI: Morehouse, 1935), xxii.

as justice and mercy in this context. However, regarding Scripture, theology, and salvation, this moderating principle is not the model for the English Reformation. More quotes, for example, the seventeenth-century English Reformer Thomas Fuller, who said that "moderation is not a halting betwixt two opinions, when the thorough believing of one of them is necessary unto salvation." Nor is it a matter of "luke-warmness" in matters divine.[4] That is, in the areas of theology and liturgy, Anglicanism is not a political model of compromise.

A third meaning of *Middle Way* for the English Reformers was that of comprehensiveness, not compromise. More develops how this model originated with the early church fathers in dealing with heresy, turning to the crisis over the issue of the relation of Christ's Divinity and Humanity. He says, "The Church, by the Definition of Chalcedon, simply thrust its way through the middle by making [recognizing] the personality of the Incarnate so large as to carry with it *both* natures." More adds, "Evidently in this case at least the principle of measure does not produce a diminished or half-truth, but acts as a law of restraint preventing either one of two aspects of a paradoxical truth from excluding the other. Nor is the middle way here a mean of compromise, but a mean of comprehension."[5]

A fourth way that English Reformers used the terminology of Middle Way was in distinguishing between what More calls "fundamentals and accessories."[6] Again, he turns to Richard Hooker who distinguished between "things necessary for salvation and things convenient in practice." The middle was to distinguish between that which was essential to salvation and things non-essential. The English Reformers applied this understanding to Roman Catholics as well as to Protestants. On the Roman Catholic side, they addressed the dogmas required by their Church. On the Protestant side, they implemented the distinction with issues such as excessive sabbath-keeping laws.[7]

In none of these English Reformational uses of *Middle Way* do we find what came to be the more modern understanding of a halfway point between two polarities. The problem with the latter approach is that the extremes have been arbitrarily constructed by scholars. Some of these ends of the continuum have been generally accurate, but they

---

[4] More and Cross, *Anglicanism*, xxiii.

[5] Ibid., xxiv.

[6] Ibid., xxiv–xxv.

[7] Perhaps a fifth usage of *Middle Way* can be found in Hooker. He devotes considerable time to explain the relationship of reason to Scripture and tradition. The recognition of the role of the mind in Scripture had been a hallmark (even a charism or gift) of Western Christianity. Augustine had observed that the mind is the chief faculty of a human reflecting the *imago Dei*, the image of God. He illustrated with the analogy that when a human stands, his mind is closer to God than any other part of the anatomy. In English Christianity this distinctive had been developed by Anselm. By Hooker's time, the Western Church was not only struggling to sort out the relationship between Scripture and tradition, but the connection between both of these and reason. The approach of the late Middle Ages was to submit reason entirely to Scripture and tradition. This model collided the geocentric versus heliocentric cosmologies in the Copernican Revolution. Therefore, it can be recognized in Hooker that he offers a middle way by speaking of Scripture, tradition, and reason. This has been called his "three-legged stool" hermeneutic. In fairness to him, however, he never suggests that the three are equal in authority. Scripture is always the primary authority (*Prima Scriptura*) with tradition being secondary for him. Nevertheless, he does offer a middle way referring to them as having complementary value under the primary authority of Scripture without excluding tradition. It's been called the view of "Scripture and *its* tradition and *its* reason."

do not provide a clear definition of Anglicanism. Some scholars, for example, place the middle way between Luther and Calvin or even somewhere in the middle of Puritan and Anglican. At certain times in history these observations have been accurate, but they do not define *Anglicanism*. At other times, this approach to the Middle Way has shifted to opposites between Latitudinarianism and Confessionalism, High Church and Low Church, Evangelical and Anglo-Catholic, Liberal and Conservative, and so forth. Each time the polarities are moved to something different, the middle goes with them, along with an understanding of the Middle Way and eventually the definition of *Anglicanism*. The term *Anglicanism* is left with vague, vacillating, and even contradictory definitions. To apply the phrase in any strict liturgical and theological manner has only resulted in a quite ineffectual and confused approach to understanding Anglicanism. Moreover, as we shall see, it is not the model of the English Reformers' view of Anglicanism.

Reformed Anglicanism

A second model often used to define Anglicanism is with the word *reformed* by itself as an adjectival modifier: *Reformed Anglican*. Such an approach, though not the one taken in this book, can bring helpful insights in some ways to comprehend better the Anglican Way. It draws on the primary themes of the sixteenth-century Reformation of the Western Church to guide its emphases.

For one, this model has focused on the authority of Scripture. This aspect has had the effect of producing many excellent Bible expositors and teachers together with important commentaries on Scripture. Two, the Reformed Anglican approach has also had a high view of God, particularly his Sovereignty. This is one of the leading themes of the Holy Scriptures. When Israel collapsed into a syncretistic amalgamation of the Biblical religion to merge it with neighboring pagan religions, God raised up mighty prophets to bring God's people back to the True God. Time and again they appealed to God's sovereignty as a leading and distinct part of his character. Three, the Reformed Anglican paradigm has emphasized the Scriptural teaching of salvation by grace through faith. By including this Biblical teaching with the proclamation of the Gospel, it has generated many converts and evangelistic fervor. Evangelical missionaries have been among the most dedicated in the spread of the Good News of Christ's death and resurrection for the salvation of the world. Their ministries have swelled the membership of all churches and especially Anglican ones. Thus, the Reformed Anglican definition is far superior to the placid, shifting *via media* approach to Anglicanism. There is greater clarity and less equivocation. In a day when the Western world has collapsed into all manner of darkness, the leading elements of the authority of Scripture and salvation by grace remain necessary to reach a lost world.

At the same time, if the *via media* approach is too broad with its middle between two (ill defined) ends of a spectrum model, the Reformed Anglican definition is too narrow by missing the full breadth of the English Reformers. It has tended to narrow the understanding of Anglicanism to the point of the church losing its identity. This happened historically in a tragic way in the seventeenth century. In the sixteenth century the word *reformed* was broader in meaning, as the English Church was called *The Reformed Church of England*. Whether more on the Lutheran, Calvinist, or even the emerging Arminian side, the followers all claimed some variation of the famous Reformation slogans, "By Faith Alone," "By Scripture Alone," "By Grace Alone," "By Christ Alone," and "To the Glory of God Alone."

Toward the latter half of the sixteenth century the meaning of the adjective *reformed* was narrowed around one segment of the Reformation following the teachings of Swiss reformer John Calvin.[8] The Calvinist movement co-opted the word to describe their theological views based on the doctrine of the invisible church, which is the belief that the true Church on earth consists of only the elect predestinated by God. The visible Church of the baptized is not considered the true church. This theology compels those who believe it to seek for this invisible true church according to their definition of *reformed*. It further tends to fragment the Church, when those who believe themselves to be the elect separate from the visible who are not elect. The question always arises with this theology, however, "How do you know the elect?" The answers center around models of purity but without the word *catholic* to broaden to a more accurate Biblical and ancient understanding. Thus, lacking the other modifier of *catholic*, the meaning of *reformed* toward the end of the sixteenth century began to shift the definition of *Anglican* toward the word *Puritan*. In the seventeenth century, the word *Anglican* was completely excluded from any association with *reformed*.

The Calvinist party in the English Reformation became the Puritan Movement. For a while, the word *reformed* remained an adjective modifying *Anglican*. The Puritans, some more Presbyterian, Congregational, or Baptist, remained within the Church of England. After decades of struggle in the seventeenth century, the Puritans rejected Anglicanism, resulting in its momentary death. The Puritan rebellion led by Oliver Cromwell executed the Archbishop of Canterbury and the King of England. Bishops were removed from their Sees. A new Presbyterian *Westminster Confession of Faith* replaced the *Thirty-Nine Articles*. Eventually, however, with the death of Cromwell and his son, Anglicanism was restored along with bishops, the *Book of Common Prayer*, and the *Thirty-Nine Articles of Religion*. The return of the original Anglican formularies reintroduced the broader views of the English Reformation in the Church of England. The word *reformed* remained associated with the Calvinist segment of Anglicanism. Yet, as a stand-alone noun or modifier of *Anglicanism*, it was no longer comprehensive enough to define *Anglicanism*. The Calvinists were not the only ones in the Church of England who believed in the authority of Scripture and salvation by grace through faith. Furthermore, the non-Calvinists not only had a hefty view of Scripture, but they also embraced a high understanding of the Sacraments. They were reformed catholic.

Theologically, the narrowing effect of the word *reformed* without the other modifier *catholic*, has tended to lose the sacramental and liturgical priorities of the English

---

[8] The Dutch Calvinists were provoked into cataclysmic controversy by one of their theologians named Arminius. He argued for a broad interpretation of Calvin while also advocating significant modification in the great reformer's teachings. Arminius proposed five points: incomplete depravity leaving the human will free to choose, predestination/election based on foreknowledge, unlimited atonement for the whole world, the possibility of grace given but able to be resisted, and the possibility of falling from grace. The opponents of Arminius argued at the Synod of Dort 1618–1619 with a more consistent interpretation of Calvin to counter with five points around the acronym TULIP: total depravity, meaning humans do not have free will; unconditional election not originating with the knowledge of what humans will do; limited atonement for the elect only; irresistible grace such that if given it cannot be refused; and the perseverance of the saints, meaning the saved cannot fall from grace. The latter group prevailed at the synod embracing the word *Calvinist* with their fivefold response. The Church of England sent bishops to the Synod of Dort, but the Anglican Church never adopted these *Canons*.

Reformers. The word *catholic*, as understood in its ancient and early church sense, included not only Word but Sacrament as well as liturgy. The Reformed, by elevating Word over Sacrament, not only moved away from the sacramental system in Scripture but also from the liturgy. Very simply, it takes a liturgy of some sort to conduct the Sacraments. By abandoning the Sacramental emphases, the liturgy is eventually lost. For Anglicans, this liturgy is the *Book of Common Prayer*. When catholic and sacrament are minimized, the pattern among the reformed Anglicans has been often to reduce the liturgy to the point of losing the prayer book. Once this happens, the meaning of Anglicanism becomes confused. It can even be lost.

Also, the other reformed emphasis of salvation by faith has had a pattern of excluding the Biblical and prayer book connections between the Sacraments and salvation. It is true that Scripture teaches salvation is by grace through faith and not works (Eph 2:8–9). Faith is necessary for the Sacraments to be effectual, but that is not the same as saying salvation and Sacrament have no association in Scripture. The Word of God in fact connects the Sacraments to the Gospel and forgiveness. Jesus said one must be born of water (baptism) and the Holy Spirit to be born again (John 3:1–5). He commanded making disciples by baptizing them with water in the Name of the Blessed Trinity (Matt 28:19–20). St. Peter told the early converts at Pentecost to "repent and be baptized for the forgiveness of sins" (Acts 2:38–39). Turning to the Sacrament of Holy Communion, Jesus said at the Last Supper that the Cup He mystically declared to be His Blood is to be received for the "forgiveness of sins" (Matt 26:26–28). St. Paul spoke of the Gospel as so imbedded in the Eucharist that the Sacrament "proclaims His [Christ's] death until He comes" (1 Cor 11:26).

The Anglican *Book of Common Prayer* consistent with the sacramental teaching of Scripture does not distance the Sacraments from salvation. They are very much a part of the meaning of the word Anglican. The historic Anglican Catechism, for example, teaches that the Sacraments are "generally necessary for salvation."[9] The historic Anglican *Office of Baptism* produced by the German Reformer Martin Bucer and brought into the *Book of Common Prayer* by Cranmer speaks of baptismal regeneration based on the Scriptural teachings of Jesus and St. Paul (John 3:1–5; Titus 3:5). The service of Holy Communion refers to the Sacrament as being received by faith for the "remission of sin" in its Prayer of Dedication. In the Post Communion Prayer of Thanksgiving, assurance of salvation is tied to the reception of the Sacrament. The *Book of Common Prayer* prevents theological shrinkage of the Scriptural doctrine of salvation that separates it from sacramental theology.

---

[9] The word *generally* is used because there is one example in the New Testament of a person being saved without Baptism: the thief on the cross who was crucified with Christ. He confessed faith and Jesus said that he would be with Him in paradise. There are no other examples in the New Testament of a person accepting Christ without also receiving the Sacrament of Baptism. Salvation and Sacrament are generally associated with one another. Nevertheless, the Church through the ages based on the example of the thief and the sacramental theology of Scripture has recognized the "Sacrament of desire" when a person believes but is not able to receive the Sacrament due to circumstances. These are situations such as martyrdom or sickness. Even in these instances such as in the administration of Holy Communion to the sick in the *Book of Common Prayer*, the person is said to "receive the Body and Blood of our Savior Christ profitably to his soul's health, although he doth not receive the Sacrament with his mouth." The connection between salvation and Sacrament is retained.

Thus, without the word *catholic* accompanying the term *reformed*, Anglicanism cannot be fully understood. At times the effect of this approach has ended up abandoning Anglicanism altogether. For the most part, the Reformed Anglican approach either misses or does not include the English Reformers' patristic catholic model to circumscribe a definition of *Anglicanism*. The latter is the predominant model among Anglicans during the sixteenth- and seventeenth-century English Reformation and at other times of reform.

Reformed Catholic Anglicanism

The reformed catholic definition of Anglicanism appears succinctly in Canon 6 of the 1571 *Canons of the Church of England* quoted at the beginning of this chapter. The Canon sets the parameters for what preachers are to teach. These boundaries are "what is agreeable to *the teaching of the Old or New Testament, and what the Catholic fathers and ancient bishops have collected from this selfsame doctrine*" (emphasis mine). The standard is Scripture and the early church fathers. The statement, "collected from this selfsame doctrine," refers back to the "Old and New Testament."

For the early church fathers, and Anglicans following them, the Word of God written was the location of doctrine. This conviction is most clearly demonstrated at the First Ecumenical Council of Nicaea in 325, out of which the *Nicene Creed* was produced and eventually adopted at the Second Ecumenical Council of Constantinople in 381. At Nicaea, the Bishops sat in a circle around the Emperor Constantine's throne. But the emperor was not on the throne. A copy of the Scriptures was placed on his seat. Presumably it was one of the fifty copies of the Bible Constantine had produced for the council. The entire scene exemplifies that the early church fathers including the emperor saw the Bible as the locus for doctrine to address the heresy of Arianism. Since the council at Nicaea was a gathering of the whole (that is catholic) Church, this was the Scriptural source of doctrine to which the English Reformation returned as expressed in Canon 6.

Nevertheless, the Canon also emphasizes the teachings of Scripture as collected by the "Catholic fathers and ancient bishops." The early church fathers are the primary guide for understanding the Scriptures. The Canon does not mention contemporary reformers like Luther or Calvin. The English Reformers read and considered the teachings of other reformers in their time, but only in so far as they held what has been called the *ad fontes* "back to the sources" model. The English Reformers as stated in Canon 6 were to measure what they considered to be true to the Word of God based on how the other reformers handled Scripture and the early church fathers. In this sense, the reformers in England by the time of 1571 were reforming the Roman Catholic Church according to a reformed catholic template.

Canon 6 does refer to two documents produced by the English part of the Reformation. They are the 1571 *Thirty-Nine Articles* "of the Christian religion to which assent was given by the bishops in lawful and holy synod convened and celebrated by command and authority of our most serene princess, Elizabeth, ... collected from the holy books of Old and New Testament, and in all respects agree with the heavenly doctrine which is contained in them." The other document is the "the book of public prayers [*The Book of Common Prayer* revised in 1559], and book of the consecration (*inauguratio*) of archbishops, bishops, priests, and deacons [*Ordinal*] contain nothing contrary to this same doctrine." Both books were combined into one prayer book. In these statements about the documents, the same emphasis carries through of Scripture as the source of "doctrine." However, upon examination of these works as we will see later in additional chapters, they follow the leading guide of Canon 6 of the Scriptures of the "Old and New Testament" and the "Catholic fathers and ancient bishops." The *Articles* and the prayer book do reflect certain statements concerning needed correction to aberrant teachings in the late Medieval Church. Nevertheless, they were not intended to deviate from the ancient model.

One other critical statement is made in Canon 6 confirming the reformed catholic approach. It says that preachers "shall not teach vain and old wives' opinions and heresies, and papal errors, abhorrent to the teaching and faith of Christ, nor anything at all whereby the unlearned multitude be *inflamed to love of novelty* or contention" (emphasis mine). The word *novelty* eschews new doctrine but goes further, speaking of "inflaming to love novelty" in the Church. It is not simply that there should not be novelty of teaching, but "an inflamed love" for it. This language reinforces the model of an "old" in contrast to "new" standard of the Holy Scriptures and the early church fathers. The phrasing also implies that whatever is contained in the Reformation documents of the *Articles of Religion* and *Book of Common Prayer*, they were not intended to introduce anything novel, as we will see more fully developed in later chapters. This rejection of novelty, however, appears time and again in the English Reformers. It is a reforming of the late Medieval Western Church back to a Biblical, patristic, creedal, and conciliar understanding of Catholic in the first centuries of Christianity.

The *Catholic* of Reformed Catholic: Scriptural, Patristic, Creedal, and Conciliar

The English Reformation lasted for well over a hundred years from the first third of the sixteenth century to the end of the seventeenth century. It even had its first dawning much earlier, with the fourteenth-century Oxford scholar John Wycliffe; he was called the "Morning Star of the Reformation." After England was no longer under the authority of the Pope in 1534, the English Reformers pointed out that though the Roman Catholic Church is part of the whole, it had never been the entire Catholic Church. Furthermore, since the division of East and West in 1054, the Roman Church had developed apart from the whole Church to introduce some peculiar novelties. To correct them, the English Reformers appealed to the ancient catholic Church as their model. They were seeking to restore the catholic Church in England without being Roman Catholic. This is demonstrated by many English Reformers in the writings, especially in their understanding of the word *catholic* to which they appealed.

The word *catholic* is derived from a Greek prepositional phrase (κατὰ ὅλος *kata holos*) meaning "according to the whole." The seventeenth-century English Reformer John Pearson indicates this understanding of *catholic* in his classic commentary on the *Apostles' Creed* called *An Exposition of the Creed*.[10] He traces the origin of the application of the word *catholic* to the Church to the description of an officer in the Roman Empire called a *Catholicus*. He "collected the Emperor's revenue in several provinces ... therefore

---

[10] John Pearson, *An Exposition of the Creed*, ed. Edward Burton (Oxford, [1659] 1864), 589–620. Burton was the Regius Professor of Divinity in Oxford. He brought the classic work of Pearson back into print with a meticulous translation of the Latin version that appeared in 1691.

called the *Catholicus*, as the general Procurator of them all, from whence that title was transferred upon the Christian Patriarchs." Pearson notes that this definition of the word in the sense of the "whole or universal" was first "most anciently in use among the primitive Fathers" in reference to books in the New Testament such as "the Epistles of St. James, St. Peter, St. John, St. Jude, the *Catholic Epistles*, because when the Epistles written by St. Paul were directed to particular Churches congregated in particular cities, these were either sent to the Churches dispersed through a great part of the world, or directed to the *whole Church of God* [emphasis mine] upon the face of the whole earth." He concludes, "We observe the Fathers to use the word *Catholic* for nothing else but general or universal, in the ordinary or vulgar sense, as the catholic resurrection is the resurrection of all men, the catholic opinion the opinion of all men."

Pearson adds that though the word *catholic* is not in Scripture, as neither is the word *Trinity*, it came to be used in the ancient Church to describe the whole. He says,

> That Church which was built upon the Apostles as upon the foundation, congregated by their preaching and their baptizing, receiving continued accession, and disseminated in several parts of the earth, containing within it numerous congregations, all which were truly called Churches, as members of the same Church; that Church, I say, was after some time called the *Catholic Church* ... taken in the large and comprehensive sense, by as large and comprehensive name, the Catholic Church.

It is this ancient model of the Catholic Church to which the English Church attempted to return at the time of its Reformation. Pearson concludes,

> The Church alone which first began at Jerusalem on earth will bring us to the Jerusalem in heaven; and that alone began there which always embraceth the *faith once delivered to the saints*. Whatsoever Church pretendeth to a new beginning pretendeth at the same time to a new Churchdom, and whatsoever is so new is none, so necessary it is to believe in *the Holy Catholic Church*.

The English Reformers did not have in mind to raise up some kind of new "Anglican denomination." They were only seeking to remain what had once been the Catholic and Undivided Church of the ages of ages in a particular English region of the world with the same Catholic "faith once delivered to the saints." Hence, the reformed catholic English Reformation did not begin a new church and certainly not a new faith.

Severed from Rome, the reformed catholic model of the English Church included the Apostles and their teachings (Holy Scripture), the ancient church fathers, the Catholic Creeds (*Apostles'*, *Nicene*, and *Athanasian*), and the Ecumenical (worldwide, as in Catholic) Church Councils. One of the clearest summaries of this catholic commitment is in a statement made by James I, King of England (1609). He said the following:

> I will never be ashamed to render an account of my profession and of that hope that is in me, as the Apostle prescribeth. I am such a CATHOLIC CHRISTIAN as believeth in the Creeds, that of the Apostles, that of the Council of Nice, and that of Athanasius, the two latter being periphrases of the former. And I believe them in that sense as the ancient Fathers and Councils that made them did understand them, to which three Creeds all the ministers of England do subscribe at their Ordination. And I acknowledge for Orthodox all the other forms of Creeds that either were derived by Councils or particular Fathers, against such particular

heresies as most reigned in their times.... For whatsoever the Fathers for the first five hundred years did with unanimine consent agree upon, to be believed as necessary for salvation, I either will believe it also, or at least will be honorably silent, not taking upon me to condemn them.... I will therefore in that case follow St. Augustine's rule in judging of their opinions as I find them agree with the Scriptures. What I find agreeable thereunto I will gladly embrace. What is otherwise I will (with their reverence) reject.[11]

King James adds, "But if the Romish Church hath coined new Articles of Faith, never heard of in the first 500 years after Christ, I hope I shall never be condemned for an heretic, for not being a Novelist." James I therefore claimed to be first and foremost a "Catholic Christian." He understood *catholic* as what was believed in the first half millennium of the Church. The primary authority by which all is "judged" is the Holy Scriptures, what he refers to as "St. Augustine's rule in judging of their [church fathers] opinions as I find them agree with the Scriptures." Next, he cites the early church fathers, creeds, and councils.

Scripture, Early Church Fathers, and the Creeds

The primary authority of Scripture is combined with the secondary authority of the early church fathers expressed in the creeds they produced out of their historic ecumenical councils. He calls them the "ancient Fathers and Councils." James refers to two of the councils, "Nice" (Nicaea) and "Athanasius." The citation of "Athanasius" is probably a reference to the *Athanasian Creed* based on the Fourth Ecumenical Council of Chalcedon in 451, since all the ancient Catholic creeds and councils of the first five hundred years are included with his statement, "all other forms of Creeds ... derived by Councils ... for the first five hundred years." Therefore, the standard of "Catholic Christian" was the way of identifying the English Reformation. This same Catholic standard appears all through the writings and the documents of the English Reformation.

For example, the Bishop of Ely, Francis White (1564–1638), echoes James I when he writes,

> The Church of England in her public and authorized Doctrine and Religion proceedeth in manner following: It buildeth her faith and religion upon the Sacred and Canonical Scripture of the holy Prophets and Apostles, as upon her main and prime foundation. Next unto the Holy Scriptures, it relieth upon the consentieth testimony and authority of the Bishops and Patrons of the true ancient Catholic Church; and it preferreth the sentence thereof before all other curious and profane novelties.

The bishop adds, "The first of these, namely the Holy Scripture, it is the sovereign authority and for itself worthy of all acceptation." The "voice and testimony of the Primitive Church, is a ministerial and subordinate rule and guide, to preserve and direct us in the right understanding of the Scriptures."[12]

---

[11] James Montague, *Works, A Premonition to all Most Mighty Monarchs, Kings, Free Princes, and States of Christendom* (London: 1616), 302–308. Montague was Bishop of Worcester. This work was sent to Emperor Rudolph II.

[12] Francis White, *A Treatise of the Sabbath Day, Containing a Defense of the Orthodoxal Doctrine of the Church of England against Sabbatarian Novelty* (London: 1635), 11ff.

The bishop spells out, however, the relationship of Scripture and the church fathers. He speaks of the Word of God as the "prime foundation." With this phrase he presents the sense in which the popular Reformation phrase *Sola Scriptura* was meant. Holy Writ is "sovereign authority" as the source of doctrine. It is *sola* in this sense of the meaning of the word as "only." However, *sola* was not understood by the English Reformers to mean "only" as "by itself," as indicated by the phrase "prime foundation." The idea is more along the lines of conceiving of *sola* like the sole of a shoe. (The sole is the main point of a shoe, protecting the foot from the ground, but the rest of the shoe is needed to keep the sole in place for it to function as it is intended.)

Bishop White says of the Church of England, "Next to the Holy Scriptures, it relieth upon the *consentient testimony and authority* of the Bishops and Patrons of the true ancient Catholic Church." He even uses an analogy to explain the relationship of Scripture to the early church fathers: "The Holy Scripture is the fountain and lively spring." He continues in referring to the ancient church that it is, "the consentient and unanimous testimony of the true Church of Christ, in the Primitive Ages thereof, is *Canalis*, a conduit pipe to derive and convey to succeeding generations the celestial water contained in the Holy Scripture." Gerald McDermott presents the *Prima Scriptura* view of the English Reformers and the early church fathers in his chapter in this volume; he also writes in another chapter on authority and Holy Tradition.

The English Reformation hermeneutic is not an unmediated approach to the Scriptures that attempts to go around historic interpretation. It is an understanding of the Word of God as mediated through the "conduit" of the early church fathers. Put another way, the English Reformers did not have what could be described as a "helicopter" approach of rising out of the sixteenth century to drop into an interpretation of the Scriptures around and past how the Word of God had been historically understood. No doubt, any believer is supposed to read and study the Word of God by the power of the Holy Spirit. But the Spirit created the Church to whom the Holy Scriptures were revealed. The Word of God is within the Holy Tradition of the Church. It is precisely because the Word of God is given within and to the Church that she cannot change the Holy Scriptures. Furthermore, the English Reformers rejected tradition not because they were against the Holy Tradition of the Scriptures given to the Church. Rather, they opposed unbiblical tradition that was contrary to the Scriptures.

The bishop addresses anything outside of the Scriptures and the "conduit" of the early church fathers as producing "profane novelties." This theme in Canon 6 of the *Canons of the Church of England* surfaces in White as well as other English Reformers. "Novelty," if it is not supported by Scripture and the ancient Church, is again expressed as detrimental to Biblical authority and teaching.

Resistance to Novelty

The leading example among the English Reformers, the Bishop of Salisbury John Jewell (1522–1571), defended the Church of England against the charge by Roman apologists that the Church of England was something "new." He offers this defense followed by others who, as we have already seen, also reject the notion of creating something new. Jewell was asked by Queen Elizabeth to produce a defense of the Church of England against late Medieval Roman Catholic criticism that the English Church was no longer catholic. He produced perhaps the most definitive and extensive development of a reformed catholic model of Anglicanism in his classic work, *An Apology of the Church of England.*

In defending the English Reformation of the sixteenth century against the charge of Roman apologists that a novel church and doctrine were being established, Jewell categorically states that the church of the English Reformation was not something "new." He says,

> Thus you see, good Christian reader, how it is no new thing though at this day the religion of Christ [in the Church of England] be entertained with its despites and checks being lately restored and coming up again anew ... and [the English Reformers] have returned again unto the primitive church of ancient fathers and apostles, that is to say, to the beginnings of things as to the very foundations and headsprings of Christ's Church ... as the holy [church] fathers in former time, and as our predecessors have commonly done, we have restored our churches.[13]

In one sense, Jewell lays out the complete English Reformation model in this statement. We find the same emphases of James I, Bishop White, and many others to follow. Jewell says that the Church of England was not attempting to make a "new faith or a new church." He refers to the effort of the English Reformation as a return to "the primitive church of ancient fathers and apostles." The English Reformation was going back to the "beginnings of things as to the very foundations and headsprings of Christ's Church." By *headsprings* he means the ancient Scriptures, the "apostles," and the "holy fathers" of the early church. Jewell adds,

> We do show it plain that God's Holy Gospel, the ancient bishops, and the primitive church, do make our side, and that we have not without just cause left these men [the Roman Church], and rather have returned to the apostles and the old catholic fathers ... and if they themselves [Roman Catholic defenders] which fly our doctrine and would be called catholics shall manifestly see how these titles of antiquity, whereof they boast so much, are quite shaken out of their hands, and that there is more pith in this our cause than they thought.[14]

With such a statement and many proofs, Jewell turned the Roman objections of novelty against them. The Anglican argument is the important insight that it was the Roman Church who had innovated with new dogmas in the Middle Ages.

Jewell appeals to the same *Prima Scriptura* view of *Sola Scriptura*. Holy Scripture is the locus of doctrine, but it was not to be interpreted apart from the ancient church fathers. Notice how he weaves together this *Prima* view of *Sola* with the secondary authority of the early church fathers when he writes:

> Thus did the holy fathers always fight against the heretics with none other force than with the Holy Scripture. St. Augustine when he disputed against Petilian, an heretic of the Donatists: "Let not these words," quoth he, "be heard between us," "I say" or "you say": let us rather speak in this wise: "Thus saith the Lord" [Scriptural refrain]. There let us seek the church: there let us boult out our cause. Likewise, St. Jerome: "All those things" saith he, "which without the testimony of the Scriptures

---

[13] John Jewell, *An Apology of the Church of England*, ed. John E. Booty (New York: Church Publishing, 2010), 134–135.
[14] Ibid., 17.

are holden as delivered from the apostles be thoroughly smitten down by the sword of God's word." St. Ambrose also to the Gratian emperor: "Let the Scripture," saith he, "be asked the question, let the apostles be asked." For at that time made the catholic fathers and bishops no doubt but that our religion might be proved out of the Holy Scriptures.[15]

These references from a King of England and two leading English Reformation Bishops cite consistent elements in their catholic standard. They are the Holy Scriptures, and the early church fathers including the ancient creeds and councils.

The Ecumenical Councils

The authoritative place of the ancient ecumenical councils was also part of the catholic standard for the English Reformation. As we've seen, the first five hundred years in which the first four of these councils took place put the latter in a special category. They were considered to be the foundation for the other three councils. However, the first four being consistently mandated and referenced for this reason, it is sometimes assumed that the English Reformers completely rejected the last three councils.

The important late sixteenth-century English Reformer Richard Field addresses the topic of councils in his multi-volume work, *Of the Church*. Field was a contemporary of and friends with Richard Hooker, and his work is considered as important as Hooker's definitive *Of the Laws of Ecclesiastical Polity*. The difference between the two men's focus is that Hooker mainly addressed the Puritan situation. Field, however, continued the role of Jewell in defending the English Church against Roman apologists.

Concerning councils, Field cites St. Gregory, who "professed that he honoureth the first four Councils as the Four Gospels; and that whosoever admitted them not, though he seem to be a stone elect and precious, yet he lieth beside the foundation and out of the building."[16] St. Gregory's comment provides the basis and rationale for the English Church holding the first four councils in special regard.

However, Field adds that "of this sort there are only six." He means that the first six are doctrinal. He explains,

> The First, defining the Son of God to be coessential, coeternal, and coequal with the Father. The Second, defining that the Holy Ghost is truly God, coessential, coeternal, and coequal with the Father and the Son. The Third, the unity of Christ's person. The Fourth, the distinction and diversity of His natures, in and after personal union. The Fifth, condemning some remains of Nestorianism ... and accusing the heresy of Origin and his followers touching the temporal punishments of devils and wicked castaways. And the Sixth, defining and clearing the distinction of operations, actions, powers, and wills in Christ, according to the diversity of His natures.

Field sums up these councils as "Lawful General Councils" in terms of their "beginning, and proceeding, and continuance that ever were holden in the Christian Church

---

[15] Jewell, *Apology*, 19.

[16] Richard Field, *Of the Church, Book V* (London: 1606), chapters xlviii–lii. See also *Ecclesiastical History Society* (Cambridge: 1852), Vol. IV, 2–11, 15–18, 24, 43–48, 51, 59–63, 64–68. These excerpts are also found in More and Cross, *Anglicanism*, 142–160.

touching matters of faith." Field says of the Seventh Council, however, that "it was not called about any question of faith but of manners."[17]

Concerning the English Church's acceptance of all seven ecumenical councils, Field states, "So that there are but seven general councils that the whole Church acknowledgeth called to determine faith and manners."[18] He then further clarifies that he understood his own church to be part of the "whole Church." He says, "Lawful general [ecumenical] councils ... we do more honour and esteem and *more fully admit all the general councils that hath ever hitherto been holden*."[19] Note that Field uses the pronoun "we" in reference to his church. He even emphasizes that the English Church "more fully admits" (i.e., accepts) all the councils. It is a more consistent conciliar church in his view than the late Medieval Roman Church, whom he considered in his book to be an "adversary."[20] The English Reformation Church recognized the first four councils as the "foundation of the building," yet this view of the first four did not reject the last three, as indicated by the leading English Reformer Richard Field.

Another leading bishop and theologian in the early seventeenth century, Archbishop of Canterbury William Laud (1573–1645), spoke to the matter of all seven. His comments are in context of addressing the Roman Catholic Council of Trent convened in the early stages of the English Reformation. This local council was an attempt to counter the Reformation and more specifically the English part of it. To refute the council, Laud draws on Article 21 from The *Thirty-Nine Articles of Religion* adopted in 1571. The Article says that when councils "be gathered together, (forasmuch they be an assembly of men, whereof all be not governed with the Spirit and Word of God), may err and sometimes have erred. Whereby things ordained by them as necessary to salvation have neither strength nor authority, unless it be declared that they be taken out of holy Scripture." He draws on this article to reject the conclusions of Trent saying it did not have "The written

---

[17] By "manners," Field refers to the council's Scriptural concern to distinguish the improper "adoration and worship" of images (idolatry) from "honorable reverence" of pictures and icons of Christ and saints. C. B. Moss, *The Church of England and the Seven Ecumenical Councils* (London: Faith Press, 1957; Project Canterbury Edition, 2003), 11–13. The council supported this distinction by noting the way that Scripture sometimes uses different words to distinguish the reverencing or honor directed toward a created being from worship. The Greek words involved are προσκύνησις (*proskunesis*) and λατρεία (*latreia*). *Proskunesis* may mean honor (Gen 23:12; 2 Sam 1:2) or worship (Matt 4:10). Thus, it is possible to show reverence toward someone or something without worshipping it. But the term *latreia* only refers to worship, meaning to serve God alone (Matt 4:10). Field implicitly supports of this conclusion, warning against the possible abuse of such a distinction. Echoing the council's language, he states that the seventh council "condemns the religious adoration and worshipping of pictures ... to allow no other use of them but ... in permitting men by outward signs of *reverence and respect* towards the pictures of saints" (Book IV, 61–62). He adds that this difference between adoration/worship and reverence/respect "may seem to have given some occasion" to idolatry. Since Field has already established that the "whole Church"—including his church—"admitted" all the councils, his concern was not to deny distinguishing between reverence and worship, in principle, but rather to warn against how such a distinction could become cause for abuse.

[18] Field, Book IV, 61.

[19] Ibid., 62. Brackets and italics mine.

[20] Ironically, the term *adversary* used by Field in reference to the Roman Church, in his discussion of iconoclasm and the Seventh Council, also would have applied to the Puritans. Their opposition to the Church of England grew partly because the Church allowed the use of pictures and images in worship.

Word of God for warrant either in express letter or necessary sense or deduction." Laud further condemned the council as "only local and not represented by the whole such as Eastern Orthodox Bishops, not attended by the Pope, the French condemned it, and the Spanish were 'unworthily overborne.'"[21]

Laud then adds a statement that explains the meaning of the other statement in Article 21 that councils "may err, and sometimes have erred." To be sure, the Article does not say that all councils have and always do err. Laud, however, says, "as all unerring councils have had, and as all that must have that [the warrant of Holy Scripture] will not err." Laud maintains that there were "unerring councils" concerning their doctrinal conclusions such as Nicaea, Chalcedon, and so forth in that their judgements were "taken out of holy Scripture" and adopted by the whole "Catholic Church." Putting his comments together with Richard Field, these were the seven ecumenical councils. Again we see that the English Church though emphasizing the first four never rejected all seven councils.

Therefore, the catholic of reformed catholic included Scripture, the early church fathers, their creeds, and councils. Holy Scripture is considered primary as the source of doctrine. The early church fathers are the "conduit" through which the Word of God is to be understood. The Catholic Creeds as a product of the ancient Church by the power of the Holy Spirit in Ecumenical Councils are based on Scripture as indicated with the phrase in the *Nicene Creed*, "according to the Scriptures." Consistent with the Word of God, these statements and their councils are also part of the ancient Catholic model. These combined elements explain the English Reformers' understanding of *catholic* in the phrase *reformed catholic*.

The *Reformed* of Reformed Catholic
Correcting the Present with the Past: *Ad Fontes*

Turning to the adjective *reformed*, it is consistent with and not antithetical to the other word, *catholic*. To use the title of the 1985 movie, reform for the English Reformers meant "Back to the Future." In general, they were not attempting novelties. They were trying to reform the late Medieval Western Church with Scripture and the early church fathers. During the second generation of the Reformation, new views and practices sprang forth. Even then, these changes were more often than not necessitated by circumstance than conviction. Such was the case with developing models of church polity without bishops.[22]

The English Reformation was different. Its church entered the Reformation with bishops, priests, and deacons. It did not seek, nor did it claim novelty as indicated by others quoted earlier along with Bishop Jewell in his *Apology*. They did have to make corrections, yet when we examine how they sought to introduce change, it was from previous sources of the past: the Scriptures and the early church fathers. No doubt, the English Reformers

---

[21] More and Cross, *Anglicanism*, 160–161.

[22] See Geddes MacGregor, *Corpus Christi* (Philadelphia: Westminster, 1958). He points out that even Calvin in his *Institutes* never rejected bishops. The Swiss reformer only advocated for "godly bishops," a phrase he uses often. He also notes that the author of a Presbyterian system of government without bishops, John Knox, primarily did so out of necessity. Knox participated in the consecration of an archbishop in Scotland, but when no bishops were available, he devised a Presbyterian system with "superintendents" who functioned like bishops.

did learn from and interact with contemporary Reformers in Europe. However, it is important to recognize that even these leading Magisterial scholars were initially working with the same reformed catholic, "back to the future" model.

The initial motto of the Reformation was derived from the Renaissance: *ad fontes*. The Latin means "back to the sources." The sources for the leading Magisterial Reformers were the same as their English counterparts: Holy Scriptures *and* the early church fathers. The Reformation scholar Timothy George, former Dean of Beeson Divinity School, refers to the *ad fontes* model when speaks of the Reformation as having become a "period of virtual patristic *ressourcement*." He adds,

> In that first age of printing, we have not only the first critical edition of the Bible, Erasmus's Greek New Testament of 1516, but also the first critical and printed editions of the church fathers ... Augustine, Jerome, and Origen, edited by Erasmus himself, as well as numerous other editions by Protestant and Catholic scholars alike. Philip Melanchthon was one of the great patristic scholars of the age, and John Calvin was not far behind him. In some respects, the Reformation was as much a debate about the church fathers as it was about the Bible itself: "Whose Cyprian?" "Which Augustine?" "My Chrysostom, not yours!"[23]

Archbishop Thomas Cranmer of the English Reformation should be added to the list. He had the most extensive patristic library of all the Reformers.

The English Reformers in particular used an *ad fontes* approach to reform the Roman Catholic Church. Bishop John Jewell in his *Apology*, for example, refers to areas in need of correction, but in addressing them he follows through tenaciously with a reformed catholic approach. As for recognizing the need to correct or to reform theological problems, he says, "Thus you see, good Christian reader, how it is no new thing though at this day the religion of Christ be entertained with its *despites and checks* being lately restored and coming up again anew."[24] Specifically, among the "despites and checks" in need of correction in the late Middle Ages, he speaks of the weak doctrine of salvation in the Western Church.

Jewell's method, however, is not only to go to the Scriptures, but to the early church fathers to establish that justification by faith "only" was not a new teaching.[25] He turns to the necessity of faith in receiving the Blessed Sacrament according to the "word of the Gospel and the expounding of the Law and the Scriptures,"[26] yet he argues that justification by faith (necessary for the Sacrament to be efficacious) is not a new teaching. He appeals to the early church fathers when he says,

> For it is our faith that applieth the death and Cross of Christ to our benefit, and not the act of a Massing priest. "Faith had in the sacraments," saith St. Augustine, "doth justify and not the sacraments." And Origen saith, "Christ is the priest, the propitiation, the sacrifice; which propitiation comes to everyone by means of faith."

---

[23] Timothy George, "The Reformation and the New Ecumenism," in *Protestantism After 500 Years*, eds. Thomas Albert Howard and Mark A. Noll (New York: Oxford University Press, 2016), 323. Quote adapted for the publication, *First Things*.

[24] See Jewell's reference to which I referred earlier, *Apology*, 134.

[25] The *Thirty-Nine Articles*, XI On the Justification of Man, states, "justified by faith only."

[26] Jewell, *Apology*, 28.

> So that by this reckoning we say that the sacraments without faith do not profit those that be alive; a great deal less do they profit those that be dead.[27]

His point is that without faith the Sacraments though valid are not effectual unto salvation. Masses for the dead cannot save.

Jewell reaches back to the early church fathers' commitment to the authority of Scripture to establish that the Faith of the reformed catholic church of the English Reformation is founded on the Word of God and the early ancient Church's understanding of it. Notice importantly how he *doesn't* refer to other reformers of the Reformation for his defense of the necessity of faith. He could have appealed to so many references in Luther and others contemporary to his time. He surely knew of them and would have acknowledged their veracity on many matters. Nevertheless, he turns to the Scriptures and the early church fathers.

Furthermore, the English Reformers retained an early patristic Incarnational model of salvation while addressing justification by faith. It appears in the *Litany of the Book of Common Prayer*. Following the prayers, "By the mystery of thy Holy Incarnation; by thy holy Nativity, and Circumcision; by thy Baptism, Fasting, and Temptation," is the response, "Good Lord, deliver us." The whole life of Christ, every major event of His Incarnation, is understood to be part of our deliverance or salvation. Thus, salvation is presented as more than the doctrine of justification by faith though true and important. Faith is the instrumental means for entering a relationship with Jesus Christ, but it is not the whole doctrine of salvation. In a later chapter of this book, Hans Boersma will develop this point. However, the Incarnational approach of the English Reformers was derived directly from the Scriptures and the early church fathers. The issue of justification by faith alone did need to be addressed correctly with Scripture, but the English Reformers knew that there was much more involved in the doctrine of salvation. It's why in the *Thirty-Nine Articles of Religion* the word *alone* is not used. Rather, Article 11 says, "We are justified by Faith only." The word *Faith* is capitalized but adjoined to *only*. This language more accurately reflects the Incarnational teaching of salvation in Scripture and the early church that provides the foundation not only for faith but a theology of works so essential to what St. James says is a "living faith" when he writes, "faith without works is dead" (James 2:19). This fulsome kind of Incarnational understanding of salvation is but one example of the reformed catholic foundation that English Reformers sought to correct the doctrinal problems in the Medieval Church.

In this example of justification by faith and the doctrine of salvation, we see that English Reformers like Jewell were more consistent with and followed through on the *ad fontes* methodology, while the Continental Reformers did not always stay with the model. They began to introduce novelties that the ancient Church did not believe nor practice. They also at times influenced English Reformers in a similar direction. In the chapter "The Sacraments: Both Which is Both," I will point out how Archbishop Cranmer adopted a German Reformer's (Oecolampadius) modified view of two early church fathers (Hilary and Cyril) on how Christ comes to the faithful recipient of the Blessed Sacrament. The archbishop expresses this perspective in his writings and somewhat reflected it in the first edition of the *Forty-Two Articles of Religion*. However, it should be noted that the issue was over views of the early fathers. Cranmer, being a foremost

---

[27] Jewell, *Apology*, 36.

patristic scholar, took and remained committed to the *ad fontes* approach, even though he was willing to embrace a contemporary reformer's new interpretation of these early church fathers. Nevertheless, in the final edition of the *Thirty-Nine Articles*, Cranmer's original articles on sacramental presence were modified back in the direction of the early church fathers' belief. The bishops of the Church of England (as well as Parliament) restored a more ancient catholic view of real presence by returning to a more consistent reformed catholic approach on this sacramental point.

In the chapter on the *Book of Common Prayer*, we will see that even the English Reformers were lured from their *ad fontes* approach at points, such as in the second revision of the prayer book in 1552. It was due to the allowance of the more European model of the Reformation to enter the process of revision. However, we will also find that after the short life (less than a year) of the 1552 *Book of Common Prayer*, the next 1559 revision returned to the model that Jewell presents in his *Apology*.

In these examples, we see two different meanings of *reformed* in the Reformation. In the English Reformation we find a meaning retained as "reformed back to the Scriptures and the early church fathers." In the Continental part of the Reformation, it became an understanding of reform back to the Scriptures, accompanied by a willingness to abandon the early church fathers. The English Reformation did not follow the latter, even though on some occasions there was acquiescence. Still, as we will see throughout this book, the English Reformers and their successors repeatedly in other times of reform returned to the reformed catholic model established at the beginning of their part of the Reformation.

Thus, the English Reformers, by returning to the Scriptures and the church fathers over the century-long history of the Reformation in their country, demonstrate the guiding principles of a back-to-the-sources paradigm in the ways that they sought to reform. It was reform of Medieval Roman Catholicism with the ancient Biblical and patristic sources. To be reformed was to be Catholic in the ancient sense. This is why we find the English Reformers of this period simply calling themselves as well as their Church, "catholic." In their minds, whether bishop, scholar, or monarch, that is what it meant to be reformed, yet to be ancient catholic included being scriptural and adhering to the creeds and councils of the early church fathers.

To sum up, the English Reformer Bishop of Lincoln Robert Sanderson (1587–1683) expresses this catholic understanding of "reformed" when he writes,

> And here I do profess, that I have lived, so I desire and, by the grace of God, resolved to die in the Catholic Church of Christ, and a true son of the Church of England; which as it stands by law established, is the truth in *doctrine* [the *Articles*] *and Worship* [the *Book of Common Prayer*] agreeable to the Word of God, and in the most agreeable points of both, conformable to the faith and practice of the goldy churches of Christ in the *primitive and purer times* I do firmly believe.[28]

Bishop Sanderson joins with James I and others in seeing themselves as "Catholic Christians" first and foremost. They even demonstrate this reformed catholic understanding when they refer to their sixteenth-century documents on the "doctrine

---

[28] Robert Sanderson, *Nine Cases of Conscience Occasionally Determined* (London: Brome, Wright, & Wilkinson, 1678). Referred to by Christopher Wordsworth in his translation in the Preface. See reference in More and Cross, *Anglicanism*, 15. Brackets and emphasis mine.

[*Articles*] and Worship [Prayer Book]" of the Church of England. They speak of them as "agreeable to the Word of God" and to "primitive and purer times." Notice the twofold catholic source of the Scriptures and the early church. Thus, the leading authoritative sixteenth-century standards of the *Book of Common Prayer* and the *Articles* taken together are understood to mirror these ancient sources of the Holy Scriptures and the Primitive Church of the first five hundred years. Later chapters in this book will substantiate these points. For now, however, this chapter has laid the foundation for an understanding of Anglicanism as reformed catholic, and the meaning of these terms as originally understood by the English Reformers.

The Value of Two Adjectives Together

A definition of Anglicanism with two adjectives together provides a number of benefits. It offers a more accurate meaning. The word *catholic* gives the central point of the definition indicating that the Anglican Way is more than a Medieval version of Roman Catholicism. The catholic is the ancient, early church version prior to the western Church being called Roman Catholic.

At the same time, the word *reformed* has an important place alongside *catholic*. It serves to remind the Church that she can and has drifted from Scripture and the ancient Church. Anglicanism is honest about the need for *ecclesia semper reformunda*, that is "the church must always be reforming." The word *reformed* alerts to the possibility that if the faith once delivered to the saints is confused, the Gospel is ultimately at stake. If the Gospel is lost, so is the Church. Thus, reforming is necessary at times in history, but it should be with a reformed catholic model of back-to-the-sources as it was with the English Reformers.

A further benefit of the two adjectives understood together can also help to overcome divisions that took place between Catholic and Evangelical Anglicans in the nineteenth century. In the early 1800s, a reforming movement arose among a group of Anglican scholars at the University of Oxford. Their concern was what they saw as the increasing secularization of the Church of England. It began with the Enlightenment in Europe in the middle of the previous century (specifically in 1755). This movement had elevated reason above the authority of Scripture and its holy traditions in the Church. A scholar priest named John Keble, therefore, preached his famous "Assize Sermon on National Apostasy" marking the beginning of the Oxford Movement. In it, he called for a return to the apostolic teaching of Scripture and the "Successors of the Apostles" (i.e., the early church fathers). Therefore, these initial leaders of Oxford returned to reformed catholic emphases of the Scriptures and the early church fathers, both of which included sacramental and liturgical teaching. And since the Anglican formularies were reformed catholic documents, Oxford movement leaders like Pusey (and so forth) appealed to them for support of their positions.[29]

---

[29] For example, Pusey appealed to language in the "Postscript" of the *First Book of Homilies* authorized in the *Thirty-Nine Articles* for support of his objective view of real presence. The "Postscript" says, "the Body and Blood of Christ are received under the forms of bread and wine."

The movement however passed through several stages, gradually drifting from the reformed catholic model of the Oxfordian founders.[30] Unfortunately, John Henry Newman gave up on the English Church, abandoning the reformed catholic model and Anglican formularies. When he left, over six hundred Anglican priests followed him to the Roman Catholic Church. The effect of this leader and so many others leaving the Church of England for Rome subtly shifted the Oxford Movement from reformed catholic back in the direction of a more Roman version of catholicism. Much of the movement remained on the reformed catholic side, while other aspects of it morphed into excessive ritualism and even liberalism, called "affirming Anglo-Catholicism" in the twentieth century.[31]

Even within Anglo-Catholicism this movement had variations. Charles Gore, Edward Pusey's successor at Pusey House in Oxford, for example, strongly disagreed with Benediction of the Blessed Sacrament. He even unsuccessfully attempted to have a canon required by the Church of England to prevent the practice. Other Anglo-Catholics disagreed, embracing Eucharistic Adoration. Therefore, the two adjectives *reformed* and *catholic* together can help to direct the Anglo-Catholic Movement back to the intent of its founders.

The reformed catholic model can serve another purpose for the evangelical and low church opponents of Anglo-Catholicism. In some respects, their reaction to Anglo-Catholicism in its ritualistic phase was justified. After Anglo-Catholicism slid into a more papal direction following Newman's departure to Rome, Anglo-Catholics in the late nineteenth and early twentieth centuries embraced the Neo-Thomist movement in Rome and begin to use terms and views of real presence such as transubstantiation which Pusey, Keble, and the early Newman never did. Given the departure of Newman into the Roman Church, many in the Church of England and in the Protestant Episcopal Church in America became convinced that the catholic emphases of the movement were not ancient but Roman. As John Shelton Reed (in his important survey of the history of Anglo-Catholicism, *Glorious Battle*) demonstrates, they were correct—given the turn by some Anglo-Catholics toward a Roman model of catholicism in the late nineteenth century. Unfortunately, the Evangelical reaction failed to recognize the distinction between the reformed catholic approach of the original Oxford Movement leaders and what aspects of Anglo-Catholicism later became.

Since both sides of the Evangelic and Anglo-Catholic division had drifted from the reformed catholic model, increasingly neither lived up to the original model of the English Reformers. As one reads the arguments of the late nineteenth-century Anglo-Catholic and Evangelical debates, it is apparent that the reformed catholic understanding of the Anglican formularies had been lost. The Evangelicals' arguments would have been much more effective in countering the Roman version of Anglo-Catholicism, if only they had adopted the reformed catholic approach that was at the heart of their own heritage. After all, John Jewell and other English Reformers had

---

[30] See John Shelton Reed, *Glorious Battle: The Cultural Politics of Victorian Anglo-Catholicism* (Nashville: Vanderbilt University Press, 2000).

[31] Charles Gore, successor to Edward Pusey, once said, "Let the Germans have the Bible as long as we can keep the Divine Liturgy." Such views probably explain the prevalence of higher critical approaches to the Bible among some Anglo-Catholics in the twentieth to twenty-first centuries.

presented and ably defeated the Roman model with the Scriptures and the early church fathers. As we will see in later chapters, the *Book of Common Prayer* and the finally approved version of the 1571 *Thirty-Nine Articles of Religion* are reformed catholic. They follow an *ad fontes* approach back to the Scriptures and the ancient Church. Instead, late nineteenth-century Evangelicals tended to use an extreme Protestant view of these formularies. They are neither the Protestantism of the general Reformation nor Roman Catholicism. The result was that Evangelicals did not resist the growing Anglo-Catholic Movement's dominance in the Church of England. It would not be until after WWII that Evangelicalism would have a resurgence in the Church of England.

With the loss of the historic understanding of Anglicanism, therefore, the Anglo-Catholic and Evangelical debates of the late nineteenth and early twentieth centuries become—as the saying goes—"ships crossing in the night." Even more tragic, while Anglo-Catholics and Evangelicals fought with each other, liberalism swept in and captured the western and northern parts of the Anglican Communion.

If Evangelicals can re-embrace the reformed catholic approach, and if the Anglo-Catholics can do the same by returning to the original vision of the Oxford Movement, perhaps the two sides might find the true common ground in their mutual heritage of the English Reformation for the sake of the Gospel. No doubt, there will still be differences of conviction about churchmanship (low and high) and vestments, but the strength of the reformed catholic model, as is developed in this book, is that it appeals to the Scriptures and the early church fathers' version of early catholicism to deal with the extremes both of Rome and of Protestantism. The English Reformers were primarily concerned with restoring the ancient Catholic Church in Word, Sacrament, worship, theology, and spirituality.

Thus, the reformed catholic model can serve to restore the heart of the matters of the English Reformation more accurately than any other approach to Anglicanism. With the new opportunities for Anglo-Catholics and Evangelicals to work together in the realignment of Anglicanism, this historic approach can provide a way forward for both to find a new level of unity. Hopefully the reformed catholic understanding of Anglicanism presented in this volume can in some way help Evangelical, Reformed, and Catholic Anglicans find their common roots in the sources of the Scriptures and the early church fathers. It is not so much that the Scriptural and Evangelical or the sacramental and ecclesiastical focal points emphasized by one side or the other are wrong; it is rather that they tend to be excluded from one another in their reactions to each other, when in fact all these aspects are part of the reformed catholic paradigm of the English Reformation. They are all biblically necessary and can complement one another in the way of the ancient Catholic and Undivided Church. Perhaps this work will help to bring the two adjectives of reformed and catholic together, for they have stridently differed from one another in the past. Today the situation is so much different for both groups, who in reality believe in the Lord Jesus Christ, His infallible Word, the Catholic Creeds, and the Anglican formularies. It is a new day with new opportunity to regroup together to build the Kingdom of God.

Caveat Preemptor

Before concluding this introduction, I should offer three points by way of a *caveat*. First, the authors in this book are clergy and laity representing many jurisdictions and dioceses. No one author or jurisdiction is to be held responsible for, nor assumed to believe, what any other author presents. This work generally reintroduces a reformed catholic model. It should not be treated, however, as a "confessional statement." There is range of conviction of higher and lower churchmanship, some with more of an Augustinian/Calvinist or Arminian soteriology, different schools of spirituality, some more on the Eastern or Western sides of Catholicism, and so forth. Even with all these variations, however, the reformed catholic Anglican model of Scripture and the early church fathers reveals that the authors agree in the main on many points. It is just that it should not be assumed that all views in the book are shared by every author.

Second, any attempt to define a position forces the need to contrast it with other views. In this chapter we have seen how the English Reformation had to distinguish itself from late Medieval Roman Catholicism and even aspects of Protestantism in the sixteenth-century Reformation. The contrasts, however, are not intended to unchurch any of God's people. Even though Anglicans differ with their Roman Catholic, Protestant, and Eastern Orthodox brothers and sisters in Christ on many issues (while agreeing with them at many points), the Anglican way still recognizes these other parts of God's Church as believers in the Lord Jesus Christ. Furthermore, the twenty-first century is quite different from the religious climate of sixteenth-century Europe. For example, there has been in the Roman Catholic Church a second Vatican council in the mid-twentieth century. It has resulted in important ecumenical dialogue between Roman Catholic and Anglican brothers and sisters in Christ. It has done the same for all other churches in Christendom. There has also been the important *Nouvelle Theologie* Movement within the Roman Church, which attempts to get behind the Reformation and even the Thomistic philosophy/theology of the thirteenth century to return to the Scriptures and the early church fathers. Sound familiar? Though not entirely the same, it is remarkably similar to the reformed catholic model which also feeds greater ecumenical dialogue and even *rapprochement*.

Much has also happened between the Eastern Orthodox Church and the Anglican Communion by way of ecumenical dialogue in the post-WWII decades. Historic agreed-upon statements have been produced. The Lambeth meetings of Anglican bishops have agreed that the original *Nicene Creed* without the *filioque* clause ("and the Son") should at least be allowed in Anglican worship. It is agreed that eventually the Western Church should return to the initial creed approved by the whole Church. In the meantime, the agreed-upon statements between Anglicans and Orthodox have clarified that the Anglican Church, when using the Western version of the creed, does not mean that God is binary nor that there are two ways to God. The *filioque* does not speak of ontology but the economy of the Trinity, as in the Spirit proceeds from the Father "through" (not literally "and") the Son.

In addition, since the English Church passed through the Reformation, biblical and confessional Anglicanism has been able to find extended levels of Gospel unity with orthodox Protestant denominations. There has even been a huge liturgical and sacramental movement within Evangelicalism for the past forty years leading many toward the historic expressions of the Church including Anglicanism. This liturgical movement among Protestants has led many of them into the historic Catholic expressions of the Church, especially the Anglican branch. Thus, for all these reasons, whatever contrasting and comparing with other parts of Christianity that may occur as this book attempts to clarify the reformed catholic understanding of Anglicanism, these types of arguments should not be taken in any triumphal or exclusive sense. One of the great charisms (gifts) of the Anglican way is that it does not see itself as the one true or only Church.

Thirdly, this book covers many different topics, but it is not exhaustive. In the following pages there are chapters on such subjects as spirituality, hermeneutics, liturgy, Sacrament, music, art, science, literature, major leaders and movements that at times endeavored to recover a reformed catholic understanding Anglicanism, and so forth. In this regard, the book is unique. It puts in one place extensive presentations to develop the reformed catholic Anglican model, but so much more needs to be done. Hopefully, therefore, this book will not be considered the last word. May it be the beginning of much more research! Further work needs to be done for a complete reintroduction of the invaluable reformed catholic understanding of Anglicanism to the current unprecedent realignment of the Anglican Communion.

Conclusion

This introductory chapter has offered a summary of a reformed catholic meaning of *Anglicanism*. I began by presenting two other definitions, the Middle Way and the Reformed Anglican models. In explaining a third, reformed catholic understanding of Anglicanism, I developed a section on the "catholic" side, focusing on the inheritance from the undivided early Church. I followed with the next major portion of the chapter about the adjective *reformed*, which focuses on correcting the present with the past, pursuing a strategy of *ad fontes*.

Perhaps now by way of drawing together the elements of a reformed catholic Anglican definition, a statement given by the twentieth-century Archbishop of Canterbury Geoffrey Fisher (1945–1961) can leave us with a helpful encapsulation. He said:

> The Anglican Communion has no peculiar thought, practice, creed, or confession of its own. It has only the Catholic faith of the ancient Catholic Church, as preserved in the Catholic creeds, and maintained in the Catholic and Apostolic constitution of Christ's Church from the beginning. It may licitly teach as necessary for salvation nothing but what is read in the Holy Scriptures as God's Word written or may be proved thereby. It therefore embraces and affirms such teachings of the ancient Fathers and Councils of the Church as are agreeable to the Scriptures, and thus to be counted apostolic. The Church has no authority to innovate; it is obliged continually, and particularly in times of renewal or reformation, to return to "the faith once delivered to the saints."[32]

---

[32] *The Church Times* (Feb. 1951): 1.

The *Book of Common Prayer*

The Most Rev. Dr. Ray R. Sutton

There was never any thing by the wit of man so well devised, or so sure established, which in continuance of time hath not been corrupted: as, among other things, it may plainly appear by the common prayers in the Church, commonly called the Divine Service: the first original and ground whereof, if a man would search out by the ancient fathers, he shall find, that the same was not ordained, but of a good purpose, and for a great advancement of godliness.

Thomas Cranmer, Preface, First *Book of Common Prayer* 1549

Archbishop Cranmer's Preface to the first edition of the 1549 *Book of Common Prayer* captures in these few words the intent not to be a new form of worship while at the same time needing to reform the liturgy of the late Medieval Western Church. He states that "the first original and ground" of this "Divine Service" was "never anything by wit of man so well devised, or so sure established." "In the continuance of time," however, it had been "corrupted." The basis for Archbishop Cranmer's assessment is the liturgical plumb line of those to whom he refers as the "ancient fathers."

According to Cranmer's own words, therefore, the best phrase to describe the Anglican *Book of Common Prayer* is "reformed catholic." This liturgy is one more key aspect for understanding Anglicanism as reformed catholic and not something else. As overviewed in the "Introduction" to this book, Anglicanism is not simply a halfway point between Protestant and Roman Catholic, a *via media*. Neither is the prayer book. The late nineteenth-century Anglican scholar Evan Daniel negates such an inaccurate approach when he summarizes Cranmer's and other English Reformers intents concerning worship as follows:

> The principles which guided the prayer book revisers were simple. In doctrinal matters they took for their standard of authority the Bible and the belief of the Church for the first five centuries; in framing formularies for the conduct of public worship they retained whatsoever they could from the older service books; in ritual matters they continued to follow the traditions of their own Church ... their object was not to revolutionize but to reform; not to get so far away as possible from the Church of Rome, or from any other Church, but, by retracing the steps whereby the primitive Church of England had "fallen from herself" to return to Catholic faith and practice.[1]

The English Reformers were not striving to find some mythical halfway point, nor were they attempting to "get so far away as possible from the Church of Rome, or from any other Church, but, by retracing the steps whereby the primitive Church of England had 'fallen from herself' to return to Catholic faith and practice." The latter is what Cranmer

---

[1] Evan Daniel, *The Prayer-Book: Its History, Language, and Contents* (London: Wells, Gardner, Darton & Co., 1880), 26. See reference in C. Arthur Lane, *Illustrated Notes on English Church History: From the Earliest Times to the Reformation* (London: SPCK, 1901), 322–323.

mentions in his Preface as the liturgies of the "ancient fathers." This language is anything but an expression to find some "middle way."

The prayer book "revisers" were returning to something ancient for their model. Queen Elizabeth I declared as much in a letter to Roman Catholic princes when she said "that there was no new faith propagated in England; no new religion set up but that which was commanded by our Saviour, practiced by the primitive Church, and approved by the fathers of the best of antiquity." As mentioned in the Introduction, Elizabeth was politically concerned to find a middle way for her country, but this was not her understanding of the Church of England, its beliefs, and certainly not its worship.

Concerning Elizabeth's and the Church of England's view of worship, they are best summarized in the *Canons of the Church of England*. The 30th *Canon Ecclesiastical* summarizes:

> So far was it from the purpose of the Church of England to forsake the churches of Italy, France, Spain, Germany, or any such-like churches, in all things which they held or practiced, that, as the Apology of the Church of England [Reference to Bishop John Jewell's classic work defending the Church of England] confesseth, it doth with reverence retain those ceremonies which doth neither endanger the Church of God, nor offend the minds of sober men; and only departed from them in those particular points, wherein they were fallen from themselves in their ancient integrity, and from the Apostolical Church, which were their first founders. (Brackets mine)

Thus, as Daniel observes the "object" of the English "revisers" was not "to revolutionize but to reform." However, as I further developed in the Introduction, these English Reformers' understanding of *reformed* was not without its other modifier *catholic*. Even if they did use the word *reformed* as a modifier without the other adjective, as in "Reformed Anglican," their view was still reformed catholic. *Reformed* for them meant back to, not away from, the ancient Catholic.

We meet the English Reformation understanding of reformed catholic in an illuminating letter from Queen Elizabeth to the Archbishop of Canterbury, Matthew Parker, Cranmer's successor. She uses the word *reformed* in a "back to" sense. The context of the communication was the late sixteenth-century anti-ritual attempts of the Puritans in the Church of England to strip the liturgy of ornaments, vestments, and ceremonies. Elizabeth is so concerned that she appeals to Archbishop Parker to "reform" what the Puritans are doing back to liturgical practice and theology according to their original design and content. She writes the following:

> We, to our no small grief and discomfort, do hear that ... for lack of regard given thereto in due time, by such superior and principal officers as you are, being the Primate, and other Bishops of your province, ... there is crept and brought into the Church ... an open and manifest disorder and offense to the godly wise and obedient persons, by diversity of opinions, and specially in the external, decent, and lawful rites and ceremonies to be used in the Churches ... We ... have certainly determined to have all such diversities, varieties, and novelties ... as breed nothing but contention, offence, and breach of common charity, and are also against the

laws, good usages, and ordinances of our realm, to be *reformed* and repressed and brought to one manner of uniformity through our whole realm and dominions.[2]

The irony of the Queen's use of the word *reformed* is that she addressed Protestant movements that considered themselves "reformed" but in a different sense. The latter group attempting to alter the liturgy away from ceremony and vestments understood *reformed* in a non-Catholic sense. The Queen's application of the term was back to the ancient and catholic. She meant by her use "reformed catholic." In this statement, she reflects the English Reformation meaning of *reformed* even though the word *catholic* is not mentioned. It is a reforming as stated in Cranmer's Preface to the "ancient fathers" of the historic Catholic Church.

Evan Daniel further clarifies this catholic sense of *reformed* when he corrects the overly reductionistic mischaracterization of the English Reformers as simply "Protestant." He states,

> We do the Anglican reformers a certain injustice in designating them by the negative name of Protestants. They did, indeed, *protest* against many Romish errors; but their main object in all they did and wrote was to affirm positive truth; and they only protested against error for the sake of more clearly defining the truth: so that the name Protestant is not so much inapplicable as inadequate. The Prayer-book is not a mere negation of Romish doctrine and practice. It is Catholic in its essence, and only Protestant by temporary necessity. Its doctrines date from a period when Romish errors had not come into existence; and it is therefore as great an anachronism to call it by the name of Protestant as it would be to call the Church of the Apostles by that name. The best name, and the grandest name that can be bestowed on the Anglican reformers, is that which they themselves rejoiced in—the name of Catholics. It keeps before our minds not a passing phase in the history of our Church, but its permanent and most essential characteristic.[3]

Daniel correctly notes that the word *Protestant* was a designation characteristic of a period of history in reforming the Church. It is not a complete enough term, however, to explain what he says is the "permanent and essential characteristic" of the English Reformers and their liturgy. They saw themselves as returning to what was truly and historically Catholic in reforming the Roman Catholic Church.

In this chapter, therefore, I present the *Book of Common Prayer* as a reformed catholic Anglican liturgy. To develop this thesis, I start by presenting the ancient apostolic and catholic liturgical origins of the services of worship in old Britain until they were corrupted in the late Medieval English Church. Second, I develop how the compilers of the *Book of Common Prayer* in the sixteenth century used the ancient catholic services as their model to return fully to worship in Word and Sacrament. Third, I will contrast the English Reformational liturgical and ceremonial model of reform with the Continental Reformation's regulative principle for reforming worship. In all these introductory ways we find that services of the Anglican prayer book are not simply a halfway house between

---

[2] John Henry Blunt, *The Annotated Book of Common Prayer* (New York: Longman, Green, & Co., 1892), 65.

[3] Daniel, *The Prayer-Book*, 26–27.

Protestant and Catholic, nor are they reformed in the sense of non-Catholic. Rather, they are reformed catholic in the great Anglican tradition of worship going all the way back to the ancient apostolic liturgies for their model.

The Ancient Apostolic and Catholic Origins of the Book of Common Prayer

The liturgy of the *Book of Common Prayer* did not begin with the Roman Catholic Church of the Middle Ages. The prayer book was not crafted *de novo*. Rather, as Cranmer says in his Preface to the first edition, the "first original and ground whereof" is the "ancient fathers." It has liturgical roots predating Medieval services by nearly fifteen hundred years, dating back to the early Church.

The Traditional History of the Liturgy

The nineteenth-century Anglican liturgical history scholar John Henry Blunt summarizes the origins of the *Book of Common Prayer* in the following chart.[4]

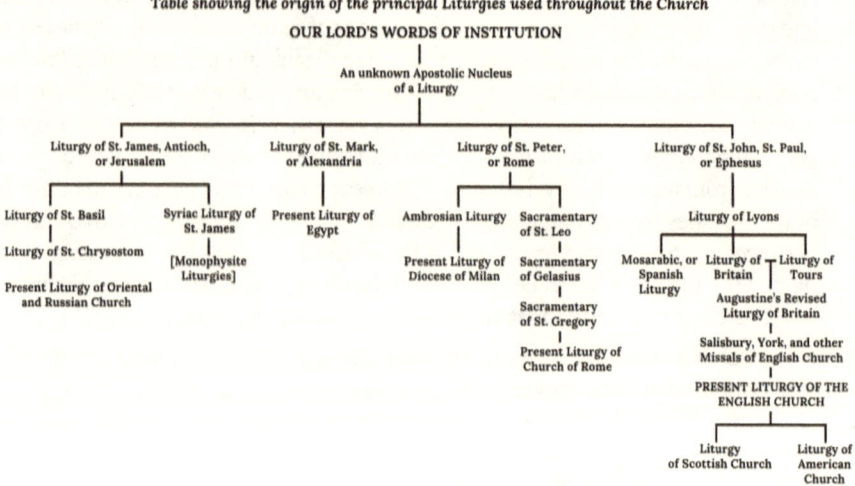

As one may detect from this liturgical summary of the history of the great liturgies of the ancient church, there were four originating from the apostolic community of the first century. The ancient view of worship was that some of the apostles (and their associates like St. Mark) composed the original liturgies on which all others are based in the history of the Church.

The apostles and their apostolic company practiced liturgical worship from the beginning of the Church. They followed the liturgical model of Holy Scripture and their Lord and Master Jesus Christ, who was thoroughly ceremonial in His commitments to worship. The largest corpus of literature in the Bible is a book of worship, the Psalms. The feasts all had set liturgies. According to the Gospels, the Lord Jesus Christ kept all

---

[4] Blunt, *Annotated BCP*, 147.

these patterns of worship. As Blunt says, "Our Lord came, not to abolish, but to transfigure the old Ritual; not to diminish, but to increase its glory; to breathe into its dead forms a Divine and Life-giving Energy. Christian worship, at its first introduction, was not designed to supplant, but to supplement, the ancient Ritual."[5]

To demonstrate our Lord's commitment to the "transfiguration" and not the "abolishing" of Old Covenant patterns and principles of worship, Blunt turns to what he calls the "first Christian Service." It took place on the "eve of our Lord's Passion, and in 'the large Upper Room'—hereafter to become the first Oratory of the Christian Church." It was in the liturgy of the Jewish festival of Passover that Jesus Christ instituted the Eucharist on the night in which He was betrayed. Blunt poignantly summarizes the liturgical transformation:

> Here we witness the meeting point of two Dispensations; the virtual passing away of the Law, and its transfiguration into the Gospel; the solemn Paschal close of the Old Economy, the Holy Eucharistic inauguration of the New. Here we see the whole Representative Church assembled together with its Divine Head.[6]

Blunt continues by detailing what he refers to as "every essential element of Christian Worship introduced and blessed by Incarnate God Himself. The grand central feature of the Service is the Eucharist." Blunt adds,

> Clustering round, and subsidiary to it, we find supplication, intercession, exhortation, benediction, excommunication, and Holy Psalmody: "after they had sung (ὑμνήσαντες), they went out to the Mount of Olives." Here, in the solemn Eucharistic Anthem which accompanied the first Celebration;—the Celebrant, God Incarnate, "giving Himself with His own Hands"; and the Leader of the Holy Choir, God Incarnate, fulfilling His own gracious prediction, "In the midst of the Church will I sing praise to Thee (ὑμνήσω σε)—do we behold the Divine Source of that bright and ever-flowing stream of "Psalms, Hymns, and Spiritual Songs," which was to "make glad the City of God."[7]

Blunt then summarizes the liturgical actions of Christ at the Last Supper:

> In this august and archetypal Service, then, we see all those venerable *essentials* of Christian Worship which it would afterwards devolve upon the Church, under the guidance of the indwelling Spirit, to embody and express in her solemn Liturgies; and for the clothing and reverent performance and administration of which it would be needful for her, under the same Holy Teaching, to borrow and adapt from the Divine Storehouse of Ritual which God had provided in the ancient Ceremonial.[8]

Thus, at Pentecost when the New Covenant Church is born and after three thousand are baptized, we find the apostles following the "Holy Teaching" and liturgical model of the Lord. St. Luke records, "And they devoted themselves to the Apostles' teaching and fellowship, to the breaking of bread, and to the prayers" (Acts 2:42). This passage

---

[5] Blunt, *Annotated BCP*, 52.
[6] Ibid.
[7] Ibid.
[8] Ibid.

mentions two types of liturgical services. The "breaking of bread" is a reference to the Eucharist, as seen elsewhere in the Book of Acts (Acts 20:7–11; 27:33–38). The second service is mentioned in the phrase, "the prayers." These prayers would have been ones used in Temple and Synagogue worship. They became the basis for the daily prayers in the Ancient Church and the Offices of Morning and Evening Prayer in the *Book of Common Prayer*.

Based on these liturgical patterns of the Lord and His Apostles, we find liturgies emerging from the early church. They are presented in the chart above. They are all quite similar as we would expect since they originated with the Apostolic community. All four, however, probably came to have some level of bearing on the worship in the ancient Church of Britain.

On the far right hand side of the chart, we see a liturgy composed by St. John in Ephesus. It was spread through missionary expansion into southern Europe (France) to become the *Gallican Liturgy*. This liturgy migrated into Spain (and Britain), where it was called the *Mozarabic Rite*. This liturgy was undoubtedly the primary service of worship in Britain. As such, it provided the standard for the formation of the *Book of Common Prayer*. It is documented by the first committee as the major ancient source for their reforming of the late Medieval Mass of the Western Church.[9]

The second ancient Apostolic liturgy that had early influence on the worship in Britain was the *Liturgy of St. James*. The first Christians in Britain came directly from Jerusalem. It is documented that the Church was fully established by A.D. 200. Some scholars believe the early Christians in Britain were slaves from the Roman Empire, probably from the Land of Palestine. Other scholars corroborate interesting tradition that may indicate Christians fleeing persecution in Jerusalem (as recorded in the Book of Acts) fled to the southwestern coast of Britain in Cornwall and the vicinity of Glastonbury. These Christians would have brought the early *Liturgy of St. James* in Jerusalem with them in some seminal form. As we will see in a moment, the *Liturgy of St. James* is almost identical to the Eucharistic Service in the *Book of Common Prayer*. Some scholars believe for this reason that the *Liturgy of St. James* has been more influential on the formation of the English liturgy than any other ancient one.

A third ancient liturgy that may have had some bearing on the early worship of Britain is the *Liturgy of St. Mark* from Northern Africa. There is significant evidence that the spirituality of the early Desert Fathers had predominant influence on the Celtic (British) saints. The famous Celtic-Knot symbol of two worlds intersecting one another is also found among the Desert Fathers.

The fourth ancient liturgy that entered the worship of England is the *Liturgy of St. Peter* (Rome). This is documented when the Pope of Rome, St. Gregory, sent a missionary named St. Augustine of Canterbury,[10] to Britain in the late sixth century. Gregory had developed a love for the people of this land when he saw little blond-haired slave children from Britain. He referred to them as appearing to be "Angels," a pun on their ethnicity of

---

[9] Blunt, *Annotated BCP*, 15–16.
[10] Not to be confused with the fourth-century St. Augustine of Hippo.

"Angles."[11] After Gregory became Pope of Rome, he was concerned that the Barbaric Saxons (and Angles) had driven Christianity from the land. He sent St. Augustine to re-evangelize Britain.

When Augustine arrived in Britain, he discovered that the Celtic Church still existed with its own liturgy for worship. He was unfamiliar with it. He wrote to St. Gregory asking for guidance on how to incorporate the *Petrine Liturgy* with theirs. The Pope's response to Augustine was the following:

> You my dear brother are acquainted with the customs of the Roman Church in which you were brought up. But it is my pleasure that if you have found anything either in the Roman or the Gallican or any other Church which may be more acceptable to Almighty God, you carefully make choice of the same; and sedulously teach the Church of the English, which is at present new in the Faith, whatsoever you can gather from the several Churches. For things are not to be loved for the sake of places, but places for the sake of good things. Select, therefore, from each Church those things that are pious, religious, and correct; and when you have made these up into one body, instill this into the minds of the English for their Use.[12]

St. Gregory's counsel is quite enlightening about the ancient liturgies of the English Church. For one, the Pope was aware of the real possibility that the Celtic Service was probably the *Gallican (Mozarabic) Liturgy*. However, for another he acknowledges that it could have been one of the other ancient liturgies. Most significantly, he encouraged Britain weaving the Celtic together into "one body" with the *Petrine Liturgy*. This is indeed what happened in subsequent centuries.

St. Gregory's wise counsel was partially accomplished by St. Osmund Bishop of Salisbury (Sarum) Cathedral in the eleventh century. He drafted the Sarum Rite. It was a combination of the ancient Celtic and Petrine liturgies. Though there were other liturgies at York, London, and elsewhere, the Sarum Rite prevailed as the predominant liturgy of the English Church through the Middle Ages in England before the erosion of this convergence of ancient worship called for reform.

Dom Gregory Dix's Model of Liturgical Revision

Before considering the Cranmerian revisions that returned the worship of England to the ancient Catholic Church, the twentieth-century revisionist theory of Dom Gregory Dix should be addressed. His influential work *The Shape of the Liturgy*—although it has much helpful information—is flawed in its overarching premises used to overturn the Cranmerian model of liturgy.[13]

Chief among these assertions, Dix argues that there was one ancient liturgy on which all the others are based. Dix asserts that it is the liturgy described in the *Apostolical Constitutions*, which he believed was authored by Hippolytus in the second century. Given

---

[11] As in "Angle-Land" (England), East Anglia, and Anglo-Saxon. The Angles were a Germanic tribe from the southern Jutland peninsula, who (together with the Saxons, also from northern Germany) began invading Britain in the fifth century, pushing the Celtic Britons to the west.

[12] St. Gregory, *Opera*, 2:1151. Venerable Bede, *Ecclesiastical History*, 1.27. See citation in Blunt, *Annotated BCP*, 2.

[13] Dom Gregory Dix, *Shape of the Liturgy* (London: Dacre, 1945).

this early date for the liturgy supposedly recorded by Hippolytus, it was plausible that this was a common liturgy on which the others were based. The presumption of Dix is therefore that this liturgy is the model for all other later liturgies. Furthermore, it is this liturgy that should inform all liturgical revision occurring in the mid- to late-twentieth century. The same view was adopted in the twentieth century by virtually all liturgical scholars across Roman Catholic and Protestant lines. Since this supposedly ancient liturgy predated all others, it became the model for liturgical revision. Concerning Anglican liturgical revision in the twentieth century, this assumption provided Dix with the tool he needed to abandon the traditional Cranmerian liturgy of the historic *Book of Common Prayer*, since he argued that what mattered was not the specific wording of the liturgy but merely its overall shape. This reductionistic view enabled revisions of the Anglican liturgy that differed significantly from the Cranmerian service. Thus, liturgical revision of twentieth-century Anglicanism essentially abandoned the Cranmerian and (for that matter) the historic understanding of the ancient origins of the English liturgy. The result was that—in the name of returning to the more ancient liturgy—a modernistic, social justice model was ushered into the revisionary work of new prayer books of Anglicanism, particularly in the northern and western parts of the Communion.

However, liturgical and historical research upended Dix's leading premise.[14] Subsequent scholars discovered that the *Apostolical Constitutions* was not a second- but a fifth-century work and was, in fact, not composed by St. Hippolytus. Therefore, the so-called archetypal liturgy was a fiction, and Dix's premises were destroyed. Simply stated, there was not one common liturgy that "shaped" all the rest. At least, if there was a converging of liturgies it happened late not early. The older view of four basic liturgies from the Apostolic company forming and informing, and not simply shaping, the historic liturgies of the Church East and West remains historically plausible. For Anglicans, the more current and accurate research supports the view that one or more of these ancient liturgies did not simply shape but actually constituted the Services of the Celtic Church. Furthermore, it means the sixteenth-century compilers of the Cranmerian prayer book were more precisely modelling their revisions on ancient precedent. As Cranmer says in his Preface to the prayer book, their work was based on the liturgies of the "ancient fathers."

The Cranmerian *Book of Common Prayer*, therefore, is a return to the worship of the Apostolic Church and the early church fathers. It is a reforming of the late Medieval Roman Catholic liturgy according to the ancient Catholic liturgies. This was the intent and work of the revisers who produced the *Book of Common Prayer*. To demonstrate this reformed catholic Anglican effort, let us consider therefore some of the specifics as a second part of this chapter.

---

[14] See Maxwell E. Johnson, "The Apostolic Tradition," in *Oxford History of Christian Worship*, eds. G. Wainwright and K. B. Westerfield Tucker (Oxford: OUP, 2005), 32–75.

The Ancient Catholic Influence on the *Book of Common Prayer* in Word and Sacrament

As a second aspect of this chapter, I turn to some of the leading ways in which the prayer book is a restoration of the ancient Catholic liturgies. They start with the intent stated in a direction from the King of England. The Crown (Henry VIII) formally tasked in 1542–1543 a Convocation (committee) of bishops and scholars chaired by Archbishop Cranmer with reforming the late Medieval Mass, Breviary, and other liturgical manuals, according to a Biblical and early-Church standard. He sent them a letter directing

> that all Mass-books, Antiphoners, *Portuises* [abridged Breviaries[15]], in the Church of England should be newly examined, corrected, reformed, and castigated from all manner of mention of the Bishop of Rome's name, from all apocryphas, feigned legends, superstitious orations, collects, versicles, and responses; that the names and memories of all saints which be not mentioned in *the Scriptures or authentic doctors* should be abolished and put out of the same books and calendars, and that the service should be made out of *the Scripture and other authentical doctors*.[16]

The king's directive is quite telling. Twice he mentions the standard by which the Medieval services are to be reformed, "the Scriptures and the authentic doctors." The Word of God and the early church fathers were the sources for revising worship in the Church of England.

The Convocation carrying out the Crown's directive lasted seven years. Ironically, it could not fully implement the king's wishes because the *Six Articles* enacted by him prevented much of what he later wanted. After his death in 1548, however, the prayer book was completed. In it we find that the committee reformed worship with the reformed catholic model of "Scripture and the authentic doctors." We see it in the two comprehensive aspects of ancient catholic worship in Word and Sacrament in the prayer book.

The Ancient Primacy of the Word in the Liturgy

First, the ancient catholic primacy of the Holy Scriptures is returned to the liturgy. Everything about the liturgy was founded in the Scriptures, and it is important not to overlook the historic place of Scripture and its reading in the early liturgies of the Church. In the mid-second century, Justin Martyr in his classic work, the *Apology*, observes concerning worship,

> On Sunday, as the day is called, the inhabitants of the town and country assemble together, and the memoirs of the Apostles and the writings of the Prophets are read as long as the time permits. When the reader has finished, the presiding brother makes a discourse, exhorting us to the imitation of those worthies. Then we stand up and pray, and when the prayers are done, bread and wine are brought ... and he who presides sends up thanksgivings and prayers as well as he is able, and the people answer, Amen.

---

[15] Cf. *Oxford English Dictionary*, s.v. "Porteous"; *A Dictionary of the Older Scottish Tongue (up to 1700)*, s.v. "Portu(o)us, -e(o)us, -(o)us." www.dsl.ac.uk/entry/dost/portuous.

[16] Blunt, *Annotated BCP*, 9. Brackets and italics mine.

Notice how the entire service begins with and is built on the Word of God. It was this fundamental catholic commitment of worship that the *Book of Common Prayer* restored.

The most obvious place we find this emphasis in the *Book of Common Prayer* is in the extensive lectionary re-created for all the services. The ancient Church followed a lectionary system based on the one in the Old Covenant. The New Testament books and letters were written to be read in conjunction with these appointed Scripture readings. By the time of the late Middle Ages in the Western Church, however, the lectionary readings had been greatly reduced, to the point where many services did not require reading from the Word of God. The lectionary of the *Book of Common Prayer* corrects this deficiency by calling for Old and New Testament readings for every day, week, and feasts or saints' days. So extensive is the lectionary in the prayer book that if followed, the Bible is read through at least once a year.

Furthermore, every service in the prayer book either begins with Scripture reading (e.g., Confirmation, Baptism, etc.) or includes appointed lessons elsewhere. The Daily Offices of Morning and Evening Prayer are essentially formed as an extension of the Psalms. The largest book of Scripture, Psalms, is understood as the foundation of all worship. It presents the view that Scripture is prayer and to be prayed in worship. The remaining bulk of these morning and evening services is the reading Psalms, the Old Testament, New Testament, and the Apocrypha. They are followed by canticles from the Word of God to be said or sung in response. Scripture is responded with God's Word. The concluding prayers are shaped and driven by Scripture as well.

The effect of the extensive lectionary system requiring so much Scripture to be read as part of Anglican worship and the overall pervasiveness of the Word of God is that it is commonly remarked by someone from a non-Anglican tradition attending a service, "I've never participated in a worship service with so great an amount of Scripture reading." No other liturgical tradition Catholic or Protestant involves the amount of Scripture reading in their worship.

In addition, new set prayers of the prayer book—though there are only a few of these—are founded upon and even quote the Scriptures. The most famous one in the prayer book is the "Prayer of Humble Access." It appears in the Eucharistic service either before or after consecration of the elements. It is based on the Syrophoenician woman, who appealed to Jesus for the crumbs from under the table (Matthew 15).

The primacy of Holy Scriptures in the ancient liturgies is fully recovered in the *Book of Common Prayer*. Matching this ancient commitment to the Word of God, and based upon it, the historic liturgies were sacramental. Thus, we find the sacramental model of the ancient liturgies restored in the *Book of Common Prayer* in its structure as well as in its specific service of Holy Communion.

Ancient Sacramental Order and Theology in the Prayer Book

Second, the ancient centrality of the Sacrament along with the Word is fully restored in the prayer book with the reformed catholic model of worship. To begin, it should be recognized that the overall order of the prayer book follows the seven Sacraments. After the Daily Offices of Morning and Evening Prayer, the Eucharistic service appears toward the beginning in most editions of the prayer book. In other versions it follows the Eucharistic propers of collects and Scripture readings for Holy Communion. Whether before or after, the Eucharist is placed with its propers in such a location in the prayer book that it becomes the foundational sacramental service of worship.

In the remainder of the prayer book, the order is shaped by the other sacramental services. They are Baptism, Confirmation, Marriage, Unction for reconciliation in relation to the service for Divine healing, and the Litany of Last Rites. The prayer book concludes with the Ordinal, the seventh Sacrament. Taken as a whole, the *Book of Common Prayer* is book-ended with the Sacrament of Holy Communion at the beginning and the Ordinal at the end. Thus, like the ancient liturgies, all of the *Book of Common Prayer* literally has a sacramental cast to it.

Furthermore, since the Eucharistic service was the primary liturgy among the services of the ancient Church, the rite of Holy Communion particularly evidences a return to historic worship. It was particularly necessary since the late Medieval Mass had been so corrupted over time, indicating primary departure from the early liturgies in many ways. As developed in the chapter "Re-Formed Catholic Anglicanism on the Sacraments," a novel and exclusive view of a transubstantiated real presence and the theology of re-sacrificing of Christ in the Eucharist had been injected into the Eucharistic service of the Western Church in the Middle Ages. The effects were devastating for the Church and the laity. With a theology of automatic grace (*ex opere operato*) whereby faith was not necessary for the Sacrament to be effectual, the Church manipulated grace via the Sacrament. Magical and superstitious practices were able to enter the Church, centering around the Eucharist.

In addition, the effects of these novelties had virtually eliminated lay participation in the Eucharist. A lay person only watched the priest through holes in large rood screens between the altar and the congregation as the priest consecrated and received the Sacrament. Lay people typically never actually received the Sacrament. As a result, the Medieval lay person may have partaken of Holy Communion just three times in his life: confirmation, marriage, and last rites. Even at that, given the superstition that had arisen due to a transubstantiated view of real presence, whereby it averred that the elements are physically transformed into the Body and Blood of Christ, the chalice had been removed from lay participation. The layman only received Holy Communion in one kind, the Host, because of a superstitious fear that a lay communicant might spill the physical Blood of Christ. Also, children had been removed from receiving the Eucharist, lest they spill, drop, or mishandle the elements. In both cases, infrequent Communion and only with one element, these alterations were over superstitious fears. None of these practices and the theology behind them existed in the apostolic and early church.

The Ancient Liturgical Order in the Prayer Book

Therefore, the Eucharistic service of the *Book of Common Prayer* abandons all of the late Western Medieval novelties. Frequent Communion in both kinds is restored, along with a return to the liturgies of the "ancient fathers." However, an overview of the complete restructuring of the Eucharist as well as significant theological changes and additional prayers via the ancient model reveals the extensive reach of the reformed catholic liturgical effort back to the early church liturgies.

Concerning the re-ordering of the Eucharistic service, for example, if we compare the ancient *Gallican* or *Mozarabic* liturgy with the *Book of Common Prayer*, we see below the similarity. The following is the order of *The Gallican Liturgy*.

1. A lesson from the Old Testament
2. A lesson from the Epistles
3. Benedicite (Gradual)
4. The Gospel
5. Sermon
6. Prayers for the people
7. Dismissal of catechumens
8. Address to the people on the subject of the day
9. Offertory, accompanied by an anthem
10. The elements placed on the holy table and covered with a veil
11. Recitations of the tablets called diptychs, containing the names of living and departed saints
12. Salutation or kiss of peace
13. Collect "*Ad pacem*"
14. Sursum Corda: "Lift up your hearts"
15. Preface or Thanksgiving, the people joining, at the proper place, in singing the Tersanctus (Holy, Holy, Holy)
16. Commemoration of the Lord's words and manual acts at the institution of the Sacrament
17. Collect, often containing an oblation of the elements, and a prayer of sanctification by the Holy Spirit
18. Breaking of bread
19. The Lord's Prayer
20. Benediction of the people
21. Communion accomplished with the singing of a psalm or anthem
22. Thanksgiving [17]

The Anglican scholar Daniel concludes, "Let the reader compare this outline [of the Gallican liturgy] with our own Communion Service, and he will at once see that in all essential matters the mode of celebrating the Holy Eucharist in the ancient Gallican Church is identical with that of the Church of England."[18] Specifically in this overall structure, the Gallican service included what was called the *Mass of the Catechumenate* with the *Mass of the Faithful*. Note that the catechumens are released before the sacramental part of the liturgy, indicating that they participated in the service before that point. The Holy Communion service of the *Book of Common Prayer* restores the

---

[17] William Palmer, *Origines Liturgicae: Or Antiquities of English Ritual and a Dissertation on Primitive Liturgies* (Oxford: Oxford University Press, 1839), 1:158.

[18] Daniel, *The Prayer-Book*, 10.

complete liturgy by following this ancient pattern. Cranmer wanted the catechetical ministry of the Word to precede the Sacrament as did the early liturgies.

Like the ancient liturgies, the prayer book Eucharistic service combines the *Mass of the Catechumenate* with the *Mass of the Faithful*. The first half of this liturgy called ante-communion, centers around the Word prayed, read, preached, and the confession of the faith with ancient Nicene Creed. The second, sacramental half of the service begins with the offerings and prayers of the people leading into confession of sin, consecration, and reception of the Sacrament. Thus, the order of the service of Holy Communion in the prayer book was a complete recovery of the *Gallican Liturgy*.

Two Differences

However, there were two significant places where the Cranmerian prayer book makes some alteration. They are the addition of the Ten Commandments at the beginning of the service and the placement of the *Gloria in Excelsis* after the reception of the Sacrament. Nevertheless, neither was without some liturgical and theological basis founded in the ancient liturgies.

Concerning the inclusion of the Ten Commandments in the first half of the service, it appears to have precedent in ancient worship. An early opponent to Christianity named Pliny the Younger wrote a letter to his Emperor, Trajan, in the early second century. He was governor of Pontus/Bithynia from AD 111–113. In the letter, he tells of interviews with Christians, his torture of them, and observations regarding their worship. He writes,

> They asserted, however, that … they were accustomed to meet on a fixed day before dawn and sing responsively a hymn to Christ as to a god, and to bind themselves by oath, not to some crime, but not to commit fraud, theft, or adultery, not falsify their trust, nor to refuse to return a trust when called upon to do so. When this was over, it was their custom to depart and to assemble again to partake of food—but ordinary and innocent food.[19]

Notice Pliny's record of how the early Christian worship involved "to bind themselves by oath." It was part of a pre-service of catechesis, the *Mass of the Catechumenate*, that was joined with a following liturgy for the reception of the Sacrament, *The Mass of the Faithful*.

The details of the oath included "not to commit fraud, theft, or adultery, not to falsify their trust, nor to refuse to return a trust when called upon to do so." This form of oath renewal was perhaps a reference to oath renewal with the Ten Commandments. In Holy Scripture, renewing the covenant was by reaffirmation of the oath to God by means of Ten Commandments. They are actually called the covenant (Deut 4:13). Thus, when the covenant was restored with the people of God before they entered the Promised Land, they engaged in a liturgical oath renewal ceremony. The priests stood on one mountain as the people were on another mountain opposite it. The priests read the commandments with their curses and blessings as the people answered antiphonally in response their "Amen." Then they stood before Moses pledging anew their commitment

---

[19] Pliny, *Letters*, 10.96–97.

to the Lord by taking an oath before the covenant representative via liturgical rehearsal of the Ten Commandments. Deuteronomy records,

> And Moses summoned all Israel and said to them, … Keep the words of this covenant and do them, that you may prosper in all that you do. You are standing today, all of you, before the LORD your God: the heads of your tribes, your elders, and your officers, all the men of Israel, your little ones, your wives, and the sojourner who is in your camp, from the one who chops your wood to the one who draws your water, so that you may enter into the sworn covenant of the LORD your God, which the LORD your God is making with you today, that he may establish you today as his people, and that he may be your God, as he promised you, and as he swore to your fathers, to Abraham, to Isaac, and to Jacob. It is not with you alone that I am making this sworn covenant, but with whoever is standing here with us today before the LORD our God, and with whoever is not here with us today. (Deut 29:2, 9–15, ESV)

Given that the covenant was summarized in the Ten Commandments, the Israelites would have recited them as the means of oath renewal. It is therefore reasonable to assume that what Pliny observed in early Christian worship was something similar. It is further understandable that, since Cranmer and his revision committee researched the "ancient fathers," they would have come across reference to the use of the Ten Commandments in worship.

Whether or not the Convocation compiling the *Book of Common Prayer* was aware of Pliny's statement or another ancient resource, the replacement of the *Mass of the Catechumenate* in the Eucharistic service is the strongest reason for understanding why Cranmer and the revisers restored the Ten Commandments to the Mass. The Ten Commandments, along with the Lord's Prayer and Creed, have always been essential pieces to catechesis. The ancient catechisms included them. Thus, their recitation would have been involved no doubt in the *Mass of the Catechumenate.* Cranmer was self-consciously restoring the *Mass of the Catechumenate.* Given that the Lord's Prayer and the Creed were brought back in this context, the catechesis of the revised service of *Holy Communion* would have been deficient without the inclusion of the Ten Commandments. It is easy to see why in Cranmer's mind it would have been necessary to complete the ancient standards of catechesis. The Ten Commandments also join with the Lord's Prayer and the Creed to inform better a fuller foundation for moral theology according to Scripture and the early church fathers. The addition of them is perfectly consistent with a reformed catholic liturgy.

Regarding the placement of the *Gloria* at the end of the service of Holy Communion in the *Book of Common Prayer,* this alteration reflected what has been described as Cranmer's theology of ascent in the liturgy. This view is based on ancient understanding of the liturgy as mystically transporting the congregation into heaven. All the ancient liturgies embody this theology of ascent. The liturgy is understood from the very beginning as ascending the people of God on earth into heaven. The culmination of this ascent is expressed in words said or sung as part of all these liturgies with specific language. What is called the anaphora begins when the priest says the *sursum chorda,* "Lift up your hearts." The congregation responds, "We lift them up unto the Lord." Then follow versicles with the Eucharistic word *thanks* (the meaning of the term εὐχραριστία *eucharistia*). The priest states, "Let us give thanks unto the Lord." The people answer, "It is meet and right so to do."

The priest continues with an exchange that leads to direct quotation of Scripture from heavenly scenes of worship. He says, "It is very meet, right, and our bounden duty, that we should times and in all places give thanks (εὐχαριστεῖν *eucharistein*) unto thee, O Lord, Holy Father, Almighty, Everlasting God." Then the assumption of having ascended into heaven is expressed as the priest says, "Therefore with angels and archangels and all the company of heaven, we laud and magnify thy glorious Name, evermore praising thee and saying ..." At that point, the congregation joins in response singing the very words of Scripture that Isaiah heard from the lips of the seraphim (Isa 6:3) and which St. John heard echoed by angels, archangels, and departed saints when he had visions of heaven (Rev 4:8), "Holy, Holy, Holy, Lord God of hosts; heaven and earth are full of thy Glory: Glory be to thee, O Lord Most High. Amen."

This language is virtually a direct quote from Isaiah's and St. John's record of heavenly worship (Isa 6; Rev 4–5). The heavenly exchange is further understood to take place in earthly worship as the writer to the Hebrews says, "therefore seeing we also are surrounded with so great a cloud of witnesses" (Heb 12:1).

Based on these Scriptures and ancient liturgies, Cranmer wanted to restore the early view that worship is ascending up to Christ to commune with Him. It countered the late Medieval emphasis of bringing Christ down to the altars of earth as the elements were falsely presumed to be transubstantiated.

Significantly, the language of glory brought into the *Sanctus* mentioned above is also identical to what the angels sing around the shepherds when Christ is born. It is a convergence of heaven and earth as a "multitude of heavenly hosts" sing, "Glory to God in the highest" (Luke 2:13). Therefore, the revisers of the prayer book with their ancient theology of ascent, placed the *Gloria* nearest to the reception of the Sacrament to emphasize the high point of traversing the heavenly Mount Zion to the heavenly Jerusalem to commune with the Lord (Heb 12:22). It is true that this was a shift in actual placement of the *Gloria*. The ancient liturgies put it at the beginning of the service to underscore the same theology. Though in a different location in the liturgy, nevertheless, the early church theology of ascent is retained. Moreover, by placing the *Gloria* at the highest point of this liturgical ascent immediately after receiving Holy Communion, Cranmer undoubtedly thought to make ascent in the liturgy even more emphatic. However, in the history of the prayer book, virtually all later editions of it allow for the *Gloria* to be sung at the beginning. Either way, the conviction of ascending into heaven in the liturgy is an essential part of the Eucharistic service in the *Book of Common Prayer* with the Biblical and ancient song of the angels.

Thus, the early church sacramental order and theology of the Eucharist is restored in the prayer book. Not only do we find ancient precedent in the restructuring of the Eucharistic service of the prayer book, we also see the same approach to reform in the particular prayers and theology related to the Canon of the Mass, or the consecration of the bread and the wine in Holy Communion.

The Ancient Prayers of Consecration in the Prayer Book

Concerning some of the particulars, although the scope of this chapter does not permit a complete analysis, brief comment should be made about the prayer book's Canon of Consecration and other prayers restored by following ancient liturgies. The Canon of the Mass in the late Medieval Western Church had deviated considerably from the early church.

The most important aspect of the ancient consecration that is restored in the prayer book is the Biblical view of sacrifice to the Eucharist. In the Middle Ages, the consecration of the elements was understood to be a re-sacrifice of Christ on the altar. In the prayer book service, any sense of re-sacrifice foreign to the early church is removed. F. E. Brightman in his work, *The English Rite*, explains how the Roman Canon was "adjusted" in the prayer book consecration and other prayers. He refers to a threefold sense of sacrifice as "(a) a commemoration of our Lord's *historical* self-oblation in his death on the cross; (b) as a sacrifice of praise and thanksgiving for the benefits of redemption so secured, and (c) as the offering of the Church, of ourselves, our souls and bodies."[20] These three aspects of sacrifice are restored in the Prayers of Consecration, Oblation, and Dedication in the prayer book.

As for the restoration of the Eucharist as a "commemoration" in the Prayer of Consecration, the Canon of speaks of the "once for all sacrifice of Christ" commemorated in the Eucharist. Blunt has this to say:

> The Priest stands there as the vicarious earthly representative of the invisible but one true and only Priest of the Heavenly Sanctuary: acting "in His Name," and "by His commission and authority" (Article xxvi of the *Articles of Religion*), he brings into remembrance before the Eternal Father the one and only everlasting sacrifice which was once for all made and "finished upon the Cross" [Article xxvi], but is perpetually pleaded, offered and presented, by the One Everlasting Priest in heaven. For Christ as our Great High Priest, who "ever liveth to make intercession for us," and Who is the ever-acceptable Victim and Propitiation for our sins, doeth indeed no more that which He pronounced to be "finished" on Calvary, but evermore pleadeth for our sake that which He did.[21]

The twentieth-century Anglican theologian Eric Mascall adds,

> It is in the sacramental order that the Mass is a sacrifice. That is to say, it is a sacrifice not because Christ is dying at a particular time on a particular altar, as he died once at a particular time on a particular cross, but because the elements of bread and wine which are at that time on the altar are the divinely appointed [commemorative] signs of the sacrifice ... The Mass is therefore neither a new sacrifice nor a part of the one Sacrifice; it is the one Sacrifice in its totality, present under a sign ... Nothing happens to Christ in the historical order as a result of the Eucharistic consecration. What happens in the historical order as a result of the Eucharistic consecration happens to the bread and the wine; which become not by

---

[20] Frank Edward Brightman, *The English Rite: Being a Synopsis of the Sources and Revisions of the Book of Common Prayer* (London: Rivingtons, 1915), 1:cvi (brackets mine).

[21] Blunt, *Annotated BCP*, 390.

change of physical properties but by sacramental causality, the Body and Blood of Christ, so that the one Sacrifice is made present in the Church as the ground of the Church's existence and the source of the Church's life.[22]

Mascall makes the important observation that the restoration of Eucharist as a commemorative sacrifice restores the sense of "sign," what he calls "sacramental causality." He elaborates on the meaning of *sacrament* as a sign "of a very special kind.... The purpose of a sign is to represent; and the purpose of that kind of sign which is a sacrament is to re-present, to make present, to effect, that which is represented.... A sacrament is a sign which has effective causality, a sign which brings about what it signifies."[23]

Mascall's explanation of *sacrament* helps us to understand the ancient Hebrew meaning of another commemorative sacrificial term in Christ's Words of Institution quoted in the consecration. The word is *remembrance* (Greek ἀνάμνησις *anamnesis*), but it is used with a Jewish understanding. A remembrance in the Old Testament was a memorial sacrifice that commemorated an event. Passover for example was a memorial sacrificial meal commemorating a once for all, unrepeatable event. However, J. Leenhardt in an essay, "This is My Body," found in a small book, *Essays on the Lord's Supper*, develops the Jewish meaning of memorial sacrifice or remembrance as "bringing the past into the present." He writes of St. Paul, "Remembrance was not for him mental recollection, an evocative thought. Remembrance was for him the restoration of the past situation which has for the moment disappeared. To remember is to make present and actual."[24] This understanding of *remembrance* in every Jewish celebration of Passover reflecting the view that in partaking the meal "you were there."

Thus, the consecration of the Eucharist as a commemorative sacrifice is not a re-sacrifice, nor a representation; it is sacramental participation in the once for all sacrifice of Christ. As the French Protestant theologian, Frère Max Thurian develops the commemorative nature of the Eucharist in his *L'Eucharistie*,

> It is the sacramental *presence* of the sacrifice of the Cross by the power of the Holy Spirit and the Word, and the liturgical *presentation* of this sacrifice of the Son by the Church to the Father, as a *thanksgiving* for all his blessings and in *intercession* for their continuation. It is the *participation* by the Church in the intercession of the Son before the Father in the Holy Spirit, for the application of salvation to all men and the coming of the Kingdom in glory. It is the *offering* which the Church makes of herself to the Father, united to the sacrifice and intercession of the Son, as her supreme *adoration* and her perfect *consecration* in the Holy Spirit.[25]

Geddes MacGregor in his book, *Corpus Christi: The Nature of the Church according to the Reformed Tradition* summarizes well the participatory nature of the Eucharistic sacrifice in the once for all sacrifice of Christ. He says,

---

[22] Eric L. Mascall, *Corpus Christi: Essays on the Church and the Eucharist*, 2nd ed. (London: Longmans, Green, & Co., 1965), 135–136.

[23] Ibid., 132.

[24] Ibid., 158.

[25] Ibid., 162–163.

> Because Christ, in surrendering himself completely, has offered up the only worthy sacrifice, there is no sacrifice or oblation or gift that a Christian may dare to offer to God *except* by participation in the Church, the Body of Christ, which being united to Christ its Head, participates in the sacrifice since he has graciously willed to unit it himself as his Body ... The Church, in receiving Christ in the Sacrament, offers itself with Christ.[26]

Thus, the commemorative emphases of the Prayer of Consecration in the Canon convey the sense of uniting with Christ. Through the consecratory prayer, the Church unites with and participates in Christ's once for all sacrifice.

A second prayer in the prayer book Eucharistic service offers another sense of sacrifice. It is the prayer of oblation. Blunt summarizes it when he says, "The Priest makes the Oblation actually and verbally when he says, 'Do this,' etc. and afterwards verbally, and with greater fulness, in the 'Prayer of Oblation' which follows the actual [consecration] or communion."[27] An oblationary sacrifice in Scripture is a thanksgiving memorial. It too was of a participatory nature. It is a kind of thanksgiving that participates in a previous sacrifice.

The Anglican theologian C. B. Moss explains that the sacrificial language Jesus used in His Words of Institution is that of the oblationary sacrifice in the Old Testament called a peace offering. Jesus' statement, "For this is My blood of the Covenant, which is poured out for many" is taken from Moses' use of the same language in another sacrificial scene in Exodus 24. Moses offers sacrifices and throws the blood on the altar and the people. After casting the blood on the people, he says, "Behold the blood of the covenant" (Exod 24:8). Moss points out that the passage specifically says that the sacrifices were "whole burnt and peace offering" (Exod 24:5). A peace offering was a sacrifice that followed others. It was unique in that the priest and the offeror's family ate the sacrifice together; it was a sacrificial meal. Importantly, it was not the sin, or propitiatory, offering that atoned for sin. Moss refers to the "Holy Eucharist, corresponding to the feast upon the sacrifice which belonged to the peace-offering."[28] Thus, the Prayer of Oblation memorializes by way of giving thanks for Christ our Peace.

A third Prayer of Dedication offers specific "praise and thanksgiving." Mascall states that

> the prayer of oblation in the English Prayer Book meant by "this our sacrifice of praise and thanksgiving" a sacrifice in which praise and thanksgiving are what we offer, and this interpretation is often supported by the exhortation in Hebrews xiii, 5, "Through him then let us continually offer up a sacrifice of praise to God, that is, the fruit of lips that acknowledge his name."[29]

This is the subjective aspect of the praise and thanksgiving. However, Mascall also indicates that there is an objective aspect as well. He says,

---

[26] Geddes MacGregor, *Corpus Christi* (Eugene, OR: Wipf & Stock, 2004), 247.

[27] Blunt, *Annotated BCP*, 390.

[28] C. B. Moss, *The Christian Faith* (London: SPCK, 1943), 368–369.

[29] Mascall, *Corpus Christi*, 189.

The phrase "sacrifice of praise," *thusia aineseos*, is used in the Septuagint of Leviticus for the sacrifice of the peace-offering, the *thusia soteriou*, which occurs also a verse or two later in the combined form "peace-offering of praise"; we may note that in the Hebrew text the word is not "praise" but "thanksgiving" (*todah*). [Lev. vii, 2, 3, 5, LXX; vii, 12, 13, 15, E.V.V.] What Hebrews, then, is telling Christians to offer with their lips is not their own praises but the sacrifice of the peace-offering, the one sacrifice which would continue in the Messianic kingdom; and this is in its Christian context is nothing other than the sacrifice of Christ, who is "our peace."[30]

These points match Moss's observation of the sacrificial language of Christ's words being that of peace offering.

The Prayer of Dedication uses the language of another Old Testament sacrifice called the whole-burnt offering. This sacrifice entailed the burning of the whole animal to represent the complete dedication of the offeror's life. The prayer says, "And here we offer and present unto thee, O Lord, ourselves, our souls and bodies, to be a reasonable, holy, and living sacrifice unto thee." This statement is based on St. Paul's exhortation, "Present yourselves as a living sacrifice, holy and acceptable, which is your spiritual service" (Rom 12:1). Participation in Holy Communion was also considered to be the sacrificial dedication of oneself to the Lord.

Thus, all of these Biblical and ancient understandings of sacrifice are restored in the Eucharistic prayers of consecration, thanksgiving, and dedication. They replace the false view of the Eucharist as re-sacrifice. Mascall refers to a helpful insight by C. W. Duggmore in his book, *The Mass and the English Reformers*. Duggmore refers to how some early English Reformers

> in casting off the medieval notion of daily pleading before God of the sacrifice of Christ by the celebrating priest, they also jettisoned the wholly scriptural belief in the High Priestly work of Christ, himself pleading before God his sacrifice upon the Cross. Though they believed in the mystical union betwixt Christ and his Church, they were, therefore, unable to see that this belief must logically include the idea of the Church as the mystical Body of Christ, through Christ its Head, pleading in the heavenly places the sacrifice once offered on the Cross. This theological blind spot was to mar the Reformed Catholic position in England until after the danger of a papal Counter-Reformation under Elizabeth had passed, and the Caroline divines had recovered something that was lost.[31]

From this statement we see that there was a reformed catholic commitment involved in restoring the ancient Eucharist, but it took the complete century of the English Reformation.

Moving from the prayers of consecration related to sacrifice, one final prayer needs to be considered that was included from the ancient liturgies. It is the Prayer of Invocation called the *epiclesis*. This ancient prayer invokes the Holy Spirit to the elements and to the people. As indicated in the *Gallican Liturgy* it was part of the ancient service. However, the Medieval Western liturgy had over time dropped the epiclesis. It is not part

---

[30] Mascall, *Corpus Christi*, 189–190.
[31] Ibid., 184.

of the Roman Eucharistic service. It is re-introduced in the 1549 Anglican liturgy by invoking the Holy Spirit to "these thy creatures of bread and wine." It "occurs in the ancient Catholic liturgy of both East and West, excepting only the Roman, and those derived from it."[32] Subsequent revision in the 1552 and the 1662 liturgies changed the wording to invoke the Holy Spirit to the people receiving the Sacrament.[33] Nevertheless, Blunt argues that the intent of invoking the Holy Spirit to the elements is still "implied" even though the wording is altered. He says, "The clause in our present [1662] Office continues as implied or oblique invocations of the Holy Ghost, since it is only through His Divine operation that we, by receiving God's 'creatures of bread and wine' can 'be made partakers of Christ's most Blessed Body and Blood." He adds, "But we may be allowed to wish, with Bishops Horsley and Wilson, and the best informed English Divines, that the direct Invocation had been left untouched."[34] Blunt along with many "English Divines" regretted that the 1662 BCP modified the epiclesis.

However, not all parts of Anglicanism opted for an "implied epiclesis." The Scottish liturgy of 1637 maintained the original, explicit epiclesis invoking the Holy Spirit to the elements. It was this epiclesis that was brought into the first American prayer book adopted in 1789. It has remained in this Eucharistic liturgy of the prayer book. Thus, whether implicit following the 1552/1662 modified version of the epiclesis or adhering to the explicit invocation in relation to the elements according to the first 1549 BCP, the ancient prayer invoking the Holy Spirit to the Eucharist was restored in the *Book of Common Prayer.*

Therefore, in form and specific detailed aspects of the service of Holy Communion in the *Book of Common Prayer,* this liturgy restored the early church liturgy of the Eucharist. Many other points could be made in support of how the revisers fulfilled the ancient model. However, the ancient catholic approach to reform was challenged shortly after the first 1549 edition of the prayer book. For a brief period of time, another version revised the revision. In this we see a struggle introduced over the model of reforming worship. Nevertheless, it affords the opportunity to learn how the revisions of the prayer book over time end up sustaining a reformed catholic approach.

The Reformed Catholic Approach to Correcting Errors

As was noted in the Introduction of this book, the reformed catholic Anglican model differed from some of the other approaches to reforming corrupted Medieval theology and practice at the time of the Reformation. We see this particularly regarding two basic models of worship between the European and English Reformers.[35] However, the difference in approach had little bearing on the first *Book of Common Prayer.*

Blunt summarizes the reason when he says, "Cranmer had much in correspondence with Melanchthon and some other German divines ... but these foreign reformers had scarcely any influence upon the Prayer Book of 1549." Melanchthon and Bucer did assist the Archbishop of Cologne, Hermann, in reforming the liturgy. They drew on some of

---

[32] Blunt, *Annotated BCP,* 389.

[33] Some ancient liturgies invoked the Holy Spirit to the people.

[34] Blunt, *Annotated BCP,* 389.

[35] The Lutheran model for reforming worship was quite similar to the English approach.

Luther's work, especially his Baptismal Office. Blunt observes, however, "This volume [Hermann's Book] contributed little to our Prayer Book beyond a few clauses in the Litany and some portions of the Baptismal Service; and it is somewhat doubtful whether in the case of the Litany our English form was not in reality the original of that in Hermann's book." Blunt expresses the English perspective, therefore: "Most likely the latter [Hermann's liturgy] was translated and brought before Convocation [the prayer book revisers chaired by Cranmer] with the hope that it would have much influence. But the Committee of Revision were too wise and too learned in Liturgical matters to attach much importance to it."[36]

Blunt concludes in a footnote to his comments, "Foreigners were very forward in interfering, but their suggestions were civilly put aside at this time."[37] He importantly goes on to explain the reason for putting aside the suggestions of foreigners. He says, "The Reformation [in England] had been strictly Catholic in its origin and in its official progress, and the repudiation of foreign interference with the Church of England had been one of its main features."[38] That is, the English Reformers were largely objecting to the late Medieval liturgy because it was a foreign service originating in Rome that had taken over the historic worship practiced in Britain, the *Gallic Liturgy*. It too was foreign, but it had been part of English Christianity from the beginning of its Church. As has been pointed out, the Convocation revisers were primarily applying Cranmer's principle expressed in his Preface to the first prayer book to return to the liturgies of the "ancient fathers."

Unfortunately, however, the guiding principle of restoring the worship of the early church fathers was relaxed in the second revision of the prayer book. Almost immediately after the first edition was approved in 1549, Continental reformers like Calvin in Geneva and others began criticizing the Anglican liturgy. Blunt states that "foreign interference now arose from a different quarter, Calvin and his associates endeavoring ... to bias the mind of England towards Genevan Presbyterianism rather than Anglican Catholicity." He further documents that "Calvin himself thrust a correspondence upon the Protector Somerset, upon the young King [Edward VI], and upon Archbishop Cranmer ... in which he urges the Protector to push the Reformation further than it had hitherto gone." The German Reformers Peter Martyr and Martin Bucer, neither of whom Blunt says, "could understand the English language were placed in the most important positions at Oxford and Cambridge by Somerset."[39]

Cranmer also unwittingly contributed to what became a problem for him by graciously housing for six months in his own home another European reformer name John à Lasco. He became part of a schismatic center in London opposing the Catholic model of the English Reformation. Another European reformer from Geneva, Poullain, was allowed to settle in Glastonbury with similar opposing views to the first prayer book. Blunt insightfully assesses the effect when he says,

---

[36] Blunt, *Annotated BCP*, 16.
[37] Ibid., 16 n. 3.
[38] Ibid., 19.
[39] Ibid.

These appointments shew what manner in which the Church of England was sagaciously leavened with the foreign Protestantism by those who wished to reduce its principles and practices to their own low ritual and doctrinal level; and they are but a few of the many indications which exist that the Puritanism by which the Church was so imperiled during the succeeding hundred and twenty years arose out of foreign influences thus brought to bear upon the young Clergy and Laity of that generation.[40]

What Blunt refers to as Continental, foreign influence to "push the Reformation further" included the "reduction of the [liturgical] principles" used by the original reformed catholic revisers of the prayer book. The different model of reform emerges over the second revision of the prayer book in 1552. Quite tellingly, it appears when certain Lords in England push Cranmer to go beyond what he was willing to accommodate in this revision. It concerns a last-minute attempt before the newly approved revision was to be printed. Certain European reformers not mentioned by name wanted to remove the requirement of kneeling to receive Holy Communion. In Cranmer's objection to the Lords who had requested this alteration, he summarizes the leading liturgical principle for objecting to kneeling that exposes the completely different approach to worship from that of the English Reformation, an approach called the regulative principle of worship.

Cranmer summarizes this principle and his objections in his letter to the lords. He states the objectionable regulative principle as, "'But' say they, 'It is not commanded in the Scripture to kneel, and whatsoever is not commanded in Scripture is against the Scripture, and utterly unlawful and ungodly."[41] This is the principle of worship that only what is commanded explicitly in Scripture is to be done in worship. Cranmer says that this is "the chief foundation of the Anabaptists and of other diverse sects." This was true, but Cranmer knew that more than the Anabaptists used this principle. The regulative principle of only doing in worship what is commanded was in fact the leading maxim for determining what should be done in worship by the Continental reformers such as Calvin and others. It became the controlling principle of the Puritans in their objections to prayer book worship. As Cranmer rightly observes, if the regulative principle is true then "take away the whole [prayer] book of service," which is precisely what the Puritans and the Presbyterians did by implementing their non-liturgical, regulative maxim of worship.

The regulative principle sounds Biblical, when in fact it is not. No doubt what is commanded should be done, but where in Scripture does it say that only what is commanded is to be observed? There is no such statement. The regulative principle is a contrived canon of persuasion foisted on the Bible in the name of the Bible. Simply put, the regulative principle of only doing in worship what is explicitly commanded is nowhere to be found in the Bible. Rather, what we find in Scripture is that the worship of the New Testament continued what had been previously commanded and patterned in Temple worship, as well as including new commandments and practices taught by

---

[40] Blunt, *Annotated BCP*, 19.

[41] Ibid., 21. Blunt has the complete letter of Cranmer to the Lords of England, who were supporting the removal of the requirement for kneeling.

Jesus and the apostles. The early church drew on the whole Bible's system of worship to form the first ancient liturgies.

We have seen this in the worship of our Lord and the Apostles. They held to the Old Covenant Tabernacle/Temple commandments and patterns of worship in the New Covenant. Christ came not to abolish but to fulfill the law and the prophets, which would include the Temple model of worship (Matt 5:19–20). Furthermore, the New Testament reveals in the Book of Hebrews that the earthly Temple worship in Scripture was a mirror image of the archetypal worship of heaven that we see in the eternal scenes of worship in the Old and New Testaments (cf. Ezek 1 with Rev 4–5; see also Heb 10–12). The heavenly Temple transcends all earthy worship and is the model for it. Christ taught in His model prayer, "on earth as in heaven." The regulative principle (of commandment only) completely misses fullness of the Biblical liturgical principles and practices.

Furthermore, the regulative principle fails even to adopt one of the leading New Testament commandments regarding worship. St. Paul says, "I appeal to you therefore, brothers, by the mercies of God to present your bodies as a living sacrifice, holy and acceptable to God, which is your spiritual worship" (Rom 12:1, ESV). This commandment calls for the whole body to be involved in worship. It is this physical participation in worship of all five senses (taste, touch, sight, hearing, and smell) that calls for extensive ceremony and ritual in worship. This bodily engagement in worship is rooted in the Incarnation. For, "The whole scheme of redemption is based on a principle which shows that God establishes communion between Himself and mankind to a great extent through the body and bodily acts, and not purely through mental ones, as the exercise of thought and will."[42]

The Incarnation proves this physical aspect of the spiritual. Blunt remarks:

> For when a perfect unimpeded spiritual intercourse was to be renewed between the Creator and His fallen creatures, God, Who, "is a Spirit," took upon Him a bodily nature, "of a reasonable Soul and Human Flesh subsisting," and by means of it became a Mediator, through Whom that intercourse could be originated and maintained. For the particular application, also, of the benefits of His mediation, Christ ordained Sacraments, which are outward and visible signs endowed with the capacity of conveying inward and spiritual grace to the soul through the organs of the body.[43]

Since, therefore, God ordained becoming physical to restore communion, the whole body is to be involved in worship. As St. Chrysostom says, "Hadst thou been incorporeal, Christ would have given thee His incorporeal gifts pure and simple; but as the soul is bound up with a body, He gives thee spiritual things in sensible forms."[44] This is the liturgical principle and commandment expressed in St. Paul's exhortation to the Romans. They were to worship God with their whole body.

Whole body worship calls for ceremony and ritual as is expressed in not only Scripture but in the ancient liturgies. It was precisely this kind of worship that was restored in the *Book of Common Prayer.* But it collided with a more cerebral approach to

---

[42] Blunt, *Annotated BCP*, 44.

[43] Ibid.

[44] Chrysostom, on Matthew 26. See reference in Blunt, *Annotated BCP*, 44.

worship from parts of the European side of the Reformation. This influence eventually became an entire movement called Puritanism. Ignoring the implications of St. Paul's commandment to worship with the whole body, the focus was on commandments dealing with preaching. The sermon, not the Sacrament, became the center of the liturgy leading to an intellectualizing of worship in terms of the mind. The rest of the body was excluded from worship. In the service of Holy Communion, we find the regulative principle, cerebral approach, playing out in the resistance to the overt bodily action of kneeling to receive the Sacrament. The argument was that Scripture does not command kneeling, therefore kneeling should not be required.

However, the Anglican view—also based on Scripture—defended kneeling with the conviction that not only is there precedent for kneeling for prayer in the worship of the Bible, but also on the belief that Christ is truly present in the Eucharist. As such, he should be met the way he is met in the Holy Scriptures, by falling down and kneeling before him. This is exemplified in the scene of the healing of the ten lepers. The text says that one returned and "gave thanks" (Luke 17:16, Greek εὐχαριστέω *eucharisteo*). This is the same term used in the consecration of the Sacrament, "gave thanks" (Matt 26:27), hence the designation of Holy Communion as the Eucharist (giving thanks). Based on this Biblical connection and belief in the real presence of Christ at the Eucharist, kneeling became a common practice for receiving Holy Communion. It became particularly prevalent in the Western tradition of the ancient Church. Therefore, according to Romans 12:1–2 calling for "spiritual things in sensible forms," and ancient liturgical practice in keeping with this Scriptural theology, the first prayer book had required kneeling to receive Holy Communion. The second edition of the prayer book had fallen prey to an innovative model alien to Scripture and the "ancient fathers." In Cranmer's mind as indicated in his response to the lords, the entire prayer book principles of Biblical and ancient worship were in jeopardy if kneeling was forbidden.

Cranmer was willing to work with the foreign reformers perhaps to unify the Reformation until he ran into the objection to kneeling to receive Holy Communion. In his letter he only points to the absurdity and inherent contradiction of objecting to kneeling, by noting it is neither expressly stated in Scripture that Christ "ministered it standing or sitting." The Presbyterians and Puritans argued that Holy Communion should be received sitting in chairs and at tables. Cranmer points out that in fact Scripture accords with the ancient Eastern tradition of eating "lying on the ground" in a reclining posture, so in fact it should be argued that the Eucharist should be celebrated reclining, if indeed the regulative principle were true. Yet no Presbyterian or Puritan proposed such a posture for receiving Holy Communion. The inherent contradiction of the fallacious regulative principle of worship on which these groups opposed kneeling to receive Holy Communion received strong objection by the normally irenic Cranmer. He so opposed such a regulative principle view of worship that he says in his letter, "I will set my foot by this, to be tried by fire, that this doctrine is untrue; and not only untrue, but also seditious and perilous to be heard of any subjects."

History records that Cranmer's letter was effective. Kneeling was not prohibited in the second revision of the prayer book of 1552. A Black Rubric was added denying that kneeling indicated belief in the "real and substantial presence of Christ in the Sacrament." Many other changes were made reflecting the influence of the European

Reformers. Consequently, this version of the prayer book presents a mixed approach to revising the liturgy different from the first reformed catholic prayer book founded on the liturgies of the "ancient fathers."

However, the 1552 BCP was short lived. Within only a few months of its approval, King Edward VI died in 1553. Blunt notes that the implementation of the revised prayer book was so short that most parishes continued to use the first prayer book. The second edition simply did not have enough time to be fully put into practice. After Edward VI's death, his Roman Catholic sister Mary came to the throne. She reinstituted the Roman liturgy and removed the *Book of Common Prayer*. Her reign also was not long. She died within five years. Her sister Elizabeth acceded to the throne of England in 1558. She restored the *Book of Common Prayer* and called for a third revision of the prayer book in 1559.

The most notable alterations in the 1559 BCP are the Words of Administration and the removal of the Black Rubric. Regarding the Words of Administration, the 1552 prayer book had dropped the sentence in the 1549 edition said by the priest when the Sacrament was offered to the recipient, "The Body of Christ which is given for thee preserve thy body and soul unto everlasting life." Such language implied that Christ was objectively present prior to reception. The 1552 BCP substituted the words, "Take and eat this, in remembrance that Christ died for thee, and feed on Him in thy heart by faith, with thanksgiving." This sentence emphasized that Christ was not received apart from faith. However, in the 1559 BCP the original line was restored but with the 1552's additional sentence. The objective sense of Christ's presence in the first sentence was returned, recognizing at the same time that apart from faith the Sacrament is not effectual.

The 1559 prayer book survived for nearly a hundred years with only minor revisions in 1603–1604, until there came an interruption to prayer book worship. The Puritans removed the prayer book in 1640. Twenty years later, the King of England returned to the throne along with Anglicanism. The epic 1662 prayer book revision took place, resulting in the major liturgy for the Anglican Communion to this day. The Black Rubric was restored but with significant changes in wording. Whereas the original had denied the "real and substantial" presence of Christ in the Eucharist, the new version of the rubric rejects the "corporal [physical] presence." This modification actually allowed for belief in the "real and substantial" presence while rejecting the doctrine of transubstantiation.

Later Prayerbook Revisions

Thus, these revisions of the prayer book, viewed as a whole over the hundred-plus years of English Reformation history, evidence that the liturgical instinct of Anglicanism is reformed catholic. In spite of the Protestant overreach of the 1552 BCP, and the complete cancellation of the prayer book under Mary and the Commonwealth, subsequent revisions returned to Cranmer's leading Catholic principle of the Scriptures and the "ancient fathers" stated in his Preface to the first prayer book. This is graphically illustrated when the prayer book is restored after what tragically happened when in the seventeenth century the Puritan party prevailed with its regulative principle approach to worship. The prayer book and the model of worship on which it is based were restored with a vengeance after the Cromwellian era. A new revision of the prayer book approved in 1662 moved much more back to Cranmer's original "ancient fathers" standard expressed in the first edition. Significantly, catholic revival of worship in the following three centuries—the Non-Jurors (late seventeenth century), the Wesleys (eighteenth century), the Oxford Movement (nineteenth century)—all worshipped with the 1662 BCP as they called for continued return to the ancient liturgies of the early church. The liturgical trajectory for the centuries after the 1662 prayer book is back to—not away from—early church liturgies.

In the twentieth and twenty-first centuries in America we find a microcosm of the prayer book revision cycle of return to the ancient model of liturgy, away from it, and then back to it. The 1928 edition of the American prayer book in the first quarter of the twentieth century was a virtual restoration of the original 1549 edition. With the rise of secularism after WWII, however, the Episcopal Church succumbed to the temptation of being like the world to grow the Church. It revised the 1928 BCP with a new liturgical model. Ironically, the revisers used the Dix theory to bring in the secular in the name of returning to a more ancient liturgy. As was mentioned earlier, Dix based his revisionist view on the liturgy found in the *Apostolic Constitutions*, operating on the premise that this work dated to the second century. It was later proven to be fifth century. Nevertheless, by appealing to this allegedly earlier liturgy, he ironically used the Cranmerian principle of the "ancient fathers" to undermine the Cranmerian prayer book. The age-old Anglican model of worship that was originally founded on and did restore the ancient liturgies was abandoned with the 1979 prayer book of the American Church. Even more tragic, this insidious approach to revisionism allowed for all kinds of secular theological seeds and alien social justice theories to be woven into the modern liturgy. Sadly, it was symptomatic of the complete secularization of Western Anglicanism. The historic liturgical principle of *lex orandi lex credendi* ("the law of praying is the law of believing," or "how you worship is what you believe") was proven in the negative. In the years following the liturgical revisionism of the 1970s producing the 1979 prayer book, the Episcopal Church collapsed into heresy and immorality.

However, that was not the end of the liturgical story in American Anglicanism. As God always does, he raises up new generations of faithful Anglicans by the power of the Holy Spirit. In the early twenty-first century, thousands of Episcopalians, led by a number of their bishops, left the Episcopal Church and joined with other Biblical Anglicans such as the Reformed Episcopal Church. At the direction, call, and sponsorship of many Primates of Anglican Provinces in the orthodox Global South portion of the Anglican Communion, these faithful Anglicans formed the Anglican Church in North America in 2009. This new Anglican province eventually produced the 2019 *Book of Common* Prayer. As witnessed time and again in the revision of the prayer book, this version returned to the *ad fontes* model of the English Reformation of the Scriptures and early church liturgies. The Cranmerian model was restored. A reformed catholic instinct re-emerged.

The Fundamental Principles

Some final points need to be made to conclude this section dealing with the ancient reformed catholic model for correcting errors. For one, the question could be raised, "If the reformed catholic Anglican prayer book is true to the Scriptures and the ancient fathers, why the need in history to return it to this standard?" The short answer is that humans are sinful. Even in the Holy Scriptures, the Old Covenant people in Israel fell into sin and abandoned the worship God had revealed. This happened while Moses was receiving the Ten Commandments on Mt. Sinai. The people at the foot of the mountain became impatient and disbelieving. The first thing they did in their doubt and unbelief was to call for a return to the pagan worship of Egypt. They even convinced the High Priest Aaron to make an idol in the form of a golden calf. The longer answer is, therefore, that as long as there is sin in the world, God's people will always be tempted to abandon God's Word and his worship. They have been and will be lured by various sinful deceptions and techniques to depart from the Scriptures and the worship of the ancient fathers rooted in the apostolic liturgies of the early church.

The previous question leads to a further query as to whether the Divine Liturgy can be changed. Yes, it can, but only according to the standards of the Word of God and the early church fathers. Scripture is the primary standard for correction. The apostolic liturgies are the secondary authority. Within this authoritative framework is the guide for any change in the liturgy. This is the standard we see in the reformed catholic approach to revision based on the Scriptures and the early church liturgies.

First and foremost, any change should be based on the liturgy revealed in Holy Scripture on earth and in heaven. Where there is specific wording such as the Baptismal formula and the Words of Institution, these cannot be altered. Other wording provided by the Lord and the Scriptures such as the Psalms, the Lord's Prayer, and the antiphonal responses witnessed by St. John in heaven (Rev 4–5; cf. Isa 6) also cannot be changed. The Biblical liturgical formulae are a given and set. Correction is to be driven by returning the liturgy to the Scriptures.

Secondarily, any change should be guided by the apostolic liturgies. It is significant that there was not a single liturgy emerging from the apostolic community. Even if there were initially one liturgy from which the others came, it is not extant. The four major liturgies arise under the early apostolic tradition. They reflect numerous apostles in varying cultures and parts of the world. From this we see that there is legitimate room for liturgical variation within this apostolic model. The cultural variations share a common Biblical and apostolic framework. As such, culture is not the final determiner of liturgical practice. Again, we see the validity of the English Reformation model of returning to the Scriptures and the early church liturgies. They applied this model to their own English culture of the sixteenth century. Others converted by the Gospel through this church in other parts of the world translated the *Book of Common Prayer* into their own cultures. As this has been done, modifications have been made. The model should be the same as the original standard for the prayer book, however, Scripture and the early church fathers.

A last point about correcting liturgies is that change should be within a conciliar model of the Church. That is, the bishops in council do the revising. Liturgical revision is not the work of only one man or one congregation. God may use one bishop or theologian to do much of the initial crafting of the liturgy, but his work must be edited and approved by the bishops in council with one another. This is precisely what happened with the process for adopting the prayer book.

Therefore, the final section of this chapter summarizes how faithful Anglicans resisted alien models of revision to return to the true model of reform. It is reformed catholic. We have seen challenges from the Protestant regulative principle approach to revising the second edition of the prayer book, as well as from the twentieth-century secular approach in the 1979 BCP of the American Episcopal Church. Time reveals, however, that when the grace of God works through the power of the Holy Spirit, a reformed catholic liturgical instinct reappears among Biblical and faithful Anglicans. They do as orthodox believers have always done through history. They return to the Holy Scriptures and the early church fathers.

Conclusion

This chapter has attempted to present the Anglican *Book of Common Prayer* as a reformed catholic expression of liturgical worship. I began with a quote from Cranmer's Preface to the first prayer book, which spells out in detail that the model for revision was the liturgies of the "ancient fathers." I have demonstrated how this intent was embedded in the work of the original revisers of the prayer book who were chaired by Archbishop Thomas Cranmer.

I have presented how the prayer book accomplishes this intent in Word and Sacrament. The *Book of Common Prayer* is dominated by the Word of God. Its lectionary and the services are governed by Holy Scripture. The *Book of Common Prayer* is also thoroughly sacramental according to the ancient liturgies. In both its overall sacramental structure and services, and particularly in the rite of Holy Communion, the Scripture and liturgies of the early church inform and influence the prayer book.

Finally, I presented how a reformed catholic model persisted even when editions of the prayer book fell away from the reformed catholic approach. It is a testimony to the faithfulness of God to His people and what happens when they are renewed by His power. The only conclusion that can be drawn is that when the Holy Spirit truly revives His Church, reformed catholic worship reappears according to the Scriptures and the early church fathers. In Anglicanism, God's reviving work has led to a reformed catholic *Book of Common Prayer*.

Chapter 3

The Sacraments: Both Which Is Both

The Most Rev. Dr. Ray R. Sutton

Sacraments are the powerful instruments of God unto eternal life. For as our natural life consisteth in the union of the body with the soul, so our life supernatural in the union of the soul with God. And forasmuch as there is no union of God with man *without that mean between both which is both* it seemeth requisite that we first consider how God is in Christ, then how Christ is in us, and how the Sacraments do serve to make us partakers of Christ ... because it pleaseth Almighty God to communicate by sensible means those blessings which are incomprehensible.

Richard Hooker, *Of the Laws of Ecclesiastical Polity*, V.51.1[1]

The sixteenth-century English Reformer and theologian Richard Hooker captures with one profound phrase the view of re-formed catholic Anglicanism on the Sacraments. It is, "the mean between both which is both." Although there would be various understandings among Anglican Reformers of the "mean between both which is both," they all essentially follow this model.

The beginning for this phrasing undoubtedly reaches back to a sixth-century hymn composed by the Bishop of Poitiers, St. Venantius Fortunatus. The title is *Pange lingua gloriosi proelium certaminus*, meaning, "Sing my tongue, the glorious battle." The following lines continue, "Sing the ending of the fray; Now above the cross the trophy; Tell how Christ, the world's redeemer; As a victim won the day." The last line speaks of Christ in a twofold way by referring to Him "as a victim who won the day." That is, Christ is a "Victim," through His death, and He is "Victor" to win the day. Victim and Victor: He is "both which is both."

The reality of "both which is both" in the Incarnation is extended to the Blessed Sacrament by medieval, Anglican, and other theologians and hymnists. Thomas Aquinas (1225–1274) adapted the hymn for the Feast of Corpus Christi. [2] His version of *Pange lingua* within a Eucharistic setting (i.e., the Feast of Corpus Christi) concludes with the statement, "to the One who proceeds from Both be equal praise."[3] This refers to the Holy Spirit, through the mystery of "both which is both" in the Holy Trinity. A previous verse in the hymn indicates the "both-ness" of the Incarnation and the Sacrament: "The Word-made-flesh, true bread by his word made into flesh."[4] Aquinas intends us to see the

---

[1] John Keble, ed., *Works of Richard Hooker* (Oxford: Clarendon, 1838), II:220 (emphasis mine).

[2] Thomas Aquinas' version begins, *Pange, lingua, gloriósi*, translated, "Sing, my tongue, the Saviour's glory," literally, "tell, tongue, the mystery."

[3] The Latin is, *Procedénti ab utróque Comparo sit laudátio*. In the sacramental context, the hymn was later sung on Maundy Thursday during the last act of stripping the chancel, as the Blessed Sacrament was processed to a side altar to be in repose for Holy Communion on Good Friday at the early Mass of the Pre-Sanctified Gifts.

[4] The Latin of the beginning of verse 4 is, *Verbum caro, panem verum Verbo carnem éfficit*. Compare the end of verse 3: *Cibum turbæ duodénæ Se dat suis mánibus*, "To the gathered Twelve, as food he gives himself with his own hands."

parallel of the mystery of "both which is both," and later theologians—especially Anglicans—would interpret this hymn by applying the doxological "both" language also to the Sacrament. For the medieval theologian, Christ's oneness with the Sacrament involved a material change in the elements of bread and wine to the physical Body and Blood of Christ (transubstantiation). He used the Greek philosophy of Aristotle to explain his version of transubstantiation.[5]

As we'll see later in this chapter, English Reformers like Richard Hooker, Bishop Lancelot Andrewes, and so forth did not agree with Aquinas' view of transubstantiation or the use of philosophy to explain Christ's real presence in the Eucharist. Yet, these Anglican Divines did recognize that Holy Scripture speaks of a mystical "oneness" between Christ and the Sacrament while rejecting that the elements cease to exist. Holding Passover bread and wine, the Lord instituted His Holy Supper with the words, "This is My Body.... This is My Blood" (Matt 26:26–28). There was no physical change, yet the bread and wine were both body and blood for Christ's "is" to be truly "is." St. Paul even more specifically states, "The cup of blessing that we bless is it not a participation in the blood of Christ? The bread that we break, is it not a participation in the body of Christ?" (1 Cor 10:16–17). Based on such Biblical statements, therefore, English Reformers acknowledged Christ's oneness with the Sacrament within a range of views from subjective (recipient only), to instrumental (elements as means), to objective (with or in the elements prior to reception). Whether Christ's oneness with the Sacrament was in relation to the recipient, elements, or a combination of them, the maxim could be maintained, "both which is both."

However, Anglican Divines had a different understanding of Christ's oneness with the Sacrament from late medieval views of transubstantiation. Rather than a physical change in the elements, or the use of Greek philosophy to explain with metaphysics Christ's real presence, they appealed to the Biblical model of oneness without confusion of the two natures of Christ in the Incarnation to explain His mystical union in the Sacrament. They used Christology instead of philosophy. We see this approach in Hooker's statement. He parallels three relationships in which there is a oneness. He says, "It seemeth requisite that we first consider how God is in Christ, then how Christ is in us, and how the Sacraments do serve to make us partakers of Christ."[6] The key to all three unions that are both which is both starts with the first one, "how God is in Christ." For Hooker, "how God is in Christ" in the relationship between His Deity and Humanity explains not only "how Christ is in us" but also "how the Sacraments do serve to make us partakers of Christ." In other words, the Incarnation is the correct Biblical model for understanding the Sacraments.

Therefore, in this chapter I present how the English Reformers used the Christology of the Scriptures as articulated by the early church fathers to arrive at their understanding of Christ's real presence in the Sacrament. With views rooted in the ancient Church, Anglican

---

[5] There have been many interpretations of transubstantiation in the history of this view of real presence. See John Bramhall, *An Answer to M. de la Milletiere, His Impertinent Dedication of His Imaginary Triumph*, in *Works*, ed. Arthur West Haddan, Library of Anglo-Catholic Theology (Oxford: John Henry Parker, 1842) I:7–23. See excerpt in Paul Elmer More and Frank Leslie Cross, *Anglicanism* (Milwaukee: Morehouse, 1935), 481–482.

[6] Richard Hooker, *Of the Laws of Ecclesiastical Polity*, V.54.5 (*Works*, II:220).

theologians attempted to reform the Roman Church of their sixteenth-century day. As was presented in the introduction to this volume, in this period English Divines argued that the Western Medieval Church had deviated not only from Scripture but the early church fathers of the Undivided Church. They corrected with a reformed catholic model. In this chapter, I present the way that English Reformers applied the Incarnational Christology of the early church fathers to the Sacrament of Holy Communion.

The Christology of St. Irenaeus in Lancelot Andrewes' Sacramental Theology

Famous for his role in chairing the translation committee for the King James translation of the Bible, Lancelot Andrewes was contemporary with Richard Hooker. He was fluent in fifteen languages and accomplished as a Biblical and patristic scholar. For four centuries since the Reformation, he has been studied by Anglican, Orthodox, Roman, and Protestant scholars as the foremost English Reformation authority of his day regarding the early church fathers and their theology.[7]

Bishop Andrewes' Eucharistic theology follows Hooker's Christological approach to the Sacraments. His model appears prominently in his legendary Christmas Day sermons: He preached seventeen of them on the Nativity of Christ. He observed in Jesus' birth parallels to His visitation in the Sacrament. So influential was this event for his understanding of the Sacrament that he hung a symbol of the star of Bethlehem directly over the altar of his private chapel. His Christmas Day sermons are therefore particularly full of sacramental teaching. They are classic examples of understanding the Sacraments based on Scripture and the Christology of the church fathers.

Andrewes' *Sermon of the Nativity* (XVI) preached on Christmas Day 1623 is perhaps the clearest instance of his Incarnational approach. He draws on early church fathers' Christology to explain Christ's relationship to the Sacrament. He specifically mentions second-century St. Irenaeus and his theology of the Incarnation. He says,

> There we do not gather to Christ or of Christ, but we gather Christ Himself. For as there is a recapitulation of all in Heaven and earth in Christ, so there is a *recapitulation of all in Christ in the Holy Sacrament*. You may see it clearly. There is in Christ the Word eternal for things in Heaven; there is also flesh, for things on earth. Sembiably ["In a resembling manner"], the Sacrament consisteth of a Heavenly and a terene part (It is Irenaeus' own words); the Heavenly there the Word too; the abstract of the other; the earthly the element. (Emphasis mine)

The key statement in Andrewes' comments is, "For as there is a recapitulation of all in Heaven and earth in Christ, so there is a *recapitulation of all in Christ in the Holy Sacrament*." The bishop cites a key word used by the early church father to describe his view of the Incarnation, *recapitulation*. He then applies this concept to the Eucharist. We must therefore consider Irenaeus' use of *recapitulation* to describe the Incarnation to be able to follow how Andrewes relates it to the Sacrament.

---

[7] Bishop Andrewes answered the objections to the English Reformation offered by the famous Roman apologist Bellarmine. So effective were Andrewes' rejoinders defending the English Reformation as standing on the side of Scripture and the ancient Catholic Church, that Bellarmine and other Roman apologists were silenced for decades to come.

Irenaeus meant by *recapitulate* to "sum up." He explains how Christ's Incarnation is a recapitulation or summing up when he says,

> [Christ] was in these last days, according to the time appointed by the Father, united to His own workmanship, inasmuch as He became a man liable to suffering.... He commenced afresh [recapitulated] the long line of human beings, and furnished us, in a brief, comprehensive manner, with salvation; so that what we had lost in Adam—namely, to be according to the image and likeness of God—that we might recover in Christ Jesus.... He has therefore, in His work of recapitulation, summed up all things, both waging war against our enemy, and crushing him who had at the beginning led us away captives in Adam.... The enemy would not have been fairly vanquished, unless it had been a man [born] of woman who conquered him.... And therefore does the Lord profess Himself to be the Son of man, comprising in Himself that original man out of whom the woman was fashioned, in order that, as our species went down to death through a vanquished man, so we may ascend to life again through a victorious one; and as through a man death received the palm [of victory] against us, so again by a man we may receive the palm against death.[8]

Irenaeus based his language of summing up or recapitulation on St. Paul's description of the Incarnation in his Epistle to the Ephesians: "That ... in the fullness of times he might gather together [sum up] in one all things in Christ, both which are in heaven and which are on earth" (Eph 1:10). The Greek word translated "gather together" in the King James version has the sense of "sum up." For Irenaeus it means "to recapitulate," in that Christ's life is a "brief," a "comprehensive manner, with salvation." And since Christ's life is a "comprehensive of salvation," the Lord is the Second Adam who "commences afresh the long line of human beings." Irenaeus means by this language that the life of Christ relives or sums up in His Incarnation to redeem or reverse the sin of the first Adam at two levels.

For one, Christ in His Incarnation becomes like the first Adam but without sin so that unlike the first man, he "wages war with our enemy, and crushes him who had at the beginning led us away captives in Adam." In this way, every event in the life of Christ is simultaneously a reliving of the first Adam's sins and its consequences but without failure to prove that he is a Second Adam. In this sense, the recapitulation of the first Adam in the second Adam, Christ, is both which is both.

At another level, therefore, Irenaeus saw Christ's life as a reliving of all of the ages of a human. He says,

> Being a Master, therefore, He also possessed the age of a Master, not despising or evading any condition of humanity, nor setting aside in Himself that law which he had appointed for the human race, but sanctifying every age, by that period corresponding to it which belonged to Himself. For He came to save all through means of Himself—all, I say, who through Him are born again to God—infants, and children, and boys, and youths, and old men. He therefore passed through

---

[8] Irenaeus, *Against Heresies*, 3.18.1, 5.21.1. See A. Roberts and J. Donaldson, eds., *The Writings of Irenaeus* (Edinburgh: T & T Clark, 1869), 2:110–111.

every age, becoming an infant for infants, thus sanctifying infants; a child for children, thus sanctifying those who are of this age ... a youth for youths ... an old man for old men."

He concludes, "Wherefore also he passed through every stage of life, restoring to all communion with God."[9] Thus Christ lived the full life cycle of humanity in the events of His life to save every age of humanity.

With this understanding of Irenaeus' doctrine of recapitulation, we can now begin to see how the English Reformer Lancelot Andrewes extended this concept to the Sacrament. Just as the Incarnation of Christ is Divine and Human, he speaks of the Sacrament being "Heavenly" and "terene" or earthly. He says, "The Heavenly there the Word too; the abstract of the other; the earthly the element." He uses *abstract* in the sense of a summary of the whole. The "Heavenly there the Word too" is a reference to Christ. In the Sacrament, he is a summary of what is revealed by means of the earthly element. Andrewes states it as the *"recapitulation of all in Christ in the Holy Sacrament."*

Furthermore, Andrewes sees a recapitulation or summary of Christ's birth in Holy Communion on Christmas Day. The Nativity of Christ is revealed in the Sacrament. Christ is born in a manger, a feeding trough. Lying there He appears as the food of the world, the Bread of Life. The bishop says,

> And in the elements, you may observe there is a fulness of the seasons of the natural year; of the corn-flour or harvest in one, bread; of the wine-press or vintage in the other, wine. And in the Heavenly, of the "wheat-corn" whereas He compareth Himself, bread, even "the Living Bread [or, Bread of Life] that came down from Heaven;" the true Manna, whereof we may each gather his gomer (John 12:24; 6:51; 6:49; 15:1). And again, of Him, the True Vine (as He calls Himself) the blood of the grapes of that Vine. Both these issuing out of this day's recapitulation, both *in corpus autem aptasi Mihi* ["the same body prepared for me"] of this day (Ps 40:6).

Thus, the Incarnate Christ born on the first Christmas Day is the same "Heavenly Word" present with the "earthly element." Andrewes uses the phrase, "this day's recapitulation." As Christ came at His birth to the world, He comes in the Sacrament. Both occur. Andrewes concludes his statement with the Hooker type of phrasing, "Both in the same Body prepared for me." That is, "the mean between both which is both."

The Christology of Saints Hilary and Cyril in the Sacramental Theology of the English Reformers

Bishop Andrewes also draws on the Christology of the two natures of Christ called the *hypostatical union* to explain His presence in the Sacrament. With this theology, he also corrects ancient aberrations of Christology that he believes have been the incorrect late medieval understanding of Christ's real presence called transubstantiation. He says of Christ's relation to the Sacrament,

> And the gathering or vintage of these two in the Blessed Eucharist is, as I may say, a kind of hypostatical union of the sign and the thing signified, so united together, as are the two natures of Christ. And even from this Sacramental union do the

---

[9] *Against Heresies*, 2.22.4; 3.18.7.

Fathers borrow their resemblance, to illustrate by it the personal union in Christ,—I name Theodoret for the Greek, and Galasius for the Latin Church, that insist upon it both, and press it against Eutyches, that even as in the Eucharist neither part is evacuate or turned into the other, but abide each still in his former nature and substance, no more is either of Christ's Natures annulled, or one of them converted into the other, as Eutyches held, but each Nature remaineth still full and whole in his own kind. And backwards as the two Natures in Christ, so the *signilium* and the *signatum* in the Sacrament *e conversio* ["the sign and the thing signified without conversion"]. And this latter device, of the substance of the bread and the wine to be flown away and gone, and in the same room of it a remainder of nothing else but accidents to stay behind, was to them not known, and had it been true, had made for Eutyches and against them. And thus for the likeness of union in both.[10]

There is much in this further statement of Irenaeus about the relationship between Christology and Eucharistic theology. He speaks of the "hypostatical union" of Christ's Deity and Humanity as a model for Christ's Sacramental presence. In this, he applies the same approach of Richard Hooker quoted at the beginning. Hooker said, "There is no union of God with man *without that mean between both which is both*." The "mean" to which he refers is the Incarnation and the Sacrament. He expresses the relationship in the rest of the statement: "it seemeth requisite that we first consider how God is in Christ, then how Christ is in us, and how the Sacraments do serve to make us partakers of Christ ... because it pleaseth Almighty God to communicate by sensible means those blessings which are incomprehensible."

In Hooker's writing, where he discusses the Sacraments and makes these comments, he follows with a brief section on the relationship of the Persons of the Godhead in the Holy Trinity. He then develops extensively how the fourth-century church fathers Cyril and Hilary dealt with the heresy of Nestorius.[11] This heretic believed the Deity and Humanity of Christ were in two Persons that were separated from one another. The late J. I. Packer used the analogy of two people in a party horse or dragon costume. One is in the head and the other in the tail as they walk around. Hooker explains how Cyril and Hilary provided insight about the relationship between the two natures (Deity and Humanity) of Christ in one Person. They played an influential role in the results of the Fourth Ecumenical Council in 451. This council concluded the denunciation of Nestorius that began at the Third Ecumenical Council in Ephesus in 431.

The effect of this errant Nestorian Christology was he would not acknowledge Blessed Mary as *Theotokos*, "God-Bearer." He would only say she *was Christotokos*, "Christ-Bearer." With his separation of Christ's Deity from His Humanity, God was not in Mary's womb. Thus, Nestorianism reintroduced all the ancient heresies through the backdoor of his own false teaching. If the Deity of Christ is separated from His Humanity, the effect is that He only appears to be Divine when, in fact, His Body is not. It's a form of Docetism that said Christ only appeared to be human. The effect is the same. Deity and Humanity are separate. The error of Nestorianism is that it's all the ancient

---

[10] Lancelot Andrewes, *Works*, The Library of Anglo Catholic Theology (Oxford: John Henry Parker, 1841), I:281ff.

[11] Hooker, *Laws*, V.51.1–52.3 (*Works*, II:220–255).

Christological heresies rolled into His one essential flaw of separating Deity from Humanity in the Incarnation.

Saints Hilary and Cyril each made significant contributions to correct the deviant Christology of Nestorius. The fourth-century St. Hilary based his understanding of the relation of the two natures of Christ on Christ's statement, "I am in the Father and the Father is in me" (John 14:10–11).[12] Jesus says elsewhere, "I and the Father are One" (John 10:30). Christ is the "mean between both which is both." In explaining how the Son could be in the Father and the Father in the Son, Hilary crafted the phrase "mutual indwelling." This "mutual indwelling" he applied to the relationship of Christ's Deity to His Humanity. He did not see this union as a kind of crass sticking of one Person to the Other like a three-legged race where two legs are tied together to run a foot race at picnics. The union is deeper. St. Paul refers to the marital union as the "mystery" (Eph 5:22). It is like the inter-penetration of man and woman in their physical union. That is the best comparison in all the mystical relations in Scripture: the Persons of the Godhead, the two Natures of Christ, and union of Christ with His Church called a marriage between God the Groom and His Bride, the people of God. Specifically, two become one without ceasing to be two, yet they are one such that they can be called "One Flesh" (Gen 2:24; Mark 10:8–9). How a man and a woman become "one flesh" in the mystery of marriage is unfathomable. Their union is the "mean between both which is both." Archbishop Thomas Cranmer crafted his Eucharistic phrase, "He in us and we in Him," based on Hilary's mutual indwelling theology.

St. Cyril of Alexandria supplies additional language and insight to explain the relation of the two Natures of Christ. He bases it on the same John 14 passage that influenced St. Hilary. Cyril produces the phrase *communicatio idiomatum* to bring light to the mystical relation of Christ's Humanity and Deity. The Latin words mean "the communication of properties." The relation of Christ's Natures is a distinct union that is so intimate the property of One is communicated to the Other. In Cyril's description of the "communication of properties," we see that he does not mean the two natures of Christ are joined together like two legs bound in what is called a three-legged sack race. Nor, as Hooker points out, is the union of mutual participation the infusion of one nature into the other. Rather, it is a mystical union like marriage where two become one without being dissolved or comingled.

The Christology of these two church fathers therefore profoundly influenced early Ecumenical Councils. They are the Third Ecumenical Council at Ephesus in 431 and the Fourth Ecumenical Council of Chalcedon in 451. The Holy Spirit led the Council of Chalcedon to arrive at the prescient verbiage concerning the two natures of Christ as "united but not comingled or mixed." The *Athanasian Creed* is the confessional articulation of the conclusions of the Council of Chalcedon. It says in describing the mystical union of Christ's Humanity and Deity without confusing or confounding them:

> Although he is God and human, yet Christ is not two, but one. He is one, however, not by his divinity being turned into flesh, but by God's taking humanity to himself.

---

[12] St. Hilary, *On the Trinity*, III.1–4 (NPNF[2] 9:62–63). See also John of Damascus, *An Exact Exposition of the Orthodox Faith*, IV.13 "Concerning the Holy and Immaculate Mysteries of the Lord" (NPNF[2] 9b:81–84).

He is one, certainly not by the blending of his essence, but by the unity of his person. For just as one human is both rational soul and flesh, so too the one Christ is both God and human.

The *Creed* states that there are two Natures, yet they are One. Their Oneness, however, is not by the dissolving of either Nature, "Divinity being turned into flesh." Neither is the unity a "blending of His essence." This blending of essence would mean that the natures are dissipated in their union. Rather, it's a unity of two Natures in one Person that, in the final analysis, is a great mystery. It is this mystery that Nestorius violated when He pushed the distinction of the Natures of Christ to the point of separation into two Persons.

The same church fathers, Hilary and Cyril, extended their insights about the union of the two Natures of Christ to the Sacraments. They applied the mystical union of Christ's Deity and Humanity to His mystical presence in the elements of Bread and Wine as His Body and Blood. The same categories of Christology as expressed at the Council of Chalcedon and the *Athanasian Creed* extend to their explanations of His real presence. Christ, in His full Humanity and Deity, becomes one with the Bread and the Wine. When Cyril applied his understanding of the communication of properties to the Sacraments, he did not mean as some have mistakenly described it as "consubstantiation."[13] It was understood to be a mystical union of oneness without mixture of Him and the elements in the Sacraments.

Just as His two Natures are not "blended" such that one is dissolved by the other, neither does Christ's presence in the Eucharist eradicate the elements of bread and wine. His Body and Blood are one such that the Sacrament can be called by their Name. At the same time, the consecrated Bread and Wine are not destroyed. In the words of St. Thomas Acquinas, "Grace perfects nature; it does not destroy it."[14] Just as in the Incarnation Jesus' Humanity is "both which is both is one," so the Sacrament is the "mean between both which is both."

Furthermore, there is the additional Christological insight of the mystical in the John 14 passage expanded to Christ's presence in the Eucharist. Not only does Jesus say, "I am in the Father and He is in Me," but He states in the same passage, "I go to the Father" (John 14:12). How can the Two be in Each Other, and yet One goes to the other? How can they not be separate—in each other—and yet one journey to the other? We don't know. However, what we are led to see is that the traversing of the Son to the Father is not bound by any laws of nature. The Two are One such that there is no spatial distance between them, but the physically resurrected Son mystically goes to the right hand of the Father.

Based on this Christology, Hilary and Cyril maintain that Christ is One with the Sacrament without destroying the elements. After all, "Grace perfects nature; it does not destroy it." This Christological model of the early church fathers is the one to which Bishop Lancelot Andrewes and Hooker appeal to explain Christ's oneness with the

---

[13] Luther's understanding of real presence was based on the Christology of Hilary and Cyril. It has wrongly been called "consubstantiation." But this is to misunderstand the early church fathers as well as Luther. Neither Luther nor any Lutheran scholar have described their understanding of real presence as consubstantiation.

[14] *Gratia non tollit naturam, sed perficit*, Thomas Acquinas, *Summa Theologiae* I.1.8; cf. St. Basil, *On the Holy Spirit*, 16.38, 26.61.

Sacrament. Hooker calls it real participation without Christ being in the elements.[15] Andrewes left it at the level of a more mystical relationship without explanation. Other English Reformers generally draw on this Incarnational approach, although some will disagree with aspects of it. Most of all, however, they applied the ancient Christological approach to the Sacraments to refute the late medieval doctrine of transubstantiation.

Sacramental Theology by Christology, Not by Philosophy

Not only do we find in Bishop Lancelot Andrewes a positive model of how the Christology of the "Fathers" informs sacramental theology, but the bishop specifically rejects with this approach the late medieval view of transubstantiation. He denies "the substance of bread and wine to be flown away and gone" (dissolved or ceased to exist), and the "accidents to stay behind." This is a reference to the thirteenth-century Thomas Aquinas' philosophical categories in explaining the doctrine of transubstantiation. The latter is the belief that the bread and the wine become physically the Body and Blood of Christ.

Rather than using the Christology of the early church fathers, Aquinas explained how the bread and the wine could become the corporal Body and Blood of Christ by means of the Greek philosophy of Aristotle. He specifically built his sacramental theology on Aristotle's categories of form and matter. His use of the word *form* is a bit misleading to modern ears. To us today the word *form* implies "shape." For Aristotle, it meant the essence or being of a thing as distinguished from the matter or material. For example, according to Aristotle the matter of a chair is the wood or stone from which it's made. The form is the essence or being of the chair. He would call this essence or form the "chair-ness" or being in the chair. Based on such Aristotelian distinctions, Aquinas applied these categories to the Sacrament. He said the matter such as the bread and the wine are the "accidents." And he designated the form or the essence of the bread and the wine their "incidents."

However, with these distinctions between the incidence/substance/essence and accidence/matter, Aquinas significantly modified Aristotle to explain the sacramental view of transubstantiation. The medieval theologian said that the essence of a thing could be changed and therefore alter the physicality of an object. That is, the essence of the bread and the wine could become the substance or essence of Christ to make the physical element into His Body and Blood. Aristotle had never averred such a view. He never suggested that the substance of a chair could be changed and therefore make the object into something different. That would be like saying the essence or form of a chair could be transformed into the substance of an elephant and thereby make the chair physically into a pachyderm. The latter was Aquinas' novel view of not only Aristotle but of Eucharistic theology.

Nevertheless, Aquinas used a philosophical modification of Aristotle to rationalize how bread and wine could become the Body and Blood of Christ. The problem with the Thomistic metaphysical/philosophical explanation is that the physicality of the bread and the wine do not change into the material Humanity of Christ. In their shape they in some sense remain the same elements. The Host or Bread does not bleed if one sticks a knife in it. For this reason, Aquinas spoke of the presence of Christ under the forms of

---

[15] Hooker, *Laws*, V.67.2 (*Works* II:349).

Bread and Wine. But the doctrine of transubstantiation actually went further saying the Bread and the Wine are physically the Body and Blood. Therefore, the dilemma for Aquinas' philosophical approach is that the fullness of Christ's Humanity is not complete in the Sacrament if the forms are actually bread and wine.

For Andrewes and the English Reformers, this metaphysical approach was not only contrary to the Scriptures and early church fathers' model of sacramental theology, but it was fraught with a major Christological error. Andrewes asserts in the statement above that Aquinas' sacramental view commits the Christological heresy of Eutychianism. It was also known as the "real Monophysitism."

Monophysitism means "one (*mono*) soul (*physeis*)." The fifth-century Monophysites believed that Jesus did not have a human soul but only one Divine nature. His Humanity was *absorbed* into His Deity to have one Divine soul. He only appeared to be fully Human. Hence, Christ was not completely Human according to this approach to Christology. Andrewes and the English Reformers accused Aquinas of committing the same Christological fallacy with his metaphysical/philosophical approach to the Sacrament. That is, if the bread and the wine do not physically become flesh and blood, since they remain in form bread and wine, the Humanity of Christ is absorbed into His essence or substance in the Sacrament. Hence, the fullness of Christ's Humanity cannot be in the Sacrament. It is therefore a sacramental form of Monophysitism.

Bishop Andrewes and English Reformers concluded that Aquinas's metaphysical sacramental theology was in sharp disagreement with the ancient Christological understanding and approach to the mystery of Christ's real presence in the Sacrament. The church fathers had applied to the Sacrament the way that the Divine and Human natures of Christ communicate their properties to each other without the essence of either being dissolved. That is, as the *Athanasian Creed* says of the two Natures of Christ, "He is one, certainly not by the blending of his essence, but by the unity of his person," the same kind of mystical union occurs between the elements of bread and wine and the Body and Blood of Christ in Holy Communion. Through this mystical union, the faithful recipient of the Sacrament partakes of Christ.

Thus, when Aquinas wrote about Christology *per se*, he was orthodox. But his sacramental view of transubstantiation, according to Lancelot Andrewes, Hooker, the English Reformers, and later nineteenth-century catholic Anglicans such as C.B. Moss, became a Monophysite view of the Sacraments.[16] Thus, the Anglican approach returned to the Christology of Scripture and the ancient church fathers to describe Christ's relationship to the Sacrament and the faithful recipient. And they used this Chalcedonian theology to critique what they saw as an aberrant medieval doctrine of transubstantiation to explain real presence. Furthermore, they objected to reducing any explanation of this mysterious relationship of Christ to the Sacrament to one dogma as the Medieval Western Church had done. As we'll see, just as the Undivided Church explained the mystical union of Christ's real presence in the Sacrament with various explanations, so did the English Reformers.

---

[16] C. B. Moss, *The Christian Faith*, 364. See also, Charles Gore, *Dissertations on Subjects Connected with the Incarnation* (London: John Murray, 1895), 229–289.

The Incarnational Sacramental Theology of the English Reformation

The sixteenth-century Reformation in general addressed the incorrect medieval view of transubstantiation various ways. The Reformers were all trying to avoid the faulty consequences of this dogma. They understood that if the elements of the Sacrament become automatically the physical Body and Blood of Christ, then grace could be manipulated. They also recognized that much superstition had arisen around what they deemed a "magical" approach to Holy Communion. Yet, there was a range of approaches to correct the view of transubstantiation.

Some reformers referred to the sacraments as "effective signs." Others spoke of the sacraments as a "means of grace," or "signs and seals of the covenant of grace." Others in the Reformation so unfortunately overreacted to the theology and effects of transubstantiation in the medieval period that they resisted using the word *sacrament*. For them even this word was too closely associated with the transubstantiated view of real presence. They abandoned any sense of realism, not being able to accept other definitions of it in terms of holy mystery. They understood Baptism and Holy Communion as symbols only and called them ordinances or commandments but not sacraments. The Swiss Reformer Ulrich Zwingli, for example, denied that the "thing signified is in the sacrament."[17] Thus, different from the metaphysical transubstantiated view of real presence, some Reformers separated Christ from the elements and the Eucharist completely.

The English Reformation, however, was significantly different in the way it returned to mystery with various views. It has the means of grace emphases of the European (Calvin, Zwingli, etc.) side of the Reformation, but the instrumentality of the Sacraments is presented with Incarnational language. The English Reformation defines a Sacrament as an "outward and visible sign of an inward and spiritual grace." The catechetical *Offices of Instruction* say, "The outward part or sign of the Lord's Supper is, Bread and Wine.... The inward part, or thing signified, is the Body and Blood of Christ, which are spiritually taken and received by the faithful in the Lord's Supper." This language expresses some kind of Incarnational relationship between grace and the elements, "outward and visible, inward and spiritual grace." Some Anglicans, as we'll see, understand this Incarnational relationship at the point of reception. Others explain it in connection with the elements prior to reception. Either way, there is participation in Christ by means of the Sacrament.

Though initially cautious with the phrase "real presence," the English Reformation restored it with a different but earlier church understanding. The seventeenth-century Anglican Henry Aldrich, Dean of Christ Church, Oxford, explains this reluctance at first but the return to the use of real presence when he writes, "[At the beginning of the English Reformation] the Church of England [had] ... wisely forborn to use the term of *Real Presence*.... Yet it must not be deny'd, but the term may be safely us'd amongst Scholars and seems to be grounded upon the language of Scripture it self."[18]

---

[17] Huldrich Zwingli, "Of Baptism," in *Zwingli and Bullinger*, ed. Geoffrey Bromiley, Library of Christian Classics (Louisville, KY: Westminster John Knox, 2006), 129–175. See also, Michael Allen, "Sacraments in the Reformed and Anglican Reformation," in *The Oxford Handbook of Sacramental Theology*, ed. Hans Boersma and Matthew Levering (Oxford: Oxford University Press, 2015), 283–297.

[18] Henry Aldrich, *A Reply to Two Discourses* (Oxford: At the Theater, 1687), 15.

At the same time, the English Reformation always emphasized mystery. Bishop Lancelot Andrewes once commented in a sermon, "Christ said, 'This is my body.' He did not say 'This is My Body *in this way*.'"[19] In other words, it's a mysterious reality because He didn't go further. He didn't explain the how.

Yet in preserving the Biblical and patristic use of mystery, the English Reformation avoided the temptation to define real presence the way the medieval theologians had done. The seventeenth-century Archbishop William Laud states that the "Body and Blood of Christ are [given] to us; but are not transubstantiated in themselves into the Body and Blood of Christ, nor that there is any Corporeal Presence in or under the elements."[20] The seventeenth-century Bishop John Bramhall concludes similarly, saying, "This was the belief of the Primitive Church ... but we dare neither screw up the question [of the mode of real presence] to such a height, nor dictate our opinions to others so magisterially as articles of Faith."[21] He continues that not one argument "comes home to Transubstantiation, but only to true, Real Presence; which no genuine son of the Church of England did ever deny."[22] English Reformation theologians and Anglican scholars, as we have seen, draw upon the ancient Christology of Saints Hilary and Cyril for their understanding of Christ's presence in the Supper of the Lord or even in the elements.

While rejecting any sense of a physical change in the elements, the English Reformers hold to a "participationist" view of real presence in a variety of ways. They understand real participation in Christ in Holy Communion either at reception only, through the elements, in the elements, or simply affirming the reality left without explanation as holy mystery. With these views, they hold in common the following points: 1) They rely on the Christology of the Scriptures and the early church fathers to develop their understanding of union with Christ in or at the reception of the elements; 2) The faithful recipient participates in the full Humanity and Deity of Christ; 3) Faith is necessary for the Sacrament to be effectual; 4) And like the Undivided Church, they reject any one dogma for understanding Christ's mystery of real presence.

The Four English Reformation Models of Real Presence according to Early Church Christology

First, the mystery of Christ's presence has been understood by many Anglicans as *simultaneous* upon faithful reception/ingestion of the sacrament. Sometimes it's been called a subjective view of real presence for the emphasis on the faithful reception of the sacrament by the person and not Christ's presence in the elements prior to receiving them. Archbishop Thomas Cranmer is the preeminent representative of this view. He did say, "I never said that Christ is utterly absent," and he even called the sacrament "mystical bread," as in consecrated for sacred use. Yet he meant that Christ is "truly and spiritually present and truly and spiritually exhibited unto godly receivers." Given some of Cranmer's language, Anglican scholars such as Basil Hall believe that Cranmer

---

[19] Lancelot Andrewes, *Responsio*, C.I.1.
[20] William Laud, *Works*, ed. James Bliss, *Library of Anglo-Catholic Theology* (Oxford: John Henry Parker, 1853), III:353–355.
[21] John Bramhall, *Works*, I:22.
[22] Ibid., 8.

retained an objective aspect in his understanding of real presence. Others disagree such as the pre-eminent Cranmer scholar Ashley Null.[23]

Cranmer based his understanding of a simultaneous reception on the leading church fathers, Hilary and Cyril. However, he arrived at a different conclusion from them about Christ's Humanity and Deity being in the sacraments. He followed Oecolampadius, a German reformer, in his interpretation of these church fathers. Oecolampadius believed that the mutual indwelling of the total Christ is not in the elements but in the believer by means of the Holy Spirit. Like Calvin, he emphasized that Christ's Life and Virtue encompass both natures. His view is that since the Body of Christ is in heaven and Holy Communion is on earth, the fullness of His Life and Virtue (Deity and Humanity) is imparted parallel to faithful reception of the sacrament by the Holy Spirit working in the believer. There is also a perpendicular aspect. The believing recipient is lifted in heart and mind in faithful remembrance (memory) through the Spirit into complete union with Christ's full Humanity and Deity. Therefore, this complex of sacramental theology is a mystery expressed in a simple but beautiful nuptial phrase in the communion service of the *Book of Common Prayer*, "He in us and we in Him." Christ participates in the believer and the recipient in Him by the power of the Holy Spirit at the moment of faithful reception. It is the simultaneous mystery of real presence in the Anglican Way.

Excursus on the Expanded Views of Real Presence after Cranmer

Before mentioning the other views of real presence in the Anglican Way, it is important to explain some background that allowed additional variations of real presence beyond the Cranmer's simultaneous understanding. There were historical developments after Cranmer was martyred in 1556 by the Roman Catholic Queen Mary and Elizabeth I came to the throne in 1558.

The first major development was the revision of the 1552 *Book of Common Prayer* in 1559. In many respects, this revision completely reversed the Continental reformed edits to Cranmer's first 1548 prayer book. Among them was the removal of the Black Rubric that had been part of a 1552 version of the prayer book. This rubric (fine print instructions in the prayer book) attempted to distance the practice of kneeling for communion from any overly realistic view of Christ's presence in the sacrament. It

---

[23] Thomas Cranmer, *Defense of the True and Catholic Doctrine of the Sacrament of the Body and Blood of our Savior Jesus Christ*, ed. J. E. Cox (London: Parker Society, 1844), I:46, 127, 366. Basil Hall, "Cranmer, the Eucharist and the Foreign Divines in the Reign of Edward VI," in *Thomas Cranmer Churchman and Scholar*, Paul Ayris and David Selwyn, eds. (Woodbridge: The Boydell Press, 1993), 232–233. Hall suggests that Cranmer was not exclusively a subjectivist. He offers that the archbishop also expresses an objective aspect in some of his comments, though certainly not in any transubstantiated sense. Hall laments that Cranmer did not develop them. Ashley Null, *Thomas Cranmer, Christian Theologies of the Sacraments: A Comparative Introduction* (New York: NYU Press, 2017), 227, presents a parallelist approach of real presence in Cranmer. He notes Brian Gerrish, "Sign and Reality: The Lord's Supper in Reformed Confessions," *The Old Protestantism and New: Essays on the Reformation Heritage* (London: T&T Clark, 1982), 118–130. See also where Null explains how Cranmer was influenced by Saints Hilary and Cyril's insights about Christology and the sacraments. In particular, Cranmer adopted another reformer's (Oecolampadius) modification of Cyril. Null further describes Cranmer's explanation of how the spiritual involves being united to the whole Christ, Humanity and Deity, as mystery (226).

rejected that there is in "the Sacramental bread or wine there bodily received, or unto any *real and essential presence* there being of Christ's natural flesh and blood." When this language was removed from the prayer book in 1559, some Anglican scholars could embrace views of "real and essential presence" associated with the elements as long as the elements were not believed to be transubstantiated.

The *1662 Book of Common Prayer* did restore the Black Rubric but with a significant modification. It did not return to the denial of a "real and essential presence" but changed the phrase to "corporal presence," meaning the disallowance of belief in the physical presence of Christ in the elements. While rejecting that Christ is corporally present in the sacrament, Anglicans could still believe in a "real and essential presence." This explains how some Anglican scholars could reject transubstantiation but maintain an understanding of Christ's presence in relation to the elements. They did so based on the Christological and Incarnational models of real presence. Christ is mystically present, though the elements did not cease to exist. With this view they do not worship the elements but only Christ who is present, a view that reflects a participationist ontology rather than a physical change.

The second major development was the revision of Cranmer's *Forty-Two Articles* to the *Thirty-Nine Articles of Religion* adopted in 1571. As I explain in the chapter on The Reformed Catholic *Thirty-Nine Articles of Religion*, this doctrinal document written by Cranmer is reduced and edited to be more consistent with reformed catholicism. A new paragraph and Article XXVIII on the Lord's Supper were crafted by Bishop Edmund Guest (Gheast), Bishop of Salisbury.[24] Significantly, he held to a more objective understanding of Christ's presence in the elements reflected in the paragraph that says, "The Body of Christ is given, taken, and eaten in the Supper, only after an heavenly and spiritual manner. And the mean whereby the Body of Christ is received and eaten in the Supper, is Faith." This wording is not the same as Cranmer's *Forty-Two Articles*. Article XXVIII of the *Thirty-Nine Articles* asserts that Christ is given before being taken and taken before being eaten. It does not speak of Christ as only present when "received" at the point of consumption. Nor does it advocate any transubstantiated means of real presence. The same article clearly denies it. Rather, the new Article XXVIII associates His presence with the elements in some manner for His Body to be given and taken through these multiple actions before the sacrament is eaten.

The article follows the three verbs *"given, taken*, and *eaten"* with "in an *heavenly and spiritual manner."* For Guest, this language should be understood with the Christological/Sacramental views of the early church fathers Hilary and Cyril in the background. Engraght says of Guest's wording,

> The author of the 28th Article, says of the Real Presence, not merely that "Christ's Body is in the Sacrament," or that It is present "under the form of bread and wine"; but he says that "Christ's Body" *"is undoubtedly in the bread,"* and that *"It is presented in the bread (as questionless It is),"* and that *"It is presented in the accidents of the bread."* He [Guest] says the "Presence of Christ's Body in the Bread" may be explained by "the

---

[24] *Calendar of State Papers, (Domestic)*, 78.37. See reference in Dom Gregory Dix, *Shape of the Liturgy* (New York: Seabury, 1982 [1942]), 675–676.

personal presence of Christ's Godhead in His Manhood," and "the presence of the soul in the body."[25]

Enraght refers to Guest's correspondence with a "Bishop of Gloucester" that confirms Guest's intent and meaning in Article XXVIII. Bishop Cheney of Gloucester wrote a letter "having been offended by the word 'only' in the 28th Article ['the Body of Christ is given, taken, and eaten, in the Supper, only after an heavenly and spiritual manner'] as seeming [by some] to 'take away the presence of Christ's Body in the Sacrament.'"[26] Bishop Guest responded in explanation to Bishop Cheney,

> that this word *only* in the foresaid Article did not exclude the Presence of Christ's body from the Sacrament, but only the grossness and sensibleness in the receiving thereof: For I said unto him, *though he took Christ's Body in his hand, received it with his mouth, and that corporally, naturally, really, substantially, and carnally*, as the doctors do write, *yet did he not for all that see It, feel It, smell It, nor taste It.*[27]

Guest's version of Article XXVIII was combined with the removal of Article XXIX in the *Forty-Two Articles*. Cranmer's original Article XXIX had said,

> Forasmuch as the truth of man's nature requires that the body of one and the self-same man cannot be at one time in diverse places, but must needs be in some one certain place, the body of Christ cannot be present at one time in many and diverse places. Because (as Holy Scripture does teach) Christ was taken up into heaven, and there shall continue unto the end of the world, a faithful man ought not, either to believe or openly to confess the real and bodily presence (as they term it) of Christ's flesh and blood in the Sacrament of the Lord's Supper.

This Article states that Christ cannot be at the right hand of God the Father and also "in diverse places." However, given the view expressed by Guest in the new Article XXVIII of the *Thirty-Nine Articles*, Cranmer's original Article XXIX was inconsistent with it. In fact, the removal of this Article in the *Thirty-Nine Articles* further proves that Article XXVIII presents a different view of real presence. If Christ is objectively present with the elements in some heavenly and spiritual sense, then he can be mystically present at the right hand of the Father and in the Eucharist. As we shall see, Anglicans who held to an objective presence explained in various ways how Christ could be at both places. Nevertheless, given Cranmer's views as expressed in his *Forty-Two Articles*, the new Article XXVIII is a significant change. Dix concludes, "Bishop Guest's interpretation of his own doctrinal Article is fully as relevant as Archbishop Cranmer's interpretation of his own liturgy in determining the sense of Anglican eucharistic belief."[28]

Yet, others holding to Cranmer's position interpreted the actions in Article XXVIII as intended to mean simultaneous upon reception, although this was not Guest's position. They point out that the second sentence of the article only says, "received and eaten" by faith. They explain that if Christ is only received and eaten by faith then He is not present until eaten. This receptionist view, though not exactly Cranmer's, allows for

---

[25] R. W. Enraght, *Real Presence and the Holy Scripture* (London: G. Wakeling, 1872), Appendix A.
[26] Ibid.
[27] Enraght, *Real Presence*, Appendix A.
[28] Dix, *Shape*, 676.

the archbishop's view. Yet, the Cranmerians take the reference to "heavenly and spiritual manner" to speak of the Holy Spirit's work in keeping with Cranmer's position.

Other Anglicans differed, maintaining that Guest's language intends the second sentence to be a shortened form of multiple actions. He still uses two verbs, "*received* and *eaten*," indicating Christ is received in hand before being eaten. The purpose of the second sentence for Guest, however, is to emphasize that Christ is only received by faith even though He may be present in relation to the elements. Nevertheless, we can begin to see how the article led one group of Anglicans to understand it as referring to Christ's Body in the elements as well as at reception in faith. Another group took Article XXVIII to mean only at faithful reception, in line with Cranmer's interpretation. Therefore, both groups use Scripture, the *Articles of Religion*, and the prayer book to advocate their position.

The combination of changes in the *Thirty-Nine Articles* with the removal of the Black Rubric in the *1559 Book of Common Prayer*, therefore, further opens the door for some Anglicans to understand Christ's Body in relation to the elements by means of the Spirit prior to reception. Furthermore, the bishops in the Church of England permitted additional views of real presence to Cranmer's understanding, as long as they did not violate Scripture, the theology of the prayer book, or the *Articles*.

Also, after 1571, when the final version of the *Articles* was adopted with its sacramental modifications, in addition to changes in the 1559 prayer book, the bishops did not mandate any one dogma on real presence. They maintained rejection of a transubstantiated interpretation and that the sacraments are "only badges or tokens [signs] of Christian men's profession" (Article XXV). The result was that their concluding theological statement in the *Thirty-Nine Articles* reflects expanded sacramental views to Cranmer's between the two extremes of transubstantiation and the elements as only symbols with no connection to Christ at reception or in the elements. We can now consider the other three views of real presence in the Anglican Way beyond Cranmer's.

Three Other Christological Approaches to Real Presence

Instrumental Participation

The second approach to the mystery of real presence in the Anglican Way emerged in the second half of the sixteenth century and is called an instrumental view. The Anglican scholar Richard Hooker represented this understanding of real presence with what Diarmaid MacCulloch describes as a greater "hospitality towards sacramental modes of thought." Hooker speaks of the elements of the sacrament as "in verity and truth unto faithful receivers *instrumentally* a cause of that mystical participation."[29] Christ gives them "in hand an actual possession of all such saving grace," which is "*to* them *and in them* Christ's Body." He adds that the elements are "hallowed food" and an "instrumental cause" by "concurrence of divine power." Hooker, however, specifically says that Christ is not in the elements. Yet, he speaks of the elements as an instrumental means of "mystical participation." This is a participationist sacramentology based on the Christology expressed at the Council of Chalcedon.

---

[29] Hooker, *Laws*, V.67.12 (*Works*, II:359ff).

The key Biblical term for Hooker is *participation*, rooted in the language of St. Paul. The apostle says, "The cup of blessing that we bless is it not a *participation* in the Blood of Christ? The bread that we break is it not a participation in the Body of Christ?" (1 Cor 10:16–17). For Hooker, this language is consistent with the *Articles of Religion*, in which this verse is quoted from the apostle with the word *partake*.[30] He therefore adopts an even more self-conscious participationist understanding of St. Paul, as has been noted, based on the Christology of the Council of Chalcedon. For this reason, he is called a "Chalcedonian theologian." He summarizes his Chalcedonian approach by saying,

> That Christ assisting this heavenly banquet with His personal and true presence doth by his own divine power add to the natural substance thereof supernatural efficacy, which in addition to the nature of those consecrated elements changeth them and maketh that to us which otherwise they could not be; that to us they thereby make such instruments mystically yet truly, invisibly yet really, work our communion or fellowship with the person of Jesus Christ as well as in that he is man as God, our *participation* also in the fruit, grace and efficacy of his body and blood, whereupon there ensueth a kind of transubstantiation in us, a true change both of body and soul.[31]

In Hooker, Christ is present in the Eucharist "through instruments mystically," "in that he [Jesus Christ] is man as God." In this correlation we see the Chalcedonian influence. A union is formed between the faithful recipient and Christ by means of the elements analogous to Jesus' two natures mutually indwelling one another in His Person. Just as Christ's Person is the means for uniting his two natures, the consecrated elements function the same way in the Eucharist as a believer participates in Christ through their reception. Hooker speaks of a change, but not such that the elements cease to exist, nor that Christ is in the elements. The change is that the blessed bread and wine are transformed into instruments for participating in Christ. And furthermore, a kind of transubstantiated change is in the transformation of the person, not the elements. The Anglican's "real participation" understanding in this regard has been described as a *dynamic* conception of real presence. Hooker also asserts that communion is with the "whole" Christ in the fullness of His Deity and Humanity. He therefore represents one way the Anglican understanding of real presence builds on and expands beyond Cranmer while holding to Scripture, the prayer book, and the *Thirty-Nine Articles of Religion*. It's an instrumental view of the mystery of real presence in the Anglican Way that returns to a participationist Christology expressed in Scripture and the church fathers.

Objective Participation

Third, Christ's presence was also understood as *objective* in relation to the elements themselves by other Anglicans after Archbishop Cranmer. The seventeenth-century Bishop George Bull wrote

> that by or upon sacerdotal benediction, the Spirit of Christ, or a divine virtue from Christ, descends upon the elements, and that therefore they are said to be,

---

[30] Article 28.
[31] Hooker, *Laws*, V.67.11 (*Works*, II:357–358).

and are the body and blood of Christ; the same Divinity, which is hypostatically united to the body of Christ in heaven, being virtually united to the elements of bread and wine.[32]

Anglicans with this objective understanding at the same time reject that Christ's presence is corporal, physical, or local, resulting in the elements ceasing to exist. Nor does the objective approach maintain that Christ conveyed in the bread and wine can be received apart from faith. Again, it is real presence by means of participation, but which is an expanded view beyond Cranmer and even Hooker. It actually returns to more of Bishop Guest's original intentions in Article XXVIII of the *Thirty-Nine Articles*. Appeal is therefore made to Scripture and the church fathers as well as *The Articles of Religion* for support of the objective position on a participationist ontology.

As for Scripture, these Anglicans, in addition to Jesus' realist language in the Lord's Supper—"This is My Body; This is My Blood"—turn primarily to His teachings after He miraculously fed the multitudes. He said, "Truly, truly I say to you, unless you eat the flesh of the Son of Man and drink His blood you have no life in you.... For my flesh is true food, and my blood is true drink" (John 6:53–55). Some evangelicals, though not all, interpret his graphic terminology of "flesh and blood" as a description of the Incarnation and not as a reference to the Eucharist. They note Christ's later statement, "The flesh is of no avail" (John 6:63). They also point to the Lord's earlier comment, "This is the work of God, that you believe in Him whom He has sent" (John 6:29). They conclude that Christ in this passage is only describing His Incarnation as the "true manna" sent by the Father in whom they are to believe.

Those with an objective view of the sacrament respond to the non-sacramental interpretation of John 6 that Christ's instruction includes the Incarnation. But by using the language of "eat my flesh and drink my blood," He is speaking of how His Incarnate presence extends sacramentally in the elements to a recipient by faith. They cite that the entire context in John 6 is "eating" what God provides: Christ's feeding of the multitudes and reference to the Old Testament parallel of manna in the wilderness. They also note that Jesus begins His teaching section of the passage talking about the food of eternal life, "which the Son of Man *will give to you*" (John 6:27). It's a future tense sense of "giving" this food. Christ elaborates that "the bread that I *will* give for the life of the world is my flesh" (John 6:51). This takes place subsequently as He later explains at the Last Supper with almost identical language to John 6, "This is My Body; This is My Blood." And as for Christ's comment in John 6 that "the flesh is of no avail," it would additionally apply to the Incarnation if that were His intent. If the statement is categorically rejecting His flesh in the sacrament, it would also be denouncing it in the Incarnation. In fact, early Christological heretics such as the Docetists used this same verse to advocate that Christ only appeared to be fully Human. But the full statement is, "It is the Spirit who gives life; the flesh is of no avail." Jesus is not arguing against the flesh regarding the Incarnation or the sacrament, both of which are accomplished by the work of the Holy Spirit. His point is that the flesh without the Spirit avails nothing, not that the flesh has no importance. Therefore, according to an objective approach to real presence, Christ is

---

[32] George Bull, *Works* (London: John Ernest Grabe, 1703), I:254ff.

presenting in John 6 that He "will give" His Incarnational flesh and blood in the Eucharist.

In addition to Scripture, Anglican scholars have pointed to the objective sacramental language in the early church fathers. One example is the fourth-century St. Ambrose. Of the consecrated elements, he says,

> Let us be assured that this is not what nature formed, but what the blessing consecrated, and that greater efficacy resides in the blessing than in nature, for by the blessing nature is changed.... Surely, the word of Christ, which could make out of nothing that which did not exist, can change things already in existence into what they were not. For it is no less extraordinary to give things new natures than to change their natures.... Christ is in that Sacrament, because it is the Body of Christ; yet, it is not on that account corporeal food, but spiritual. Whence also His Apostle says of the type: "For our fathers ate spiritual food and drank spiritual drink." [1 Cor 10:2–4] *For the body of God is a spiritual body.*[33]

Christ is understood by Ambrose to be objectively present in the sacrament, though not corporeally. Christ is present by a mystical participation spiritually or supernaturally in the elements. Many Anglican theologians agreed by emphasizing Christ's objective presence through the elements.

Concerning the *Thirty-Nine Articles of Religion*, some Anglican scholars, following Bishop Guest's position on Article XXVIII discussed earlier, maintained that the Article supports an objective view of real presence. The seventeenth-century John Cosin (Bishop of Salisbury) said, "*In* the sacrament ... the body and blood of Christ ... are indeed really present ... and really united to the sacramental signs which not only signify but convey.... Yet ... in a way mystical, heavenly, and spiritual, as is rightly laid down in our Articles."[34]

The nineteenth-century Oxford Hebrew and Old Testament scholar Edward Pusey also appealed to the *Articles of Religion* for support of an objective view of real presence.[35] Concerning Article XXVIII, he was convinced that Guest intended it to mean Christ is present in or under the elements. Pusey also supported this understanding with the *Postscript* at the end of the *First Book of Homilies* mentioned in Article XXXV of the *Articles of Religion*. The *Postscript* speaks of an objective real presence as, "the due receiving of his blessed body and blood *under* the form of bread and wine."[36] This language of "under" is

---

[33] St. Ambrose, *On the Mysteries*, 9.50–52, 58 (emphasis mine).

[34] John Cosin, *Praelectiones*; cf. H. R. McAdoo and Kenneth Stevenson, *The Mystery of the Eucharist in the Anglican Tradition* (Norwich, UK: Canterbury, 1997; Eugene, OR: Wipf & Stock, 2008), 14.

[35] Tobias A. Karlowicz, *The Sacramental Vision of Edward Bouverie Pusey*: T&T Clark Studies in English Theology (New York: T&T Clark, 2021).

[36] John Griffiths, ed., *The Homilies*, revised (Herefordshire, UK: Preservation, 2006), 109. Edward Pusey, *The Real Presence of Christ in the Holy Eucharist* (London: James Parker, 1871), 1 n. 2. This sermon with notes builds on, explains further, and defends an earlier sermon he had preached, *The Holy Eucharist a Comfort to the Penitent* (London: James Parker, 1843). He prefaced this sermon with a quote from the *Sermon on the Worthy Receiving and Reverent Esteeming of the Sacrament* in the *Book of Homilies*, in which the Eucharist is referred to as a "deifical communion": *The Homilies*, 323. The objective presence approach using the *Formularies* of the English Reformation also

continued

similar to Aquinas' terminology but with a different meaning. The English Reformers rejected the doctrine of transubstantiation, maintaining according to Scripture and the church fathers that the elements did not cease to exist nor become the corporal presence of Christ. That is, unlike Aquinas, the English Reformers did not believe that Christ was somehow physically under the elements. And although, as I noted in Part One of this chapter, the view of transubstantiation in the sixteenth century had reverted away from Aquinas' nuanced approach to it, the English Reformers did not believe the elements corporeally changed. As I have explained, their use of *under* in the Postscript would have only been understood according to a participationist, not a conversionist ontology.

Pusey, in his reference to the Postscript's use of the word *under*, followed this participationist approach but with an objective view of it. He, too, denied any belief in transubstantiation. Yet he believed that Christ is objectively present in relation to the elements, albeit mystically "under" them, supernaturally participating in and conveying Christ to the faithful recipient by them. He also further reinforces his difference with Aquinas' transubstantiated view in that the medieval theologian believed the grace of the sacrament was automatic, "from the work performed" (*ex opere operato*). For Aquinas, grace came to the recipient irrespective of faith. If Anglicans, including Pusey, sacramentally agree on anything based on Scripture, it is that grace is only operative in the person by reception in faith and not by consecration of the sacrament alone.

A major counter to the objective view by evangelicals of the nineteenth century, however, is *Christ being seated at the right hand of God the Father* after the Ascension.[37] It was argued that in His Humanity, He could not be in two places at once. Pusey and others, in what came to be known as the Anglo-Catholic Movement in the Church of England and America, answered the objection much the way Lutherans did. Since Christ's resurrected body is supernatural, a spiritual body, it is not subject to natural laws. It is like all miracles that do not operate by natural law. Though in heaven, Christ could also be supernaturally present in some way at all the altars where Holy Communion is observed. Christ is not bound by natural law. Even in the current views of quantum physics, quite different from the old Baconian understanding of natural law, there is the law of entanglement whereby two protons are connected no matter how great a distance between them.

---

appears in Pusey's discussions about the Black Rubric that was added to the 1552 *Book of Common Prayer* and altered in the later 1662 edition. The 1552 version of the Black Rubric says that "lest the same kneeling might be thought or taken otherwise, we do declare that it is not meant thereby, that any adoration is done, or ought to be done, either unto the Sacramental bread or wine there bodily received, or unto any *real and essential presence* there being of Christ's natural flesh and blood." The 1662 prayer book removed the language of "real and essential presence," substituting the word *corporal*. For this reason, Pusey and others believed and used the words *real and essential* to explain the presence of Christ. At the same time, they understood the word *corporal* as denying that the "natural flesh and blood" of Christ are present in some crass and material sense. In other words, they interpreted the Black Rubric to be a denial of the sixteenth-century notion of transubstantiation that the *Articles* repudiate. In this way, Pusey could embrace the language of the *Postscript* to the *First Book of Homilies*, "The body and blood of Christ received under the form of bread and wine." Christ is therefore objectively present in this sense.

[37] Christopher J. Cocksworth, *Evangelical Eucharistic Thought in the Church of England* (Cambridge: Cambridge University Press, 1993), 80–81.

Others, however, have pointed to Scripture that teaches heaven and earth are mysteriously woven together or participate in one another in the Eucharist.[38] According to the writer to the Hebrews, worshipping believers on earth are surrounded by a "cloud of witnesses in heaven" (Heb 12:1). Something similar happens at Deacon Stephen's martyrdom and St. Paul's conversion, where Christ in heaven appears on earth. Scripture says, "heaven opens," by which Christ is present in the merger of heaven and earth (Acts 7:55–56, 9:3–4; 22:6–7). Some Anglicans with the objective understanding of real presence therefore believed that Christ does not have to leave His throne to be present in His Deity and Humanity at every altar. Christ is present, participating in consecrated elements and faithful recipients if one realm intersects the other. This is the third (objective) view of the mystery of real presence in the Anglican Way with a participationist ontology.

Real Presence Affirmed Without Explanation

A fourth way Anglicans have expressed the mystery of real presence is *affirmed without explanation*. By this I mean some Anglicans have advocated Christ as truly present in the Supper of the Lord but have not attempted to go any further. They offer no qualification. They acknowledge that when the Lord says, "This is My Body; This is My Blood," His presence is real but incomprehensible and unexplainable with any of the above views. "Is" means "is" for Scripture to be true to Christ's words, but according to Lancelot Andrewes, referenced earlier, we do not know how. At the same time, this view rejects a transubstantiated presence or any other attempt to comprehend the mystery of real presence. There is a mystical participation in Christ in the Eucharist that cannot be explained nor understood. It is left fully as a mystery. Perhaps the sixteenth-century Anglican Queen Elizabeth I provides the best example of this fourth approach. She is reported to have said, "Twas the Word that spake it; the same took bread and brake it; and as the Word did make it; so I believe and take it." The poetic verse also appears in slightly modified form in John Donne's seventeenth-century *Divine Poems on the Sacraments*.

To summarize, all four views are brought together without requiring any one dogma of real presence by the Words of Administration in the *Book of Common Prayer*. As the minister gives the sacrament in both kinds to an individual, he says first of the host/bread, "The Body of Christ, which was given for thee, preserve thy body and soul unto everlasting life." He says the same with the cup. The inference is the Body and Blood

---

[38] Will Spens, *Essays Catholic and Critical* (London: S.P.C.K., 1926), 441–443. See also Hans Boersma, *Heavenly Participation: The Weaving of a Sacramental Theology* (Grand Rapids: Eerdmans, 2011). The Black Rubric rejects that "Christ's true natural body, to be in more places than in one at one time." However, it should be realized that even the understanding of "natural law" in the sixteenth century was influenced by a Baconian kind of physics. This was a type of physics in terms of cause and effect, space, and matter. This meant that physical matter, heaven, and earth could only be conceived in isolation from one another. However, given the more current natural law of quantum physics—wave, particle, and field all at the same time—Bacon's model of matter and energy is no longer accurate, and therefore obsolete. We now actually can better understand the reality of Hebrews 12:1 because science has caught up with Scripture. That is, with quantum physics we can begin to fathom how two worlds separated by time and space can come together at the same time. Thus, Christ can be at more places at the same time because more places come before Him as "we are surrounded by a great cloud of witnesses."

of Christ are "given before taken." Yet, the second sentence in the Words of Administration says, "Take and eat this in remembrance that Christ died for thee and feed on him in thy heart by faith with thanksgiving."[39] The subjective or simultaneous understanding is expressed with the words "in thy heart by faith with thanksgiving."

Conclusion

I began the chapter with a classic quote from Richard Hooker where he says, "the mean between both which is both." This statement of how the Sacraments are one with Christ while still retaining the physicality of bread and wine is founded on the Scriptures and the Christology of the early church fathers. It is a reformed catholic approach. Relying on the Scriptures and the Christology of the ancient Church, the English Reformers refuted the medieval view of transubstantiation that had been defended in the thirteenth century with the metaphysics of Greek philosophy. Yet like the undivided church, the English Reformation theologians understood this mystical two-yet-one sacramental relationship in various ways, best described as a participationist view of real presence. Some Anglicans understood the mystical participation in terms of the faithful recipient and not the elements. Others interpreted it instrumentally and objectively in relation to the bread and the wine. Additional Anglican scholars only affirmed Christ's real presence based on Christ's statement, "is," and left it unexplained.

Therefore, in Anglicanism there are different views of the mystery of real presence according to Scripture, the Christology of the early church fathers, and Anglican standards. Like the Undivided Church, however, Anglicans did not require only one way or dogma for understanding real presence. Also, the undivided church that existed for a millennium with varying views of real presence was unified, so unity in diversity is possible for Anglicans. This, too, is part of the reformed catholic model of the Sacraments.

The seventeenth-century Anglican Bishop Jeremy Taylor expresses the need for unity when he says to "gather together into a union all those several portions of the truth, differing apprehensions of the mysteriousness." Like the early church, there are "apprehensions," various ways of understanding the mystery while affirming it. But Taylor also appeals to "gather together into a union ... differing apprehensions of the mysteriousness" without requiring any one view (dogma) concerning it.[40] To this end, I have summarized in this chapter how Anglicans have relied on the Christology of the Scriptures and the early church fathers to understand Christ's participation in the Supper of the Lord. It is a reformed catholic approach to the Sacraments. In the words of Richard Hooker, it is the "mean between both which is both." Hopefully, this effort to understand the reformed catholic sacramental model of the English Reformers will serve to unify "differing apprehensions of the mysteriousness."

---

[39] *1662/1928 Book of Common Prayer*, 82–83. These Words of Administration are found in more contemporary language in the *Book of Common Prayer 2019*, 120.

[40] Jeremy Taylor, *The Worthy Communicant* (1.I–II), in *Works*, ed. Reginald Heber, (London: Ogle, Duncan, & Co., 1822), XV:404–421, esp. 407, 410.

Chapter 4

Spirituality

The Rev. Dr. Greg Peters

Introduction

Any intellectually honest Christian will acknowledge that Christianity did not fall from heaven to earth whole cloth. Moreover, the same intellectually honest Christian will also admit that the earliest followers of Jesus borrowed from what had come before. An obvious example is Acts 2:42, 46–47a: "And they [the first Christians] devoted themselves to the apostles' teaching and the fellowship, to the breaking of bread and the prayers.... And day by day, attending the temple together and breaking bread in their homes, they received their food with glad and generous hearts, praising God and having favor with all the people." Notice that the first Christians, as converted Jews, continued worshipping in the Temple according to the practices associated with Second Temple Judaism. Thus, when it comes to considering a Re-formed Catholic Anglican spirituality, we are not surprised to see that it heavily depends on what has come before it, including not only Jewish precedents but also elements of Greek and Roman philosophy that were adopted by the early Church fathers and mothers.

Is there a unique Re-formed Catholic Anglican spirituality? If so, how is it Re-formed and Catholic? If not, then how should Anglicans think about the work of the Holy Spirit in the life of the baptized believer? Further, what is the role, if any, of the Sacraments in Re-formed Catholic Anglican spirituality?

Defining Spirituality

Let us begin with a definition. A very misunderstood word among Christians is spirituality. In fact, scholars have spilled a lot of ink trying to arrive at an agreeable definition. The well-known historian of Christian spirituality, Bernard McGinn, claims to have turned up thirty-five different definitions of spirituality without making an exhaustive search.[1] He suggests three approaches to the study of spirituality in an attempt to make sense of these many definitions: the theological approach, the anthropological approach, and the historical-critical approach. Another well-known writer on spirituality, Walter Principe, also sees a threefold element to spirituality: the real or existential level, the level of formulating a teaching about the lived reality (e.g., *Anglican* spirituality), and the level at which scholars study the first and second levels.[2] Though much more could be said, it seems that the theological approach is the most important. First, this is the perspective most consistent with the Christian faith for two reasons: 1) all of life is theological for we are theological beings and the world itself is theological (that is, created by and under the providential hand of God); and 2) theological encompasses "anthropological" and "historical-contextual." Anthropology needs to be a subcategory of "theological," as a purely anthropological approach to

---

[1] Bernard McGinn, "The Letter and the Spirit: Spirituality as an Academic Discipline," *Christian Spirituality Bulletin* 1.2 (Fall 1993): 4.

[2] Walter Principe, "Toward defining spirituality," *Religion/Sciences Religieuses* 12 (1983): 135–137.

spirituality will miss out on some important biblical-theological claims, such as original sin and *imago Dei*. The historical-contextual approach is a subcategory of theological, inasmuch as we are talking about God's work in the world (currently and historically) by way of the Holy Spirit.[3] Thus, we must understand spirituality in a theological way but not to the neglect of the anthropological (i.e., the real or existential level) or historical-critical (i.e., the lived reality). Simply put, spirituality is "the lived experience of Christian belief in both its general and more specialized forms" or "the effort to appropriate Christ's saving work in our lives."[4]

Anglican Spirituality

Is there a unique Re-formed Catholic Anglican spirituality? Working from this perspective then, we are led to the conclusion that when we use the phrase "Re-formed Catholic Anglican spirituality," we are at first acknowledging that we are formulating a teaching about the lived reality of a particular group of people, which, in this case, are those who worship in Anglican contexts using the *Book of Common Prayer*.[5]

What is this lived reality? Let us begin with what it is *not*. In 1895, Charles Gore (d. 1932), then Principal of Pusey House in Oxford, published the book *Dissertations on Subjects Connected with the Incarnation*, wherein he wrote, concerning Anglican theology, that the "characteristic of the Anglican Church has been from the first that of combining steadfast adherence to the structure and chief formulae of the Church Catholic with the 'turn to Scripture' which was the central religious motive of the Reformation."[6] This sentiment was echoed in 1938 by the Doctrine Commission of the Church of England:

> There is not ... a system of distinctively Anglican Theology. The Anglican Churches [*sic*] have received and hold the faith of Catholic Christendom, but they have exhibited a rich variety in methods both in approach and of interpretation. They are the heirs of the Reformation as well as of the Catholic tradition; and they hold together in a single fellowship of worship and witness.[7]

Thus, the lived reality, what we would call "Anglican spirituality," is not anything different than the living of the Christian life as it has always been led by faithful, Catholic Christians throughout the centuries. It is appropriate, if not a bit redundant, to speak of a "Catholic Anglican spirituality," but it is properly referred to as "Re-formed," for both Gore and the Doctrine Commission note that Anglicanism, as an expression of the Catholic tradition, has been impacted by the sixteenth-century Reformation. Gore called

---

[3] Greg Peters, "On Spiritual Theology: A Primer," *Journal of Spiritual Formation and Soul Care* 4.1 (2011): 19–26.

[4] Bernard McGinn, "Introduction," in *Christian Spirituality: Origins to the Twelfth Century*, ed. Bernard McGinn, John Meyendorff and Jean Leclercq (New York: Crossroad, 1985), xv–xvi.

[5] Perhaps it is naïve to define *Anglican* in such a simplistic manner, but it suffices for the current purpose. For more detailed discussion see Anthony Milton, "Introduction: Reformation, Identity, and 'Anglicanism,' in *The Oxford History of Anglicanism, Volume I: Reformation and Identity, c. 1520–1662*, ed. Anthony Milton (Oxford: Oxford University Press, 2017), 1–27.

[6] Charles Gore, *Dissertations on Subjects Connected with the Incarnation* (London: John Murray, 1895), 196.

[7] Cited in G. R. Evans and J. Robert Wright, eds., *The Anglican Tradition: A Handbook of Sources* (Minneapolis: SPCK/Fortress, 1991), 401.

it the "turn to Scripture" and the Doctrine Commission acknowledges that Anglicanism is an heir of the Reformation. Hence the use of *Re-formed*. It would seem, then, that the answer to our first question "Is there a unique Re-formed Catholic Anglican spirituality?" is "yes." There might not be "Catholic Anglican spirituality" *per se*, but there is a "Re-formed Catholic Anglican spirituality."

Re-formed and Catholic

We can now move to the second question: How is it Re-formed and Catholic? Right away in his preface to the first Book of Common Prayer (BCP) of 1549, Thomas Cranmer (d. 1556), principal architect of the BCP, wrote, "There was never any thing by the wit of man so well devised, or so surely established, which (in continuance of time) hath not been corrupted."[8] As surely as the sun sets each day, Cranmer is certain that in time everything is corrupted, in that it strays from its original form. Cranmer goes on to name these corruptions in the daily worship of the Catholic Church:

> But these many years passed this Godly and decent order of the ancient fathers, hath been so altered, broken, and neglected, by planting in uncertain stories, Legends, Responds, Verses, vain repetitions, Commemorations, and Synodals,[9] that commonly when any book of the Bible was began: before three or four Chapters were read out, all the rest were unread.[10]

He also notes that the number of psalms appointed for each daily office by the ancient fathers had been radically reduced and the worship books had become overly complex and, therefore, difficult to use. Thus, for Cranmer, the BCP was an attempt to restore Christian worship to its original form: "These inconveniences therefore considered: here is set forth such an order, whereby the same shall be redressed." This redress will include taking "out many things, whereof some be untrue, some uncertain, some vain and superstitious."[11] Though the immediate context of Cranmer's comments is the recitation of the entire Bible in the Daily Office, his comments also lend themselves to the whole of a Re-formed Catholic Anglican spirituality since the Daily Office (and the Holy Eucharist) are the backbone of this spirituality, a point that I will return to below.

Cranmer believed that the BCP, especially reading the whole Bible (or nearly all of it) every year, stirred up its users to love: "The people (by daily hearing of holy scripture read in the Church) should continually profit more and more in the knowledge of God, and be the more inflamed with the love of his true religion." The whole purpose of Anglican worship was "for a great advancement of godliness."[12] Simply put, the BCP is a spirituality, a Re-formed Catholic Anglican spirituality, to be exact. In the astute words

---

[8] Joseph Ketley, ed., *The Two Liturgies, A.D. 1549, and A.D. 1552: With other Documents Set Forth by Authority in the Reign of King Edward VI* (Cambridge: University Press, 1864), 17; modernized.

[9] Charles Wheatly, *A Rational Illustration of the Book of Common Prayer of the Church of England* (London: Henry G. Bohn, 1852), 139–140: "These were the publication or recital of the provincial constitutions in the parish-churches. For after the conclusion of every provincial synod, the canons thereof were to be read in the churches, and the tenor of them to be declared and made known to the people; and some of them to be annually repeated on certain Sundays in the year."

[10] Ketley, ed., *The Two Liturgies*, 17; modernized.

[11] Ibid., 18; modernized.

[12] Ketley, ed., *The Two Liturgies*; modernized.

of Anglican pastoral theologian Martin Thornton (d. 1986), "The Book of Common Prayer is derived from a long line of ancestors" and it is "designed to regulate the total life of a community, centered on the Divine Office, the Mass, and continuous devotion as daily, domestic life unfolds." It is "concerned with common, even 'family' prayer, ... prayer for the united Church or community."[13] Thornton has put his finger right on the pulse of the BCP and the spirituality that it espouses and promotes: the threefold order of Daily Office, Holy Eucharist, and private devotion. With Cranmer we would say that each of these foci include or—perhaps more rightly—are designed to facilitate our reading of the Holy Scriptures, for our Re-formed character, in the words of Gore, is rooted in our "turn to Scripture." Thus, let us focus on this quintessential feature of Re-formed Catholic Anglican spirituality, which is rooted in the Catholic Christian tradition, of course.

From the beginning of the Church's existence there was an expectation and a focus on the reading of God's words. Already in the Old Testament we have reference to the fact that the Jews, the people of God, were expected to read and meditate on the Law: "This Book of the Law shall not depart from your mouth, but you shall meditate on it day and night, so that you may be careful to do according to all that is written in it" (Josh 1:8). The words of God were thought to be a "lamp to [one's] feet and a light to [one's] path" (Ps 119:105). That is, they helped the disciple of God follow the commandments of God so as to please him and fulfill his Law.

This focus on the word(s) of God continued into the New Testament era. By this time the writings from before the time of Christ (i.e., the Old Testament) were collected and available to be read and were regularly read during public worship: "Devote yourself to the public reading of Scripture, to exhortation, to teaching" (1 Tim 4:13). This public reading of the Scriptures was valued because "whatever was written in former days was written for our instruction, that through endurance and through the encouragement of the Scriptures we might have hope" (Rom 15:4). In other words, the early Christians read the Scriptures so that they would be instructed and encouraged, especially as they awaited the second coming of Jesus Christ. The Scriptures were also valued because they were not like other writings, such as the epics of Homer or the philosophy of Plato and Socrates. No, the Christian Scriptures were "breathed out by God and profitable for teaching, for reproof, for correction, and for training in righteousness, that the man of God may be complete, equipped for every good work" (2 Tim 3:16–17). Further, these writings were "living and active, sharper than any two-edged sword" so that they could pierce the reader's conscience, showing readers their true selves (Heb 4:12). The Scriptures act as a kind of mirror so that when one reads them, one is looking into a mirror, seeing a reflection of oneself.

In the earliest Church the reading and preaching of the Scriptures continued to be highly valued, and this reading was explicitly tied to holiness (i.e., spirituality).[14] Let us take the second-century theologian Irenaeus of Lyons' *Demonstration on the Apostolic*

---

[13] Martin Thornton, "The Anglican Spiritual Tradition," in *The Anglican Tradition*, Richard Holloway (London and Oxford: Mowbray, 1984), 74.

[14] Hughes Oliphant Old, *The Reading and Preaching of the Scriptures in the Worship of the Christian Church*, Volume 2: The Patristic Age (Grand Rapids: Eerdmans, 1998).

Preaching as an example. Irenaeus wrote this work prior to the finalization of the canon of Christian Scriptures.[15] Though individual books were available, there was no "Bible" as such. Hence, Irenaeus focuses on the apostolic preaching, since that would have been the main way that the truths of the Christian faith (i.e., the so-called "rule of faith"[16]) were communicated to the earliest Christians. According to Irenaeus, "The prophets announced and Christ confirmed and the apostles handed over and the Church ... hands down to her children."[17] In the end we have the Bible, the Christian Scriptures.[18] Moreover, the purpose of these writings is to strengthen the faith of its readers or hearers. By way of this teaching the Christian is given illumined sight to see in a "single and upward" way, leading to the "kingdom of heaven, uniting man to God."[19] Keeping "the faith in God whole" leads to "holiness of soul."[20] For Irenaeus, right thinking that results from an illuminated reading of the Holy Scriptures leads to holiness. Thus, the reading of the Bible is the foundation of a Catholic spirituality and, thereby, of a Re-formed Catholic Anglican spirituality.

Returning to the sixteenth century, we should not be surprised to see a similar Iranaean thread in some of the earliest Anglican formularies and writings, especially given the fact that Cranmer and other early Anglican theologians (such as Nicholas Ridley [d. 1555], Hugh Latimer [d. 1555] and John Jewel [d. 1571]) were students of the patristic writers.[21] What Clifford Dugmore says about Cranmer et al. on the Holy Eucharist seems to be true of their Re-formed Catholicism in general: "One is so tired of reading that everything said by Cranmer or Ridley, Frith or Latimer or Jewel was derived from Luther, Zwingli or Calvin, as if they had no theological training, no knowledge of the Schoolmen or the Fathers and were utterly incapable of thinking for themselves."[22] We can expect, then, to find Catholic sensibilities in early Anglican writings on the Holy Scriptures and spirituality. In the *Thirty-Nine Articles of Religion*, we read that "Holy Scripture contains all things necessary to salvation" (Article VI). Likewise, the homily "A

---

[15] On the formation of the canon of Scripture see Craig D. Allert, *A High View of Scripture? The Authority of the Bible and the Formation of the New Testament Canon* (Grand Rapids: Baker Academic, 2007).

[16] Everett Ferguson, *The Rule of Faith: A Guide* (Eugene, OR: Cascade, 2015).

[17] Irenaeus of Lyons, *Demonstration of the Apostolic Preaching* 98, in *St Irenaeus of Lyons: On the Apostolic Preaching*, trans. John Behr (Crestwood, NY: St Vladimir's Seminary Press, 1997), 100.

[18] This process also results in the Christian "tradition," which contains elements of Christian faith and practice not explicitly cited in the Holy Scriptures.

[19] Irenaeus, *Apostolic Preaching* 1; Ibid., 39–40.

[20] Irenaeus, *Apostolic Preaching* 2; Ibid., 40.

[21] See G. V. Bennett, "Patristic Tradition in Anglican Thought, 1660–1900," *Oecumenica* (1971–72): 66–76; and Robert D. Cornwall, "The Search for the Primitive Church: The Use of Early Church Fathers in the High Church Anglican Tradition, 1680–1745," *Anglican and Episcopal History* 59 (1990): 303–329. Nonetheless, Cranmer is clear that the writings of the fathers is always secondary to the primacy of the Holy Scriptures. See Thomas Cranmer, "A Confutation of Unwritten Verities," quoted in Chapter 2: "That the Writings of the old Fathers, without the written Word of God, are not able to prove any doctrine of religion," in *Miscellaneous Writings and Letters of Thomas Cranmer*, ed. John Edmund Cox (Cambridge: University Press, 1846), 22–36.

[22] C. W. Dugmore, *The Mass and the English Reformers* (London: Macmillan/New York: St Martin's, 1958), vii.

Fruitful exhortation to the reading of holy Scripture," written by Cranmer and published in 1547 in the *First Book of Homilies*, states,

> There is no truth nor doctrine necessary for our justification and everlasting salvation, but that is or may be drawn out of that fountain and well of truth. Therefore as many as be desirous to enter into the right and perfect way unto God must apply their minds to know holy Scripture; without the which they can neither sufficiently know God and his will, neither their office and duty. And, as drink is pleasant to them that be dry, and meat to them that be hungry, so is the reading, hearing, searching, and studying of holy Scripture, to them that be desirous to know God or themselves, and to do his will. And their stomachs only do loathe and abhor the heavenly knowledge and food of God's word, that be so drowned in worldly vanities, that they neither savour God nor any godliness: for that is the cause why they desire such vanities rather than the true knowledge of God.[23]

The language of salvation, of course, is also the language of spirituality, for the Christian life is nothing other than one's justification that results in one's conformity to Christ or, to use an Irenaean phrase, the union of man to God. Ashley Null has summarized Cranmer's doctrine of justification this way:

In justification God pardoned sin by imputing Christ's alien righteousness to the ungodly, not by infusing in them an inherent personal merit. Concomitant with this externally based justification was an intrinsic renovation of the will and its affections by the indwelling of the Holy Spirit. Nevertheless, the Spirit's presence and the love he stirred in the believer's heart did not constitute a personal righteousness meritorious *de con-digno*. When used in a broader sense to refer to both pardon and renewal, justification could be said to make the ungodly "right-willed" but never inherently righteous.[24]

What is the "renovation of the will and its affections by the indwelling of the Holy Spirit" other than an apt description of *spirituality*? Recall the definition from McGinn quoted above, *spirituality* is "the effort to appropriate Christ's saving work in our lives." It seems right and good then to conclude that we are made holy, we live out a Re-formed Catholic Anglican spirituality when we read the Holy Scriptures, for this is truly, in part, what makes us Re-formed. But what is the role, if any, of the Sacraments in Re-formed Catholic Anglican spirituality? It is to this question that we now turn.

The Sacraments?

What is the role, if any, of the Sacraments in Re-formed Catholic Anglican spirituality? According to the *Thirty-Nine Articles of Religion*, "There are two Sacraments ordained of Christ our Lord in the Gospel, that is to say, Baptism and the Supper of the Lord" (Article XXVI). And these two dominical sacraments are necessarily connected

---

[23] John Griffiths, ed., *The Two Books of Homilies appointed to be Read in Churches* (Oxford: Oxford University Press, 1859), 7.

[24] Ashley Null, *Thomas Cranmer's Doctrine of Repentance: Renewing the Power to Love* (Oxford: Oxford University Press, 2000), 158–159.

together, in that those who approach the Lord's Supper are baptized Christians.[25] In one sense, then, to talk about the Lord's Supper includes baptism. Let us recall, with Martin Thornton, that the Anglican *regula* is the Daily Office, Holy Eucharist, and private devotion. Given its centrality in creating the unity of the Body of Christ and expressing it, we can conclude that the Holy Eucharist is the center of the life of the Church, and it is that to which the Daily Office prepares and from which personal devotion flows. To quote the Second Vatican Council, the Eucharist is "the source and summit of the Christian life,"[26] primarily because as a sacrament it conveys grace.[27] The Collect for Maundy Thursday says,

> Almighty Father, whose dear Son, on the night before he suffered, did institute the Sacrament of his Body and Blood; Mercifully grant that we may thankfully receive the same in remembrance of him, who in these holy mysteries giveth us a pledge of life eternal; the same thy Son Jesus Christ our Lord, who now liveth and reigneth with thee and the Holy Spirit ever, one God, world without end. *Amen.* (BCP 1928)

Christ instituted the Eucharist as a sacrament, and according to the *Thirty-Nine Articles of Religion*, sacraments are "ordained of Christ ... as not only badges or tokens of Christian men's profession, but rather they be certain sure witnesses, and effectual signs of grace, and God's good will towards us, by the which he doth work invisibly in us, and doth not only quicken, but also strengthen and confirm our Faith in him" (Article XXV: "Of the Sacraments"). Notice that the Eucharist is a sure witness and effectual sign of grace. As an "effectual sign" it rightly and accurately points to the greater reality, which in the Holy Eucharist is the literal body and blood of Jesus Christ: "This *is* my body.... This cup *is* ... my blood." As witness it testifies to the presence of grace in God's economy of salvation, and grace is the very thing (res) that we need to be in relationship to God; it is "the inward working of God's free mercy" that seals "in our hearts the promises of God."[28] It also effects "our holiness and joining in Christ."[29] Accordingly, the role of the sacraments is to make us holy by joining us to Christ; therefore, they have a central role to play in a Re-formed Catholic Anglican spirituality.

Because the Eucharist is a sure witness and effectual sign of "God's good will towards us," there is an intimacy to the Holy Eucharist—it is God's good will toward his Church. God's good will is evidenced by his desire that all people be saved for God "is patient toward [us], not wishing that any should perish, but that all should reach repentance" (2

---

[25] Despite contemporary arguments to the contrary, this was the mind of the earliest Christians. For example, see *Didache* 9.5: "let no one eat or drink from the Eucharist except those who are baptized in the name of the Lord" (Shawn J. Wilhite, *The Didache: A Commentary* [Eugene, OR: Cascade, 2019], xxxviii).

[26] Vatican II, *Lumen Gentium* 11; and *Catechism of the Catholic Church* 1324.

[27] That the sacraments convey grace is indicated in the *Thirty-Nine Articles of Religion* not only by the phrase in Article XXV that they are "effectual signs of grace" but also in Article XXVI ("Of the unworthiness of the Ministers, which hinders not the effect of the Sacraments") wherein the effect of the sacraments is not altered by the unholiness of the priest administering the sacrament for "the grace of God's gift" is not "diminished," assuming that the sacrament is rightly received. Sacraments convey grace, it is what they do as instruments of God's good will toward the Church.

[28] "Of Common Prayer and Sacraments" in *The Two Books of Homilies*, 353.

[29] Ibid., 355.

Pet 3:9). In the words of the great spiritual theologian Thomas à Kempis (d. 1471): "I have given my very Body and Blood to be your food, that I may be all yours, and that you may be mine for ever."[30] God wants his followers to be sanctified, made holy for "this is the will of God, your sanctification" (1 Thess 4:3). Thomas Cranmer says it this way: "Christ ordained the sacrament to move and stir all men to friendship, love, and concord, and to put away all hatred, variance, and discord, and to testify to brotherly and unfeigned love between all them that be the members of Christ...And that finally by his means they may enjoy with him the glory and kingdom of heaven."[31]

This is accomplished by the Eucharist because it works invisibly by quickening, strengthening, and confirming our faith. Regarding our quickening, the Apostle Paul says to the Christians at Corinth, "The first man Adam was made a living soul; the last Adam was made a quickening spirit" (1 Cor 15:45). The context here is resurrection and life. Thus, the believer is quickened when given resurrection life; that is, made like Jesus Christ, for faith is made alive. Regarding strengthening, the follower of Jesus "can do all things through him who strengthens" him (Phil 4:13). The Christian is strengthened in order to do the work that he or she has been given to do, for a living faith orients the direction of lives of service: "we humbly beseech thee, O heavenly Father, so to assist us with thy grace, that we may continue in that holy fellowship, and do all such good works as thou hast prepared for us to walk in" (BCP 1928). Lastly, regarding confirming, the Apostle Paul writes to the church in Corinth:

> Grace to you and peace from God our Father and the Lord Jesus Christ. I give thanks to my God always for you because of the grace of God that was given you in Christ Jesus, that in every way you were enriched in him in all speech and all knowledge— even as the testimony about Christ was confirmed among you—so that you are not lacking in any gift, as you wait for the revealing of our Lord Jesus Christ, who will sustain you to the end, guiltless in the day of our Lord Jesus Christ (1 Cor. 1:3–8).

Though one's faith may be shaky at times, God's will is that a Christian's faith be firm and unwavering, and it is the Eucharist and its operative grace that effects the confirmation of our faith. The whole reason that Christ instituted the Holy Eucharist, writes Cranmer, is to "confirm [our] faith and hope of eternal salvation."[32]

A Re-formed Catholic Anglican spirituality sees several things occurring at the Holy Eucharist. First, the humble elements of bread and wine betray the great riches of the Eucharistic feast but also serve as an image of the Christian's need to come to the Lord's Table humbly. The humble nature of the elements themselves are reflected in the priest's prayer over the offering, which goes back to Jewish practice: "Blessed be thou, Yahweh, our God, King of the universe, who givest us this fruit of the vine"; and "Blessed be thou,

---

[30] Thomas à Kempis, *The Imitation of Christ*, trans. Leo Sherley-Price (London: Penguin, 1952), 198.

[31] Thomas Cranmer, *Defensio verae et catholicae doctrinae de sacramento* 1.7; Henry Wace, ed., *Archbishop Cranmer on the True and Catholic Doctrine and Use of the Sacrament of the Lord's Supper* (London: Chas. J. Thynne, 1901), 10–11.

[32] Cranmer, *Defensio verae et catholicae doctrinae de sacramento* 1.Pref.; Wace, ed., Archbishop Cranmer, xxii.

Yahweh, our God, King of the universe, who bringest forth bread from the earth"[33] or, in modern Christian parlance, "Blessed are you, Lord God of all creation, for through your goodness we have received the bread we offer you: fruit of the earth and work of human hands, it will become for us the bread of life"; and "Blessed are you, Lord God of all creation, for through your goodness we have received this wine we offer you: fruit of the vine and work of human hands, it will become our spiritual drink." Through the very common elements of bread and wine God works his Eucharistic miracle. The communicant must, however, receive in a worthy manner, which includes, among other things, humility in imitation of Jesus who "humbled himself by becoming obedient to the point of death, even death on a cross" (Phil 2:8). In the words of Cranmer, we "ought ... to approach to this heavenly table with all humbleness of heart, and godliness of mind."[34]

Second, and very obviously, humans are sinners before God in that they are born in original sin and continue to sin against God through actual sins. Nonetheless, "as in Adam all die, so also in Christ shall all be made alive" (1 Cor 15:22) for the sacramental grace makes its way through every part of a person: inwardly in the soul and outwardly in the body.[35] It transforms the whole person, for God cares about our souls and bodies: "Grant us therefore, gracious Lord, so to eat the flesh of thy dear Son Jesus Christ, and to drink his blood, that our sinful bodies may be made clean by his Body, and our souls washed through his most precious Blood" (Prayer of Humble Access). The grace of the sacrament nourishes and strengthens every part of the baptized Christian.

Third, because Christ is spiritually present in the bread and the wine, the division between the body and soul, the material and the immaterial has been overcome, the key that unlocks the door has been used.[36] This is why the immaterial grace of the Eucharist effects a change in embodied sins and offenses, and this is made possible, of course, by

---

[33] Louis Boyer, *Eucharist: Theology and Spirituality of the Eucharistic Prayer* (Notre Dame: University of Notre Dame Press, 1968), 70–80.

[34] Cranmer, *Defensio verae et catholicae doctrinae de sacramento* 4.6; Wace, ed., Archbishop Cranmer, 218.

[35] See the Collect for the Second Sunday in Lent: "Almighty God, who seest that we have no power of ourselves to help ourselves; Keep us both outwardly in our bodies, and inwardly in our souls; that we may be defended from all adversities which may happen to the body, and from all evil thoughts which may assault and hurt the soul; through Jesus Christ our Lord. *Amen*" (BCP 1928).

[36] See stanzas 4–5 of George Herbert's (d. 1633) "The Holy Communion":

> Onely thy grace, which with these elements comes,
> > Knoweth the ready way,
> > And hath the privie key,
> Op'ning the soul's most subtile rooms;
> While those to spirits refin'd, at doore attend
> > Dispatches from their friend.

> Give me my captive soul, or take
> > My bodie also thither.
> Another lift like this will make
> > Them both to be together.

the fact that Jesus is both a man and God. The ineffability of the hypostatic union leads to the ineffability of the real presence. It is the incarnation of Jesus Christ at a particular time and in a particular place that is the foundation of all sacramental theology. Without the Incarnation there would be no sacramental grace by way of the material bread and wine. Thus, a Re-formed Catholic Anglican spirituality will encourage frequent Communion so that the communicant continues to receive the grace of God in order to experience the "effectual working of his power" (Eph 3:7, KJV).

Fourth, it is by sacramental grace that God has made it possible for the Christian to leave earth for heavenly discourse with God—a movement of theosis and union with God. In the words of Anglican theologian and priest Edward Pusey (d. 1882),

> The gift vouchsafed in the Holy Communion must be altogether of a different kind, because it is not the stirring up of the human spirit, but the union of the Divine, the Presence of the Redeemer within the soul, when the soul is silent, not acting upon itself, but 'caught up', present with its Lord, because 'one with Him,' penetrated with Him and His Divinity, when in solemn words which have been used, the soul is 'transfigured' by His Holy Presence in it.[37]

In short, in receiving Christ's body sacramentally, communicants receive into their body Christ's life and divinity that leads to their own transformation or *theosis*. Further, Pusey says that Christ's "life... is transmitted to us also, and not to our souls only, but our bodies also, since we become flesh of His flesh, and bone of His bone."[38] Through Eucharistic grace we are "caught up within the influence of the mystery of [God's] ineffable love."[39] It is by sacramental grace that we are not only brought into a saving relationship with Jesus Christ, but we are made one with the Holy Trinity—as we grow in love we are joined to God who is Love for anyone "who does not love does not know God, because God is love" (1 John 4:8).

Though the *Thirty-Nine Articles of Religion* only refer to baptism and the Holy Eucharist as dominical sacraments, the Anglican Church in North America's *To Be a Christian: An Anglican Catechism* states that "Other rites and institutions commonly called sacraments include confirmation, ordination, marriage, absolution, and the anointing of the sick. These are sometimes called 'sacraments of the Church.'"[40] These sacraments "were not ordained by Christ as necessary to salvation, but arose from the practices of the apostles and the Early Church, or were blessed by God in Scripture. God clearly uses them as means of grace."[41] Because these sacraments are also "means of grace," they contribute

---

[37] Edward Bouverie Pusey, *A Letter to the Right Hon. and Right Rev. the Lord Bishop of London, in Explanation of Some Statements Contained in a Letter by the Rev. W. Dodsworth* (Oxford: John Henry Parker, 1851), 155–156.

[38] Edward Bouverie Pusey, *The Holy Eucharist a Comfort to the Penitent* (Oxford: John Henry Parker, 1843), 11.

[39] Ibid., 14.

[40] *To Be a Christian: An Anglican Catechism* (Wheaton, IL: Crossway, 2020), 56; scripture references removed.

[41] Ibid., 56. The language of "clearly uses them as means of grace" seems to go beyond what is stated in Article XXV: "Those five commonly called Sacraments, that is to say, Confirmation, Penance, Orders, Matrimony, and Extreme Unction, are not to be counted for Sacraments of the

continued

to the believer's growth in holiness and, therefore, are spiritual aids. It is proper in a Re-formed Catholic Anglican spirituality to hold to these five sacraments, given that they meet the criteria for catholicity ("arose from the practices of the apostles and the Early Church") but also are Re-formed in that they "were blessed by God in Scripture." Like the Holy Eucharist, these sacraments are God's means to unite us to himself through our participation in the life of the Holy Trinity. Like baptism and the Lord's Supper, these sacraments play an essential role in the life of the believer, leading to salvation, which is holiness.

In particular, the sacrament of absolution (i.e., Confession or the "Reconciliation of Penitents") seems most useful in a Re-formed Catholic Anglican spirituality. Though the BCP 1549 did not have a specific rite for Confession, there was the following instruction for the "Visitation of the Sick": "Here shall the sick person make a special confession, if he feel his conscience troubled with any weighty matter. After which confession, the priest shall absolve him after this form: and the same form of absolution shall be used in all private confessions."[42] From this we can conclude that Cranmer assumed that sick persons near death would desire to confess their sins but it also assumes "private confessions." In his *Questions and Answers concerning the Sacraments* from 1540, Cranmer says, "A man is not bound by the authority of this scripture[43]... and such like, to confess his secret deadly sins to a priest, although he may have him."[44] Nonetheless, if one chooses to confess one's sins to a priest, Cranmer emphasized that it was most valuable because of the need in the spiritual life for true contrition: "The Scripture speaketh not of Penance, as we call it a sacrament, consisting in three parts, contrition, confession, and satisfaction; but the Scripture taketh Penance for a pure conversion of a sinner in heart and mind from his sins unto God."[45] Though there is a psychological benefit to Confession (naming one's sins aloud to another person) that may help the confessant resist sin, the true end of the sacrament is genuine contrition so that one may sin less and grow in holiness. In the words of the Collect following the absolution in the BCP 1549:

> Most merciful God, which according to the multitude of thy mercies, does so put away the sins of those which truly repent, that thou remember them no more: open thy eye of mercy upon this thy servant, who most earnestly desires pardon and forgiveness: Renew in him, most loving father, whatsoever hath been decayed by the fraud and malice of the devil, or by his own carnal will, and frailness: preserve

---

Gospel, being such as have grown partly of the corrupt following of the Apostles, partly are states of life allowed in the Scriptures; but yet have not the like nature of Sacraments with Baptism and the Lord's Supper, for that they have not any visible sign or ceremony ordained of God." It appears that Article XXV is *not* closed to these sacraments being used of God as a means of grace, but they do not do so by virtue of being sacraments. Article XXV's reluctance seems to go back to the anti-Roman Catholic posture of the *Thirty-Nine Articles of Religion*. *To Be a Christian* restores the catholicity of the "commonly called Sacraments."

[42] Ketley, ed., *The Two Liturgies*, 138.

[43] John 20:23: "If you forgive the sins of any, they are forgiven them; if you withhold forgiveness from any, it is withheld."

[44] Cox, ed., *Miscellaneous Writings and Letters*, 117.

[45] Cox, ed., *Miscellaneous Writings and Letters*, 116.

and continue this sick member in the unity of thy Church, consider his contrition, accept his tears, assuage his pain, as shall be seen to thee most expedient for him. And forasmuch as he puts his full trust only in thy mercy: Impute not unto him his former sins, but take him unto thy favour: through the merits of thy most dearly beloved son Jesus Christ. Amen.[46]

Conclusion

The contemporary Church, at least in North America among Protestants, needs renewal, perhaps even reform like that of the sixteenth century, which gave birth to a Re-formed Catholic Anglican spirituality. The days of vapid lyrics set to unsophisticated music and therapeutic preaching must end if the Church is to live not only into her mission of making disciples of all nations (Matt 28:19) but to foster the holiness of her members (1 Thess 4:3). There must be a "turn to Scripture" so as to enliven the Church and bring about a renewed appreciation of and celebration of the Holy Sacraments. In this way, Re-formed Catholic Anglicanism has much to offer, rooting followers of Christ in the Catholic tradition while also remaining faithful to the teachings of the Holy Scriptures.

---

[46] Ketley, ed., *The Two Liturgies*, 138–139.

Chapter 5

Asceticism

The Rev. Dr. Greg Peters

Introduction

The content of this chapter necessarily grows out of the previous chapter on Re-formed Catholic Anglican spirituality. In many ways, asceticism is the flip side of the coin of spirituality, inasmuch as asceticism is a necessary component of the spiritual life. In fact, the centrality of asceticism in world religions and schools of philosophy shows that ascetical practices are part of what it means to be a human. The historian of ancient philosophy Pierre Hadot has shown how even Greco-Roman philosophy was essentially a form of asceticism,[1] and questions of embodiment are often cast in the terms of asceticism.[2] Though I doubt if she has ever used the word *asceticism*, Marie Kondo's philosophy of organization and "tidying up" is a kind of asceticism[3] as are Greg McKeown's ideas on essentialism.[4] It seems obvious to anyone with the eyes to see that asceticism is necessary today to counteract the materialistic perspective that permeates world cultures. Moreover, within the Christian Church there is a functional, if not implicit, Pelagianism, that humankind's perfection depends on our efforts and nothing else, a view that reduces salvation to a kind of asceticism. Ascetical practices, and the corresponding discipline of ascetical theology, show that this is not the case.

This chapter, then, seeks to answer the following questions: What is the role of asceticism and ascetical practices in a Re-formed Catholic Anglicanism? What ascetical practices have developed in the history of the Church that may need to be re-introduced or discarded from a Re-formed Catholic Anglican perspective? How is asceticism an outgrowth of Holy Baptism and related to the other Sacraments?

Defining Asceticism

The earliest use of ἄσκησις (*askēsis*) occurs in Homer's *Iliad* (c. eighth century BC) where it expresses the idea of artistic work: "His chariot is fairly ornate [ἤσκηται] with gold and with silver" (10.438); or it describes the technique used to produce such work: "Lakedaimon made beautiful things [ἤσκειν] out of wool" (3.388).[5] Subsequently, the word began to be used in three ways: 1) physical, 2) moral, and 3) religious. From the Homeric idea of "practicing an art" it is not hard to see how the idea of exercising the body came to the fore. For example, the historian and philosopher Xenophon of Athens

---

[1] Pierre Hadot, *Philosophy as a Way of Life: Spiritual Exercises from Socrates to Foucault* (Oxford: Blackwell, 1995).

[2] Mary G. Winkler and Letha B. Cole, eds., *The Good Body: Asceticism in Contemporary Culture* (New Haven: Yale University Press, 1994).

[3] See Marie Kondo, *The Life-Changing Magic of Tidying Up: The Japanese Art of Decluttering and Organizing* (Berkeley: Ten Speed, 2014); and *Spark Joy: An Illustrated Master Class on the Art of Organizing and Tidying Up* (Berkeley: Ten Speed, 2016).

[4] Greg McKeown, *Essentialism: The Disciplined Pursuit of Less* (New York: Crown Business, 2014).

[5] Richard Lattimore, trans., *The Iliad of Homer* (Chicago: University of Chicago Press, 2011), 248 and 360.

(d. 354 BC) wrote, "And while the enemy were said to be approaching but had not yet come, Cyrus tried to develop [ἀσκεῖν] the physical strength of his men, to teach them tactics, and to steel their hearts for war."[6] Morally, the word came to be used by philosophers characterizing the effort put forward by the soul to gain wisdom and/or virtue. To quote Xenophon again, this time from his *Memorabilia*,

> But many self-styled philosophers may reply: A just man can never become unjust; a prudent man can never become wanton; in fact no one having learned any kind of knowledge can become ignorant of it. I do not hold with this view. I notice that as those who do not train [ἀσκοῦντας] the body cannot perform the functions proper to the body, so those who do not train [ἀσκοῦντας] the soul cannot perform the functions of the soul: for they cannot do what they ought to do nor avoid what they ought not to do. That is why fathers try to keep their sons, even if they are well behaved, out of bad company: for the society of honest men is a training [ἄσκησιν] in virtue, but the society of the bad is virtue's undoing.[7]

Aristotle says something very similar in his *Nicomachean Ethics*: "Good people's life together allows the cultivation [ἄσκησις] of virtue."[8] Lastly, ἄσκησις was used to refer to the practice of one's religion: "for Busiris established for [the Egyptians] numerous and varied practices of piety [ἀσκήσεις τῆς ὁσιότητος]"[9]; or, "For I know well that they will not only not be worsened, but actually bettered, through the persistence of their worship and through practising piety [εὐσέβειαν ἀσκήσαντες] pure and undefiled."[10]

By the time of the New Testament, the moral usage had become predominant. When he testified before Felix, the governor of Judea, the Apostle Paul assured him that he worshipped "the God of our fathers, believing everything laid down by the Law and written in the Prophets, having a hope in God, which these men themselves accept, that there will be a resurrection of both the just and the unjust." Paul swore that he believed what the Jews believed and was not attempting to stir up a crowd but was attempting to do the opposite, confessing, "I always take pains to have a clear conscience toward both God and man" (Acts 24:14–16).[11] The phrase "take pains" is the word ἀσκῶ, from ἀσκέω (*askeō*), which at that time had come to mean "to exercise or to practice."[12] Thus, Paul uses ascetical practices to have a "clear conscience" before God and others. Further, Paul, like the philosophical tradition before him,[13] connects ἀσκέω to bodily exercise and training: "For this is the will of God… that each one of you know how to control his own body in

---

[6] Walter Miller, trans., *Xenophon: Cyropaedia, Books 1–4*, LCL 51 (Cambridge, MA: Harvard University Press, 1914), 145.

[7] E. C. Marchant and O. J. Todd, trans.; Jeffrey Henderson, rev., *Xenophon: Memorabilia, Oeconomicus, Symposium, Apology*, LCL 168 (Cambridge, MA: Harvard University Press, 2013), 27.

[8] Terence Irwin, trans., *Aristotle: Nicomachean Ethics*, 3rd ed. (Indianapolis: Hackett, 2019), 177.

[9] Isocrates, *Busiris* 26; Van Hook, La Rue, trans., *Isocrates: Volume III*, LCL 373 (Cambridge, MA: Harvard University Press, 1945), 117. Isocrates was an Athenian rhetorician who died in 338 BC.

[10] Philo of Alexandria, *On Abraham* 129; F. H. Colson, trans., *Philo: Volume VI*, LCL 289 (Cambridge, MA: Harvard University Press, 1935), 67.

[11] Unless otherwise noted, all Scripture references are from the English Standard Version.

[12] Hermigild Dressler, *The Usage of Ἀσκέω and its Cognates in Greek Documents to 100 A.D.* (Washington, DC: Catholic University of America, 1947), 71–73.

[13] Dressler, *The Usage of Ἀσκέω*, 36.

holiness and honor" (1 Thess 4:3–4); and, "Do you not know that in a race the runners all compete, but only one receives the prize? Run in such a way that you may win it. Athletes exercise self-control [ἀγωνιζόμενος πάντα ἐγκρατεύεται] in all things; they do it to receive a perishable wreath, but we an imperishable one" (1 Cor 9:24–25).

It is this understanding that continues into the wider Christian tradition, demonstrating that asceticism is part of the Catholic tradition in that ascetical practices have always been part of the warp and woof of Christian living. The early Church father Clement of Alexandria (d. c. 215), in a chapter of his *Stromata* titled "Description of the Perfect Man, or Gnostic,"[14] gives a list of biblical commands and then concludes, "Such are the preparatory exercises of gnostic discipline [ἀσκήσεως]."[15] In his *Paedagogus* Clement says that the patriarch Jacob is an example of a Christian ascetic/athlete: "See how the Educator follows a just man, anoints the athlete [ἀσκητήν], and teaches him to overcome his adversary."[16] Origen of Alexandria (d. c. 253), in his *Homilies on Jeremiah*, says that he will "describe something which happens with ascetics [ἀσκηταῖς]." He continues by listing a number of common ascetical practices: celibacy, bodily mortification through fasts, and abstinence from certain foods. He concludes that each person has an option to either call upon faithfulness or call upon misery,[17] or, in imitation of the prophet Jeremiah, to "*call upon faithfulness*... but also let him *call upon misery* through ascetical practices [ἀσκήσεσι]."[18] What Origen is getting at here is that one can adopt ascetical practices in a way that makes them miserable (i.e., disciplined living through rigorous and continual asceticism) or that makes them faithful (i.e., disciplined living through occasional asceticism). This sets a proper vision for the way that asceticism has been practiced throughout the Christian Catholic tradition, with an asceticism of misery pertaining in particular to monastics and an asceticism of faithfulness being proper to all non-monastic Christian disciples.

We, however, are concerned with not only a Catholic asceticism but a Re-formed Catholic Anglican asceticism. Let us turn to the thinking of Charles Gore, who says that what makes Anglicanism Re-formed is its "turn to Scripture."[19] Thus, we might say that a Re-formed Catholic Anglican asceticism is not only an asceticism born out of the Catholic tradition but also rooted in the Scriptures. That is, some ascetical practices stem directly from the Holy Scriptures (e.g., fasting) while others emerge from the practices

---

[14] Clement is using the word *gnostic* here not to refer to some kind of heretic as it was often used but as a way of talking about a Christian who is thoroughly catechized into the mysteries of the Christian faith.

[15] Clement of Alexandria, *Stromata* 4.21; William Wilson, trans., *Ante-Nicene Fathers* (Buffalo, NY: Christian Literature, 1885), 2:433.

[16] Clement of Alexandria, *Paedagogus* 1.7.57; Simon P. Wood, trans., *Clement of Alexandria: Christ the Educator* (Washington, DC: Catholic University of America Press, 1954), 52.

[17] This distinction comes from a Geek rendering (the Septuagint recension) of Jer. 20:8 in Origen's *Hexapla*: ὅτι πικρῷ λόγῳ μου γελάσομαι, ἀθεσίαν καὶ παλαιπωρίαν ἐπικαλέσομαι (Frederick Field, ed., *Origenis Hexaplorum* (Oxford: Clarendon, 1875), 2:624.

[18] Origen, *Homilies of Jeremiah* 20.7; John Clark Smith, trans., *Origen: Homilies of Jeremiah, Homily on 1 Kings 28* (Washington, DC: Catholic University of America Press, 1998), 237.

[19] Charles Gore, *Dissertations on Subjects Connected with the Incarnation* (London: John Murray, 1895), 196.

of the Church (e.g., use of a hair shirt). For example, the Apostle Paul provides a good illustration of this principle in 1 Cor 7:3–5:

> The husband should give to his wife her conjugal rights, and likewise the wife to her husband. For the wife does not have authority over her own body, but the husband does. Likewise the husband does not have authority over his own body, but the wife does. Do not deprive one another, except perhaps by agreement for a limited time, that you may devote yourselves to prayer; but then come together again, so that Satan may not tempt you because of your lack of self-control.

Celibacy within marriage was not unheard of in pre-Christian philosophy and other religions. Though quite crass, Aristophane's *Lysistrata* depicts a group of women choosing to forsake sex with their husbands in order to bring a quicker end to war. There was also the annual Greek religious festival *Thesmophoria* wherein husbands and wives forsook sex for a season. The sixth-century BC philosopher Pythagoras taught that sex within marriage should only be for procreation and only during certain times of the year.[20] Thus, the Apostle Paul was perhaps merely suggesting an ascetical practice that was common, but he places value on this time of marital celibacy not because of the absence of sex *per se* but because the absence of sex leads to something else, in this case devotion to prayer. A Re-formed Catholic Anglican asceticism, then, needs not only to be ascetic but scriptural in that ascetical practices should not be pursued merely for their own sake but for the sake of godliness: "Train [γύμναζε] yourself in godliness, for, while physical training [σωματικὴ γυμνασία] is of some value, godliness is valuable in every way, holding promise for both the present life and the life to come" (1 Tim 4:7–8).

Role of Asceticism

This leads us to ask, What is the role of asceticism and ascetical practices in a Re-formed Catholic Anglicanism? Anglican pastoral theologian Martin Thornton (d. 1986) wrote that "the Book of Common Prayer is not a list of Church services but an ascetical system for Christian living in all of its minutiae."[21] This being the case, the Anglican who makes full use of the *Book of Common Prayer* (BCP) is engaging in a full ascetical system inasmuch as it offers a full regimen for the Daily Office, Holy Eucharist, and private devotion.

Moreover, particular ascetical practices are a part of this system. In 1549, Thomas Cranmer (d. 1556), architect of the BCP, included a catechetical note for the celebration of Ash Wednesday. Having just prayed the Litany, the priest instructs the congregation that in the primitive church, during Lent, "notorious sinners, were put to open penance, and punished in this world, that their souls might be saved in the day of the Lord; and that other, admonished by their example, might be more afraid to offend."[22] In this way, Cranmer was emphasizing the Catholic understanding that Lent was a season to restore sinners to the Church and because of this, Ash Wednesday was the day wherein Anglicans would begin their own journey of penance and reconciliation: "Let us... return

---

[20] Elizabeth Abbott, *A History of Celibacy* (Cambridge: Lutterworth, 2011), 32–45.

[21] Martin Thornton, "The Anglican Spiritual Tradition," in Richard Holloway, ed., *The Anglican Tradition* (Wilton, CT: Morehouse-Barlow, 1984), 87.

[22] Joseph Ketley, ed., *The Two Liturgies, A.D. 1549, and A.D. 1552: With other Documents Set Forth by Authority in the Reign of King Edward VI* (Cambridge: Cambridge University Press, 1864), 150.

unto our Lord God, with all contrition and meekness of heart, bewailing and lamenting our sinful life, knowledging and confessing our offences, and seeking to bring forth worthy fruits of penance."[23] This was possible because of God's "infinite mercy"[24] but was enacted through ascetical practices: "Turn thou us, good Lord, and so shall we be turned: be favourable (O Lord) be favourable to thy people, which turn to thee in weeping, fasting and praying: for thou art a merciful God, full of compassion, long suffering, and of a great piety [or, pity]."[25] Note, the ascetical practices of weeping,[26] fasting, and prayer.

Just a few years later, in the BCP 1552, a rubric was inserted into the Communion service instructing the celebrant to "declare unto the people whether there be any holy days or fasting days the week following."[27] It assumes that a) fasting is an acceptable ascetical practice; and b) that there are already appointed fast days observed by the Catholic Church.[28] *The Primer*, published in 1553 states that prayer "with temperate fasting and charitable alms" is good.[29] Fasting is biblical (Matt. 6:17) and, therefore, not controversial; and the same can certainly be said for prayer and for almsgiving (Luke 18:22), but early Anglican theologians also saw value in other ascetical practices and even wrote a series of homilies to explain them and encourage their use in Anglican churches.

Anglican historian and theologian Gerald Bray writes, "Along with the Thirty-Nine Articles, the Book of Common Prayer and the Ordinal, the two books of Homilies, first issued in 1547 and 1563 respectively, form part of the basic formularies of the Church of England. They are therefore of considerable importance for understanding both its history and its doctrine."[30] Nevertheless, as Bray notes, they are seldom read today even though Article XXXV of the *Thirty-Articles of Religion* says, "The second Book of Homilies … doth contain a godly and wholesome Doctrine, and necessary for these times… therefore we judge them to be read in the Churches by the Ministers, diligently and distinctly, that they may be understood by the people." Of particular interest is the *Second Book of Homilies* that contains a series of sermons that form a Re-formed Catholic Anglican ascetical theology: Sermon 4 on "Good works, especially fasting"; Sermon 5 "Against gluttony and drunkenness"; Sermon 6 "Against excess of apparel"; and Sermon

---

[23] Ketley, ed., *The Two Liturgies*, 151.

[24] Ibid., 153.

[25] Ibid., 154.

[26] On weeping as an ascetical practice, see Kallistos Ware, "'An Obscure Matter': The Mystery of Tears in Orthodox Spirituality" and Kimberley Christine Patton, "'Howl, Weep and Moan, and Bring It Back to God': Holy Tears in Eastern Christianity," in *Holy Tears: Weeping in the Religious Imagination*, ed. Kimberley Christine Patton and John Stratton Hawley (Princeton: Princeton University Press, 2005), 242–273.

[27] Ketley, ed., *The Two Liturgies*, 269.

[28] That particular days of the week (esp. Wednesday and Friday) would be fast days goes back to the early third century, at least. See Tertullian, *On Fasting* 8.2.3, for example, and compare *Didache* 8.1. But it was only at the Council of Coyanza in 1050 that legislated year-round fasting on Friday. See Francisco Javier Fernández and Xosé Lluis García Arias, "Concilium Coiacense y Conceyu de Coyanza / Concilium Coiacense and Council of Coyanza," *Lletres Asturianes* 123 (2020): 192.

[29] Ketley, ed., *The Two Liturgies*, 377.

[30] Gerald Bray, ed., *The Books of Homilies: A Critical Edition* (Cambridge: James Clarke, 2015), ix.

11 on "Alms and acts of mercy."[31] The authors of these homilies are not known with certainty but the point of the homilies in general was "to provide a more extensive commentary on certain aspects of Christian doctrine than was possible within the constraints of a single paragraph" in the Articles.[32] From these homilies we can understand the role of asceticism and ascetical practices in a Re-formed Catholic Anglicanism.

The fourth homily takes up the biblical discipline of fasting,[33] stating that there are two kinds of fasting, "the one outward, pertaining to the body; and other inward, in the heart and mind."[34] The homily understands fasting in a traditional sense, as a "withholding of meat, drink and all natural food from the body for the determined time of fasting."[35] And there "are three ends or right uses of fasting": 1) "to chastise the flesh"; 2) "that the spirit may be more fervent and earnest in prayer"; and 3) "that our fast be a testimony and witness with us before God of our humble submission to his high majesty when we confess and acknowledge our sins unto him and are inwardly touched with sorrowfulness of heart." The homily says that the first end is "most properly to private fast; the other two are common as well to public fast as to private."[36] The homily goes on to recognize that there are better times to fast than merely observing a kind of continual fast, especially since a proper fast is not only of the body but of the soul. After an examination of biblical instances of fasting, the homily concludes that "there are many more causes of fasting and mourning in these our days than hath been of many years heretofore in any one age." Therefore, Anglicans need "diligently to exercise this godly exercise of fasting in such sort and manner as the holy prophets, the apostles and divers other devout persons for their time used the same."[37] Simply put, fasting is expected, it is done both outwardly and inwardly and done at particular times to gain the favor of God.[38]

The fifth homily against gluttony and drunkenness is an extension of the homily on fasting: "Ye shall hear how foul a thing gluttony and drunkenness is before God, the rather to move you to use fasting more diligently." The homily notes that gluttony and drunkenness are kinds of excess that offend the majesty of God. These sins grow out of the human need for food and drink, but they are the fruit of "immoderate abuse."[39] In a good Re-formed Catholic way, the homily states that they are listed by the Apostle Paul

---

[31] The connectedness of these homilies, forming a mini-treatise on asceticism, is found in Homily 5 where it makes a connection to fasting (Homily 4) but then states that gluttony and drunkenness are kinds of excess that offend God just like "costly and sumptuous apparel, treated in Homily 6. See Bray, ed., *The Books of Homilies*, 311.

[32] Bray, ed., *The Books of Homilies*, x.

[33] Ibid., 299: "that we ought to fast is a truth more manifest than that it should here need to be proved."

[34] Ibid., 298.

[35] Ibid., 300.

[36] Ibid., 303.

[37] Ibid., 310.

[38] It should be noted that by the time of the publication of the American BCP 1928, there were about 75 days of either a partial or full fast prescribed by the BCP. That number was modified by subsequent revisions of the BCP.

[39] Bray, ed., *The Books of Homilies*, 311.

(Gal 5:19–21) among the worst crimes one could commit against God, equated with even the sin of murder. By being gluttonous or drunk, Christians are defiling their own bodies and submitting themselves through "beastly banqueting" to the "belly gods." Through "bibbing and banqueting" and "feasting and banqueting" we are giving in to pleasure, making us forgetful of our duties to God and "not respecting the sanctification which is by the Word of God and prayer."[40] The homily then proceeds to provide examples of God's commandments not to overeat and over-drink, followed by biblical and non-biblical (e.g., Alexander the Great) examples of those who sinned in this way. The point is to "restrain our raging lusts and greedy appetites," but, assuming that might not be enough, the homily continues by considering "the manifold mischiefs that proceed thereof," such as "sudden death by banqueting"[41] and the risk of being "stricken with frenzy of mind" leading to "mere madness."[42] In other words, eating too much and drinking too much is not only a violation of God's commandments, and a violation of godly examples, it is also a great risk to the body and the mind. Accordingly, the homily concludes with this exhortation:

> Let us therefore, good people, eschew, every one of us, all intemperancy; let us love sobriety and moderate diet, oft give ourselves to abstinence and fasting, whereby the mind of man is more lift up to God, more ready to all godly exercises, as prayer, hearing and reading of God's Word, to his spiritual comfort. Finally, whosoever regardeth the health and safety of his own body, or wisheth always to be well in his wits, or desireth quietness of mind and abohorreth fury and madness, he that would be rich and escape poverty, he that is willing to live without the hurt of his neighbour, a profitable member of the commonwealth, a Christian without slander of Christ and his church, let him avoid all riotous and excessive banqueting, let him learn to keep such measure as behoveth [sic] him that professeth true godliness, let him follow Saint Paul's rule, and so "eat and drink to the glory" and praise "of God," who "hath created all things to be" soberly "used with thanksgiving."[43]

The sixth homily (against excess of apparel), like Homily 5 on drunkenness and gluttony, begins by stating that it is a continuation of the previous one. The goal of this homily is to "consider the end and purpose whereunto Almighty God hath ordained his creatures" so as to "easily perceive that he alloweth us apparel not only for necessity's sake, but also for an honest comeliness." Not only has God given humanity things to use, he has also endowed these necessities with "pleasant sight and sweet smell to delight us" and "to refresh our sense with an honest and moderate recreation."[44] That does not mean, of course, that the Christian is at liberty to advance himself "in sumptuous apparel."[45] The homily then gives four reasons for restraint in one's dress: 1) make no provision for the flesh (Rom 13:14); 2) any inordinate care and affection withdraws the person from contemplation of "heavenly things and consideration of our duty towards

---

40 Bray, ed., *The Books of Homilies*, 312.
41 Ibid., 316.
42 Ibid., 317.
43 Ibid., 319, quoting 1 Cor 10:31 and 1 Tim 3:3–4.
44 Ibid., 320.
45 Ibid., 321.

God"; 3) contentment with "base and simple attire" is proper; and 4) one's clothing out to be consistent with one's "degree and office" that are given by God.[46] Then, like Homily 5, a number of biblical commandments and examples (biblical and non-Christian) are provided so as to illustrate the four points. In the end, the person who dresses modestly is behaving in a way that "becometh Christians," showing thankfulness to God for giving his provision of daily bread.[47]

The last sermon to consider briefly, Homily 11 on almsgiving and mercy toward the poor and needy, lays out its case in three points: 1) the biblical basis for almsgiving; 2) how profitable it is for one to give alms; and 3) that the one who gives generously will not lack in life. As is the case with the other sermons, we see a Re-formed Catholic Anglican approach: look at what the Church and the Scriptures teach on an issue and admonish contemporary Christian believers to follow their good example. This approach works well with those disciplines rooted in the Scriptures, such as the aforementioned prayer, fasting, simplicity in dress, and almsgiving. On the other hand, this says nothing about those ascetical practices rooted in the tradition that were discarded by the early Anglican reformers.

Other Ascetical Practices

Are there ascetical practices that have developed in the history of the Church that may need to be discarded from or re-introduced into a Re-formed Catholic Anglican perspective? Without a doubt, there is a history in the Christian Church of interesting ascetical practices, such as sitting for long periods of time in freezing cold water. For example, the great English saint Cuthbert (d. 687) would go "into the deep water [of the North Sea] until the swelling waves rose as far as his neck and arms" spending "the dark hours of the night watching and singing praises to the sound of the waves."[48] The wearing of hair shirts was a Christian ascetical practice, going all the way back to the early church, but it became much more common in the eleventh century.[49] In fact, Edward Pusey (d. 1882), leader of the Oxford Movement, himself wore a hair shirt with some regularity.[50] Evagrius of Pontus (d. 399) followed a very strict diet of uncooked food, even though it ultimately led to his death.[51]

On the other hand, there are also deeply disturbing ascetical practices that have emerged throughout Christian history: "Angela of Foligno drank the water left over from washing the sores of lepers. Catherine of Siena drank pus from the wounds of the sick

---

[46] Bray, ed., *The Books of Homilies*, 321–322.

[47] Ibid., 328.

[48] Venerable Bede, *Life of Saint Cuthbert*, 10; Bertram Colgrave, trans., *Two Lives of Saint Cuthbert: A Life by an Anonymous Monk of Lindisfarne and Bede's Prose Life* (Cambridge: Cambridge University Press, 1940), 189.

[49] D. Alexander, "Hermits and hairshirts: the social meanings of saintly clothing in the *vitae* of Godric of Finchale and Wulfric of Haselbury," *Journal of Medieval History* 28 (2002): 208.

[50] Henry Parry Liddon, *Life of Edward Bouverie Pusey* (London: Longmans, Green, & Co., 1894), 3:100.

[51] Palladius, *Lausiac History* 38.12–13; W. K. Lowther Clark, trans., *The Lausiac History of Palladius* (London: SPCK, 1918), 137.

she tended, and Catherine of Genoa ate lice."[52] Simeon Stylites (d. 459) lived on top of a pillar for nearly forty years and he was not alone in living in this way.[53] A monk of the eleventh century named Dominic wore a *lorica* (ascetic chainmail) for fifteen years[54] and whipped himself excessively.[55] I do not bring these examples up to be perverse, but to show that there is a history of extreme, excessive and, one might add, unbiblical asceticism in the Christian tradition. Thus, these practices would fail Gore's "turn to Scripture" test. These practices, of course, should be discarded.

Nevertheless, there are a host of other ascetic practices that have not factored largely into Re-formed Catholic Anglican asceticism that should be re-introduced. One example will suffice: celibacy.

Many of the earliest Protestant reformers were former monks and, therefore, lived under vows requiring celibacy. Once these men left their religious orders and married, they often advocated for the superiority of the married life. Martin Luther (d. 1546) was persuaded that only those with a divine gift for celibacy should remain unmarried, coming to value greatly marriage and family life,[56] and he was not alone.[57] Further, clerical celibacy had been an ideal of the early and medieval Church (even if it had never quite been achieved) but it was rejected by Anglican theologians from the start: "Bishops, Priests, and Deacons, are not commanded by God's Law, either to vow the estate of single life, or to abstain from marriage: therefore it is lawful for them, as for all other Christian men, to marry at their own discretion, as they shall judge the same to serve better to godliness" (Article XXXII). Thus, with the dissolution of the monasteries in the nascent Anglican church and with a non-obligatory clerical celibacy (except for the unmarried, of course), the ascetic practice of celibacy came to be devalued or ignored. Some early Anglican theologians remained unmarried and, thus, celibate (e.g., Lancelot Andrewes [d. 1626] and William Laud [d. 1645]) but many, if not most, married.

By the mid-seventeenth century there was a growing appreciation of celibacy, so much so that it came to be called the "angelic life," a phrase for celibacy (and the monastic life) whose origins goes back to at least Augustine of Hippo (d. 430) and Jerome (d. 420).[58]

---

[52] Madeleine Pelner Cosman and Linda Gales Jones, *Handbook to Life in the Medieval World* (New York: Facts on File, 2008), 422.

[53] See Robert Doran, trans., *The Lives of Simeon Stylites* (Kalamazoo, MI: Cistercian, 1992); Elizabeth Dawes and Norman H. Baynes, trans., *Three Byzantine Saints: Contemporary Biographies of St Daniel the Stylite, St Theodore of Sykeon and St John the Almsgiver* (Crestwood, NY: St. Vladimir's Seminary Press, 1977).

[54] See Peter Damian, *Vita venerabilis viri Dominici loricate* 6 and 8; Alexander, "Hermits and hairshirts," 208.

[55] Wm. M. Cooper, *Flagellation and the Flagellants: A History of the Rod* (London: John Camden Hotten, 1869), 49.

[56] See Greg Peters, *The Monkhood of All Believers: The Monastic Foundation of Christian Spirituality* (Grand Rapids: Baker Academic, 2018), 167–169; Trevor O'Reggio, "Martin Luther on Marriage and Family," *History Research* (2012): 195–218.

[57] See R. V. Young, "The Reformations of the Sixteenth and Seventeenth Centuries," in Glenn W. Olsen, ed., *Christian Marriage: A Historical Study* (Herder & Herder, 2001), 269–301; and Peter Coleman, *Christian Attitudes to Marriage: From Ancient Times to the Third Millennium* (London: SCM Press, 2004), 175–197.

[58] Suso Frank, *Angelikos bios: Begriffsanalytische und begriffsgeschichtliche Untersuchung zum "engelgleichen Leben" im frühen Mönchtum* (Münster: Aschendorff, 1964).

Celibacy was ubiquitous throughout the history of the Church, mostly associated with the monastic life.[59] In fact, celibacy became one of the standard monastic practices, and then a vow in its own right. Scripturally, celibacy is required of the unmarried, a teaching upheld by Re-formed Catholic Anglicans; and it can also be entered into for a season by those who were married (cf. 1 Cor 7:3–5). But celibacy, as a state of life, was not highly valued by early Anglicans in the same way it had been in the early and medieval Church, likely because of the dissolution of the monasteries and disavowal of consecrated religious life,[60] but it never vanished wholly from the Re-formed Anglican faith. For example, Anna Collett (d. 1638), of the semi-monastic Little Gidding community, made a vow around 1631 to "end [her] days in a Virgin's Estate."[61]

A more thorough treatment of celibacy came from the pen of Thomas Culpeper (d. ca. 1697), a graduate of Oxford, who published a collection of homilies entitled *Morall Discourses and Essayes, upon Severall Select Subjects* (1655). One of these, entitled "Of Cœlibacy, or Single Life," argues for celibacy as a state of life. Culpeper rightly notes at the outset that celibacy is a "state of Abstinence, both from the unlawful and lawful Bed." It differs from continence, which is *not* a state of life but a "habit of the Mind," and from chastity, "For that is not confined to abstinence, but extends to lawful and regular use."[62] Celibacy as a state of life is an "Angelical Estate" for it "seems to share in honour with Martyrdom, for it bids defiance to Lust, It plucks up Avarice and Ambition, by the Root, It ... pursues even [the Gospel's] Counsels and intimations, And that it may not miss of happiness, aims at Eminency."[63] Culpeper notes that the "Ancients [i.e., the Romans] esteemed no greater hinderance of heroic achievements then Marriage" for the married person will "always float betwixt Virtue and Nature" (cf. 1 Cor 7:32–35). Nonetheless, Culpeper notes that many cannot receive Christian teaching on celibacy because they do not have "the Power of receiving it" and merely think that an argument in favor of celibacy is an argument against marriage. With this mindset, says Culpeper, both celibacy and marriage are cancelled. Rather, he writes, celibacy should be seen as possible and profitable as a "help to devotion" and an aid to "Perfection in Virtue."[64]

Culpeper was not unique in his positive valuation of celibacy, for Jeremy Taylor (d. 1667), bishop of Down and Connor, voiced a similar sentiment around the same time in his *Holy Living* (1650): "*Virginity* is a life of Angels, the enamel of the Soul, the huge advantage of Religion, the great opportunity for the retirements of devotion." Taylor says that the natural condition of virginity is "not a state more acceptable to God: but that which is chosen and voluntary ... is therefore better than the married life, not that it is more holy, but that it is a freedom from cares, an opportunity to spend more time in spiritual employments," for "if it be a chosen condition to these ends, it containeth in it a victory over lusts, and greater desires of Religion, and self-denial, and therefore is

---

[59] Abbott, *A History of Celibacy*, 47–161.

[60] James G. Clark, *The Dissolution of the Monasteries: A New History* (New Haven: Yale University Press, 2021).

[61] A. L. Maycock, *Nicholas Ferrar of Little Gidding* (Grand Rapids: Eerdmans, 1980), 184.

[62] Thomas Culpeper, *Morall Discourses and Essayes, upon Severall Select Subjects* (London: Charles Adams, 1655), 88–89.

[63] Ibid., 89; spelling modernized.

[64] Ibid., 90; spelling modernized.

more excellent than the married life, in the degree in which it hath greater religion, and a greater mortification, a less satisfaction of natural desires, and a greater fulness of the spiritual."[65]

Though much more could be said, and though counter-arguments could be mustered, there is a rich Re-formed Catholic Anglican ascetical theology that places great value not only on traditional ascetical practices but also on those more common in the early and medieval Catholic tradition. These practices, like celibacy, are not contrary to the Scriptures;[66] therefore, they can be re-introduced into Re-formed Catholic Anglicanism. These ascetical practices are done because they are aids to devotion and contribute to sanctification, but they are also a natural outgrowth of baptism, and strengthened by the Sacraments, particularly the Holy Eucharist.

Asceticism and the Sacraments

How is asceticism an outgrowth of Holy Baptism and related to the other Sacraments? In the sixteenth century, theologians advocating for reform of the Church recovered a doctrine commonly referred to as the "priesthood of all believers." This doctrine, rooted in the Scriptures (cf. 1 Peter 2:4–9, Rev 1:6, 5:10), was embraced by Cranmer but he refused a "radical application of universal priesthood." Indeed,

> Cranmer understood the priesthoods of people, ministers, kings, and Christ to function in a cooperative harmony: Christ's eternal priesthood entailed his constant intercession on our behalf. The kings' priesthood coordinated and defended the harmony of church and society. The ministers' priesthood was to teach, lead an exemplary life, and administer sacraments. The people's priesthood was to labor within their distinct vocations and offer spiritual sacrifices both in worship and at other times.[67]

This common priesthood is rooted in baptism, and it is in baptism wherein a believer is endowed (i.e., ordained = ordered) with the priesthood appropriate to his state in life. Cranmer did not reject the particular, ordained priesthood (like the Anabaptists) in favor of a priesthood of all believers. Rather, he gave the laity a role in the making of priests but still saw that priestly ordination required the laying on of hands by a bishop.[68] Cranmer thought that one's universal priesthood was exercised according to one's vocation: "It is further lawful for all Christians, each according to his own rank and condition, following the laws of God and of princes, and the honest customs of particular countries, to occupy and exercise such offices and duties by which this mortal life either continues, or is graced or is preserved."[69] Thus, it is the priesthood of all believers, which

---

[65] Jeremy Taylor, *The Rule and Exercises of Holy Living* (London: William Pickering, 1847), 85–86.

[66] In fact, celibacy may be traced back to the Apostle Paul's own example: e.g., 1 Cor 7:7, 25–35; 9:5.

[67] Malcolm B. Yarnell III, *Royal Priesthood in the English Reformation* (Oxford: Oxford University Press, 2013), 227.

[68] Thomas Cranmer, "The Institution of a Christian Man," in *Formularies of the Faith put forth by Authority during the Reign of Henry VIII*, ed. Charles Lloyd (Oxford: Oxford University Press, 1856), 109.

[69] "The Thirteen Articles, with Three Additional Articles, 1538," in *Documents of the English Reformation*, ed. Gerald Bray, 3rd ed. (Cambridge: James Clarke & Co., 2019), 181.

derives from baptism, that empowers one to live out their Christian vocation in society. Since every baptized Christian is called to holiness in those vocations, then the believer's ascetical life is rooted in and is an outgrowth of baptism.

Furthermore, from the start, baptism in the Anglican tradition entailed a promise to live an ascetical life: "Dost thou forsake the vain pomp and glory of the world...? Dost thou forsake the carnal desires of the flesh?"[70] The answer, of course, is "I forsake them." It is in this forsaking of the world and the desires of the flesh that the newly baptized followers of Jesus confirm their intent to live an ascetical life, for, as stated above, asceticism is bodily exercise and training for the purpose of growth in holiness and purity of life, rejecting those things that appeal to our flesh. Lastly, this journey is aided by the grace that comes by way of the Holy Eucharist: "Assist us with thy grace, that we may continue in that holy fellowship, and do all such good works, as thou hast prepared for us to walk in."[71] Not only are ascetical practices preparatory to the worthy reception of the body and blood of Christ but the grace received thereby contributes to the empowerment for further ascetical practices, that in turn lead again to worthy reception. The cyclical nature of the ascetical life is fixed on the still point of the Holy Eucharist.

Conclusion

A Re-formed Catholic Anglican asceticism will look remarkably like that which came before it in the Christian tradition: prayer, fasting, and almsgiving. However, it can and should look like the full Catholic tradition, embracing some ascetical practices that may have fallen out of fashion, like celibacy. Whatever ascetical practices a Re-formed Catholic Anglicanism embraces, they need to be rooted in the Holy Scriptures to be properly "Re-formed," and they must also be an outgrowth of the Christian's baptismal life and vows, empowered by the grace of the sacraments and the ministrations of the Holy Spirit. Thus, let us discipline ourselves for the purpose of godliness (1 Tim 4:7).

---

[70] Ketley, ed., *The Two Liturgies*, 111.
[71] Ibid., 94.

Chapter 6

The *Thirty-Nine Articles*

The Most Rev. Dr. Ray R. Sutton

The sixteenth century was marked by a general upheaval and unsettlement in religious matters, a state of things owing partly to the revival of learning, which had caused men to contrast the Church of the New Testament with medieval Rome and to think for themselves, and partly due to ecclesiastical abuses. At this crisis, especially in the countries where a breach with Rome had taken place, a definition of doctrine became necessary. It had to be made clear how far the Church was at one with the Church of the past, how it differed from the Church of Rome on the one hand, and from other Reformed bodies on the other hand. Thus, at the period of the Reformation we find the various parts of Christendom putting forth more or less complete confessions of faith.

Speaking quite generally, there is this broad distinction between our English Articles and the formularies of foreign Protestant or Reformed bodies. The latter exhibit a more uniform body of doctrine than the Articles of the English Church, a result to which several causes contributed ... [because] they owe so much more to individuals [and less to national feelings and the various forces at work in the nation.] ... Our *Articles* ... are not [systematic, nor do they] elaborate a logically complete theory of God's dealings with men.[1]

The author of this quotation is E. Terrell Green, a late nineteenth century Anglican author of a commentary on the *Thirty-Nine Articles of Religion*. He makes the important observations that in the sixteenth century English Reformation, "where a breach with Rome had taken place, a definition of doctrine became necessary." The "definition of doctrine" to which Green refers is the *Thirty-Nine Articles of Religion* approved in 1571. He then adds importantly, "It had to be made clear how far the Church was at one with the Church of the past." This "Church of the past" was the ancient Catholic Church of the early fathers.

Green's assessment regarding the *Articles of Religion* further confirms what the Introduction and the contents of this book present as a re-formed catholic Anglicanism. It is the approach of reforming the English Church "with the Church of the past," to use Green's phrasing. This model of correcting the late medieval Roman Catholic Church with the "Church of the past" has been explained as the method of *ad fontes* or back to the sources. These sources for the English Reformers, and initially the other Magisterial Reformers, were the Holy Scriptures and the ancient church fathers. The Continental or European Reformation in various parts did not maintain this model. The English Reformers did with their primary documents: *The Book of Common Prayer* and the *Thirty-Nine Articles of Religion*. They further explained this re-formed catholic rationale in their writings.

---

[1] E. Terrell Green, *The Thirty-Nine Articles and the Age of Reformation* (London: Wells Gardner, Darton, & Co., 1896), 1–2.

In this chapter, I will develop that the leading doctrinal statement of the English Reformation called the *Thirty-Nine Articles of Religion* adheres to a re-formed catholic approach. They express the doctrinal commitment of the English Reformation according to the Scriptures and the early church fathers. They offer no new doctrine alien to the theology and practices of the first centuries of Christianity. In so doing, however, they attempt to correct aberrant and abusive doctrines and practices in the medieval Roman Church by appealing to "the Church of the past."

Background and General Commitment to the Reformed Catholic Model

The English Church began with *Forty-Two Articles of Religion* during the reign of Edward VI. Archbishop Thomas Cranmer was the primary architect of them, although he worked with a committee of bishops. This first edition was not initially approved by all the Church of England but only by a small group of the bishops.[2] Fifteen years after Cranmer's martyrdom, however, in 1571 his *Forty-Two Articles* were amended to *Thirty-Nine Articles*. The shaping and production of the final version was done by others under the oversight of the new Archbishop, Matthew Parker.

Importantly, Bishop John Jewell was the major editor of the *Thirty-Nine Articles*. He died in 1571 around the time that they were approved. It was the last of his many great contributions to the English Reformation. His influence would have been consistent with his understanding of Anglicanism. As is mentioned in the introduction to this volume, he was the primary defender of the English Reformation in dealing with Roman Catholic objections. His approach articulated a re-formed catholic model of Anglicanism in his classic defense called the *Apologia of the Church of England*. In this seminal work, he outlines the "back to the sources" model of appealing primarily to the Scriptures and the ancient church fathers. As we shall see, the final version of the *Articles* reflects more his reformed catholic apologetic. Nevertheless, Cranmer's *Forty-Two Articles* statement of doctrine for the most part is also re-formed catholic. Before considering some of the differences between Cranmer's first version and the final 1571 *Thirty-Nine Articles* edition, it's necessary to recognize how both versions of the *Articles* generally reflect a re-formed catholic approach.

First, the *Articles of Religion* are built on a re-formed catholic foundation at the beginning of the document by establishing that the Trinitarian formulae of the ancient creeds are the same basis for theology as they were for the early church. The specific ancient catholic character of the *Articles* appears in the first five, concerning the Doctrines of the Holy Trinity and the Incarnation of Jesus Christ. They are not like the other later reformed confessional documents such as the *Westminster Confession of Faith* that begin with statements on the Holy Scriptures and then move to the Trinity. It's not that the *Thirty-Nine Articles* lack commitment to the authority of Scripture. They do endorse the primary standard of the Word of God in Articles VI–VII. However, the *Articles of Religion* are set in the context of the Trinitarian God who reveals the Scriptures. This is the approach of the ancient catholic Church.

Second, the ancient catholic model also appears in how the *Articles* state the authority of Scripture. The primacy of the sixty-six books of the Old and New Testament is

---

[2] Diarmaid McCulloch, *Thomas Cranmer* (New Haven: Yale University Press, 1996), 536–537.

endorsed with the statement, "of whose authority was never any doubt in the Church." They are stated as "authority," but the added, "never any doubt in the Church," points back to an ancient catholic standard of the relationship between the Church and the Scriptures. St. Paul says, "the church of the living God, the pillar and ground of the truth" (1 Tim 3:15). The Word of God does not stand apart from the Church. It is organically connected as the "pillar" upholding and under the "truth." To be precise, the Church was birthed at Pentecost before the New Testament was revealed. Community preceded canon. The same was true of the Old Testament. The people of God existed before his revelation. We see therefore that Scripture is the primary and ultimate authority, while the Church via the early church fathers is the secondary and also an essential authority for interpretation.

Given this ecclesial connection to the Scriptures, Article VI states what the Church has historically recognized. In fact, the list of the Books of Scripture in the Article is essentially identical to one produced in the early church by St. Athanasius.[3]

The early church approach to the Scriptures in Article VI also continues with reference to the *Apocryphal Books*. The Article retains their place in the life of believers and even provides the rationale for why the lectionary in the *Book of Common Prayer* includes them in the readings of Scripture for worship. The Article refers to them as "Books," with uppercase "B." In addition, it quotes the early church father St. Jerome's principle for retaining these Books: "the Church doth read for example of life and instruction of manners; but yet doth it not apply them to establish any doctrine." Thus, this is the ancient church model of the Scriptures and the early church fathers expressed all through the English Reformation. In the introductory chapter of this volume, I noted *Canon 6 of the Canons of the Church of England*, where reference is made to the *teaching of the Old or New Testament, and what the Catholic fathers and ancient bishops have collected from this selfsame doctrine*. I also pointed out how this Canon applied the dual standard to the *Book of Common Prayer* and the *Articles*.

In addition, Article VI on the Scriptures deals with the problem of requiring additional documents and dogmas to be believed for salvation. Therefore, the Article points out that only the Word of God "containeth all things necessary for salvation." Further, nothing should be "thought requisite or necessary to salvation" that "is not read therein, nor may be proved thereby." This emphasis also proves why no other document except the Scriptures, or the Catholic Creeds written "according to the Scriptures," can be made into a confession unto salvation. This is why the next section of the *Articles* following the first eight speaks to salvific issues such as original sin, faith, and salvation (Articles IX–XVIII).

Third, the re-formed catholic foundation of the *Articles of Religion* appears in the way that Article VIII refers to the ancient catholic creeds as the confession of faith for an Anglican. Harold Edward Browne in his *An Exposition of the Thirty-Nine Articles* writes, "Our own Church requires of its *lay* members no confession of their faith, except that contained in the Apostles' Creed."[4] Browne speaks of this creed as the one that must be

---

[3] Athanasius, *Thirty-Ninth Festal Epistle*, AD 367.

[4] Harold Edward Browne, *An Exposition of the Thirty-Nine Articles: Historical and Doctrinal* (London: Longmans, Green, & Co., 1894), 11.

confessed in the *Baptismal Office* for acceptance of Christ by faith unto salvation. Article VIII says, "The Three Creeds, *Nicene* Creed, *Athanasius* Creed, and that which is commonly called the *Apostles* Creed, ought thoroughly to be received and believed: for they may be proved by most certain warrants of Holy Scripture."[5] No other Article calls for it "thoroughly to be received and believed." The *Articles*, as important and Scriptural as they are, are not to be "thoroughly received and believed" for salvation. Only the Creeds provide the content of what is necessary as the *sine qua non* for salvation.

Strictly speaking, the *Articles* are not the confession of faith. The laity were not required to believe them for salvation. The clergy on the other hand had to subscribe to the *Articles* as "doctrinal principles" to guide their teaching.[6] Perhaps the early seventeenth-century Bishop John Bramhall, Archbishop of Armagh, Anglican apologist and theologian, best summarizes how he says, "We do not suffer any man 'to reject' the Thirty-nine Articles of the Church of England 'at his pleasure'; yet neither do we look upon them as essentials of saving faith or 'legacies of Christ and His Apostles'; but in a mean, as pious opinions fitted for the preservation of unity: neither do we oblige any man [of the laity] to believe them, but only not to contradict them."[7]

Bramhall's comments reflect the view that the *Articles* are attempting to correct doctrinal issues in the late medieval Western Church. For example, even the *Articles'* opening statements about the Trinity are phrased in such a way as to be correcting a current theological concern. It was a resurgence of the ancient heresy of Sabellianism that denied the doctrine of the Trinity. It was a redux of the ancient heresy of Arianism sweeping across the Western Medieval Church. The *Articles* state up front that the doctrine of the English Church remains true to the ancient Trinitarian and creedal formulae to counter these heresies.

Fourth, the ancient catholic approach of the *Articles of Religion* does not attempt to be a "whole body of divinity," like other sixteenth-century Reformational doctrinal statements. As E. Terrell Green, quoted at the beginning of this chapter, writes in his commentary on the *Thirty-Nine Articles*:

> Speaking generally, there is this broad distinction between our English Articles and the formularies of foreign Protestant bodies. The latter contain a more uniform body of doctrine than the Articles of the English Church, because they owe more to individuals…. As might be expected from this fact, our *Articles* are not systematic; they do not evolve a logically complete theology of God's dealings with man.[8]

Green adds, "One sometimes hears the *Articles* spoken of as 'containing a whole body of divinity.'" He rejects this view with an important footnote, "The *titles* of the various English formularies indicate that it was not at any time the intention of the English Reformers to draw up a complete confession of faith."[9] He continues,

---

[5] Brian Cummings, ed., *The Book of Common Prayer: The Texts of 1549, 1559, and 1662* (New York: Oxford University Press, 2011), 676.

[6] See for example the Anglican Church in North America's *Constitution and Canons*.

[7] John Bramhall, *Works*, ed. Arthur West Haddan, Library of Anglo-Catholic Theology (Oxford: John Henry Parker, 1842), II:470.

[8] Green, *Thirty-Nine Articles*, 2.

[9] Ibid.

What the Church of England does claim is that they [the *Articles*] are a fair Scriptural account of the doctrines of Christianity, set out in a way especially suited to the needs of the time when they were composed, together with a condemnation of prevalent errors, both of the Roman Church and of Protestants [i.e., Zwinglians, Anabaptists, and so forth]. Many subjects are unnoticed in them, but as far as the *Articles* go, they are a legal definition of the doctrines of our Church, though it is to the Prayer-Book, together with the Articles, that the English Churchmen look for the genuine expression of their faith.[10]

Green supports his conclusion that the *Articles* are not a "complete confession of faith" by pointing out what they do not address, namely, topics such as, "(1) The work of the Son of God in creation. (2) The work of the Holy Spirit in nature. (3) The intercession of the ascended Christ. (4) The nature and office of Holy Angels. (5) The resurrection of men in general, the everlasting life of the *righteous* and everlasting punishment of the wicked. (6) We may also add that the devil is only once mentioned (in Art. XVII) as thrusting men to desperation and unclean living."[11] The *Articles* are not a complete body of Divinity, and therefore not strictly speaking a "confession of faith."

Green also makes the important point that in Anglicanism the "Prayer-Book together with the Articles" are the "genuine expression of faith." In Anglicanism like the ancient Church, the liturgy including the Catholic Creed is the central defining document for dogma. The *Articles* were never intended to be a stand-alone confession of faith apart from the prayer book; they were not to be interpreted by themselves. They are to be understood with the controlling Divine Liturgy of the *Book of Common Prayer*. Numerous commentaries on the *Articles* have unfortunately not taken this approach. The result is that the *Articles* end up being slanted in one interpretative direction or the other, usually following one version of Reformation theology. However, when allowed to be understood with the re-formed catholic model of the English Reformers of prayer book and *Articles* together, the more accurate ancient catholic perspective is seen to be prevalent.

The English Reformer Bishop Lancelot Andrewes sums up perhaps best the body of theology maintained by the English Reformation in its prayer book and the *Articles* as "the Vincentian Canon and the claims of the Primitive Undivided Church."[12] The Vincentian Canon stated the doctrine of the Church as that "believed everywhere, at all times, by all." The *Articles* should be taken together with the *Book of Common Prayer* to be the re-formed catholic doctrinal statement of the English Reformation.

Therefore, the *Articles of Religion* are generally a re-formed catholic document. They set out Scripture and the early church fathers' approach from the beginning. They follow this template in addressing a range of key doctrinal issues in the late Middle Ages. Yet in the final 1571 *Thirty-Nine Articles* version, we see an even more specific re-formed catholic approach in the way in which the Bishops of the Church of England amended Cranmer's *Forty-Two Articles*.

---

[10] Green, *Thirty-Nine Articles*, 2–3 (brackets mine).

[11] Ibid., 3 n. 1.

[12] See reference in Paul Elmer More and Frank Leslie Cross, *Anglicanism*, (Milwaukee: Morehouse, 1935), liv. The reference is to Andrewes, *Responsio ad Apologiam Cardinalis Bellarmini* (London: Robert Barker, 1610).

The *Thirty-Nine Articles* Not Reduced to One Theologian or System

The *Thirty-Nine Articles* do not allow any one Reformer or his theological system to dominate this doctrinal statement. Green points out that

> Lutheranism is a system gathered around the doctrine of justification, and other doctrines having a place as they bear on it. Calvinism, again, is a system turning on election and reprobation, other doctrines being subordinated to or influenced by them. But the problem taken up by the English Church in the articles is reformation of abuses, the organic identity of the Church before and after the Reformation is assumed, the old creed is assumed, and the abuses corrected.[13]

Green's insight is that the *Articles* resist being formed around any one main doctrine addressed by the Reformation.

Concerning the German Reformation, it is true that the *Articles of Religion* rely heavily on the *Augsburg Confession*. However, it is important to note that this confession is reformed catholic and does not organize according to justification. Lutheranism later developed its theology around the "doctrine of justification," but its central confession does not. Instead, the document is an episcopal, non-papal doctrinal statement of ancient catholic Christianity. It simply maintains Scripture and the early Christian teachings while addressing certain errors of the medieval period. It reflects Luther's important emphasis on justification without ordering all theology in terms of it. In this regard, the *Articles* follow this confessional model but do not become *per se* "Lutheran."

Regarding the great Swiss reformer John Calvin, Green observes that the *Articles* do not become exclusively Calvinistic. He says for example of Calvinism that the center of this theological system became "election and reprobation."[14] Article XVII "Of Predestination and Election" does affirm "election unto life," but it does not go as far as Calvin's double election that included predestining reprobation.

The final version of Article XVII also makes a significant modification. It does not mention at the end the "secret decrees" of God as do the *Forty-Two Articles*. This theme in Calvin became much of the basis for his "invisible Church" doctrine. Calvinists emphasize that the true church is the invisible elect. By the time of the final version of the *Articles* the Calvinistic emphasis on the invisible Church was growing among the nascent Puritan movement in the Church of England. The *Articles* nowhere advance an "invisible Church" theology, but any statement such as the "secret decrees" in Article XVII that might become foundational to such teaching is removed from the *Thirty-Nine Articles*.

Furthermore, to the point that the *Articles* do not organize around any one Reformational doctrine such as predestation, Green recognizes that this Biblical

---

[13] Green, *Thirty-Nine Articles*, 4.

[14] Some Calvinists prefer to say that the central organizing doctrine of their confessions is the "glory of God." It's true that the Presbyterian *Shorter Catechism* begins, "What is the chief end of man?" with the answer, "Man's chief end is to glorify God and enjoy Him forever." However, the predominant theme throughout Reformed confessions and catechisms is predestination. This doctrine together with its parallel of reprobation is presented throughout these documents as explaining how God glorifies Himself. Anglicans while not accepting the double predestination of Calvin generally agree, but they do not see predestination as the central organizing doctrine of the faith.

doctrine virtually never receives attention in the rest of the *Articles*. Nor is it central to the theology of the prayer book. This doctrine though biblical is simply not understood as the organizing point of theology around which every other doctrine is ordered.

Article XVII even emphasizes that predestination is not to become a point of controversy, clearly referring to how it had become so divisive during the Reformation. On the point of the *Articles* not being polemical regarding predestination, John Bramhall, Bishop of Derry (1634) similarly refuted that the Anglican Church was exclusively Calvinist in "a polemical treatise" he wrote against a Jesuit, Sylvester Norris. In this work he "defended the Anglican Articles of Faith, and the validity of her orders." He produced this defense "while an exile [from the Puritan takeover of the Church of England] in France during the Commonwealth." In this writing, "he had an opportunity to prove to De la Milletiere, a French lay convert to Roman Catholicism, that the Church of England was not a Calvinist body, although she differed in much from the Church of Rome, as, for instance, in repudiating the doctrine of Transubstantiation, and reverting to the more primitive and scriptural doctrine of Real Presence."[15] Thus, though there is evidence of an Augustinian influence in the Articles, there is a Calvinisitic as well as an Arminian neutrality about the way the Article is stated.

This is not to say that the Calvinist or the Arminian views of salvation are prohibited by the *Articles of Religion*. It's that the English doctrinal statement rises above theological systems developing out of other parts of the Reformation, such as the systems of Calvinism and Arminianism congealed at the 1618–1619 Synod of Dort fifty years after the final version of the *Articles of Religion* are approved in 1571. A Dutch theologian name Jacob Hermann (Arminius) had proposed five Remonstrances modifying Calvinistic teachings. The Synod countered with five points of Calvinism (later associated with the acronym TULIP). Anglican bishops were at the Synod. Yet the Church of England never adopted the Canons of Dort (the five points of Calvinism) even though there were many Calvinists in the Church of England by the time of the seventeenth century. Neither system emerging around the Synod of Dort, however, is intended by the *Thirty-Nine Articles* to be taken exclusively as the interpretation of them.

The *Articles* have been interpreted in support of both systems. Arminians for example interpret the statements on predestination as based on God's foreknowledge. The article does not mention foreknowledge, but the Scriptures do (Rom 8:28–30). The view is that God knows who will believe and predestinates on the basis of the "pre" information.

Calvinists do not understand foreknowledge as information when the direct object of *predestine* is a person, as is the as case in Romans 8. Although they agree that God knows everything and even what will happen, the foreknowledge in relation to predestination in Scripture is understood to be an intimate knowledge as in a personal knowing before the relationship begins. It is the knowing of a person as in the early Biblical reference, "Adam knew Eve" (Gen 4:1). Calvinists interpret the word *foreknowledge* in Scripture to be some kind of relational predisposition to love as the basis of God's election. As a result of the different ways of interpreting Article XVII, eighteenth-

---

[15] Paul Elmer More and Frank Leslie Cross, eds., *Anglicanism: The Thought and Practice of the Church of England, Illustrated from the Religious Literature of the Seventeenth Century* (Milwaukee: Morehouse Publishing, 1935), lv.

century Calvinists like George Whitefield and Arminians such as John Wesley both dutifully subscribed to it. These great Anglican evangelists each claimed that it supported their theology. They were also friends.

Therefore, the articles on the subject of predestination are kept within a re-formed catholic, biblical, and Augustinian framework of soteriology without delineating Calvin's or Arminius' particular views on the subject. The soteriological model instead is that of the Scriptures and the early church fathers.

Reformed Catholic Amendments to the 1571 *Thirty-Nine Articles*

Furthermore, the revisions of Cranmer's first *Articles* demonstrate a re-formed catholic process at work. Clearly, the *Articles of Religion* were revised. As has been noted, fifteen years after Cranmer's martyrdom in 1556, his *Forty-Two Articles* are revised and approved by the entire Synod of Bishops and Parliament as the *Thirty-Nine Articles of Religion*. The *Forty-Two Articles* were therefore not the final version adopted in 1571 as the *Thirty-Nine Articles*. Though quite similar, there were significant re-formed catholic alterations.

Where we most detect a decisive ancient catholic mindset in the final edition of the *Articles* is in the Sacraments sections both in what was removed from Cranmer's first version and by what was added in the *Thirty-Nine Articles*.

As to what was added in the *Thirty-Nine Articles*, a new Article XXVIII says, "The Body of Christ is given, taken and eaten, in the Supper, after an heavenly and spiritual manner. And the mean whereby the Body of Christ is received and eaten in the Supper, is Faith." This is quite different from Cranmer's phrasing. Cranmer had expressed a more subjective understanding of how a person is united with Christ upon faithful reception of the Sacrament simultaneous with the working of the Holy Spirit.

With a different view of real presence, the English Bishop of Salisbury Edmund Guest wrote the new Article intending to communicate that Christ is objectively and really present in relation to the elements prior to reception. For the bishop, this was a mystical relationship, but it did not involve the elimination of the elements through their being transubstantiated. The Article says, "The Body of Christ is given, taken, and eaten." Lest there is any doubt about what Guest meant, he explained his meaning in correspondence to a Bishop Cheney of Gloucester as not excluding "the Presence of Christ's body from the Sacrament, but only the grossness and sensibleness in the receiving thereof." He even adds, "For I said ... 'though he [the recipient] took Christ's Body in his hand, received it with his mouth, and that corporally, naturally, really, substantially, and carnally,' as the doctors do write, 'yet did he not for all that see It, feel It, smell It, nor taste It.'"[16]

Guest intends the Article to mean that Christ is mystically present in relation to the Sacrament prior to reception, without the elements ceasing to be bread and wine. The remainder of Article XXVIII rejects the doctrine of transubstantiation (which is a false view of real presence based on the bread and the wine molecularly changing to be the physical Body and Blood in some material sense). Such a view means the elements are dissolved to become something other than they are. Rather, the new Article XXVIII of Guest expresses a "heavenly and spiritual" mystical presence without the elements being

---

[16] R. W. Enraght, *Real Presence and the Holy Scripture* (Brighton: Wakeling, 1872), Appendix A.

destroyed or removed. Yet, the article though stating a mystical presence of Christ in relation to the elements, retains that He is only received effectually by faith.

Guest further elaborates in his correspondence that his view of Christ's real presence in the Sacrament is according to the Christology of the Council of Chalcedon in 451. Guest on this point articulates what was the Christological approach to the Sacraments by the English Reformers. In the chapter "Re-formed Catholic Anglicanism on the Sacraments," I explain this in greater detail. Here, a brief summary will suffice.

The Christology of the Council of Chalcedon in 451 understood the two natures of Christ—his deity and his humanity—as being united but not comingled in his person. This is the Christology of Holy Scripture articulated by two leading fourth-century church fathers, St. Hilary and St. Cyril. They applied their Biblical understanding of Christology to sacramental theology. That is, they concluded that the relationship of the two Natures of Christ explained Christ's presence in the bread and the wine of the Eucharist. Though a mystical union, he was really present in relation to the elements. Importantly, Cranmer had used the same two church fathers to arrive at a different subjective view of real presence by relying on a German Reformer's (Oecolampadius) alternate interpretation of them.[17] Cranmer did not believe Christ was present in the elements. Rather, parallel to the reception of the elements the Holy Spirit brought the full Humanity and Deity into union with the believer. Nevertheless, what Guest intended with the new Article XXVIII in the *Thirty-Nine Articles* was language more consistent with the ancient catholic understanding of real presence based on Hilary, Cyril, and what became Chalcedonian Christology.

As to what was removed from Cranmer's sacramental section in his *Forty-Two Articles*, his original Article 29 had said,

> Forasmuch as the truth of man's nature requires that the body of one and the self-same man cannot be at one time in diverse places, but must needs be in some one certain place, the body of Christ cannot be present at one time in many and diverse places. Because (as Holy Scripture does teach) Christ was taken up into heaven, and there shall continue unto the end of the world, a faithful man ought not, either to believe or openly to confess the real and bodily presence (as they term it) of Christ's flesh and blood in the Sacrament of the Lord's Supper.

This was a standard argument against transubstantiation and any non-transubstantiated, objective real presence view. If Christ is seated at the right hand of God the Father since His Ascension, it is presumed that He cannot also be present at Holy Communion. Yet, given the language of Guest's Article XXVIII and his stated meaning, he believed that Christ in his glorified, resurrected "spiritual body" could miraculously be present at both places. This was his meaning of the phrase, "heavenly and spiritual." Christ is heavenly and spiritually present. We can understand therefore why with the new addition of Guest's Article XXVIII, Article 29 of the *Forty-two Articles* was removed from the *Thirty-Nine Articles*. Its removal further substantiates a return to an ancient church fathers' view of real presence.

---

[17] For Oecolampadius, the Holy Spirit not the elements communicated the full Humanity and Deity of Christ simultaneously in parallel upon reception by faith.

The result is a sacramental viewpoint in the *Thirty-Nine Articles* that, while not prohibiting Cranmer's version of receptionism, is reformed catholic.[18] Article XXVIII in the final *Thirty-Nine Articles* version actually expands beyond Cranmer's views, and opens the way for an objective understanding of real presence to be held by English Reformers in the late sixteenth through seventeenth centuries, as well as by others later to come (the nineteenth through the twentieth centuries).

In summary, if we understand accurately the sacramental modifications of the final version of the *Articles of Religion*, they are much more in line with the view of the real presence of Christ in the Eucharist that was held by the ancient catholic, Undivided Church. They are reformed catholic. The 1571 *Thirty-Nine Articles* shifted in their Eucharistic theology to a more objective understanding of real presence. This view in the new Article XXVIII of the *Thirty-Nine Articles* is further supported by the removal of Article XXIX in the *Forty-Two Articles*. It spoke of Christ's presence being confined to the right hand of God the Father. The *Thirty-Nine Articles* do not. They allow for Christ to be present at God's right hand and mystically also in the Sacrament.

Yet even with these changes, Cranmer's views were still permitted. He believed that the faithful recipient of the Sacrament mystically comes into union with the "total Christ" by the power of the Spirit. It is a form of receptionism (Union with the Body and Blood of Christ when the elements are received in faith). Though Cranmer's position was not precisely what Bishop Guest's Article XXVIII says, it is a form of realism. Thus, we see from the sacramental changes in the *Thirty-Nine Articles* that multiple beliefs about real presence are permitted in the Anglican Way.

Re-formed Catholic in Correction of Late Medieval Spirituality

Another way in which we find the re-formed catholic model in the *Thirty-Nine Articles* is the specific manner of correcting late medieval abuses of the Sacraments and spirituality. These statements in the *Articles* concerned Eucharistic practices and prayers to the saints. Yet, upon close analysis it is important to understand what is and what is not being said, allowed and disallowed in particular articles. I note the following examples.

Article XXVIII

First, the *Articles* offer correction to abuses of devotion to the Sacraments that had become prevalent in the late Middle Ages. Article XXVIII mentioned above concludes with a paragraph, "The Sacrament of the Lord's Supper was not by Christ's ordinance reserved, carried about, lifted up, or worshipped." In considering this final paragraph of the Article, there are two important contexts to be understood for a correct interpretation, as well as the actual wording regarding what it does and does not say.

As for the contexts, for one we should not forget what has already been developed about the Scriptural and ancient sacramental theology expressed by Bishop Guest who

---

[18] Article XXVIII did not totally exclude Cranmer's sacramental views. The language of "heavenly and spiritual" allowed interpreters to understand "spiritual" to be a reference to the Holy Spirit, which would have fit with Cranmer's understanding of how Christ's full Humanity and Deity are communicated to the faithful recipient. See chapter three in this book for a more detailed explanation of Cranmer's views on real presence.

wrote it. Given this re-formed catholic context, the last paragraph should be seen as flowing from and consistent with what has preceded. That is, the final paragraph addresses late medieval practices that were not part of the ancient church, pointing to a second contextual consideration.

The other context in understanding the final paragraph of Article XXVIII is the actual worship services in the late Middle Ages that the Article says were not "Christ's ordinance." The Article indicates with the verb *worshipped* that it is speaking of certain kinds of acts associated with specific services called *Benediction*. These services involved lifting and venerating the Host. And there were particular Western Medieval liturgies in which the Sacrament was consecrated and reserved for these purposes.

Unfortunately, by the late Middle Ages such practices involved worshipping the elements of the Sacrament because of the transubstantiated understanding of real presence. If the elements physically turned into the Body and Blood of Christ, then the Sacrament would be inescapably worshipped if lifted up or carried about. Further abuse resulted when such views of the Body and Blood of Christ led to taking the Sacrament into warfare. The priests carried the Sacrament before soldiers going into battle like a magical talisman, with the belief that the Lord would magically grant victory.

As the article states, Christ did not institute the Sacrament for such purposes. Neither are these kinds of services found in the ancient Church. The Eastern Church never has practiced this kind of Eucharistic devotion. Nevertheless, the actions of "lifting up," "reserved," and so forth were understood in pastoral ways and with the ancient view of real presence such that they were continued. The sacramental history in the Church of England illustrates how the Article was observed while the practices remained.

For example, concerning reserving the Sacrament for pastoral purposes in the Church of England, it was never understood as prohibited if the article was interpreted by the prayer book. Reservation had to do with the priest's consecration of more Sacrament than was distributed in a communion service for the purpose of its being used for ministering to the sick at other times than worship. Important to note, the first two editions of the prayer book, 1549 and 1552, permitted reserving the sacrament to take to the sick who could not attend worship. The rubric in the 1549 *Book of Common Prayer* says:

> If the same day there be a celebration of the Holy Communion in the Church, then shall the priest reserve (at the open communion) so much of the sacrament of the Body and Blood as shall serve the sick person, and so many as shall communicate with him (if there be any). And as soon as he conveniently may, after the open Communion ended in the Church, shall go and minister the same, first to those that are appointed to communicate with the sick (if there be any), and last of all to the sick person himself. But before the curate distribute the Holy Communion, the appointed General Confession must be made in the name of the communicants, the curate adding the Absolution, with the Comfortable Sentences of Scripture following in the open Communion, and after the Communion ended, the Collect, *Almighty and everlasting God, we must heartily thank thee, etc.*[19]

---

[19] Charles Harris, *Liturgy and Worship: A Companion to the Prayer Books of the Anglican Communion*, Ed. W. K. Lowther Clarke (London: SPCK, 1932), 551.

The rubric provides administration of the reserved Sacrament for a sick person who gave notice within hours of the worship service. A second rubric was added for the Sacrament to be given at other times. In it, the minister is directed to conduct actual consecration if possible. Yet it was not always possible. The rubric includes language such as, "And having a convenient place in the sick man's house (where he may reverently celebrate) ... he shall there celebrate Holy Communion." However, the Anglican scholar Charles Harris qualifies the word *convenient* by explaining, "If this living room [or a place in the house] were too small, too dirty, or otherwise not 'convenient,' he [the priest] would bring the Reserved Sacrament with him from the church." Harris concludes, "Their avowed object was to do all things according to the 'laudable custom of the Primitive Church.'"[20] Since the Sacrament had been reserved for the sick and for Last Rites (the viaticum) from the earliest days of Christianity, the English Reformation Church made the same provision.[21] Thus, the first prayer book provided for reservation of the Sacrament, meaning the language in the *Articles* was not forbidding this specific act.

In addition, the more Protestant second edition of the 1552 *Book of Common Prayer* continued to allow these rubrics permitting the reservation of the Sacrament with an even stronger commitment to the practice. Harris points out that the second rubric in the 1552 prayer book did not even require "consecration" when taking communion to the sick. This version only uses the word "minister," which meant "distribute," the Holy Communion. It thereby indicated reservation of the Sacrament had occurred. Harris further proves this meaning by referring to Martin Bucer's, Calvin's, and other Reformers' favorable views toward reservation.[22]

Bucer for example was the German Reformer who offered the extensive Protestant critique of the 1549 prayer book in his writing, *Censura*, consisting of 28 chapters. Harris notes, "Commentators on the Prayer Book have mostly failed to notice that though Bucer detected numerous and grievous faults in nearly every other part of this Book, he found nothing whatever to censure in the Service for the Sick Communion, though this prescribed Reservation as the normal method to be used."[23] To be certain, the other Protestant critic of the prayer book, Peter Martyr, objected strongly to the practice. It presented a problem for the revisers as expressed in the *Reformatio Legum*. It should not be overlooked that Bucer's conclusion of his version of the prayer book commended in his *Censura*, however, was "sufficiently in agreement with the Divine Scriptures." Harris says that he "made his opinion known to the 1552 revisers" gathering Calvin's and other Reformers' support for the practice under pastoral circumstances for the sick. In the end, even though many disliked the practice, Bucer's view of reservation was upheld in the rubrics of the 1552 *Book of Common Prayer*. Thus, the practice of reservation continued

---

[20] Harris, *Liturgy and Worship*, 552 n. 1. (brackets mine).
[21] Harris provides extensive proof of the early church's practices of reserving the Sacrament to help the sick and dying. See Ibid., 543–549.
[22] Ibid., 578–579.
[23] Ibid., 559.

in the English Reformation down to the present, though not all English Reformers agreed that it was always necessary.[24]

The other verbs in Article XXVIII refer to the service of Benediction of the Blessed Sacrament. As stated, at the time of the Reformation these types of liturgies were perceived as involving the worship of the Sacrament due to the particular view of real presence at the time. The English Reformation restored the ancient model of Christ's mystical presence without destroying the elements. This made it possible for later nineteenth-century Anglo-Catholics to maintain that Benediction could be observed without idolizing the Sacrament. They argued that Christ is being worshipped when the Host is elevated not the elements themselves. They therefore revived this form of Eucharistic devotion. Even so, the effort was not without great controversy even among the Anglo-Catholics. Charles Gore, Edward Pusey's successor at Pusey House, so opposed the restoration of the practice that he proposed that a Canon should be instituted in the Church of England prohibiting it.[25] C. B. Moss also objected to it.

In fairness to those who revived the service of Benediction, another important aspect of Anglican hermeneutics should be remembered: "what is not expressly forbidden in Scripture may be allowed." This is quite different from other views in the Protestant Reformation stating that "what is not expressly commanded may not be allowed." The English Reformers clearly had the former approach, explaining why some Anglicans believed that Benediction may be practiced if medieval abuses are removed. If read literally, Article XXVIII only states that Benediction is not among "Christ's ordinances." In other words, Scripture is silent on the matter. Therefore, some Anglicans have understood that although Christ did not command such practices, neither did he explicitly forbid them. At the same time, they would acknowledge that based on what Jesus did command, normal observance of the Sacrament should be to take and eat it.

Consequently, Bishops in the Anglican Communion have allowed or disallowed the practice according to their understanding of the Article. Nevertheless, when permitted, it is an adiaphora service offered not at the main worship on Sunday but at optional times (usually in the evening on certain days of the week). Others have maintained that the service in and of itself violates the Scripture and the Article. Regardless, both understandings admit that the way the medieval Roman Church had come to use the Sacrament with practices related to Benediction was wrong.

I offer this discussion of the final paragraph in Article XXVIII to demonstrate how the re-formed catholic approach in the *Articles* corrected abuses without necessarily removing Eucharistic pastoral care and devotion. Yet even when addressing medieval corruption, the English Reformers remained faithful to the guiding principles of the Scriptures and the early church fathers. Their Eucharistic theology and practice were part of the *ad fontes*, re-formed catholic model of back to not only the Scriptures but the early church fathers.

---

[24] See Lancelot Andrewes, *Two Answers to Cardinal Perro and Other Miscellaneous Works*, ed. James Bliss, Library of Anglo Catholic Theology (Oxford: John Henry Parker, 1854), 17–19. Andrewes appeals to the validity of the Sacrament of Desire. This is included in the prayer book service for the Sick and Dying. It states that a person who cannot receive the Sacrament due to illness still by faith receives the Body and Blood of Christ.

[25] See Harris, *Liturgy and Worship*.

Article XXII

A second place in the *Thirty-Nine Articles of Religion* where we find correction to specific late medieval spirituality is in Article XXII "Of Purgatory." It states, "The Romish Doctrine concerning Purgatory, Pardons, Worshipping and Adoration, as well as of Images and Relics, and also Invocation of the Saints, is a fond thing, vainly invented, and grounded upon no warranty of Scripture, but rather repugnant to the Word of God." Without the ancient history of the practices condemned, one might read this Article as saying all of them are inherently Roman Catholic and medieval. For some of them this is true. Yet, given what we know was the re-formed catholic model of the English Reformers in going back to the Scriptures and the ancient church fathers, the designation "Romish Doctrine" is key to the proper interpretation of what is being prohibited. It indicates that there may be earlier ancient Catholic views of such practices differing from what they became in their corrupted form in the late Middle Ages of the Roman Church.

Although time and space do not permit complete analysis of the Article in this brief introductory chapter on the re-formed catholic nature of the *Articles*, I can state that there was no precedent in the Scriptures or the ancient Church for a view of purgatory as a *limbus partum* state between heaven and hell that became known in the Middle Ages of the Western Church. There was the understanding of the growth of the departed saints in heaven after death and before the Second Advent. This ancient view is reflected in the "Prayer for the Whole State of Christ's Church" in the 1549/1928 editions of the *Book of Common Prayer*. Not all Anglicans agreed, which explains the other version of it in the 1662 BCP, the "Prayer for the Whole State of Christ's Church Militant." With either prayer, however, there is no suggestion of "pardon" after death, also mentioned in the Article.

Concerning the worship or adoration of saints and their relics, the ancient Church did neither. They recognized the power of their relics based on Scripture. When a dead man fell on Elisha's bones he was raised (2 Kings 13:21). Nevertheless, the Seventh Ecumenical Council distinguishes between worshipping and reverencing images. It denounces the former while permitting the latter, given the proper understanding of what was allowed. The early church therefore respected and reverenced the saints of God. However, at the time of the late Middle Ages, the Western Church had more shrines to the saints than they did to Jesus Christ. Invocation of the saints in the Roman sense had displaced the centrality of Christ's intercession. Instead of petitioning Christ, saints were being invoked for what only God could provide. This was clearly a departure from the ancient Church. It is this aberration that Article XXII seeks to correct.

Regarding the "invocation of the saints" there was clearly a difference between what the early church practiced and what was being done in the late medieval church. It needed correction for the people of God to return to Him for their petitions. It is on this point in particular that we see the re-formed catholic approach of the English Reformers. The Article condemns the Roman practice, but it does not exclude the early church's understanding of invocation as expressed by views articulated by some of the leading English Reformers.

The late nineteenth-century Anglican Darwell Stone fully explains and distinguishes the ancient understanding of invocation of the saints articulated by leading Anglican Divines in the Reformation period, and the medieval Roman view as it had come to be popularly practiced.[26] The difference is quite significant. Since the English Reformation understanding of the invocation of saints is rooted in early church, *vis a vis* a re-formed catholic approach, the ancient practices of prayer should be understood.

Stone summarizes with numerous examples how initially the early church practiced the "comprecation" of the saints. This was the view of asking God to have the saints join with their prayers. He cites, for example from the *Gallican Sacramentary* (Liturgy), a prayer offered on St. Stephen's Day. It says, "Almighty and Eternal God, who didst dedicate the first fruits of the martyrs in the blood of thy holy deacon St. Stephen, grant, we beseech thee, that he who made supplication for his persecutors may stand before thee as our intercessor."[27] This type of comprecation of the saints was based on the Scriptural teaching that the departed saints are "conscious" and living souls. As the Book of Revelation reveals, they pray for God's kingdom on earth (v. 7). They are present in worship surrounding the people of God as a "great cloud of witnesses" (Heb 12:1). Stone concludes, "In the early Church it does not appear to have been ever doubted that in the case of the holy dead to retain consciousness was to retain the power of prayer."[28] Therefore, the Lord could be petitioned to have the departed saints pray for the people of God on earth.

Stone then develops how within the third century of the Church, the practice of comprecation expanded to Christians on earth asking the saints of God to pray for them. Stone provides numerous examples. St. Ambrose, by whose ministry St. Augustine was converted, once offered the following comment on prayer:

> Martyrs are to be besought, whose patronage we seem to claim for ourselves by having their bodies as a kind of pledge. They who washed away whatever sins they had in their own blood are able to entreat for our sins; for they are God's martyrs, our leaders, the spectators of our life and actions. Let us not be ashamed to employ them as intercessors for our weakness, because they themselves have known the weakness of the body, even when they overcame.[29]

The prevalence of the practice of asking for the prayers of the saints was such that Stone summarizes, "It was the ordinary Christian belief in the East and in the West, that it is lawful and expedient to address to the saints' supplications for the benefit of their prayers to Almighty God."[30]

However, Stone observes the important distinction that appears in the English Reformation. He mentions how some have tried to minimize statements like the one above from St. Ambrose by noting that the same early church fathers "speak elsewhere of the necessity of prayer being addressed to God."[31] This is true, but Stone points out that "these other statements refer to prayers for direct help as distinguished from

---

[26] Darwell Stone, "The Invocation of Saints," *Church Quarterly Review* 47/94 (Jan. 1899): 273–301. Originally anonymous; reprinted Darwell Stone, *The Invocation of Saints* (London: Longmans, Green, & Co., 1903).

[27] Stone, "Invocation," 275.

[28] Ibid., 276.

[29] Ibid., 281.

[30] Ibid., 282.

[31] Stone, "Invocation," 282.

requests for prayer for the help of God."[32] The distinction is that only God can answer prayer, and therefore He is the only One to whom a Christian should pray. However, that is not the same as asking a fellow believer to pray. It's just that the early Christians, with their view of the nearness of heaven, believed they could ask departed saints as well as those on earth for prayer. Stone concludes, "In any case, it has been allowed that the testimony of St. Basil, St. Gregory of Nyssa, St. Ephraim the Syrian, and St. Augustine in favor of the practice of invocation [prayer requests] is 'unshaken.'"[33]

Therefore, when we come to the English Reformation, we discover that the same kind of distinction between prayer to God and prayer requests to departed saints was restored according to the early church fathers' understanding of the invocation of the saints. We should not be surprised given the *ad fontes*, back to the sources, reformed catholic model of the English Reformers.

In 1537 and 1543 a Convocation of English Bishops, chaired by Archbishop Thomas Cranmer, composed and edited in final form *The Institution of a Christian Man*. On the subject of the invocation of the saints, it makes the early church distinction saying, "So we esteem not or worship not them [departed saints] as givers of those gifts [from God], but as intercessors of the same." Stone explains the meaning of this statement as, "It was declared to be unlawful to seek from the saints those good things which can only be given by God; it was declared to be lawful to ask them for prayers."[34] Cranmer even included the following invocation of the saints in his 1544 Litany after the opening invocation of the Trinity:

> Holy virgin Mary, Mother of God [and] our Saviour Jesus Christ, *pray for us.*
> All holy angels and archangels, and all holy orders of blessed spirits, *pray for us.*
> All holy patriarchs and prophets, apostles, martyrs, confessors, and virgins, and all the blessed company of heaven, *pray for us.*

Nevertheless, in the subsequent revisions of the prayer book, these prayers were removed from public worship. In Cranmer's first version of the *Forty-Two Articles*, Article 23 stated the following: "The doctrine of the schoolmen concerning ... invocation of the saints is a fond thing vainly feigned and grounded upon no warrant of Scripture but rather repugnant to the word of God." The "schoolmen" were early medieval Western scholars who had failed to maintain the distinctions of invoking saints that is found in the early church fathers. The intent of Article 23 was to reject only prayers to saints, not prayer requests of them.

However, in the final version of the 1571 *Thirty-Nine Articles of Religion*, a significant change of wording occurs in the revision (Article XXII). Instead of "schoolmen," the phrasing is altered to "the Romish doctrine." Stone cites that this different wording from "schoolmen" to "Romish Doctrine" had already been approved at two synods of English Bishops in 1563. The words *Romish doctrine* were put into the Article to emphasize that it is addressing "the popular current teaching of the Romish theologians at the time."

---

[32] Stone, "Invocation," 282.

[33] Ibid. (brackets mine).

[34] Ibid., 291 (brackets mine).

Archdeacon Hardwick refers to this group as the "extreme Medieval party."[35] Stone underscores that whereas the "schoolmen" distinguished between prayer to God and prayer requests to saints, by the time of the late Middle Ages in the sixteenth century, the "Romish theologians" of the "extreme Medieval party" were failing to make the distinction. There was a burgeoning "cult of the saints." Saints and angels were being worshipped at shrines. They were being asked to grant things that only God could give. It was this kind of aberrant approach to the invocation of the saints that Article XXII was rejecting. Therefore, Stone concludes, "The Article ... was intended ... to leave open the right or the wrong of the limited practice of asking the saints for the help of their prayers."[36]

When Stone says, "leave open the right or the wrong," he indicates that the English Reformation Church that approved the *Thirty-Nine Articles* in 1571 wanted to let the matter of issuing prayer requests to the saints reside at the level of personal conviction. These prayers were not included in the public prayers of the prayer book. Thus, there were those who took Article XXII to condemn not only prayers to but prayer requests of the departed saints. At the same time, there were others who wanted to make the distinction. In fairness to Article XXII, however, based on the change in wording and how the English Reformers interpreted it, the Article did not disallow asking the saints for prayer.

For proof that there were English Reformers who understood Article XXII as not necessarily forbidding prayer requests to the saints, two helpful citations should be noted. Archbishop James Ussher, who was more on the Protestant (even Calvinistic) side of Anglicanism, speaks to the matter of the invocation of the saints in his *Answer to a Jesuit Challenge* published in 1624. In it he denotes the difference of "addresses to the saints similar in wording to the adoration which we render to God," and "formal and absolute prayers ... tendered to the saints," and "requests for the prayers of the saints," as "requests of the same nature with those which are in this kind usually made unto the living."[37] The archbishop, in a re-formed catholic manner, recognizes the same distinctions as the early church fathers. As a fervent defender of the *Thirty-Nine Articles*, he could have only done so with the view that Article XXII was not prohibiting prayer requests offered to the saints. The Article addresses medieval failure to make the ancient differences.

Bishop William Forbes (1585–1633) similarly recognizes the same kind of statement in his *Considerationes Modeste et Pacificae*. He makes the distinction between, "religious invocation or such prayer as can be rightly addressed only to God, and mere invocation or addressing angels and saints to pray with us and for us, a practice which is not to be condemned either as unlawful or as useless."[38] Forbes' use of the word *unlawful* is significant. At the time, the Anglican Formularies, including the *Book of Common Prayer* and the *Thirty-Nine Articles of Religion*, were law in the Church of England. His reference

---

[35] Stone, "Invocation," 294. Stone prefers the phrase "extreme Medieval party" noting that there were Roman theologians such as Bellarmine who also opposed the failure to distinguish prayers to God and prayer requests to the saints. Even the Council of Trent made this point. Nevertheless, this only proves that there was indeed a problem. Certainly, the popular understanding and spirituality of the late Middle Ages did not make the ancient distinction nor that of the "schoolmen."

[36] Ibid., 294–295.

[37] Ibid., 293.

[38] Ibid., 301.

to asking "angels and saints to pray with and for us" as not being "unlawful" meant that Article XXII of the *Thirty-Nine Articles* did not prohibit these kinds of prayers.

I provide this explanation of Article XXII to demonstrate how the English Reformers maintained their *ad fontes*, re-formed catholic approach, to the final version of Article XXII in the *Thirty-Nine Articles*. The critical change in wording from "the doctrine of the schoolmen" in the *Forty-Two Articles* to "Romish Doctrine" in the *Thirty-Nine Articles* was to clarify that they were intending to condemn current late medieval abuses. Concerning the invocation of the saints, they were not necessarily outlawing prayer requests to the saints, but only the corruption of the early church distinctions. The Article only condemns praying to the saints in place of petitioning God, asking them to do what only he can do. An example of the latter abuse would be like asking a saint to "heal me," or to "give me a new house," as opposed to, "pray for my healing," and so forth.

To be sure, there were and are many Anglicans who hold the conviction that departed saints should not be asked to pray for anything. Only saints on earth may be given such requests. These faithful Anglicans understand the Article to condemn all attempts to address heavenly saints in prayer. This has always been an acceptable conviction within Anglicanism. Yet, it is clear from a careful reading and comparison in the change made in the final version of the Article, combined with writings of English Reformers contemporary to that time, that the Article does not go as far as to remove the early church distinction between prayers to God and prayer requests to the saints. As a result, there are also many in the history of Anglicanism down to the present who practice the spirituality of asking departed saints to pray for them. What is certain is that such prayers are not in the public liturgies of the prayer book so as to bind consciences one way or the other. The matter is left to the personal convictions of a believer in his prayer closet.

To sum up this section, I have presented how two of the *Articles* (XXVIII and XXII) in the *Thirty-Nine Articles* in the context, writings, and practices of the English Reformation sustain a re-formed catholic *ad fontes* approach. In either Article, none of the practices are mentioned in the Scriptures. Yet is clear that aspects of these Articles, properly interpreted according to the English Reformers' understandings of the early church fathers, were permitted and practiced. What could be done consistent with the ancient teachings was distinguished from late medieval abuses. Such an approach could have only been taken with a re-formed catholic model.

Conclusion

Therefore, the *Articles of Religion* in general, and in particular, the final *Thirty-Nine Articles* revision of Cranmer's original *Forty-Two Articles*, are re-formed catholic. Cranmer approached necessary corrections to late medieval doctrinal aberration with an overall re-formed catholic mindset. He did allow some views of contemporary reformers into his first edition. However, years after his death, when the entire House of Bishops revised Cranmer's work, the *Articles* are pulled back from the influence of any one reformer. Instead, they return to a more consistent re-formed catholic model according to Scripture and the early church fathers. Parliament approved the *Thirty-Nine Articles*. The stage was set for the English Church throughout its history to follow this re-formed catholic approach of the *Thirty-Nine Articles of Religion*.

Chapter 7

Hermeneutics

The Rev. Dr. Gerald McDermott

Hermeneutics is the fancy theological term for how we know what we know. For Christians it means two things, how to interpret the Bible and then how to see through Scripture to interpret life under the Triune God. The question addressed in this chapter is, How do Anglicans interpret the Bible and reality? What is their particular way of interpreting the Bible and life? Let's start with a thought experiment.

Think back to when you were a new believer. Perhaps you wanted to learn all you could about the Bible. You realized it is the Word of God, and somewhere you heard that you can only know God to the extent that you know his Word.

You also knew there was an old man down the street who was renowned for his intimate walk with God. He had been studying the Bible since he was a boy and learning from the early church fathers how to understand God's Word and therefore all of life.

But you also heard that tradition is a bad thing, that it is the word of men as opposed to the Word of God, and that the priesthood of every believer means you should read and interpret the Bible for yourself and not be influenced by anyone else—which means by someone else's tradition.

So you refuse to visit this old man and ask him to tutor you in the Bible or in anything about God. Over the years you come to conclusions that differ from what you have heard that the church fathers taught in the first millennium. But you don't care, because what you have heard about their teachings doesn't make sense to you. For you know that God really cares about equality, and not everything they wrote seems to agree with what new books about equality and equity teach. And you have learned that God is love, and not everything the fathers wrote about love agrees with what you feel *love* must mean.

Good and Bad Tradition

Is there something wrong with this picture? No doubt. But this is the approach taken by many evangelicals. They have read in Matthew 15 that Jesus criticized the Pharisees for making void the Word of God because of their tradition. They have read Paul telling the Colossians to beware of philosophy and human deceit "according to human traditions" (2:8). So they have concluded that all tradition is bad in and of itself, and therefore all of the teaching of the great men and women of God over the last three millennia should be avoided lest they miss the direct insight they can get from reading the Bible on their own.

They have missed what Paul wrote about *good* tradition and the context of Jesus' teaching about tradition. First, Paul. The apostle praised the Corinthians for "maintain[ing] the *traditions* even as I delivered them to you" (1 Cor 11:2 ESV).[1] He warned the Thessalonians to "stand firm and hold to the *traditions* that you were taught by us, either by our spoken word or by our letter" (2 Thess 2:15). He instructed Timothy to pass on the tradition he had taught Timothy (remember, this was before there was New Testament teaching in print, as it were): "What you have heard from me in the presence

---

[1] Unless otherwise noted, all Scripture translations are the author's.

of many witnesses entrust to faithful men who will be able to teach others also" (2 Tim 2:2). He passed on to the Ephesian elders a saying of Jesus from the oral tradition, never recorded in the gospels, "It is more blessed to give than to receive" (Acts 20:35).

And think back to what Jesus said in Matthew 15 about the bad tradition of the Pharisees. Notice why it was bad: it "makes void the word of God." God had told all his people to honor their parents, which included caring for them when they need it. But the Pharisees were teaching in their bad tradition that their followers could make contributions to the Temple in a way that would exempt them from supporting their parents. Most evangelicals and other Christians miss the fact that Jesus actually praised other traditions of the Pharisees when he told his disciples in Matthew 23:3 to "practice and protect whatever [the Pharisees] teach you." Why would Jesus praise *these* traditions? Because they supported and helped interpret the Word of God rather than making it void.

For Jesus, then, as for Paul, there are two kinds of tradition: bad tradition that makes void the Word of God and good tradition that supports and helps us understand the Word of God.

Let's see two more things. First, that the early Church used tradition to defend biblical teaching against heresy. Second, that there is no way for us to avoid using *some* tradition when interpreting the Bible. The only question is whether the tradition we use is bad or good.

Tradition in the Early Church

The early fathers showed the necessity of good tradition or interpreting the Bible in their battles with the Gnostics, who together mounted the greatest challenge to orthodoxy in the early centuries of Christianity. The Gnostics whom the Church battled claimed to be Jesus followers and quoted the Bible, both Old and New Testaments, to teach their false Jesus and false salvation. Their Jesus, they said, denounced the God of the Old Testament as an evil God who had created an evil world of matter. This Jesus was never a real man and so was never born in flesh and blood and never died on a bloody cross. Nor was he raised in a flesh and blood body, for matter is evil and the true God has nothing to do with something as crass as dirty matter. The Gnostic Jesus saves not by his death and resurrection in a body, for he doesn't have one, but by giving people special, secret knowledge in the mystical and spiritual vision that comes by going to the gnostic churches.

Irenaeus (c.130–c.200), one of the great early fathers of the Church, taught that the Scriptures contain the truth about God, Jesus, and salvation, but that Christians must listen to the teaching of the bishops of the orthodox churches that had been given by tradition from the apostles in order to understand the Bible rightly. Tertullian (c. 155–c. 220 AD), another early father fighting the Gnostics, said the "rule of faith" given in the creeds contained the proper interpretation of Bible. So both of these fathers insisted that Christians need tradition taught in the orthodox churches and summarized in the orthodox creeds in order to interpret the Bible rightly and gain true salvation. The gnostic teachers twisted the scriptures to teach a false God and false salvation.

Our Anglican fathers have said the same as the early fathers. Article VIII tells us "the three Creeds ... ought thoroughly ... to be believed" and Article XX that "the Church hath power to decree Rites and Ceremonies and [has] authority in Controversies of Faith" over how to interpret the Bible. The preface to the Ordinal says that our polity "is evident unto all men, diligently reading the Holy Scripture and ancient Authors." The preface "Concerning the service of the Church" proclaims that our worship is "much agreeable to the mind and purpose of the old Fathers." Moreover, the preface "Of Ceremonies" in the 1662 BCP advised critics of liturgy to "have reverence unto [these ceremonies] for their antiquity" and warned against "innovations and newfangleness."

Evangelicals and Tradition

Many evangelicals insist they read the Bible without being influenced by tradition. They have not noticed what Alister McGrath calls "the evangelical tendency to cite the interpretations of earlier evangelical writers in weighing up how a given biblical passage is to be interpreted." Nor have they noticed how their own understandings of a host of issues—women in ministry, marriage roles, usury, charismatic gifts, what happens in communion and baptism, the nature and sequence of the end times—have all been influenced by the communities of interpretation in which they have been reared or schooled.

Thus, the real question is not whether tradition influences our interpretation of the Bible, but which tradition does so. And the best way to judge the tradition we allow to influence us is to regularly compare it to the Great Tradition—which is the voice of the "great cloud of witnesses" down through the centuries.

For the last two centuries liberal Protestants tried to free themselves from all tradition in order to get back, they thought, to Jesus' simple gospel—before it was corrupted by umpteen layers of church tradition. They waved the flag of *sola scriptura*, imagining they stood above or outside tradition—after swallowing the dogmas of their own Enlightenment tradition. They were blind, as many evangelicals are, to what could be called the Heisenberg uncertainty principle of hermeneutics. This is based on the widely accepted conclusion that all research and interpretation are affected by unproven assumptions and personal involvement. It was no surprise that in their quests for the historical Jesus these liberal interpreters painted pictures of Jesus that looked surprisingly like themselves.

Anglican Tradition

So how can Anglicans find good tradition to be sure they are interpreting the Word of God correctly? The best answer is to turn to the greatest theologian of the English Reformation in the sixteenth century, Richard Hooker (1554–1600). Now, many Anglicans think Thomas Cranmer (1489–1556) was our first principal theologian, but this is a confusion of categories. Cranmer was a brilliant liturgist, but his only theological treatise was on the Lord's Supper. Most historians have rightly recognized Hooker as the towering genius at the end of the sixteenth century who produced a massive compendium of Anglican thinking on Scripture and life that has guided much of the best Anglican thinking ever since. And among other things, Hooker showed us Anglican hermeneutics, the Anglican way of reading Scripture and life: to read the Bible and understand the Tradition while sitting at the feet of the fathers.[2]

In Hooker's classic *Of the Laws of Ecclesiastical Polity*, which has justly been called Anglicanism's *Summa*, Hooker principally battled Puritans who thought the Anglican way had imported too much extra-biblical baggage from Catholic worship. Over and over again, Hooker appeals to the fathers of the church to support Anglican liturgical worship. For example, in Book V he cites Jerome's defense of special vestments for ministers and their ceremonies against Pelagius' complaint that "the glory of clothes and ornaments was a thing contrary to God and godliness." Jerome asked, "[I]f a Bishop, a Priest, a Deacon, and the rest of the ecclesiastical order come to administer the usual sacrifice in a white garment, are they hereby God's adversaries?" Hooker adds, "By which words of Jerome we may take it [that he meant Pelagius was] condemning by so general a speech even the neatness of that very garment itself, wherein the clergy did then use to administer publicly the holy Sacrament of Christ's most blessed Body and Blood."[3]

Puritans also criticized the reading of long passages of different Scriptures in the same Anglican worship service, sometimes without a sermon or with only a short sermon. Hooker went for justification to Cyprian's observation that people are blessed simply by hearing the Word of God read.[4]

Hooker turned to the fathers 774 times in his *Laws*, as often to the Latin as the Greek and African fathers, but Tertullian and Augustine were his favorites. To the great Bishop of Hippo, Hooker appealed ninety-nine times, either to justify an Anglican practice or to interpret a controverted passage of Scripture.[5] In one of his most important arguments against Puritans, for example, Hooker argued against the regulative principle that everything in church government and worship must have an explicit biblical—preferably New Testament—prooftext. Augustine recognized, according to Hooker, that while the most important Christian doctrine is clear in Scripture to those willing to see, many matters of church polity and worship are either unclear or not addressed. Therefore, church leaders are free to use reason and charity to keep traditional practice that does not violate the clear teaching of Scripture. Augustine wrote, "The custom of the people of God and the decrees of our forefathers are to be kept, touching those things whereof the Scripture hath neither one way or other given us any charge."[6] Hooker then interprets Augustine as follows: "St. Augustine's speech therefore doth import, that where we have no divine precept, if yet we have the custom of the people of God or a decree of our forefathers, this is a law and must be kept."[7]

---

[2] In one sense, the church fathers *are* the best of tradition. But when Hooker, for example, argued with the Puritans about the tradition of using set prayers and the sacramental traditions that the prayer book mediated, he went to the fathers often for support and interpretation. In that sense he read both the Bible and the tradition at the feet of the fathers.

[3] Hooker, *Laws*, 5.29.2.

[4] Ibid., 5.22.13.

[5] John K. Luoma, "Who Owns the Fathers? Hooker and Cartwright on the Authority of the Primitive Church," *Sixteenth Century Journal* 8/3 (1977): 57.

[6] Augustine, Letter 36.2.

[7] Hooker, *Laws*, 4.5.1.

This is not, for Hooker, tradition simply for the sake of tradition—keeping what was done in the past because change is anathema. No, it is a recognition of what could be called the providential ordering of Christian faith and worship, and a sense that there was a divine rationality in the ways that worship unfolded over the centuries, even if there was also need for continual attention to how Scripture and reason should guide that unfolding.

The fathers were necessary for Hooker because he saw Scripture operating at different levels. At its highest are the things which "Scripture plainly doth deliver." Then there are deductions made from Scripture by "force of reason." But "after these the voice of the Church succeedeth" because there are many things in Church life which Scripture does not explicitly address (4.14.5). Here, as C. S. Lewis writes, "[I]t is in Hooker's nature to listen to this voice very lovingly—to 'uniform practice throughout the whole world' (7.9.2), 'the use of the people of God' or 'ordinances of our fathers' (3.11.15) which it would be 'hathenish petulancy' to 'trample under foot' (5.65.9)."[8]

Now Hooker did not accept every tradition, nor did he agree with the primitivist conviction that the earliest is always the best (5.20.4). For circumstances change and the shape of tradition sometimes must be adjusted to accommodate new contingencies. But, as Lewis saw, Hooker would countenance adjustment "only of order not doctrine, the one mutable, the other not, because truth does not change and convenience does (5.8.2)."[9]

Hooker set a pattern which the best Anglican thinking has followed ever since—interpreting Scripture and Church tradition with the help of the fathers. He recognized that there is no such thing as Scripture without tradition, that every person reads Scripture through some tradition or other, whether he realizes it or not. Even Jehovah's Witnesses, proud proclaimers of appealing to the Bible only, use a hermeneutical tradition—in their case—that which interprets Christological passages in an Arian framework. So the question is not *whether* we use tradition to understand Scripture, but *which* tradition has guided our interpretation. Hooker used sixteen hundred years of patristic, medieval, and Reformation tradition for his interpretation, but privileged the patristic tradition.

Lewis points out that while previous English controversialists used tactics, Hooker was the first to add strategy.[10] His principal Puritan opponent, Thomas Cartwright, claimed to find only Puritan worship in the New Testament, but Hooker showed that Cartwright was cherry-picking the New Testament and advocating worship practices that could not be found there. In other words, Cartwright was using *Puritan* tradition, not Scripture alone, to draw Puritan conclusions about worship. The Puritans, who criticized Anglicans for using tradition to interpret Scripture and order worship, were

---

[8] C. S. Lewis, *English Literature in the Sixteenth Century* (Oxford: Oxford University Press, 1973), 456.

[9] Ibid., 455.

[10] Ibid., 459. By this he means that long before he fights the Puritans in close quarters in Book V, he has already undermined their position in Books I and II by asking and answering questions they never considered but which "are fatal to their narrow scripturalism." The result is that his final refutation of their position is "a very small thing, a by-product" of what was a long developing argument.

using their own tradition to read the Bible and order their worship. Hooker turned the tables on them, and established a method that many later Anglican thinkers used to great profit: interpreting the Bible and ordering their lives and worship after patristic patterns.[11]

Historic Anglicanism is re-formed catholicism, where the second word means not "Roman," but "the undivided, universal (hence catholic) church of the first millennium." *Re-formed* refers in part to the Reformation emphasis on Scripture to correct, principally but not solely, semi-Pelagian tendencies in the late medieval period. We have just seen that the greatest Anglican theologian of the sixteenth century, Richard Hooker, read Scripture and tradition at the feet of the Fathers. Therefore, his theological method was not *sola scriptura* but *prima scriptura*—Scripture as primary, but interpreted by the light of tradition, especially that of the Fathers.

Hooker was watching what the fathers themselves did. Athanasius, for example, was a thoroughly biblical theologian who recognized that the Bible will be interpreted rightly only if it is read with help from Church tradition, which is the accumulated wisdom of the Jesus community going back to the apostles and their predecessors in Israel. It was this tradition that had been asserting, long before Athanasius, that Jesus Messiah was fully God, and that the Holy Spirit was too, as Athanasius later argued. It took Athanasius and the Cappadocian Fathers to work out the precise ways in which the divine Persons were three and one at the same time. But they were all working with previous theological and liturgical tradition that had been insisting back since the first century AD that the divine Word became flesh and dwelt among us.

The Arians, like the Gnostics before them, refused to grant weight to tradition. They wanted to read the Bible in their own idiosyncratic ways, with an ear to elite cultural presumptions rather than the teaching of the historic Church. Athanasius recognized that permitting private interpretations of the Bible was the road to heresy if it did not listen to the historic teaching of the Church. Inevitably, private interpretation would be formed by surrounding culture and read those cultural biases into its interpretation of Scripture.

Conclusion

In conclusion, Anglican hermeneutics is a simple but all-important principle: to discern the meaning of life and how to live under the Triune God by reading the Bible at the feet of the fathers. As we re-formed catholic Anglicans do this in the years to come, we will discover new joy and power that will give us the strength to weather the storms that lie ahead.

---

[11] The previous eight paragraphs are borrowed from McDermott, "An Anglican Theologian: An Ancient-Future Anglicanism," in *The Future of Orthodox Anglicanism*, ed. McDermott (Wheaton: Crossway, 2020).

Chapter 8

Justification[*]

The Rev. Dr. Hans Boersma

In this chapter I will focus on our understanding of justification, and I will draw on the late-second-century church father Irenaeus to retrieve what I think is a helpful way of approaching this doctrine. Particularly if we are perhaps used to treating justification as the core of our theology of salvation, or if we think of justification being by faith alone, Irenaeus may challenge us. As we will see, for Irenaeus justification is one aspect of a larger understanding of salvation as participation. It is this key notion that I want to look at with you, since I have become convinced that an Irenaean way of treating justification as an aspect of participation pays huge dividends for the renewal of Anglican theology, as long as we are willing to accept the challenge that such a retrieval entails.

Justification by faith is not the very center of the doctrine of salvation; rather, justification is one aspect of participation in Christ's recapitulation and as such serves to uphold and strengthen our deifying union with God in Christ. This is perhaps the most significant insight to be drawn from Irenaeus's exposition on justification. One reason we should not ask the doctrine of justification to do too much of the soteriological heavy lifting is its relatively minor place within Irenaeus's theology. Ben Blackwell rightly comments, "Like many Greek fathers, Irenaeus does not use the language of justification frequently, nor does he find it necessary to explain it in depth when he does."[1]

To be sure, the Bishop of Lyons does devote one important section of his main work, *Against Heresies*, to the doctrine of justification (*haer.* 4.12–17),[2] but even here it is not justification as such, but the role of the law, that is central. Irenaeus simply does not concern himself with the debates that would later rage in the Western church between Augustine and the Pelagians, between Catholics and Protestants, or between "old" and "new" perspectives on Paul. This is not to deny that Irenaeus addresses some of the same questions that would come up also in these later Western debates; it is fairly evident that he does. But we must recall that Irenaeus devised *Against Heresies* to do battle with the Gnostics and that justification played a subordinate role within Irenaeus's broader theology of salvation.

Put differently, while I believe that St. Irenaeus does shed light on key questions regarding justification such as the relationship between faith and works, the Pauline "works of the law," and the role of imputation in justification, he frames his approach to these issues not as part of a debate on the "mechanics" of justification. Instead, over against the Marcionite separation between old and new covenants, Irenaeus presents a plea for unity: the redeemer God is also the creator God, so that we dare not introduce

---

[*] An earlier version of this essay was published in *International Journal of Systematic Theology* 22 (2020): 169–190.

[1] Ben C. Blackwell, "Paul and Irenaeus," in *Paul and the Second Century: The Legacy of Paul's Life, Letters, and Teaching*, ed. Michael F. Bird and Joseph R. Dodson, Library of New Testament Studies 412 (New York: T & T Clark, 2011), 190–206, esp. 205.

[2] Irenaeus, *Against Heresies* (*haer.*), in *Ante-Nicene Fathers*, ed. Alexander Roberts and James Donaldson (1867; Peabody, MA: Hendrickson, 1994), 1:315-567.

two (or more) gods; and the new covenant is the legitimate continuation and unfolding of the old, so that it would be erroneous to suppose that God saves his people differently today than he did in days of old.

Recapitulation and Participation as Framework for Justification

Nowhere does this emphasis on unity come to the fore more clearly in Irenaeus's thought than in his confession of Christ as the one who "unites all things in him, things in heaven and things on earth" (Eph 1:10).[3] Irenaeus takes the verb used here for "uniting" all things—ἀνακεφαλαιόω in Greek, or recapitulare in Latin—as the starting point for his soteriology (and also his doctrine of justification). It is Irenaeus's theology of recapitulation (objectively speaking) and our participation in God through Christ (subjectively speaking) that together form the proper framework within which to understand Irenaeus's doctrine of justification.

Attacking his Gnostic opponents, Irenaeus puts forth a ringing affirmation that all created things are united (or, are recapitulated) in the Incarnation, in Jesus Christ: "There is therefore, as I have pointed out, one God the Father, and one Christ Jesus, who came by means of the whole dispensational arrangements [connected with Him], and gathered together all things in Himself (omnia in semetipsum recapitulans)" (3.16.6).[4] The Bishop of Lyons echoes here the Pauline language of recapitulation and treats it as the key to a biblical soteriology. The paradoxical language that Irenaeus employs—"the invisible becoming visible, the incomprehensible comprehensible, the impassible passible, and the Word man"—alludes to the reality of the Incarnation and to the corresponding impossibility of separating created human existence from the being of God. In Christ, God has really and ontologically, not just nominally and externally, identified with us.[5]

For Irenaeus Christ's recapitulation of Adam is inclusive in character. By that I mean that recapitulation is not something that takes place outside us, apart from us, yielding a righteousness that would then notionally or forensically be imputed to us. What Christ does in his recapitulation, ontologically affects us. Just as we are all included in the first Adam, so too we are all included in the second Adam. By taking on human flesh, the second Adam establishes a real connection with us, and it is that real link that enables us, through adoption, to share in Christ's sonship. Christ's recapitulation establishes a real or ontological communio with humanity. As the second Adam, he enters into communion with us.

---

[3] All Scripture passages cited in this chapter are from the English Standard Version (ESV).

[4] Square brackets original.

[5] The juridical element is muted in the Greek fathers, including Irenaeus. The reason is that justification is encapsulated within a broader soteriology of recapitulation and deification, which is ontological in character. Valerie A. Karras exaggerates the opposition between ontological and juridical categories, however, when she argues that that the Greek fathers operate only with ontological or existential categories and not with juridical categories Valerie A. Karras, "Beyond Justification: An Orthodox Perspective," in *Justification and the Future of the Ecumenical Movement: The Joint Declaration on the Doctrine of Justification*, ed. William G. Rusch (Collegeville, MN: Liturgical, 2003), 99–131, esp. 111, 115.

In no way, therefore, should we think of the link between Christ and humanity as merely an external or nominal connection. Recapitulation (from the perspective of what Christ does, objectively) and participation (in terms of our subjective transfiguration in and through Christ) are real, ontological categories. And even in the subjoined doctrine of justification, a forensic imputation of Christ's righteousness has no place in Irenaeus's teaching.[6] We are restored to communion with God inasmuch as Christ's recapitulation has forged a bond of communion between us and himself.

For Irenaeus, then, Christ's recapitulation unites us to God. The reason is that the Son of God has become the son of man, in order that the sons of man might share in the Son of God and through this adoption might be divinized. Communion with God implies, on Irenaeus's understanding, participating in divine characteristics, most notably life and incorruption.

The bishop complements the objective element of recapitulation with a subjective aspect: we are called to make Christ's recapitulation our own. This tension between the objective (Christological) aspect of recapitulation and the subjective (anthropological) element of participation or deification comes out beautifully when Irenaeus comments that Christ came "to save all through means of Himself—all, I say, who through Him are born again to God" (2.22.4). It is true that Christ makes himself present objectively through recapitulation, but it is equally necessary—and indispensable—for those who have witnessed him to put their faith in him and to follow him.[7] That, after all, is what Abraham did. In that sense, we could say: for Irenaeus, Christ's recapitulation includes only those who *want* to be included, those who put their faith in Christ.[8]

Justification: Continuity and Discontinuity with the Law

It is at this point that we must begin our reflections on the inner workings of the doctrine of justification—keeping in mind our caveats (1) that it lies encapsulated within the broader framework of recapitulation and participation; and (2) that Irenaeus does not develop the doctrine of justification at length and that when he does discuss it, he does

---

[6] D. H. Williams, though he does not discuss Irenaeus *per se*, similarly argues, "Instead of mitigating the contributions of the pre-Augustinian legacy, we may rather observe the ways in which it may serve to balance the Protestant insistence that the doctrine of justification is expressed only as the imputation of an alien or external righteousness to the sinner." "Justification by Faith: A Patristic Doctrine," *Journal of Ecclesiastical History* 57 (2006): 649–667, esp 667.

[7] To be sure, while a strict application of the logic of recapitulation might lead to universalism, Irenaeus nonetheless insists on a final judgment with eternal consequences. Cf. Terrance L. Thiessen, *Irenaeus on the Salvation of the Unevangelized*, ATLA Monograph Series 31 (Metuchen, NJ: Scarecrow, 1993), 161–162.

[8] Karras comments, "Whether or not human beings avail themselves of the redemption and restoration offered in Christ is dependent on how they exercise their human freedom by responding positively to union with Christ. "Beyond Justification," 116. In general terms this seems right to me—though for Irenaeus the language of "offered" may be too limiting with respect to Christ's work of recapitulation—as if he merely made it *possible* for us to be united with Christ. For Irenaeus, it is precisely by uniting himself with human nature in the Incarnation that he saves us. The result is that Irenaeus is genuinely paradoxical: recapitulation saves all (objectively) but participation is equally dependent on active human participation (subjectively) in faith and works. Cf. the discussion in Hans Boersma, *Violence Hospitality, and the Cross: Reappropriating the Atonement Tradition* (Grand Rapids: Baker Academic, 2004), 126–132.

so in the course of his treatment of the law in the service of his broader anti-Gnostic and anti-Marcionite train of thought. Irenaeus follows St. Paul in treating Abraham as the primary example of one who put his faith in Christ and so was justified. Faith is what justified Abraham, and we, following Abraham's faith, can also have our faith counted "for righteousness" (ad justitiam) (4.5.5).

Irenaeus discusses Abraham here as part of his argument that one and the same God makes himself known in both old and new covenants. Making his way toward the section where he discusses justification in greater detail than anywhere else—chapters 12–17 of book 4—Irenaeus thus starts building his case against Marcion: by pitting the new over against the old, Marcion places Abraham with the old and thus cannot avoid excluding him from salvation.

Irenaeus's theology of recapitulation works on the assumption that Christ is the great archetype on which the various scriptural types are modeled. Thus, although *chronologically* the second Adam follows the first, *theologically*, for Irenaeus, the second Adam precedes the first. As Irenaeus famously puts it: "For inasmuch as He [i.e., Christ] had a pre-existence as a saving Being, it was necessary that what might be saved should also be called into existence, in order that the Being who saves should not exist in vain" (3.22.3). Adam as a type was patterned on Christ as the archetype. Adam was created in the image of Christ, who in turn was the original, true image of God.[9] On Irenaeus's understanding, therefore, the Incarnation is not dependent on sin. While Irenaeus does employ the juridical language of remission and justification, this discourse lies anchored within a broader perspective: ever since creating Adam, God aimed at human maturation or participation in Christ and so at a deifying union with God. The juridical element merely serves to get the initial project of "Christification" back on track.

If, theologically speaking, the second Adam precedes the first, then Irenaeus has every reason to see Christ as always already present in the Scriptures of the old covenant. Christ, Irenaeus claims elsewhere, "is the treasure which was hid in the field, that is, in this world (for 'the field is the world' [Matt 13:38]); but the treasure hid in the Scriptures is Christ, since He was pointed out by means of types and parables (διὰ τύπων καὶ παραβολῶν; per typos et parabolas)" (4.26.1). The Son of God spoke with Abraham and ate with him, gave Noah the dimensions of the ark, inquired after Adam, brought judgment on Sodom, directed Jacob on his journey, and spoke with Moses. The continuity or unity of the old and the new is predicated on the Word of God being the author and the content of both.

The typological connection between old and new (with Christ being the archetypal reality always already present in the ancient Scriptures) allows Irenaeus to posit not just continuity but also discontinuity. After all, the archetype is greater than the types that foreshadow it. This means that the recapitulation principle functions to hold at bay not only Marcionite opponents (who accept only the new), but also Jewish antagonists (who

---

[9] Cf. *haer.* 5.16.2: "For in times long past, it was *said* that man was created after the image of God, but it was not [actually] *shown;* for the Word was as yet invisible, after whose image man was created. Wherefore also he did easily lose the similitude. When, however, the Word of God became flesh, He confirmed both these: for He both showed forth the image truly, since He became Himself what was His image; and He re-established the similitude after a sure manner, by assimilating man to the invisible Father through means of the visible Word" (brackets original).

simply insist on the old).[10] Christ's work of recapitulation implies not only continuity but also discontinuity.

How exactly Irenaeus understands the element of discontinuity is important, for it is here that he makes some of the key decisions in connection with justification. The first thing to observe is that Irenaeus in no way opposes faith to works. The two invariably go together. They did so for Abraham, they did so under the Mosaic dispensation, and they still do so in the new covenant. To be sure, a caveat is in order. Irenaeus highlights faith in connection with Abraham. Referring to Romans 4:3, Irenaeus explains that Abraham believed God and that his faith was imputed to him for righteousness (4.5.3). Faith in Christ is key to one's justification. Irenaeus repeatedly argues along with St. Paul (Rom 3:30) that God justifies both the circumcised and the uncircumcised through faith (3.10.2; 4.22.2; 5.22.1). Each time, the Bishop of Lyons uses this as evidence that there is only one Father; he justifies people through faith in both the old and the new covenants. We may even go so far as to suggest that in an important sense, justification, for Irenaeus, is by faith alone (*sola fide*). It is faith, not any of our actions, that initially unites us to Christ.

Irenaeus does not, however, play off this faith against love or a Christian walk of life. After mentioning justification by faith in 4.5.3, he immediately proceeds to discuss the righteous walk of life, both of Abraham and the patriarchs and of Christian believers: "Righteously (δικαίως; juste), therefore, having left his earthly kindred, he [i.e., Abraham] followed the Word of God, walking as a pilgrim with the Word, that he might [afterwards] have his abode with the Word. Righteously (δικαίως; juste) also the apostles, being of the race of Abraham, left the ship and their father, and followed the Word. Righteously (δικαίως; juste) also do we, possessing the same faith as Abraham, and taking up the cross as Isaac did the wood, follow him" (4.5.3–4). Similarly, on one of the few occasions where Irenaeus actually speaks of forgiveness—in the context of a discussion of the healing of the paralytic (Matt 9:1–8)—Irenaeus makes a point of arguing that the forgiveness and the healing of the paralytic were intertwined. The paralysis was a "consequence of sins" (5.17.2), so that "by remitting sins, He did indeed heal man" (5.17.3). Irenaeus does not isolate forgiveness from renewal.[11]

---

[10] When in *haer.* 4.26.1, Irenaeus has made the point that Christ is the treasure hidden in the Scriptures (cf. Matt 13:44), he quite naturally proceeds with an anti-Jewish argument. To the Jews, he claims, the law is "like a fable; for they do not possess the explanation of all things pertaining to the advent of the Son of God, which took place in human nature."

[11] As part of a broader argument that numerous patristic notions anticipate the Reformation teaching of justification, Nick Needham quotes a section from *haer.* 5.17.4 in support for his view that "Irenaeus interprets the nonimputation of sin as the remission and forgiveness of sin and debt." "Justification in the Early Church Fathers," in *Justification in Perspective: Historical Developments and Contemporary Challenges*, ed. Bruce L. McCormack (Grand Rapids: Baker Academic, 2006), 25–53, esp. 32. Needham overlooks, however, Irenaeus's linking forgiveness with healing, and he fails to allude either to the underrepresentation of forgiveness in Irenaeus or to his broader understanding of righteousness in believers' lives.

Justification by Faith, Not by the Law

Irenaeus's argument, therefore, is not that of the Reformation against Catholic teaching. He does not oppose justification by works as such (though he repeatedly speaks of justification by faith and never mentions justification by works). Rather, he specifically opposes justification by *certain kinds* of works: works of the law. In other words, for Irenaeus it is not faith versus works *per se*, but faith versus the law.

In articulating his position, Irenaeus focuses on three aspects. First, he reiterates over against the Marcionites that the law itself was never a problem in the first place. God is the one who gave it, and so "the law does indeed declare the Word of God from the Father" (5.21.3). Even if the law does not perfectly set forth God's will (since, as we will see, it accommodated the Israelites' immaturity), it nonetheless was God's own, good gift to his people. Irenaeus, therefore, does not object to the law as such. Instead, he objects to specific traditions the Jews subsequently added to the law. As he discusses Jesus's healing on the Sabbath of a bent-over woman unable to straighten herself (Luke 13:10–17), Irenaeus points out that "the law did not prohibit men from being healed upon the Sabbaths" and merely prohibited "servile work" and "worldly business" (4.8.2). Irenaeus points out that Jesus chastised the Pharisees for breaking the law while at the same time adding the so-called "tradition of the elders": "Desiring to uphold these traditions, they were unwilling to be subject to the law of God, which prepares them for the coming of Christ" (4.12.1). Irenaeus explains St. Paul's comment that the Jews sought to establish their own righteousness while not submitting to God's (Rom 10:3) as referring, not to an attempt to earn one's own salvation—a common reading within Protestant thought[12]—but to the practice of adding to the law the "tradition of the elders," which he says "they had invented," and through which "they made the law of God to none effect" (4.12.4).[13]

Second, Irenaeus argues at some length that circumcision, Sabbath, and sacrifices have all been abolished. Circumcision and Sabbath were never meant as the "completer of righteousness" (4.16.1). Instead, both functioned as "signs" (signa) (Gen 17:11; Exod 31:3) that "were not unsymbolical" (non sine symbolo): circumcision of the flesh typified (praefigurabat) spiritual circumcision (Col 2:11), and the Sabbaths taught symbolically that we should continually be consecrated to God (Rom 8:36) and abstain from avarice (Matt 6:19), while awaiting the eternal rest of God (4.16.1). Irenaeus appeals to Abraham,

---

[12] Calvin, *Comm.* Rom 10:3, contrasts the righteousness of men ("that which they derive from themselves, or believe that they bring before God") with the righteousness of God (which people put on "when the righteousness of Christ is imputed to them"). Cf. also John Piper, *The Future of Justification: A Response to N. T. Wright* (Wheaton, IL: Crossway, 2007), 191–195.

[13] Michael Jin Choi, in an argument that tries to pit Irenaeus over against the new perspective on Paul, argues that Irenaeus objects to "zeal or self-achievement apart from God." "Irenaeus on Law and Justification," 130/2 *Expository Times* (2018): 53–61, esp. 58. Choi appeals to *haer.* 4.11.4, where Irenaeus argues against "those who pretend that they do themselves observe *more than what has been prescribed (plus quam quae dicta)*, as if preferring their own zeal (diligentiam suam) to God Himself, while within they are full of hypocrisy, and covetousness, and all wickedness ...." However, it should be clear that what Irenaeus has in mind with people's "own zeal" is the addition of human tradition (*plus quam quae dicta*), so that this zeal is problematic inasmuch as it is their own. Nowhere does Irenaeus allude to the danger of "self-achievement."

Lot, Noah, and Enoch, who were all justified without circumcision or Sabbath (4.16.2). God never really wanted the sacrificial system, argues Irenaeus, since—having in himself "all the odour of kindness, and every perfume of sweet-smelling savours"—God has no need for sacrifices (4.14.3). The Bishop of Lyons quotes numerous biblical passages in support of his conviction that God does not desire offerings but wants a sacrifice of obedience or of praise instead.[14]

Throughout this discussion, Irenaeus treats circumcision, Sabbath, and sacrifices as identity markers.[15] He speaks of circumcision as something that allowed others to recognize the "race of Abraham" (genus Abrahae) (4.16.1; cf. 3.12.11).[16] And he maintains that the combination of faith and obedience—which he sees as following the law of liberty (libertatis lex; 4.34.4)—abolishes these Mosaic regulations.[17] For Irenaeus, the question of justification is closely tied up both with hermeneutics and with ecclesiology: it is not those who circumcise, observe Sabbath, and offer sacrifices, but those who through faith (and obedience) identify with Christ, that read the Scriptures aright, and that will be saved.[18]

Irenaeus's opposition to law observance is not limited, however, to the identity markers of circumcision, Sabbath, and sacrifices.[19] These Mosaic requirements are merely the most obvious indications that the Mosaic law *as a whole* has been rendered inoperative—at least, in terms of its external, prescriptive character.[20] This is the third key element of Irenaeus's opposition to justification by the law. One cannot be justified by the Mosaic law, because in an important respect the whole thing has been abolished. God "does not wish those who are to be redeemed to be brought again under Mosaic legislation," insists Irenaeus, "for the law has been fulfilled by Christ."[21] The reason he

---

[14] Irenaeus quotes 1 Sam 15:22; Pss 40:6; 51:17; 50:9, 14–15; Isa 1:11; Jer 6:20; 7:2–4, 21–24; 9:24; Isa 43:23–24; 66:2; Jer 11:15; Isa 58:6–9; Zech 7:9–10; 8:16–17; Ps 34:12–14; Hos 6:6; Matt 12:7 (*haer.* 4.17.1–4).

[15] James D. G. Dunn and N. T. Wright both treat the Pauline "works of the law" (Rom 3:20, 28; Gal 2:16; 3:2, 5, 10)—which they argue refers to circumcision, Sabbath, and food laws—as Jewish identity markers, so that Paul's rejection of justification by works would be an ecclesiological statement: the Christian identity marker would be faith rather than "works of the law." See James D. G. Dunn, *The New Perspective on Paul*, 2nd ed. (Grand Rapids: Eerdmans, 2008), 111; N. T. Wright, *Justification: God's Plan and Paul's Vision* (Downers Grove, IL: IVP Academic, 2009), 116–117.

[16] Cf. Matthew J. Thomas, *Paul's "Works of the Law" in the Perspective of Second Century Reception* (Heidelberg: Mohr Siebeck, 2018), 199.

[17] Cf. *haer.* 4.16.5: "These things, therefore, which were given for bondage (*servitutem*), and for a sign (*signum*) to them, He cancelled (*circumscripsit*) by the new covenant of liberty."

[18] Cf. Irenaeus's polemic against "Marcion and his followers when they [seek to] exclude Abraham from the inheritance ...." *haer.* 4.8.1; brackets original.

[19] Irenaeus uses the expression "works of the law" only once (*haer.* 4.21.1), and he gives no indication that only, say, circumcision, Sabbath, and sacrifices are to be considered "works of the law."

[20] Choi correctly points out that in *Epid.* 35 and in *haer.* 4.34.2, Irenaeus takes St. Paul's "law" in Rom 3:21 and 4:13 as referring not to specific identity markers but to the Mosaic law as a whole. "Irenaeus on Law and Justification," 56–58.

[21] Irenaeus, *Proof of the Apostolic Preaching* (*Epid.*) 89. I quote from the translation by Joseph P. Smith, Ancient Christian Writers 16 (New York: Paulist Press, 1952).

gives for this supersession of the law is the gift of the Spirit under the new covenant, in which the Lord writes the law on people's hearts (cf. Jer 31:31–34) (*Epid.* 89–90).

Again, Irenaeus does not suggest that the law itself was problematic. It was simply part of God's pedagogy in maturing humanity and became superfluous once God had reached the purpose of his training. Irenaeus's treatment of redemptive history as a pedagogical process is closely linked to the way he treats justification. Adam and Eve were created as infants, and it is only through a long history of training, culminating in Christ, that they would attain to maturity and immortality in the vision of God (cf. *haer.* 3.22.4; 4.20.5; 4.38.1–4; *Epid.* 14–15).[22] This pedagogical approach features prominently when Irenaeus discusses the role of the law. On his reading, the law, while it is God's own gift to his people, marks a regression of sorts. Prior to the law, the patriarchs "had the righteousness of the law in themselves" (4.16.3), and so they had no need for a law to restrain them. But the law became necessary when the Israelites lapsed into idolatry:

> When they turned themselves to make a calf, and had gone back in their minds to Egypt, desiring to be slaves instead of freemen, they were placed for the future in a state of servitude suited to their wish,—[a slavery] which did not indeed cut them off from God but subjected them to the yoke of bondage. (4.15.1; brackets original)[23]

So, while Abraham had not been in need of the law, the Israelites coming out of Egypt were slaves, and as such they did need the law as "bondage" (servitus) until Christ would come to set us free.[24] In short, for Irenaeus the law was a gift of God suited to the immature, servile character of the ancient Israelites and was always meant to be superseded once the divine pedagogy had reached its aim.

The language of "bondage" (servitus) draws attention to the external and restrictive character of the Mosaic law. In no way does Irenaeus suggest that this external bondage of the law implied legalism, in the sense of a system that requires one meritoriously to establish one's own salvation.[25] The reason we no longer need the law today is simply that

---

[22] See further Hans Boersma, *Seeing God: The Beatific Vision in Christian Tradition* (Grand Rapids: Eerdmans, 2018), 401–404.

[23] Cf. *haer.* 4.16.5: "The laws of bondage (*servitutis*), however, were one by one promulgated to the people by Moses, suited for their instruction or for their punishment."

[24] Cf. *haer.* 4.13.4: "But this is our Lord, the Word of God, who in the first instance certainly drew slaves to God, but afterwards He set those free who were subject to Him, as He does Himself declare to His disciples: 'I will not now call you servants, for the servant knoweth not what his lord doeth; but I have called you friends, for all things which I have heard from My Father I have made known' [John 15:15]. For in that which He says, 'I will not now call you servants,' He indicates in the most marked manner that it was Himself who did originally appoint for men that bondage (*servitutem*) with respect to God through the law, and then afterwards conferred upon them freedom."

[25] Choi suggests that when under the old covenant people did not turn to Christ, their religion turned to legalism. "Irenaeus on Law and Justification," 60–61. Irenaeus, however, merely describes the problem as adherence to a system of 'bondage'; in other words, the problem is that of holding to an external guide after the internal gift of the Spirit has been made. Depending on one's definition, I suppose one may call this 'legalism,' but in that case *all* obedience to the law under the old covenant would have to be termed 'legalism.' Irenaeus's objections to the law as 'external' do not imply a religion of "self-achievement" ("Irenaeus on Law and Justification," 58) or

continued

its aim—love of God and love of neighbor—has been reached. Now that we have the Lord of the law, we no longer need the external regulations and restrictions.

The law as a whole has been superseded; circumcision, Sabbath, and sacrifices in particular no longer pertain. Still, Irenaeus is careful how he articulates this abolition of the law. He insists, at least for the most part, that this supersession of the law does not pertain to the Decalogue. The Decalogue functions for Irenaeus as an exception to the general rule that the law has been abolished. The reason is that the Decalogue is close to being identical to natural law and to the twofold-love command that is the fulfilling of the law.

Even the Decalogue, however, has something of the law's external, prescriptive character. But rather than suggest that also the Decalogue is *abolished*, Irenaeus argues that it is extended or deepened.[26] When Jesus says that to look at a woman lustfully is already adultery (Matt 5:27–28), that it's not just murder but even just anger that makes one liable to judgment (Matt 5:21–22), and that we should not merely avoid swearing falsely but should not take an oath at all (Matt 5:33–37), Irenaeus concludes: "All these do not contain or imply an opposition (contrarietatem) to and an overturning (dissolutionem) of the [precepts] of the past, as Marcion's followers to strenuously maintain; but [they exhibit] a fulfilling (plenitudinem) and an extension (extensionem) of them" (4.13.1).[27] Irenaeus seems to have in mind that the extension or fulfilling of the Decalogue takes us beyond its external, prescriptive character, so that much like Abraham, we again have the law written on our hearts.[28]

Conclusion

It would be difficult precisely to align Irenaeus's views with the approaches of Catholics, traditional Protestants, or adherents of the new perspective. Perhaps this is not a bad observation to begin with in our conclusion, since an Anglican *via media* is typically difficult to slot into any of the traditional theological categories. The first thing to note is that Irenaeus does not hold to a forensic imputation of Christ's righteousness. When

---

an attitude in which people merely "pay their dues" ("Irenaeus on Law and Justification," 60). Thomas rightly comments, therefore, that "'legalism' would not accurately characterize the significance of observing works of the law according to Irenaeus." *Paul's "Works of the Law,"* 200.

[26] Irenaeus is not entirely consistent here. Because the Decalogue is nearly identical to the laws of nature, he insists on it being extended rather than set aside. However, in *Epid.* 96, Irenaeus uses the Sermon on the Mount to argue that "we have no need of the law as pedagogue" and that the law no longer tells us not to commit adultery, to kill, to covet, etc. The reasons he gives here are very similar to the ones he gives in *haer.* 4.17 for arguing that the sacrificial system is done away with. In other words, in *Epid.* 96 Irenaeus treats the Decalogue in the same way he treats sacrifices elsewhere—as an external prescription that is no longer needed.

[27] Cf. *haer.* 4.13.3. Cf. also 4.16.4: "The Lord Himself did speak in His own person to all alike the words of the Decalogue; and therefore, in like manner, do they remain permanently with us, receiving by means of His advent in the flesh, extension and increase, but not abrogation (*extensionem et augmentum, sed non dissolutionem*)."

[28] Irenaeus mentions that prior to Moses, "the righteous fathers had the meaning of the Decalogue written in their hearts and souls" (*haer.* 4.16.3), and that with the gifting of the Spirit the promise of Jer 31:33 (that God would write the law on people's hearts) has been fulfilled (*Epid.* 90). Irenaeus refers to this fulfillment when he mentions "barbarians who believe in Christ" and have "salvation written in their hearts by the Spirit, without paper or ink (*haer.* 3.4.1).

he uses the imputation language of Romans 4:3 and Galatians 3:6, it is clear that he holds that it is faith, not Christ's righteousness, that God imputes to us (4.5.3; 4.8.3; 4.16.3). In traditional dogmatic language, we could say that it is faith as our own inherent righteousness that Irenaeus believes God (juridically) imputes to us. In terms of this key issue between Catholicism and Protestantism, Irenaeus would unambiguously seem to side with the Catholic position, and I think that as Anglicans, we should do so, as well.

Second, when we ask whether there is also a justification by works for St. Irenaeus, the answer is slightly more complex. Irenaeus nowhere speaks of being justified by works. Nor does he distinguish clearly between initial and continuing justification—the former perhaps being by faith only and the latter also by works.[29] Irenaeus does, however, speak of Abraham "righteously" (juste) following the Word of God (4.5.3) and makes clear that both the patriarchs and we today have the "righteousness of the law" written on our hearts (4.16.3; cf. 3.4.1). Clearly, Irenaeus would not have had any difficulty accepting that God also imputes this righteousness to us—even if he does not use the language of justification by works. To be sure, the absence of "merit" discourse in Irenaeus holds some significance. Unlike the later Catholic tradition, Irenaeus does not suggest that we merit eternal life condignly or properly.[30] Because the notions of recapitulation and participation form the broad framework within which Irenaeus expounds his doctrine of justification, our righteousness is always a (partial) participation in God. The language of condign merit does not fit well within such a participatory framework.

Third, Anglicans should welcome at least aspects of the new perspective on Paul, since it retrieves a genuine patristic insight when it describes St. Paul's "works of the law" as Jewish identity markers. For Irenaeus, the main identity markers are circumcision, Sabbath, and sacrifices. At the same time, however, for Irenaeus it is not *only* these three elements that are "works of the law" and that function as identity markers. Rather, he treats the entire law (except the Decalogue) as an identity marker, and presumably he would have regarded *any* observance of the law as observance of works of the law (or, we could say, as an attempt to be justified by works of the law). For Irenaeus, it is faith (in Christ) and love (of God and neighbor) that mark the identity of

---

[29] The distinction between initial and ongoing justification plays an important role in ecumenical discussion. Reformed theologians commonly taught a "twofold righteousness." John Calvin, for instance, recognizes, a "works righteousness," as long as one understands it as included under faith and subordinated to it. *Institutes of the Christian Religion*, 2 vols., trans. Ford Lewis Battles, ed. John T. McNeill (Philadelphia: Westminster, 1960), 3.17.9–10. And Martin Bucer speaks of a *secundaria iustificatio* as a result of works. See Brian Lugioyo, *Martin Bucer's Doctrine of Justification: Reformation Theology and Early Modern Irenicism* (New York: Oxford University Press, 2010), 178. Not surprisingly, the notion of a "twofold righteousness" was the key to the agreement reached at the Regensburg Colloquy. See Anthony N. S. Lane, "Twofold Righteousness: A Key to the Doctrine of Justification? Reflections on Article 5 of the Regensburg Colloquy (1541)," in *Justification: What's at Stake in the Current Debates*, ed. Mark Husbands and Daniel J. Treier (Downers Grove, IL: InterVarsity; Leicester, UK: Apollos, 2004), 205–224.

[30] Thomas Aquinas argues that we merit eternal life condignly, not "as regards the substance of the work, and inasmuch as it springs from the free-will," "because of the very great inequality." But he goes on to suggest that when we consider that the Spirit makes us "a partaker of the Divine nature," we should understand eternal life as the outcome of condign merit (*ST* I-II, q. 114, a. 3).

Christians and that constitute true fulfillment of the law. In no way, then, does Irenaeus worry that Jewish law observance might imply reliance on human achievement or merit.[31] The problem with law observance is, instead, (1) that it puts us back into an earlier, inferior stage of the divine pedagogy; and (2) that it would probably also entail the observance of additional manmade laws and traditions.

Everything I have said so far about justification by way of conclusion must be refracted through the lens of the two key concepts of recapitulation and participation. Irenaeus, rightly I think, does not treat justification as the central category by which to understand salvation. Protestantism does generally treat justification in this manner, but it seems to me that Anglicans should avoid it. The reason is this: the central soteriological concept is not justification but recapitulation (by which Christ, objectively, incorporates humanity in his salvific life), along with participation or deification (by which we, subjectively, are conformed through faith and love to the character of God in Christ). Justification, in other words, while it retains a juridical aspect, is for Irenaeus one element within a broader soteriology, which as a whole is ontological in character. Our faith and righteousness enable us to share in Christ as the new humanity, the second Adam. And by sharing in Christ, we are made alive and so rendered immortal; in other words, we are divinized as children of God. This means salvation is not an external or nominal affair but is a matter of real or ontological participation in the life of God.

Our brief excursus into the second-century insights of Irenaeus offers a challenge both to Catholics and to Protestants, urging us that divisions that we often think of as unbridgeable may look different in the light of patristic theology. At the least, Irenaeus enables us to take the sharp edges off some of the debates surrounding faith and works. Here, Anglicans can perhaps be of help in mediating between Catholic and Protestant extremes. On the one hand, Catholics could perhaps become somewhat more cautious with regard to the language of meriting eternal life. The Christian pilgrimage of love is, after all, simply an initial participation in God's own character by virtue of Christ's recapitulation. In no way are works autonomous human achievements. Although Catholic theology recognizes this—it is important, for example, to recall that Aquinas's talk of condign merit occurs in the context of deification—nonetheless, a preponderance of merit discourse may serve to highlight the juridical at the cost of the ontological. Justification (and the language of merit) should play only a subservient role in the doctrine of salvation.

On the other hand, traditional Protestants should also take note. Yes, forensic imputation of Christ's righteousness foregrounds a sensibility that is entirely legitimate—namely, that it is only by seeking refuge in Christ that we can be saved. But the logic of forensic imputation is not the right instrument to shore up this valid concern. After all, St. Paul does not use the language of imputation in connection with Christ's righteousness but employs to it to articulate the imputation of the righteousness

---

[31] Human achievement and merit are not the same. Irenaeus is a strong adherent to free-will. See, for instance, *haer.* 4.37.1–5; 4.38.4; 4.39.3. Cf. Hans Boersma, "Accommodation to What? Univocity of Being, Pure Nature, and the Anthropology of St Irenaeus," *International Journal of Systematic Theology* 8 (2006): 266–293, esp. 287–288. Thus, the language of "human achievement" may in some sense be appropriate to describe Irenaeus's understanding of salvation: Irenaeus is a synergist. But he does not suggest that we can merit our salvation.

of our own faith (Rom 4:3; Gal 3:6).[32] Theologically, what is at stake here is the recognition that when God justifies us, he transfigures us. The language of *simul iustus et peccator* (righteous and sinner both at once) is particularly troubling—at least, whenever it is meant to imply that Christ's righteousness simply covers over our own continuing sinfulness. Such a strictly forensic imputation is also at odds, I think, with some of the better Reformation insights, which recognize that it is by means of genuine union with Christ that we are justified and sanctified.[33] The focus on union with Christ would, if consistently maintained, lead to a retrieval of the Irenaean notions of recapitulation and divinization. Re-formed Anglicanism, therefore, needs the patristic doctrine of deification. Irenaeus, I think, had it right: justification is a subset of our deifying union with God in and through the recapitulation of humanity in Christ.

---

[32] Cf. Robert Gundry's laconic comment: "If Paul had meant that the righteousness of Christ replaces our sins, we would expect him to have said so." "The Nonimputation of Christ's Righteousness," in *Justification: What's at Stake in the Current Debates*, ed. Mark Husbands and Daniel J. Treier (Downers Grove, IL: InterVarsity; Leicester, UK: Apollos, 2004), 17–45, esp. 42.

[33] For John Calvin, faith leads to union with Christ, which then gives the believer the twofold grace (*duplex gratia*) of justification and sanctification. J. Todd Billings rightly points out: "Although the righteousness that the believers come to possess is formally external to themselves, Calvin uses the images of union, adoption, engrafting, and participation to describe Oxford this 'wondrous exchange' so that the imputation is not from 'a distance' but from union with Christ." *Calvin, Participation, and the Gift: The Activity of Believers in Union with Christ* (: Oxford University Press, 2007), 106–107. The tension in Calvin's thought seems palpable at this point. After all, for Calvin, God's acceptance of us in justification "consists in the remission of sins and the imputation of Christ's righteousness" (*Inst.* 3.11.2). It is not clear how this external justifying righteousness fits with Calvin's robust theology of union and participation.

Chapter 9

The Church

The Rev. Dr. Gerald McDermott

What is the Church? The Bible tells us it is a sheepfold (John 10:1–15), a vineyard (John 15:1–10), a building built by God (Matt 21:42; 1 Cor 3:9; 1 Pet 2:5), the house of God in which his family dwells by the Holy Spirit (Hag 2:4–5; Eph 2:19; 1 Tim 3:15), the dwelling place of God among men (Eph 2:22), the holy temple (Eph 2:20), the bride of Christ (Eph 5:22–33; Rev 21:9), the body of Christ (Eph 1:22–23; 1 Cor 12:18–20), the temple of the Holy Spirit (1 Cor 3:16), and the kingdom of God (Matt 16:18–19).

This chapter will outline a reformed catholic Anglican theology of the Church. It will argue that the Church came before and in fact gave us the Bible, is essential for our salvation, and was given a structure by Jesus. It explains what the Creed means by its being one, holy, catholic, and apostolic, and contends that God's kingdom and Church are visible phenomena and not just invisible. It also maintains that the Body of Christ is not the New Israel but comes in two expressions, the Gentile Christian Church and the assembly of messianic Jews.

Church before Scripture

Many of us have been told that Scripture formed the Church and therefore the Bible is prior to the Church and more authoritative than the Church. There is a certain truth here: as the Fathers regularly put it, Scripture is the Word of God that continually informs and guides the Church, and the Church must never accept any doctrine that cannot be proved by Scripture (Article VI). On the other hand, Scripture itself testifies that God's people were gathered by God before there was Torah (Gen 4:26; 9:8–17; 12:13), that the Church is prior to the New Testament (Acts 2:42–47; 4:32–37), and that the orthodox Church must guide our interpretation of the Bible (John 14:26; 16:13; 1 Cor 11:2; 2 Thess 2:15; 2 Tim 2:2).

Jesus told his apostles that he would teach them all things after he left the earth, that over the years he would bring to their remembrance everything he had said to them and guide them into all the truth (John 14:26; 16:13). Long before the Church had assembled all the New Testament documents, Jude wrote that the Church already possessed "the faith once delivered to all the saints" (Jude 3). Before some of the New Testament documents were written and long before the whole New Testament was assembled, Paul declared that the Church "is the Church of the living God, the pillar and ground of truth" (1 Tim 3:15). Notice the implication: to believers wondering where to go for authoritative teaching about the true God and salvation, Paul counseled truth-seekers to go not to written scriptures, as critically important as they are, but to their authoritative interpreter, the Church of the apostles.[1]

Even after the New Testament was completed, the Fathers counseled the same. Irenaeus wrote that the source of life for believers is not the Bible *per se* but the Church: "They are nourished into life from the mother's [the Church's] breasts, [and they] enjoy

---

[1] Acts 17:11 does not alter this typical pattern.

that most limpid fountain which issues from the body of Christ."[2] Cyprian of Carthage also referred to the Church as the "mother" of true believers whose guidance is necessary to avoid the error that comes inevitably from private judgment on the Scriptures. As he famously wrote in his treatise on the unity of the Church, "He can no longer have God for his Father who has not the Church for his mother."[3]

Not Optional

For many in American churches, participation in any church is considered a nice option but not necessary for salvation. All that is important is a personal relationship with Jesus; warm fuzzies for Jesus render superfluous sacraments in a Church with apostolic succession and orthodox doctrine. Such notions, however, are wrong and dangerous. Paul wrote that God judges those outside the Church (1 Cor 5:13), and that only in the ark of the Church, as Peter and Tertullian called it,[4] can one be assured grace and truth. Augustine referred to the Church as *Totus Christus*, the whole Christ. This phrase suggests that the Messiah is not complete without his Body. He is its head, but without all its members the Messiah's Body is incomplete. So the "whole" Messiah is the Messiah joined to all the saints in heaven and on earth. And apart from that Body a man is without Christ at all, without his graces, and risks damnation. The Church is the highway of grace, as Anglican Vernon Staley has called it, the sure road along which we travel to heaven and glory, for it is in the Church that the Lord Jesus carries on his work of saving men and fitting them for heaven.[5] The upshot of all this is that the Church is no more optional for heavenly life than food and air are optional for earthly life.

Structured

Today we hear frequently in the media that many Americans want to be spiritual but not part of "organized religion." Many just want to do "me and Jesus" up on a local mountain, apart from churches that are too structured for them. The problem is Jesus said he came not simply to get souls to heaven but to "build [his] church" (Matt 16:18), and the purpose of that Church was to extend his incarnation through time, as we have just seen. The mechanism he chose for this was for the apostles to choose their successors, that is, bishops, who would be responsible to teach and guard apostolic faith. He told the apostles—not the disciples generally—that he was giving them authority to forgive sins, preside over the Eucharist, teach the nations everything he commanded them, and rule the Church. Jesus would be present in this Church through its bishops, priests, and deacons. Already at the beginning of the second century Ignatius said this was the Church order recognized throughout the world: bishops, priests, and deacons extending the incarnation of the Messiah. In Ignatius' words, "Without these three orders no church has any right to the name."[6]

---

[2] Irenaeus, *Against Heresies* 3.24 (ANF 1).

[3] Cyprian, *On the Unity of the Church* 6 (ANF 5).

[4] 1 Pet 3.21; Tertullian, *On Idolatry* 24 (ANF 3).

[5] Vernon Staley, *The Catholic Religion* (Harrisburg: Morehouse, 1983 [orig. 1883]), 34.

[6] Ignatius, *The Epistle to the Trallians* 3, in *Early Christian Writings*, ed. Andrew Louth (London: Penguin, 1987).

The bishops—that is, those who traced their lineage back to the apostles—were the backbone of the early Church and its source of unity. Ignatius wrote to the church of Philadelphia, "Every man who belongs to God and Jesus Christ stands with his bishop."[7] Tertullian challenged the leaders of gnostic churches who taught a different Jesus, "[If they want to prove their own validity,] let them unfold the roll of their bishops ... to show [that their first bishop was ordained by] one of the apostles."[8] He knew they could not, and that clinched his argument: the true Church is based on apostolic succession. Irenaeus said the same, tracing the bishops of Rome back through Clement, Anacletus, Linus, and Peter and Paul.[9]

The English reformers were insistent that the apostolic succession continued in their portion of the Church. They made sure that Archbishop Parker who succeeded Cardinal Pole was consecrated by four bishops, two of whom had been consecrated with the Latin rite under Henry VIII. It was then Parker who oversaw the consecrations of the next generation of Anglican bishops.[10] The Ordinal in all the prayer books perpetuated the catholic order of ministry—bishop, priest, and deacon. The 1662 *Book of Common Prayer*, which until 2000 was the only official version in the Church of England, refused Presbyterian pressure to change the word from *priest* to *pastor*.

So Jesus set up a structure—centered on the bishops in apostolic succession—to ensure that the incarnation of the Son of God would come to us. What of other churches—such as the Episcopal Church—that also claim apostolic succession but have changed historic orthodox doctrine? Jesus prayed to the Father that his apostles would be "sanctified in the truth" and explained that the Father's "word" which he had come to reveal "is truth" (John 17:17). So when the Episcopal and other mainline Protestant churches reject God's Word on marriage, the principal metaphor in Scripture for his relationship to his people, they forfeit their claim to remain in the apostolic succession which requires both God's order and his truth.

The Creedal Description

The Church Is One

What do we confess in the Creed about the Church? First, that it is one, united by one faith, common sacraments, and apostolic succession. As we have seen, the Fathers considered the bishops the principal of unity because they were in a succession going back to the apostles who taught the faith to the Church. Much of the Church is now in heaven, and that means our unity comes from the bishops of church history who were— and are—in unity about our one calling, one Lord, one faith, one baptism, one God and Father of all (Eph 4:4b–6). They gave us our creeds, which was the "rule of faith" by which the Fathers interpreted the Bible. Thus, the center of our unity is still the bishops, most of whom are in heaven cheering on the earthly bishops and all their flocks who still walk in the order and truth our Lord Jesus gave to the apostles.

---

[7] Ignatius, *The Epistle to the Philadelphians* 3, in *Early Christian Writings*.

[8] Tertullian, *The Prescription Against Heretics* 32 (ANF 3).

[9] Irenaeus, *Against Heresies* 3.3.3 (ANF 1).

[10] J .L. C. Dart, *The Old Religion: An Examination into the Facts of the English Reformation* (Eugene, OR: Wipf & Stock, 2016; orig. 1956), 49–51.

The Church Is Holy

The Creed calls the church holy, which in Hebrew (*kadosh*) means "set apart." Jesus died to set his elect apart from the rest of the world. When he ascended to the right hand of the Father, he sent down upon them the gift of the Holy Spirit, so the church is the holy people of God filled with and therefore set apart by the Holy Spirit. This is why the members of the Church are called "saints," from the Latin word *sanctus* for "holy" because they are set apart by their filling with God's Holy Spirit.

The Church Is Catholic

When we say every Sunday that the Church is catholic, we use a word derived from the Latin *catholicus*, itself derived from the Greek *katholikos*, with the etymology *kata* "according to" and *holos* "the whole." This is the faith of the whole world. We catholic Anglicans think particularly of the faith and worship of the whole world in the undivided church of the first millennium, when churches both East and West used the same creeds and substantially similar liturgy, and when they believed and worshiped and lived as catholic Christians in the same ways. We confessed the same creeds, participated in the same sacraments, and were served by bishops, priests, and deacons who could be traced in a succession going back to the apostles. The English church made sure to continue this faith through the Reformation and beyond, and many have kept it to this day.

Our prayer book professes this catholic faith. The collect for the feast day of Sts. Simon and Jude uses traditional catholic language for the Church: "God himself has built his Church upon the foundation of the Apostles and Prophets." At the Reformation, the Protestant communions abandoned bishops and priests, made of the sacraments something new, and rejected the apostolic succession. but our prayer book kept the old order of bishops and priests, and states on its title page that it administers the sacraments and rites and ceremonies of "the Church," by which it meant the universal catholic Church with its sacraments that make effectual what they promise because they are administered by bishops and priests in the apostolic succession.

So do the *Thirty-Nine Articles*. Article XIX begins, "The visible Church of Christ is a congregation of faithful men," repudiating the Protestant view that the true Church is *in*visible with its members known only to God. (More on visible and invisible in a bit.) Article XXXIV says "private judgment" is not sufficient to "break the traditions and ceremonies of the Church, which be not repugnant to the Word of God."

For Anglicans, *catholic* does not mean Roman Catholic, though we happily say the Romans are among the great catholic churches of the world, along with the Eastern Orthodox. We also say there is historical reason for not holding to the primacy of Rome. Peter was the leader, not lord of the twelve apostles. He was the first among equals. The power of the keys was given to all the apostles in Matthew 18:17 and to all except Thomas in John 20:21–24. The Fathers stressed the equality of the apostles. Cyprian, for example, wrote that "the rest of the apostles were ... the same as was Peter, endowed with a like partnership both of honour and power."[11] St Augustine, perhaps the greatest of the Fathers, said at the end of his life that Peter was not the rock in Matthew 16 but Christ, and that he was wrong to hold earlier in his life that it was Peter. This suggests that

---

[11] Cyprian, *On the Unity of the Church* 4 (ANF 5).

Augustine did not think Petrine or Roman primacy was a significant doctrine. Gregory the Great (d. 604) wrote in a letter to the patriarch of Alexandria that he shared the Petrine office with him and the patriarch of Antioch, since Peter was the bishop of Antioch and sent Mark to found the church in Alexandria.[12] He chided the bishop of Alexandria for calling him "universal Pope," told him to "do this no more" and insisted he did not have authority to "command" him because "in position you [and other patriarchs] are my brethren."[13] The early councils gave first place to the bishop of Rome among five patriarchs, but it was a place of honor rather than lordship. Staley compares it to the foreman of a jury, first among equals.[14]

Our own reformers made clear that they were not Roman but catholic nevertheless. As J. L. C. Dart has argued, in Elizabethan days *Protestant* meant "not papist," not anti-catholic.[15] For Jewell, Hooker, and Andrewes, it meant Catholicism without the pope.[16] Later Anglicans have found more reason to be catholic but not Roman. Pusey argued that Rome brought changes to the catholic faith by its doctrines of transubstantiation and a juridical version of purgatory.[17] Anglicans have long venerated Mary but objected to Roman innovations of her immaculate conception and assumption. The Anglican Newman was disturbed by the emerging doctrine of papal infallibility. St. Peter, he wrote, was not infallible at Antioch when St. Paul disagreed with him, nor was Liberius, the bishop of Rome, when he excommunicated Athanasius.[18]

The Church Is Apostolic

For catholic Anglicans, the apostolicity of the Church has two meanings. First, our prayer book and Articles are devoted to the Word of God as interpreted by the Church of God. The Church gave us the Word of God which was delivered to us by the apostles. They gave us the Old Testament and told us it is the Word of God, and they authorized the eventual writing and authorization of all the New Testament. So *apostolic* means a faith founded on the foundation of the apostles and the Scriptures that have come from them. As Article VI teaches, "Whatsoever is not read [in the Holy Scriptures], nor may be proved thereby, is not to be required of any man, that it should be believed as an article of the Faith."

Second, our catholic Anglican doctrine of Holy Order is the catholic one, which means it is descended in power from the succession going back to the apostles. Our Ordinal teaches this, that "from the Apostles' times there have been these Orders of Ministers in Christ's Church, Bishops, Priests, and Deacons."

---

[12] Gregory the Great, *Epistle XL* (NPNF² 12).
[13] Gregory the Great, *Epistle XXX* (NPNF² 12).
[14] Staley, *The Catholic Religion*, 40.
[15] Dart, *The Old Religion*, 12–13.
[16] Ibid., 18.
[17] Edward Pusey, *Anglican Doctrine: Notes and Questions on the Catholic Faith and Religion*, ed. Ben Jefferies (Nashotah: Nashotah Press, 2018), 144–49, 296–301.
[18] John Henry Newman, *Certain Difficulties Felt by Anglicans in Catholic Teaching*, 2 vols., 256–258; cited in Ian Ker, *John Henry Newman: A Biography* (New York: Oxford University Press, 1988), 689.

A Visible Church

The Reformed tradition has tended to refer to the true Church as invisible and known to God alone. Calvin wrote in the *Institutes* that true Christians in the visible church are "a small and contemptible number ... a few grains of wheat ... covered by a pile of chaff" (4.1.2). But as Anglican Claude Moss has written, for Sts. Paul and John, the Church is a visible society. "They knew who was a member, and who was not" (1 Cor 5.12–13; 12:12ff; 1 John 2:19; 1 Tim 1:20).[19]

Jesus' church was a visible thing. One could see its apostolic leaders and successors, who later came to be its bishops. One could see its priests and bishops and deacons on the Lord's Day as they led believers in celebration of the Eucharist. They gathered together visibly for daily prayer and teaching and eucharistic worship (Acts 2:42), both in the Temple and in homes. When they disciplined wayward members, they sometimes banned them from visible fellowship in the hope that they would repent and return to that visible fellowship (1 Cor 5).

In the New Testament, the concept of God's kingdom is visible and political, not merely a matter of the heart. After all, as the *Dictionary of Biblical Imagery* observes, if God is king then Caesar is not. Neither is his client-king Herod. When Jesus tells Pilate that his kingdom is not of this world, he explains that his disciples were not revolutionaries "fighting" his arrest (John 18:36). His kingdom would not come by military force. Yet it was not without its visible presence in the world. Apostles and their churches, with martyrs and bishops, could be seen and heard in the world, especially when they defied political authorities with the spirit of the apostles, "We must obey God and not men!" (Acts 5:29). Paul's witness was heard at the center of the Roman empire, and the church in Rome had outsized influence until Constantinople challenged its primacy in the fourth century. As time went on, whole civilizations were changed by the gospel message. The movement of the Spirit was invisible, but his effects on people and their institutions were visible. Not all that became visible was Spirit-inspired, but there is no doubt that the Spirit revival that was early Christianity became a visible kingdom that changed the world.

It is significant that the Reformation Anglican documents refer only to the visible church, never to the invisible. It is also significant that the primary sign of the universal Church, its bishops, is always visible, and it is this critical sign that Anglicans recognize and most Reformed deny. Catholic Anglicans have acknowledged, as did Richard Hooker, that the visible Church is always full of wheat and tares. But the wheat is always visible eventually, and the tares are often invisible, at least for a while.[20]

Israel and the Church

Did the Church begin at Pentecost? Or did it exist in another form long before? What about Israel and the Chosen People? Where do they fit?

Let us first think about the way the Church has been described for more than sixteen hundred years, as the New Israel. After the Holocaust, theologians and Bible scholars

---

[19] Claude Beaufort Moss, *The Christian Faith* (London: SPCK, 1954), 243.

[20] Richard Hooker, *Of the Laws of Ecclesiastical Polity* 3.1.8–11, ed. Michael Russell (Scotts Valley, CA: CreateSpace, 2004).

asked themselves how this could have happened in the most Christianized country in history, Germany, the birthplace of the Reformation with its close attention to the Bible. The great New Testament scholar C. E. B. Cranfield wrote that Romans 9–11 "emphatically forbid us to speak of the church as having once and for all taken the place of the Jewish people."[21] Cranfield, like many other scholars and theologians in the last few decades, cited Romans 11:2 where Paul writes of Jews who had not yet accepted their Messiah, "God has not rejected his people whom he foreknew" (NRSV). The formidable biblical theologian W. D. Davies had already pronounced that "Paul never calls the Church the New Israel or the Jewish people the Old Israel."[22] Others have noted that the word *Israel* appears 77 times in the New Testament, and in every single case it refers to the Jewish people, their polity, or the land called by that name.[23]

One of the other discoveries by scholars in the last sixty years was that Paul was referring to the majority of his Jewish brothers who had not accepted Jesus when he wrote in Romans 11:28 that "they are beloved [by God] for the sake of their fathers [Abraham, Isaac, and Jacob]." That is, God still loves the Jewish people because of the promises he made to the patriarchs about their seed. He wrote in the same passage that "the calling of God" to be his Chosen People is "irrevocable" (Rom 11:29), which means never revoked, even if they do not accept Jesus as their Messiah. This does not mean that Paul thought every Jew is guaranteed salvation, for he wrote shortly before this that "not all who come from Israel are of Israel" (Rom 9:6). It does mean, however, that the Jewish people are still beloved of God. They are still his Chosen People. When we think of the Church, we must reckon with God's calling of Israel, and try to think of the relation between the two.

One way of doing this is to realize that we can speak of all of God's chosen from Adam and Eve and their descendants as in God's Church, and of the Jews who followed the Spirit's leading as God's Jewish Church, as Jonathan Edwards and Anglican theologians like Staley have called them. We should join Staley in recognizing that God did not set up his Church polity without precedent, for he had previously set chief priests and priests and Levites over Israel. The new polity of bishops, priests, and deacons was his way of baptizing the polity he had given to his Jewish flock in Israel.

We do not have time or space to develop these thoughts here. Suffice it to say that we can infer from Romans and other Pauline letters such as Ephesians that the Body of Christ—who is the Jewish Messiah!—comes in two expressions. One is the Gentile Christian Church that is the assembly of the faithful from the nations who are joined to Israel through the Jewish Messiah. The other is the assembly of Jewish believers in Yeshua (Jesus' Hebrew name). Together they constitute the one Body of Messiah, a

---

[21] C. E. B. Cranfield, *A Critical and Exegetical Commentary on the Epistle to the Romans* (Edinburgh: T&T Clark, 1979), 2:448.

[22] W. D. Davies, *The Gospel and the Land: Early Christianity and Jewish Territorial Doctrine* (Berkeley: University of California Press, 1974), 182.

[23] Galatians 6:16 is the only source of dispute on this, and even here there are several interpretations that are more plausible than thinking that "the Israel of God" means the Church as a New Israel. See Gerald McDermott, *Israel Matters: Why Christians Should Think Differently about the People and the Land* (Downers Grove, IL: InterVarsity Press, 2017), 26–27, 66.

community of Jews and Gentiles who in their distinctions and mutual blessings anticipate the shalom of the renewed earth to come.

This is probably what Paul means in Ephesians 2, where the Gentiles are "no longer strangers and sojourners, alienated from the commonwealth of Israel, but fellow citizens with 'the separated ones' [the literal meaning of τῶν ἁγίων tōn hagiōn, probably referring to Jewish Yeshua believers] and members of the household of God" (Eph 2:19–20). Paul here makes clear that Gentile believers do not become Israelites *per se* but associate members of the commonwealth of Israel. Particularity, not universality or sameness, is the mark of Paul's ecclesiology. Just as men and women retain their different sexes after becoming one in marriage, so Jews and Gentiles remain as Jews and Gentiles after sharing in the commonwealth of Israel because of their oneness with the Jewish Messiah. This divine diversity is not a vestige of remaining sinfulness but an original divine intent. God always intended to have Gentiles join Israel without becoming Jewish, just as he always intended marital unity with distinctions to mirror the Messiah's unity with the Church without collapsing distinctions between a holy Messiah and his unholy Church.[24]

Conclusion

What have historic Anglicans believed about the Church? For most of the last two thousand years Anglicans have known that the Church is more than what happened at their parish. They have known it is a gigantic organism—not organization—that includes all the angels, all the cosmos, and the living and the dead. It has three parts, the Church Militant here on earth, the Church in the intermediate period awaiting their complete sanctification, and the Church Triumphant in heaven who will be revealed at the Messiah's second coming. They have known implicitly that the Church transcends time. It includes the Old Testament saints and some outside Israel like Job who looked forward to him and therefore were part of his Body, the Church.

They have also known that the Church is still full of spots and wrinkles. It has been a testing ground or even stone of stumbling in times of bad leaders, heresies, and divisions. Theologians and preachers have often likened the Church to a moon with its waxing and waning, sometimes reflecting the light of the sun (Son) and sometimes obscured in darkness. Some have quoted St. Augustine of Hippo who wrote that the Church is pure and shining because the Messiah illuminates her, but ugly and sinful in herself, yet she can become beautiful once again, Augustine continued, when she confesses her sins and weeps penitent tears.

In the meantime, we continue to confess that the Church is a divine society that is one, holy, catholic, and apostolic. It is God's plan for salvation. It gave us the Scriptures. It is a visible people God has gathered to himself from outside of Eden through the history of Israel and now these last two thousand years of the Church. We Anglicans are the English way of being catholic, the Anglican way of being the historic Church.

---

[24] This last paragraph is adapted from my forthcoming book on the history of redemption at Baker Publishing.

Chapter 10

Holy Orders

The Rev. Dr. Gerald McDermott

Why do Re-formed Catholic Anglicans have a separate order of ministers set apart in special ways? Why is that order limited to bishops, priests, and deacons? What special authority do they have? Why are they only men? And is Rome right to say their orders are void?

These are the questions I will try to answer in this chapter. But let me first say that this doctrine of Holy Order is the key to the state of Anglicanism worldwide. For it has fractured worldwide over the dogmas of marriage and Holy Order, and the latter is the key to the first.

Why do I say that? Because it was setting aside the universal, more than three-thousand-year tradition of Holy Order that led to setting aside the equally hoary doctrine of Christian marriage between a man and a woman. How so? Because once Anglicans allowed themselves to depart from the plain sense of the biblical text on Holy Order, their brains were then rewired to permit *another* departure from the Bible and tradition—that on marriage—and all the sexual perversions that flow from rejecting Christian marriage.

Scripture

As Aidan Nichols has put it, holy Tradition is the reading of the Bible by the Church's eyes of faith.[1] This is why Scripture and tradition are mutually informing. The Word of God in Scripture is our ultimate authority, but we can be sure of our interpretation of Scripture only when we follow the Great Tradition's reading of it. In this chapter I will explicate how the early fathers and the Anglican tradition have interpreted Scripture on Holy Order.

When we go to Scripture, not only the New Testament but also the Old Testament—which we should remind ourselves was Jesus' Bible and constitutes 77% of the Protestant Bible and 80% of the Catholic and Anglican Bibles—we find that the Holy Order that emerges in the second century was foreshadowed not only in the developing polity of the New Testament but also in the three degrees of Holy Order found in the Old Testament: chief priests, priests, and Levites.

From Jewish Israel, Jesus and the apostles—who we should remind ourselves were all Jews—drew the rabbinic notion of שָׁלִיחַ *shaliach*, "the one sent," who was identical to the sender. So, when Jesus told the apostles, "As the Father has sent me, so I send you," and then breathed on them and declared, "Receive the Holy Spirit" (John 20:21–22),[2] he was sending them as שְׁלִיחִים *shlichim*, his representatives in whom he dwelled and through whom he ministered. This is why he said, "He who receives you, receives me" (Matt 10:40), and "He who hears you, hears me, and he who despises you, despises me" (Luke 10:16).

---

[1] Aidan Nichols, OP, *Holy Order: Apostolic Priesthood from the New Testament to the Second Vatican Council* (Eugene, OR: Wipf and Stock, 2011 [orig. Veritas, 1990]), 4.

[2] Unless otherwise noted, all Scripture translations are the author's.

As Jesus the Messiah was prophet, priest, and king, he gave the apostles his same threefold priestly ministry. They shared his prophetic priesthood as preachers and teachers ("he who hears you hears me"). They shared his priestly priesthood declaring his absolution of sin, grafting new members into his body, and celebrating the ἀνάμνησις *anamnesis*[3] of his sacrifice in the Eucharist ("what sins you forgive, they are forgiven"; "baptizing them in the name of the Father, Son, and Holy Spirit"; "This is my Body.... Do this in *anamnesis* of me" [John 20:23; Matt 28: 19; Luke 22:19]). They also shared his kingly priesthood by presiding over the Church ("whatever you bind on earth shall be bound in heaven, and whatever you loose on earth shall be loosed in heaven" [Matt 18:18]).

Jesus also taught, "I will be with you until the end of the age" (Matt 28:20). But how will he do that if in his body he is in heaven at the right hand of the Father? The answer to that question was his consecration of the apostles by filling them with his Spirit and teaching them to lay hands on their successors to pass down their authority as שְׁלִיחִים *shlichim*, so that Jesus' threefold ministry would continue in the Church. In Acts of the Apostles we see the apostles doing just this in Samaria (Acts 8:17) and elsewhere. These Jewish apostles perpetuated the Old Testament Holy Order of chief priests, priests, and Levites by a renewed[4] covenant Holy Order of bishops, priests, and deacons. Paul acted as an archbishop to all the churches he planted and helped, and he treated Timothy and Titus as bishops who were consecrated to ordain priests and deacons in their networks of churches.

The Fathers

Already by Ignatius at the beginning of the second century (about 112), the church fathers are referring to one holy order in three degrees. In his epistle to the church at Smyrna (now the modern Turkish city of Izmir), Ignatius wrote, "Follow your bishop ... as Jesus Christ followed the Father. Obey your presbyters too, as you would the apostles; give your deacons the same reverence that you would to a command from God."[5] Only priests who were ordained by bishops in the succession from the apostles were validly ordained. Before the end of the first century, about 95, Clement the bishop of Rome wrote, "Christ therefore was sent forth by God, and the apostles by Christ.... [T]hey appointed the first fruits [of their labours]—having first proved them by the Spirit—to be bishops and deacons of those who should afterwards believe.... They appointed those [ministers] already mentioned, and afterwards gave instructions that when these should fall asleep, other approved men should succeed them in their ministry."[6] A century later Tertullian

---

[3] ἀνάμνησις *anamnesis* is the Greek word for the Jewish concept of liturgical זִכָּרוֹן *zikkaron*, in which the past is brought into the present.

[4] There is no separate word for "renewed" in Hebrew, but the same Hebrew word חָדָשׁ *chadash* was used for both "new" and "renewed." Since the renewal of the covenant was a repeated event in the Old Testament, and usually in deeper ways, it is plausible that the meaning of Jeremiah's "new covenant" in Jeremiah 31, which Jesus and the New Testament authors repeat, is a renewal of the covenant by the Messiah at a higher and deeper level. See McDermott, *Israel Matters* (Grand Rapids: Brazos, 2017), 96–98.

[5] Ignatius, *The Epistle to the Smyrnaens* 8, in *Early Christian Writings*, ed. Andrew Louth (London: Penguin, 1987), 103.

[6] *The First Epistle of Clement* 42 and 44 (ANF 1:16–17).

made this a test of orthodoxy: "[If they want to prove their own validity,] let them unfold the roll of their bishops ... to show [that their first bishop was ordained by] one of the apostles."[7] Obviously the Gnostic Christians could not do so; they were celebrating Gnostic Eucharists with Gnostic priests ordained outside the apostolic succession.

The fathers saw ordination as a sacrament because they saw the Church as a sacrament of salvation. Only in the orthodox Church could be found salvation from sin, death, and the devil—by the Church's Sacraments. And the Sacraments were valid only if they were administered by priests ordained by bishops who could trace their lineage back to the apostles. These priests were given by ordination what the fathers said was a new bond with the Spirit and the Son that empowered them to confer the Sacraments full of divine power. This new bond that was printed on the soul of the priests at ordination was called a *character* by medieval theologians. It did not make the priest a better person, but it changed him into an "icon of Christ" as the fathers put it.[8] He was not put into a privileged caste separated from the community of believers but became forever changed by the sacrament so that the Messiah could minister sacramentally through him as *repraesentatio Christi capitis* (representative of Christ the Head).[9] This did not mean that as a priest he had a right to domineer or bully a church. Augustine said the one marked at ordination was not to be *over* others in a worldly way but *for* others as a servant. Especially if he were to receive the higher degree of Holy Order to become a bishop: "A man may know himself to be no bishop if he loves to precede rather than to profit others."[10]

Anglican Tradition

The last two millennia of Anglican tradition have accepted the church fathers' consensus on Holy Order, that it is a sacrament that sets apart men as bishops, priests, and deacons and confers on them an indelible mark with sacramental power. The *Articles* declare "it is not lawful for any man to take upon him the office of publick preaching, or ministering the Sacraments in the Congregation, before he be lawfully called" (Article XXIII). Several articles refer to "Bishops, Priests, and Deacons" as the only clergy (XXXII, XXXVI), and the Preface to the Ordinal of the 1662 prayer book starts with the pronouncement, "It is evident unto all men diligently reading holy Scripture and ancient Authors, that from the Apostles [sic] time there have been these Orders of Ministers in Christs [sic] Church; Bishops, Priests, and Deacons."[11] The prayer book also affirms the ontological character of Anglican ministry by adding the Bishop's prayer for a priest at the laying on of hands, "Receive the holy Ghost for the Office and work of a priest in the Church of God .... Whose sins thou dost forgive, they are forgiven; and whose sins thou dost retain, they are

---

[7] Tertullian, *The Prescription Against Heretics* 32 (ANF 3:258).

[8] Gerhard Müller, *Priesthood and Diaconate: The Recipient of the Sacrament of Holy Orders from the Perspective of Creation Theology and Christology*, trans. Michael J. Miller (San Francisco: Ignatius, 2002), 126.

[9] Ibid., 64.

[10] Augustine, quoted by Müller, 170–171.

[11] *The Preface* to *The Book of Common Prayer, 1662* in *The Book of Common Prayer: The Texts of 1549, 1559, 1662*, ed. Brian Cummings (Oxford: Oxford University Press, 2011), 622.

retained. And be thou a faithful Dispenser of the Word of God, and of his holy Sacraments."[12]

Richard Hooker, the preeminent Anglican theologian of the English Reformation, affirmed both the threefold order and the ontological character of ordination for "clergy" who are "either presbyters or deacons"[13]: "Christ hath imparted power ..., a kind of mark or character and acknowledged to be indelible ..., and maketh them a special *order* consecrated unto the service of the Most High in things wherewith others may not meddle ...; they are a distinct *order*."[14]

The 2019 prayer book suggests the same impartation of sacramental character in its ordinal for both deacons ("Receive the Holy Spirit for the Office and work of a Deacon") and priests ("Receive the Holy Spirit for the office and work of a Priest in the Church of God. If you forgive the sins of anyone .... If you withhold forgiveness .... Be a faithful minister of God's holy Word and Sacraments.")[15]

Women Priests?

The besetting question dividing churches all over the world, including the Anglican Church in North America (ACNA), is that of ordination for women. Since the 1960s, which not coincidentally was the time of the rise of the Sexual Revolution, many have suspected that Holy Order in Christian churches—and the Jewish Church before that— was withheld from women because of misogyny and that women have never been allowed to use their God-given gifts for ministry.

Both claims are untrue. While the Gnostics ordained women but believed them a lesser form of humanity because they were closer to matter, which they considered evil, the fathers limited Holy Order to men not because of a low view of women but because of a high view of Jesus's will and practice. They pointed to Jesus' setting apart twelve men as apostles and seventy men as disciples, and many remarked that while Mary was obviously superior in many ways, Jesus nevertheless limited ordained ministry to men. Far from being misogynists, the fathers often praised women for their spiritual sensitivities and gifts. John Chrysostom, for example, commented as follows on Priscilla teaching Apollos:

> Let the men hear, and let also the women listen to these things! We are told of these holy ones so that we might emulate their race and kind, and also lest the women appear to be the weaker. For who among us has defense, who receives pardon, when such women demonstrate such eagerness and such philosophy, while we [men] remain continually bound to the cares of the world?[16]

---

[12] *Book of Common Prayer*, 1662, 642.

[13] Richard Hooker, *Of the Laws of Ecclesiastical Polity and other works as edited by John Keble*, arranged by Michael Russell, vol. 2 (Scotts Valley, CA: Create Space Independent Publishing, 2010) 5.78.2; 5.77.2 (pages 469 & 456).

[14] Hooker, *Laws*, 5.77.2, emphasis original.

[15] *The Book of Common Prayer, According to the Use of the Anglican Church in North America* (Huntingdon Beach, CA: Anglican Liturgy, 2019), 480, 493.

[16] John Chrysostom, "Greet Priscilla and Aquila," 1.4, quoted in David C. Ford, *Women and Men in the Early Church: The Vision of St. John Chrysostom*, rev. ed. (South Canaan, PA: St. Tikhon's Seminary Press, 2017), 67.

The fathers pointed to Scripture, which pointed in turn to creation. They were impressed that Paul appealed to the created order <u>before</u> the Fall: women were not to teach authoritatively or exercise authority over a congregation because *Adam was formed first, then Eve* (1 Tim 2:13). Women were to *pray or prophesy* with their heads covered because *man was not made from woman but woman from man. Neither was man created for woman but woman for man* (1 Cor 11:8-9).

For the fathers reading Paul, then, male authority in the Church derives not from a fallen order but from the creation order. Male headship is not from *sinful* patriarchy but because of God's original order for humanity. In fact, the form of the Fall reinforces male headship. Eve took the initiative rather than Adam, and did not consult with Adam. Adam should have protected her from Satan and reminded her of God's commands. Men are appointed heads in the home and church not because of biological or spiritual superiority but because God has ordered his creation and Church after the relation between Christ and the Church: Christ as the God-man is the head of his Church which is the feminine Bride. Woman represents "the bridal response of faith and love made by the Church."[17]

Clement, the first-century bishop of Rome, wrote to the church at Corinth that the apostles gave orders that *proven men* should succeed them as bishops and hand this ministry on to *other proven men*.[18] Irenaeus, Hippolytus, Clement of Alexandria, Origen, Tertullian, and Cyprian said the same.[19] Here is Chrysostom again: "When someone has to preside over the Church and be entrusted with the care of so many souls, then let all womankind give way before the magnitude of the task—and indeed most men also. Bring before us those who far excel all others and are as much above the rest in spiritual stature as Saul was above the whole nation of the Hebrews in bodily stature."[20]

But what about women's gifts? Cannot they be used for ministry? They can, and they were, in the early church. Baptized women prophesied, supported the apostles financially, and helped in myriad ways behind the scenes, served the sick and needy, evangelized both inside and outside the Church, instructed their husbands and children, and the older women taught the younger women. They showed what has been called the Marian charism (as opposed to the Petrine and Pauline charisms of leadership and church-planting) of special spiritual openness exemplified by the Virgin Mary and Mary of Bethany, service as spiritual mothers, works of charity and mercy like those of Tabitha and Dorcas, faith and evangelism as seen in Martha and Mary Magdalene, hospitality like that of Martha and Mary, and special gifts of prayer like those of the women at the cross and in the upper room.[21]

These various feminine gifts of the Marian charism continued to be part of the Church's ministry through the post-apostolic age and into the second millennium. Up to the time of the Reformation in the West, there were numerous influential ministries

---

[17] Müller, *Priesthood and Diaconate*, 103.

[18] *The First Epistle of Clement* 44 (ANF 1:16).

[19] Müller, *Priesthood and Diaconate*, 150.

[20] Ford, *Women and Men in the Early Church*, 159–160.

[21] On the Marian and Petrine charisms, see the chapter by Barbara Gauthier and Gerald McDermott, "Women and Men in Ministry," originally published in *North American Anglican* (Oct 14, 2022), https://northamanglican.com/women-and-men-in-ministry.

exercised by laywomen in the Church: Macrina (theologian with Gregory of Nyssa), Olympias (deaconess to John Chrysostom), Dominca (spiritual mother, lifelong service to the Christian community, gifts of healing prayer and prophecy), Hilda of Whitby (educator and diplomat), Walburga (missionary work with Boniface), Milburga of Shrewsbury (abbess, gifts of evangelism, pastoral care, physical healing, and spiritual deliverance from sin's power), Clare of Assisi (foundress of Franciscan order to care for the poor), Hildegard von Bingen (mystic, herbalist, spiritual writer, composer), Catherine of Siena (mystic author, nurse of the critically ill, catalyst for reformation of the papacy), Teresa of Avila (mystic, reformer of the Carmelite order, businesswoman, prolific author on prayer).[22]

Deaconesses But Not Female Deacons

Both the discipline and the liturgy of the Church throughout its early history insisted on a very clear distinction between male deacons and female *deaconesses*.[23] Based on this early Church model of ministry, women cannot be ordained as deacons but may be set apart for ministry as deaconesses. They would exercise a variety of ministries under the authority of the rector or bishop, such as pastoral care, counseling, caring for the sick and poor, teaching, spiritual formation, prayer ministry, preparing candidates for baptism and confirmation, assisting at baptisms, leading Morning and Evening Prayer, and conducting other forms of social and educational work.

Scripture speaks of Phoebe as a διάκονος *diakonos* or servant (Rom 16:1) but limits the diaconate to men: deacons are to be *husbands of one wife* (1 Tim 3:12). The γυναῖκας *gynaikas* in 1 Timothy 3:11 have different qualifications from those of deacons, are evidently doing something other than what male deacons do, and so are best translated by the plain sense "wives."[24] The word διάκονος *diakonos* is used by Paul to refer to the office of deacon only in Philippians 1:1 and 1 Timothy, where it is used in conjunction with ἐπίσκοπος *episkopos*. Elsewhere it is the generic term for "servant" or "helper" (Rom 15:8; Gal 2:17; 1 Thess 3:2; Col 1:7, 23, 25; 4:7; Eph 3:7; 6:21; 1 Cor 3:5; 2 Cor 3:6; 11:15, 23; 1 Tim 4:6; Titus 1:9).

In the early Church, the ministry of deaconesses was separate from that of deacons. They were not ordained as deacons but were set apart as deaconesses for ministries in keeping with their Marian charism. This continued after the apostolic era. In the *Apostolic Tradition* (c. 215), only bishops, priests, and deacons were ordained by the laying on of hands. All other ministries—widows, lectors, virgins, subdeacons, and those with healing gifts—were expressly forbidden to receive the laying on of hands because

---

[22] This paragraph and the following section were adapted, with permission, from "Women and Men in Ministry." See that chapter for further discussion.

[23] Aimé Martimort, *Deaconesses: An Historical Study*, trans. K.D. Whitehead (San Francisco: Ignatius, 1986; orig. *Les Deaconesses* [1982]); see chs. 1–7, especially "The Liturgy for the Ordination of Deaconesses." This sums up his study: "However solemn may have been the ritual by which she was initiated into her ministry, however much it may have resembled the ritual for the ordination of a deacon, the conclusion nevertheless must be that a deaconess in the Byzantine rite was in no wise a female deacon" (156). Deaconesses had no strictly sacramental office and were not near the altar during a Eucharist when a priest was presiding.

[24] Besides, as the NET Bible notes, "It would be strange for the author to discuss women deacons right in the middle of qualifications for male deacons."

"ordination is for clerics destined for liturgical service." The diaconate was limited to men. Women in other ministries were set apart for service to the Church by the bishop with prayer only and were excluded from liturgical functions.

At the Council of Nicaea (325), Canon 19 (on receiving Paulinists back into the Church) states, "Clergy must be rebaptized and then ordained by a bishop of the Catholic Church.... The same thing must be done with respect to the deaconesses [but] they have received no laying on of hands and are thus therefore to be counted among the laity."

Later ordinations made very clear distinctions between the ordinations of deacons and deaconesses, using different prayers and ordination rubrics for each order to specifically identify and distinguish their different charisms and ministries.[25] Only the heretical Montanist sect ordained women to the same diaconate, presbyterate, and episcopate as men.

The Conciliar Model[26]

A last word on the ordination of women: it violates the conciliar model which has been passed down through the ages from the early church and ratified in our Anglican formularies. The Jerusalem Council in Acts 15 is the biblical model for resolving disputes about new rites in the Church. Some Christians wanted new rites for the circumcision of gentile believers. There was much debate. Paul and Barnabas were appointed to discuss this question with the apostles and elders in Jerusalem (v. 12). Resolution was gained only when it seemed good to the Holy Spirit and to us (v. 28), to the whole church (v. 22).

The rule for the early Church in resolving disputes was to accept only rites that agreed with Scripture as understood by the whole Church. The early church leaders believed not only that Scripture was the Word of God, but also that the Church of the living God [is] a pillar and buttress of truth (1 Tim 3:15). Their criterion was Scripture as understood by the whole Church.

Rites for women's ordination have been approved without the consent of the whole Church. They have come from a minority of the world's churches, and from churches that are heretical and dying. This is a new and (mostly) Western development. The ACNA College of Bishops conceded this in 2017 when it concluded that women's ordination was a "recent innovation" with "insufficient scriptural warrant."[27] This new way of understanding man and woman in the Bride of the Messiah deviates from the way the one, holy, catholic, and apostolic Church has understood Holy Order for two millennia.

It also deviates from the conciliar model endorsed by our Anglican formularies. The Anglican Ordinal and canons seek to replicate the conciliarism of the early church where disputes were settled in councils with apostles and elders deciding as a group, with no leader given dictatorial authority. This is why Anglicans cannot accept a papacy with juridical authority over all other churches. At Jerusalem Peter did not preside. He and

---

[25] Martimort, *Deaconesses*, 146–64.

[26] This section is adapted from "Women and Men in Ministry." See further discussion in that chapter.

[27] "A Statement from the College of Bishops on the Ordination of Women," Sept. 7, 2017, anglicanchurch.net/college-of-bishops-statement-on-the-ordination-of-women.

James were first among equals, and the body of apostles and elders came to agreement. In Anglican polity as determined by the Ordinal and canons, the whole Church works together by representation from laity, clergy, and bishops. The Archbishop is first among equals but does not have absolute authority to dictate to all. This model is taken in part from the Council of Nicaea (325) where the emperor stepped off the throne and the bishops sat in a semi-circle facing the throne with the Scriptures sitting on it.

Null and Void?

In 1896 Pope Leo XIII issued a papal Bull called *Apostolicae Curae*, in which he declared that Anglican orders are null and void because they changed the "intention" of previous Catholic ordinals and contained "defect of form."[28] In short, the pope claimed that the Ordinal in the 1552 *Book of Common Prayer* no longer intended to continue the Roman ordination to the priesthood, and the form of the ordination itself was defective because it did not mention explicitly that the central act of a priest is to offer the "sacrifice" of the Mass.

Was Pope Leo right? Are Anglican orders null and void, which would mean they are not in the apostolic succession and our sacraments do not convey what our prayer book claims?

No. Leo was wrong. And it is not difficult to show why he was wrong. In short, both the 1552 and 1662 prayer books in their Prefaces say they intend to "continue" the offices of Bishop, Priest, and Deacon they had inherited from the universal Church. Earlier in this chapter I quoted those words. The pope claims that Cranmer, the primary author of the 1552 prayer book, privately had different intentions. That may or may not be true, but it does not matter. At no time has the Church ever given credence to private opinions of theologians when it comes to Church doctrine. Only public formularies matter, and in this case the Preface to the Ordinal in every Anglican Prayer Book proves Leo's claim was wrong.

Second, Leo argued that the form of the ordination rite should have contained mention of the sacrifice of the Eucharist as the principal work of the priest. But none of the Catholic ordinals in its first millennium of the Church contained mention of the sacrifice of the Eucharist.[29] Were their priesthoods and sacraments invalid? Leo would never have conceded that. The 1552 ordinal contained what all the ordinals in the first millennium contained by way of form: the laying on of hands and prayer for the Holy Spirit to confer the power to loose and retain sins from John 20. In fact, just twelve months before Cranmer put together the 1552 ordinal, the Council of Mainz declared that this form—laying on of hands and the formula from John 20—was the essential "form" of the sacrament.[30] And in 1895, the year before Leo's Bull, "Roman opinion had markedly swung around to the idea that imposition of hands with prayer for the gift of

---

[28] Pope Leo XIII, *Apostolicae Curae: On the Nullity of Anglican Orders*, www.papalencyclicals.net/leo13/l13curae.htm.

[29] Dom Gregory Dix, *The Question of Anglican Orders: Letters to a Layman* (Westminster: Dacre Press, 1944), 44–58.

[30] Ibid., 67.

the Holy ghost were the essential 'Matter' and 'Form' of the Roman rite."[31] As Gregory Dix put it, "These had been the Anglican 'Matter' and 'Form' all along."[32]

Why This Is Important

In closing, I would submit there are five reasons why Holy Order is critical for us to embrace in this turning point in the history of redemption.

For the first time in the last three thousand years, *patriarchy* is treated as a dirty word. But God invented it. The word means "the rule of fathers," and for a Christian this means the rule of our heavenly Father over us, the spiritual leadership of families by husbands, and the servant leadership of the Church by male bishops, priests, and deacons. We should refuse the guilt trip which our culture has imposed on us for accepting godly patriarchy.

Secondly, understanding Holy Order means rejecting the Marxist view of history as a "battle of the sexes for predominance and prestige."[33] The true view of history, suggested by the sacrament of Holy Order to bring salvation to the world, is of a "history of love" for which God designed man and woman as types of his relation to the Church.[34]

Holy Order also shows us that only within this sacramental understanding of the Church and its ministry can man and woman be understood. Men and women in the Church have their own ministries from the sacraments of baptism, confirmation, and Eucharist. The Church is a divine society conferring divine power to every member of the Body through its sacraments, which makes it obvious that it cannot be treated like a political party, pushed and pulled by trends and opinion polls.[35]

Modern agendas for equal rights and opportunities for women could never have been conceived without the earlier Christian doctrine of equal dignity for man and woman in nature and grace.[36] But these recent agendas have now turned Gnostic because they despise sexual difference and treat it as non-essential. Yet male and female are not what philosophers would call accidental differences such as race, color, age, and state of health.[37] They are fundamental and necessary differences, essential to sacramental marriage and Christ's communion as a husband with his bride the Church. Holy Order's essential connection to marriage and salvation shows that Christian orthodoxy is more woman-friendly and human-friendly than current programs for self-liberation by self-creation.[38]

Thank God that three dioceses in the ACNA now have orders of deaconesses. Let us strengthen these three orders and start more around the ACNA and Anglican Communion. Here is found a restored arena for ministry for women serving with their gifts of hospitality, evangelism, service, and catechesis. May these show Anglicans that

---

[31] Dix, *The Question of Anglican Orders*, 81.
[32] Ibid.
[33] Müller, *Priesthood and Diaconate*, 26–27.
[34] Ibid.
[35] Ibid., 77.
[36] Ibid., 80–81.
[37] Ibid., 164.
[38] Ibid., 167.

the answer for women's ministry is not by ignoring sexual difference but by recognizing the biblically authorized areas of ministry entrusted to women.

Chapter 11

Women and Men in Ministry*

Dr. Barbara Gauthier and The Rev. Dr. Gerald McDermott

In 1970 the Episcopal Church USA (ECUSA) eliminated the canon for deaconesses and included women in the canon on deacons. In 1976 its General Convention approved the ordination of women to both the diaconate and priesthood. Eastern Orthodox Churches and the Roman Catholic Church condemned both moves, protesting that these changes were made unilaterally and against the ecumenical pattern of waiting until there was consensus among the oldest Churches.

One could say the ECUSA innovations were understandable if not acceptable. For they were responding to several centuries of clericalism, where the only ministry was for what we call the "Petrine charism" and required a collar around one's neck. Several millennia of diverse and vigorous women's ministry using the "Marian charism" were suppressed and ignored. The result was that gifted women, called by God to ministry, concluded that the only way to use their gifts was to be ordained and imitate the Petrine charism.

In this chapter we will explain the Marian charism as illustrated in both Scripture and Church history, show the evidence for traditional Holy Order in Scripture and tradition, and then consider the most common objections to the tradition.

Different Charisms

In the beginning, "The LORD God took the man and put him in the garden of Eden to work it and keep it" (Gen 2:15).[1] Woman was made as a "helper fit for him" (Gen 2:20–23) and was given the name "Eve, because she was the mother of all living" (Gen 3:20). Adam's task of working and keeping the land was different from the two tasks given to Eve: to be a fit helper for the man in his work and also to mother and care for the living who were born to her. A similar distinction of divinely appointed tasks can be seen in the New Testament Scriptures, with men and women receiving different charisms to accomplish what was needed for the successful proclamation of the gospel and building up of the Church.

The Petrine Charism

Jesus trained his disciples by providing them with very specific on-the-job instruction. On the shore of the Sea of Galilee, Jesus commissioned Peter to feed his lambs and tend his sheep (John 21:15–17), to be the shepherd of his flock: to protect them, lead them, take care of them, and serve them even as he himself had done (John 10:14–16). At his ascension, Jesus instructed all of his disciples to go and make disciples of all nations, baptizing them and "teaching them to observe all that I have commanded you" (Matt 28:16–29).

By the power and leading of the Holy Spirit, Peter and his fellow disciples were empowered to proclaim the gospel and shepherd Christ's flock, the Church. This Petrine

---

* An earlier version of this chapter was published in *The North American Anglican*, Oct. 14, 2022, northamanglican.com/women-and-men-in-ministry/.

[1] All Scripture passages cited in this chapter are from the English Standard Version (ESV) unless otherwise noted.

charism can be seen throughout the rest of the New Testament. Peter, as leader of the disciples, provided leadership for the Church (Acts 1:15–26), preached and baptized those who were being saved (Acts 2:1–41), healed the infirm (Acts 3:1–10), and administered discipline (Acts 5:1–11; 8:20–24).

Through the teaching and leadership of Peter and the other apostles, the Church was unified in fellowship and fed through the breaking of the bread and the prayers (Acts 2:42). Deacons were raised up to help with administration and service, making sure that physical needs of the expanding flock were being met (Acts 6:1–6). They were also commissioned by the Holy Spirit to preach (Acts 7:1–53; 8:4–13) and evangelize (Acts 8:26–40) under the supervision of Peter and the apostles in Jerusalem (Acts 8:14–17).

The ministry of Paul (Acts 13ff.) expanded the structure and leadership of the Church through the planting of new churches, preaching and teaching new converts, and establishing local leadership in his fledgling congregations. His letters to these new leaders gave episcopal instruction on how to shepherd the flock and build up the Church in love. He provided both doctrinal teaching and practical guidance on the right ordering of church relationships, discipline, church practice, and liturgy. He also gave instruction on leadership roles.

The pastoral epistles document the passing of this Petrine charism on to the next generation of church leadership, with counsel on the qualities and responsibilities of ordained leadership, the necessity for sound doctrine, the right ordering of church relationships, and roles within the Church.

In the West, especially among the churches of the Reformation, virtually all ministry in the church came to be defined exclusively in terms of this Petrine model of ordained church leadership based on scriptural precedent. The Protestant pastor was always a man, whose ministry consisted of providing leadership; running the church; administering the rites of baptism, communion, marriage, and burial; tending to the spiritual needs of the flock through preaching and teaching; and administering discipline when necessary.

Clericalism merely amplified this understanding—that in order to exercise any recognized ministry in the Church, one had to be ordained according to the Petrine model of ministry. Thus, if women were to exercise a ministry in the Church, then they too had to be ordained.

Gifted women came to believe that limiting the ordained ministry to men was depriving women of their own spiritual callings and preventing them from exercising their gifts for building up the Church. The problem was defining women's ministry based on a Petrine model of ordination, which narrowly limits the scope of women's ministry. It inevitably tries to shoehorn women into what is essentially a male charism for ministry. It is not a comfortable fit.

If Scripture is to be the basis for determining how the Church should best function, what does the New Testament tell us about women's ministry? The ministry of the Marian charism is far broader than the Petrine ministry. It tends to rise organically and, unlike the disciples, women are not told specifically as a group what their ministry will be. Their participation is more fluid, and they receive their callings and instructions through the spiritual gifts they receive. The many things they do to minister to Jesus and his Church seem to flow effortlessly out of their natural gifting for nurturing and providing support, given to them from the beginning.

The Marian Charism

The Marian charism is multi-faceted and multi-dimensional. It builds on gifts not exclusive to women but innate in them to a greater extent. The praiseworthy woman described in Proverbs 31 exercises a wide variety of gifts in ministry both to her family and the world around her. In the Gospels, this feminine charism is exemplified by Mary the Mother of Jesus and many other women.

As a "handmaid of the Lord" (Luke 1:38, RSV), the Virgin surrenders herself completely to the Lord and to a life of spiritual openness (Luke 1:38) and worship (Luke 1:46–55). She exercises the gift of prophecy along with her cousin Elizabeth (Luke 1:41–45). As a woman of deep prayer, she "treasured up all these things, pondering them in her heart" (Luke 2:19, 51). Other women share in her charism of spiritual openness. Mary of Bethany sits at the feet of Jesus, listening to the Lord (Luke 10:42). On the morning of the resurrection, it is only the women who see the angels and encounter the risen Jesus (Matt 28:2–10; Mark 16:5–9; Luke 24:4–7; John 20:11–18).

A second vital aspect of the Marian charism is ministering directly to the body of Christ as spiritual mothers: nurturing adults and children and showing mercy to those in need. In the Gospels, they minister to the physical body of Jesus himself. His mother Mary carries him, gives birth to him, nurtures, and teaches him, raising him up in the fear of the Lord and in godly obedience to the Law (Luke 2:51–52). The sinful woman washes Jesus' feet with her tears and anoints them with ointment, pouring out her great love for him (Luke 7:36–50). Just before His passion, another woman anoints Jesus' head with expensive perfume, and he commends and praises her for having done "a beautiful thing" for him in preparing his body for burial (Matt 26:6–13).

The women of the Gospels have particular gifts of faith and evangelism. They bear witness to the truth of who Jesus is, they point people to the Lord, and their personal testimony brings others to faith and obedience. At the wedding in Cana, Mary addresses the servants in faith, pointing to Jesus and exhorting them, "Do whatever he tells you" (John 2:5). The Samaritan woman hurries to her neighbors, exclaiming excitedly, "Come, see a man who told me all that I ever did" and she brings a whole village to Jesus (John 4:28–30). Martha is put forward as the model of faith, confessing to Jesus: "Yes, Lord, I believe that you are the Christ, the Son of God" (John 11:27). Outside the empty tomb Mary Magdalene encounters the risen Jesus, who sends her to the disciples as an eyewitness to proclaim to them the good news of the resurrection: "I have seen the Lord!" (John 20:18).

The gifts of hospitality and helps of many women, known and unknown, were vital to the ministry of Jesus, providing necessary practical support for him and his disciples. Martha and Mary welcomed Jesus into their home whenever he was in Jerusalem (Luke 10:38). The women at the cross with Jesus provided crucial behind-the-scenes support for his ministry: "When Jesus was in Galilee, they used to follow him and minister to him" (Mark 15:40–41 NASB). While Jesus was ministering to the crowds, these women were busy taking care of his needs. They also provided financial support: "Joanna and Susanna and many others who were contributing to their support out of their private means" (Luke 8:3, NASB).

These same gifts are evident in the New Testament church as well. At the beginning of Acts, the women were gathered with the disciples in the upper room and "with one accord were devoting themselves to prayer" (Acts 1:14). The deacon Philip had four daughters who prophesied (Acts 21:9). In the pastoral epistles, the widow who has set "her hope on God and continues in supplications and prayers night and day" is honored (1 Tim 5:5).

Women continued to minister to the body of Christ, now present in his Church, through corporal works of mercy. In the town of Joppa, Tabitha was a pillar of the church, "abounding with deeds of kindness and charity which she continually did" (Acts 9:36–39, NASB). When she died, Peter was called, and the weeping widows showed him all the tunics and outer garments she had made for them. When Tabitha was raised from the dead, many believed in the Lord. In the pastoral epistles, elderly widows are to be supported who have brought up their children, shown hospitality, relieved the afflicted, and devoted themselves to doing good in every way (1 Tim 5:9–10).

Other gifts involve teaching, raising up the next generation of believers, and mentoring younger women as spiritual mothers in the Church. In Corinth, Priscilla and her husband Aquila explained more accurately the way of God to the eager preacher Apollos, who had known only the baptism of John (Acts 18:24–26). Timothy, who had a Gentile father, was commended by Paul for the "sincere faith" instilled in him by his Jewish mother Eunice and his grandmother Lois and now dwelling in him as well (Acts 16:1; 2 Tim 1:5). Titus is told to bid the older women in his church "to teach what is good and so train the young women to love their husbands and children" and contribute to the growth of healthy families (Titus 2:3–4).

Wealthy women were generous in supporting the ministry of the Church. When Lydia was baptized as one of the first converts in Philippi, she begged Paul to stay at her house, supplied hospitality for his ministry, and helped catalyze the founding of a new church (Acts 16:14–15). Nympha provided her home as a meeting place for the church in Laodicea (Col 4:15).

These various feminine gifts of the Marian charism continued to be part of the Church's ministry through the post-apostolic age and into the second millennium. Up to the Reformation in the West, there were numerous influential ministries exercised by laywomen in the Church: Macrina (theologian with Gregory of Nyssa), Olympias (deaconess to John Chrysostom), Dominica (spiritual mother, lifelong service to the Christian community, gifts of healing prayer and prophecy), Hilda of Whitby (educator and diplomat), Walburga (missionary work with Boniface), Milburga of Shrewsbury (abbess, gifts of evangelism, pastoral care, physical healing, and spiritual deliverance from sin's power), Clare of Assisi (foundress of Franciscan order to care for the poor), Hildegard von Bingen (mystic, herbalist, spiritual writer, composer), Catherine of Siena (mystic author, nurse of the critically ill, catalyst for reforming the papacy), and Teresa of Avila (mystic, reformer of the Carmelite order, businesswoman, prolific author on prayer).

Embracing Both the Petrine and Marian Charisms

After the Reformation, these Marian charism ministries were mostly lost in the Protestant world, leaving only one model of ministry in Church, that of ordained Petrine ministry. Whatever women did for the Church often consisted of such tasks as caring for the children, cleaning, cooking, preparing bulletins, washing altar linens, singing in the choir, tidying up afterwards, and other similar duties as assigned. Women were discouraged or even prevented from doing anything considered "ministerial"—that was the work of men—and the message they received was that their mostly mindless work might be necessary for the Church but was not esteemed or honored.

Western society came to hold the same views of the types of work that were appropriate for women. By the mid-twentieth century, gifted women in secular society were pushing back against the limitations that had been imposed on them. They sought to be treated as equal to men in all areas of life: jobs, education, family roles, and social relationships. This feminist pushback spread also to the churches. Women's rights were soon piggybacked onto civil rights as a first-order justice issue. For women to use their gifts fully in the Church, they said, they must be ordained just like men, in order to do what men do. What was missing from this equation was the Church's recognition, acceptance, and blessing of the Marian charism of women, without which the Church is incomplete.

Both Petrine and Marian charisms are needed for the Church to be a complete and healthy body. We tend to focus on what can be seen in the Body—the feet, hands, ears, eyes, and noses (1 Cor 12:12–26)—and often forget that it is the internal organs, the unseen ministries, that enable the external members of the Body to function well. In God's economy, what is hidden and modest is deemed most valuable and given the greater honor (1 Cor 12:24b–26).

This notion is counter-cultural in a society which values "men's work" as a "real job" and denigrates "women's work" of nurturing, providing support, caring for the physical and emotional needs of others, raising children, and attending to the spiritual formation of the next generation. It was not so in Jesus' day, when rabbis exempted Jewish women from all positive commandments with a specific requirement of time, because whatever they would be doing at that time was more valuable to God and to society.

The concept that men's and women's ministries are not the same and not interchangeable is also counter-cultural in today's world. In the beginning, Adam's task of tending and keeping the garden was a visible work needed to bring forth fruit in the present. The two tasks given to Eve were less visible. She was to provide helpful support for Adam in his work. As mother of all living, her focus was also to be on the future, successfully raising the next generation. Men are called to build up the Church in the present. Women are called to support that work and plant for the future, laying the foundations of faith for the next generation to build on.

What would the Church look like if it were to restore the fullness of the Marian charism, with its ministries flowing like water throughout the body of Christ? What would happen if the Church began to encourage and honor all the gifts that women have been given to build up the Church and to lay foundations for the future? In reserving to men the Petrine charism specific to sacramental ordained ministry, the Church can make space for gifted lay women, support the release of their gifts, and encourage them to create their own fruitful ministries in service to the Church, in their own families and within the larger family of God. Their ministries, carried out in partnership with men, both lay and ordained, would reflect more fully the order of God's creation and build up the Church both now and for the generations to come, enriching and strengthening the life and witness of the Church in the world.

A Male-Only Presbyterate

Paul is the most insistent New Testament proponent of a male-only presbyterate (1 Cor 14:33–35; 1 Tim 2:11–14; 3:1–2, 12; Titus 1:5–6). Since Paul makes much use of the Genesis 2 account of the creation, we will start there and note its emphasis on male leadership. First, "the LORD God commanded the man" (v. 16) and not the woman, suggesting here what is stated elsewhere in Scripture (Eph 5:22)—that the man is head of the family. Second, the woman is a "helper" to the man to assist him in obeying God's command to work and keep the garden, and to be fruitful and multiply and steward the creation (1:28). Third, the woman is made from man—ἐξ ἀνδρός *ex andros* "out of man" as Paul says in 1 Cor 11:8. Fourth, man takes the lead in marriage: "a man shall leave his father...." (Gen 2:24).

Paul does not "permit a woman to teach or to exercise authority over a man" (1 Tim 2:12), which according to the tradition has meant teaching authoritatively from the pulpit, celebrating the Eucharist, and presiding over a congregation. A πρεσβύτερος *presbyteros* is to be "the husband of one wife" (Titus 1:5–6), which is the same requirement for the ἐπίσκοπος *episcopos* or overseer and the διάκονος *diakonos* or deacon (1 Tim 3:2, 12).

Paul is adamant that these are not just his own opinions but come from the Lord Jesus. When he writes to Corinth that women should not "speak in church" authoritatively as leaders of a congregation, he adds, "If anyone thinks that he is a prophet, or spiritual, he should acknowledge that the things I am writing to you are a command of the Lord. If anyone does not recognize this, he is not recognized" (1 Cor 14:35, 37–38). Nor, according to Paul, was it a local policy to address a merely local problem. Women were not to lead congregations or preach authoritatively "as in all the churches of the saints" (1 Cor 14:33).

Paul also made clear that these rules were not remedial measures for a fallen creation. He appeals to events before the Fall: women were not to teach authoritatively or exercise authority over a congregation because "Adam was formed first, then Eve" (1 Tim 2:13). Women were to "pray or prophesy" with their heads covered because "man was not made from woman but woman from man. Neither was man created for woman but woman for man" (1 Cor 11:8–9).

For Paul, then, male authority in the Church derives not from a fallen condition but from the creation order. Male headship is not sinful patriarchy but God's original order for humanity. In fact, the form of the fall reinforces male headship. Eve took the initiative rather than Adam and did not consult with Adam ("who was with her" Gen 2:6). Adam should have protected her from Satan and reminded her of God's commands.

Corroborating Evidence

Because Anglicans have been living with female bishops, priests, and deacons for a half-century, we tend to forget that this is a recent innovation without Biblical support against a tradition that stretches back more than three thousand years into our Jewish roots. Therefore, it is easy to miss the numerous corroborations in Scripture that are on the plain surface of the text.

For example, *God's names*. God names himself in Scripture as a "he." In the Old Testament *YHWH* is masculine in reference. In the New Testament God's name is Father, Son, and Holy Spirit. The Father and Son are obviously masculine. The Spirit, while grammatically neutral, often takes a masculine pronoun. Feminine pronouns are never used for God in the Bible. While males and females are both made in the image of God and God therefore has female aspects, they are still "his" aspects. He is never said to be a "she." Jesus says he would have liked to gather Jerusalem to himself as a mother hen gathers her brood (Matt 23:37), but he never calls God "mother."

Adam names. As the great OT scholar Gerhard von Rad observed, naming in the biblical world was an act of authority. Adam was chosen to name the animals, and God brought Adam to Eve to give her a name. These were symbolic actions that people in the ancient world understood to be signs of Adam having authority over Eve.

Adam, not Eve, represents the human race. Throughout Scripture it is Adam who represents all of God's human creation. Christ is the second Adam (1 Cor 15:45); "in Adam all die" (Rom 5:12, 14; 1 Cor 15:22). God uses a man, not a woman, to represent humanity—both in creation and sin, and in redemption and righteousness: "Just as sin came into the world through one man ... much more will those who receive the abundance of grace and the free gift of righteousness reign in life through the one man Jesus Christ" (Rom 5:12, 17).

Junia (Rom 16:7): Some think of Junia as a female apostle because Paul says Junia and Andronicus are ἐπίσημοι ἐν τοῖς ἀποστόλοις *epistemoi en tois apostolois*. The ESV translates this phrase, "well known to the apostles." Paul might have been using ἀπόστολς *apostolos* here to mean "messenger," as he did in 2 Corinthians 8:23 ("as for our brothers, they are messengers [ἀπόστολοι *apostoloi*] of the churches") and Philippians 2:25 ("I have felt it necessary to send Epaphroditus ... your messenger [ἀπόστολον *apostolon*] and minister to my need"). The NRSV rendering "Andronicus and Junia ... are prominent among the apostles" conflicts with every other reference in the New Testament to apostles as males, and translations such as the ESV make better sense of the literary and theological contexts.

Of course, there are difficult situations, both in Scripture and modern life, where spiritual headship seems ambiguous. Because Barak was not willing to lead without the help of Deborah, she—the prophetess, judge, and mother in Israel—reluctantly joined Barak when he routed Sisera and all his chariots (Judg 4–5). There is no indication that Deborah fought in battle, but she clearly strengthened Barak when he needed it. Timothy's mother apparently gave young Timothy spiritual direction because her husband was not a believer (2 Tim 1:5; Acts 16:1). There are difficult and extraordinary situations where women must exercise spiritual headship, but the home and Church should always try to return to the biblical order. Hard cases make bad law, and abnormal situations should not dictate regular order.

The Divine Pattern: Family

Scripture makes clear that Holy Order reflects a pattern of *family* that stretches from heaven to earth, from the Trinity to the home and Church. God the Father is the head of the divine family that is the Trinity, the father and husband is called to head the family in the home, and the male Messiah Jesus (Christ) is the head of his Body, the Church.

Paul deliberately connects the words for Father and family to show that family is the connecting pattern and male leadership is the norm: "For this reason I bow my knees before the Father [πατέρα patera], from whom every family [πατριά patria] in heaven and on earth is named" (Eph 3:14–15).

Once again, Paul indicates that the ordering of headship in this pattern of family goes back before the Fall. The headship of the husband in the nuclear family, which is a type of Christ's headship of the Church family that is His body, is rooted in creation, not the fallen order. After saying that wives are to submit to their husbands because the husband is the head of the wife as Christ is the head of the Church, his Body (Eph 5:22–23), Paul grounds this in Genesis 2 given before sin entered the picture: "'Therefore a man shall leave his father and mother and hold fast to his wife, and the two shall become one flesh.' This mystery is profound, and I am saying that it refers to Christ and the church" (Eph 5:31–32).

Scripture's point, taught by the tradition for three thousand years, is that God has revealed himself as a divine family headed by the Father, and that this pattern of male headship is replicated in the families of the home and Church.

Principal Objections

Mark Twain reportedly said that it was not the parts of the Bible that he couldn't understand that bothered him but the parts that he did understand. Similarly, it is not difficult to see that Scripture and the tradition teach male headship in the family of the home and the family of the Church, both patterned after God's Fatherhood in the Trinity and his creation. The problem is not that these texts are unclear but that it is impossible to square them with the modern rejection of hierarchy in the home and Church.

Moderns often presume that headship is arbitrary and will always oppress because it involves power. While painful experience in a fallen world might point to this as conclusive, all this changes in Christ's relationship with his Church. Christ is the Head of the Church, and as she submits to his headship she grows in joy and fruitfulness. As E. L. Mascall put it, the fundamental relation of the Church to Christ

> is not one of inferiority but of membership and reception of communicated sonship. And behind St Paul's thought about the man and the woman we must surely see the story of the creation of Eve from the side of Adam, in which the fundamental relation is not one of inferiority but of mutual perfection and of derived partnership: *I will make him a helper fit for him* (Gen. 2:18).[2]

While for Mascall, Christ's headship means that male headship in home and Church is not inherently oppressive, some Anglicans disagree. Not only do they see all notions of headship as oppressive, but some suggest that any case for headship arguing from the Trinity requires an Arian view of the Son. Besides, they say, we do not know enough "about the immanent Trinity to say very much at all," and "the analogy between the divine Persons and human beings" is not "remotely apt."[3]

---

[2] E. L. Mascall, *Women and the Priesthood of the Church* (London: The Church Literature Association, 1960), 33–34.

[3] "The Holy Orders Task Force Final Report," for the ACNA College of Bishops, 2017, anglicanchurch.net/wp-content/uploads/2020/07/HolyOrdersTaskForce-printable.pdf, 266.

We agree that "models of the Trinity" have sometimes been used mischievously, and that these models have been constructed in ways remote from the clear testimony of Scripture, but we believe that while the Trinity is a mystery beyond human comprehension, Scripture makes clear some things that we can know about the relations among the Father, Son, and Holy Spirit. Among these is the Father's headship over the Son and the Spirit. It was the Father who sent the Son, not vice-versa (John 4:34; 5:36; 6:38; 8:29; 14:24; 17:8). The Spirit proceeds from the Father (John 14:26).[4] As both the Creed and Scripture tell us, Jesus' kingdom shall have no end (Luke 1:33; Rev 11:15), but after the end of history the Father is still head: "Then comes the end.... When all things are subjected to him, then the Son himself will also be subjected to him who put all things in subjection under him, that God may be all in all" (1 Cor 15:24, 28). Jesus told the disciples at the Last Supper that he would not drink of the fruit of the vine again until "I drink it new with you in my Father's kingdom" (Matt 26:29). Paul tells us, "The head of Christ is God" (1 Cor 11:3). Elsewhere he suggests the Father's headship of the Trinity (Eph 1:3; 4:6), as does Peter (1 Pet 1:2). In Revelation, the Lamb is distinguished from the One who sits upon the throne (Rev 4:2; 5:1, 6–7, 13). Scripture makes clear what the Creed pronounces, that the Son is "God from God, Light from Light, true God from true God ... one in being with the Father." We reject Arian views of the Son, as Scripture and tradition do.

The upshot, then, is that there is a relation of eternal headship in the Trinity, where the Father is always the head over the Son and the Spirit, with the second and third Persons equal in essence and nature but under the Father's headship. This, unsurprisingly, is reflected in the home and Church.

Just Local Problems

Anglicans have also objected that Paul's strictures on ministry were simply "correctives to specific abuses in the early Christian movements."[5] That is, they were local or temporary problems. The women in Corinth and Timothy's churches were interrupting and asking inappropriate questions. They were not willing to learn in silence. They were insisting on teaching in a formal manner that would usurp local authority or lord it over men.

Yet, as we have seen, Paul wrote that these were his rules in all (not just some) churches, and this was from the Lord not himself. In some circumstances, women could speak (prophesying in Corinth, e.g.) and teach (Priscilla and Aquila teaching Apollos, e.g.), but not in a way that would exercise authority over a congregation. There is no suggestion in Scripture that these rules were merely temporary. Instead, their foundation is God's creation order.

Concessions to Greco-Roman Patriarchy

Proponents of women's ordination have also argued that New Testament restrictions were "tactical and temporary concessions to the ambient Greco-Roman patriarchy in the first century."[6] That is, patriarchy was the order of the day in ancient culture. Paul and

---

[4] Sometimes Scripture refers to the "Spirit of the Son" (e.g., Rom 8:9), but it also testifies that the Son sends the Spirit "from the Father" (John 15:26; Acts 2:33).

[5] "The Holy Orders Task Force Final Report," 263.

[6] "The Holy Orders Task Force Final Report," 263.

Jesus knew of no other social or religious possibility, and both realized that gender egalitarianism would ruin the Church's chances for growth, but their revolutionary treatment of women pointed to future egalitarian roles in the Church.

This objection makes sense if Paul, for example, did not know of other possibilities. But he did. The ancient world was full of altars and shrines with priestesses. Ephesus was dominated by an enormous temple to Artemis (Diana), led by a female priest and her female assistants. Thus, female presbyters in the early Church would not have been revolutionary. They were all over the Mediterranean world, and particularly in the backyard of one of the early Church's most important centers, yet none of the elders in the church at Ephesus was female (Acts 20:17–38); all the articles and pronouns designating the elders are masculine. Moreover, as we have seen above, every instruction about headship in the church limits it to males. There is not one female priest or elder in either the Old or New Testament. The only female priests we know in the early Church were in its heretical branches—among the Montanists and Gnostics.

Jesus was revolutionary indeed, permitting women to sit at his feet learning from him, to travel with him, to talk with him in public in ways that broke social conventions, and to be his first public witnesses. He could have appointed a woman as one of the Twelve, but he did not. To ordain a woman to headship in the Church, suggests not only that Christ was wrong to choose only male apostles but also that God was wrong to have chosen his Son to become a man and not a woman. In sacramental ministry the celebrant at the Eucharist stands *in persona Christi* (in the person or place of Christ), reenacting the Last Supper. As C. S. Lewis argued, to say that a woman can represent Christ at the altar is to deny that Scripture is inspired when it taught us to speak of God with masculine imagery.[7]

Would Jesus have approved of women as heads in the home or Church if ancient culture had changed its approach to patriarchy? Not likely, because ancient culture already accepted goddesses and female priests. Furthermore, if the Bible had grounded its rules for leadership in the fallen order, then an argument for female headship might have worked, but the Bible grounds these rules for the family and Church in creation and makes it clear that these reflect an eternal order.

The Diaconate

The tradition has taught that there is one Holy Order in three degrees. It is ontological: it changes the inner being of those on whom it is conferred. This is true of deacons no less than priests or bishops, and it is one reason why the tradition has restricted all three degrees to men.[8]

Richard Hooker, the preeminent Anglican theologian of the Reformation period, affirmed this ontological character of ordination for "clergy" who are "either presbyters or deacons" (*Laws of Ecclesiastical Polity* 5.77.8): "Christ hath imparted power ... a kind of mark or character and acknowledged to be indelible ... and maketh them a special *order*

---

[7] C. S. Lewis, "Priestesses in the Church?" in Ben Jefferies, ed., *No Other Foundation: Essays on Women's Ordination in the Anglican Church* (Omaha: North American Anglican Press, 2021), 47.

[8] Aidan Nichols, *Holy Order: Apostolic Priesthood from the New Testament to the Second Vatican Council* (N.p.: Dominican Council, 1990; reprinted by Wipf and Stock, n.d.).

consecrated unto the service of the Most High in things wherewith others may not meddle.... They are a distinct *order*" (*Laws* 5.77.2).

The Ordinal in the 1662 *Book of Common Prayer* affirmed this ontological character of Anglican ministry by adding the Bishop's prayer for a priest at the laying on of hands, "Receive the holy Ghost for the Office and work of a priest in the Church of God.... Whose sins thou dost forgive, they are forgiven; and whose sins thou dost retain, they are retained. And be thou a faithful Dispenser of the Word of God, and of his holy Sacraments."

The 2019 BCP suggests the same in its Ordinal for both deacons ("Receive the Holy Spirit for the Office and work of a Deacon") and priests ("Receive the Holy Spirit for the office and work of a Priest in the Church of God. If you forgive the sins of anyone.... If you withhold forgiveness.... Be a faithful minister of God's holy Word and Sacraments.")

Both the discipline and the liturgy of the Church throughout its early history insisted on a very clear distinction between male deacons and female deaconesses.[9] Based on this early Church model of ministry, women cannot be ordained as deacons but may be set apart for ministry as deaconesses. They would exercise a variety of ministries under the authority of the rector or bishop, such as pastoral care, counseling, caring for the sick and poor, teaching, spiritual formation, prayer ministry, preparing candidates for baptism and confirmation, assisting at baptisms, leading Morning and Evening Prayer, and conducting other forms of social and educational work.

Scripture speaks of Phoebe as a διάκονος *diakonos* or servant (Rom 16:1) but limits the diaconate to men: Deacons are to be "husbands of one wife" (1 Tim 3:12). The γυναῖκας *gynaikas* in 1 Timothy 3:11 have different qualifications from those of deacons, are evidently doing something other than what male deacons do, and so are best translated by the plain sense "wives."[10] The word διάκονος *diakonos* is used by Paul to refer to the office of deacon only in Philippians 1:1 and 1 Timothy, where it is used in conjunction with ἐπίσκοπος *episkopos*. Elsewhere it is the generic term for "servant" or "helper" (Rom 15:8; Gal 2:17; 1 Thess 3:2; Col 1:7, 23, 25; 4:7; Eph 3:7; 6:21; 1 Cor 3:5; 2 Cor 3:6; 11:15, 23; 1 Tim 4:6; Titus 1:9).

In the early Church, the ministry of deaconesses was separate from that of deacons. They were not ordained as deacons but were set apart as deaconesses for ministries in keeping with their Marian charism. This continued after the apostolic era. In the *Apostolic Tradition* (c. 215), only bishops, priests, and deacons were ordained by the laying on of hands. All other ministries—widows, lectors, virgins, subdeacons, and those with healing gifts—were expressly forbidden to receive the laying on of hands because "ordination is for clerics destined for liturgical service." The diaconate was limited to

---

[9] Aimé Martimort, *Deaconesses: An Historical Study*, trans. K. D. Whitehead (San Francisco: Ignatius, 1986; orig. *Les Deaconesses* [1982]); see chapters 1-7, especially "The Liturgy for the Ordination of Deaconesses." This sums up his study: "However solemn may have been the ritual by which she was initiated into her ministry, however much it may have resembled the ritual for the ordination of a deacon, the conclusion nevertheless must be that a deaconess in the Byzantine rite was in no wise a female deacon" (156). Deaconesses had no strictly sacramental office and were not near the altar during a Eucharist when a priest was presiding.

[10] Besides, as the NET Bible notes, "It would be strange for the author to discuss women deacons right in the middle of qualifications for male deacons."

men. Women in other ministries were set apart for service to the Church by the bishop with prayer only and were excluded from liturgical functions.

At the Council of Nicaea (325), Canon 19 (on receiving the followers of Paul of Samosata back into the Church) states, "Clergy must be rebaptized and then ordained by a bishop of the Catholic Church.... The same thing must be done with respect to the deaconesses [but] they have received no laying on of hands and are thus to be counted among the laity."

Later ordinations made very clear distinctions between the ordinations of deacons and deaconesses, using different prayers and ordination rubrics for each order to distinguish their different charisms and ministries.[11] Only the heretical Montanist sect ordained women to the same diaconate, presbyterate, and episcopate as men.[12]

The Biblical Model for Resolving Church Disputes

How should we resolve the dispute over women in ministry? The Jerusalem Council in Acts 15 is the biblical model for resolving disputes about new rites in the Church. After much debate whether gentile believers must be circumcised, Paul and Barnabas were appointed to discuss "this question" with "the apostles and elders in Jerusalem" (v. 12). Resolution was gained only when it "seemed good to the Holy Spirit and to us" (v. 28), to "the whole church" (v. 22).

Thus, the rule for the early Church in resolving disputes was to accept only rites that accorded with Scripture as understood by the whole church. The early Church leaders believed not only that Scripture was the Word of God, but also that "the Church of the living God [is] a pillar and buttress of truth" (1 Tim 3:15).

Rites for women's ordination have been approved without the consent of the whole Church. They have come from a minority of the world's churches, and from churches that are heretical and dying. This is a new and (mostly) Western development.

The Anglican Church in North America (ACNA) College of Bishops conceded this in 2017, when it concluded that women's ordination was a "recent innovation" with "insufficient scriptural warrant."[13] This new way of understanding men and women deviates from the way the one, holy, catholic, and apostolic Church has understood Holy Order for two millennia. For these reasons, women's ordination has been divisive, and will prevent Anglican churches who embrace it from full communion with the largest and oldest Christian churches in the world. We make our argument, then, not only for the sake of fidelity to Scripture but also for the sake of unity in God's Church.

---

[11] Martimort, *Deaconesses*, 146-64.

[12] Regarding vestries, however, we agree that since the vestry is responsible for "the temporalities of the congregation" and not "spiritual leadership" (ACNA Constitution and Canons 6.5), women may serve on them.

[13] "A Statement from the College of Bishops on the Ordination of Women," Sept. 7, 2017, https://anglicanchurch.net/college-of-bishops-statement-on-the-ordination-of-women.

Chapter 12

Hierarchical Power[*]

The Rev. Dr. Hans Boersma

Introduction

Hierarchy is in trouble. I am not telling you anything new. We all know our society is strictly egalitarian; so, unfortunately, is much of the church. Anglicans, too, are often wary of hierarchy, or, at the very least, they find it difficult to justify hierarchy in the face of objections. The reasons for this state of affairs are fairly straightforward: we tend to associate hierarchy with medieval feudalism, obscurantism, unfairness, and, especially, oppressive power and violence. As moderns, we celebrate the equal opportunity that a non-stratified, egalitarian society offers, and we take courage from the horizontalizing or flattening of its horizons, for it treats everyone as equals and hence offers protection against arbitrary power from above—or so we think. In short, modernity associates hierarchy with imposition of power and aims to eradicate this evil by replacing hierarchy with equality, vertical stratification with horizontal relationality.

In this chapter, I will examine the presuppositions underlying this critique of hierarchy. To do so is imperative for a variety of reasons. At a fundamental level, hierarchy would seem to be endemic to a Christian metaphysic: God transcends angels, who transcend human beings, who transcend animals, who transcend plants, who transcend inanimate objects. It is not a coincidence, I think, that the egalitarianism of modernity has coincided, historically, with the substitution of reason for revelation and human authority for divine authority. What is more—speaking as an Anglican among Anglicans—we cannot understand the nature of the Church without the concept of hierarchy. The very structure of our episcopal system—laity, deacons, priests, bishops— is hierarchical. To let go of hierarchy is to let go of the very structure of the Church as the tradition has passed it on to us. (Of course, to some this might not seem all that tragic, but regardless of our evaluation of such a loss, the truth is that it would result in a different ecclesial structure than the one we have inherited. And to me, at least, it would be an intolerable break with tradition.) The priority of revelation and divine authority and our ecclesial structures are probably the most obvious issues at stake in how we deal with hierarchy.

Here I aim to investigate the principles that undergird a hierarchical metaphysic. I will do so by turning to the sixth-century Syrian monk Dionysius, in part because he was the first to use the term *hierarchy* and wrote extensively about its relation to power, and in part because Dionysius thought deeply about hierarchy both in terms of the structures of reality in general and in terms of ecclesial structures. I hope to show that the Dionysian hierarchy, which undergirded church and society in the Middle Ages, did indeed have the functioning of power at its center, but not the kind of power that violently imposes itself upon the disenfranchised and marginalized but the kind that lovingly lifts others into the very heart of God. I will also try to turn the tables on

---

[*] This article was first published in adapted form in *Touchstone: A Journal of Mere Christianity* 36/2 (March/April 2023): 24–30.

modernity by briefly comparing the implications of an egalitarian, nominalist metaphysic with those of a hierarchical, participatory metaphysic. My basic argument is that when power is embedded within a hierarchical, participatory metaphysic, it serves to uplift others into God himself. By contrast, the modern atomizing and mapping of creaturely beings onto a strictly horizontal map of creaturely beings requires centralized power structures to manage and control individual beings. Put differently, within a hierarchical view of reality, power serves to lift up rather than to oppress, whereas within an egalitarian view of reality, power naturally oppresses people rather than lifting them up.

The Purpose of Power

Dionysius, through much of the Christian tradition identified with Dionysius the Areopagite mentioned in Acts 17 as being converted through Saint Paul's sermon on Mars Hill, articulates his theology mainly in four books: *The Divine Names (DN)*, *The Mystical Theology (MT)*, *The Celestial Hierarchy (CH)*, and *The Ecclesiastical Hierarchy (EH)*. The first two are in some ways markedly different from the last two, as the titles intimate: *The Divine Names* and *The Mystical Theology* discuss the question of how it is that we can name God, considering his transcendence, while *The Celestial Hierarchy* and *The Ecclesiastical Hierarchy* deal with the divinely ordered structures of angels and of the church. Still, the two are closely linked. To understand how Dionysius viewed hierarchical power, we need to look at his discussion of angelic and ecclesial hierarchies against the backdrop of the participatory metaphysic that he outlines in *The Divine Names* and *The Mystical Theology*.

Before we ask after the role of power in Dionysius's hierarchies, we should investigate what he meant by *hierarchy*. He defines it in chapter 3 of *The Celestial Hierarchy* as

> a sacred order (τάξις ἱερὰ) and knowledge and operation, assimilated, as far as attainable, to the likeness (ἀφομοιουμένη) of God, and lifted up (ἀναγομένη) to the illuminations granted to it from God, according to capacity (ἀναλόγες), with a view to divine imitation. Now the God-befitting Beauty, as simple, as good, as source of initiation, is altogether free from any unlikeness (ἀνομοιότητος), and it imparts its own proper light to each according to their worth (ἀξίαν), and harmoniously perfects through divine initiation the form, indistinguishable from itself, of those who are being initiated.[1]

A little further in the same chapter, Dionysius ventures a second attempt at defining the term:

---

[1] *CH* 3.1 (164D). The most well-known translations of Dionysius's works are the following three: *The Works of Dionysius the Areopagite*, trans. John Parker, 2 vols. (London: James Parker, 1897–1899); *Pseudo-Dionysius: The Complete Works*, trans. Colm Luibheid; ed. Paul Rorem, Classics of Western Spirituality (New York: Paulist Press, 1987); and *The Divine Names and The Mystical Theology*, trans. and ed. John D. Jones, Mediæval Philosophical Texts in Translation 21 (Milwaukee, WI: Marquette, 2011). I use Parker's translation, while throughout I make significant changes to it, without indicating this each time.

He, then, who mentions hierarchy, denotes a certain altogether sacred arrangement (ἱεράν ... διακόσμησιν), an image of the supremely divine blossoming, ministering the mysteries of its own illumination in hierarchical ranks and understandings, and assimilated to its own proper head as far as lawful.[2]

Hierarchy, for Dionysius, is a sacred order or arrangement. The order contains members with varying degrees of dissimilarity to God. These members of the hierarchy are meant to be lifted up (ἀνάγειν), each in accordance with the mode of its own being (according to its own capacity or ἀναλογία), toward the simple Beauty or Goodness of God, in the process more and more being assimilated to God, whose perfection implies that he has no unlikeness at all. Dionsyus, then, repeatedly uses the language of being lifted up (ἀνάγειν) or, as Dionysius also calls it, being hierarchized (ἱεραρχεῖσθαι).

It is crucial to observe that to hierarchize does not mean to control or to rule. To be sure, hierarchies and hierarchizing have everything to do with order and ranks. But when a hierarchy hierarchizes, this simply means that, in line with their created distinctiveness, the various beings are lifted up, so as to become more like God. This means that the role of the various hierarchies is mystagogical. Dionysius writes his book *The Ecclesiastical Hierarchy* for "those who have been initiated with the initiation of the sacred mystagogy (μυσταγωγίας), derived from the hierarchical mysteries (μυστηρίων)."[3] The role of a mystagogue is to initiate others into certain religious mysteries.[4] For example, in the centuries preceding Dionysius, mystagogical catechesis served to explain to newly baptized Christians the meaning of the mysteries enacted in the liturgy.[5] Dionysius puts it this way: "Let us view our hierarchy, conformably to ourselves, abounding in the variety of the sensible symbols, by which, in proportion to our capacity, we are conducted, hierarchically (ἱεραρχικῶς ... ἀναγόμεθα) according to our measure, to the uniform deification (θέωσιν)—God and divine virtue."[6] The aim of every hierarchy is for the members to be lifted up into God—deification.

Power, on a Dionysian hierarchical understanding, serves only one purpose: to facilitate the mystagogical return (ἐπιστροφή) of creatures to God, from whom they have come by way of procession (πρόοδος). Power serves not to put down or to oppress; it serves the process of returning to God. A telling section in the fifth chapter of *The Ecclesiastical Hierarchy* discusses the power (δύναμις) of the sacraments, the ministers, and the initiates. Sacraments have three powers (δυνάμεις): purification of the uninitiated, illumination of those who are purified, and perfection of those being instructed. Ministers, too, have three powers: purification of the uninitiated through the sacraments; illumination of those purified; and perfection of their understanding. Finally, the initiates themselves have three powers: the power of being purified, of being

---

[2] *CH* 3.2; 165B.

[3] *EH* 1.1; 372A.

[4] Cf. Alexander Golitzin with Bogdan G. Bucur, *Mystagogy: A Monastic Reading of Dionysius Areopagita*, ed. Bogdan G. Bucur, Cistercian Studies Series 250 (Collegeville, MN: Liturgical, 2013).

[5] Cf. Enrico Mazza, *Mystagogy: A Theology of Liturgy in the Patristic Age* (New York: Pueblo, 1989). See also the recent book by Hanna Lucas, *Sensing the Sacred: Recovering a Mystagogical Vision of Knowledge and Salvation*, Veritas 48 (Eugene, OR: Cascade, 2023).

[6] *EH* 1.2; 373B.

illuminated, and of perfecting the understanding.[7] In short, power is the ability to guide or be guided through the process of purification, illumination, and perfection.

True, Dionysius's hierarchies offer a dazzling outline of heavenly and ecclesial structures: angels are divided into three hierarchical groupings of three: seraphim, cherubim, and thrones; dominions, powers, and authorities; and, finally, principalities, archangels, and angels. The church is structured by way of hierarch, priest, and deacon; monks, laity, and uninitiated; and, within that last group, catechumens, penitents, and demon-possessed. The overall structure looks something like this:

Diagram 1: Celestial and Ecclesiastical Hierarchies

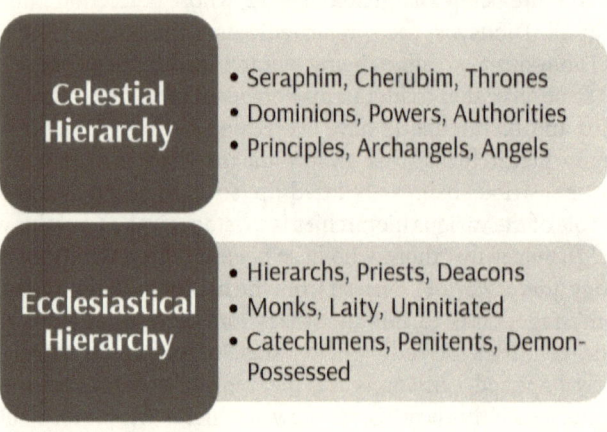

To a modern mindset, what is perhaps most troubling about this structure is its seemingly static character. We insist on equal opportunity; we want a chance to advance. Dionysius's categories seem static and do not seem to allow for this kind of upward mobility. The criticism is partly on-target: once an archangel always an archangel; archangels do not become seraphim. The heavenly hierarchy does not change. On the other hand, within the ecclesial hierarchy, some degree of movement is possible. Deacons can become priests and hierarchs. Catechumens have the intention of advancing to the rank of the laity, and some of them may end up becoming deacons or priests. Some, mostly limited, upward mobility is possible, at least within the ecclesial hierarchy.

Dionysius, however, does not even discuss such upward mobility. What matters for him is to move up into God. To give but one example, for Dionysius, if I am a priest, my aim is not to become a bishop. That might, for a variety of reasons, be a terrifying prospect.

Dionysius describes the role of priests as follows:

> The illuminating rank (τάξις) of the priests conducts those who are being initiated to the divine visions of the mystic rites [i.e., the Eucharist], doing so under the rank (τάξει) of the inspired hierarchs, hierarchizing (ἱερουργοῦσα) its own hierarchies

---

[7] *EH* 5.1.3; 504A–B.

(ἱερουργίας) in co-operation with them. Whatever then this rank may do, by showing the works of God through the most holy symbols and by perfecting (ἀποτελοῦσα) those who draw near in the divine contemplations, and in communion of the holy rites, it yet refers to the hierarch those who desire an understanding of the sacred rites contemplated.[8]

The role of the priest is to prepare catechumens for the celebration of the Eucharist, to give them a proper understanding of it, so they may properly contemplate what they are about to celebrate. This very process of instruction not only perfects the initiates but also leads to the priests' own hierarchizing. In other words, their service to the rank below them allows them to engage more fully themselves the deifying process of returning to God. Precisely by knowing our place within the hierarchy, by accepting and inhabiting it—the aspects that most bother moderns for their static implications—we unleash the dynamism inherent within the hierarchy.

God Beyond Being

As we will see momentarily, to be lifted up or hierarchized is to participate more intensely or deeply in the Being, Life, and Wisdom of God. Before I explore what Dionysius writes about this, we need to reflect on God's own relationship to the cosmos and its various hierarchies. Dionysius comes closest to sketching an overall metaphysic in *The Divine Names*, where he discusses what it is that we do when we name God. Our ability to do so is a pressing issue for Dionysius because of an unprecedented emphasis on God's transcendence in his theology. Western theologians are accustomed to talk about God as Being. We speak about him primarily in positive or kataphatic language. We recognize, of course, that such language does not adequately capture what God is. We, therefore, build in caveats, particularly that of analogy: God is wise *in a unique fashion*; Socrates was wise *in a human mode*. God is being itself—*esse ipsum subsistens*, in Thomas Aquinas's celebrated phrase—so that his very essence is to be or to exist.[9] By contrast, we merely participate in creaturely being—*esse commune*—which makes us contingent, ephemeral beings; for us, existing or being is by no means our essence. Put differently, God's being or existing is divine; ours is human. This built-in caveat of analogy lets us use positive language about God: God *is* wisdom; God *is* being—all the while recognizing that because of the dissimilarity inherent in analogy, we are limited in understanding what this actually means.

For Dionysius, it was not enough to speak of God in terms of being. Influenced as he was by the Neoplatonic philosophers Plotinus and Proclus, Dionysius foregrounded negative or apophatic language about God. Time and again, the Areopagite speaks of

---

[8] *EH* 5.1.6 (505D–508A).

[9] Alan Philip Darley is rightly critical of recent readings of Thomas Aquinas that read him through a Dionysian lens, insisting that Aquinas's "primary perfection term is Being which, in contrast to the Dionysian God 'beyond being,' applies to God literally and pre-eminently." "'We Know in Part': How the Positive Apophaticism of Aquinas Transforms the Negative Theology of Pseudo-Dionysius," *Heythrop Journal* 63 (2022): 583–612, esp. 583.

God as Beyond Being (ὑπερούσιος).[10] He freely uses terms such as the One (τὸ ἕν) Goodness (τἀγαθόν), and Beauty (τὸ κάλλος) to refer to this God Beyond Being.[11] But even these exalted Plotinian terms, which reach beyond the realm of being, do not adequately capture who God is. We use these names, not because we thereby capture God; rather, we speak of God as One to indicate that, in a unique manner, he is all things and is the cause of all things, without losing his own oneness (DN 13.2; 977C). And we speak of him as Goodness and as Beauty to make clear that he is the cause of every good and beautiful thing. "This," writes Dionysius, "the one Good and Beautiful, is uniquely the cause of all the many things beautiful and good" (DN 4.7; 740B). But because God is actually beyond any of these concepts, we have to negate even these concepts of One, Goodness, and Beauty or, rather, move beyond them. The hidden God is Beyond Oneness (τὸ ὑπερηνωμένον) (DN 13.3; 981A)—at least, the way we commonly understand oneness. Similarly, he is Beyond Good (ὑπεράγαθόν) (DN 4.2; 696C–D). And he is Beyond Beauty (ὑπέρκαλον) (DN 4.7; 701D).

It should be obvious that, for Dionysius, the language of *esse* will not do to describe God. The philosophical tradition, beginning already with Parmenides, taught Dionysus that being implies intelligibility.[12] To say that God is Being would mean, for Dionysius, that our concepts can encapsulate God. Such a God could not possibly be transcendent. Dionysius, therefore, relegates Being to the Plotinian realm of Intellect (νοῦς), which is a step down from the utterly unknowable and ineffable deity. For Dionysius, when we move into the darkness beyond Intellect (ὑπὲρ νοῦν), we end up with complete speechlessness (ἀλογία) and unknowing (ἀνοησία).[13] The concluding paragraph of *The Mystical Theology* is far-reaching in its apophatic claim. The cause of all, suggests Dionysius,

> is neither soul, nor mind, nor has imagination, or opinion, or reason, or conception; neither is expressed, nor conceived; neither is number, nor order, nor greatness, nor littleness; nor equality, nor inequality; nor similarity, nor dissimilarity; neither is standing, nor moving; nor at rest; neither has power, nor is power, nor light; neither lives, nor is life; neither is essence nor eternity, nor time; neither is its touch intelligible, neither is it understanding, nor truth; nor kingdom, nor wisdom; neither one, nor oneness; neither deity, nor Goodness; nor is it Spirit according to our understanding; nor Sonship, nor Paternity; nor any other thing of

---

[10] The term ὑπερούσιος is difficult to translate. I follow John Jones, who translates it as "beyond being." John Parker uses the term "superessential." The difficulty with this is twofold: (1) "super" may seem to convey intensification, as if God were *notably* essential; and (2) the word "essence" may seem to indicate the form or essence of a thing, perhaps to be distinguished from its act of being. Dionysius does not have any such thing in mind, though he does distinguish God's οὐσία from his Being, Life, Wisdom, and the like, which refer to God in his providential or economic dealing with the world. Mostly, when he wants to highlight the transcendence of God as imparticipable, he speaks of God as ὑπερούσιος, though he once uses the term ὑπὲρ τὸ εἶναι (EH 4.1; 177D).

[11] See especially the discussions in DN 4.1–7 (693B–704C); 13.2–3 (977C–981B).

[12] Eric D. Perl, *Thinking Being: Introduction to Metaphysics in the Classical Tradition*, Studies in Platonism, Neoplatonism, and the Platonic Tradition 17 (Leiden: Brill, 2014), 7.

[13] MT 3; 1033C.

those known to us, or to any other existing being; neither is it any of non-existing nor of existing things, nor do things existing know it, as it is; nor does it know existing things, as existing; neither is there expression of it, nor name, nor knowledge; neither is it darkness, nor light; nor error, nor truth; neither is there any definition at all of it, nor any abstraction.[14]

Nothing positive can be said about the beyond-*esse* cause of all things. We must negate even our negative statements about God. Because he is Beyond Being, creatures cannot participate in him. Creatures participate in the Being of God, but not God as Beyond Being (ὑπερούσιος). The upshot is that to Dionysius, God is radically transcendent, and—with respect to God as ὑπερούσιος—we simply do not participate in him.

God Beyond Hierarchy

This unprecedented emphasis on God's transcendence means he cannot possibly be part of any hierarchy. He does not even occupy a place at the very top. Hierarchies have to do with being, whereas the Dionysian God Beyond Being transcends all this. Let me illustrate the importance of this claim by depicting two possible approaches to hierarchy and participation.

Diagram 2: God within Hierarchy

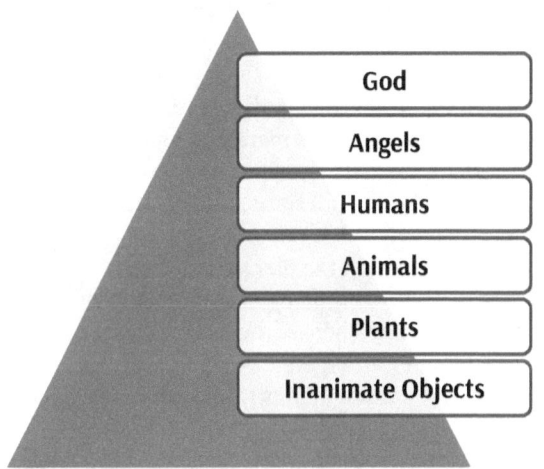

This diagram treats God as the highest level of a hierarchy. This does two things. First, it turns this God into one being among many beings. After all, here God is depicted as one item among many. The others may be much lower than he, but no matter where they are located, they, together with God, are so many links within the one chain of being.

Dionysius emphatically rejects the notion that God would be *a* being, one among many, for it would mean that within the chain of being, God and his creatures competed, as it were, for space. It would mean that whenever God exercises power in a certain

---

[14] *MT* 5 (1045D–1048B).

activity, he exercises this power instead of creatures. And, of course, the obverse would be true as well: when creatures exercise their power in a certain activity, they thereby foreclose the exercise of divine power. In other words, God's relationship with other beings would be a zero-sum game: what God does, other beings cannot do, and what they do, God cannot do. Such competition would endanger the radical alterity or transcendence of God, and Dionysius avoids this by treating God and creatures as being in a non-competitive relationship.

A non-competitive relationship gives genuine power to creatures. Human beings can cooperate with God in the process of lifting up or hierarchizing. Dionysius explains this as follows:

> Each of those who have been called into the hierarchy, finds his perfection in being carried to the divine imitation in his own proper degree (ἀναλογίαν); and, what is more divine than all, in becoming a fellow-worker (συνεργὸν) with God, as the Oracles say, and in showing the divine energy (ἐνέργειαν) in himself manifested as far as possible. For it is a hierarchical regulation that some are purified and that others purify; that some are enlightened and others enlighten; that some are perfected and others perfect; the divine imitation will fit each one in this fashion.[15]

As God enlightens creatures, each in its own way imitates God according to its creaturely capacity (ἀναλογία). God's activity (ἐνέργεια) is at work in them, so that God does what they do, and they do what God does. The creature becomes God's fellow worker (συνεργός) (cf. 1 Cor 3:9; 1 Thess 3:2). "The essence of hierarchy," explains Eric Perl, "is the sacramental principle of co-operation, or synergy. This means not merely that the creature and God 'work together' as though the creature were another being, additional to God, or that the creature's operation is merely by courtesy attributed to God, but that the activity of the creature, by participation, truly is that of God."[16] For Dionysius, synergy is possible because God is both transcendent and immanent at the same time: he is not one item within the hierarchy.

Treating God as one item within the hierarchy—at the very top, to be sure—has an additional adverse effect: God would be present directly only to the level immediately below him. Perhaps we might think here of the seraphim, cherubim, and thrones, God's highest creatures. They might participate directly in God, since they would be located immediately below him, but human beings would not; nor would elephants, let alone oak trees or rocks.

On a Dionysian understanding, no matter where a creature is located within the overall hierarchical scheme, and no matter the generous mediation offered by higher to lower levels (say, that of a priest to a catechumen), creatures nonetheless always directly participate in God, while God is directly present to them. We may perhaps picture the relationship as follows:

---

[15] CH 3.2 (3.165B).
[16] Eric D. Perl, "Hierarchy and Participation in Dionysius the Areopagite and Greek Neoplatonism," *American Catholic Philosophical Quarterly* 68 (1994): 15–30, esp. 23.

Diagram 3: God Beyond Hierarchy

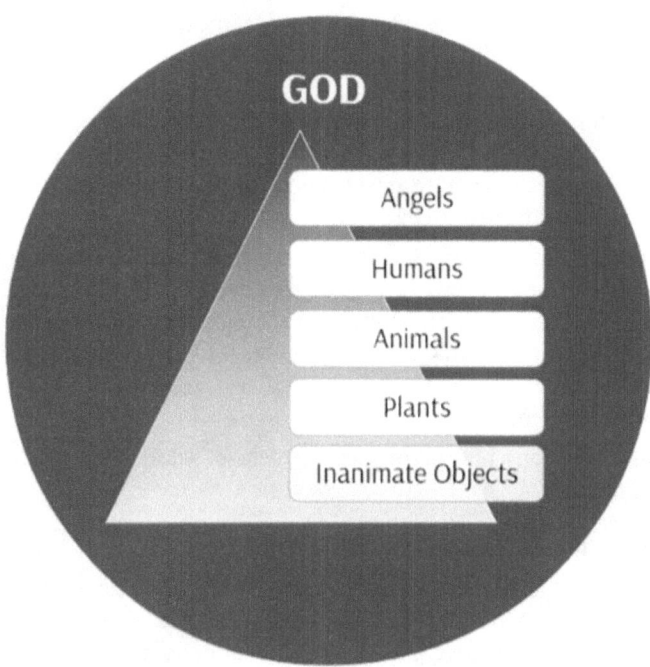

We see here that God is utterly transcendent: he is not part of the hierarchy but transcends it. He is not one being among many. That is why the diagram places God beyond the hierarchical triangle. To be sure, transcendence implies sovereignty. Scripture often does use hierarchical terminology to speak about God, employing metaphors such as king or father. Hence, also in a Dionysian hierarchy, God is "higher" than creatures.[17] After all, Dionysius speaks of God's power "lifting up" or "hierarchizing" creatures. Anagogical discourse—language of ascending to God—intimates that God is "higher" than creatures. But such vertical discourse (along with hierarchical metaphors) does not adequately capture or comprehend God. While creatures are bounded or limited (indicated by the rectangular boxes), God is unbounded or infinite (something no diagram can adequately depict). God is not part of the created hierarchy.

Because God is not circumscribed in any way and is not a being, present within the created hierarchy, he is omnipresent. He is present to every creature, and every creature participates in him—which the diagram depicts with the circle that surrounds each creature. Each creature within the hierarchy participates in the Being of God, though the different shades of green indicate varying degrees of participation. The God Beyond Being is not only radically transcendent, but he is also—precisely because of his

---

[17] I am grateful to my colleague Travis Bott for assistance in refining Diagram 3 and helping me think through my articulation of God being "higher" than creatures while at the same time being beyond every hierarchy.

transcendence—immanent to the entire created order, every level of the hierarchy. Eric Perl puts it this way: "The One *immediately* produces and is present to the *entire* sequence of hierarchical mediation. As the productive power of the whole, it is present throughout the whole."[18] For Dionysius, divine transcendence and immanence are in no way opposed to each other.

The reason Dionysius manages to combine divine transcendence and immanence is that he doesn't treat God as one of many beings. God himself is Beyond Being (ὑπερούσιος), so that he does not, in any way, need to either crowd out or make room for the beings that proceed from him. Perl writes:

> God is not a being, the first link in the great chain, standing at the summit of the cosmic hierarchy. If he were, he would be a determinate being, a member of the cosmos, one existing thing among other existing things. Rather, as the determinate being of all things, himself beyond being, God is at once transcendent and immanent, beyond the entire hierarchy of creatures and permeating the whole from top to bottom.[19]

God, according to Dionysius, permeates the whole without being any one of its constituent elements.[20]

Modern Hierarchies

The world is hierarchically structured, inescapably so. True, modernity has lost the notion of participation. As a result, we insist on strictly egalitarian social arrangements. It is not, however, like we no longer have any hierarchies. It is just that they are socially constructed and are strictly functional. My dean still tells me when to teach a course, army captains still issue military orders to their lieutenants, and in low-church settings, the pastor still writes up the mission statement, and it is with him that the buck stops. All of these, however, are functional rather than ontological hierarchies. They are the result of various social contracts rather than being grounded in the nature of things. We need these social contracts because life together would be impossible without power or hierarchy. Power, in modernity, is the result of the way in which we construct relationships. In other words, the modern social web, including its power relations, is grounded in a nominalist (constructivist) understanding of reality rather than in a realist (participatory) metaphysic.

Let me offer one final diagram, which approximates the way moderns view power—whether in church or more broadly in society:

---

[18] Eric D. Perl, *Theophany: The Neoplatonic Philosophy of Dionysius the Areopagite* (Albany: State University of New York, 2007), 77.

[19] Perl, "Hierarchy and Participation," *American Catholic Philosophical Quarterly* 68 (1994): 18.

[20] See, e.g., *DN* 5.4 (817C): "God is not somehow Being (οὐ πώς ἐστιν ὤν), but simply and unboundedly, comprehending and anticipating the whole Being in himself." Cf. also Vladimir Lossky's comment that for Dionysius, "God is not an object of knowledge; he is not even an *object*; God makes himself known in theophanies, manifesting himself diversely in the creatures that participate in his perfections." "La Notion des 'analogies' chez Denys le Pseudo-Aréopagite," *Archives d'histoire doctrinale et litteraire du moyen age* 5 (1930): 279–309, esp. 298.

Diagram 4: Modern Power

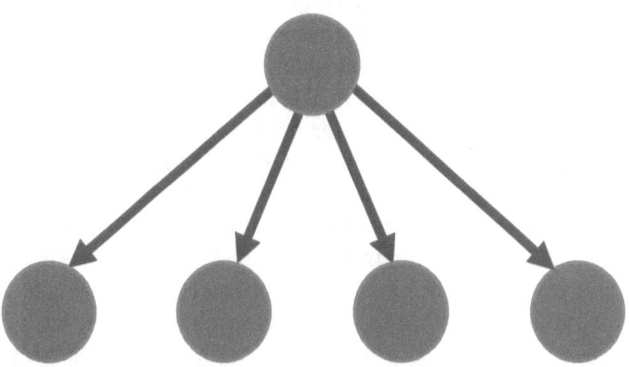

The face of power, in modern settings, purports to be much gentler than that of ancient and medieval societies. Earlier societies, so we tend to think, were brutal in their exercise of power; whereas in our enlightened world, we recognize the equality of all, so that we give power to people or institutions by assigning particular functions to them.

The reality, however, is much different. The structure in this final diagram is strictly this-worldly. The top circle is Jeff Bezos or Bill Gates or Klaus Schwab—not God. We have, at best, bracketed God and removed him from the picture. We no longer need God for power to function well, or so we think. In other words, we have a thoroughly non-participatory, nominalist universe, which for its functioning depends upon the way we structure our power relationships. The result is a voluntarist arrangement—voluntarism being a word that derives from the Latin *voluntas*—will. The Hobbesian and Lockean social contract—articulated in detail in Hobbes's *Leviathan* (1651) and Locke's *Two Treatises of Government* (1689)—depends upon the human will, which (purportedly) has agreed to yield certain powers to those in control. But the increasing power of companies such as Google, Facebook, and X makes more and more evident that large masses of people are virtually powerless in the face of the powers that impose, exclude, and censor at will. It is often the *voluntas* of one or a few individuals at the top that predetermines the outcome of our social debates.

I suspect that Charles V, Holy Roman Emperor at the time of the Reformation, would have been green with envy at the power at Bill Gates's disposal. The reason for the emperor's comparative lack of power should be obvious: Charles V functioned within a hierarchical feudal system with mediating powers, such as monarchs, nobles, knights, and peasants, as well as a variety of often pesky ecclesial figures—monks, priests, bishops, popes. These mediating and overlapping powers stood in the way of any emperor who would attempt arbitrarily or unilaterally to impose his will.[21] Voluntarism—as depicted in diagram 4—knows no mediating powers. And where they do continue to exist, they have largely been robbed of genuine influence. An egalitarian society is one that, in principle, has opened itself up to totalitarian rule—something that today only those willfully blind are still not able to see.

The most important difference, however, between power in a traditional hierarchical system and power in egalitarian societies does not concern the question of *where* power is situated—whether throughout the hierarchies (including their mediating people and institutions) or only at the top (particularly among global elites)—though that is an important difference. The greatest difference has to do with *what* we understand power to be. Egalitarians construe power as a means of control. Power is a functional thing, after all; it is something we give to people who we think will get the job done. The result is that we link power with control, whether subtle or harsh. For Dionysius, and for the Christian tradition in his wake, power is an ontological thing; it is something rooted in the nature of reality. As a result, for Dionysius, power is mystagogical in character, facilitating the return of created beings to God himself. Modern egalitarians use power to oppress and put down; Dionysian mystics use it to hierarchize and lift up.

I know, also within traditional hierarchies, power has been misused; while modern egalitarian structures witness shining examples of selfless service. How come? Sinful behavior negatively affects even the best of structures, while the image of God continues to shine no matter how confused and messed-up our structures become. Counterexamples are hardly surprising. But that, nonetheless, Christian hierarchies lift us up to heaven while modern hierarchies bring us down to hell is nothing new to those who have read and compared the founding documents of the Christian and the modern, liberal traditions.

---

[21] William T. Cavanaugh comments, "The rise of the state was not necessitated by the 'Wars of Religion'; rather, these wars were the birth pangs of the state, in which the overlapping jurisdictions, allegiances, and customs of the medieval order were flattened and circumscribed into the new creation of the sovereign state (not always yet nation-state), a centralizing power with a monopoly on violence within a defined territory." "Beyond Secular Parodies," in *Radical Orthodoxy: A New Theology*, ed. John Milbank, Graham Ward, and Catherine Pickstock (London: Routledge, 1998), 191.

Part II
Luminaries of the Tradition

The School of Christ: The Benedictine Spirit of Re-Formed Catholic Anglican Spirituality

The Rev. Michael Vinson

St. Benedict writes in the prologue to the monastic *Rule*[1] attributed to his name,

> Therefore, we must establish a school for the Lord's service. In its organization, we have tried not to create anything grim or oppressive. In a given case, we may have to arrange things a bit strictly to correct vice or preserve charity. When that happens, do not immediately take fright and flee the path of salvation, which can only be narrow at its outset. But as we progress in the monastic life and in faith, our hearts will swell with the unspeakable sweetness of love, enabling us to race along the way of God's commandments.[2]

I begin here because I believe our English Reformers shared a similar vision for laity and clergy alike: a vision for "Everyday Monks" to live the Christian life within a local parish as a kind of domestic monastery, a "School of Christ" for every baptized believer to be conformed into the *imago Dei*. Underlying this idea of "the monkhood of every believer,"[3] is the Rule of Benedict, the spirit and regulating principle of what we would call prayer book spirituality. The intent of this chapter is to develop and present what I believe is fairly obvious: the Benedictine Spirit of Re-formed Catholic Anglican Spirituality. We will begin by introducing St. Benedict and the Catholic *Regula*, then proceed to highlight the pivotal role of the three-fold Rule as the bedrock of Prayer Book Spirituality. Finally, we will make a compelling case for the Benedictine spirit as the connective tissue of Re-formed Catholic Anglican spirituality, tracing its influence from its origins to the present day.

Although this infallible and living test of orthodoxy is infrequently applied, living by this Rule of trinity-in-unity, consisting of Mass, Office, and Personal Devotion, is crucial to claiming any allegiance to historical Christian orthodoxy. Thus, the Rule of Benedict has regulated and guided Christian spirituality for over sixteen centuries, making it the foundational ascetical scheme of Western spirituality.

St. Benedict of Nursia

In the early fifth century, a young man named Benedict made a life-changing decision to abandon his studies in Rome and pursue a life of solitude in the countryside. Having "given over his books, and forsaking his father's house and wealth, with a mind only to serve God, sought for some place where he might attain to the desire of his holy

---

[1] Terrance G. Kardong, trans., *The Rule of St. Benedict in Latin and English with Notes* (Collegeville, MN: Liturgical, 1981).

[2] *Rule*, Prologue, 45–49.

[3] See Greg Peters, *The Monkhood of All Believers: The Monastic Foundation of Christian Spirituality* (Grand Rapids: Baker, 2018).

purpose."[4] At the age of twenty, Benedict made the bold decision to leave behind the prospect of secular success and pursue a life of seclusion in the village of Enfide, located in the Simbrucini mountains outside Rome.

There he performed his first miracle, which unfortunately brought him unwanted attention and notoriety. "But Benedict more desirous to suffer afflictions than covetous of praise; and rather willing to undergo labors for the honor of God, than to be extolled with the favors of this world, fled secretly from his nurse to a remote place in the desert called Subiaco, distant about forty miles from Rome."[5] The young man was more interested in suffering for the honor of God than in receiving praise from the world and fled to a cave in the desert of Subiaco, where he lived as a hermit for three years.[6] Despite his isolation, his reputation for holiness and his miraculous gifts drew people to him, and soon he had many devoted disciples. Benedict's example of selflessness and devotion to God inspires people today, demonstrating the enduring appeal of a life of faith and service.

Benedict's reputation for holiness and miracles grew so strong that nearby monks from a monastery pleaded with him to become their abbot after their own abbot passed away. Benedict reluctantly agreed, but upon arriving at the monastery, he found the community in disarray and resistant to his efforts at reform. In fact, they even attempted to poison him. Faced with such opposition, Benedict returned to his cave and continued to offer spiritual guidance to those who sought him out. Over time, he founded twelve monasteries and placed twelve monks under an Abbott.[7] He also founded a thirteenth monastery where he presided as Abbott over all of the communities he had founded. After twenty years at Subiaco, Benedict fled to Monte Cassino to escape persecution from a jealous local priest.[8]

Benedict and his disciples climbed to the highest point in the mountains at Monte Cassino, where a temple dedicated to the heathen God Apollo stood. Led by a processional cross, they cleared the woods surrounding the temple and destroyed its pagan statuary and altars. In their place, Benedict founded the Abbey of Monte Cassino, which became famous throughout Europe for its holiness and devotion to God. While there, Benedict wrote his famous *Regula, The Rule of St. Benedict*, which provided guidelines for monastic life and became a cornerstone of Western monasticism.

After his experience at Subiaco, Benedict gained vast insight into human nature and the challenges of monastic life. He knew that few people could succeed in such a rigorous lifestyle without guidance and support. Drawing on his own ascetic practices and

---

[4] Pope Gregory I, *Dialogues*, ed. and trans. Edmund G. Gardner (London: Phillip Lee Warner, 1911), 51.

[5] Gregory, *Dialogues*, 52.

[6] St. Benedict's three-year hermitage occurred sometime between AD 502 and 507.

[7] From AD 507 to 529.

[8] Pope Gregory I, known as Gregory the Great, in his biography of St. Benedict, tells the story of a priest named Florentius who was consumed by bitterness and envy upon seeing the success of Benedict. Florentius was a greedy man who coveted the gifts and reputation of Benedict's holiness. In an attempt to murder Benedict, Florentius offered him a poisonous loaf of bread. However, a crow swooped down and snatched the bread from Benedict's hand, saving his life. Upon learning that Benedict had been driven out, Florentius climbed to his balcony to witness the departure of the saint. But his joy was short-lived, as the balcony collapsed, burying the wicked priest in its ruins. This account can be found in *Dialogues* II.viii.

spiritual insights, he set out to create a *Regula* or Rule that would provide practical guidance for all members of the monastery community, regardless of their background or level of spiritual development: spiritual amateurs and proficients, clergy and lay brothers, the young and the old, the educated and ignorant. His little handbook for his monks was, in his own words, written as a "modest sketch for beginners" to "arrive at the higher peaks of doctrine and virtue" to attain "the heavenly homeland."[9]

In AD 529, St. Benedict compiled his *Regula* to govern the school of Christ at Monte Cassino, which brought together the various emerging monastic expressions of his time.[10] This *Regula* solidified the three-fold Rule of prayer, which serves as the foundation of all Catholic spirituality and is essential to the reformed-catholic spirituality of classical Prayer Book Anglicanism. Martin Thornton's book, *English Spirituality*, refers to the three-fold Rule as the greatest Benedictine achievement and *the basic Rule of the Church, shared by the East and West,* monastic and secular, and all individual schools without exception.

> Here is the basic Rule of the Church, which, varying in detail, is common to the East and West, monastic and secular, to all the individual schools without exception, and which forms the overall structure of the Book of Common Prayer. Amongst all the tests of catholicity or orthodoxy, it is curious that this infallible and living test is so seldom applied.... We fail to see that no group of Christians is true to orthodoxy if it fails to *live* by this Rule of trinity-in-unity: Mass, Office, and Devotion.[11]

Although this infallible and living test of orthodoxy is infrequently applied, living by this Rule of trinity-in-unity, consisting of Mass, Office, and Personal Devotion, is crucial to claiming any allegiance to historical Christian orthodoxy. Thus, the Rule of Benedict has regulated and guided Christian spirituality for over sixteen centuries, making it the foundational ascetical scheme of Western spirituality.

The Re-Formed Catholic *Regula* and the Book of Common Prayer

The concept of *regula*, or Rule, was central to Benedict's vision of monastic life. *Regula* is the Latin rendering of the English word *rule*, or simply the way or means by which something is ordered and regulated. He saw the Rule as a means of ordering and regulating spirituality, providing a framework for individuals to enter and participate in the Divine Trinitarian life. Benedict organized the monastic day around a three-fold trinitarian pattern of spirituality, which included the common Daily Office (*opus Dei*), personal prayer (*orationes particulares*), and weekly Eucharist (*Divina liturgia*).

The prayer book and St. Benedict's Rule stem from this ancient threefold Rule of the Catholic Church. For Anglicanism, it is crucial that its spirituality is directly linked to apostolic origins. The *Book of Common Prayer* is a remarkable example of ascetical construction, representing centuries of spiritual development. Its ascetical theology is almost as Benedictine as the *Regula* itself. The prayer book is a significant component of

---

[9] *Rule of St. Benedict*, Rule 73.

[10] St. Benedict relied heavily upon *The Rule of the Master*, a sixth-century monastic document of unknown origin, which he adapted to create his Rule.

[11] Martin Thornton, *English Spirituality* (London: SPCK, 1963), 76.

all periods of Anglican spirituality and embodies the culmination of the biblical and patristic tradition, the spirituality of the undivided Church.

Paul F. Bradshaw notes that "while the compilers of the Prayer Book believed that they were returning to the spirit and forms of prayer used in the early Church, they were actually restoring the spirituality of the fourth-century desert. This spirituality was primarily focused on personal ascetical growth, rather than on praying as a Church for the sake of the world."[12] Here Bradshaw sheds light on a key tension in the English Reformation. While the reformers sought to return to the practices and beliefs of the early Church, they did so through a lens colored by their own context and concerns. The emphasis on personal spiritual growth and the monastic way of doing things may have been well-suited to the challenges of the Reformation era, but it also represented a departure from the communal and outward-facing approach of the early church.

And yet, the Benedictine *Regula* remained the organizing principle of reformed Anglican spirituality, as evidenced by Bishop Joseph Hall, who in 1808 emphasized the three main components of God's service that Anglican spirituality is built upon: prayer, reading and hearing the holy Word, and the reception of the Sacraments. Hall writes: "There are three main businesses, wherein God accounts his service, here below, to consist. The first is, our Address to the Throne of Grace and the pouring out of our souls before him in our Prayers; the second is, the Reading and Hearing his most Holy Word; the third is, the receipt of his Blessed Sacraments; in all which, there is place in use for a settled devotion."[13] Joseph Hall's assertion is one of many examples of the three-fold Benedictine nature of re-formed catholic spirituality highlighting the importance of a settled devotion in all three areas, which remain essential for Anglican spiritual growth and stability.

The 1928 *Book of Common Prayer*, as the inheritor of re-formed catholic Anglicanism, is structured around the three-fold Rule of prayer, which consists of the Daily Offices, private devotion, and Eucharist. The Daily Offices, which include Morning and Evening Prayer, begin on page three of the Prayer Book. Additional prayers are included after the Daily Offices. Then, the Order for Holy Communion, also known as the Eucharist, begins on page sixty-seven of the prayer book. Archbishop Cranmer and the English Reformers were keen to continue the Benedictine emphasis of daily prayer, private devotion, and weekly observance of the Eucharist into the worship and spiritual lives of post-Reformation Anglicans.

The Daily Office

The structure of the monastic day, with its set times of communal prayer, was a distinctive feature of the monastic way of life. The Rule of St. Benedict codified this practice and provided guidelines for organizing the monastic day around common

---

[12] P. F. Bradshaw, *Daily Prayer in the Early Church* (London: SPCK, 1981), 73–74.
[13] *The Works of Joseph Hall*, 12 vols. (Oxford: Talboys, 1837), 6:494, google.com/books/edition/The_Works_of_Joseph_Hall/DICMkEryntUC?hl.

prayer. The seven prayer offices mentioned in Rule 16[14] were held at specific times throughout the day, with *Lauds* being the first service at daybreak, followed by *Prime, Tierce, Sext, Nones, Vespers*, and *Compline*. Each service had appointed prayers, hymns, and readings designed to help the monastic community cultivate a spirit of devotion and mindfulness of God's presence throughout the day.

Despite not being a monk, Archbishop Thomas Cranmer recognized the value of the monastic approach to prayer and spiritual discipline as he compiled the *Book of Common Prayer*. And it was through the creation of the *Book of Common Prayer* that Cranmer aimed to normalize and simplify the liturgy throughout the Anglican Church, with the monastic office at its heart. Cranmer took the seven times of day that monks and nuns prayed and reduced it to two, Morning and Evening Prayer. This made the monastic approach to prayer accessible to the laity and expected of the clergy, with the Daily Office becoming a central aspect of the Christian life for everyone. In fact, Cranmer obligated every Anglican clergyman to recite the Daily Offices of Morning and Evening Prayer, a vow he lived by, not simply because of any spiritual preference in personal piety, but as a duty becoming of the clergy.[15]

Personal Devotion

In addition to the seven Benedictine daily prayer offices, monks would also set aside time to read and study Scripture and for personal prayer and contemplation (*Orationes Particulares*). *Lectio Divina*, the traditional way of reading the Holy Scriptures, became the determining discipline of monastic devotion. By incorporating regular communal prayer

---

[14] *Rule of St. Benedict*, Rule 16: "The Prophet says: Seven times a day have I praised you (Ps 118[119]:164). We will fulfill this sacred number of seven if we satisfy our obligations of service at Lauds, Prime, Terce, Sext, None, Vespers and Compline, for it was of these hours during the day that he said: Seven times a day have I praised you (Ps 118[119]:164). Concerning Vigils, the same Prophet says: At midnight I arose to give you praise (Ps 118[119]:62). Therefore, we should praise our Creator for his just judgments at these times: Lauds, Prime, Terce, Sext, None, Vespers and Compline; and let us arise at night to give him praise (Ps 118[119]:164, 62)."

[15] "Private individual recitation of the Divine Office became obligatory for the clergy in the Fifth Century. In the Sixth Century numerous councils reenforced previous enactments, or inflicted penalties on clergy who failed to say their Office. In 528, Justinian I decreed that 'all clerics appointed to Churches shall themselves sing the Morning and Evening Office.' These regulations, re-enforced by the Quinisext Council *in Trullo*, still bind the clergy of the Eastern Orthodox Church. Legislation in the West took final shape in the Thirteenth Century, at the Council of the Lateran, in the form of a canon requiring all clerks in Holy Orders to recite the Divine Office each day, either in Church or in private. Such obligation had been laid on the clergy of England by the Canons of Aelfric, as early as the Eleventh Century. The legislation of the Lateran Council remains in force in the Roman Catholic Church today, while the requirements of the Canons of Aelfric still bind all Deacons and Priests of the English Church, by virtue of explicit reaffirmation by the Church of England in 1552, 1559, and 1662. The present form of this requirement, as it stands in the Preface to *The Book of Common Prayer ... according to the Use of the Church of England* is as follows: 'All Priests and Deacons are to say daily the Morning and Evening Prayer, either privately or openly, not being hindered by sickness or some other urgent cause' (Preface *Concerning the Service of the Church*). The principles and implications underlying the legislation of the Catholic Church, in its various formulations, Eastern, Latin, and English, make it clear that every Priest and Deacon is under grave obligation to say the Divine Office." Thomas J. Williams, "The Obligation of the Clergy to Recite the Divine Office," *The American Church Quarterly* 27 (1930): 119–124.

and devotion into their daily routines, the monks sought to cultivate a sense of community and shared purpose to deepen their individual relationships with God. As regulated by the Rule, monastic life was an ordered pursuit of increasing devotion and furthering participation in the Divine life. When not engaged in personal devotion, the monks typically engaged in manual labor, such as farming or craftwork, during the daytime between the liturgical services. Yet even their daily *labora* was an offering unto the Lord and means of spiritual contemplation and personal devotion.[16]

Despite Henry VIII's dissolution of the monasteries in England, the characteristics of monastic spirituality and theology continued to influence the development of post-Reformation English piety. Thomas Cranmer had a deep understanding of the Rule of Benedict. His sister, Alice, was a Cistercian nun at Stixwould, which was suppressed in 1536. However, Cranmer supported his sister's religious vocation by installing her at the Benedictine priory in Sheppey. He even unsuccessfully tried to obtain a royal grant for the priory. This act may have been motivated more by his desire to support his sister than promoting monasticism. Nevertheless, it does show that Cranmer did not want to eliminate every trace of monasticism from England.

Cranmer's famous Collect for the Second Sunday of Advent echoes the monastic tradition of *lectio divina* as personal devotion. Cranmer exhorts the Church to "hear ..., read, mark, learn, and inwardly digest [the scriptures]," which is clearly an allusion to the monastic practice of "chewing" or meditating upon the words of holy writ and digesting them into the mind and soul.[17] In fact, at the conclusion of his Homily, *A Fruitful Exhortation to the Reading and Knowledge of Holy Scripture* (1547), Cranmer urges supplicants to "ruminate" or "chew" the Scriptures to extract their "sweet juice, spiritual effect, marrow, honey, kernel, taste, comfort, and consolation." Cranmer's metaphor of eating and drinking is in keeping with the monastic tradition, which believed the Scriptures were not just to be studied but fully consumed and digested.

When Cranmer issued injunctions to the Benedictines of Worcester Cathedral Priory, he demonstrated his knowledge of the Rule. He mandated that the monks attend daily Scripture reading following "the rule of [their] Religion," which refers to the Rule of St. Benedict. While this does not necessarily mean that Cranmer had a favorable view of the Rule of Benedict as a whole, it does indicate that he recognized and respected Benedict's significant emphasis on reading Scripture. Cranmer's appeal to the Rule of Benedict as an authority of the past further shows his approach to Reformation, which often involved drawing on established traditions and practices. By requiring the monks to follow the Rule of St. Benedict's guidance on Scripture reading, he demonstrated a willingness to incorporate elements of monastic spirituality into the Church of England. This nuanced approach to reform suggests that Cranmer was not simply seeking to erase

---

[16] In the early Middle Ages, the monasteries became the prominent centers of learning and scholarship. Monks were responsible for preserving and transmitting knowledge, and the production of manuscripts was a key part of this task. In time, the monastic scriptorium became the preferred place of daily labor.

[17] The Collect for the Second Sunday in Advent resonates with the teachings of Guigo II, the fourteenth-century Carthusian monk who wrote extensively on the practice of contemplative prayer thus producing a final synthesis of the monastic practice of *lectio divina*.

all aspects of monasticism from English society but rather to reform and adapt its practices to better suit the changing times.

Although the monasteries were dissolved, their legacy lived on in the hearts and minds of the English people, and their practices continued to shape the nation's spirituality. The emphasis on deep reflection and contemplation of Scripture, which is at the heart of monastic spirituality, was embraced by the Church of England and became a vital part of Anglican piety. In this way, the dissolution of the monasteries failed to eradicate the influence of monastic spirituality and theology from English culture. Instead, it became integrated into the fabric of Anglican spirituality, providing a rich and enduring legacy that remains to this day. The echoes of the monastic tradition can still be heard in the liturgy and practices of the Church of England and in our American prayer book of 1928, reminding us of the profound impact that the monasteries had on Anglican spiritual life.

Weekly Eucharist

While the Rule of Saint Benedict doesn't explicitly reference the Divine Liturgy or service of Holy Communion, it is nearly impossible to imagine the brothers at Monte Cassino excepting the weekly observance of Holy Communion from the Rule. True, Benedict only touches upon the Sunday Eucharist in his *Regula* and usually in relation to other communal concerns. For instance, in Rule 38, he suggests asking for prayers after Mass and Communion on Sunday instead of allowing anyone to read during meals. Despite the lack of explicit instructions, the weekly receiving of Holy Communion on the Lord's Day was undoubtedly the focal point of the three-fold Rule of prayer, [personal or private] devotion, and Eucharist.

The Lord's Supper was paramount to Thomas Cranmer's liturgical reforms. At the time, it was common for the Eucharist to be celebrated infrequently, often only a few times a year. Cranmer believed that this practice did not align with the teachings of Scripture and the early church, which emphasized the centrality of the Eucharist to Christian worship and the importance of regular participation in the Sacrament. Cranmer argued that weekly Communion would help to foster a deeper sense of community among the faithful and strengthen their spiritual lives.

He believed that by regularly partaking in the Eucharist, Christians could experience a more profound sense of Christ's presence and be better equipped to serve God in their daily lives. To support this reform, Cranmer revised the Church of England's liturgy to emphasize the Eucharist. He also encouraged priests to preach on the importance of the Sacrament and to make it more accessible to the laity. This included introducing the practice of receiving Communion in bread and wine rather than just the bread alone.

Cranmer's emphasis on the breaking of the bread and the prayers, in that specific order, revealed the weekly Holy Communion as the primary devotion of the three-fold Rule encompassing the common offices and personal devotion which flow out of and return to the Eucharist. Cranmer believed that Holy Communion informed devotion rather than the other way around. It is important to note that each part of the *Regula* is an integrated system necessary for Anglicans. However, the Holy Communion defines the entirety of the Rule. Therefore, Anglicans faithfully celebrate the Eucharist on a weekly basis, reflecting Cranmer's belief in the vital importance of regular participation in this Sacrament.

At the heart of the English Reformation stands neither a key theological position nor dogmatic insistency. Absent is the towering theologian in the continental Reformation (Luther or Calvin). No, at the center of re-formed catholic Anglicanism is the *Book of Common Prayer* which rendered the essential aspects of the Benedictine rule and spirit to the entire Western Church, thus continuing the pre-reform monastic spirit to this day.[18]

The Benedictine Spirit of Re-Formed Catholic Anglican Spirituality

As a fundamental practice of monastic asceticism, the Rule was written for a specific community of monks residing in geographical monasteries, and it followed a common rule of prayer, work, and spiritual reading. Benedict would never have conceptualized the creation of his Rule as a universal monastic document to guide and regulate Western monasticism. And yet, as Thornton rightly observes, the "genius of St. Benedict cannot be confined within the walls of Monte Cassino or any other monastery; the *Regula* is not only a system of order, but also a system of ascetical theology, the basis of which is as applicable to modern England as it was to the sixth century Italy."[19]

Re-formed catholic Anglican spirituality happily embraces the monastic patrimony of the pre-reform Church in England, all the way back to its Celtic origins. "The [Anglican] has never imagined that the Reformation was anything but a Reformation. It was in no sense a new beginning. The English Churchman regards himself as standing in the fullest fellowship and continuity with Augustine and Ninian and Patrick and Aiden and Cuthbert and, perhaps most of all, the most typically Anglican of all saints, the Venerable Bede."[20] All of these were monks; Bede was a Benedictine monk who lived, studied, and died within the walls of St. Paul's monastery at Jarrow, founded by St. Benedict Biscop, who decided that the Rule of Benedict should govern the house.

The Benedictine monastic charism profoundly influenced the development of Christianity in England and, thus, upon English spirituality. The Anglican Church has been influenced by this spirit throughout its history and is presently influenced as lay and clergy alike live out the spirit of the Benedictine *Regula* through the exercise of Prayer Book spirituality. It is safe to say that the monastic spirit constitutes the heart of the Anglican Church through historical insistence and continuity with its monastic roots and experience.[21]

---

[18] Robert Hale keenly observes that the English reformation preserved the Benedictine charism in the Church through its Prayer Book. Robert Hale, "The Benedictine Spirit in Anglicanism," *Christian* 5, no. 3 (1980); *The American Benedictine Review* 30, no. 3 (1979): 226–248. Available online: babel.hathitrust.org/cgi/pt?id=mdp.39015077514324.

[19] Thornton, *English Spirituality*, 76.

[20] Stephen Neill, *Anglicanism* (Middlesex: Penguin, 1990), 419, quoted in Hale, "The Benedictine Spirit in Anglicanism," 227.

[21] "To return to the people's faith in the Middle Ages. If we look for the heart of the Church, in the days before it was transformed by the impact of heresy, Islam, and its own reforming movements, we shall find it in the cloister. This is a fact of quite exceptional importance: up to the middle of the twelfth century the leadership of Christendom was largely in the hands not of Popes, canon lawyers and university-trained theologians, but of monks." Friedrich Herr, *The Medieval World: Europe 1100—1350* (Cleveland: World, 1961), 39.

Domesticity

The Benedictine Rule, which forms the basis of prayer book spirituality, emphasizes daily prayer, personal devotion, and communal celebration of the Eucharist as the means for individuals to grow in holiness and become more like Christ. But this rule is always lived through community in a particular geographical location, not only ordering communal and individual life, but also setting an environment, an ethos, if you will, of the School of Christ. I'd like to briefly touch upon two important characteristics of the Benedictine nature which greatly influence English prayer book spirituality: (1) The *domestic* nature of Benedictine spirituality and (2) its inherent *moderation* when it comes to the spiritual life.

The revisers of the prayer book presupposed parish life to be like Benedict's monastic community—comparatively small, domestic, and very stable, and a common *school of Christ* for both laity and clergy. This helps to foster a sense of belonging and shared purpose among parishioners. For clergy, the *Book of Common Prayer* guides their congregations in worship and spiritual formation. By modeling the three-fold Rule of prayer, personal devotion, and weekly Eucharist, clergy can help their parishioners to grow in their faith and become more deeply committed to the life of the Church. But this *Regula-shaped* telos is the same for clergy.

The Benedictine Rule emphasizes the importance of obedience, renouncing one's own will, and putting on the armor of obedience to fight for the Lord Christ. The common life it envisions is smallish, intimate, and homely, rather than the idea of a large Christian community. *Little Gidding* was a religious community formed in the mid-1620s by Nicholas Ferrar and his extended family at the manor house of Little Gidding in Huntingdonshire and is a wonderful example of Anglican domesticity embracing the quasi-monastic life. Ferrar and about thirty souls dedicated themselves to a common liturgical life, and "like the majority of medieval choir monks and nuns, the community knew the entire Book of the Psalms."[22] Whether in the parish or the home, the goal of Prayer Book spirituality is for all its members to become "little Christs" and to attain the beatific vision of beholding the face of God. This vision is rooted in the belief that all faithful people have the potential to grow in holiness and become more like Christ through the regular practice of prayer, personal devotion, and participation in the Eucharist.

Moderation

"Yet let all things be done in moderation on account of the faint-hearted."[23] Anglican prayer-book piety enjoys the Benedictine ethos of moderation, which is reflected in the *Regula* because it is written for imperfect saints; Benedict is keenly aware of man's inabilities, weaknesses, and limitations. The *Regula* was not meant to be a strict set of rules to be followed blindly but rather a flexible framework that could be adapted to the needs of the individual and the community. Benedictine spirituality encourages a balanced approach to life and faith by emphasizing the importance of spiritual discipline and community. The *Book of Common Prayer* shares this Benedictine ethos. The preface to

---

[22] Hale, "The Benedictine Spirit in Anglicanism," 240.
[23] *Rule of St. Benedict*, Rule 48.

the 1662 *Book of Common Prayer* states that the Church of England has always sought to strike a balance between rigidity and flexibility in its liturgy. This principle of moderation is at the heart of Anglicanism and reflects the Benedictine spirit that has influenced the Church throughout its history.

As Anglicans continue to seek a deeper understanding of their faith and their place in the world, the Benedictine spirit of moderation remains a vital guiding principle. The Benedictine approach to moderation is not about avoiding extremes for their own sake but rather about finding a balance that allows for growth and transformation. It encourages a balanced approach to life and faith grounded in spiritual discipline and community, and it has helped shape the Church's liturgy and practices over the centuries.

Conclusion

The Benedictine spirit that carried through the English Reformation remains a critical influence on how Anglicans approach prayer, worship, and community simply because Anglicanism is the inheritor of the Benedictine Regula. During a time when Europe was overrun by pagan barbarian tribes and Christianity seemed to be on the brink of collapse, Benedict created a short and simple yet comprehensive rulebook that allowed his monasteries to keep the faith alive. Charlemagne later encouraged the spread of these monasteries, which kept theology and culture alive during centuries of widespread illiteracy. This Benedictine spirit has had a significant influence on Anglican spirituality, particularly in the areas of monasticism and contemplative prayer.

Many Anglican religious communities follow the Rule of St. Benedict, incorporating regular times of prayer and meditation, a commitment to living in community, and a focus on hospitality and service to others. Anglican liturgy and hymnody have also been shaped by the Benedictine tradition, reflecting a contemplative and meditative approach to worship. Additionally, the Benedictine emphasis on hospitality and service has inspired Anglicans to work for social justice and advocacy, promoting peace, environmental stewardship, and the well-being of marginalized and oppressed members of society.

Those who practice the prayer book *Regula* of the Daily Office, personal devotion, and weekly Eucharist are merely walking the same path traversed by so many English monks, scholars, historians, kings, missionaries, and martyrs who were either Benedictine themselves or directly shaped by it. In a time when holding the Anglican Communion together is becoming more difficult to do, common, communal prayer and life remain its organizing principle, as it does for Benedictine communities. Although the majority of Anglican Churchmen will practice their "monkhood" within the life and worship of the local parish, we are "all Benedictines," and a sixth-century monk named St. Benedict remains a trustworthy guide enabling us to race along the way of God's commandments.

Chapter 14

The Catholicity of the Vernacular: The Venerable Bede (672/3–735)

The Rev. Dr. Peter Johnston

The focus of the 2023 Anglican Way Institute conference was on the unity of the Anglican Way, as both a Reformed and Catholic tradition. This unity is demonstrated by tracing continuities between pre- and post-Reformation eras. To this purpose, the majority of presentations brought out the Catholic elements in the Reformed era, i.e., the continuity of the universal church into the sixteenth-century Reformation and thereafter. In a similar vein, my chapter traces a continuity between these two eras, but it does so in the converse. Rather than finding Catholic principles in the Reformed era, I find what we typically consider a Reformed principle already present in the Catholic era.

Specifically, I explore the emergence of Biblical translation in the Anglo-Saxon period. I focus on Bede's account of Cædmon, and trace two trajectories of poetic paraphrase and translation proper into the vernacular of Old English. My contention is that this historical and literary analysis demonstrates the catholicity of the vernacular. In this light, the priority of the vernacular in the sixteenth-century English Reformation is revealed to be deeply continuous with the historic Anglican Way, even in its earliest forms.

The Origins of the Old English Language

Old English was the spoken language of the Angles, Saxons, and Jutes, the Germanic tribes who displaced the Britons in England in the fifth and sixth centuries. The earliest written form of the language was a system of runes, preserved in incomplete stone inscriptions from the sixth and seventh centuries. Sometime in the eighth century, Anglican monks created a new form for written Old English, using Latin letters and a typographic system from the Irish called "Insular Script."

Bede wrote his *Ecclesiastical History of the English People* in the early eighth century, completing it in 731. This, like all of Bede's written works, was in Latin. If we ask why Bede did not write in Old English, the most common explanation is that Latin was the language of monastic learning, of the written scriptures, and of all the historical texts on which he modeled his history. But what is also true, and often unmentioned, is that Old English only existed as a written language in its most rudimentary form, if at all! Thus, even had Bede wanted to write his *Ecclesiastical History* in Old English, it likely would not have been possible.

Yet it is clear that Bede knew the Old English spoken language, not only because it was his mother tongue, but also because he also refers to it in his *Ecclesiastical History*, notably in the story of Cædmon. Moreover, Bede's presentation of the story of Cædmon lays a conceptual foundation for the importance of the vernacular, and of translation to the vernacular as a strategic missionary work. Indeed, if the monks had not yet developed their written version of the Old English vernacular, Bede's account of Cædmon offers the most likely rationale for its invention.

Translation by the Grace of God

Bede tells the story of Cædmon in his *Ecclesiastical History*, in Book IV, Chapter 24.[1] The account begins as if an afterthought, concerning a "certain brother" who is not yet named, from the monastery of Abbess Hilda. This unnamed brother seems especially insignificant in contrast to Hilda, the much-renowned hostess of the Synod of Whitby, an account of which Bede previously related in Book III, Chapter 25.

Though he does not immediately name this "certain brother," from the start Bede uses the language of grace to set this "brother" apart. He was "specially marked out by the grace of God" to "compose godly and religious songs." These songs would be "learned from the Holy Scriptures by means of interpreters" and then "turned into extremely delightful and moving poetry, in English, which was his native tongue." While other poets composed similar poetic translations later on, "none could compare with him," because "he received the gift of song freely by the grace of God." In other words, Bede is not only telling the origin story for the translation of the Bible in the vernacular, he is also explicitly attributing the new genre to the grace of God.

Moreover, in Bede's account of the first such translation, he sets the scene in such a way to emphasize God's grace. This "brother" was "advanced in years" and "had never learned any songs." Thus, when he was gathered with a group for a "feast," and they decided to "sing in turn," he left the feast before it was his turn. He is unnamed, unlearned, and too shy to sing, which sets forth all the more the grace of God which will give him the power of Biblical song using the vernacular language.

Called by Name

When Bede finally reveals this brother's name, he does so through the Biblical motif of a divine call. Having left the feast, this brother goes to a cattle barn, lies down, and falls asleep. Then in a dream, "someone stood by him, saluted him, and called him by name: Cædmon." Whether this "someone" is God or an angel, what really leaps off the page is the name "Cædmon," not only because this is its first appearance, but also because it is situated in the Biblical pattern of a divine call at night.

In *The Art of Biblical Narrative*, Hebrew literary critic Robert Alter develops the concept of "type-scenes" or sets of stories with common structural elements but variation of detail. Alter gives special attention to the *romance at the well* "type-scene," analyzing the cases of Abraham's Servant meeting Rebekah (Genesis 24), Jacob meeting Rachel (Genesis 29), and Moses meeting Zipporah (Exodus 2). Though Alter does not extend his analysis to the New Testament, we could include the account of Jesus meeting the Samaritan Woman (John 4).[2]

I would suggest that another Biblical "type-scene" is the *divine call at night*. Cases include God calling to Jacob in night visions (Genesis 46), God's call to Samuel when he had laid down to sleep (1 Samuel 3), and the angel's call to Joseph (Matthew 1–2). Each of these characters is called by name at night, and then given a specific revelation: Jacob is

---

[1] See e.g., Bertram Colgrave and R.A.B. Mynors, eds., *Bede's Ecclesiastical History of the English People* (Oxford: Clarendon, 1969), 415–421 (iv.24), archive.org/details/x-bede-s-ecclesiastical-history.

[2] Robert Alter, *The Art of Biblical Narrative*, revised and updated ed. (New York: Basic Books, 2011), 55–78.

sent to Egypt, Samuel is given a prophecy concerning the house of Eli, and Joseph is told to keep Mary as a wife because her child is by the Holy Spirit.

The story of Cædmon follows the form of this Biblical type-scene. As a result, when reading the account of Cædmon, we not only get the feeling of Cædmon as a Biblical character being used by God, we also expect that something momentous is about to be revealed.

Singing Creation

"Cædmon, ... sing me something," this someone told him. Cædmon was incredulous: "I cannot sing; that is why I left the feast and came here, because I could not sing." Cædmon's double insistence that he cannot sing heightens the sense of miraculous grace in what follows. "Nevertheless you must sing," the someone told him, "sing ... about the beginning of created things."

Cædmon then sings about creation, and Bede includes the text of this *Cædmon's Hymn*, albeit in Latin rather than Cædmon's original Old English. As discussed above, Bede may not have had a written alphabet for the Old English language.

We do however have the Old English text of *Cædmon's Hymn*, which was added to manuscript copies of Bede's *Ecclesiastical History*, beginning in the mid-700s, about two decades after Bede completed his *History*. Twenty-one copies of the manuscript exist with the added Old English text of *Cædmon's Hymn*. Though the text has multiple forms, representing multiple Old English dialects and perhaps also multiple memories, a complete early version, with my interlinear translation, is as follows:

Nū scylun hergan   **hefaenrīcaes Uard,**
Now we should praise   *heaven-kingdom's Ward,*

metudæs maecti   **end his mōdgidanc,**
the measurer's might   *and his mind-purpose,*

uerc Uuldurfadur,   **suē hē uundra gihwaes,**
the work of the Glory-father   *when he of wonders all,*

ēci dryctin   **ōr āstelidæ**
ageless Lord,   *the beginning established;*

hē ǣrist scōp   **aelda barnum**
he first shaped   *for the sons of men*

heben til hrōfe,   **hāleg scepen.**
heaven as a roof,   *the holy shaper.*

Thā middungeard   **moncynnæs Uard,**
Then middle-earth   *Mankind's Ward*

eci Dryctin,   **æfter tīadæ**
the ageless Lord,   *after made*

firum foldu,   **Frēa allmectig.**
For men the earthfields   *The Master Almighty*[3]

---

[3] I created this interlinear compilation with the Old English text from the Moore Bede and my own word for word translation. See the Moore Bede: Cambridge, University Library, MS Kk. 5. 16, as referenced in "Cædmon's Hymn," en.wikipedia.org/wiki/Cædmon%27s_Hymn.

Bede's Latin translation depicts *Cædmon's Hymn* it in its "general sense" but not "in the order of the words" that Cædmon sang:

> Now we must praise the Maker of the heavenly kingdom, the power of the Creator and his counsel, the deeds of the Father of glory and how He, since he is the eternal God, was the Author of all marvels and first created the heavens as a roof for the children of men and then, the almighty Guardian of the human race, created the earth.[4]

Poetic Paraphrase

From a modern perspective, we would not call *Cædmon's Hymn* a Biblical translation. Rather, we would characterize it as a selective poetic paraphrase of a Biblical text—in this case, Genesis 1:1–13. The key ideas that this paraphrase captures from that Biblical text are an Almighty God, who creates the heavens and the earth in the beginning, with the order of creating heaven first, and then creating the earth. Thus, there is more focus on the second and third days of creation, with no discussion of the light created on the first day.

On the other hand, there are formal features of *Cædmon's Hymn* which capture the Biblical Creation narrative better, in some ways, than modern translations. First, its poetic structure, especially in its alliteration and its rhythm, lends it a dignity and weight appropriate to the Biblical text. Bede himself points out that "it is not possible to translate verse, however well composed, literally from one language to another without some loss of beauty and dignity."[5] Less literal translations, then, are sometimes better able to capture the sense, albeit not the words, of an original text.

Second, *Cædmon's Hymn* gestures toward the sixth day of creation with the explanation that this creation is being made for mankind, incorporating a key aspect of the Creation narrative in its shortened form. Indeed, by referring to God's "mind purpose," *Cædmon's Hymn* adds an interpretive gloss to the fact of creation, incorporating a theology of God's purpose in its account of creation.

Third, the text offers multiple terms for God, drawing upon the variety of ways God is described Biblically and in the Anglo-Saxon imagination. He is the Ward, the Measurer, the Glory-Father, the Ageless Lord, the Holy Shaper, and the Master Almighty. The literary term for this descriptive variation is apposition, setting multiple terms for the same thing next to each other. This poetic elaboration has the effect of helping the reader to enter into the mystery of God as Creator.

In light of its content and formal features, another helpful way to think of *Cædmon's Hymn* is as a theologically informed expansion of Genesis 1:1 (rather than a selective compression of Gen 1:1–13). The key concepts are the beginning, God, creation, the heavens, and the earth. Everything else is the theological and poetic elaboration of these themes.

Trajectory 1: Old English Biblical Poetic Paraphrase

The following morning, Cædmon shared his song with Hilda.[6] Hilda assembled a group of "learned men" to determine the "nature and origin" of his song, and after hearing Cædmon's story and song, "it seemed clear to all of them that Lord had granted him

---

[4] Colgrave and Mynors, *Bede's Ecclesiastical History*, 417 (iv.24).

[5] Ibid.

[6] Ibid.

heavenly grace." Hilda therefore directed Cædmon to "take monastic vows," to be "instructed in the whole course of sacred history," and to turn it into metrical verse.[7]

Bede explains that Cædmon did so, creating poetic paraphrases into Old English, from many parts of the Bible:

> He sang about the creation of the world, the origin of the human race, and the whole history of Genesis, of the departure of Israel from Egypt and the entry into the promised land, and of many other of the stories taken from the sacred Scriptures: of the incarnation, passion, and resurrection of the Lord, of his Ascension into heaven, of the coming of the Holy Spirit, and the teaching of the apostles. He also made songs about the terrors of future judgment, the horrors of the pains of hell, and the joys of the heavenly kingdom.[8]

Remarkably, the extant corpus on Old English Biblical Poetic Paraphrase largely maps onto the categories enumerated by Bede. In addition to *Cædmon's Hymn*, we have *Genesis A* and *Genesis B*, which recount stories from Genesis from the Creation to stories about Abraham. We have *Exodus* which covers the story of Moses through the deliverance of Israel through the Red Sea. We have *Daniel* with aspects of both the Daniel narrative and apocalyptic. There are multiple Old English poems about Christ: *Christ I* focuses on the incarnation, *Christ II* on the Ascension, and *Christ III* on the Last Judgment. Multiple shorter poems, including the *Dream of the Rood*, address the Crucifixion. The *Fates of the Apostles* depicts Acts and the early church, *Christ and Satan* depicts Satan in Hell.[9]

Today scholars doubt that it was Cædmon himself who wrote all of these poems. But the close alignment of Bede's list with the extant corpus makes clear that, at the very least, it was Cædmon's example, and Bede's list, which laid out the program for Old English Biblical Paraphrase.

Trajectory 2: Biblical Translation

And what of Biblical translation proper? We have already seen, above, how Biblical poetic paraphrase can at times capture the form and feeling of the Biblical text even better than direct translation. Nevertheless, it is only a short step from seeing the value of poetic paraphrase, to seeing the value of direct translation.

Indeed, it was not long after the eighth century work of Biblical paraphrase that interest began to build for direct translation. This came especially through the efforts of King Alfred in the ninth century, who put royal resources behind the work of translation into Old English, and even created his own translation of Gregory the Great's *Pastoral Rule*.[10]

We do not know if Alfred commissioned a Biblical translation, but someone around that time was organizing a systematic effort. The result was a complete translation of the gospels into Old English, completed by the mid tenth century. This translation was

---

[7] Colgrave and Mynors, *Bede's Ecclesiastical History*, 419 (iv.24).

[8] Ibid.

[9] For the text of these poems see the website of the *Old English Poetry in Facsimile Project* oepoetryfacsimile.org/; for a facsimile of the main manuscript Junius 11, see digital.bodleian.ox.ac.uk/inquire/p/82365036-24f3-4c43-95fe-0a4a4d94d90a; G.P. Krapp, ed., *The Junius Manuscript*, Anglo-Saxon Poetic Records 1 (New York: Columbia University Press, 1931).

[10] See e.g., Sarah Foot, "The Making of Angelcynn: English Identity before the Norman Conquest," *Transactions of the Royal Historical Society* 6 (1996): 25–49, doi.org/10.2307/3679228.

added to the Lindisfarne Gospel book, the Old English text added between the lines of the eighth century Latin text, by a monk named Aldred. Thus, from Caedmon and Bede to Aldred, we see the development of a vernacular tradition, first in Biblical paraphrase, and finally in direct Biblical translation.[11]

In this regard, a helpful analogy to the literary work of Bede and his community of scholar monks is the pioneering mission of Cyril and Methodius, ninth-century Byzantine monks from northern Greece who invented the Cyrillic alphabet to give written form to the vernacular of the Slavic peoples and translated selections of the scriptures and the liturgies into the Slavonic language. This, together with the creation of an autocephalous Bulgarian Church, in what we might call the "Reformation of the East," was accomplished by the end of the ninth century.[12]

The development of the Old English translations, however, was soon interrupted by military and political developments. Viking raids led to massive disruption, especially of monastic communities. Lindisfarne itself was evacuated, the monks saving only their most prized possessions, including the Lindisfarne Gospels and the relics of Cuthbert. And then the eleventh-century Norman Conquest brought the most significant disruption of all, in the change of the language itself. Norman French became the language of the aristocracy, beginning the process of changing Old English into another language entirely. Thus, Old English lost its aristocratic patrons and sense of future value, and no one really knew what the vernacular would become. Though there were still some translations into Old English being completed in the eleventh and twelfth centuries, notably of the Psalms, it gradually became clear that Old English was becoming obsolete. Translations into Old English could no longer be called translations into the vernacular!

Conclusion

In the broader scope of Anglican history, we can see that translation into the Old English vernacular is a story of arrested development. What began as Biblical poetic paraphrase, and then turned into direct Biblical translation, would very likely have turned into a complete Biblical text in the Old English vernacular. But when the vernacular itself changed, the program of translation lost momentum. It would take a few centuries for the vernacular to find its new and settled form and the genius of Wycliffe and Tyndale to pick up on tradition begun by Cædmon and Bede.

Nevertheless, in light of this history, the work of Wycliffe and Tyndale cannot be considered a disruption to the historic and catholic Anglican Way. On the contrary, Wycliffe and Tyndale drew deeply on the literary and missionary impulse of historic Anglicanism, restoring the native Anglican tradition of translation into the vernacular.

---

[11] See e.g., Robert Stanton, *The Culture of Translation in Anglo-Saxon England* (Cambridge: D. S. Brewer, 2002); David C. Fowler, *The Bible in Early English Literature* (London: Sheldon, 1977); Geoffrey Shepherd, "English versions of the Scriptures before Wycliff," in *The Cambridge History of the Bible*, ed. G. W. H. Lampe (Cambridge: Cambridge University Press, 1969), 2:362–387; Bruce M. Metzger, "The Anglo-Saxon Version," in *The Early Versions of the New Testament* (Oxford: Clarendon, 1977), 443–455.

[12] See e.g., George C. Soulis, "The Legacy of Cyril and Methodius to the Southern Slavs." *Dumbarton Oaks Papers* 19 (1965): 19–43, doi.org/10.2307/1291224; Francis Dvornik, "The Significance of the Missions of Cyril and Methodius," *Slavic Review* 23, no. 2 (1964): 195–211, doi.org/10.2307/2492930; and Horace G. Lunt, "The Beginning of Written Slavic," *Slavic Review* 23, no. 2 (1964): 212–19, doi.org/10.2307/2492931.

Chapter 15

Thomas Cranmer (1489–1556) and the Church Fathers: A Test Case on the Descent

The Right Rev. Dr. Charles F. Camlin

Introduction

Archbishop Thomas Cranmer, at his degradation speech before being burned at the stake, articulated his commitment to the church fathers when he said:

> And touching my doctrine of the sacrament, and other my doctrine, of what kind soever it be, I protest that it was never my mind to write, speak, or understand any thing contrary to the most holy word of God, or else against the holy catholic church of Christ; but purely and simply to imitate and teach those things only, which I had learned of the sacred scripture, and of the holy catholic church of Christ from the beginning, and also according to the exposition of the most holy and learned fathers and martyrs of the church.[1]

Even though Cranmer was primarily defending his view of the Eucharist, he says here that he sought to make all of his doctrine consistent with what was taught in scripture "according to the exposition of the most holy and learned fathers and martyrs of the church."[2]

I intend to provide a test case concerning one particular doctrine that was highly disputed at the time of the Reformation: the descent of Christ into hell. The prominence of the doctrine in the ancient Church is evident by the fact that it is included in two of the ancient Creeds (the Apostles' and Athanasian). Despite this, reformation scholars offered a spectrum of views, which ranged from reinterpreting the article from the Creeds or denying it altogether. Two examples of reinterpretation were offered by Martin Bucer and John Calvin. Bucer was brought to England by Cranmer and was appointed Regius Professor of Divinity at Cambridge.[3] In his work on the Psalter, translated into English by George Joye, Bucer offers the following on Psalm 16:10: "For thou wilt not leave me in my grave: nor suffer thy dear beloved holy one to be corrupted."[4] Likewise, in Psalm 30, he writes, "Lord thou hast called me again from my grave."[5] In both places, he uses *grave* to translate the Hebrew word *Sheol* (which referred to the abode of the dead,

---

[1] John Edmund Cox, ed., *The Works of Thomas Cranmer, Archbishop of Canterbury, Martyr, 1556*, The Parker Society (Cambridge: The University Press, 1846), 2:227.

[2] Some of the material in this lecture is derived from my unpublished doctoral thesis: "He Descended Into Hell: An English Reformation Controversy" (London School of Theology/Middlesex University, 2022).

[3] For a summary of Bucer's work in England, see Basil Hall, "Martin Bucer in England," in *Martin Bucer: Reforming Church and Community*, ed. D. F. Wright (Cambridge: Cambridge University Press, 1994), 144–160.

[4] George Joye, *Dauids Psalter, Diligently and Faithfully Tra[n]Slated by George Ioye, with Breif Arguments before Euery Psalme* (Antwerp: Maryne Emperowr, 1534), fol. 18a–b.

[5] George Joye, *Dauids Psalter*, fol. 40a. In the Latin text, Bucer substitutes *inferis* (below) for the Vulgate's *inferno* (hell). *S. Psalmorum Libri*, 155.

situated below the earth).[6] The standard way of reading the Psalms at the time was to interpret the words of David as prophecies of Christ (following the manner that Peter interpreted Psalm 16 in Acts 2:25-31).[7] In some ways, Bucer was modifying this, but he would have been well aware of this interpretive tradition.[8] So when he substitutes *grave* for *Sheol*,[9] he demonstrates that he has adopted the view that Christ's descent was nothing more than his burial.[10]

John Calvin, who went another route, was highly critical of this "descent as burial" view for the phrase in the Creed. He wrote:

> How careless it would have been, when something not at all difficult in itself has been stated with clear and easy words, to indicate it again in words that obscure rather than clarify it! Whenever two expressions for the same thing are used in the same context, the latter ought to be an explanation of the former. But what sort of explanation will it be if one says that "Christ was buried" means that "he descended into hell?"[11]

Calvin adds that it is unlikely that "a useless repetition" would have crept into this summary of our faith which is stated in the "fewest possible words." Justin Bass writes: "To equate the Descensus with Christ's burial was nothing more than a pre-Bultmannian attempt to demythologize the NT text because Bucer and those who followed him could no longer accept an underworld beneath the earth."[12]

Calvin took the doctrine of Christ's descent in a different direction. He argues against removing the article when he says: "This much is certain: that it [the descent] reflected the common belief of all the godly; for there is no one of the fathers who does not mention in his writings Christ's descent into hell, though their interpretations vary."[13] He acknowledges that all of the fathers taught the doctrine, but he opens the door for his own interpretation by saying that "their interpretations vary," which is an exaggeration. It should be noted that none of the fathers taught his view. He writes succinctly in his Catechism:

> Concerning the expression that [Christ] descended into hell, it means that he was afflicted by God and that he has felt and endured the horrible rigor of his judgment in order to shield us from his wrath and to satisfy his justice for us. Thus he has

---

[6] The word *Hades* is used in the Greek translation of the Old Testament (LXX) to translate *Sheol*.

[7] On this topic, see Herman J. Selderhuis, *Psalms 1–72*, Reformation Commentary on Scripture (Downers Grove, IL: InterVarsity, 2015), xlvi–lii.

[8] R. Gerald Hobbs, "How Firm a Foundation: Martin Bucer's Historical Exegesis of the Psalms," *Church History* 53 (1984): 477–491.

[9] Bucer uses the Latin word *sepulchrum* in place of the Vulgate's *inferno*. *S. Psalmorum Libri*, 89–94.

[10] Cf. Constance I. Smith, "Descendit Ad Inferos—Again," *Journal of the History of Ideas* 28 (1967), 87. Theodore Beza, Calvin's successor, would also propound this view later.

[11] John Calvin, *Calvin: Institutes of the Christian Religion*, ed. John T. McNeill, trans. Ford Lewis Battles, (Philadelphia: Westminster, 1967), 2.16.8.

[12] Justin Bass, *The Battle for the Keys: Revelation 1:18 and Christ's Descent into the Underworld* (Eugene, OR: Wipf & Stock, 2014), 18.

[13] Calvin, *Institutes*, 2.16.8.

suffered and borne the penalties due to our iniquity and not to him who was without sin and without stain.[14]

Here he locates Christ's descent into hell on the cross. Elsewhere, he appeals to Christ's quotation of Psalm 22:1, "My God, My God, why hast thou forsaken Me?" as the moment of this "descent." Thus, Calvin asserts that Christ experienced hell while on the cross. And the purpose of this "descent" was "to shield us from [God's] wrath and to satisfy his justice for us."[15] Plumptre offers a succinct critique of these two reinterpretations when he writes: "We may be quite sure that no Jew or Greek in the apostolic age would ever have thought that the words 'He descended into Hades' meant only that the body of Christ had been laid in the grave, or that His soul had suffered with an exceeding sorrow in Gethsemane and on the cross."[16]

Others at the time of the reformation wanted to strike the *descensus* clause from the Creeds altogether. One example is a man named Christopher Carlile, who was bold enough to make this proposal as a graduating student at Cambridge University in 1552. This was a bold move for at least two reasons. First, an English bishop named Reginald Pecock (ca. 1395–ca. 1460) had lost his bishopric for denying the descent of Christ into hell less than a hundred years before this. Second, in 1549, a man named Putto had been censured by Archbishop Cranmer for denying that Christ descended into hell.[17] Carlile vehemently denied the *descensus* clause and wrote a treatise to this effect during Elizabeth's reign. The treatise was in the form of a dialogue with Richard Smith, a Roman Catholic controversialist.[18] Carlile took contrary positions on a number of biblical texts which the church fathers had employed in affirming Christ's descent. This background concerning how this doctrine was being debated in the sixteenth century is important as we consider what Cranmer believed and taught.

The Teaching of the Church Fathers on the Descent

Space will not permit a thorough articulation of the patristic doctrine of the descent. But we can produce a sampling of texts from the fathers on this doctrine from the earliest centuries of the Church's history. Suffice it to say that virtually all of the fathers affirmed Christ's descent. Contrary to Calvin's assertion quoted above, they did not all differ. Some emphasized different aspects of Christ's descent, but all agreed that following his death, Jesus descended into Sheol, the abode of the dead. Once there, he brought some benefit to those faithful ones who had died in faith prior to his earthly ministry. Whereas some modern authors acknowledge that there may be two or three passages of Scripture

---

[14] James T. Dennison, Jr., ed., *Reformed Confessions of the 16th and 17th Centuries in English Translation*, (Grand Rapids, MI: Reformation Heritage, 2008), 1.374.

[15] Dennison, *Reformed Confessions*, 1.374.

[16] E. H. Plumptre, *The Spirits in Prison and Other Studies on the Life after Death* (New York: T. Whittaker, 1894), 102.

[17] On both controversies, see chapter 2 of my doctoral thesis.

[18] Christopher Carlile, *A Discourse, Concerning Two Diuine Positions* (London: Roger Ward, 1582).

which hint at the descent,[19] the church fathers found the doctrine alluded to in dozens of texts. We will see some of the major texts in the quotes below.[20]

Ignatius, the bishop of Antioch in the early second century, provides us one of the earliest witnesses to the descent of Christ outside of the New Testament. In his epistle to the Trallians he wrote:

> He was crucified and died under Pontius Pilate. He really, and not merely in appearance, was crucified, and died, in the sight of beings in heaven, and on earth, and under the earth [Phil 2:10]. By those in heaven I mean such as are possessed of incorporeal natures; by those on earth, the Jews and Romans, and such persons as were present at that time when the Lord was crucified; and by those under the earth, the multitude that arose along with the Lord. For says the Scripture, 'Many bodies of the saints that slept arose,' their graves being opened [Matt 27:52–3]. He descended, indeed, into Hades alone, but He arose accompanied by a multitude; and rent asunder that means of separation which had existed from the beginning of the world, and cast down its partition-wall [Eph 2:14].[21]

Ignatius' immediate concern in this context is to argue for the reality of Christ's humanity (probably against Docetists)[22] Ignatius says that Christ's crucifixion and death happened "not merely in appearance" but in the sight of beings in heaven, on earth, and under the earth.[23] The third category of beings, "those under the earth," were delivered from Hades by Christ at his descent. The statement "Many bodies of the saints that slept arose" is a quotation of the enigmatic passage in Matthew 27 which describes how the saints, "coming out of the tombs after [Christ's] resurrection ... went into the holy city and appeared to many" (Matt 27:52–53). Ignatius believes that this is a reference to Christ's resurrection after His descent in which He rescued all of the Old Testament saints from Sheol. The phrase "He descended, indeed, into Hades alone, but He arose accompanied by a multitude" offers a concise explanation regarding the purpose of Christ's descent and could be considered as a virtual motto for the patristic doctrine.

In the third century, Melito, bishop of Sardis, offers some intriguing references to the descent in his famous Paschal Homily. Melito imagines Christ explaining to his hearers what he had accomplished in his descent:

> [And he] arose from the dead and cries thus [to you]: "Who is he that contendeth against me? Let him stand before me. I freed the condemned, I made the dead to live again, I raise him who was buried. Who is he who raises his voice against me? I," he says, "am the Christ, I am he who put down death, and triumphed over the

---

[19] Ps 16:10; Acts 2:24–31; Eph 4:9.

[20] For a full list of Biblical texts, see Appendix I of my doctoral thesis. I have inserted some of the biblical texts found in the quotes into brackets.

[21] Ignatius of Antioch, "The Epistle of Ignatius to the Trallians," 9 (*ANF*, 1.70). This passage is found in the longer version of the epistle but not the shorter version.

[22] Docetism "considered the humanity and sufferings of the earthly Christ as apparent rather than real." F. L. Cross and Elizabeth A. Livingstone, eds., *The Oxford Dictionary of the Christian Church* (New York: Oxford University Press, 2005), 496.

[23] Another allusion to Phil 2:10.

enemy, and trod upon Hades, and bound the strong one and brought man safely home to the heights of the heavens; I," he says, "Christ."[24]

Here, Melito echoes texts from Isaiah (49:25; 50:8) and uses triumphant imagery for the descent. He personifies death and Hades and says that Christ was victorious over them, likely drawing upon Revelation 1:18, where Christ tells John that He has the keys to Death and Hades (implying that by defeating Death, he opened Hades).[25] Where Melito has Christ saying that He "bound the strong one," he is alluding to Jesus' story about the stronger man who enters into the strong man's house to plunder his goods.[26] The fathers interpreted this text as essentially Christ's prophecy about what He would do to the devil at the descent, when he entered the realm of death, he effectively bound the devil, and released those who were imprisoned. Melito concludes by saying that Christ brought those he delivered "safely home to the heights of heaven."[27]

In the fourth century, Ambrose, the bishop of Milan, affirmed the descent by calling Christ the "Vanquisher of Death" and saying that in his resurrection, Christ "burst the bonds of hell and exalted the souls of the godly." He asserts that before Christ ascended into heaven, no one had gone there (alluding to John 3:13); this included Enoch and Elijah, who had both apparently escaped death. Ambrose uses Psalm 24 to describe Christ's ascent into heaven with the host that He had released from Sheol where he writes:

> And therefore [the angels] descrying the approach of the Lord of all, first and only Vanquisher of Death, bade their princes that the gates should be lifted up, saying in adoration, "Lift up the gates, such as are princes amongst you, and be ye lifted Up, O everlasting doors, and the King of glory shall come in."[28]

Ambrose's conclusion was that heaven was shut to humanity until the ascension of Christ.[29] Thus, the purpose of Christ's descent was to rescue the Old Testament saints and to deliver them into heaven.

One witness from the fifth century is the great bishop of Hippo and doctor of the church, Augustine. Augustine's most extensive work on the subject is in a letter responding to Evodius, a fellow bishop, who posed a question about the interpretation of 1 Peter 3:18–22. In the opening response, Augustine acknowledges that this text "is wont to perplex me most seriously." He even says, "I therefore refer this question back to yourself, that if either you yourself be able, or can find any other person who is able to do

---

[24] Campbell Bonner, ed., *The Homily on the Passion by Melito Bishop of Sardis and Some Fragments of the Apocryphal Ezekiel* (University of Pennsylvania Press, 1940), 180.

[25] Bass writes: "Melito is the first to use the battle imagery for Christ's descent that will become commonplace throughout the Fathers and the medieval period. It is difficult to find a better Scripture than Revelation 1:18 for the background to Melito's belief that Christ conquered Death and Hades. Where else in the NT are Death and Hades personified and brought together in this way?" *Battle For the Keys*, 11.

[26] Matt 12:29; Mark 3:27; Luke 11:21–22.

[27] Melito of Sardis, *On Pascha: With the Fragments of Melito and Other Material Related to the Quartodecimans*, trans. Alistair Stewart-Sykes (Crestwood, NY: St Vladimir's Seminary Press, 2001), 64–65.

[28] Ambrose, "Exposition of the Christian Faith" (*NPNF²*, 10.263).

[29] A concept which is found in the ancient hymn, the *Te Deum:* "He opened the kingdom of heaven to all believers."

so, you may remove and terminate my perplexities on the subject." Then he adds, "In the meantime, I will communicate to you the things in the passage which occasion difficulty to me, that, keeping in view these remarks on the words of the apostle, you may either exercise your own thoughts on them, or consult any one whom you find competent to pronounce an opinion."[30] We should note that Augustine is tentative in his interpretation.

Augustine acknowledges his belief in Christ's descent when he writes: "It is established beyond question that the Lord, after He had been put to death in the flesh, 'descended into hell.'"[31] He appeals to the prophecy of Psalm 16:10 which was quoted in Peter's Pentecost sermon (Acts 2): "For you will not leave my soul in Sheol." The real conundrum for Augustine is the interpretation of the text from 1 Peter which says that the Lord made proclamation to "the spirits in prison" (3:19) and preached "to the dead" (4:6). In his letter to Augustine, Evodius had claimed that some were teaching that Christ descended to Hades to preach and thereby, to empty it (meaning, all in Hades embraced his preaching and were delivered by Christ to heaven).[32] Augustine offers an alternative view of the text, giving a spiritual interpretation. He believes that when the text talks about Jesus going to make proclamation to "the spirits in prison" or preaching to "the dead," that these are references to those who were alive but imprisoned by sin or spiritually dead (meaning, they were not in Hades). Furthermore, since the text references "the days of Noah," Augustine asserts that the preaching noted took place through Noah, who spoke to his generation by the Spirit of Christ who was in him.[33] In the final analysis, Augustine offered a novel interpretation, denying that the Petrine texts referred to the descent at all, even though the earlier fathers had asserted that it did.[34]

This smattering of texts from the first centuries of the Church should suffice to give us the broad outlines of how Christ's descent was understood in this era. Three central tenets come through in these texts. First, when Christ died on the cross, his soul departed to Sheol like every other human being before him. However, Christ was no ordinary human being: he was the Son of God. Death could not defeat him, and Hades could not hold him. Second, while Christ's death on the cross looked like a defeat, the descent made it evident that it was anything but that. Christ's death opened the way for him to appear in Hades; but his stay there would be brief. The fathers envisioned the descent as the beginning of Christ's victory. This culminated in his resurrection from the dead, and his delivery of the saints who had been held in Hades with him.

Third, contrary to modern scholarship, the fathers believed that the descent of Christ into hell was alluded to in many biblical texts. Some modern scholars, particularly those

---

[30] Augustine of Hippo, "Letters of St. Augustin," 164.1 (*NPNF*[1], 1.515).

[31] "Letters of St. Augustin," (*NPNF*[1], 1.515–516).

[32] Augustine considered those who held this position to be misguided and devoted two chapters (18 and 24) of Book 21 in *The City of God* to refuting their views. See Richard Bauckham, "Augustine, the 'Compassionate' Christians, and the Apocalypse of Peter" in *The Fate of the Dead*, 149–59. This implicit universalism was roundly denounced in the ancient Church though it has found many proponents in our own time.

[33] "Letters of St. Augustin" (*NPNF*[1], 1.517–520).

[34] For some examples, see Gerald Bray, ed., *James, 1–2 Peter, 1–3 John, Jude*, Ancient Christian Commentary on Scripture NT 11 (Downers Grove, IL: InterVarsity, 2000), 106–108; 113–114.

who appeal narrowly to the historical-grammatical method of interpretation, would question the use of certain biblical texts, but the fathers were operating with a different hermeneutic. N. T. Wright, in his monumental work on the resurrection, quotes Paul's statement that "the Messiah was raised on the third day according to the scriptures"[35] and then notes how that concept is not easily found at first glance in the Hebrew scriptures (to which Paul was referring). Then he asserts that later Jewish and Christian exegetes "became skilled at discovering covert allusions which earlier readers had not seen."[36] This same principle is applicable to the doctrine of the descent, and the church fathers drew upon both the Old and New Testaments to propound this doctrine.[37]

The Formularies of the Church of England Developed under Cranmer on the Descent

With this background, we can now turn our eyes to the earliest period of the English Reformation to see how the doctrine of Christ's descent was taught, looking particularly at some of the formularies that were developed under the watchful eye of Thomas Cranmer. We will begin by examining one work issued during the reign of Henry VIII before turning to the formularies issued under Edward VI.

In 1537, Archbishop Cranmer and his fellow bishops issued a work which was officially called *The Institution of a Christian Man* but was commonly known as *The Bishops' Book*. Bray describes the work as "a practical textbook outlining the Church's beliefs, within the recognized framework of traditional catechetical instruction."[38] The work was primarily intended to guide the future ministers of the Church of England in their preaching and teaching (and could be read as sermons from the pulpit).[39]

In the exposition of the *Apostles' Creed*, it offers a concise teaching on Christ's descent:

> I believe assuredly in my heart, and with my mouth I do profess, that this our Saviour Jesu Christ, after he was thus dead upon the cross, he descended immediately in his soul down into hell, leaving his most blessed body here in earth, and that at his coming thither, by the incomparable might and force of his Godhead, he entered into hell. And like as that mighty man, of whom St. Luke speaketh, which entering into the house of another strong man, first overcame him, and bound him hand and foot, and afterward spoiling him of all his armour and strength, wherein he trusted, took also away from him all the goods and substance he had; and like as strong Samson slew the mighty lion, and took out of his mouth the sweet honey: even so our Saviour Jesu Christ, at his said entry into hell, first he conquered and oppressed both the devil and hell, and also death itself, whereunto all mankind was condemned, and so bound them fast, that is to say, restrained the power and tyranny which they had before, and exercised over all

---

[35] 1 Cor 15:4.

[36] N. T. Wright, *The Resurrection of the Son of God* (Minneapolis, MN: Fortress, 1994), 85.

[37] For a creative and fuller view of how Christ's descent was understood in the Patristic Era, see the apocryphal work *The Gospel of Nicodemus*, which was immensely popular in medieval England. H. C. Kim, ed., *The Gospel of Nicodemus* (Toronto: Pontifical Institute of Mediaeval Studies, 1973).

[38] Gerald Bray, ed., *The Institution of a Christian Man* (Cambridge: James Clarke, 2019), 2.

[39] Diarmaid MacCulloch, *Thomas Cranmer: A Life* (New Haven: Yale University Press, 1996), 206.

mankind, that they never had sith that time, nor never shall have any power finally to hurt or annoy any of them that do faithfully believe in Jesu Christ; and afterward he spoiled hell, and delivered and brought with him from thence all the souls of those righteous and good men, which from the fall of Adam died in the favour of God, and in the faith and belief of this our Saviour Jesu Christ, which was then to come.[40]

This explanation of the descent is entirely consistent with what we saw from the patristic era, employing many of the same biblical passages. Christ's descent is envisioned as the stronger man entering the strong man's house and plundering his goods (even likening Christ to Samson as many of the fathers had done). The descent amounted to a rescue mission in which Jesus gathered and "brought with him" (presumably, to heaven) all of the righteous who from the fall of Adam had died in favor with God.

We now shift to some of the works issued by Cranmer and his associates during Edward's reign. In 1548, Cranmer issued a catechism which was his revision and translation of a work by Andreas Osiander. Cranmer's Catechism has the following statements on Christ's descent: "And as man he suffered death for us, and descended into hell. But as naturally God he loosed the bands and pains of hell, he destroyed the kingdom of death, he rose from death to life, and so paid ransom for our sins, and took away the guiltiness of the same."[41] A bit later in the same sermon regarding our redemption, Cranmer adds, "And when our Savior Jesus Christ had thus satisfied for our sin, and so overcame death and hell, then like a valiant conqueror he ascended into heaven."[42] One more line is worth noting: "And although we be never so much afraid of the sorrows and pains of hell, yet they shall not be able to hold us, because to them that be his servants, he hath broken hell, and set open the gates thereof."[43] The language here is quite traditional and pastoral in intent. As a man, Christ suffered death and descended to hell; but as God, he was victorious over hell, and opened its gates (presumably to release those who had been held captive) and to spare all who belong to Him from fear of going there.

A second catechism that came out during this period was the work of John Ponet, one of Cranmer's chaplains and later, Bishop of Winchester. The work was issued in 1553 along with the *Forty-Two Articles of Religion*. The section on the descent was brief but was consistent with Article III which will be discussed later. After rehearsing the *Apostles' Creed*, the "Scholar" goes on to explain the significance:

> Then he truly died: and was truly buried: that by his most sweet sacrifice, he might pacify his Father's wrath against mankind: and subdue him by his death, who had authority of death, which was the devil: forasmuch not only the living, but also the

---

[40] Charles Lloyd, ed., *Formularies of Faith Put Forth by Authority During the Reign of Henry VIII* (Oxford: The University Press, 1856), 40–41.

[41] Edward Burton, ed., *A Short Instruction into Christian Religion, Being A Catechism Set Forth by Archbishop Cranmer* (Oxford: Oxford University Press, 1829), 114. The language from this work has been slightly updated.

[42] Cranmer, *A Short Instruction*, 116.

[43] Ibid.

dead, where they in hell, or elsewhere, they all felt the power and force of his death: to whom living in prison (as Peter sayeth) Christ preached, though dead in body, yet alive in Spirit.[44]

The most significant aspect of this quote is that the 1 Peter 3 text (which Augustine had reinterpreted) is employed in reference to the descent. The ensuing section on the resurrection also contains allusions to Christ's descent:

> For to die is common to all men: but to loose the bonds of death, and by his own power to rise again, that properly belongeth to Jesus Christ the only begotten Son of God, the only author of life. Moreover it was necessary, that he should rise again with glory, that the sayings of David and other prophets of God might be fulfilled, which told before: that neither his body should see corruption: nor his soul be left in hell.[45]

Reference here is made to "David and other prophets of God," specifically to Psalm 16 (quoted in Acts 2), that Christ's soul would not be left in hell.

For liturgical references to the descent, we turn to the *Book of Common Prayer* which Cranmer issued in two editions during Edward's reign (1549 and 1552). The average layperson would have heard about Christ's descent in almost every encounter with the prayer book. At every baptism, they would have heard the priest ask the godparents, "Doest thou beleue in Jesus Christ hys onely begotten sonne our lorde ... that he went downe into hel?"[46] (The same credal statement would be confessed at every Confirmation service as the confirmands rehearsed the Catechism). At every service of Matins or Evensong that they attended, they would have confessed that Christ "descended into hell," using either the *Apostles'* or *Athanasian Creeds*. And on their sick beds, the minister would recite the *Apostles' Creed* and they would be expected to assent.[47]

The theme of Christ's descent was also prominent in the appointed services around Easter. Those who attended the Easter Even service would have recited Psalm 88, which was frequently linked with the descent by the fathers. The psalmist, or according to the fathers, Christ himself says, "For my soule is full of trouble: and my lyfe draweth nye unto hell," but then he adds that he is "free among the deade."[48] Immediately after the conclusion of this Psalm, the worshiper would have heard in the Epistle the words of 1 Peter 3, that Christ "went and preached unto the spirits in prison."[49] It should be noted here that this was a change from *The Sarum Missal* which preceded it, for the Epistle Lesson for Easter Eve there was Colossians 3:1-4 (this text was moved to Easter Day in the BCP).[50] By using the text from 1 Peter 3 on Holy Saturday, the prayer book clearly sets forth this text as an allusion to Christ's descent. This is reinforced by the fact that the

---

[44] John Ponet, *A Short Catechisme, or Playne Instruction, Conteynynge the Su[m]me of Christian Learning*, (London: Iohn Day, 1553), xx–xxii. Language slightly updated in this work.

[45] Ponet, *A Short Catechisme*, xxiii–xxiv.

[46] *The First and Second Prayer Books of Edward VI* (New York: Dutton, 1949), 244.

[47] Ibid., 262.

[48] Ibid., 108.

[49] Ibid., 108–109.

[50] *The Sarum Missal in English*, (London: The Church Press, 1868), 172.

same text is referenced in the *Articles of Religion* (see below) and its accompanying Catechism by Ponet (noted above).

The English church saw fit to devote an entire article to Christ's descent in the *Forty-Two Articles of Religion* (1553). Article III said:

> As Christ died, and was buried for us: so also it is to be believed, that he went down in to hell. For the body lay in the sepulcher, until the resurrection: but His Ghost departing from him, was with the Ghosts that were in prison, or in hell, and did preach to the same, as the place of S. Peter doth testify.[51]

This version was actually a slight recension of Article III in the Forty-Five Articles signed by six royal chaplains in 1552. The one change from that version was the elimination of a single phrase at the end: "But Christ the Lord freed no one from prison or torment by his descent into Hell."[52] At first glance, this seems rather odd given the fact that it follows after the 1 Peter 3 text which talks about Christ preaching to the spirits in prison, but it was likely inserted to guard against what was perceived as a heresy in the West, the idea that Christ would deliver any of the wicked from hell (those in "prison or torment"—the righteous were perceived as being in Abraham's bosom, the compartment for the righteous in Sheol, following Jesus' story in Luke 16).[53] This line may have been proposed to deal with Augustine's concerns over employing the Petrine text in association with the descent because of the perception that some might think that Christ emptied hell. Regardless, the line was excluded from the 1553 Article (probably because this was not a perceived threat at the time).

This Article, as it was set forth, taught the fact of Christ's descent into hell subsequent to death, as well as the purpose for his descent: namely, to "preach to the spirits in prison." The 1 Peter 3 text provided the biblical rationale for this. Article III would undergo a more extensive recension during Elizabeth's reign, removing the allusion to the Petrine text, despite the strenuous objection of Bishop William Alley of Exeter.[54] In spite of this removal, as noted above, 1 Peter 3 remained as the epistle reading on Holy Saturday, the Church's central moment for reflecting on Christ's descent.

For those subscribing to the *Articles of Religion*, this Article would have prohibited them from denying Christ's descent altogether. The Article would also prohibit adopting Bucer's view that the descent clause was merely a restatement of His burial. The Article says that Christ's "body lay in the sepulcher, until the resurrection: but His Ghost" departed from Him into hell. The Article would also argue against Calvin's view that the *descensus* clause in the Creed was a reference to Christ's cry of abandonment from the cross (Ps 22:1). The Article obviously references what happened after His death, not while suffering on the cross.

---

[51] Charles Hardwick, *A History of the Articles of Religion* (London: George Bell & Sons, 1881), 292. Language slightly updated.

[52] The line in Latin was: "*At suo ad inferos descensu nullos a carceribus aut tormentis liberavit Christus Dominus.*" Edgar C. S. Gibson, *The Thirty-Nine Articles of the Church of England*, Fifth (London: Methuen, 1906), 159. See also Hardwick's *History of the Articles*, 278–79.

[53] Luke 16:19–31.

[54] John Strype, *Annals of the Reformation and Establishment of Religion, and Other Various Occurrences in the Church of England, During Queen Elizabeth's Happy Reign* (Oxford: Clarendon, 1824), 1.1.519.

Conclusion

Having surveyed the formularies produced by Thomas Cranmer and his associates during the successive reigns of Henry and Edward, we would conclude that the teaching of the re-formed Church of England on Christ's descent into hell was broadly consistent with what had been taught by the church fathers. The exposition of the credal article in *The Bishops' Book* is closest to the fathers' use of the Scriptures in teaching the descent and its purpose, but the formularies produced under Edward are not vastly different. There is a clear and consistent line of interpretation which runs through the *Forty-Two Articles of Religion*, the *Book of Common Prayer*, and the catechisms quoted. The official teaching on this matter is that after his death on the cross, Christ descended into hell, where he made proclamation of his victory to those therein (alluding to 1 Peter 3), and then arose from death and hell as a valiant conqueror over the devil.

One important aspect of this doctrine from the patristic era that is not explicitly stated is the deliverance of the Old Testament saints. However, it would appear that even though this concept is not explicitly stated, it continued to be held for three reasons 1) the Petrine text which was used for biblical support had long been held to refer to Christ's proclamation of victory to those in Sheol who had longed for his appearing; 2) reference is made to Christ's breaking and opening of the gates of hell; 3) there are several references to Christ loosening "the bonds of death."

So in this brief test case, we have seen that Cranmer and his associates, in spite of the reinterpretation of Christ's descent offered by other reformers, maintained a close view with the fathers. The Anglican church today would do well to return to these sources and to the teachings of the fathers to clarify what we believe concerning a greatly misunderstood doctrine.

Chapter 16

Catholic Doctor:
John Jewel (1522-1571)

Mr. James Syrow

The question of how to maintain catholicity amidst reform was perhaps the greatest question for the sixteenth-century Anglican Divines. It is not an exaggeration to say that modern Anglo-Catholics think about catholicity only with a fraction of the attention, research, and interest it received during the English Reformation.

This assertion may come as a surprise to those who consume secondary scholarship, written by seemingly reputable modern historians; but let us remember that our era no longer holds it disreputable to filter historical research through one's own biases and prejudices. Diarmaid MacCullough's history of the Reformation omits the fact that the Anglican Divines were more interested in catholicity than any contemporary Roman Catholic theologians. A top living expert on John Jewel is a Reformed Baptist, and Jewel's interest in catholicity will be found nowhere in his work. In fact, Jewel is a good case study of the misrepresentation inflicted upon the whole scope of the English Reformation. As much as Thomas Cranmer has been mistreated, no one more than Jewel has been a victim of recent historic distortion. One recent book referred to him as a Calvinist, despite the fact that there is no trace of Calvin in any of his writings. Another recent book[1] calls him an "arch-protestant," without defining the term. While Jewel was certainly a fierce and implacable opponent of the Church of Rome, so was William Laud; and Jewel in fact wrote more on catholicity than Laud ever did. Thus, our church history has become distorted and divided against itself, by the sloppy biases of recent (mostly non-Anglican) scholars. I propose that we sweep all of them aside, and consider John Jewel on his own terms and in his own words. Studying our great bishop as an individual will then serve as a bridge for us to grasp the English Reformation as a whole.

So then, who was John Jewel? Among sixteenth-century Anglican reformers, Jewel was perhaps the strongest contender for catholicity. He taught Anglicans what it means to be Catholic without the Pope, and thus became our *Doctor Catholicus*.

This article will walk through the key moments of Jewel's life and work, tracing his lifelong effort to refine and articulate catholicity in the absence of the Papacy. The concept which he formulated in the back-breaking trials of the sixteenth century has left a lasting legacy in Anglican self-identity.

Early Life and Exile

John Jewel was born in 1522. In the 1540s he received a bachelor's and a master's from Oxford. He distinguished himself through diligent learning and the study of the classics; his biography says that "he was a great admirer of *Horace* and *Cicero*, and read all Erasmus's works, and imitated them too, for it was his custom to write something every day.... He affected ever rather to express himself fluently, neatly, and with great weight

---

[1] Kenneth Fincham and Nicholas Tyacke, *Altars Restored: The Changing Face of English Religious Worship, 1547-c.1700* (New York: Oxford University Press, 2008).

of Argument and strength of Reason, than in hunting for the Flowers of Rhetorick and Cadences of Words."[2] His later writings undoubtedly derive their power and force from the training he received in the classical studies.

In 1551, when Jewel was 29, he was ordained and given a vicarage at a village near Oxford, frequently preaching both at his parish and the university. However, in 1553 his career was cut short by the accession of Bloody Mary, whereupon he was expelled from his vicarage and all university positions. Aged 32 and reduced to extreme poverty, Jewel wrote in his farewell message:

> Pardon me my Hearers, if grief has seized me, being to be torn from that place against my will, where I have passed the first part of my Life, where I have lived pleasantly, and been in some Honour and Employment. But why do I thus delay to put an end to my Misery by one word? Woe is me, that (as with my extreme sorrow and resentment I at last speak it) I must say farewel my Studies, farewel to these beloved Houses, farewel thou pleasant Seat of Learning, farewel to the most delightful Conversation with you, farewel Young men, farewel Lads, farewel Fellows, farewel Brethren, farewel ye beloved as my eyes, farewel ALL, farewel.[3]

Forced to leave England, Jewel fled to a city that was then taking refugees, Frankfurt, and joined the English colony of refugees there.

It is in Frankfurt, in 1554, that we come to Jewel's first debate on catholicity, for there was another personality present there: John Knox. This John Knox, upon his arrival at Frankfurt, observed something strange: these refugees from Roman persecution were for some reason worshipping in the Roman fashion! All the clergy wore vestments, not just at the divine service but while walking the streets, doing their grocery shopping, and at all other times outside the home. The order of worship followed a lengthy pre-written liturgy, likely chanted, with formulaic litanies, responses, and all the gestures of bowing and crossing oneself. When it came time for Communion, he saw them kneel in order to receive the Sacrament of the blessed Body and Blood. To the English Catholiques, as the refugees at Frankfurt styled themselves, there was nothing unusual here; this was simply Christianity as it has always been, everywhere and at all times, for there was not yet any other form of Christianity, anywhere on the planet. This universal form of Christianity they identified as Catholic, and indeed Edward VI was called a Catholic Prince and a Catholic King; the reforming bishops were called Catholic bishops who helped correct the errors of Rome. Thomas Cranmer entitled his treatise the *Defense of the Catholic Doctrine of the Body and Blood of Jesus Christ*, and the reforms conducted during Edward's reign were called the Catholic Reformation. To the Edwardian reformers, then, the Reformation was an *ecclesiastical* movement, by the Churchmen within the wider One True Church. But to the Scots and some reformers on the Continent it seemed to be an *eschatological* movement, something like one last and final battle against the Devil and all his works.

---

[2] Anon., *The Life of the Right Reverend Father in God, Dr. John Jewel, Lord Bishop of Salisbury, Collected and Written by a Person of Quality* in *The Apology of the Church of England and an Epistle to One Seignior Scipio, a Venetian Gentleman, Concerning the Council of Trent* (London, 1685), 5, google.com/books/edition/The_Apology_of_the_Church_of_England/W2I9AQAAMAAJ?hl.

[3] *Life*, 9.

When Knox arrived in Frankfurt, then, he was scandalized by the English ceremonial; taking it as compromise and not as timeless Christianity, he set upon agitating the people to abandon their church calendar, put aside their liturgies and observances, and adopt the new piety that was found in Geneva. He ceaselessly reminded them that the Genevans did not persecute them like the adherents of Rome did, and they should leave behind the ritual that resembled their enemies.

Knox's arguments had an air of plausibility, and he began to gather adherents. This was the founding moment of the Puritan movement. As Heylyn writes, "They reject[ed] the whole Frame and Fabrick of the Reformation made in England in King Edward's time, and conformed themselves wholly to the fashions of the Church of Geneva."[4]

In time the orthodox party began to answer these challenges, led by Richard Cox, the exiled Canon of Windsor and Dean of Westminster. Together with the young John Jewel and other orthodox divines, they sought to persuade the radicals that their proposals were not Catholic or compatible with the timeless Christianity. However, without the Pope it was not clear what that word meant, for the Roman church had spent the previous several centuries teaching that it was the Popes who created catholicity in those who submitted to them. The radicals rejected the term *Catholic* as irrelevant, dangerous, and at any event incompatible with the Reformation. Here then, Jewel for the first time was confronted with the problem: *was* there anything special about the form of Christianity that the English refugees brought with them? Or was Knox right that it was just an accident of history, artificially imposed under the domination from Rome?

These struggles exposed the reality that the Reformation was a battle on two fronts, not just one. In his later years he would blast the early Puritans well.[5] How he would refer to the secular historians and his reformed Baptist biographers today, we can only guess.

Eventually Richard Cox and the orthodox party succeeded in pushing Knox out of Frankfurt, who with his adherents resettled in Geneva and went on to give birth to Puritanism. What remained bothersome, however, is how the orthodox prevailed: they relied exclusively on statutory law. They fell back on a venerable English custom which went back in time; and the statutory authority of the prayer book was authorized by law under Edward VI, as if mere passage by parliament were enough to quell all doubts about the book's catholicity. However, as any sagacious observer could see, neither of these pillars was absolute; ancient churches could and did err, and the laws of the Realm certainly could and did err. Even worse, the Church of Rome, which did claim to be absolute, was constantly changing its doctrine, the number of sacraments, the purpose of Mass, the definition of mortal sin, the theology of purgatory, and many other loci of theology. Christian teaching somehow had to be put on an absolute foundation, to prevent internal schisms like that of Knox; and yet avoid the example of the Roman church where truth was a flexible concept.

---

[4] Peter Heylyn, *Ecclesia Restaurata: The history of the Reformation of the Church of England*, 3rd ed. (London: Twyford, 1674), 232.

[5] Jewel certainly preached passionately against prideful divisions in the church; see, e.g., Sermon XIII in Richard William Jelf, ed., *The Works of John Jewel*, 8 vols. (Oxford: Oxford University Press, 1848), 7:558-571. archive.org/details/ofjohnjeweljelf07jeweuoft.

Two key texts provided the first hints of an answer to this. The first was Philip Melanchthon's pioneering book, *De ecclesiae autoritate / On the Authority of the Church and the Writings of the Ancient Fathers* (1539), recently described as follows: "Few texts of the Reformation period state so clearly the principles according to which the Fathers and the councils of the church may be considered authentic sources for Christian doctrine."[6] The other was Thomas Cranmer's vast *Defence of the true and catholike doctrine of the sacrament of the body and bloud of our sauiour Christ* (1550), in which he marshaled 4 volumes of arguments and testimonies from the church fathers to demonstrate the novelty of Roman transubstantiation. Cranmer also linked patristic testimony to catholicity—as if catholicity did not have to be Papal or even *recent*, in order to be valid or binding. Clearly there was something there, and it had something to do with the church fathers. But more questions were created than answered. If the church fathers were authoritative, didn't that diminish the authority of Scripture? Could the Reformation really hitch its wagon to the utterances of the fathers, in case they too fell into error? Cranmer's book seemed to show that on the Eucharist, at least, the fathers were safe, but what about all the other points of Christianity?

Jewel saw that in order to defend the English piety (or perhaps abandon it if it were in error), there had to be a better justification than long custom, or legal backing. What if the critics were right that the English 'way' was just a transplant from Rome, with all the attendant complexities that would entail?

A wide-reaching effort needed to be made, both to recover pure Christianity from centuries of Papal imposition, and to protect it from self-willed radicals. If the church fathers offered help in this, then it was imperative to become a scholar of patristics, and check whether they really could become the fortress and castle in defense of Scripture. The resources available to Jewel at Frankfurt, being a penniless refugee, were simply unequal to the task. His friend Peter Martyr Vermigli, in Zurich, called for his help in a major new undertaking: to publish significant new editions of the fathers. Here was a prime opportunity, and Jewel took it. He traveled to Zurich and spent the next four years living in Vermigli's home, with his family, taking advantage of the Zurich academic archives to read everything the church fathers had ever written.

Return to England

At the end of 1558, the English communities suddenly learned that Bloody Mary had passed away, and the hundreds of executions had come to an end. Questions immediately arose around the shape that the Church would take under Elizabeth. Jewel, now a seasoned man nearing 40 years old, on his return was immediately pulled into controversies with Roman Catholics, who resumed the polemic of catholicity as the exclusive gift of the Popes. In Jewel, however, they found a fundamentally different man from the freshly ordained vicar just before exile. By now he had read just about everything the church fathers had written. He confirmed that catholicity did not have to be recent in order to be valid and binding; and Scripture would not be diminished, if this reliance on the fathers was rightly understood. What Thomas Cranmer did in showing

---

[6] Ralph Keen, "Political Authority and Ecclesiology in Melanchthon's '*De Ecclesiae Autoritate*,'" *Church History* 65, no. 1 (March 1996): 1.

the safety of the fathers on the Eucharist could be applied to *every* topic of Christianity: justification, Papacy, sin and grace, communion in two kinds, images in worship, liturgy, the ceremonial, and ethical questions. The doctrine of the Church of England, as reformed under Edward VI, appeared to be a carbon copy of the ancient Church (undoubtedly the legacy of Archbishop Cranmer, perhaps the greatest Patristic scholar of *his* generation, with a personal library larger than that of Oxford[7]). What Cranmer had done implicitly, Jewel could bring out into the open explicitly; hitching the Elizabethan Settlement to the church fathers would require no changes in doctrine at all. The first generation of Anglican reformers had done their job well; left now was a wide-ranging justification of that doctrine by references to the Patristics, in defense from both the Popes and the Knoxes of the world.

In the spring of 1559, Jewel took part in the "Westminster Disputation," the first official Elizabethan dialogue between followers of the Church of Rome and that of the Church of England. The statement to which Jewel signed his name reads, in part, as follows:

> Christ is our only master, whom the Father hath commanded us to hear: and seeing also his word is the truth, from the which it is not lawful for us to depart not one hair breadth, and against the which, as the apostle saith, *we can do nothing* ... And forasmuch as we have for our mother the true and catholic church of Christ, which is grounded upon the doctrine of the Apostles and Prophets, and is of Christ the head in all things governed; we do reverence her judgement; we obey her authority as becometh children.[8]

Here was an explosive statement. The catholic church as mother? Reverence her judgment? Obeying her authority as children? We do not know if Jewel had a direct role in drafting those words, but they match what he would go on to say for years to come.

The Roman Catholic theologians in England challenged these claims, stating that the Church of Rome, *the* Catholic Church, stands against them. Nonetheless, by this stage in his career, Jewel was deeply studied in the fathers, seeing them again and again espouse beliefs oddly similar to the English Church, and confirm little of what was then being ratified at the Council of Trent. He therefore gave a sermon, which history has called the "Challenge Sermon," wherein he gave his first substantial statement on catholicity. He listed Roman Catholic doctrines, and challenged his audience to find any ancient support for them, putting his name and reputation on the line:

> If any learned man of all our adversaries, or if all the learned men that be alive, be able to bring any one sufficient sentence out of any old Catholike Doctor, or Father; Or out of any old general Council; or out of the holy Scriptures of God; or any one example of the Primitive Church, whereby it may be clearly and plainly proved, that [...], or that [...], or that [...]. If any man alive were able to prove any of these articles,

---

[7] Cf. David G. Selwyn, "Cranmer's Library: Its Potential for Reformation Studies," in *Thomas Cranmer: Churchman and Scholar*, eds. Paul Ayris and David Selwyn (Woodbridge, UK: Boydell, 1993), 58-59.

[8] John Strype, *Annals of the Reformation and Establishment of Religion, and Other Various Occurrences in the Church of England, during Queen Elizabeth's Happy Reign : Together with an Appendix of Original Papers of State, Records, and Letters* Vol 1, Part 2 (Oxford: Clarendon, 1824), 465.

by any one clear or plain clause, or sentence, either of the Scriptures, or of the old
Doctors, or of any old general Council, or by any example of the Primitive Church:
I promised then that I would give over and subscribe unto him.

If any one of all our adversaries be able clearly and plainly to prove by such
authority of the Scriptures, the old Doctors, and Councils, as I said before, that [...],
or that [...], or that [...]. If any one of all our adversaries be able to avouch any one of
all these articles, by any such sufficient authority of Scriptures, Doctors, or
Councils, as I have required; as I said before so I say now again, I am content to yield
unto him, and to subscribe.

Several points are significant here, such as the confidence with which Jewel could claim
the testimony of antiquity better than all Roman theologians put together. More
significantly, here for the first time he drew an explicit link between the church fathers
and catholicity.

Until that time, and indeed in our own day as well, catholicity was attached to the
edicts of the Roman Catholic Church. After all, the word *Catholic* is in its title! Whatever
the Councils of Florence or Constance decreed and ratified by the Pope was *ipso facto*
Catholic; whatever Trent decreed was *ipso facto* Catholic, from the authority of the Popes
who made it so. In one year, the number of sacraments was such, and in another year
that number became different—all fine because the Pope made it so. What counted as a
mortal sin changed from decade to decade, the Popes adding or subtracting from that
category as suited their plans (or financial needs). Catholicity, Catholic-*ism*, then, was
something of a moving target, its contents quite expansive and stretchable throughout
the ages. If the Popes wanted to raise money for a new art gallery, they would invent a
new category of sins cleansed in Purgatory, and offer a merciful dispensation from 700,
or 900, or 9000 years of Purgatory torture, if the person sent in an extra silver florin to
the church Collector. Indeed, St. Peter's Basilica was financed through this kind of selling
of Monopoly Bucks to the desperate and destitute peasants. Even the Eucharist could be
altered at will, with the wine and sacred Blood having been no longer offered for
centuries. When Jan Huss raised a cry of reform against these abuses, he was promised
safe passage to make his case at the Council of Constance; when he arrived, he was
promptly seized and burned at the stake.

To say that the Church was in highest disrepute, the Popes being repeatedly put in
the lowest rungs of Hell by the likes of Petrarch and Dante, is to say too little. If this was
the Catholic Church, then it could be reasonably concluded that "catholicity" described
all that was spiritually evil in the world, and the reformation was indeed some sort of
eschatological Final Battle against the Antichrist. It is therefore a great marvel that the
Anglican Divines like Jewel charged into the breach and spent their lives defending the
word *Catholic*, even against impossible odds.

Was catholicity stretchable, or fixed for all time? Who determined its contents? Could
a minority of Christians be more Catholic than the vast majority? Was catholicity
necessarily a function of the present living Church?

The teaching of Vincent of Lérins was perhaps instrumental here, that catholicity at
least resides in the past, whether or not it resides in the present. Drawing from Vincent,
Melanchthon, and Cranmer, John Jewel came to the felicitous insight: the way to affirm

catholicity safely was to make the church fathers its source and definition. The edicts of today's church may or may not be catholic, regardless of how solemnly they were promulgated. The catholicity they possess can only be derivative, not intrinsic, deriving it only from a pre-existing objective standard, and not the church's fiat and authority. The church cannot create new catholic truths, but only draw from the existing "treasury" of catholicity, in order for its edicts to have validity.

The Challenge Sermon created a sensation throughout Europe, taking catholicity out of the Pope's living power and depositing it with the long-deceased church fathers. Jewel writes:

> Good people, there is now a siege laid to your walls; an army of Doctors and Councils show themselves upon a hill. The adversary who would have you yield, makes you think that they are his soldiers and stand on his side. But keep your hold: the Doctors and old Catholike Fathers, in the points that I have spoken of, are yours.

The Apology

In 1560, aged 38, Jewel was made bishop in the See of Salisbury, which he found impoverished by the rapacious John Capon, his predecessor and bishop of Salisbury under Queen Mary. In parallel with working overtime to restore the dilapidated parishes under his charge, Jewel set about to prepare the most famous work associated with his name: *An Apology, or Answer in Defence of the Church of England*, published in 1562. Although removed from us by nearly five centuries, this remarkable book feels like it could have been written today, so remarkably was it written, perhaps the most readable book of the sixteenth century. His biographer states that it was immediately

> published by the Queen's Authority, and with the advice of some of the Bishops, as the Publick Confession of the Catholick and Christian Faith of the Church of England... This Apology being published during the very time of the last meeting of the Council of Trent, was read there, and seriously considered, and great threats made that it should be answered; and accordingly two Learned Bishops, one a Spaniard and the other an Italian, undertook that task, but neither of them did any thing in it. But in the mean time the Book spread into all the Countries in Europe, and was much applauded in France, Flanders, Germany, Spain, Poland, Hungary, Denmark, Sweden and Scotland; and found at least a passage into Italy, Naples and Rome itself; and was soon after translated into German, Italian, French, Spanish, Dutch, and last into the Greek Tongue.[9]

This book has many merits, but for our purposes it shows a further refinement in Jewel's thought: whether catholicity embodies the views of the largest body of Christians at any given time. How could Anglicans pretend to have the fullness of the Catholic truth if they were locked away on their island? Surely it is more reasonable to take a statistical average from Christendom at large. Yet, any student of church history and the Arian controversy knows the folly of treating numerical advantage as a proxy for the truth. Jewel writes:

> It has been a Complaint through all ages, from the Patriarchs and Prophets, down to us, and confirmed by the Histories of all Times and Places, that Truth has been a

---

[9] *Life*, 31–32.

Stranger upon Earth, and that she has met with many among the ignorant sort of men who have Hated and Reviled her.... [Jesus] when he taught the Truth, was esteemed as a Cheat, and an Evil-doer; a Samaritan; the Prince of the Devils; a Seducer of the People; a Drunkard, and a Glutton. Who does not know, that St. Stephen [...] was immediately arraigned and condemned for a wicked Blasphemer of the Law, of Moses, of the Temple, and of God? ... Who knows not what Calumnies were formerly cast upon our Fathers, the first Professors of Christianity? [Calling them] conspirators that held secret cabals against the State, and for that reason used to assemble before it was Light? That they murdered Children, eat their Flesh, and, like Wild Beasts, drank their Blood?... That they were an Impious, Irreligious, Atheistical Sect, Enemies to Mankind, not fit to Live and Enjoy the Common Benefit of Light? ...

These were the scandalous Reproaches that were at that Time thrown upon the People of God, upon our Saviour Jesus Christ, St. Paul, St. Stephen, and upon all who in the first Ages embraced the Truth of the Gospel, and were content to be known by the Then Universally hated and despised Name of Christians. And tho' these Stories were false, yet the Devil gained his Ends, if he could at least cause them to be believed, and the Christians to be publickly hated, and generally persecuted. Hereupon, Kings and Princes, induced by Insinuations of this kind, put all the Prophets to Death; condemned Esaia to be saw'd in pieces, Jeremy to be stoned, Daniel to be devoured by Lions, Amos to be broken with an Iron Bar, Paul to die by the Sword, Christ to be crucified, all Christians in general to be imprisoned, tormented, hanged on Gibbets, thrown in headlong from Rocks and Precipices, torn in pieces by Wild Beasts, and burned.... This has been the Reception which the Authors and Professors of the Truth have ever met with.[10]

Therefore, if the fullness of the truth is likely to be in minority at most times, catholicity must not depend on current statistics in the Christian population.

All men, may see what are our Sentiments of every part of the Christian Religion, and may themselves determine, whether that Faith which they shall see confirmed by the Words of Christ, the Writings of the Apostles, the Testimonies of the Catholick Fathers, and the Examples of many Ages, be only the Extravagant Notion of Madmen, and the Conspiracy of Hereticks.[11]

The *Apology* is a short work, and yet the word *Catholic* is used over thirty times, and the church fathers are cited hundreds of times; demonstrating how in this or that point the Church of England espoused a key truth, or the Church of Rome has departed from the Catholic faith. The explosive impact of this work was unequalled in the sixteenth century. Church historian Thomas Fuller says that "[the Roman Catholic apologists] came off so poorly, and Jewel on the contrary so amazed and confounded them with 'a

---

[10] John Jewel, *The Apology of the Church of England*, trans. Thomas Cheyne (London, 1719), 1–6, books.google.com/books?id=X9ksAAAAYAAJ&newbks.

[11] Ibid., 19–20.

cloud of witnesses' in every point in question, that as Bishop Godwin upon good ground affirmeth, no one thing in our age gave the Papacy so deadly a wound."[12]

At the Peak

By the mid-1560s, references to the non-Papal Church of England as being Catholic were the default mode of Anglican address and self-identity. The Declaration of Doctrine officially promulgated in 1559 said: "We have neither swerved from the Infallible Truth of God's written Word, neither yet from the Doctrine and Confession of Christ's Catholick Church; as we by God's Grace shall be able and ready at all times evidently to shew unto all Men."[13]

Queen Elizabeth wrote in a letter to Emperor Ferdinand II (Nov. 3, 1563): "England embraceth no new or strange Doctrine, but the same which Christ hath commanded, the primitive and Catholike Church hath received, and the antient Fathers have with one voyce and minde approved."[14]

Of her own power and royal prerogative, she wrote as follows:

> [We do not] challenge or take to us (as malicious persons do untruly surmise) any superiority to ourselves to define decide or determine any article or point of the Christian faith and religion, or to change any ancient ceremony of the Church from the form before received and observed by the Catholic and Apostolic Church, or the use of any function belonging to any ecclesiastical person being a minister of the Word and Sacraments in the Church.[15]

The official 1571 Church Canon on Preachers said:

> Chiefly they shall take heed, that they teach nothing in their preaching, which they would have the people religiously to observe, and believe, but that which is agreeable to the doctrine of the old Testament, and the new, and that which the catholike fathers, and ancient Bishops have gathered out of that doctrine.

Thomas Bilson wrote: "the things refourmed in the Church of England by the Lawes of this realme are truely Catholike."[16]

There are hundreds of other such references, not least of which are the texts in the 1559 prayer book:

> More especially we pray for the good estate of the Catholic Church; that it may be so guided and governed by thy good Spirit, that all who profess and call themselves Christians, may be led into the way of truth, and hold the faith in unity of spirit, in the bond of peace, and in righteousness of life.
>
> ... of the sundry Alterations proposed unto us, we have rejected all such as were [...] of dangerous consequence, as secretly striking at some established Doctrine, or

---

[12] Thomas Fuller, *Abel Redivivus* (London: John Stafford, 1651; William Tegg, 1867), 360.

[13] Strype, *Annals*, Vol 1, Part 1, 170.

[14] William Camden, *The History Of The Most Renowed and Victorious Princess Elizabeth, Late Queen of England*, 4th ed.(London, 1688), 32.

[15] William Edward Collins, "Queen Elizabeth's Defence of her Proceedings in Church and State" (London: SPCK, 1899).

[16] Thomas Bilson, *Christian Subjection* (Oxford: Joseph Barnes, 1585).

laudable Practice of the Church of England, or indeed of the whole Catholick Church of Christ.

Catholicity was thus returned to its original usage, a concept with a fixed meaning not open to future revision or update. A church today could only lay claim to being Catholic insofar as she partook of that initial primordial catholicity. This was the great insight which Jewel spent his life formulating, and then defending. In this form, catholicity was not dangerous for the likes of John Knox to accept (that is, if they wanted to be with all the common company of Christians).

The decade of the 1560s saw Jewel at the peak of his energy and productivity. Zealously re-building the impoverished diocese of Salisbury, he ceaselessly traveled through the parishes and vicarages under his charge. His biographers record a statement that was often on his lips: "A bishop should die preaching."[17] The Roman apologists in England attacked his writings, with lengthy line-by-line refutations of his *Apology*. He responded with no less lengthy defenses of the *Apology*. His main opponent Thomas Harding tried to claim that without Papal influence, proper liturgical reverence was impossible. Jewel responded that "Kneeling, bowing, standing up, and other like," rightly understood, "are commendable gestures and tokens of devotion."[18] A nineteenth-century edition of the *Defence* describes it as follows:

> [It] is the greatest monument of his power: it evinces a more perfect mastery of his weapons, a more skilful use of his materials old and new, greater precision of argument and language, more concentration of thought, an increased consciousness of his own strength and of his opponents' weakness, proportioned to his growing confidence in the justice of his cause upon each repeated revision of the subject."[19]

There was so much work to do that Jewel slept four hours a night, tying a weight to his toes so that he would never fall asleep for too long or too deeply. Today we understand that this probably contributed to his early death in 1571, at the age of 49. For one of his sermons, he chose a line from the Psalms: "The zeal for thine House hath eaten me up" (Ps 69:9). So passionate was he for the Church and for the Truth.

Out of scraped up donations and tithings, Jewel established charitable scholarships to support poor students unable to afford University; the most famous of the students he supported was Richard Hooker. In Jewel's biography we find the following charming anecdote:

> [I]n the last year of the Bishop's Life, Mr. Hooker making this his Patron a visit at his Palace, the good Bishop made him, and a Companion he had with him, dine at his own Table with him.... The Bishop when he parted with him, gave him good Counsel and his Blessing, but forgot to give him Money, which when the Bishop bethought himself of, he sent a Servant to call him back again and then told him, *I sent for you* Richard, *to lend you a Horse which hath carried me many a mile, and I thank*

---

[17] *Life*, 36

[18] Richard William Jelf, ed., *The Works of John Jewel, D.D., Bishop of Salisbury*, Vol 2. (Oxford: Oxford University Press, 1848), 97.

[19] Jelf, *Works of John Jewel*, Vol. 1., xvi-xvii.

God with much ease. And presently delivered into his hand a walking-staff, with which he professed he had travelled many parts of Germany.

[He gave some money to him and his poor mother, saying:] ... *tell her, I send her a Bishop's Blessing with it, and beg the continuance of her Prayers for me.*[20]

Thus, receiving benediction and a Bishop's Blessing, Hooker completed his education and went on to make quite a name for himself in the following generation.

Doctor of the Church

The final years of his life saw Jewel at the peak of his theological career. He was consulted by Primates of the church and took part in the Church Convocation which formally ratified the *Thirty-Nine Articles of Religion*. The sagacity of those articles bears witness to the great restraint of the churchmen of that era, Jewel among them. He was also asked to draft some of the official Homilies, which proved of help during that era when there were almost no educated clergy to competently preach from the pulpits.

The bulk of Jewel's efforts however was dedicated to two colossal projects. The first was a massive biblical project, unfinished at his death, from which we have extant commentaries on the liturgical Epistles and Gospels; commentaries on Galatians, 1 Peter, both Thessalonians; and expositions on the Our Father, the Creed, and the Ten Commandments.

Closer to our purpose was his second project, also unfinished. By all indications it was going to be a system of dogmatic Divinity, covering all major loci of theology. However, the only sections to have come down to us are the treatises on Scripture and on the Sacraments. In both these texts Jewel put the finishing touches on his concept of catholicity.

The first text, "The Treatise on Scripture" (published 1570), addressed itself to reconciling Scripture with the doctrine of the church fathers. No doctrine of the Church of England could be catholic if it did not adhere to the fathers; but the uniqueness, centrality, and inspiration of Scripture was fundamental to all Anglican Divines, Jewel not least among them. This was a hard knot to untie, and continues to bedevil some churchmen to this day; but Jewel provided an answer to it back in 1570, and this modern summary captures the needle which Jewel successfully threaded:

> The scope and tendency of all Bishop Jewel's writings was an appeal from the novelty and corruption to the purity of earlier times. This was the general design of his life. In the Treatise of the Holy Scriptures, for example, while he fully asserts the supremacy of the written word of God, yet he expressly acknowledges and teaches, "that the Fathers are *interpreters* of the word of God; that they were learned men and learned fathers, the instruments of the mercy of God, and vessels full of grace. They were witnesses to the truth."[21]

Why read some modern interpreter, when you have an ancient one who lived closer to Christ? When put that way, the logic is inescapable.

---

[20] *Life*, 47.

[21] J. H. Parker, "Preface" in *Two Treatises: I. On the Holy Scriptures ; II. On the Sacraments* (Oxford: 1840), vi.

Jewel's other text, "A Treatise on the Sacraments" (published 1583, after his death), contains his exploration of catholicity as applied to the Sacraments, with the most strident pro-sacramental language found anywhere in the Elizabethan Church. In this his student Hooker declined somewhat from the high precedent set by his master, for Hooker's sacramental language is significantly softer, while that of Jewel could scarcely have been said more strongly. The reception of Christ's Body and Blood in the Sacrament, the washing and Regeneration of man in Baptism—these teachings thunder from across Jewel's pages. Yet it is the manner in which he teaches these doctrines that is most significant, for Jewel never rests on his own authority; by that measure his teachings could never be said to be catholic. Instead, he derives his entire teaching from the church fathers themselves:

> That which I will utter herein shall not be of myself, but of the fathers of the church: not of those which have been of later years, but of the most ancient: not of the heretics, but of the most Catholike, which ever have been the enemies and confounders of Heretikes. I will show the use, and order, and faith of the Primitive Church which was in the times of the Apostles, and of Tertullian, Cyprian, Basil, Nazianzen, Jerome, Augustine, Chrysostom, and other Catholike and godly learned Fathers. Let no man regard me, or my speech: I am only a finger: these are clear and bright stars. I do but show them unto you, and point them, that you may behold them. God give us grace that we may see them truly, and by them be able to guide and to direct our way. Let us lay aside all contention, and quietly hear that shall be spoken. Whatsoever shall be said, if it be true, if it be ancient, if it be Catholike, if it be so clear as the sunbeams, let us humble our hearts, and believe it.[22]

Legacy

Anglicans have a relationship with the church fathers not found in the other traditions. Others may certainly quote the fathers, but only those which confirm whatever they already happen to believe. Not many will be willing to chain themselves to the doctrines of the fathers and go wherever those may lead. Yet this has been precisely the mode in which Anglicanism has operated after the Reformation. Presbyterians like Jean Daille mocked the fathers; in his magnum opus, *Du vrai emploi des Pères / On the Right Use of the Fathers* (1631) he devoted hundreds of pages to blasting holes in Patristic theology and the *consensus patrum*, dismissing anyone who demanded submission to them as a guide to doctrine. Roman Catholics opportunistically cited the fathers when convenient, but were just as quick to jettison them, as seen in the following examples:

> **Belgic Index Expurgatorius:** We bear with many errors in Ancient Catholick Authors, and lessen, and excuse them, and by some cunning device often deny them, and give a more commodious sense, when they are objected to in our disputes with our Adversaries.

---

[22] Jelf, *Works of John Jewel*, Vol. 8, 19.

Maldonatus: Although I have only one Author to support my interpretation, yet I allow it, rather than those of Augustine's and others, although they are more probable, because this one of mine better contradicts the sense of the Calvinists. (*Comment. in John 6*)

Cardinal Cajetan: If we come across some fresh interpretation which, though new, yet squares with the text under discussion, with the rest of the Bible and with the Church's teachings, though differing from the TORRENT of the Fathers, we, as critics, must in fairness be prepared to render to every one his due... Let no one, then, reject some fresh interpretation merely on the grounds that it does not square with what the early Fathers have held... let him give thanks to God who has not limited interpretation of the Bible to the early Fathers.[23]

Anglicans are the only Christian body who have been bold enough to say:

These be cases not of wit, but of faith; not of eloquence, but of truth; not invented or devised by us, but from the Apostles and the holy Fathers and founders of the Church by long succession brought unto us. We are not the devisers thereof, but only the keepers; not the masters, but the students. Touching the substance of religion, we believe what the ancient Catholike learned Fathers believed: we do what they did: we say what they said. And marvel not, in what side soever ye see them, if ye see us join unto the same. It is our great comfort that we see their faith and our faith to agree in one.[24]

The legacy of this thought proved important to all subsequent Anglican self-identity. Lancelot Andrewes further built on Jewel, supplying the boundaries for who counted as a church father, in his famous formula, adapted as follows: "One canon, two testaments, three creeds, four general councils, first five centuries, form the boundary of our faith."[25]

This train of thought has been a mainstay of Anglican thought ever since, down to as recently as 1951, when Geoffrey Fisher, Archbishop of Canterbury, gave a modified formulation: "We have no doctrine of our own—we only possess the catholic enshrined doctrine of the Catholic Church enshrined in the catholic creeds, and those creeds we hold without addition or diminution."[26]

Jewel's biographer provides the following assessment of Anglicanism:

This Church hath been persecuted because she alone of all the Churches in Europe, has had the Blessing and singular Favour of God to reform with Prudence, Moderation, and an exact and regular Conduct, after great and wise Deliberations, by the consent of our Bishops, Convocations, States, and Princes, without Tumults or hasty Counsels; and accordingly here was nothing changed but upon good Advice, after the most irresistable Conviction that it was contrary to the Word of

---

[23] Cajetan, "Praef. in Pentateuchen," trans. Hugh Pope, *Blackfriars* 26 (1945): 96.

[24] Jelf, *Works of John Jewel*, Vol. 3, 499.

[25] Translation, based on Lancelot Andrewes, *Opuscula Quædam Posthuma*, J. H, Parker, ed. (London, 1852), 91.

[26] Anselm Hughes, *The Rivers of the Flood* (London: The Faith Press, 1961), 50.

God, the Sentiments of the Holy Fathers and Councils, and the Practice of the truly Primitive and Apostolical Church.[27]

Hooker sums up his legacy simply as follows: "John Jewel was the worthiest divine that Christendom hath bred for some hundreds of years."[28]

---

[27] *Life*, Preface.
[28] *Laws of Ecclesiastical Polity*, II.6.

Chapter 17

Sweet Wisdom's Order: Richard Hooker (1554–1600) and the Re-Formed Catholic Stand against Chaos

The Rev. Richard Tarsitano

In 1935, Paul Elmer More and Frank Leslie Cross produced a compilation of "the thought and practice of the Church of England, illustrated from the religious literature of the Seventeenth Century" entitled *Anglicanism*. This anthology, reprinted many times (including a new edition in 2009), includes an opening essay, by More, which seeks to define the "Spirit of Anglicanism."[1] There is one word he believes encapsulates this spirit: *pragmatism*.[2] At the heart of this pragmatist spirit is the supposed "just balance" which protects the clear-eyed modern churchman from believing in anything as simplistic or common as the infallibility of "Tradition or Scripture."[3]

In More's mind, and in the minds of the now four generations of men and women who have essentially signed up for some version of this personal, upmarket pentecostalism, the great enemy of Anglicanism's "Spirit" would be to follow either John Henry Newman or John Jewel into the ghettos of absolutism and certainty. We would do well to follow St. John the Evangelist's advice upon encountering More's pragmatic specter: "Beloved, believe not every spirit, but try the spirits whether they are of God: because many false prophets are gone out into the world" (1 John 4:1).[4] Any serious project seeking to grow and nurture a re-formed catholicism should hold these types of opinions in utter contempt and call them by the name the Beloved Disciple gave us to classify them: "antichrist" (1 John 4:3).

The irony of More, and so many who try to define Anglicanism by following his example, is not that he ignores the excellent seventeenth-century theologians, statesmen, and pastors which fill the anthology he is editing; rather, he enlists them in his revisionist project—not by claiming that their actual words match his opinions, but by divining a familiar "spirit" which only the most up-to-date and learned Endorian enchantress could possibly detect. Taylor and Hall and Laud and Cosin and Ussher and Andrewes and Donne and Hooker become zombie foot soldiers enforcing the peculiar beliefs of the liberated modern Anglican.

A spiritually nourishing alternative to this pablum is to crack open, almost at random, any passage from the writings of the great sixteenth-century Anglican divine, Richard Hooker:

> Dangerous it were for the feeble brain of man to wade far into the doings of the Most High; whom although to know be life, and joy to make mention of his name; yet our soundest knowledge is to know that we know him not as indeed he is, neither can know: and our safest eloquence concerning him is our silence, when we

---

[1] Paul Elmer More and Frank Leslie Cross, eds, *Anglicanism*, 3rd ed. (London: SPCK, 1962).

[2] Ibid., xxxii.

[3] Ibid., xxii.

[4] All Scripture passages quoted in this chapter are from the King James Version (KJV).

confess without confession that his glory is inexplicable, his greatness above our capacity and reach. He is above, and we upon earth; therefore it behoveth our words to be wary and few.[5]

Humility, we see, is an ideal for Hooker; one he does not always perfectly demonstrate, but it is humility which so often separates him from the radical puritans whose misplaced faith in their own interpretation of Scripture, particularly regarding secondary matters, made them ready to choose anarchy and chaos over peace.

The humility of Hooker, a feature so often lacking in those who would define the Anglican Way, compels him to do the hard work of manfully defending the consistency of the Anglican establishment he inherited rather than using his towering intellect to try and create a church made in his own image. This firm defense is his stated purpose as he writes in the famous opening lines of his magnum opus, *Of the Laws of Ecclesiastical Polity*: "Though for no other cause, yet for this—that posterity may know we have not loosely through silence permitted things to pass away as in a dream, there shall be for men's information extant thus much concerning the present state of the Church of God established amongst us, and their careful endeavor which would have upheld the same."[6] Hooker musters his great learning to create vast cathedrals of English prose to both educate men and honor the God who loves truth and beauty and goodness.

It is not just humility which stands behind Hooker's active and brilliant defense of the Anglican Way against puritan and papist. Indeed, it is the chaos these two groups sought to inflict on the very order of the nation which he saw as a war against the common good and the very design of God. The 1570 papal bull, *Regnans in Excelsis*, declared Elizabeth I to be not only illegitimate but also excommunicated from the supposed one, true church. Calls for assassination and rebellion followed and persisted for decades. On the other side, the radical puritans fought every aspect of the established order with an ever more malleable biblicism through which the whims and preferences of their leaders could be ill-clothed in the most threadbare prooftexts dragged out of context and genre.[7] It was Hooker who prophetically recognized the grave danger of giving way to these groups, grounding his defense of the Anglican Way in the order and law of God found both in natural and special revelation:

> God therefore is a law both to himself, and to all other things besides. To Himself He is a law in all those things which our Savior speaks of, saying, "My Father worketh even until now, and I work" (John 5:17). God works nothing without cause. He does all things with some end in mind, and the end for which each is done is the

---

[5] Richard Hooker, *Of the Laws of Ecclesiastical Polity*, I.ii.2. Hooker texts are taken from the second edition of John Keble's *The Works of that Learned and Judicious Divine Mr. Richard Hooker with an account of His Life and Death by Issac Walton* (Oxford, 1841). Citations from that edition give the books of the *Laws* in upper case Roman numerals, followed by the chapter in lower case Roman numerals, followed by the section of the chapter in Arabic numbers, e.g.: I, v, 2. To aid those less accustomed to Hooker's august prose, citations have also been provided from the fine modernized editions by Bradford Littlejohn, Brian Marr, and Bradley Belschner published by The Davenant Institute.

[6] Hooker, *Laws*, Preface i.1.

[7] Bradford Littlejohn, *Richard Hooker: A Companion to His Life and Work* (Eugene, OR: Cascade, 2015), 60.

reason he acts. He would never have created woman unless he saw that it would not be good unless she were created. "It is not good that the man should be alone; I will make a help meet for him" (Gen 2:18). God only does those things which to leave undone would not be good.[8]

Torrance Kirby summarizes the foundational argument of Hooker as, "God is law."[9] He continues, "[Hooker's] sustained effort to explore the intimate connections of pressing political and constitutional concerns with the highest discourse of hidden divine realities—the knitting together of theology and politics—is arguably the defining characteristic of Hooker's thought."[10]

Hooker's work benefits from this complex vision to provide both a context for Anglicans to understand the importance of "decency and order" in our ecclesiastical life, while also serving as a ready life raft for an American church left shipwrecked in the public sphere by an unfortunate functional reliance on Baptist political theology on the one hand and a call for "theonomy" on the other. Hooker, in a brilliant synthesis of Neo-platonic, Thomistic, and Reformed orthodoxy, writes of the law God freely binds to himself with no diminishment of his freedom or power so that "He works toward a certain end and by a certain law which constrains the effects of His power so that it does not work infinitely but only as much as necessary to reach that end: 'all things well' (Wisdom 8:1), all 'by measure and number and weight'" (Wis 11:20).[11] The laws which govern men flow from God as their perfect source, in Scripture and in nature, and have discrete functions for different tasks in an elegant hierarchy which does not need to blasphemously misuse the Bible for purposes God never intended.[12] This argument is as relevant now as it was in the sixteenth century as the Western church faces the phenomenon of functionally ultramontanist popes, who claim to be somehow defending the apostolic deposit by adding to it their own innovative conclusions, coupled with the new Montanism of popular pentecostalism whose path to prominence was paved by those who inherited and expanded the radical puritans' insistence upon the supreme value of individual interpretation against institutional authority.

So how would Hooker have us use Scripture in an ordered and judicious manner? He defends the manner prescribed in the sixth of our *Articles of Religion*:

> Holy Scripture containeth all things necessary to salvation; so that whatsoever is not read therein, nor may be proved thereby, is not to be required of any man, that it should be believed as an article of the faith, or be thought requisite or necessary to salvation.[13]

---

[8] Hooker, *Divine Law and Human Nature: Or, the first book of the Laws of Ecclesiastical Polity, Concerning Laws and their Several Kinds in General*, ed./trans. W. Bradford Littlejohn, Brian Marr, and Bradley Belschner (Landrum, SC: Davenant, 2017), 6 [I.ii.3].

[9] Torrance Kirby, ed., *A Companion to Richard Hooker*, Brill's Companions to the Christian Tradition 8 (Leiden: Brill, 2008), 251.

[10] Ibid.

[11] *Laws*, I.ii.3.

[12] *Laws*, II.viii.6.

[13] *The 1662 Book of Common Prayer: International Edition*, ed. Samuel L. Bray and Drew N. Keane (Downers Grove, IL: IVP Academic, 2021), 629.

Hooker does the hard work of defending and clarifying the meaning of this article by first responding to what we might call in our own age the "Catholic Answers" fallacy where it is claimed that the Scriptures cannot contain everything necessary for salvation because the Scriptures do not list which books count as Scripture, thus since we cannot get that list from Scripture itself, it is the papacy and magisterium who must evaluate the truth claims of Scripture and Tradition, and somehow this means the Bishop of Rome can tell you what font to use in your parish. Mind you, this oft repeated position is not what the Council of Trent or Vatican I teach about Scripture,[14] but we are not in a very sophisticated polemical age. Here is Hooker from a much more elegant one:

> We may truly reply that every field of study requires prior knowledge of some things that lie outside that field of study properly speaking. Each kind of knowledge only goes so far and takes for granted many things supplied by other fields. For instance, whoever wishes to teach the art of eloquence must explain the rules necessary to reach this end. But, since no one can speak eloquently unless he can first speak in proper sentences, it would seem such basic ability is a necessary part of the art of eloquence.... It is the same with Scripture. Even though Scripture says that it contains all things necessary for salvation, "all things" cannot be construed to mean absolutely, "all things," but all things of a certain kind, such as all things which we could not know by our natural senses. Scripture does indeed contain all these things. However, it also presupposes that we first know and are persuaded of certain rational first principles, and building on that, Scripture teaches the rest. Among the things we must first believe is the sacred authority of Scripture itself. Since we are persuaded by other means that the Scriptures are indeed the oracles of God, they teach us everything else we must know and do for salvation.[15]

Hooker maintains that "Rome teaches Scripture to be so insufficient that, without adding traditions, it would not contain all revealed and supernatural truth necessary for salvation," but, he writes, it is this opinion that is "repugnant to the truth."[16]

But equally repugnant are those who "fall into the opposite ditch—just as dangerous—thinking that Scripture contains not only all things necessary to salvation, but indeed simply all things, such that do anything according to any other law is not only unnecessary to salvation but unlawful, sinful, and downright damnable."[17] Hooker parries this dangerous radical puritan position by rightly recognizing that anything said about God or his Word which is untrue, even if meant to honor God, is still a lie and a

---

[14] "These books ['the complete books of the old and the new Testament with all their parts'] the church holds to be sacred and canonical not because she subsequently approved them by her authority after they had been composed by unaided human skill, nor simply because they contain revelation without error, but because, being written under the inspiration of the holy Spirit, they have God as their author, and were as such committed to the church." Council Fathers, "Decrees of the First Vatican Council," Session 3, Ch. 2, #6–7 (1870), Papal Encyclicals Online, https://www.papalencyclicals.net/councils/ecum20.htm.

[15] *Laws*, I.xiv.1. From *Divine Law and Human Nature*, 81.

[16] *Laws*, II.viii.7. Cited from Richard Hooker, *The Word of God and the Words of Man: Or, the Second and Third Books of the Laws of Ecclesiastical Polity*, ed./trans. by W. Bradford Littlejohn, Brian Marr, Bradley Belschner, and Sean Duncan (Landrum, SC: Davenant, 2018), 44.

[17] Ibid.

blasphemy against the true honor of God: an honor which does not need our pious exaggerations to defend it.[18] Further, to try and compartmentalize God by cutting him out of the realities which can be learned concerning his will and glory from natural revelation would be, in and of itself, an impiety of the highest order. Following Hooker, it is the Anglican who is humbly shaped and ordered by the Scriptures, recognizing their special status as the oracles of God, but also recognizing the Scriptures' function and purpose in their context and genre. This insight can be abused, as any tool can, but when it is coupled with a firm trust in the reliability of Scripture, the re-formed catholic can rightly distinguish between doctrine, discipline, and adiaphora.

Disorder creeps into this method when progressives, in the dark tradition of More and his ilk, pervert Hooker's method to raid and pillage the church for which he fought so long to defend. Justin Welby, the current embattled Archbishop of Canterbury, invoked Hooker's supposed three-legged stool of "scripture, tradition, and reason" to defend his support of the ministers of the Church of England blessing same-sex unions.[19] His crude argument is made more eloquently, if just as unconvincingly, by a number of progressive theologians looking for any weapon they can find to carve out space to bless the unbiblical demands of themselves or their straying flocks. For example, Kathryn Tanner writes that "what would need to be changed about the [marriage] rite to cover same-sex unions (e.g., changes of pronoun, of scriptural texts perhaps) arguably involves incidentals and not substance (i.e., matters with a necessary connection to ends) and therefore falls under the rubric of changeable positive law."[20] Her subtle argument is that the substance of the marriage rite itself would not be altered by adding same-sex participants, for it would simply be the inclusion of previously excluded people or elements—something, in her mind, akin to adding a wedding ring to the marriage ceremony.[21] However, one does not need too sophisticated a mind to see the weakness in an argument which presupposes that a marriage service's substance could be equally preserved if the best man forgot the wedding ring or if the bride forgot she was a man.

The grim failure of Welby and his fellow revisionists flows from their convenient leveling of the authority and meaning of Scripture, tradition, and reason. They may have many allies in this fight, but Hooker certainly is not one of them: "Whatever [Scripture] forbids, the Church must not permit, lest the path which should always be clear become overgrown with brambles and thorns."[22] In Hooker's analogy, the Church by blessing sin, even in the name of inclusion or fulfillment, would be actively choking the path of sanctification. It would be to put oneself in the same category as the first Adam, who failed to steward and protect the garden, rather than the second Adam whose death and

---

[18] *Laws*, II.viii.7.

[19] John James, "Justin Welby Appears Close to Tears during Emotional Debate about Blessing Gay Couples," *Mail Online*, February 9, 2023. https://www.dailymail.co.uk/news/article-11731077/Justin-Welby-appears-close-tears-emotional-debate-blessing-gay-couples.html.

[20] Kathryn Tanner, "Hooker and the New Puritans," in *Authorizing Marriage*, ed. Mark D. Jordan (Princeton, NJ: Princeton University Press, 2006), esp. 125.

[21] As detailed in the dissertation, now published: Philip Peter Hobday, "Relocating Richard Hooker: Theological Method and the Character of Anglicanism," (PhD thesis, Durham University, 2021), 201. Available at Durham E-Theses Online: http://etheses.dur.ac.uk/13874/.

[22] *Laws*, III.iii.3. From *The Word of God and the Words of Man*.

resurrection vindicated the true Church's call to live in loving obedience to the Father's will revealed in and through his Word. The very renewal and redemption of creation itself hangs in the balance. Any bishop who chooses to call death "life" and sin "grace" fails to love just as Adam failed to love God and Eve by participating in Eve's sin. One failure cast humanity into millennia of darkness; its modern doppelganger would be to thrust a jurisdiction into the dark without "a lamp unto my feet and a light unto my path" (Ps 119:105).

Even if one did decide to walk the dark path of establishing a jurisdiction's practice without the true light of holy Scripture aided by its traditional interpreters, Hooker also vehemently resists the idea that the natural moral law is anything but "perpetually valid."[23] In fact, it is the natural moral law's constancy and longevity which elevate it to a status whereby it can mold and shape the life and practice of the Church in areas where Scripture is silent. Disconnecting the natural law from an immutable God is inevitably to connect it to the patterns of "conjuring" and "becoming" which characterize so much of the pre- and post-Christian pagan world: a pattern we have seen in so many jurisdictions who have proven incapable of coherently defining what it means to be a man or a woman or what roles are appropriate for each sex.

On the very question of the purpose of marriage, Hooker follows St. Paul in refusing to conceive of the natural law in any such way:

> In this world there can be no society durable otherwise than by propagation. Albeit therefore single life be a thing more angelical and divine, yet [since] the replenishing, first of earth with blessed inhabitants, and then of heaven with saints everlastingly praising God did depend upon conjunction of man and woman, he which made all things complete and perfect saw it could not be good to leave man without a helper unto the fore-alleged end.[24]

Hooker synthesizes a coherent picture of the institution of marriage as the will of God in and through the Scriptural record while simultaneously respecting the enduring witness of God's order gained from observing "durable" societies. On the other hand, progressives look for durable societies not in the past but in a promised immanentized eschaton supposedly being held back by retrograde simpletons. One is cast as such a simpleton if he is not inspired by the idea that we are just one more treacly Church of England slogan away from utopia. Hooker does not at all fit into this box, for he is quite obviously not a fool, but he holds ideas which the progressive cannot help but call retrograde, and so rather than face the horrifying possibility that Hooker's actual positions present well-reasoned, enduring truth, progressive scholars attempt to transform the erudite defender of the traditional Anglican Way into something he is not. Again and again, we see that one of the enduring legacies of Hooker is in his arguments for continuity and stability, order, and decency in the face of the radical puritans, and it is this same gifted argumentation which rightly positions the re-formed catholic against those darkly puritanical emanations which ultimately result in a disdain for the past.

---

[23] Hobday, "Relocating Richard Hooker," 203.
[24] *Laws*, V.lxxiii.1.

Reason must be calibrated by grace, for only when it is made properly righteous, can it be a powerful instrument in the hands of a holy God.[25]

Hooker, far from holding the Christians of the past in contempt, constantly seeks to synthesize the thoughts of the great theologians who came before him but often in new language he deploys for greater precision, greater nuance, or even to build bridges between rival schools of thought. This terminological style leads to careful distinctions and advanced contributions to the Christian theological project, but it also leaves Hooker open to attack and misinterpretation. We see this at work, not least in his writings on soteriology.

Walter Travers, who was both jealous for being passed over for the younger Hooker as Master of the London Temple church in 1585 as well as being, unfortunately, an increasingly radical puritan himself, wrote "A Supplication to the Privy Council," in which he claimed Hooker was preaching sermons the likes of which had not been heard since to the reign of the counter-reformational Queen Mary I.[26] Quite fascinatingly, almost three hundred years later, John Henry Newman would make a similar argument in his 1837 *Lectures on Justification* (this shared verdict perhaps being the only thing Travers and Newman would ever agree upon). However, Alister McGrath spends a full twelve pages of his classic survey of justification painstakingly working through the poor scholarship and deceptive editing on Newman's part which should make trusting his writing on Hooker a perilous affair.[27]

An excerpt from a timely new printing of the very sermons Travers opposed shows just how misplaced the objections of both Travers and Newman were. Hooker writes:

> "Yea verily," says the Apostle, "I count all things to be loss for the excellency of the knowledge of Christ Jesus my Lord: for whom I suffered the loss of all things, and do count them but refuse, that I may gain Christ, and be found in him, not having a righteousness of mine own, even that which is of the law, but that which is through faith in Christ, the righteousness which is from God by faith" (Phil 3:8–9). Whether [the Church of Rome] speak of the first or second justification, they make the essence of it an inherent divine quality, that is, a righteousness which is in us. But if it is in us, then it is ours as our souls are ours, even if we have our souls from God and can possess them no longer than pleases him. For if God withdraws the breath from our nostrils, we return to dust at once. But the righteousness in which we must be found, if we are to be justified, is not our own. Therefore, we cannot be justified by any inherent quality. Rather, Christ has merited righteousness for as many as are found in him. God finds us in him, if we are faithful, for by faith we are incorporated into Christ. Thus, although we ourselves are altogether sinful and unrighteous, even the man who is himself impious, full of iniquity and sin, if he is found in Christ through faith and hates his sin in repentance, God beholds him

---

[25] *Laws*, I.vii.2, 1; I.lxxviii.3–4; I.viii.

[26] Walter Travers, "A Supplication made to the Privy Counsel," in *The Folger Library Edition of the Works of Richard Hooker, Vol 5: Tractates and Sermons*, ed. Laetitia Yeandle (Cambridge, MA: Belknap, 1990), 5:208.9–10.

[27] Alister McGrath, *Iustitia Dei: A History of the Christian Doctrine of Justification*, 3rd ed. (Cambridge: CUP, 2005), 296–307.

with a gracious eye! God puts away his sin by not imputing it to him; God takes away the punishment he justly deserves by pardoning it; God accepts him in Jesus Christ as perfectly righteous, as if he has fulfilled all that is commanded by the law, and—can it be—as more perfectly righteous than if he himself had fulfilled the whole law![28]

The entire sermon is a wonderful example of soaring rhetoric and theological clarity while maintaining a pastor's heart toward his congregation and a strong case for the Holy Spirit's continued activity and presence even within a medieval church whose official teaching became so full of accretions and innovations that she ceased to be, in Hooker's eyes, meaningfully catholic. Hooker, however, defended his conviction that it was very possible that the ancestors of his congregation were not resigned to hell fire just because of the failures of the medieval church to teach correct doctrine (a view pounced upon by Travers). It is important to note that church authorities sided with Hooker against Travers's accusations of unloyalty to the Elizabethan settlement.

Years of debating men like Travers and Thomas Cartwright (one of the main targets of opportunity throughout the *Laws*) helped Hooker to develop a series of helpful terms and concepts which, while more complex than some of the easier solutions of his puritan and papist interlocutors, keep the tensions of Scripture more faithfully taut. A good example can be found in Hooker's method of viewing human depravity through the classic Christian principal (first quoted from St. Basil): "Grace does not destroy nature but perfect it." As he puts it in the *Laws*, after considering the example of Festus from Acts 26, "This example makes clear, as the apostle teaches elsewhere, that nature has need of grace (1 Cor. 2:14), which I trust we do not contradict by saying that grace makes use of nature."[29] Within this reformed Thomistic framework, with deep roots in Lombard and Augustine, Hooker prefers to speak of Total Disability rather than Total Depravity.[30] W. David Neelands summarizes Hooker from his late work, the *Dublin Fragments*, in this way, "To do that which is acceptable to God, we must have God's preventing and helping grace, yet we have not lost the aptness of our wills, or else grace would be of no avail, though because of sin our wills have lost their ableness for good."[31] Our wills are entirely unable to choose the truly good without God's intervention, but Hooker seeks to maintain the ordered and created goodness of creation throughout history despite what he calls the devastating and tragic effects of the Fall, and following Augustine, to also make a distinction in the reception of grace between brute beasts and men.[32] By maintaining this classic Christian balance, Hooker operates in the re-formed catholic orthodoxy one finds in the ninth and tenth *Articles of Religion* while also heading off the Hyper-Calvinist intent on transforming the doctrine of Total Depravity into one

---

[28] Hooker, *A Learned Discourse on Justification*, ed. Bradford Littlejohn, Rhys Laverty, and Ken Cook (Landrum, SC: Davenant, 2022), 8.

[29] *Laws*, III.viii.6. From *The Word of God and the Words of Man*.

[30] Hooker, *Dublin Fragments 1–13*, in *The Folger Library Edition of the Works of Richard Hooker, Vol 4: Of the Laws of Ecclesiastical Polity, Attack and Response*, ed. John E. Booty (Cambridge, MA; Belknap, 1982), 4:101–113.

[31] W. David Neeland, "Predestination," in *A Companion to Richard Hooker*, ed. Kirby, William J. Torrance (Leiden: Brill, 2008), 186.

[32] *Dublin Fragments* 1; 4:101.28–31.

of absolute depravity and despair. As Hooker himself maintained again and again, these types of distinctions and amplifications were meant to strengthen the re-formed catholic position in England not to undermine it for the sake of contemporary or future critics.

We see this very focus when Hooker deals with the always difficult subject of predestination. Too often, the Hookerian position is framed as being unreformed or even in mortal conflict with Article XVII,[33] but this reduction does great damage to Hooker's actual position and the catholic comprehensiveness of Article XVII. Hooker does deviate from Calvin by more doggedly maintaining the link between providence and predestination, but this move puts him firmly in line with the reformed Augustinianism of Peter Martyr Vermigli—who of course, while teaching at Oxford, taught John Jewel who would later teach Hooker.[34] Hooker, healthily operating within the framework of Article XXVII, maintained throughout his works that the elect may resist God obstinately, but God's election in them, itself totally undeserved, will inevitably bring them to glory.[35] This positive side of election Hooker defends in his sermons as a source of comfort for the Church,[36] but he spends even more time in his later writings placing the full weight of damnation on the backs of "obdurate" sinners who have no one to blame but themselves for being permitted to choose damnation.[37] God is not the author of the evil which resides in men, and so God's decision to withhold grace is therefore a consequence of what they have made themselves, not a consequence of God's antecedent will.[38] Now, whatever God permits happens (permissive does not equal

---

[33] Article XVII reads, "Predestination to Life is the everlasting purpose of God, whereby (before the foundations of the world were laid) he hath constantly decreed by his counsel secret to us, to deliver from curse and damnation those whom he hath chosen in Christ out of mankind, and to bring them by Christ to everlasting salvation, as vessels made to honour. Wherefore, they which be endued with so excellent a benefit of God, be called according to God's purpose by his Spirit working in due season: they through Grace obey the calling: they be justified freely: they be made sons of God by adoption: they be made like the image of his only-begotten Son Jesus Christ: they walk religiously in good works, and at length, by God's mercy, they attain to everlasting felicity.

As the godly consideration of Predestination, and our Election in Christ, is full of sweet, pleasant, and unspeakable comfort to godly persons, and such as feel in themselves the working of the Spirit of Christ, mortifying the works of the flesh, and their earthly members, and drawing up their mind to high and heavenly things, as well because it doth greatly establish and confirm their faith of eternal Salvation to be enjoyed through Christ as because it doth fervently kindle their love towards God: So, for curious and carnal persons, lacking the Spirit of Christ, to have continually before their eyes the sentence of God's Predestination, is a most dangerous downfall, whereby the Devil doth thrust them either into desperation, or into wretchlessness of most unclean living, no less perilous than desperation. Furthermore, we must receive God's promises in such wise, as they be generally set forth to us in Holy Scripture: and, in our doings, that Will of God is to be followed, which we have expressly declared unto us in the Word of God.

[34] Peter Martyr Vermigli, *Predestination and Justification: Two Theological Loci*, ed./trans. Frank A. James III, Sixteenth Century Essays and Studies LXVIII (Lincoln, NE: Davenant, 2018; Kirksville, MO: Truman State University Press, 2003), 17–18.

[35] *Dublin Fragments*, 46. W. David Neelands observes that this section includes a partial appropriation of the *Lambeth Articles* of 1595.

[36] See, *Certaintie*.

[37] *Dublin Fragments* 34; 4:145.19–146.4.

[38] *Dublin Fragments* 34; 4:146.14–18.

passive with Augustine, Aquinas, or Hooker), but the perfect justice of God is maintained in the deserving state of the reprobate. As Hooker writes:

> The whole body of mankind in the view of God's eternal knowledge, lay universally polluted with sin, worthy of condemnation and death, that over the mass of corruption, there passed two Acts of the will of God. An act of favor, liberality and grace, choosing part to be made partakers of everlasting glory; and an Act of Justice, forsaking the rest and adjudging them to endless perdition, these vessels of wrath, those of mercy, which mercy is in God's elect, so peculiar, that to them and to none else (for their number is definitely known, and can neither be increased nor diminished) to them it allotteth immortality and all things thereunto appertaining, them it predestinateth, it calleth, justifieth, gloryifyeth them, it powreth voluntarily that spirit into their hearts, which spirit so given is the root of their very first desires and motions, tending to immortality; as for others on whom such grace is not bestowed there is justly assigned, and immutably to every of them, the lot of eternal condemnation.[39]

This carefully constructed position respects the biblical evidence of God's sovereignty, as recognized in the works of the catholic doctors, while also building a rhetorical wall against the blasphemous notion that God is the author of evil. Hooker's work in soteriology reveals an abundance of dynamic possibilities for engaging the theologians of the Church's past in their fullness within and through the Anglican Way's tried and trusted formularies, and we see his work reflected in the later formulations of Ussher, Davenant, Ward, and many other seventeenth-century greats whose works are resetting the scholarly consensus about what the Anglican Way has to offer in the field of soteriology.[40]

However, it is not only in soteriology where Hooker performs vital service to the reformed catholic project. His sacramentology, particularly but not limited to Holy Communion, reveals a true genius at work. Calvin once said of Vermigli, "The whole doctrine of the Eucharist was crowned by Peter Martyr, who left nothing more to be done."[41] Many conflicts and disagreements within the modern Anglican world would be solved if our clergy and laymen simply replaced Vermigli with Hooker in that sentence and acted accordingly. His grand synthesis of the best of Vermigli, Jewel, Cranmer, Augustine, and Aquinas leave the Anglican with absolutely no need to anxiously run to Lutheran or Latin sources for fear of falling into the dreaded clutches of Zwingli's bare tokenism. Rather, churchmen of every rank have been gifted a profound and balanced account of the doctrine of the real presence in Hooker.

Hooker grounds his sacramentology in his Christology, spending an enormous part of Book V of the *Laws* working through the classic definitions taught throughout the prayer book, but most especially in the *Creed of Saint Athanasius* and the *Articles of Religion*. This important groundwork allows him to show that our predestined union with Christ happens in real time as Christian men and women are effectually called and grafted into

---

[39] *Dublin Fragments* 36; 4:148.23–149.4.

[40] See especially Michael J. Lynch, *John Davenant's Hypothetical Universalism: A Defense of Catholic and Reformed Orthodoxy* (New York: Oxford University Press, 2021).

[41] J. C. McLelland, *The Visible Words of God* (Edinburgh: Oliver & Boyd, 1957), 279.

the mystical body of Christ. He writes: "The words of Adam may be fitly the words of Christ concerning His church. Flesh of my flesh and bone of my bones, a true native extract out of mine own body. So that in him even according to his manhood we according to our heavenly being are as branches in that root out of which they grow."[42] Our union with Christ occurs through his manhood in a variety of ways (imputation and infusion), but it is in the holy rituals of Christ's visible body wherein we most perfectly and necessarily participate *in Christ*.[43] This distinction protects the balance between the sovereign work of God in soteriology, while also protecting the Church from an anti-physical prejudice, often deployed as a supposed defense against Rome's innovations, which leads the unwitting adherent into the arms of an unsophisticated version of pagan Greek metaphysics (spiritual good/physical bad).

A key synthesis in Hooker's work is the Thomistic understanding of the twofold movement of procession and return expressed in the hierarchies of reality itself, which further serves as the background and frame for the sacrament of Holy Communion.[44] Stated briefly, the procession is one of God moving outward in creating, and the creation returning to the supreme beauty: God.[45] The classic prayer books of 1552–1662 (including the 1559 edition of Hooker's day) all feature a Communion service which sees as its apex a gracious journey of the justified sinner's lifted heart into the heavenly holy of holies, in true union with Christ, to pray the Lord's Prayer, to offer ourselves as a sacrifice of praise and thanksgiving through our faith in Christ's meritorious death, and to sing the song of the angels as our hearts descend back to earth—changed men and women.

Hooker sees no cognitive dissonance at all in defending the prayer book's account of the real presence because he sees it in Aquinas and John Damascene. As Aquinas writes in the *Summa*, "In Greek, moreover, [the Eucharist] is called *Metalepsis*, i.e. 'Assumption,' because, as Damascene says (*De Fide Orth.* iv), 'we thereby assume the Godhead of the Son.'"[46] Hooker is not being "uncatholic" when he says, "The real presence of Christ's most blessed body and blood is not therefore to be sought for in the sacrament, but in the worthy receiver of the sacrament."[47] Rather, he is using the grammar of classic catholic thought to reunite the mystery of the presence of Christ's sacramental body with his mystical body (the Church). By moving the focus away from the host alone, the church is better able to see the full enormity of what Christ is gifting to his people. Hooker writes:

> Again as evident it is how [the church fathers] teach that Christ is personally there present, yea present whole, albeit a part of Christ be corporally absent from thence; that Christ assisting this heavenly banquet with his personal and true presence doth by his own divine power add to the natural substance thereof supernatural efficacy, which addition to the nature of those consecrated elements changeth them and maketh them that unto us which otherwise they could not be; that to us they are thereby made such instruments as mystically yet truly, invisibly yet really

---

[42] *Laws*, V.lvi.7.

[43] *Laws*, V.lvi.11.

[44] *Laws*, VIII.ii.2.

[45] Andrew Louth, *Denys the Areopagite* (London: G. Chapman, 1989), 52.

[46] Thomas Acquinas, *Summa Theologiae*, III.73.4, www.newadvent.org/summa/4073.htm.

[47] *Laws*, V.lxvii.6.

work our communion or fellowship with the person of Jesus Christ as well in that he is man as God, our participation also in the fruit, grace, and efficacy of his body and blood, whereupon there ensueth a kind of transubstantiation in us, a true change both of soul and body, an alteration from death to life.[48]

Echoing Ignatius of Antioch, Hooker here tells us that those who faithfully receive the Holy Eucharist partake of the "medicine of immortality," in a blessed communion whose dual focus of Christ and his Body together have no need for theories of corporal consubstantiation or transubstantiation of the elements (two views Hooker goes on to say cannot be proved by Scripture and are also unprovable from the arguments for "mystical participation" one finds in the church fathers). We are left then with a dynamic presentation of old high Anglican sacramentology which if revisited and studied would alleviate much of the historical and liturgical inconsistencies plaguing our modern discourse, and in that clarity, perhaps even strengthen the bonds of fellowship and devotion.

The full legacy of Richard Hooker is, in many ways, still to be determined, but in an age so desperately in need of careful thinking, faithful courage, and judicious argumentation, it would be hard to imagine a more fitting champion than the greatest theologian the Anglican Way has ever produced. This small sampling of his genius will, God willing, encourage clergy and laymen alike to visit and dwell in the textual cathedrals Hooker constructed each night after Evensong—beautiful strongholds from which he intellectually defended and sustained a vision for a robust, re-formed catholic church strong enough to survive through trial and terror, built to prepare men for joy and glory.

---

[48] *Laws*, V.lxvii.6.

Chapter 18

The Voice of English Catholicism:
Lancelot Andrewes (1555–1626)

The Rev. Nicholas Ziegenhagen

Rare is the theologian as renowned for his sanctity as his scholarship. In the English divine Lancelot Andrewes, we encounter just such a striking blend of great learning and holiness, a union that is the particular ideal of the English pastoral tradition. His renown as a pastor, preacher, theologian, evangelist, controversialist, translator, and counsellor led to his installation to prominent bishoprics during both the reigns of Elizabeth I and James I, and to his famous role as preacher of the royal court. His influence on the history and theology of the English Church was immense, "a place second to none in the history of the formation of the English Church."[1]

Lancelot Andrewes was born in the bloody year of 1555, in which Queen Mary's persecution produced many Protestant martyrs. Though Andrewes is immortalized as a leading High Church Bishop, his early circumstance of life could easily have predisposed him towards Puritanism. He was born to parents of the merchant class and seafaring trade, most of whom at this point in England were anti-Spanish and therefore almost unanimously anti-Catholic in outlook.[2] Meeting with great success in his early education, he eventually entered Cambridge, which, at the time, was a Puritan stronghold. Yet, in spite of being raised and educated by the best that Puritanism had to offer, we find no evidence that he was ever inclined to embrace Calvinistic theology or Puritan reforms, but rather the opposite.

The most conspicuous attribute of young Lancelot Andrewes is his predilection for study. Bishop Buckeridge says of his schooldays "that from this time 'he accounted all that time lost that he spent not on his studies.'"[3] Furthermore it is said that when he entered Cambridge, he "owed little to his tutors, but most to his own pains and study."[4] He was particularly fond of languages, a love which is evident in his sermons, which are almost never without a smattering of Latin or Greek. He was reputed to know Latin, Greek, Hebrew, Chaldee, Syriac, Arabic, and fifteen modern languages. Whenever he visited his parents on breaks, he would send instructions to his father to obtain a tutor of a new language. This insatiable appetite for learning remained a mark of his person throughout his whole life.

His prestigious academic career brought him ecclesial preferment. "Andrewes was elected a fellow of Pembroke College, Cambridge, in 1575 and was ordained a deacon in 1580. His service to several parishes from 1589 was followed by consecration as bishop of Chichester in 1605 and his transfer to Ely in 1609 and to Winchester in 1619."[5]

---

[1] T. S. Eliot, "Lancelot Andrewes," in *Selected Essays* (New York: Harcourt, Brace & Co., 1950), 310.

[2] Paul Welsby, *Lancelot Andrewes 1555–1626* (London: SPCK, 1958), 8.

[3] Welsby, *Andrewes*, 10.

[4] Ibid., 12.

[5] "Lancelot Andrewes, English Theologian," *Britannica*, n.d., www.britannica.com/biography/Lancelot-Andrewes.

Bishop Andrewes was popularly beloved and known for his impressive sermons, many of which were preached at the royal court annually on the high holy days of Christmas, Easter, and Whitsunday, where he preached for King James I for twenty years. His sermons were greatly admired at the time for their depth and eloquence; they have been greatly praised in more recent times as well, most notably by T. S. Eliot.

His fame as a preacher was due largely to the seeming perfect harmony of his intellect and devotion; the power of his thought was in balance with the power of his spirit. Andrewes was not a George Whitefield who captivated his audience with an imposing boom, nor a John Wesley whose zeal electrified, but rather lacking charisma in his persona, his sermons are cherished for their stand-alone excellency—for the clarity, precision, nuance, and depth of his theological thought and presentation regarding matters essential to the Church in a time when matters indifferent were everywhere being hurled at her bulwarks.

Three theologians stand out brightest in the twilight of the Elizabethan Age: John Jewel, Richard Hooker, and Lancelot Andrewes. As the Reformation came to a close in England, the English Church settled into its own secure self-understanding as a catholic body due to the great influence of these men. Jewel defended Anglicanism against Rome, Hooker against the Puritans, and Andrewes against both from his position in the royal court. With Elizabeth and her theologians, the English Church withstands the pressure to deny her heritage and become a mere provincial and schismatic sect, and having withstood, she stands formidable intellectually against her "Continental antagonists." In the words of T.S. Eliot: "The achievement of Hooker and Andrewes was to make the English Church more worthy of intellectual assent. No religion can survive the judgment of history unless the best minds of its time have collaborated in its construction; if the Church of Elizabeth is worthy of the age of Shakespeare and Jonson, that is because of the work of Hooker and Andrewes."[6]

As the mention of Shakespeare makes clear, this was the age of eloquence, and among churchmen Andrewes was preeminent; he is the most celebrated preacher of the age. The Anglican Bishop Thomas Fuller, writing in the second half of the nineteenth century, nicknamed Andrewes, *stella predicantium*, or "star of preachers."[7]

To modern readers, the style of his sermons may seem a bit antiquated, but it was certainly in line with the medieval tradition of sermon-making. Here is an example of his rich prose about Mary Magdalene's visit to the empty tomb from one of his Easter sermons:

> The sun must scatter that cloud, and then we may. Here is an example of it. It is strange a thick cloud of heaviness had so covered her, as see Him she could not through it; this one word, these two syllables, Mary, from His mouth scatters it all. No sooner had His voice sounded in her ears but it drives away all the mist, dries up her tears, lightens her eyes, that she knew Him straight.[8]

---

[6] Eliot, "Lancelot Andrewes," 301.

[7] Jonathan Warren Pagán, "Lancelot Andrewes, The Star of Preachers," June 30, 2014, anglicancompass.com/lancelot-andrewes-the-star-of-preachers.

[8] Lancelot Andrewes, *Ninety-Six Sermons by the Right Honourable and Reverend Father in God, Lancelot Andrewes, Sometime Lord Bishop of Winchester* (Eugene, OR: Wipf & Stock, 2009), III:20–21.

It is clear that Andrewes seems to love what he is doing, evinced by his playful attitude towards words: "Let us then make this so accepted a time in itself twice acceptable by our accepting, which He will acceptably take at our hands." And yet, his wordplay is never without purpose, but part of his unique way of driving home the meaning of his text.

Notably, he never strays from his Scripture text. He never uses the Scriptures as a springboard into other matters. In fact, he does just the opposite, diving ever deeper into the text of Scripture itself, leaving nothing unexamined, seeming to wring every possible drop out of the words therein. In one of his Christmas sermons, he takes the text "For unto you is born this day in the city of David a Saviour, which is Christ the Lord" (Luke 2:11 KJV), and throughout his lengthy sermon, he never strays from this text. Here is an example of his concentration:

> Who is it? Three things are said of this Child by the Angel. (1) He is "a Saviour." (2) "Which is Christ." (3) "Christ the Lord." Three of his titles, well and orderly inferred on of another by good consequence. We cannot miss one of them; they be necessary all. Our method on earth is to begin with great; in heaven they begin with good first. First, then, "a Saviour"; that is His name, Jesus, *Soter*; and in that Name His benefit, *Salus*, "saving health or salvation." Such a name as the great Orator himself saith of it, *Soter, hoc quantum est? Ita magnum es tut latino uno verbo exprimi non possit.* "This name Saviour is so great as no one word can express the force of it."
>
> But we are not so much to regard the *ecce* how great it is, as *Gaudium* what joy is in it; that is the point we are to speak to. And for that, men may talk what they will, but sure there is no joy in the world to the joy of a man saved; no joy so great, no news so welcome, as to one ready to perish, in case of a lost man, to hear of one that will save him. In danger of perishing by sickness, to hear of one [who] will make him well again; by sentence of law, of one with a pardon to save his life; by enemies, of one that will rescue and set him in safety. Tell any of these, assure them but of a Saviour, it is the best news he ever heard in his life. There is joy in the name of a Saviour. And even this way, this Child is a Saviour too. *Potest hoc facere, sed hoc non est opus Ejus.* "This He can do, but this is not His work"; a farther matter there is, a greater salvation He came for. And it may be we need not any of these; we are not presently sick, in no fear of the law, in no danger of enemies. And it may be, if we were, we fancy to ourselves to be relieved some other way. But that which He came for, that saving we need all; and none but He can help us to it. We have therefore all cause to be glad for the Birth of this Saviour.[9]

In the words of T. S. Eliot, "When Andrewes begins his sermon, from beginning to end you are sure that he is wholly in his subject, unaware of anything else, that his emotion grows as he penetrates more deeply into his subject, that he is finally 'alone with the Alone,' with the mystery which he is seeking to grasp more and more firmly."[10]

His mastery of English prose and of other languages led to his selection as one of the chairmen and leading editor of the King James translation of the Bible. Small wonder

---

[9] Andrewes, *Ninety-Six Sermons*, I:73–74.
[10] Eliot, "Lancelot Andrewes," 308.

that he had a significant part to play in the most enduring of all monuments of the English language, the King James Version text.

This brings us to another observation of Andrewes' writings: the breadth and depth of his extensive scholarship. Andrewes was well-versed in the patristic writings, as well as the world of classical antiquity and literature. "In his three Good Friday sermons, for example, a brief list of the non-biblical references would include St. Augustine, St. Bernard, St. Chrysostom, Leo, Theodoret, the Greek Liturgy, Aristotle, Livy, and Juvenal."[11] There is a story of Andrewes, who, newly introduced to James I, engaged in a debate against the Puritans in the presence of the king and other bishops, concerning the use of the sign of the cross in baptism. Rather comically (as they were the offended party) the Puritans objected to this practice on the grounds that it was an offense to the weaker brethren. After some debate, the King finally asked for information about the antiquity of the practice. Andrewes then looked up and said, apparently entirely from memory, "It appears out of Tertullian, Cyprian, and Origen, and it was used in *immortali lavacro* [the washing of immortality]."[12]

His influence as a patristic scholar was clearly not confined to the realm of homiletics. This more than anything was his most solid and dangerous weapon as a defender of the English Church's claims to catholicity against both Romanism and Puritanism: he was a better student of church history than Rome, and a better student of Scripture than the Puritans. As his biographer, Paul A. Welsby, says, "He brought to his office learning and piety and distinguished himself as a sound theological controversialist, meeting the Roman argument from antiquity by a deeper and more thoughtful study of antiquity, and the Puritan argument from the Scriptures by an appeal to the interpretation of the Scriptures by the Church-writers of the early centuries."[13] His expert knowledge of patristic writings and his eloquence enabled him to guide the English Church into embracing the more comprehensive theological inheritance of the Church catholic, neither distinctly Roman, nor distinctly Protestant, but Christian.

The content of his theology is therefore *catholic* or *universal*. Rooted as he was in the doctrines of the historic church, he was not easily swayed by the theological controversies of the day. He was a man who, as the Gallic monk Vincent of Lérins said of the Catholic Christian, "will take care to cleave to antiquity, which cannot now be led astray by any deceit of novelty."[14] Andrewes was decidedly not fond of Calvinistic theology, over which there was much heated controversy, and maintained that a matter such as predestination is too great a mystery to be debated over.[15] As T. S. Eliot noted, "Bishop Andrewes ... tried to confine himself in his sermons to the elucidation of what he considered essential in dogma; he said himself that in sixteen years he had never alluded to the question of predestination, to which the Puritans, following their

---

[11] Welsby, *Andrewes*, 196.

[12] Ibid., 82.

[13] Ibid., 98.

[14] J. Douglas Johnson, "What is 'Mere Christianity'? *Quod Unique, Semper, et Ab Omnibus*," *Touchstone* 35, no.3, (May/June 2022), www.touchstonemag.com/archives/article.php?id=35-03-004-e.

[15] Ibid., 43–44.

Continental brethren, attached so much importance."[16] From the time of his ordination he had refrained from disputing and preaching on these points, and he advised that silence should be enjoined on both sides. Andrewes was therefore not strictly an Arminian either. He and his followers were concerned with the maintenance of other more important doctrines—the visible Church, the nature of episcopacy, the validity of rites and ceremonies—against the views of the Calvinists.[17] In the words of Marianne Dorman, "As a theologian he never spent enormous energy over religious controversies, but rather preached and lived out the Catholic faith of the early Church. For him that was always his criterion for teaching and preaching in the post-Reformation Church in England."[18]

Andrewes strongly decried the neglect of the Sacraments in England. "The Altar is neglected," he says, and "the highest and most solemn service of God fares worse than any other."[19] He denounced the Puritan over-emphasis on preaching to the neglect of the liturgy—"all our holiness is in hearing, all our service ear-service," he bemoaned, "Now is the world of sermons."[20] For someone who excelled so far above his contemporaries in preaching, he had the wisdom and humility to know that there were much more important things. His appreciation of the Sacraments is well explained by Dorman as

> his belief in the perennial Bethlehem. For you see, for Andrewes what happened at Bethlehem almost two thousand years ago still happens every day at the altar and will continue until our Lord's return to claim this world as His. Important as preaching is, the Sacrament is more important for Andrewes. Nearly all his sermons end by linking Christ in the various aspects of His life with that life being with us now in the Eucharist under the guise of bread and wine.
>
> > *For what are they, but weak and poor elements of themselves? yet in them find we Christ. Even as they did this day in the beasts' crib the food of angels; which very food our signs both represent, and present unto us.*[21]

Andrewes strongly opposed any movement to abolish the episcopacy in England and saw in the Scriptures and church history more than enough to affirm the historic episcopacy and apostolic succession.

> Touching the form of which government many imaginations have lately been bred in these our days especially. At the writing of this verse, it is certain that the government of Christian people consisted in two degrees only – of both which our Saviour Christ Himself was the Author: of the Twelve, [and] of the Seventy; both which were over the people, in things pertaining to God.
>
> These two were, one superior to another, and not equal. And that the Apostles established an equality in the Clergy is, I take it, an imagination.... Now in the place of the Twelve, succeeded Bishops; and in the place of the Seventy, Presbyters, Priests

[16] Eliot, "Lancelot Andrewes," 304.

[17] Welsby, *Andrewes*, 44.

[18] Marianne Dorman, "Lancelot Andrewes: Prelate, Preacher, Pastor," Project Canterbury, anglicanhistory.org/essays/dorman4.pdf.

[19] Welsby, *Andrewes*, 125.

[20] Ibid.

[21] Dorman, "Andrewes."

or Ministers, and that by the judgment of Irenaeus, who lived immediately upon the Apostles' age, of Tertullian, of St. Augustine. And this, till of late, was thought the form of fellowship, and never other imagined.[22]

Elsewhere, in his *Pattern of Catechistical Doctrine*, he speaks of how necessary the Apostles' ministry and graces were in their time, and then says:

> Seeing then that God has no less care for the propagation and continuance of His church than for the first settling or planting of it, it must needs follow that this power was not personal in the apostles, as tied to them only, but a power given to the church; and in them for their times resident, but not ending with them as temporary, but common to the ages after and continuing, to whom it was more needful than to them, to repress schism and to remedy other abuses. So that the very same power at this day remaineth in the church, and shall to the world's end.[23]

The people of England were seriously divided at this time. As the English Church returned decidedly to her historic catholic roots, the divide between the Anglicans and the Puritans grew, and tensions mounted and finally exploded in the next generation in the form of the English Civil War. Men like Andrewes recognized that Puritanism was only loosely connected to a specific or coherent theological framework. As one historian says, "In the case of the Roman menace, the English Elizabethan government was faced with a clear-cut issue. Regarding the Puritans, however, there was no such clarity. Puritanism defies exact definition."[24] At this time in England, before the clear delineation of Church and State, religious movements were often political movements clothed in theological controversy. Puritanism cannot be clearly defined by a doctrinal confession, and is rather a term used to describe the persons who wished to see the continued reformation of the Church of England, and who "went on to demand the replacement of the episcopate by the presbyterian form of church government, and the Book of Common Prayer for Calvin's order of public worship."[25] "All that can be said by way of generalization is that [Puritanism] represented that body of people who regarded the Reformation in England as incomplete, and who wished to purify the Church still further by action from within or from without."[26] Another historian explains that the Puritans, in the 1620's, the decade in which Lancelot Andrewes died, were those who saw the established Church and English government as barriers to the continued spiritual reformation of England, to whom, "there could be no real progress without changes in the ritual and leadership of the Caroline Church of England."[27] The same author then defines Anglicanism in the same time period, saying, "Anglicans were those more or less content with the episcopal organization and liturgy of the Church of England."[28]

---

[22] Raymond Chapman. *Before the King's Majesty: Lancelot Andrewes and His Writings* (Norwich: Canterbury, 2008), 79–80.

[23] Ibid., 81.

[24] Welsby, *Andrewes*, 4.

[25] Ibid., 5.

[26] Ibid., 4–5.

[27] J. Sears McGee. *The Godly Man in Stuart England: Anglicans, Puritans, and the Two Tables, 1620–1670* (New Haven, CT: Yale University Press, 1976), 10.

[28] Ibid.

Puritanism was therefore a movement inherently hostile to the structure of the ancient Church, and the governance in England that maintained it, and therefore is a movement better understood in a political, and not a purely theological, light.

Lancelot Andrewes and James I, as well as their successors, Charles I and the Caroline Divines, understood this. Hence so much of the efforts of Andrewes and his followers in this period were to vindicate and support the episcopacy. In tandem with Richard Hooker, he helped lay the groundwork for a distinctly Anglican mode of doing theology in contradistinction to the rising Puritan anti-ecclesiological influence in England. His theology was based on the theology of the undivided Church. During a volatile and controversial period, he anchored the English Church to its catholic theological roots—in his words: "One canon reduced to writing by God himself, two testaments, three creeds, four general councils, five centuries, and the series of Fathers in that period – the centuries that is, before Constantine, and two after, determine the boundary of our faith."[29] The reason Andrewes laid so much stress on this period in particular is because it represented the opinion of the undivided Church, and was still close enough to Christ and His Apostles to avoid gross corruption.

Theological battles were being fought over many historic doctrines and practices. Andrewes maintained the doctrine of the Real Presence in the Eucharist against both Roman transubstantiation and Protestant memorialism. He vindicated the practice of auricular confession as beneficial but voluntary, neither mandatory as Rome decreed nor wicked and superstitious as the Puritans claimed. He maintained a proper emphasis on both Word and Sacrament, against overbalances on either side. He defended the Patristic doctrine of *theosis*, or the articulation of glorification as deification. In one of his Pentecost sermons Andrewes speaks of the "royal exchange" that took place on Pentecost. He says, "Whereby, as before He of ours, so now we of His are made partakers. He clothed with our flesh, and we invested with His Spirit. The great promise of the Old Testament accomplished, that He should partake our human nature; and the great and precious promise of the New, that we should be *consortes divinae naturæ*, 'partakers of His divine nature,' both are this day accomplished."[30]

In many controversies, we see Bishop Andrewes pointing the way forward according to an English *Via Media* rightly understood not as a compromise between two doctrines, but as a more sensible and comprehensive embrace of the whole of Biblical and historical theology, against the extreme and polemical positions taken by Romans and Puritans.

Because Andrewes saw that the form, practices, and beliefs of the apostolic church were preserved in England, he maintained that the English Church was part of the historic, catholic Church. "Both Rome and Geneva would have repudiated this Anglican claim, but Andrewes and his followers asserted that the prerogative which Rome confined to the Pope and which Puritans confined to an invisible Church, belonged to the universal, historical church, and therefore to the Church of England."[31] In other words, Rome justified her catholicity through the papacy, Protestantism through the

---

[29] Andrewes, *Opuscula quaedam posthuma*, 91 [5]. Anglicancompass.com.

[30] Michael Marsh, "Theosis in the Episcopal Church," 2011, interruptingthesilence.com/2011/07/14/theosis-in-the-episcopal-church.

[31] Welsby, *Andrewes*, 156.

idea of an invisible church, but Anglicanism – with Andrewes – through the visible, historic, and universal church's apostolic ministry and rites. "On the whole Andrewes' vindication became the norm of the Anglican apologetic."[32]

Andrewes was respected by both Roman Catholic and Protestant theologians, and was considered a great controversialist, or debater, as well as a great peacemaker amongst Christians of different traditions. He was not naturally combative and kept regular correspondence with varying stripes of theologians on the Continent. Andrewes was so well respected as a theological counsellor and correspondent because of his constant emphasis on adoration, and prayer. He resisted the emphasis on systematic theology and the casuistic endeavors of both Rome and Geneva and sought to maintain a more comprehensive view of the truth, including the tension, of what, according to the historic church, are ultimately divine mysteries. "His theology was mystical rather than speculative, refusing to make a system of a mystery."[33] When Andrewes "did theology" he looked to the Scriptures and the first five centuries of the Church, asking, is this theology in the acceptable range of what the early church fathers believed, taught, or practiced? If there existed in that period a range of belief about a given matter—say about the Sacraments, or governance of the Church, or of predestination—then it was permissible to have a range of opinion on that matter in the contemporary Church—you could not claim one position as *de fide*. If, however, the contemporary Church began espousing novel or newly developed doctrines or began codifying too narrow a view on a given subject that it denied the historic breadth of patristic theology, Andrewes would point them to the church fathers for determining the acceptable range for matters *de fide*. Here, the depth and breadth of his learning was his greatest strength as a theological apologist for the Church of England.

There is one particular work of Lancelot Andrewes that gives us our greatest insight into the seriousness of his devotional life. Andrewes crafted for himself a book of private prayers, called the *Preces Privatae*, or "Private Devotions" which was published posthumously.

The *Preces* emerged out of Andrewes' personal habit of prayer. Bishop Buckeridge said that Andrewes' "'life was a life of prayer'; a great part of five hours every day, did he spend in prayer and devotion to God."[34] S. R. Gardiner described him, saying, "Going in and out amongst the frivolous and grasping courtiers who gathered round the King, he seemed to live in a peculiar atmosphere of holiness."[35] He was revered, not just for his scholarship, but for his saintliness, and in his *Private Devotions* lies a key to understanding why.

His personal ascetic was, when measured against the average Christian, intense, but Andrewes always was more of a medieval than a modern, even amongst his contemporaries. He lived a saintly, some would say a monkish, life in the midst of courtly wealth and prestige. His priorities were prayer, then study, then business. He seems to have taken to the habit of prayer and sermon writing as a fish to water. His sermons

---

[32] Welsby, *Andrewes*, 156.

[33] Chapman, *Before the King's Majesty*, 9.

[34] Welsby, *Andrewes*, 266.

[35] Ibid., 98.

exude his devotion and love of God; they reveal a man more interested in the worship and adoration of God than in theological controversy. His virtues as a godly and wise preacher and pastor could only have come from a divine source and habit of prayer such as is found in his *Private Devotions*.

This personal piety was not merely a mark of his private life. A strong case can be made that Andrewes' own devotional exercises and personal moral and ascetical theology were just as influential upon the whole English Church as was his preaching. "As a moral theologian, Andrewes was first in the line of the later Caroline churchmen," says Welsby.[36] Andrewes' influence on the later Caroline Divines is not to be understated. Upon his death, Charles I had Andrewes' sermons published as reading for the clergymen in his realm. But it was not his homiletical style that lasted, but rather his moral and ascetical theology that had the most lasting impact upon the English Church. Commenting on Andrewes early *Pattern of Catechistical Doctrine*, Welsby continues, "With regard to the other characteristics of Caroline Moral theology, Andrewes also linked moral with ascetical theology."[37]

This final statement is worth unpacking. Ascetical theology is essentially the praxis of moral theology. If moral theology tells us that formation of righteousness is reliant on a habit of prayer, ascetical theology is where the habit and rule of prayer is developed. Moral theology is interested in the nature of holiness; ascetical theology is interested in the personal and corporate progress in holiness through spiritual disciplines.

Ascetical theology therefore is the mark of a Church no longer wrestling with the issue of its own identity, no longer fighting to defend its own right to exist. There is no time for the healthy development of ascetical theology when soteriology and ecclesiology are being debated and hashed out. Ascetical theology is, in a sense, the practice and aim of a theologically stable Church. Andrewes was the first of the English bishops and theologians to emphasize the importance of ascetical theology, both corporately, in the life of the parish and the prayer book rule, and individually, in the realm of private prayer. The discipline of the Church was to be obeyed in matters such as fasting, times of prayer, confessions, and pastoral direction. And the people were to be actively and truly praying, not taking their religion passively as spectators. Andrewes therefore marks a transitional period in the English Church. His ascetical theology and personal devotion greatly influenced the next generation of Church leaders, the Caroline Divines. In the great lights of Carolingian ascetical theology and devotion, which followed directly on his heels, Andrewes' own theology and devotion is reflected.

Andrewes' influence on the English Church survives in key markers of Anglican identity: the embrace of apostolic authority and succession, a rejection of trending sectarian doctrines for a submission to the fuller practices and beliefs of the undivided Church, an insistence on sacramental and scriptural fidelity, and an emphasis on ascetic piety in the corporate and private lives of Christians. He played a pivotal role in leading the English Church back to her historic roots at a critical juncture in time. T. S. Eliot contrasts Andrewes to Hugh Latimer, another famous preacher during the initial Protestant reforms in England especially under Edward VI. He argues that what makes

---

[36] Welsby, *Andrewes*, 29.
[37] Ibid., 31.

Andrewes' words so much more compelling and enduring is not that he knew Greek or had a better homiletical style, but ultimately that Latimer "is merely a Protestant; but the voice of Andrewes is the voice of a man who has a formed visible Church behind him, who speaks with the old authority and the new culture. It is the difference of negative and positive: Andrewes is the first great preacher of the English Catholic Church."[38]

---

[38] Eliot, "Lancelot Andrewes," 302.

For further information about Andrewes, see also Benjamin Guyer, *The Beauty of Holiness* (Norwich, Canterbury, 2012).

Chapter 19

Doubt Wisely:
The Faith of John Donne (1573–1631)

Dr. David K. Anderson

John Donne preached his final sermon in 1631, before a crowd in St. Paul's Cathedral that included King Charles I. As it was the first Friday in Lent, the text was a solemn though hopeful one: "And unto God the Lord belong the issues of [*escapes from*] death" (Ps 68:20). Donne's appearance was shocking, and he meant for it to shock. He knew how cadaverous his cancer-ravaged body had become.[1] It is easy to understand how the coincidence of the Biblical text and his terrible illness prompted Donne to preach this sermon, known as *Death's Duel*, that stares at death without blinking. Donne tells us that we begin to die as soon as we are born; the very placenta that nourishes us in the womb is a kind of winding sheet. The whole world is a "common grave," he writes, and the actions of the greatest kings and generals are likened to nothing more than the shaking of buried bodies in an earthquake—a mere ripple of energy that passes in a moment.[2] A modern reader might label Donne's sermon "morbid" and push it away with distaste. But aside from the fact that we denizens of the twenty-first century would be well served by a little more sober thinking on death, the sermon crystalizes not only Donne's thought in his final weeks, but of much of his life. *Death's Duel* is a culmination of decades spent pondering on man's terrible vulnerabilities, as well as on their antidote.

His Life

First, a few words on the man himself. He was born in 1573 into an arch-Catholic family and converted in his twenties to the Church of England, at least in part to further his career. He then gained an impressive administrative appointment along with a reputation for libertinism, during which time he wrote the most scandalous and original love poetry of the era. He threw both the career and the reputation away when in 1601 he married his employer's 17-year-old niece Anne, provoking the outrage of her powerful family so that he had to face brief imprisonment and long-term financial duress. The marriage was both devoted and fruitful, though most of their children failed to survive into adulthood and Donne was devastated when Anne died after their twelfth was stillborn. Throughout, there were intermittent bursts of poetry. In the 1590s he had written of love and the world in such frank terms, and with such unexpected associations, that he can still unsettle the jaded undergraduates of the twenty-first century. Eventually, God became the subject of his verse, but once again in a register and

---

[1] Izaak Walton, Donne's first biographer, is responsible for this description of Donne at his last appearance in the pulpit: "to the amazement of some beholders, he appeared in the pulpit, many of them thought he presented himself not to preach mortification by a living voice, but mortality by a decayed body, and a dying face." See *The Life of John Donne*, in Walton's *The Lives of Dr. John Donne, Sir Henry Wotton, Mr. Richard Hooker, Mr. George Herbert* (London: Newcomb, 1670), 9–88, esp. 71.

[2] John Donne, *Death's Duel*, in *Devotions Upon Emergent Occasions and Death's Duel*, ed. Andrew Motion (New York: Vintage, 1999), 153–178, esp. 159–160.

with a battery of images that no one used to reading of divine matters would expect. As the years passed, Donne reflected deeply over whether God was calling him into the ministry.[3] He finally took Holy Orders in 1615 and was rapidly promoted, until in 1621 he received the prominent appointment of Dean of St. Paul's Cathedral, where soon he became celebrated as the greatest preacher in England.

His Faith

In what follows I will attempt to sketch the contours of John Donne's faith. I want to begin by addressing an early poem, where a disaffected and troubled young man expresses ambivalence, so striking in the early seventeenth-century, regarding the church to which he should belong.

However, Donne's suspicion of ecclesiastical partisanship springs not from an indifference to theology but from a deeply personal sense that it is Christ, not doctrine, that saves us. And so, in the remaining section of the essay I discuss what I take to be the heart of his mature spirituality. The early poem avers that we cannot rest secure in what today we might call our religious identity and this insecurity is explored in Donne's later poetry and prose which is imbued with an overwhelming awareness that death—spiritual as well as physical—makes a mockery of his moral efforts and that only the radical intervention of God can save him. Donne's commitment to the doctrine of salvation *sola gratia* is not a matter of technical theological niceties but of lived reality; it is for him a spiritual lifeline rather than an intellectual premise. He embraces it so vigorously because it tells him the truth about himself and points out the only source of hope that a dying body and a sin-sick soul can rely upon.

His Work

John Donne, sensitive, passionate, and idiosyncratic, is one of the great figures of Anglicanism's first century. No one would have expected this had they surveyed his first three or four decades. As a young man Donne looked around at a country where Catholics, Puritans, and those we anachronistically call Anglicans were engaged in a fight to the knife for control of the English church. Donne, in his own way, participated in this struggle as the years unfolded, but the principal thing he learned from the savage contest was that God was not to be placated by our confessional allegiance, nor even by fine displays of theological acuity. Without question Donne possessed a formidable, if idiosyncratic, theological mind. He was not indifferent to the question of which church God favored. However, Donne believed it is a secondary consideration. In the half-confessional, half-polemical poem known as "Satyre 3," written around the time of his conversion, Donne offers the reader a map for search for what he calls "True Religion." An odd, ungainly piece, the poem is remarkable for its comprehensive, sweeping dismissals, and for the conclusion that it draws. The speaker surveys several hypothetical partisan figures: a convinced Catholic, a committed Calvinist, and a staunch adherent of the national church. All are derided as simplistic, hidebound, unthinking. However, he

---

[3] In her recent biography of Donne, Katherine Rundell notes that he first rejected the possibility of ordination in 1607. See Katherine Rundell, *Super-Infinite: The Transformations of John Donne* (New York: Farrar, Straus, and Giroux, 2022), 193.

goes on to deride a sceptic, who assumes all churches are indelibly compromised and a syncretist who proclaims, with cretinous good cheer, that "he loves them all."[4] None of these will do. No theological allegiance offers a sure footing, and nor does a blanket rejection or blanket acceptance. It will mean nothing, Donne says, when we stand before the Judgment Seat, to tell the Lord that "a Philip, or a Gregory, / A Harry, or a Martin, taught thee this."[5] The names refer to two German theologians, a pope, and an English king. "Cannot both sides say so?"[6] he asks of a hypothetical dispute, noting that adherents of all churches cite authorities in aid of their positions.

What matters is the authenticity and fervour of the search for truth. Within the white-hot climate of Reformation England, such an idea was no platitude. Donne counsels the reader,

> Keep the truth which thou hast found; men do not stand
> In so ill case here that God hath with his hand
> Signed kings blank charters to kill whom they hate.[7]

God is here contrasted with an earthly tyrant who might leave his aides with a sheaf of signed death warrants, victims' names left out so that any emergent enemy can be eliminated at convenience. In other words, he has not entrusted the divine seals to a klatch of subordinates who will punish those who wander outside party lines. The statement "Keep the truth which thou hast found" seems to imply that to find something of God in an inferior church is better than finding none of him in a superior one. It does not make the difference between the two churches immaterial, but it does dampen the anxiety that the question is an ultimate one for the individual soul. Taking the furor over iconoclasm as an example of an issue where absolute certitude should not be claimed Donne writes,

> T'adore, or scorn an image, or protest,
> May all be bad: doubt wisely. In strange way,
> To stand enquiring right is not to stray.[8]

The opening claim seems contradictory: how can the Catholic *and* Calvinist extremes, as well as the moderate position of the Anglicans "all be bad"?[9] It is because the issue is not a black and white one, so the essential factor is the purity of one's intentions. When lost, he suggests, it is better to hold in place and try to puzzle out the map than to plunge off in a hastily chosen direction. Hence, the maxim "[D]oubt wisely" does not enjoin blanket skepticism. The doubt encouraged here is first of all directed at the self and its priorities. A decision based on external characteristics or factionalism is no better than one based on mere whim. The long, winding ascent up the mountain of truth that Donne describes

---

[4] Donne, "Satyre 3," in *The Complete Poems of John Donne*, ed. Robin Robbins (New York: Routledge, 2010), 386–396, ll. 43–68.

[5] Ibid., ll. 96–97.

[6] Ibid., l. 99.

[7] Ibid., ll. 89–91.

[8] Ibid., ll. 76–78.

[9] By "protest" Donne likely means "to be a Protestant," which he is conflating here with Anglicanism, in contrast to the iconophilic Catholics and the "scorning" Calvinists.

elsewhere in the poem both demands and engenders epistemological humility.[10] The result will not be the absolute assurance that one particular theological and epistemological model has been proved "true" but that the soul has been made ready to behold Truth itself, which is to say Christ. In Donne's later writing we can discern a cluster of positive reasons for his eventual conciliation with the national church, along with a wish that his Catholic and Puritan countrymen should likewise reconcile, even as we notice little anxiety on his part that their souls are necessarily imperiled by their refusal. Quite simply: depth and sincerity of faith matter more than confessional alignment. If this seems an obvious point today, it was not often stated so pointedly in the seventeenth century.[11]

Donne takes this position not on behalf of doctrinal laxity, but a spiritually mature ecumenicism, which presupposes that our object is not the ideal confessional framework but to draw as near as possible to Christ. Its result is an Anglicanism defined less by the *moderation* which is so often thought to characterize our church, than by *modesty*. And a man who believes what Donne believes should be modest. Death lurks somewhere up the pathway for us all. We feel its touch in the physical frailty of the body, but we can feel it just as keenly in the soul, where it goes by the name Sin. As Donne prays at the close of an undated sermon, we are "by our own faults made more wretched and contemptible, then [sic] the wormes which shall eat us, or the dust which we were, and shall be."[12] The killing wounds we commit against our own souls are the inner truth of which death is simply the outward expression. We are locked in a lifelong struggle with this two-headed monster. We might fight it to a seeming draw for a few short seasons, but it will have us before long. And mostly we work against our own interests, helping it in its program, like addicts who consume the thing that poisons their bodies and blights their happiness. "I run to death," Donne writes in one of the Holy Sonnets, the verb indicating a perverse compulsion towards destruction, like an antelope charging a lion.[13] In "A Litany," an experiment in liturgical poetics, he puts the matter even more forcefully:

> In every Christian
> Hourly tempestuous persecutions grow;
> Temptations martyr us alive; a man
> Is to himself, a Diocletian.[14]

---

[10] For Donne's description of the ascent up the mount of Truth, see lines 79–84.

[11] For a survey of ecumenical statements from the mature Donne, within the context of his pointed antipathy to the Jesuits, see Marla Lunderberg, "Protesting against Those Who Have 'Risen up against Princes': How Political Concerns Alter John Donne's Usually Ecumenical Voice," *Christianity & Literature* 70 (2021): 95–112, esp. 96. Lunderberg quotes a number of Donne's statements including the following from a 1609 letter to his close friend Sir Henry Goodyer: "You know I never fettered nor imprisoned the word Religion ... immuring it in a Rome, or a Wittemberg, or a Geneva; they are all virtuall beams of one Sun." From *Letters to Severall Persons of Honour*, ed. Charles Edmund Merrill, Jr. (New York: Sturgis & Walton, 1910), 25.

[12] From Sermon 5, *John Donne's Sermons on the Psalms and Gospels: With a Selection of Prayers and Meditations*, ed. Evelyn M. Simpson (Berkeley: University of California Press, 2003), 115–128, esp. 127.

[13] Donne, "Holy Sonnet 1," in Robbins, *Complete Poems of John Donne*, 521–523, l. 3.

[14] Donne, "A Litany," in Robbins, *Complete Poems of John Donne*, 496–416, ll. 96–99.

The Emperor Diocletian, the architect of the greatest persecution of the ancient church, lives inside of each of us. I, rather than my external enemies, am my own worst tormentor.

In *Devotions Upon Emergent Occasions*, the masterpiece of spiritual prose that Donne wrote while recovering from a near fatal illness in the last decade of his life, he reflects on his inclination to grip so tightly to the sin that pulls him down. Why, he asks, does the soul not quiver and pulsate in the presence of sin as the body does in the presence of pain? Rather, he writes,

> I stand in the way of temptations, naturally, necessarily; all men do so; for there is a snake in every path, temptations in every vocation; but I go, I run, I fly into the ways of temptation which I might shun; nay, I break into houses where the plague is; I press into places of temptation, and tempt the devil himself, and solicit and importune them who had rather be left unsolicited by me.[15]

The metaphor of the plague house suggests that sin and death are tied so tightly together in Donne's mind that any differences between them seem only to be a matter of perception. As Donne wrote these words, London was still in the grip of a harrowing outbreak of what was likely typhus. Not only did it nearly end his own life but given his role as pastor-in-chief of the city's cathedral, he had to oversee numberless funerals as the plague scythed its way through his neighborhood.[16] Yet if the speaker is wise enough not to needlessly expose himself to physical pestilence, he admits to luxuriating in the moral variety.

Donne's early days as a swashbuckling young womanizer did much for the development of English love poetry, but also gave him much to regret. In later life he made a wry distinction between scandalous young "Jack Donne" and the sober and austere "Doctor Donne" that Londoners had come to know.[17] He had no illusions, though, that the doctor was a pillar of faultless rectitude. His blood may have cooled, but the conscience is heavy. Recalling the physicians who would bleed him in his illness he writes, "There is no artery in me that hath not the spirit of error, the spirit of lust, the spirit of giddiness in it; no bone in me that is not hardened with the custom of sin."[18] Those who minister to his body may give him a respite, but the underlying condition is terminal. And yet, as he continues the passage, he asserts that there is one who can heal him. Though the cure is a fearful one, he will entrust himself to it completely.

Sin is not a series of demerits on some eternal report card. It is a fateful, savage potency, that we cannot overcome nor even effectively resist. But grace overcomes it, and grace for Donne is equally savage—a white hot cauterizing iron wielded by a surgeon who will not be content until every trace of the infection has been burned away. The relationship between Sin and Death, on the one hand, and Grace on the other is always paradoxical for Christians. But Donne saw paradoxes wherever he turned, and so that sense is heightened for him. Hating his sin and fearing his death, he is piercingly aware

---

[15] Donne, "I. Expostulation," in Motion, *Devotions*, 1–152, 5.

[16] For a discussion of Donne's life in London during plague season see John Stubbs, *John Donne: The Reformed Soul*, (New York: W. W. Norton & Co., 2007), 399–405.

[17] Donne, *Biathanatos*, ed. Ernest W. Sullivan (Newark: University of Delaware Press, 1984), 4.

[18] Donne, "IX. Expostulation," in Motion, *Devotions*, 55.

that these are the very things God can use to redeem him. When Lady Julian of Norwich declared that "sin is very befitting" she takes pains to explain that this is not because it is in itself good, but because "it purges us and makes us know ourselves and ask for mercy."[19] In confronting our sin, we are reminded of the One who bore it and thus of the value he places on us. And while Death is to be swallowed up in victory, for those of us who live between Easter and the Last Trumpet, this means not its total obviation but its transmutation. It is no longer the cancellation of life but a portal to *real* life.

Death's Duel, for all its severity, is imbued with this understanding of death. In it, Donne says, the Father "rescues his servants from the jaws of death"; the Son "rescues us by taking upon himself the issue of death"; and "between these two" the Holy Ghost "rescues us ... that what manner of death soever be ordained for us, yet...our issues of death shall be an entrance into everlasting life."[20] Only by grasping tightly to Christ, the God who died, can sin and death be overcome: "Hast thou gone about to redeem thy sin," he asks, "by fasting, by alms, by disciplines and mortifications, in way of satisfaction to the justice of God? That will not serve, that is not the right way; we press an utter crucifying of that sin that governs thee: and that conforms thee to Christ."[21]

Comfort, Donne suggests, can only be found by recognizing that God is using our very frailty, physical and moral, to make us participants in the crucifixion. "Therefore that he may raise," he writes at the end of a hymn, "the Lord throws down."[22] It is not the healthy who need a doctor, we have been told, but the sick; in his mercy he will make us feel our sickness. In "Good Friday" perhaps the greatest devotional lyric in the English canon, Donne recounts the disorientation and guilt he feels when a professional necessity requires him to make a horseback journey on the most solemn of days. His physical deportment—facing west, towards his destination, as opposed to facing the Holy Land as he would be doing were he kneeling in a traditional east-facing church— allows him to meditate both on his spiritual derangement and on how Christ may redeem him from it. After detailing the sublime and terrible sights that would have confronted him had his soul been properly fixed on Calvary, he comes to admit "I'almost be glad," to be facing away from the event, the beholding of which he knows he is not spiritually strong enough to endure.[23] We might at this point expect a humble supplication for the speaker to be gently reoriented. Instead, in a development that is as disquieting as it is unexpected, the westward-facing posture is reimagined as that of someone humbly accepting a whipping:

> I turn my back to thee but to receive
> Corrections, till thy mercies bid thee leave.
> O think me worth thine anger: punish me,

---

[19] Julian of Norwich, *Revelations of Divine Love*, trans. Bary Windeatt (Oxford: Oxford World's Classics), 20.

[20] Donne, *Death's Duel*, in Motion, *Devotions*, 156–157.

[21] Ibid., 176.

[22] Donne, "Hymn to God in My Sickness," in Robbins, *Complete Poems of John Donne*, 610–614, l. 30.

[23] Donne, "Good Friday: Made as I Was Riding Westward That Day," in Robbins, *Complete Poems of John Donne*, 562–567, l. 15.

> Burn off my rusts and my deformity;
> Restore thine image, so much, by thy grace
> That thou may'st know me, and I'll turn my face.[24]

"Think me worth thine anger." As much as he may fear the divine judge, Donne shocks us by implying that he is even more afraid of a lenient God.

C. S. Lewis writes of twentieth-century Christians that "we want, in fact, not so much a Father in Heaven as a grandfather in heaven—a senile benevolence who, as they say, liked to see young people enjoying themselves."[25] Donne fears such benevolence. Another poem describes his trepidation prior to a long voyage to the continent, with separation from the familiar world of home conjuring up fears of death and judgment. Noting that God does not compel holiness, he wonders whether God's ardor for his soul is as great as it needs to be for his salvation:

> Art jealous, Lord, so I am jealous now;
> Thou lovest not, till from loving more Thou free
> My soul ; Who ever gives, takes liberty;
>   Oh, if Thou carest not whom I love,
>   Alas ! Thou lovest not me.[26]

God's refusal to deny the speaker's "liberty" to sin is construed here as a denial of ultimate liberty—salvation. If God is not concerned with the disordered loves of the speaker, how much does he love really him? In his most famous Holy Sonnet, complaint turns to demand as the speaker presumes so far as to give God a series of orders. The nature of these orders compounds the audacity: he asks God to "batter"[27] him like an old pot that needs to be broken up, melted and remade rather than gently polished; to assault him like a walled city under foreign occupation; to "divorce" him from the devil to whom he finds himself married;[28] and finally, in the couplet, to both imprison him in aid of his true freedom and "ravish" him in order to save his chastity.[29] Begging God to assume the metaphorical malefactor's role, aside from arresting the reader's attention, allows Donne to emphasize his altogether desperate condition. If God continues to treat him with gentlemanly forbearance the speaker will one day find himself in hell.

His Legacy

> And he said, Let me go, for the day breaketh.
> And he said, I will not let thee go, except thou bless me. (Gen 32:26 KJV)

I have presented John Donne in terms that may make him appear naïve: who would not, in the abstract, prioritize sincerity of faith over confessional affiliation? The question is

---

[24] Donne, "Good Friday," 37–42.

[25] C. S. Lewis, *The Problem of Pain* (New York: Harper Collins, 1996), 31.

[26] Donne, "At the Seaside, Going Over with the Lord Doncaster into Germany, 1619," Robbins, *Complete Poems of John Donne*, 583–586, ll. 18–21.

[27] Donne, "Holy Sonnet 14," Robbins, *Complete Poems of John Donne*, 562–567, l. 1.

[28] Ibid., l. 11.

[29] Ibid., l. 13–14.

too simplistic, of course, as many in his day and some in our own would have said that faith is only sincere if it is rooted in right doctrine. However, for Donne, who subordinated the latter to the former, naivete would be assuming that there was eternal value in anything but the most ardent and all-consuming pursuit of Christ. "Without thee," he tells God in his *Devotions*, "all health is but fuel and strength to the bellows of sin."[30] We may construe "health" here as broadly or narrowly as we please: soundness neither of body nor mind, nor even an exemplary moral track record, will be sufficient, and having one's name on a parish register is not the same as having it written in the Book of Life. God must intervene, and God must stir up the heart to call out for salvation; God must show us the ugliness of sin so that his advent in the soul becomes a thing invited, longed for rather than taken for granted. Donne is so compelling to us, nearly four hundred years after he preached that last sermon, because he presents himself as a latter-day Jacob, who will not release his grip on the angelic wrestler without receiving a blessing, holding on with all his strength, indifferent to convention or to his dignity. The radical nature of our plight, as Donne understands it, demands nothing less than everything we have.

---

[30] Donne, "IV. Prayer," in Motion, *Devotions*, 23.

Chapter 20

Reformed Episcopalianism:
James Ussher (1581–1656), Irish Primate
and Apologist for Episcopacy

The Rev. Barton J. Gingerich

James Ussher was born to a prominent family in Dublin. He attended the Dublin Free School and in 1594 enrolled in the newly founded Trinity College Dublin, a Protestant school whose purpose was to better establish the reformational faith in Ireland. He was ordained in the Church of Ireland and quickly rose to prominence. He served as the chancellor of St. Patrick's Cathedral, Prebend of Finglas, and Professor of Theological Controversies at Trinity. He became Vice-Chancellor of Trinity in 1607 and Vice-Provost in 1616. He was deeply involved in the drafting of the 1615 Irish Articles of Religion. He was nominated by King James I as Bishop of Meath in 1623, became a Privy Councillor in 1623, and was nominated the Primate of All Ireland and Archbishop of Armagh in 1625 (his uncle had served in the same role some years before).[1]

Throughout his lifetime, Ussher established himself as a reputable scholar, and it was in scholarship that he was the most at home. Between 1623 and 1626, he was excused from his episcopal duties to study church history in England. He was also a collector of manuscripts, particularly Irish ones. His opinion became deeply valued in the Protestant world. For instance, he held the position now called "hypothetical universalism," which would play a significant role in guiding the English delegates to the Synod of Dort, with delegate John Davenant working to soften the language on limited atonement.[2] Ussher, it must be known, was no friend to Arminianism, yet he subscribed to a moderate form of Calvinism.

Ussher's career as an archbishop was far from peaceful. Ireland had a unique and troublesome political history, with the Normans and later the Tudor and Stuart dynasties working to establish some kind of stable rule over the kingdom. The crown's control was most firmly established in The Pale, and the king and his servants had to constantly wrestle with the vacillating "Old English" nobility of Ireland who had been present since the Norman Conquest. The conflict between the Roman Church and the Church of Ireland only exacerbated these tensions, and the ecclesio-political intrigues of Scotland and England brought even more complications for matters in Ireland. Put simply, England, Ireland, and Scotland were all headed toward the bloody conflict known as the Wars of the Three Kingdoms, and Ussher was stuck in the middle of these events as a Protestant archbishop in Ireland. Even his own family was marked by division.

---

[1] See Alan Ford, *James Ussher: Theology, History, and Politics in Early-Modern Ireland and England* (New York: Oxford University Press, 2007).

[2] "Much later, Richard Baxter thought himself to be at one with the Primate on this issue, and reported that Ussher had claimed, when Baxter had met him in the mid-1650s, that he had been the person responsible for converting not only Davenant, but also the puritan leader John Preston to hypothetical universalism. He has accordingly been seen by the most thorough study of this topic as the founder of English hypothetical universalism, offering Calvinism a more pastoral, mediatory position on the atonement." Ford, *Ussher*, 109.

While many of his relatives were prominent in the Protestant establishment, Ussher's cousin Henry Fitzsimon was a Jesuit controversialist who was both active and effective in Ireland, and Ussher's own mother had converted to Catholicism while he was away in England.

As will be covered later, Ussher desired harsh policies against Roman Catholicism and worked for the continued prominence of the Irish Articles of Religion, which were doctrinally narrower than the Thirty-nine Articles of Religion. This put him at odds with the likes of Thomas Wentworth, Archbishop William Laud, and Bishop John Bramhall. Of course, up until that time, the Church of Ireland suffered because of the widespread duplicity and corruption of various political leaders. For the most part, Wentworth, Laud, and Bramhall brought order to this chaotic situation, particularly with regard to forcing the nobility to pay what was owed the Church. Ussher had also longed for these much-needed obligations to be met. However, the Crown was willing to grant tolerance to Irish Catholics in exchange for financial, military, and other forms of support. In addition, Laud and other church leaders under Charles I were not too interested in litigating and relitigating predestinarian controversies. This clashed with Ussher's own convictions and inclinations, which will be discussed later.

The doctrinal and political disagreements manifested themselves in the context of ecclesiastical affairs. In the process, Ussher soon found himself losing *de facto* power in Ireland. He did not achieve his full desires at a 1634 convocation, which resulted in the Church of Ireland more fully conforming to the Church of England. However, he was able to hammer out various compromises.[3] He lost some control of Trinity College in the early to mid 1630s, especially with the installation of William Chappell as provost of the school, replacing Ussher's cousin Robert. While Ussher was not able to achieve all of his will at this period, he did continue in his pastoral and scholarly duties in Ireland until 1640, when he was summoned to England. Both King Charles I and Parliament sought his well-respected opinion.

Ussher would never again return to Ireland. He lost his home and income in the Irish Rebellion of 1641. He was granted a pension from Parliament while the king granted him the income and property of the See of Carlisle. He continued to preach, produce scholarly work, and counsel important figures on both sides of the English Civil War. Ultimately, Ussher sided with the Royalists, even though he was frustrated with Charles I's seeking support from the Catholics in Ireland. Amazingly, in 1642, Ussher had been nominated by the House of Commons to represent Oxford University at what would become the

---

[3] Cf. Ford, *Ussher*, 176–207. Ussher clashed with what may be described as "Laudians" in the Convocation of 1634. In the words of Ford, this became a "closely fought draw" (190). One the one hand, the Convocation struck the requirement for the Ten Commandments to be placed on the east wall of churches, mandated a silver chalice be used for Holy Communion, placed tables on the east end, and reinstated the allowance for private auricular confession. On the other hand, the Convocation did not rescind the Irish Articles. In addition, the Convocation refused bowing at the name of Jesus, kneeling for prayers, requiring university students and fellows to wear the surplice, and requiring cathedral clergy to wear the cope during Communion. Moreover, the Irish canons made no mention of the sign of the cross at baptism. Ford thinks the result of these negotiations could best be described not as greater "uniformity" between the Church of England and Church of Ireland but rather greater "congruity" (194).

Westminster Assembly, but he refused to attend a synod proscribed by the king. The Royalists lost the war, and Ussher himself witnessed the beheading of the king from the roof of Lady Peterborough's house, fainting at the sight. During the Protectorate, Ussher lost the income and property from Carlisle, since the episcopacy was disestablished, but throughout the Commonwealth years until his death, he enjoyed the patronage of Elizabeth, Dowager Countess of Peterborough.[4] He preached at Lincoln's Inn (winning approval from Parliament by a narrow margin) until 1655, a year before his death.

Through it all, Ussher proved himself a man of unimpeachable character and graciousness. He never seemed to take political and scholarly conflict personally, often to the astonishment of contemporaries. Indeed, historians today still gape in wonder at the wide diversity of Ussher's friends and lack of enemies—an exceedingly rare achievement during an era of partisanship and violence. Ussher was a staunch episcopalian, royalist, and Calvinist until the day he died in 1656, during the Protectorate and before the Restoration. Oliver Cromwell insisted that he be given a state funeral using the ceremony from the then-banned Book of Common Prayer. Ussher's remains were buried at Westminster Abbey.

Primate of Ireland

Ussher had faced immense challenges in his role as archbishop in the Church of Ireland. Leading up to his tenure, both the crown and the established church struggled with a weak control of the island. Time was not on the side of the Protestants when it came to bringing reformation to that kingdom.[5] The Gaelic common-folk and much of the Old English nobility were drawn into closer solidarity as the Protestant English attempted to exert more power in the region, often anchoring that solidarity in the form of religious identity. The Roman Catholic Church focused much energy, personnel, and effort to secure the Irish for Rome, which only ramped up with the unfolding Counter-Reformation. It must be remembered that, in 1570, a papal bull excommunicated Elizabeth I as a heretic and absolved all Catholics of their duty to obey her. The Protestants were in a distinct minority; they did not have many friends amongst the Irish common people, and the "Old English" nobility were given to vacillation if not outright antagonism.

Compounding the problem were corruption and rapacity on the part of leaders. The English often saw Ireland as a vast colony or plantation to be despoiled and exploited. Meanwhile, many of the nobility refused material sustenance to the Church of Ireland for their own benefit. They often found ways to enrich themselves off of tithes, glebes, benefices, and other properties that were meant for the Church, which left her horribly underfunded.[6]

The lack of funds, no doubt combined with other concerns and predilections, made it difficult to staff the Church of Ireland with clergymen. As a result, the Church was desperate for pastors. Many of the Puritan persuasion made their way over to Ireland to

---

[4] From a pro-Restoration Anglican perspective, members of the laity who patronized and protected the clergy are the unsung heroes of the Protectorate era.

[5] Ford, *Ussher*, 19.

[6] Ibid., 175–176.

serve, especially since the ecclesiastical leadership could be more lax with regard to uniformity and more hospitable to those with Genevan leanings. Irish leaders could turn a blind eye to liturgical deprivation if it meant staffing the church with Protestant pastors that had a strong doctrinal spine. At the same time, the plantation of Ireland was well under way, in which swathes of Irish land were granted to British settlers brought in from across the Irish Sea. Of course, the Scottish and northern English planters—known as the Scots-Irish in the United States—probably did not mind these lax dynamics, especially since the Scottish were usually Presbyterians.

The need for clergy—particularly native-born Protestant pastors—fueled the founding of Trinity College Dublin. Right off the bat, Trinity's aims and values were anti-Roman. Indeed, the Church of Ireland's character and challenges was perfectly encapsulated in the fact that Walter Travers, the infamous opponent of Richard Hooker, was Provost of Trinity College from 1594 to 1598, when James Ussher was a student there.

Unsurprisingly, the Church of Ireland's variant of Anglicanism was a "hotter" sort of Protestantism. Ussher frequently exemplified these tendencies. The Irish Articles were strongly predestinarian and Sabbatarian. Ussher opposed the theater (which was, it must be admitted, given to bawdiness at the time). Ussher clearly believed the pope to be the Antichrist, and he even saw the unveiling of the "man of sin" as one of the main themes of church history. He also sympathized with various sectarian groups that had been opposed by the Catholic Church, such as the Waldensians, although this view may have moderated in his later years.[7] While much of this historiography has fared poorly over the centuries (and was questioned by Ussher's fellow Anglican contemporaries), his criticism of Roman claims regarding papal supremacy and ecclesiastical legitimacy have fared much better. Simply put, Rome was deeply anti-Catholic, inventing and upholding novel doctrines that actively tore the fabric of Christendom.[8] Rome's false claims not only opposed the pure biblical faith of the Protestant Christians, but also severed relationships with Eastern Orthodox, Oriental Orthodox, and Coptic Christians. Roman Catholicism's errors had indeed been a long-standing problem, and they would remain so until they were abandoned. Thus, Ussher's efforts to refute Roman apologists and their doctrines had a catholic goal in mind.

Ussher sought a united front against Roman Catholicism, both in Ireland and abroad. He clearly pushed for a strong emphasis on the crown (even to the point of divine right royal absolutism) and crushing enforcement of recusancy laws. He wanted Catholicism brought to heel in Ireland under zealous religious crackdowns, which was not always congruent with the aims of the king and his advisors, who often sought cooperation and peace from the Irish through extending toleration toward Catholicism. Of course, Ussher's positions on this front have left a checkered legacy in Ireland.

---

[7] Ford, *Ussher*, 73–84.

[8] Richard Snoddy, ed., *James Ussher and a Reformed Episcopal Church: Sermons and Treatises on Ecclesiology* (Moscow, ID: Davenant, 2018), 68–71.

Ussher served as an important architect for the Church of Ireland's unique character as a non-English form of Anglicanism.[9] Ussher insisted that the Church of Ireland was a native, national church, not a Roman import. Ussher desired a truly Irish Protestant church. As Ford has pointed out, he along with others saw Ireland not so much as a colony of England but rather another kingdom entirely, whose monarch also happened also to be the ruler of England and of Scotland.[10] Ussher also welcomed a narrowing of dogmatic subscription to require more Reformed Calvinist doctrines in the Irish Articles of 1615, which not only encapsulated a narrower interpretation of soteriology than the *Thirty-Nine Articles* but also required a confession of the Pope as "that man of sin" and Sabbatarianism. Through the efforts of Wentworth, Bramhall, and Laud, greater English influence over the Church of Ireland increased, all over and against Ussher's protests. However, all of this was short-lived as the Irish revolted in 1641.

While Ussher failed in making all of Ireland Protestant, it might be said that it was a miracle that there was and is any Irish Protestantism—particularly Irish Anglicanism, if such a term is possible—at all. Ussher saw the theology and practice he advocated for as truly native to the lands of Ireland, even while he also welcomed a Reformed theology that was in keeping with significant parts of the pan-Protestant world of his time. Of course, Ussher also served as a major contributor to the troubled and troubling history of religion and politics in Ireland. On the other hand, he and his Anglican colleagues faced almost-insurmountable challenges in their effort to bring reform to his beloved homeland.

Academic

It may be that Ussher was a better academic than administrator.[11] Undeniably, Ussher served as an intellectual resource for the pan-Protestant world. Indeed, any irenicism he had toward Catholics manifested in his scholarly pursuits in the republic of letters. He was devoted to study and was a full member of the academic confraternity of his day. As an antiquary, he devoted himself to stockpiling an intellectual arsenal to build up the Church. His initial trips to England were to purchase books for Trinity's library.

As mentioned, Ussher maintained a deep and abiding interest in the study of history. To this day, he is still remembered for his *Annales*,[12] in which he calculated that the world began in 4004 BC. Most of his energy was devoted to church history. His *Brittanicarum*

---

[9] The terminology here proves tricky. In some sense, "Irish Anglicanism" is a begging of the question. Ussher insisted that the Church of Ireland's was the true Christian faith as found in Ireland's shores. It did not have complete theological dependence upon the Church of England. However, it used a *Book of Common Prayer*, had bishops, enjoyed supreme governorship from the crown, and more. In the 1630s, the Church of Ireland would go on to adopt the *Thirty-Nine Articles of Religion*.

[10] Ford, *Ussher*, 178–181.

[11] R. Buick Knox, *James Ussher: Archbishop of Armagh* (Cardiff: University of Wales Press, 1967), 191–192.

[12] *Annales Veteris Testamenti, a prima mundi origine deducti, una cum rerum Asiaticarum et Aegyptiacarum chronico, a temporis historici principio usque ad Maccabaicorum initia producto* ("Annals of the Old Testament, deduced from the first origins of the world, the chronicle of Asiatic and Egyptian matters together produced from the beginning of historical time up to the beginnings of Maccabees").

Ecclesiarum Antiquitates and other works advocated for a native British church, not a Roman import beholden to the pope. British Christianity had its own identity, history, and traditions that were 1) faithful to the catholic deposit of faith in terms of doctrine and practice and 2) not reliant upon the Church of Rome, thus undermining claims of papal authority and jurisdiction.

Not only did Ussher have a great love for Irish heroes of the faith like St. Patrick; his tone was one of deep affection and respect that contrasted with the chauvinistic attitudes of the earlier Anglo-Normans and recently-arrived English, who often dismissed the Irish, their language, and their culture as backwards and barbaric.[13] Additionally, Ussher saw the contemporary conflict over Arminianism in light of the ancient British conflict and eventual victory over the Pelagian heresy.[14]

Notably, James Ussher was probably the foremost scholar of Ignatius' writings in his day. At the time, the corpus of St. Ignatius' epistles suffered numerous problems. There were thirteen letters reported to be authored by Ignatius.[15] Critics (most famously John Milton in his *Of Prelatical Episcopacy*) pointed out anachronisms and other textual problems. Nonconformists regarded Ignatius as an unreliable historical source and thus refused to recognize him as a source of evidence in the debate over church government. Through his research, Ussher discovered that, up until AD 500, all quotations from Ignatius seemed to be from an old Latin version.[16] He deduced that only six letters of Ignatius were genuine,[17] and identified two manuscripts that contained accurate texts.[18] Modern scholars today tend to agree with Ussher's assessment, with the exception of Ussher's dismissal of Ignatius' letter to Polycarp as inauthentic.[19]

Defender of the Episcopacy

This important scholarly achievement in patristic history and textual study provided a solid foundation for what may be Ussher's most important and valuable contribution to the Reformed Catholic tradition, which is his defense of episcopacy. Put simply, while Ussher affirmed the Christian orthodoxy and ecclesiastical legitimacy of non-episcopalian Protestants, he was an insistent apologist for bishops and even metropolitans and archbishops. In this, Ussher embraced both the law and the spirit of the Anglican Reformation. He was episcopalian by conviction, not begrudgingly because of enforced conformity. His noteworthy argument for bishops did not primarily rely upon political theology. Many apologists for conformity to the established norms of the

---

[13] Ford, *Ussher*, 217–218. Notably, Ussher's colleague, William Bedell, actively evangelized and preached in the native tongue and made it a point to translate important resources into Irish, particularly the Old Testament. He faithfully served as the Bishop of Kilmore and stridently oppose non-residence and pluralities. Later on, he was imprisoned and tortured by the Catholic rebels in 1641. The deprivation led to his untimely death soon after his release in 1642.

[14] Ibid., 210–211.

[15] Knox, *Ussher*, 101.

[16] Ibid.

[17] Ibid.

[18] Snoddy, *Ussher*, xxix.

[19] Knox, 101–102; Snoddy, xxx.

Elizabethan settlement within the Church of England leaned heavily upon arguments from submission to magisterial authority.

Not so with James Ussher. While he would have no doubt affirmed such political theology, he was more interested in championing the episcopate on more basic grounds. In his *The Original of Bishops and Metropolitans* (1644), he put forth a biblically-based, historically-informed argument for episcopacy, especially in response to the "root and branch petition" of 1640.[20] For Ussher, church governance does not find justification only in the accidents of political history or national-constitutional norms, with a heavy reliance upon a Christian prince. It also takes its cues from Holy Scripture and precedents of the primitive church. While Ussher was mainly contending against Presbyterians, his argument also provides an active, relevant challenge to various Congregationalists, including Baptists and non-denominational evangelicals. Ussher does not make a full-bore *jure divino* or "divine right" case for the episcopate, neither does he see bishops as the *esse* of the Church.[21] Nevertheless, he sees episcopacy as the correct, biblical form of church government. Some scholars call this position, found also in the great Richard Hooker, as *ius divinium*. Bishops are "scriptural, apostolic and divine in origin, but it was not therefore immutable or necessary to the Church."[22]

Ussher's apology for the episcopate relies on three sources: Old Testament patterns, New Testament clues, and early church history. Starting with Old Testament patterns, Ussher begins with a prophecy. Isaiah 66:20 foretold that Gentiles will be joined to the people of Israelites as brothers. In v. 21, Isaiah then declares, "And I will also take of them for priests and for Levites, saith the LORD." Ussher sees a continuity from old covenant to new covenant ministry. He also notes the distinct, ordered nature of Old Testament ministry. As Peter Blair adeptly summarized, Ussher sees distinctions between the priests and Levites and distinctions within the priests and the Levites.[23] He also notices hierarchical oversight, especially in Nehemiah 11:22. For Ussher, the parallels between Old and New Testament ordained ministry are not neat and tidy. Instead, he is interested in establishing principles of order and hierarchy, which are found in both the old and new covenant.

Citing Deuteronomy 33:10, Ussher notes that Old Testament ministers had two distinct jobs: teaching God's people and sacrificing. The sacrifices prefigured Christ Jesus. As such, they have been fulfilled in and by Him. However, no such New Testament typological fulfillment exists for the teaching duties of ministry. Instead, teaching is the emphasis of New Testament pastoral ministry, particularly for presbyters and bishops. In other words, there is a significant continuity between the Old and New Testaments in the form of teaching. It is not at all surprising that the New Testament Church would also have order and even hierarchy as features of its ministry. As such, these principles and the structures they upheld were not the "device of Antichrist" as signatories of the "root and branch" petition insisted.[24] Instead, the crisis the Church faced was one of

---

[20] Peter Blair, *Biblical Bishops: James Ussher's Defense and Reform of Anglican Polity* (London: Latimer Trust, 2022), 20.

[21] The *esse* position would espouse the statement "no bishop, no Church."

[22] Blair, *Biblical Bishops*, 19.

[23] Ibid., 23.

[24] Ibid., 26.

faithless leaders, which is in total keeping with the warnings of Scripture as found in Jeremiah 2:21 and Matthew 15:13. Throwing out inherited—even biblical—structure would do little to assure biblical fidelity.

Surprisingly, when Ussher turns his attention to the New Testament, he focuses not on the pastoral epistles but rather on St. John's Revelation. In Revelation 1–3, the Lord addresses the "angels" of the seven churches in Asia. Ussher insists that this "angel" was in fact a pastoral leader of some kind in charge of and responsible for the Church in those seven cities mentioned in Revelation. Each city has an angel, not angels. And those stars are clearly owned by Christ.[25] This emphasizes the "divine (as opposed to human) origin of church offices and their authority."[26] Citing Reformed exegete Thomas Brightman, Ussher also draws attention to the portrait of church governance that St. Luke provides in Acts 19–20. The Church at Ephesus seemed to have a presbytery—a plurality of presbyters. This would make sense. The Church had become large enough to threaten the idol-making industry. So, when the Lord Jesus addresses the "angel" of Ephesus, was he actually addressing the "angels" of the presbytery? Brightman thought so. Ussher deemed this as built "upon a pretence of a poor show of some shallow reasons."[27] The obvious conclusion is that one man in particular exercised oversight and superintendence over the presbytery, working with them in Christian pastoral ministry. There is an obvious eminence and primacy of this officer and his authority in Christ's addresses in Revelation that cannot be reconciled with Presbyterianism. It is much simpler to concede that Christ was encouraging and rebuking "a presidential figure over each church."[28] As Ussher goes on to claim, this presidential figure operated alongside the presbytery, even while having some primacy within the presbytery.[29] In time, this figure became known as the bishop whereas, beforehand, "bishop" and "presbyter" seemed to be interchangeable terms.

Ussher thinks this finding is well supported by the testimony of the primitive church. In a long discourse, Ussher points out the fact that episcopalianism was the norm for the ancient church. He opens with two substantial examples: St. Timothy and St. Ignatius. Referencing Eusebius, Ussher observes that Timothy was understood to be the first bishop of Ephesus. It is likely that the "angel" of Ephesus was either St. Timothy or one of his immediate successors.[30]

Moreover, the authentic writings of Ignatius, bishop of Antioch, are a serious stumbling block for opponents of the episcopalian position. And this is where Ussher's Ignatian scholarship paid dividends. Ignatius clearly addresses his books to the bishops and presbyteries of various cities, and he obviously holds to a very high view of the episcopal office and its authority. Before Ussher's textual scholarship, non-episcopalians could have dismissed Ignatius out of hand as a tainted, unreliable source, but now they

---

[25] Snoddy, *Ussher*, 120.

[26] Blair, *Biblical Bishops*, 30.

[27] Snoddy, *Ussher*, 121.

[28] Blair, *Biblical Bishops*, 35.

[29] Ibid., 41.

[30] Interestingly, Ussher thinks that St. Polycarp was the "angel" of Smyrna. Snoddy, *Ussher*, 125–216.

had to contend with a legitimate primary historical witness who wrote only a few decades after the latest possible New Testament book.

This is quite a conundrum for critics of the episcopate. How quickly could the Church universally corrode into something unfaithful, abandoning primitive congregationalism or presbyterianism? Ignatius affords only a very short window of time for such a corruption—an unbelievably short window, in fact. As such, he is a true stumbling-block for the Presbyterian and Congregationalist alike. He is one of the earliest church fathers whose writings are on record, he is very clearly working within a Church characterized by episcopacy, and he holds bishops in very high regard. Of course, the rest of early church history reflects a similar picture: bishops working with their presbyteries, even while superintending the ministerial efforts of the Church.

Ussher is not content to defend the bare, minimal outlines of episcopal governance. In the geographical and historical context of the letters to the Asian churches in Revelation 1–3 and from Ignatius, Ussher discerns the seeds of diocesan and metropolitan structure, which is further established by the later conduct and wording of the patristic church.[31] Again, such structures and institutions are not an abomination of the Antichrist, as some of the more vituperative critics of primates and other bishops seemed to think.

The model of a bishop working closely with the presbytery informed Ussher's other famous treatise, *The Reduction of the Episcopacy* (1657). In it, Ussher proposes 1) a weekly meeting of the rector with the churchwardens to discuss church discipline issues, 2) increasing the number of suffragan bishops to match the number of rural deaneries, in order to assemble monthly synods with the deanery's presbyters, 3) annual or twice-annual diocesan synods, and 4) some suggestions on how to administer provincial synods. This proposal, which could potentially address the church discipline concerns of various Puritans and Separatists, did not in any way dismantle or even attack episcopalian church governance. Instead, it would revive a closer imitation to the form of governance that Ussher perceived in the ancient church. Peter Blair has convincingly suggested that the word "reduction" in the treatise's title has more to do with *reducere*: a return to ancient form.[32] While the Church of England did not embrace Ussher's ideas in his own lifetime or soon thereafter, several of his suggestions do seem to have manifested themselves in various Anglican contexts across the globe.

These days, there is no small amount of squabbling over Ussher. While Presbyterians and more Reformed Anglicans both claim Ussher and his legacy, other partisan Anglicans may turn up their noses at his zeal for Reformed theology. While he is not above criticism, Ussher is indeed an important Anglican figure in the heritage of Reformed Catholicity. Although some voices have tried to make Ussher out to be a compromised, lukewarm "prescopalian,"[33] an honest engagement with the primary sources precludes such an assertion. Simply put, Ussher was an episcopalian Protestant

---

[31] Snoddy, *Ussher*, 135–45.

[32] Blair, *Biblical Bishops*, 57.

[33] This would be the assertion that Ussher created a hybrid of episcopalian and presbyterian church governance. While Ussher proposed reforms with regard to the constitution and canons of the Church, his proposal was still an episcopalian form of church government.

by conviction, basing his views on biblical and historical argument. This contribution in particular must be gratefully appreciated by all those who call themselves Reformed and Catholic, and it remains a powerful and relevant argument for episcopalian church governance to this day.

Chapter 21

"Heaven in ordinary, man well dressed":
The Catechetical Poetics of George Herbert (1593–1633) as a Model of Reformed Catholicity*

Dr. Alex Fogleman[1]

Introduction: Varieties of Reformed Catholicity

What does it mean for Anglicanism to be a reformed and catholic tradition? We could think of at least three options. First, we could understand reformed catholicity in strictly doctrinal terms. Some doctrines are held in common with the universal or catholic Church—the great creeds of the early church, for instance—while others are uniquely reformational, such as a reformed conception of justification by faith or a rejection of transubstantiation and the papacy.

A second way to think of reformed catholicity would be in terms of both doctrine and worship. A reformed catholic tradition could be one that is reformed in doctrine but catholic in worship, or liturgical form. It holds to reformation beliefs, such as justification by faith, but maintains certain rites and practices that are more catholic in character—episcopal governance, a high regard for the Eucharist, vestments, and confession, to name a few.

Third, we could imagine reformed catholicity as a theological method. Here, reformed catholicity denotes an attempt to reform—as opposed to rejecting—traditional Christianity by returning to the sources of early Christian tradition. The way forward is not by demolition and innovation but by retrieval. This is another mode of reformed catholicity.[2]

But there are other ways as well. In this chapter, I want to let the great seventeenth-century poet-priest George Herbert help us understand what it means to be both reformed and catholic. By most accounts, Herbert would probably fit into the second model listed above. He is probably best described as a moderate Calvinist. In worship, he eschewed both popery and puritanism—landing at what one scholar has called a "sacramental puritanism."[3]

But more interesting, though, I think, is what Herbert can teach us about reformed catholicity through how poetic language functions. One of the most distinctive features of Herbert's poetry is the way in which an extraordinary depth of meaning can be encompassed in the simplest images and words. He is one of the few great poets whom the non-specialist can read with immediate profit. At the same time, his poetry contains

---

* This article was originally published in *CRUX, a Quarterly Journal of Christian Thought and Opinion* published by Regent College, under the title "'Build Up This Knowledge to a Spiritual Temple': George Herbert's Catechetical Poetics" Summer 2023, Vol. 59.2.

[1] My thanks to Ralph Wood and David Lyle Jeffrey for feedback on an earlier draft of this paper.

[2] Michael Allen and Scott R. Swain, *Reformed Catholicity: The Promise of Retrieval for Theology and Biblical Interpretation* (Grand Rapids: Baker Academic, 2015).

[3] Robert Whalen, *The Poetry of Immanence: Sacrament in Donne and Herbert* (Toronto: University of Toronto Press, 2002), 127.

a surplus of significance that leaves one constantly seeking—restless in the present age apart from God's true rest. This approach to poetic speech was intentional and, as I will try to show, deeply intwined in his understanding of the Christian life. Poetic speech, for Herbert, especially serves as a means by which the Word of God does not remain external to us but comes to dwell within. It allows holy speech, divine truth, to seep into our souls—to become assimilated to us that we may be transformed into his likeness. Herbert's poetry, in short, has a remarkable capacity to meet us where we are, in familiar words and images, and yet to provide through these very words a ladder of divine ascent. They become not only "heaven in ordinary" but also "man well dressed."[4]

In what follows, I first offer a brief introduction to Herbert's life and writings, followed by a longer exposition of what I will call Herbert's "catechetical poetics"—the way in which his poetry, like Christian catechesis, uses simple images to exact an anagogical transposition of the soul. In the end, we will revisit how this brand of catechetical poetics might offer a fresh way of understanding what it means for Anglicanism to be a reformed catholic tradition.

George Herbert: From Public Court to Country Parson

Born in Montgomery, Wales, on April 3, 1593, Herbert lived quietly amid one of the most politically and culturally tumultuous periods in English history.[5] In 1603, James VI of Scotland succeeded Queen Elizabeth to become James I of England—which was met with several attempts on his life, including most famously the gunpowder plot of November 5, 1605, celebrated today as Guy Fawkes Day. In ecclesiastical politics, Puritans and Laudians were set at odds with one another, while the great literary achievements of William Shakespeare, John Donne, Edmund Spenser, and Philip Sidney were coming to life. The year 1604 saw both a revision to the *Book of Common Prayer* as well as the commissioning of the Authorized Version of the Bible, later published in 1611 and known today as the King James Version.

Herbert's father died when George was only three, and his mother Magdalen relocated George and his nine siblings to London, where she would marry the English gentleman Sir John Danvers in 1609. That same year, George matriculated at Trinity College at Cambridge University, where he would go on to earn bachelor's and master's degrees, along with various fellowships, and was eventually promoted to the prestigious role of University Orator in 1620. His roughly twenty years affiliated with Cambridge were a highly auspicious time. It was here that he began to write poetry in earnest, while being set up for an illustrious career in public office.

But that path was not to be. Poor health, suboptimal finances, and his own vocational grappling led Herbert to cut his Cambridge ties and pursue a calling to the priesthood. In 1624, he was ordained a deacon. In 1627, his beloved mother Magdalen passed away, and the illustrious John Donne, Dean of St. Paul's Cathedral, delivered her funeral sermon. (Herbert himself published a collection of poems and elegies in her honor, *Memoriae Matris Sacrum*.) Soon afterward, he left Cambridge for good, and in 1629, he

---

[4] George Herbert, "Prayer," *The Temple* (London: Cassell, 1887), 51, line 11.
[5] For one of the best introductions to Herbert, see John Drury, *Music at Midnight: The Life and Poetry of George Herbert* (Chicago: University of Chicago Press, 2013).

married Jane Danvers, his stepfather's cousin, and the following year was ordained to the priesthood. The new pastor and his bride, with their three adopted orphaned nieces, settled into parish life in the small town of Bemerton, some 80 miles southwest of London, near Salisbury, where Herbert oversaw two rural parishes. It was to be, however, a short life in ministry. Only three years after donning the collar, declining health took its toll. Herbert died on March 1, 1633, a month shy of his fortieth birthday.

Herbert's most well-known body of literature is the collection of 167 poems entitled *The Temple*, published the year of his death by his dear friend and literary executor Nicholas Ferrar.[6] His other most important writing is a guide for parish ministry called *A Priest to the Temple: The Country Parson, His Character, and Rule of Holy Life*, which was published twenty years later, in 1652. He also left behind dozens of letters and treatises and a collection of proverbs.

Herbert has long enjoyed a celebrated reception by both Puritans and High Churchmen. In 1670, Izaak Walton published an affectionate hagiographical account of his life. The great Puritan theologian Richard Baxter described him as a man who "speaks to God like one that really believeth a God, and whose business in the world is most with God."[7] Both T. S. Eliot and C. S. Lewis considered him one of the greatest English poets and a chief influence on their work.[8] Herbert's great poem, "Love (III)," was responsible for a profound mystical experience by the Jewish philosopher, Simone Weil. During Holy Week of 1938, while suffering debilitating migraines, Weil sat amid a French Benedictine monastery hearing Herbert's great poem on love read. She later recounted in a letter that "Christ himself came down and took possession of me.... Neither my senses nor my imagination had any part; I only felt in the midst of my suffering the presence of a love, like that which one can read in the smile on a beloved face."[9]

In the Anglican tradition, Herbert's life is commemorated on February 27. The collect for that day especially commemorates his rejection of a secular career to pursue God's calling on his life as a pastor and poet: "Almighty God, who called your servant George Herbert from the pursuit of worldly honors to be a poet and a pastor of souls: Give us grace, we pray, joyfully to dedicate all our powers to your service."

Building the Spiritual Temple

Herbert's great work, *The Temple*, consists of three parts. The first is called "The Church-porch," the entryway to the church proper. It contains the long poem, "Perirrhanterium," which means "sprinkler" in Greek, and it constitutes a ponderous meditation on sin and repentance that prepares one to enter the church. The second part is, "The Church," and it contains the bulk of Herbert's poems, organized in a way to reflect both the architecture of a church building as well as the "architecture" of the Christian life more

---

[6] One other manuscript also survives, called the "Williams Manuscript," which contains 78 English and Latin poems edited in Herbert's own hand, which are thought to be an earlier draft arrangement of what was eventually produced in the published version by Ferrar.

[7] Richard Baxter, "Epistle to the Reader," in *The Poetical Fragments of Richard Baxter* (London: 1681), n.p.

[8] T. S. Eliot, *George Herbert* (Liverpool University Press, 1994); David Werther and Susan Werther, eds., *C.S. Lewis's List: The Ten Books that Influenced Him Most* (New York: Bloomsbury, 2015).

[9] Simone Weil, *Waiting for God* (New York: Harper & Row, 1951), 26–27.

generally. The third part of *The Temple* concludes with another long poem called "The Church Militant." This poem pictures life on the other side of glory, with God the King ruling all things from his heavenly throne.

It was not Herbert but Ferrar who entitled this collection *The Temple*. It is, nevertheless, a supremely fitting and significant designation. On the one hand, the image recalls the Church body—the temple of living stones built upon the foundation of Christ and the Apostles (see Eph 2:19–22, 2 Cor 6:16–7:1, 1 Pet 2:4–5). Herbert's poems, in this view, are not simply his private prayers and meditations. They belong to the whole Church as a kind of "communal spiritual exercise."[10] They are, as Herbert describes Christian prayer, "the Church's banquet."[11]

At the same time, the temple metaphor also connotes the interior temple, the temple of the heart. Greg Peters describes "an interiority to Herbert's architecture" in which "he is arranging his poetry not only by literally following the architecture of a parish church or cathedral but also by thinking of God's architecture as touching a person's inner journey to God."[12] In the poem, "Sion," for example, Herbert recounts the regal splendor of Solomon's temple, and yet he concludes by drawing attention to the architecture whose "frame and fabric is within":

> Yet all this glory, all this pomp and state
> *Did* not affect thee much, was not thy aim;
> Something there was, that sowed debate:
> Wherefore thou quitt'st thy ancient claim:
> And now Thy Architecture meets with sin;
> For all Thy frame and fabric is within.[13]

The entire structure of Herbert's poetic *oeuvre*, then, can be understood as an exercise in edifying the "spiritual temple." He devotes poems depicting nearly every feature of the physical church building, from floors to windows to altar—everything it seems except, interestingly, the pulpit—as a means of constructing the temple of the church and of the soul. Herbert neither stripped the altars[14] nor stuck to their surfaces. Rather, he allowed the church temple to become a sign and sacrament, a means of grace, for the soul's encounter with Christ in his body, the Church.

The temple image is also significant as it pertains to another key aspect of Herbert's pastoral ministry—namely, catechesis, or basic instruction in the faith. Architectural motifs have long been a staple feature of Christian catechesis. In the fourth century, the great theologian-catechist Cyril of Jerusalem made the comparison of catechesis and construction explicit:

---

[10] David Lyle Jeffrey, *Scripture and the English Poetic Imagination* (Grand Rapids: Baker Academic, 2019), 121–123.

[11] Herbert, "Prayer," in *The Temple*, 50, line 1.

[12] Greg Peters, "The Architecture of George Herbert's Poetry," *Scriptorium Daily*, January 14, 2022, www.scriptoriumdaily.com/the-architecture-of-george-herberts-poetry.

[13] Herbert, *The Temple*, 102, lines 7–12.

[14] See Eamon Duffy, *The Stripping of the Altars* about the rejection of many "catholic" forms of worship in sixteenth-century England.

Let me compare the catechizing to a building. Unless we methodically bind and joint the whole structure together, we shall have leaks and dry rot, and all our previous exertions will be wasted. No: stone must be laid upon stone in regular sequence, and corner follow corner, jutting edges must be planed away: and so the perfect structure rises. I bring you as it were the stones of knowledge; you must be instructed in the doctrine of the living God, of the Judgment, of Christ, of the Resurrection. Many things have to be said in order, which are now being touched upon at random but will then be brought together into harmonious system. Unless you achieve this unity of design, holding the beginning and the sequel in your mind together, the builder may do his best, but your house will be a ruin.[15]

Many Christian pastors and theologians in Herbert's own time made similar comparisons.[16] Herbert himself, in *The Country Parson*, alludes to this image in describing the three main duties of the pastor:

the one, to infuse a competent knowledge of salvation in every one of his Flock; the other, to multiply, and build up this knowledge to a spirituall Temple; the third, to inflame this knowledge, to presse, and drive it to practice, turning it to reformation of life, by pithy and lively exhortations.[17]

For Herbert, the first of these tasks, "infusing spiritual knowledge," is catechesis. It is the first and necessary condition for what Herbert goes on to describe as the building up of knowledge into a "spiritual Temple."

Crucial to Herbert's poetics, then, is Christian catechesis. What, though, does Herbert mean by this, and how does it inform his approach to poetic speech and the Christian life?

The Parson Catechizing

We can begin by situating Herbert within the context of Reformation-era catechesis. Amid the many and varied patterns of sixteenth-century reform, one of the most pressing was the improvement of lay Christian education. In 1529, after touring dozens of local churches throughout the German countryside, Martin Luther bewailed what he called the "deplorable, miserable condition" of so many pastors and lay people who did not know basic Christian doctrine and prayers.[18] Pastors and bishops, he lamented, had badly neglected their flocks by denying them the solid milk of the Creed, the Lord's Prayer, and the Ten Commandments—the three pillars that what would become the bedrock of Reformation catechisms.

Over the next several hundred years, across church traditions, Catholic and Protestant alike, Christians devoted an exceptional amount of energy to catechesis.

---

[15] Cyril of Jerusalem, *Procatechesis* 11, in *The Works of Saint Cyril of Jerusalem*, trans. Leo P. McCauley and Anthony A. Stephenson, Fathers of the Church 61 (Washington, DC: Catholic University of America Press, 1969), 79.

[16] For references, see Fish, *Living Temple*, 54–68.

[17] George Herbert, *George Herbert's Country Parson*, ed. H. C. Beeching (Oxford: B. H. Blackwell, 1898), 77.

[18] Martin Luther, "Luther's Preface to the Small Catechism," accessed April 5, 2024, https://bookofconcord.org/small-catechism/preface/.

Catechesis was an extension of the fervent efforts to translate the Bible into the vernacular. Reformers not only wanted people to read the Bible in a familiar tongue but also to understand and absorb the text. They wanted Christians to have a living encounter with the life-giving Word of Scripture.

This aspiration manifested in the writing of hundreds of catechisms in the following centuries. In England, a catechism was included in the first edition of the *Book of Common Prayer* in 1549 and has remained ever since. In addition, English clerics produced some 800 catechisms and question-and-answer texts over the next 200 years.[19] It is not the case, we should add, that medieval Christians had neglected lay education; teaching sound doctrine to the laity had been a major preoccupation of late medieval pastoral care since at least the twelfth century. Nevertheless, the sixteenth-century reformers, now abetted by the printing press, brought new energy to the renewal of catechesis. Pastors, theologians, schoolteachers, and parents united in a concerted effort to see Christians transformed by the Word of God.

Herbert, who died just a century after Luther had published his Small and Large Catechisms, was heir to this rich catechetical tradition. While his approach paralleled his peers in many ways, in some respects he was unique. In particular, he did not think catechesis was only necessary for children or for those preparing for the rite of confirmation. Moreover, he did not just think catechesis was about filling up empty minds. Catechesis was useful for the whole congregation as well as for the pastor himself, as it demanded concerted attention on the role of both catechist and catechumen in engaging Christian doctrine.

We see the key features of Herbert's approach to catechesis in Chapter 21 of *The Country Parson*, called "The Parson Catechizing." Here, Herbert dwells at length on the power of dialogue for enabling Christians to engage more fully with Christian teaching. After they have memorized the catechism, students engage their pastor through dialogue and well-ordered questions about what they have learned. Herbert compares this pedagogy to the famed method of Socrates. According to Herbert, Socrates believed that "the seeds of all truths lay in every body, and accordingly by questions well ordered he found Philosophy in silly Trades-men."[20] He has in mind here the Platonic dialogue *Meno*, where we read how Socrates taught high-level geometrical truths to an illiterate slave boy through a series of well-structured questions. Herbert qualifies this comparison, though, by noting that Christianity does not simply teach natural truths but "contains things above nature."[21] Nonetheless, catechesis is analogously related to the Socratic method in the way it engages pupils through dialogue to achieve a participatory acquisition of truth. More than the monological form of the sermon, dialogical catechesis requires the active engagement of the learner. As Herbert memorably puts it, "at Sermons, and Prayers, men may sleep or wander; but when one is asked a question, he must discover what he is."[22]

---

[19] Ian Green, *The Christian's ABC: Catechisms and Catechizing in England, c. 1530–1740s* (Oxford: Clarendon, 1996), 50–51.

[20] Herbert, *The Country Parson*, 80.

[21] Ibid.

[22] Ibid., 82.

Herbert finds warrant for this practice in scriptural language itself. Scripture, Herbert argues, uses ordinary images and metaphors to convey supernatural realities: "heav'n lies flat in thee / Subject to ev'ry mounters bended knee."[23] Scripture, writes Herbert, "condescends to the naming of a plough, a hatchet, a bushel, leaven, boys piping and dancing," and then through these images conveys hidden depths of meaning, showing "that things of ordinary use are not only to serve in the way of drudgery, but to be washed and cleansed, and serve for lights even of Heavenly Truths."[24]

The art of catechesis, then, with its hallmark feature of question-and-answer dialogue, is modeled on principles from both classical philosophy and Holy Scripture. When the country parson asks questions about pipes and plowshares, he provides a pathway by which their vision can be cleansed and their gaze directed to the "light of Heavenly Truths."[25] Catechetical dialogue, in other words, is a way of allowing Scripture to indwell the hearts of Christians—to get inside them and allow the light of glory to shine forth.

Herbert's Catechetical Poetics: Scripture, Church, Creation, Love

This conception of catechesis is also what undergirds Herbert's approach to poetic language. The legendary literary critic Stanley Fish has argued catechesis and poetry share many of the same goals, especially in the way they both "[involve] the reader in his own edification."[26] Herbert alludes to this similarity when he describes the value of poetry in the opening lines of "The Church-porch." The poet puts rhyme and meter to noble purpose, he says, as "bait" for the wayward soul; for "a verse may find him, who a sermon flies, / And turn delight into a sacrifice."[27] Poetic speech, like catechesis, catches the attention of the hearer and transforms the experience of delight into the obedience of sacrifice.

It is not that Herbert's poems necessarily take the form of question-asking, though sometimes they do. More importantly, Herbert's poetry draws out from the readers what they think at a presuppositional level; through surprise, challenge, and redirection, their attention can be turned toward divine truth. Poetic speech, thus, enables the Christian to internalize and wrestle with the text—to allow the poem to unearth one's preconceived notions and begin to establish a new foundation.

Consider, for example, the poem, "Love-Joy":

> As on a window late I cast mine eye,
> I saw a vine drop grapes with J and C
> Annealed on every bunch. One standing by
> Asked what it meant. I (who am never loth
> To spend my judgement) said, It seemed to me
> To be the body and the letters both

---

[23] Herbert, "The Holy Scriptures, I," in *The Temple*, 57, lines 13–14.
[24] Herbert, *The Country Parson*, 82.
[25] Ibid.
[26] Stanley Fish, *The Living Temple: George Herbert and Catechizing* (Berkeley: University of California Press, 1978), 27.
[27] Herbert, *The Temple*, 11, lines 5–6.

> Of *Joy* and *Charity*. Sir, you have not miss'd,
> The man replied ; It figures *JESUS CHRIST*.[28]

The reader sees something that gives him pause—the letters J and C on a vine dropping grapes. But then, another voice appears asking, "What does it mean?" A classic catechetical question! The question invites pause from one who is "never loath to spend judgment." What does it, in fact, mean? We, too, are invited to stop, listen, and notice. The J and C perhaps mean "joy" and "charity." The unnamed respondent though, both agrees and corrects this analysis. "Yes," is the reply. "You have not missed," and yet, in affirming this response, he invites the reader into a deeper refection: It *does* signify joy and charity, the man replies, "You have not missed.... It figures *Jesus Christ*." In this brief poem, we see how ordinary language and well-ordered questions function to draw out the deeper significance figured in the natural image of vines and grapes.[29]

Catechesis, then, is closely linked with Herbert's poetic speech. But what does this look like in practice? To fill in this sketch of Herbert's catechetical poetics, I want to examine four key motifs in his poems. These are Scripture, the Church, creation, and love.

1. Scripture

Christian Scripture is central to Herbert's poetry. *The Temple* is saturated with commentary, references, and allusions to the holy text. As David Lyle Jeffrey comments, Herbert's are "commentaries on Scripture, not so much on this biblical text or that, but on the *totem integrum* of the Word of God, ingested, digested, and now overflowing with the exuberant health of a grateful heart."[30]

Here is an important parallel to catechesis. Like this description of Scripture in Herbert's poetry, catechesis offers a distilled, collated vision of Scripture—the Creed, the Lord's Prayer, the Ten Commandments—but without dumbing down or oversimplifying the gospel. Catechesis is like a prism that allows Scripture to be seen in all its splendor. As a catechist and poet, Herbert distills Scripture in concrete yet allusive images, allowing Holy Writ to be ingested in the heart, to sustain and nourish Christian devotion.

Following a venerable tradition of spiritual reading called *lectio divina*, Herbert especially deploys images of "tasting" and "digestion" to describe the Christian posture towards the Word of God. Scripture is "infinite sweetness"—"let my heart / suck ev'ry letter, and a honey gain."[31] It is a "storehouse and magazine [i.e., artillery] of life and comfort" that the country parson "sucks and lives."[32] No doubt in the background here is one of Cranmer's greatest collects, which invites us to pray that we may "read, mark, learn, and inwardly digest" Scripture. Herbert's catechetical poetics manifests the "*totem integrum* of the Word of God," which allows readers to feast upon Christ and grow into new life.

---

[28] Herbert, *The Temple*, 111.

[29] The preceding analysis owes to Fish, *Living Temple*, 27–29.

[30] Jeffrey, *Scripture*, 125.

[31] Herbert, "The Holy Scriptures," in *The Temple*, 57, lines 1–2.

[32] Herbert, *The Country Parson*, 9.

2. Church

Second, Herbert's catechetical poetics is firmly rooted in the Church. The nature and function of the Church, it goes without saying, was a fraught matter during the Reformation. In this context, Herbert takes a classically Anglican path, espousing a high view of the church, the priesthood, and the Sacraments while issuing reserve towards the perceived extremes of Roman Catholicism.

About the Eucharist, Herbert is best understood as a moderate realist.[33] His reluctance to name the mode of presence echoes other Anglican Divines, such as Richard Hooker, who rejects both the superstitions associated with transubstantiation and the austere Puritanism of memorialism, while affirming that the body and blood of Christ are truly partaken in the sacraments.[34]

In the *Country Parson*, Herbert admits the great difficulty of the priest's position. Confronted with the absurdity of "not only to receive God, but to break, and administer him," the parson resigns himself in trust: "to throw himself down at the throne of grace, saying, Lord, thou knowest what thou didst, when thou appointedst it to be done thus; therefore doe thou fulfill what thou didst appoint; for thou art not only the feast, but the way to it."[35] In his poetry on the Eucharist, he especially highlights the medicinal and nourishing effects of the Sacrament, and the subtle interplay between the effects on soul and body:

> But by the way of nourishment and strength
>   Thou creep'st into my breast;
>   Making thy way my rest,
>   And thy small quantities my length;
> Which spread their forces into every part,
>   Meeting sinnes force and art.
>
> Yet can these not get over to my soul,
>   Leaping the wall that parts
>   Our souls and fleshy hearts.[36]

He reflects similarly on the priesthood. An unimaginable thing it is for sacred fire to touch earth and clay. But that is just what happens when God ordains a person to the priesthood:

> Their hands convey him, who conveys their hands.
> O what pure things, most pure must those things be,
>   Who bring my God to me![37]

In his understanding of the Church, Herbert begins in wonder and awe that the greatness of God can mingle with frail humanity. Nevertheless, faith and Holy Scripture

---

[33] See Brian Douglas, *Sacramental Poetics in Richard Hooker and George Herbert* (Lanham, MD: Rowman & Littlefield, 2022).

[34] Douglas, *Sacramental Poetics*, chap. 2.

[35] Herbert, *The Country Parson*, 83

[36] Herbert, "The Holy Communion," in *The Temple*, 51–52, lines 7–15.

[37] Herbert, "The Priesthood," in *The Temple*, 155–156, lines 28–30.

compel him to see God truly present in the material means of grace—the priesthood and sacraments. God's presence comes in ordinary ways but transforms our lives by his all-consuming fire.

3. Creation

Herbert's understanding of Scripture and the Church entails a commensurate doctrine of creation—and this is the third major theme of what I am calling Herbert's catechetical poetics. Herbert has an exceptional eye for beauty in the created world, especially music. Musical imagery and instrumentation resound in many of his poems. In the poem "Easter," for example, Herbert perceives the cross as a pedagogue of creation—the wood of the cross teaching the wood of the lute—and indeed all wood—to sing of Christ:

> Awake, my lute, and struggle for thy part,
> 　　　With all thy art.
> The cross taught all wood to resound his name,
> 　　　Who bore the same.
> His stretched sinews taught all strings, what key
> Is best to celebrate this most high day.[38]

In the poem "The Thanksgiving," meanwhile, music signifies the harmony of the soul and the created order attuned to the one God who orchestrates all things:

> My music shall find thee, and ev'ry string
> 　　　Shall have his attribute to sing;
> That all together may accord in thee,
> 　　　And prove one God, one harmony.[39]

By far, though, Herbert's richest meditation on the Christian life as a transfiguring vision of creation is his great poem "The Elixir"—a fascinating image that refers to the magical stone of ancient lore that would turn everything it touches to gold. Herbert perceives in this image a sign of divine grace transforming all of life into divine service:

> Teach me, my God and King,
> 　　In all things Thee to see,
> And what I do in anything
> 　　To do it as for Thee.
>
> Not rudely, as a beast,
> 　　To run into an action;
> But still to make Thee prepossessed,
> 　　And give it his perfection.
>
> A man that looks on glass,
> 　　On it may stay his eye;

---

[38] Herbert, *The Temple*, 41, lines 7–12.
[39] Herbert, *The Temple*, 35–36, lines 39–42.

> Or if he pleaseth, through it pass,
>   And then the heaven espy.
>
> All may of Thee partake:
>   Nothing can be so mean,
> Which with his tincture (for Thy sake)
>   Will not grow bright and clean.
>
> A servant with this clause
>   Makes drudgery divine:
> Who sweeps a room as for Thy laws,
>   Makes that and th' action fine.
>
> This is the famous stone
>   That turneth all to gold;
> For that which God doth touch and own
>   Cannot for less be told.[40]

In this poem, we see a particular understanding of the created world—of all things participating in the divine life. Nothing is separate from or extrinsic to God, nothing cut off from the divine life. It is like when we look at a piece of glass: our eye can remain on the glass, looking at what it is, on its own; it can also pass through the glass, beholding that which the glass mediates (see too the use of the glass imagery in the poem "The Windows"[41]).

This metaphysical vision is commensurate with a certain way of living in the world, what the reformers called the sanctification of ordinary life. The work of cooking, cleaning, building, accounting can all become sites of holiness, or what Kathleen Norris calls "quotidian mysteries."[42] For the one who learns to "heaven espy," every mundane task can be a means by which everything we do, we do for the glory of God (1 Cor 1:31). No work, no matter how crude, is transformed by this alchemical doctrine. Drudgery is made divine.

4. Love

Herbert's catechetical poetics, then, is informed by a deeply biblical, ecclesial, and creational spirituality. A fourth key theme, finally, is love, or the formation and reformation of desire.

Herbert's view of the Christian life is not all flowers, rainbows, and happily dusted furniture. Herbert is deeply attuned to the complexities and struggles of the heart, as well as the many temptations to despair and grief. One of the most striking cases in *The Temple* is a series of five poems entitled "Affliction." In the first of these poems, the poet recounts the initial joy of the Christian life. At first, everything goes well. Life is "milk

---

[40] Herbert, *The Temple*, 179, lines 28–30.

[41] Ibid., 65.

[42] Kathleen Norris, *Quotidian Mysteries: Laundry, Liturgy, and "Women's Work"* (New York: Paulist Press, 1998).

and sweetnesses ... flow'rs and happiness; / There was no month but May."[43] But with time, sorrows grow like thorns, twisting the soul into sin-sickness:

> My flesh began unto my soul in pain,
>   Sicknesses cleave my bones;
> Consuming agues dwell in every vein,
>   And tune my breath to groans.
> Sorrow was all my soul; I scarce believed,
> Till grief did tell me roundly, that I lived.[44]

In his incisive study of the affliction poems, Rowan Williams shows that such agony resists the kind of pseudo-spirituality—especially pressing in the Arminian-Calvinist debates of Herbert's time—that consider the role one's own life experience as an assurance of divine grace.[45] Rather, Herbert gives voice to the God-oriented assurance that grounds the possibility of crying to God in lament, agony, and grief.

This is why one of the central motifs of *The Temple* is the heart depicted as a broken or enfleshed stone. In the opening poem, "The Altar," the words of the poem are arranged visually into the shape of an altar.[46] Yet it becomes clear that the physical altar, and especially the Eucharist celebrated thereon, is closely linked with the altar of the heart, the stone turned to flesh by the transforming sacrifice of Christ:

> A broken A L T A R, Lord, Thy servant rears,
> Made of a heart, and cemented with tears:
>   Whose parts are as thy hand did frame;
>   No workman's tool hath touch'd the same.
>   A   H E A R T   alone
>   Is   such   a   stone,
>   As   nothing   but
>   Thy   pow'r   doth   cut.
>   Wherefore   each   part
>   Of   my   hard   heart
>   Meets   in   this   frame,
>   To praise Thy name.
>   That if I chance to hold my peace,
>   These stones to praise thee may not cease.
> O let Thy blessed S A C R I F I C E be mine,
> And sanctify this A L T A R to be Thine.

The perfectly crafted form juxtaposes the brokenness and pain of the words, and yet, through this interplay of image and word, what appears is the power of God to cut and shape stony hearts into vessels fit for Christ's sacrifice. In receiving the Eucharist on the altar, the altar of the heart is sanctified to the praise of God's name.

---

[43] Herbert, *The Temple*, 46–48, lines 19–22.
[44] Ibid., lines 25–30.
[45] Rowan Williams, *Anglican Identities* (Lanham, MD: Rowan & Littlefield, 2003), 57–72.
[46] Herbert, *The Temple*, 26.

This image runs throughout many of the poems in the *Temple*: "though my hard heart scarce to thee can groan, / Remember that Thou once didst write in stone";[47] "My heart hath store, write there, wherein / One box doth lie both ink and sin";[48] "Blest be the Architect, whose art / Could build so strong in a weak heart."[49] In the poem, "Nature," Herbert writes,

> O smooth my rugged heart, and there
> Engrave thy rev'rend law and fear;
> Or make a new one, since the old
>   Is sapless grown,
>   And a much fitter stone
> To hide my dust, than thee to hold.[50]

Writing about the heart is not incidental in Herbert's poetry. Rather, Christian desire is integral to human nature. In his great poem "The Pulley," Herbert describes restlessness in distinctively Augustinian terms as a gift from God that forestalls an idolatrous preoccupation with creaturely goods over the good Creator. He imagines God at the creation of Adam perusing the many gifts of his storehouse—strength, beauty, wisdom, honor, pleasure. The final treasure, though, is rest, and God elects to withhold this gift in the beginning.

> "For if I should," said He,
> "Bestow this jewel also on my creature,
> He would adore my gifts instead of me,
> And rest in Nature, not the God of Nature;
>   So both should losers be.
>
> "Yet let him keep the rest,
> But keep them with repining restlessness;
> Let him be rich and weary, that at least,
> If goodness lead him not, yet weariness
>   May toss him to My breast."[51]

Through several puns on the word *rest*, Herbert highlights the way in which desire for God is itself a divine gift for life in the present age—a structural feature of the architecture this side of beatitude. The gift of desire, restlessness, allows the Christian to seek God even when he is not propelled by virtue. Weariness may be more violent than the gentle persuasion of virtue, but it keeps the Christian from idolatry, the true destruction—of both self and the created world.

The culmination of Herbert's catechetical poetics of desire is ultimately a theology of love. Herbert's view of love is deeply shaped by the cross: "Love is that liquor sweet and

---

[47] Herbert, "The Sinner," in *The Temple*, 37–38, lines 13–14.
[48] Herbert, "Good Friday," in *The Temple*, 38–39, lines 23–24.
[49] Herbert, "The Church Floor," in *The Temple*, 64–65, lines 19–20.
[50] Herbert, *The Temple*, 45, lines 13–18.
[51] Ibid., 154–155, lines 11–20.

most divine, / Which my God feels as blood; but I, as wine."[52] Cruciform love transforms
the heart of stone to flesh. By feasting on Scripture and the sacraments, by learning to
"espy" God in all creation, we slowly, painfully, learn the joy of suffering love. The poem
"Discipline" conveys well the difficult, though deeply biblical, character of desiring God.

> For my heart's desire
> Unto thine is bent:
>   I aspire
> To a full consent.
>
> Not a word or look
> I affect to own,
>   But by book,
> And thy book alone.[53]

Once again, there is no sentimental piety amid life in this frail and fragile world, yet even
here, love bids him:

> Though I fail, I weep:
> Though I halt in pace,
>   Yet I creep
> To the throne of grace.[54]

Ultimately, Herbert's is a spirituality of love. Love not only pardons and forgives this
sinner, love transforms the heart.

> Then let wrath remove;
> Love will do the deed:
>   For with love
> Stony hearts will bleed.[55]

Catechetical Poetics as Reformed Catholicity

Herbert's catechetical poetics combines a biblical, ecclesial, and creational spirituality
that works to transform the desire of the heart. How does this form of catechetical
poetics serve as response to the question of what it means for Anglicanism to be a
reformed catholic tradition?

We can begin by noting that this approach encapsulates a central principle of
reformation sensibility—namely, the desire to bring Christian truth within the grasp of
ordinary believers. The reformers sought to bring heaven to earth, to sanctify ordinary
life. They wanted cobblers, millers, and bakers to read the Bible in a language they could
understand. Certain expressions of Roman Catholicism, they thought, made God too
remote, too distant. At the same time, this sanctification of ordinary life seems to be
deeply implicated in what eventually became the secularization of modern culture—the

---

[52] Herbert, "The Agony," in *The Temple*, 37, lines 17–18.
[53] Herbert, *The Temple*, 173–174, lines 5–12.
[54] Ibid., lines 13–16.
[55] Ibid., lines 17–20.

evacuation of a proper appreciation of the heavenly or transcendent dimension of the Christian faith. While it would be too simplistic to trace every deplorable feature of modern life to the Reformation, it seems incontrovertible that modernity entails certain theological commitments springing from an immanentizing framework that corresponds to the reformation impulse to accommodate divine transcendence into a this-worldly framework.

Herbert's catechetical poetics, though, point in a different direction, an equally important upward or anagogical direction, characteristic of the pre-modern catholic tradition broadly conceived. In classical Christian theology, east and west, God is understood as "that than which nothing greater can be conceived."[56] The *telos* of human life is not simply God coming down to earth but all of creation being drawn into heavenly beatitude. God transfigures the world in Christ so that all of life can radiate with the presence of Christ.

Herbert, then, teaches us what it means to be reformed in his high valuation of the earthly, ordinary means of divine presence. There is a strongly incarnational bent to Herbert's poetry that parallels God's descent into human flesh—particularly God's descent into ordinary, non-spectacular things. At the same time, however, Herbert's poetry, in a more catholic vein, draws us upward, allowing the quotidian objects of ordinary life to become means of heavenly participation. The incarnational thrust is balanced by an equally significant deifying arc. In patristic terms, Herbert's catechetical poetics mirror the logic of "God became man that man might become God"[57]—or, in Herbert's words, "heaven in ordinary, man well dressed."

Perhaps the quintessential expression of Herbert's vision of catechetical poetics as a reformed catholic sensibility appears in his best-known poem, "Love (III)," the one that led Simone Weil to a mystical encounter with Christ and which is widely recognized as one of the finest poems in the English language[58] This poem comes at the end of *The Church* and so can be understood as most closely approximating the eschatological vision of beatitude.

> Love bade me welcome. Yet my soul drew back
>   Guilty of dust and sin.
> But quick-eyed Love, observing me grow slack
>   From my first entrance in,
> Drew nearer to me, sweetly questioning,
>   If I lacked any thing.

---

[56] This turn of phrase is chiefly known as "Anselm's ontological argument for the existence of God," but I use it here to intend the broadly shared sacramental ontology of the pre-modern tradition. For this view of reality, see Hans Boersma, *Heavenly Participation: The Weaving of a Sacramental Ontology* (Grand Rapids: Eerdmans, 2011). Readers will recognize in these paragraphs my indebtedness to Boersma's work.

[57] Sometimes called "Theosis," "Deification," or "Divinization."

[58] For an excellent analysis of this poem, see Chana Bloch, *Spelling the Word: George Herbert and the Bible* (Berkeley: University of California Press, 1985), For the following, my reading of this poem is indebted to Ralph Wood. See his *Contending for the Faith: The Church's Engagement with Culture* (Waco: Baylor University Press, 2003), 196–97.

"A guest, "I answered, "worthy to be here."
    Love said, "You shall be he."
"I"—the unkind, ungrateful? Ah my dear,
    I cannot look on thee."
Love took my hand, and smiling did reply,
    "Who made the eyes but I?"

"Truth Lord, but I have marred them: let my shame
    Go where it doth deserve."
"And know you not," says Love, "who bore the blame?"
    "My dear, then I will serve."
"You must sit down," says Love, "and taste my meat."
    So I did sit and eat.[59]

Here we find a convergence of the major themes of Herbert's catechetical poetics, but especially the *telos* of life as graced friendship with God. The core image is the simplest and yet most profound—a weary traveler, a welcoming host, a shared meal. The tired pilgrim confesses his double unworthiness: mortality compounded by sin. Christ the host, however, dons the role of catechist one last time, asking a series of well-ordered questions: "Who made the eyes but I?" "Who bore the blame?" This is a catechesis of creation and redemption. The Creator's works cannot be destroyed by even the greatest misuse. The Redeemer has paid the price of sin that keeps the soul from God. The questioning grace of "quick-eyed Love" invites the restless wayfarer not only to creep to the throne of grace but to dwell, to sit, and finally, to taste the goodness of the Lord in the land of the living. At last, no longer questioning, no longer restless, the pilgrim's heart rests content: "So I did sit and eat."

---

[59] Herbert, *The Temple*, 183.

Chapter 22

Anglicanism 101: John Cosin's (1594–1672) Forgotten Guide to the English Church

The Rev. Jarrod Hill

New members present an interesting problem for parish rectors. In a landscape where biblical illiteracy and theological ignorance reign, should new member classes focus on "Anglicanism 101" or "Christianity 101"? Most newcomers understandably want to focus on learning the Anglican distinctives before joining an Anglican parish, but many still need Christian basics. A catechesis class that merely reads the Anglican Church in North America's approved catechism, *To Be a Christian*, would leave out a lot of distinctively Anglican material. On the other hand, surveys of English history, expositions of the *Articles of Religion*, or book clubs on Hooker's *Laws of Ecclesiastical Polity* are difficult to make work alongside a more comprehensive study of Christian doctrine and practice, particularly if the historic trifold framework of the *Apostles' Creed*, the Lord's Prayer, and the Ten Commandments is adopted. Such an approach would necessarily take too much time or, if abbreviated, not go deep enough to sink in. It's my conviction that a little-known work written by Bishop John Cosin in the seventeenth century could serve as a concise, historically rooted guide to Anglican distinctives, whether as a supplement to catechesis, a primer for the intellectually minded newcomer, or as a template for Anglicans seeking to succinctly summarize the "Anglican Way."

Cosin, who had perhaps the second-greatest influence on Anglican liturgy, behind only Archbishop Thomas Cranmer himself, gained notoriety for writing his *Collection of Private Devotions* in 1627 at the request of King Charles I. Upon returning from his exile in Paris during the Puritan Commonwealth government, Cosin was consecrated bishop of Durham shortly after the Restoration of Charles II in 1660. As the leading High Churchman at the Savoy Conference of 1661, Cosin helped ensure that the English Church's prayer book was not re-created in a Puritan image. The resulting 1662 *Book of Common Prayer* is still widely used throughout much of the Anglican Communion today. Between these great liturgical feats, Cosin wrote an outline of the faith and practice of the Church of England in 1652 while in exile in France. In this brief work, *The Religion, Discipline and Rites of the Church of England*[1] (called *The Religion of the Church of England* from here on), Cosin sought to explain English religion to royalty and clergy throughout the rest of Christendom. Interestingly enough, Cosin's guide was translated from Latin into several European languages before finally being published in English over two centuries later by the Reverend Frederick Meyrick in 1870. It is Father Meyrick's English translation which we will consider.

Now in the twenty-first century, Cosin's *The Religion of the Church of England* can help to introduce Anglicanism to new Anglicans, many of whom were raised Baptists, Presbyterians, and non-denominational evangelicals. His own son having converted to Roman Catholicism, Cosin clearly penned his brief guide with a great burden to show

---

[1] John Cosin, *The Religion, Discipline and Rites of the Church of England*, 2nd ed., trans. Frederick Meyrick (London: Rivington, 1882), archive.org/details/religiondisciploocosigoog.

Anglicanism's closer fidelity to the historic Christian faith as compared to the Roman Church. But given that today it's overwhelmingly evangelicals, and not Roman Catholics, becoming Anglicans, I will focus on what the former need to know about Anglicanism, organizing things around four ideas: theological method, church leadership, worship, and church life.

Theological Method

The first eight chapters of *The Religion of England* summarize the Anglican theological method. For Cosin, this starts with Holy Scripture, which "is an absolutely certain rule and test of all Church doctrine."[2] Not only does the Bible contain all things necessary to salvation, but the plain words of the Bible contain "everything that appertains to faith and practice."[3] This may at first sound like a "chapter-and-verse" approach to Scripture, which demands that some single passage explicitly and conclusively teach a doctrine or command a practice before such doctrine or practice be adopted. But Cosin knows that biblical interpretation often requires using reason to draw inferences from multiple passages to come to the most likely, even if not conclusively necessary, meaning of Scripture on a given topic. Cosin's primary point here is made more explicit later: Anglicans have "no unwritten faith as Rome has."[4] "Anglican faith and practice," particularly that which is *required* of a believer, must be grounded in Holy Scripture.

The problem today is we live in an age when most of us Christians cannot reason biblically because we do not know our Bibles. Social media and streaming services distract us from reading the Bible, and our search-engine-engineered brains often cannot retain the little that we have read. One of the best ways we might fight against these technological fetters is by embracing the Daily Office or at least its corresponding lectionary. Even cutting the lectionary in half and reading two lessons a day with Psalms would help us live up to Cosin's aspirational claim that we Anglicans keep the Holy Scriptures "constantly before our eyes," that we may not fall into error.[5]

But even if we are well-versed in the Scriptures, that does not mean we can understand it all on our own. This is where the issue of authority comes in. For Cosin, Holy Scripture is the *final* authority, but it's not the *only* authority. Some new Anglicans may have been trained in other denominations to treat the Bible as a lone authority whose meaning the individual Christian must finally determine on his own. The ultimate theological exercise under this model would be to lock yourself in a room, preferably with a nice view of nature, and spend the days in nothing but reading the Bible on your own. That way you can figure it all out—with the help of the Holy Spirit, of course. For Cosin and historic Anglicanism, though, Christians are supposed to read Scripture with the help of tradition.

Cosin lists as authorities after Holy Scripture the three Creeds, the first four Councils, and the first five centuries.[6] The three main Christian Creeds have been

---

[2] Cosin, *Religion*, 16.
[3] Ibid., 15.
[4] Ibid., 24.
[5] Ibid., 16.
[6] Ibid., 15.

retained in the prayer book tradition to this day. It's common practice for Anglicans today to read the *Nicene Creed* in Holy Communion, the *Apostles' Creed* in the Daily Office, and the *Athanasian Creed* on Trinity Sunday at minimum. Cosin notes that the first four Ecumenical Councils had such respect among the English that the substance of what the Councils taught were given the force of law in England, as in the Act of Supremacy of 1558 under Elizabeth I.[7] Today, "The Fundamental Declarations of the Province" contained in the ACNA's 2019 *Book of Common Prayer*, still affirm "the teaching of the first four Councils and the Christological clarifications of the fifth, sixth and seventh Councils, in so far as they are agreeable to the Holy Scriptures."

Applying Cosin's commitment to the "first five centuries" is as much art as science. Church fathers make mistakes, of course. You can certainly find weird and wrong beliefs in the writings of the church fathers. But Cosin says that Anglicans "regard a thing as an undoubted and settled truth if it was openly, frequently, and preservingly held and taught, not by one or two teachers only, but unanimously."[8] No one can reject such a universal doctrine "without being guilty of great arrogance and temerity."[9] The grace of the Holy Spirit was "more abundantly shed upon" the church fathers,[10] and they better understood the truth since they were nearer to the days of the Apostles. This is why the English Church urges her clergy and students to read the Holy Fathers "again and again."[11] Cosin grounds his patristic commitments on what he calls the "golden canon," which was part of the Canons of 1571.[12] The canon on preachers requires that nothing be taught to be religiously held or believed by the people, unless it be agreeable to the doctrine of the Old and New Testaments, and what the Catholic Fathers and Bishops of the ancient Church have actually gathered from that doctrine."[13] He concludes, "It is in this way that we combine Holy Scripture and tradition, making tradition always subordinate and agreeable to Scripture."[14] The Bishop of Durham would, no doubt, have us Anglicans today look to the consensus of the Fathers to understand the Scripture's teaching on raging issues such as hell, sexual ethics, and the ordination of women.

To give an example, in a letter defending the Anglican practice of Communion in both kinds (the bread and the wine), Cosin relied on patristic consensus to reject Rome's practice of lay people only receiving the bread. Cosin maintained that Jesus was speaking about the sacrament of his body and blood in John 6:54 when he said: "Whoever feeds on my flesh and drinks my blood has eternal life." Since Jesus said body *and* blood, Cosin reasoned that it is necessary to receive both in Communion. Cosin called it a "peculiar and private interpretation" to deny that John 6 spoke of the Sacrament "when the common and public known mind of all the ancient Fathers, who (without excepting any of them, that

---

[7] Cosin, *Religion*, 18.
[8] Ibid., 22.
[9] Ibid.
[10] Ibid., 19.
[11] Ibid., 20.
[12] Ibid.
[13] Ibid., 20–21.
[14] Ibid., 21.

had occasion to treat of that place,) have understood it of the Sacrament."[15] Unfortunately, too many evangelical New Testament scholars today embrace the peculiar view that Jesus did not mean to refer to Holy Communion in John 6.

It is worth noting that, although Cosin mentions only the Old and New Testaments in his guide to the English Church, he does have a high view of the Apocrypha. In his *Scholastical History of the Canon of Holy Scripture*, Cosin set out to demonstrate that the Anglican position on the Apocrypha was in fact the traditional position held by the church fathers. While not allowing for the Apocryphal books to be counted as part of the canon of Holy Scripture, Cosin grants that they should be read in church, published within the Bible, and even casually referred to under the name "Holy Scripture." Cosin maintains that sermons and theological writings can appeal to the morality and history found within the Apocrypha and that the Apocrypha can be used to help clearly explain doctrines elsewhere established in the proper canon of Holy Scripture.[16] This is all in keeping with Article VI of the *Articles of Religion* which says that "the Church doth read [the books of the Apocrypha] for example of life and instruction of manners." If we ignore the Apocrypha, then we cut ourselves off from books that the Church has always read. We will remain ignorant of the centuries of history between the Old and New Testaments, and we will miss out on heroes of the faith such as the courageous Susanna.

Cosin's sustained claim is that the Church of England had "in no way departed from the religion of our forefathers, in so far as that was Christian and Catholic."[17] On the one hand, this means the English Church has not embraced the innovations of Rome such as "mutilating" the Eucharist (i.e., only distributing the bread) or holding divine service in a language "not understood of the people."[18] Further, "unhealthy excrescences on the ancient faith" such as "the divine authority of the Roman Bishop over all Churches throughout the world" have been "utterly cut off from our Church."[19] On the other hand, Cosin says, Martin Luther was a "man of great learning" but not infallible, and John Calvin "deservedly stands high in reputation"[20] but is no way a master to Anglicans. Anglicans are "no more followers of Luther or Calvin than of the Pope" wherever they or he depart from Holy Scripture or "the old Fathers."[21]

Church Leadership

Cosin gives a brief overview of Anglican Holy Orders in chapters 9 through 13 of *The Religion of the Church of England*. For Cosin, organizing the spiritual leadership of the Church according to the three-fold ministry of bishops, priests, and deacons is more than just a matter of prudence or convenience. He maintains that "nothing can be more agreeable to the regulations of Holy Scripture and to the precedents which we find in it"

---

[15] *The Works of the Right Reverend Father in God John Cosin, Lord Bishop of Durham*, 5 vols. (Oxford: John Henry Parker, 1843–1855), 4:330–331.

[16] Cosin, *Works*, 3:9–10.

[17] Cosin, *Religion*, 26.

[18] Ibid., 24.

[19] Ibid., 24–25.

[20] Ibid., 28.

[21] Ibid., 29.

than Holy Orders as received in Anglicanism from antiquity.[22] He insists that Anglican bishops are validly consecrated and are part of a line of bishops that "has never been interrupted."[23] While Cosin does not elaborate on this point, his description of Anglican orders certainly supports the idea of apostolic succession. This doctrine holds that bishops today have inherited through the laying on of hands the office first held by the Apostles themselves and thus continue to legitimately pass on "the gift given through the laying on of hands" (1 Tim 4:14; 2 Tim 1:6). This gift is so real that Cosin preached at a bishop's consecration that "none can take away [its power] when it is once given," although its execution can be suspended.[24] Given the gravity of Holy Orders, it is appropriate that ordinations were on the Sundays immediately following the Ember Day fasts, during which time the people of God fasted and prayed for the new clergy. In our own day, ordinations have been largely separated from Ember Days, which might be part of the reason why the observance of Ember Days has dramatically fallen off.

In listing the duties of the bishop, Cosin naturally starts with ordaining priests and deacons. As the chief pastor, the bishop acts as "guide of clergy and laity in sacred things."[25] He cannot become a mere bureaucratic dispenser of ordinations since he is to be "active in preaching."[26] As an overseer of the Church, his functions include instruction of the ignorant, correction of the wrongdoer, excommunication of the obstinate, and condemnation of the heretic. Perhaps most importantly, he has to keep the Church's own house in order by disciplining "indolent, immoral, or disobedient clergymen."[27] The bishop provides an oversight that many independent churches in our own day desperately need, and wherever a bishop fails to exercise these duties of discipline, the people of God will suffer.

There are several Anglican distinctives in Cosin's outline of the priest. The priest is to preach the gospel not only on Sundays but also on Festivals, and he is to say Morning and Evening Prayer daily. This certainly exceeds the common assumption that pastors only work once a week on Sundays. Visiting the sick, comforting the afflicted, and absolving the penitent are central to the priest's vocation. Cosin adds that the priest is to wear clerical dress. Such a description unavoidably means that the priest's vocation requires every part of his life, in terms of his time, relationships, and identity. If the priest comes to your house when you are sick, he is not merely coming to be friendly; he is coming to bring you the grace of Christ through anointing, prayer, and likely Holy Communion. If you see him at the store, he won't just be "John," wearing a V-neck shirt, but "Fr. John," the priest in a collar. Expectations of clerical dress have lessened since Cosin's day, but the internal disposition symbolized by external dress is still necessary—the priest is always and everywhere a priest.

New Anglicans will likely need instructions in the duties of the deacon since Baptists and Presbyterians have different conceptions of this office. Deacons read the Scriptures in worship, assist the priest in church services, catechize the young, and inquire into the

---

[22] Cosin, *Religion*, 30.
[23] Ibid.
[24] Cosin, *Works*, 1:93.
[25] Cosin, *Religion*, 31.
[26] Ibid.
[27] Ibid., 31–32.

condition of the sick and poor. While it is vital to remember that priests and bishops do not discontinue being deacons, the limited liturgical, preaching, and teaching responsibilities of the deacon allow him greater opportunity to be the hands and feet of Christ to those in need. The deacon is the liaison between the Church and those in need.

Worship

In chapters 14 through 17, Cosin outlines the regular worship of the English Church, addressing the services in this order: the Daily Office, the litany (or Great Litany), and the Eucharist (or Holy Communion). Morning and Evening Prayer are appointed to be held every day. Two daily services at church make the priest available to his congregation for regular pastoral counsel and fellowship. Of course, most Anglican churches today do not hold Morning and Evening Prayer every day. Particularly for church plants without daily access to a building or for commuter churches where parishioners drive from some distance, a public daily office service is an impossibility or at least a great burden. Larger parishes, though, might find that their small group of clergy and staff could regularly form a critical mass which others can join less frequently as they are able. And those who cannot attend are still blessed by the prayers of the remnant who can. Cosin notes the differing capabilities of different contexts when he observes that cathedrals and collegiate churches usually chant the Daily Office, whereas parish churches simply read it. For the Anglican newcomer, it might be helpful to note, as Cosin does, that the exhortation at the start of the daily office summarizes all the elements of the rest of the service: confession, thanksgiving, praise, the hearing of Scripture, and supplication. Former evangelicals might recognize this as the reading of Scripture plus the well-known acronym for prayer, "A.C.T.S.," which stands for adoration, confession, thanksgiving, and supplication.

Cosin's outlines of the various services should be very recognizable to all Anglicans, but there are a few items that stand out in the great liturgist's summary of the Eucharist. The first is that Cosin is open to daily Eucharist. He says that Eucharist is celebrated on the greater Festivals and the first Sunday of every month, but he adds that if any desire it more often and are worthy to be communicants, then it ought to be celebrated at other Sundays, Festivals, and even weekdays. Speaking into another controversy in modern Anglicanism, Cosin writes that in the prayer before the sermon, Anglicans are not "satisfied with only commending the living to God" but that Anglicans pray "God mercifully to grant to [all who have kept Christ's faith sound] and to us a happy resurrection from the dead, a perfect consummation on the Last Day, and eternal happiness in His glorious Kingdom."[28] While a far cry from Rome's doctrine of purgatory, Cosin's description is clear support for prayer for the dead. Lastly, we would do well today to hear Cosin's mention that after the sermon, the Holy Days and Fasting Days to be observed in the following week are declared to the congregation. In the busyness of modernity, it would be a great help to the religious life of Anglican laity for clergy to embrace this practice today.

Some today might find it distasteful that at the exhortation, any who did not intend to communicate were dismissed. Everyone else, after hearing the exhortation, entered

---

[28] Cosin, *Religion*, 41.

the choir area and knelt for the confession. During the reception and "indeed to the end of the whole celebration,"[29] the communicants were to kneel in worship to Christ, not the Sacrament. Although we no longer dismiss non-communicants during the Holy Communion, it is worth appreciating the gravity of eating and drinking the body and blood of Christ. Reading the Exhortation on the first Sunday of Advent, the first Sunday of Lent, and Trinity Sunday, at the very least, can go a long way toward reminding people of the seriousness of sin and the joy of repentance.

Church Life

Chapters 18 through 22 of *The Religion of the Church of England*, along with the first three chapters of the appendix, make clear that Anglicanism is not a merely private religion. In taking up in his final chapters the subjects of baptism, confirmation, matrimony, the visitation of the sick, and the burial of the dead, Cosin shows that the Christian lives his faith, from birth to death, in the context of the Church. And in describing the feasts and fasts of the Church in the beginning of his appendix, Cosin shows that the Church guides the Christian in living out his faith throughout the year. Part of catechizing new Anglicans is to teach them that the Church offers a whole regimen of what it looks like to live as a Christian throughout one's year and throughout one's life.

Several points in these chapters show the communal nature of life within the Church. Starting with baptism, Cosin states that the godparents must educate the child in the faith and make sure that he is confirmed when ready.[30] So parents have the support of godparents in raising their children as Christians. Cosin explains that baptism is administered on Sundays and Holy Days because of the large congregations present on those occasions,[31] which implies that Anglicanism emphasizes both the sacramental and the social aspects of the Church. When someone joins the Church, they become joined to Christ, yes, but they also are joined to a whole congregation of people—some of whom they quite naturally would have invited to such an important occasion as baptism, but some of whom they may not have. Life in the Church can be messy because we do not get to choose who will live it with us. Along this line, concerning weddings, the banns of marriage must be published in worship in three Sundays or Festivals prior to the wedding.[32] Of course, this allows the opportunity for anyone in either the man or the woman's home parish to point out any civil or canonical reason why the couple should not be married. But it's also another example of the corporate reality of Church life. Not even one's wedding is just a private or family matter.

The end of life, too, requires the involvement of the Church. Our age does its best to avoid death and dying, so there is a tendency to be hidden away in one's last days. After COVID-19 restrictions were introduced in 2020, there was an increase in delaying funeral services or forsaking them altogether. But that's not how Christians have traditionally operated. If death seemed on the horizon, then the visitation of the priest allowed for the Church to physically enter into the pain and dying of the individual

---

[29] Cosin, *Religion*, 44.
[30] Ibid., 46.
[31] Ibid., 45.
[32] Ibid., 46.

Christian. According to Cosin, the visiting priest ought to minister to the dying in several ways.[33] With regard to faith, the priest "rehearses the Articles of the *Apostles' Creed* and asks the sick ... whether he ... believes them." According to finances, he asks if the sick "has made his will" and "whether he has been liberal to the poor." As for the conscience, the priest should be prepared to hear the confession of the sick and to comfort him and absolve him of his sin. And sacramentally, the priest gives the "final sacred Viaticum" of Holy Communion.

Should the sick die, the priest will preside over his proper Christian burial. The themes of the sentences of Scripture read in procession suggest the tone of Anglican funerals and burials—"the mortality and misery of men" on the one hand, and "the resurrection and eternal life of the faithful" on the other.[34] Cosin notes that prayer is made not only for the individual being buried and the living attending the burial, but also for those departed in the faith, that they would all have "perfect consummation and bliss both in body and soul in heaven."[35] Cosin allows that these words can be regarded as "pious desires, or as prayers, or as thanksgivings" and insists that they are made "in accordance with the universal custom of the ancient Church."[36] But he is sure to add that this practice does not imply a doctrine of purgatory.

The first three chapters of the appendix provide basic information about the feasts and fasts of the Church—arguably the most important information to explicitly teach to new members. Everything discussed so far should unavoidably come up either within the walls of the church or as part of the major milestones of one's life (e.g., birth, marriage, and death). But much of what constitutes the observance of feasts and fasts takes place outside the church and away from the guidance of a priest. So unless a priest announces upcoming holy days or discusses in sermons how to fast, then a person can (and many sadly have) worship weekly in an Anglican Church for decades without even encountering the concept of corporately fasting as the Church. The Christian life includes a certain tension between rejoicing over life in Christ and sorrowing over one's sin. The Christian calendar of feasts and fasts gives us appointed times to live into both sides of that tension and not slip into a shallow triumphalism on the one hand or a deep depression on the other.

Most of what Cosin has to say on the subject of feasts and fasts is readily available in the prayer book rubrics, but he does add a certain wrinkle to the practice of fasting which might be helpful. Cosin makes a distinction between fasting and abstinence.[37] Fasting is done on the days preceding certain feast days and consists of putting off food until a "frugal evening meal."[38] Abstinence—which is fitting for the season of Lent, Fridays of each week, Ember Days, Rogation days, and all the previously mentioned fasting vigils—

---

[33] Cosin, *Religion*, 47.

[34] Ibid., 48.

[35] Ibid., 48–49.

[36] Ibid., 49.

[37] It's worth noting that Cosin's distinction between fasting and abstinence, while not contained in prayer book rubrics, is consistent with certain statutes passed during the reign of Edward VI. See *The Several Statutes in Force for the Observation of Lent: And Fish-days, at All Other Times of the Year.* London: 1661.

[38] Cosin, *Religion*, 53.

requires the "greater exercise of sobriety, moderation, and temperance" and abstaining from "the ordinary eating of meat."[39] Regardless of exactly *how* we fast, it's important that Anglicans pick up this practice that has been central to historic Christian piety. By fasting, we learn our own frailty, we train ourselves in self-control (a fruit of the spirit), and we focus ourselves on prayer and almsgiving. And by fasting together, the Church protests the culture's materialism, reminding the world that there is more to life than *this* life.

Conclusion

Summarizing Anglicanism is no easy task, but Cosin can help us here. *The Religion of the Church of England* can be read by Anglican newcomers in all of thirty minutes. But it also shows Anglican clergy and catechists the right categories to use when onboarding evangelicals into Anglicanism: theological method, church leadership, worship, and church life. To be sure, these headings are artificial, Cosin not having used these terms himself, but they are faithful to Cosin's work and stand as the key areas to address with new Anglicans. Imagine a generation of evangelicals who became Anglicans and did not learn those four core areas. You would end up with an Anglican Church that sanctifies novel ideas and practices through private interpretation of Scripture, implicitly rejects sacramental authority in favor of humanistic egalitarianism, makes up worship as she goes, and tries to live a private, secular-looking faith without the aid of the Church at every step of the way. May it not be so.

---

[39] Cosin, *Religion*, 54.

Chapter 23

Holiness in Exile:
Jeremy Taylor (1613–1667)
and the Christian Life

The Rev. Hunter Van Wagenen

Although the English Reformers sought to correct the Church from its Roman (commonly called Catholic) excesses, they achieved and defended these reforms not through innovation but through appeals to Scripture and the interpretations given by ancient church writers. Much ink has been spent over the centuries reporting on the relative success (or failure) of the Anglican enterprise. Nevertheless, the Anglican enterprise itself—a catholic Christianity that is at once ancient and pioneering, founded on and guided by the Scriptures and tradition, but also sensitive to the pastoral needs of the moment, courageous enough to stand firm in the essentials and also humble enough to reform when found in error—is an enterprise worth pursuing. How, then, should the Christian who identifies as both reformed and catholic live in a present age whose spirit seeks to divide people into "camps," and immediately assumes or demands to know one's "pro-" or "anti-" sentiments?

Jeremy Taylor (1613–1667) lived in a period of English history that was similar to our own age in its fraught and fractured character. His pastoral understanding of the power of prayer, his self-understanding as a steward standing in a long line of tradition, and his deep and regular meditation upon the sacrament of Holy Communion served, by God's grace, to sustain him through intense persecution and personal pain. Contemporary Christians will do well to mark his life as they seek to live faithfully in the twenty-first century.

Taylor's early career held much promise for advancement.[1] As a young man he caught the attention of Archbishop of Canterbury William Laud, who took Taylor under his wing and gave him a number of opportunities to exercise his gift for preaching in London that would have, in a different century, led to excellent placement and a fine career. Instead, due to the tensions between King Charles I and Laud on the one side and the Puritan Parliament on the other, culminating in the Civil War that resulted in the execution of both the King and the Archbishop, Taylor's career and indeed his life were in danger of ending. After a brief imprisonment, however, Taylor found a home for several years as private chaplain to Lord and Lady Carbery in Gelli Air in Wales where he wrote his best-known works and immortalized the estate's English name of "Golden Grove."

By 1654, Puritan-ruled London had apparently relaxed its strictures against High Churchmen, for John Evelyn, one of Taylor's friends and patrons, recorded that he saw Taylor preach to a congregation. Following another imprisonment for criticizing Cromwell and some of his followers in a preface, and after losing goodwill among even his High Church friends for—as some said—countering the doctrine of original sin as

---

[1] All biographical information on Taylor comes from Thomas K. Carroll, "Introduction," in *Jeremy Taylor: Selected Works*, ed. Thomas K. Carroll (New York: Paulist, 1990), 15–85.

expressed in Article IX,[2] Taylor's ministerial life was relegated to private gatherings of High Church royalists. These years of more comfortable exile saw Taylor writing, first, an understandable plea for toleration with *A Discourse on the Liberty of Prophesying*, followed by an apology for the *Book of Common Prayer*, which had been outlawed by Parliament. While at Golden Grove, he wrote his famous manuals, *The Rule and Exercises of Holy Living* and *The Rule and Exercises of Holy Dying*, as well as publishing a year's worth of sermons, a compilation of sermons turned into a life of Jesus, a defense and description of the ordained ministry, a collection of prayers and litanies, an argument against the dogma of transubstantiation in favor of spiritual presence in the Eucharist, a discourse on the doctrine of repentance (the tendentious *Unum Necessarium*), and finally, a brief piece on friendship, among other papers and letters.

After a final imprisonment due to a published collection of prayers with an image of Christ in prayer on the cover (a breach of the second commandment to the Puritan mind), Taylor had to leave London and received the hospitality of new friends Lord and Lady Conway in Portmore, Ireland. Shortly after his arrival, however, the Restoration of 1660 drastically changed the political and social dynamics of the church, and Taylor was appointed to a bishopric at last. His episcopacy at the diocese of Down and Connor, however, was hardly an easy one. The diocese itself had been ruled by Presbyterians who had no desire for a bishop, and despite several meetings and attempts to reconcile with them, he ultimately took a firm hand, removing more than thirty of the rebellious clergy from churches in his care and appointing (or importing) High Churchmen from England.

The years as Bishop of Down and Connor, later expanded to include Dromore, seem to have been taxing on Taylor's spirit and physical health. If he had hopes for further advancement to a primate's throne, he was disappointed, and seems to have lost many of his friends due to his uncompromising stance against the Presbyterians in his diocese. While he still lent his opinions on theological matters when consulted, in Ireland he remained, publishing a work on casuistry, a manual of preparation for Holy Communion, and a polemic against the papacy. The last of these, from a modern missiological perspective, was a disastrous and ill-conceived attack on the Irish culture, language, and people themselves. In 1667, shortly after the death of his seventh son, Taylor himself took ill and died on August 13, a date still observed in Anglicanism.[3]

Taylor's gift for writing and speaking earned him the title "The Shakespeare of the Caroline Divines," and the content of his writing reveals a penetrating intellect joined to a pastor's heart and sensibility. His manuals, *Holy Living* (1650) and *Holy Dying* (1651), written in honor of his patroness and hostess Lady Carbery after her death, record the

---

[2] For a helpful treatment of the controversy surrounding *Unum Necessarium*, see the entries from August 8–12, 2022 on the blog "Laudable Practice" (laudablepractice.blogspot.com/2022/08/jeremy-taylor-week-unum-necessarium-i.html). The gist of Taylor's argument is not that Adam's sin did no damage to human nature, but that Original Sin in and of itself does not merit eternal damnation from God, but only results in the privation that all experience as a result of being cut off from the Tree of Life. Sins committed by individuals, unrepented-of, are what lead to everlasting condemnation for them. His view, he contends, actually takes the reality of sin and the need for repentance more seriously than the view which imputes Adam's guilt as well as the results of the fall to all of humanity.

[3] Carroll, "Introduction," 37.

counsel of an experienced pastor who laid out scriptural responses to the familiar struggles of Christian obedience and discipleship; he addresses such everyday experiences as the battle against lust or against distraction in prayer, as well as weightier experiences such as the death or suffering of a child. Taylor interspersed these directives for how to act in every situation, some of which might strike modern readers as clinically unemotional, with beautiful prayers for the tempted, the distraught, the distracted, and the hungry. Throughout his manuals he recognizes the human need for both prayer and for handholds to grasp in moments of struggle. The contemporary Christian would learn much in seeking virtue and preparing for eternity from this treasure trove, and the pastor would do well to emulate his courage to speak both scripturally and sensitively about painful subjects such as grief.

Taylor's keen understanding of the human need for form in prayer as a defense against weakness, distraction, and vainglory is likely what kept him fixed as a High Churchman even when it meant celebrating services in private homes. Indeed, one need go no further than the title of his 1649 *Apology for Authorised and Set Forms of Liturgy against the Pretence of the Spirit* to discover his attitude toward those who would disdain the Psalms, collects, and public services of the Church as a valid means of communion with the Lord. In addition to pointing out the problematic and indeed dangerous level of presumption involved in demanding God the Holy Spirit to inspire an appropriate offering of prayer before God's people, Taylor also points out that much of the prayer book's contents are already Scripture, which his opponents would agree is inspired by the Holy Spirit. The Holy Spirit has already provided means of worship preserved through writing. Why, then, he asks, do so many Christians ignore this provision from God and insist that praying extemporaneously is of more value?

He does not let up in his indictment of the cult of spontaneity, so familiar to contemporary Christians. Next, he turns to the objection that many Anglicans have no doubt heard, that the pastor is more able to fit the pastoral needs and feeling of his people if he prays extemporaneously, not "constrained" by the liturgy. With the precision of a surgeon and the ruthlessness of an executioner, Taylor addresses the pastoral problems evident in such thinking. First, he goes back to Scripture: there are plenty of good sermons out there that will please the sensibilities of the people more and get a better reaction from a congregation, but the words of Scripture are second to none in their power and health for God's people. Second, he questions whether the affectionate response of the people is a wise standard at all—what the pastor prays extemporaneously may bless one parishioner's heart while missing another's entirely, when a set prayer would at least have better guarantee of pleasing God. Indeed, there are plenty of examples in Scripture where the "taste" of the people is cast in severe doubt as a trustworthy guide, primary in the examples being the Israelites' demands for meat in the wilderness to add to their manna.[4]

Lest the reader think Taylor or the tradition-minded Anglican of today is allergic to prayers or liturgies composed after the sixteenth century, it should be noted that Taylor himself wrote dozens of prayers. His criticism of the pastoral objection to set prayers—

---

[4] Jeremy Taylor, *An Apology for Authorized and Set Forms of Litvrgie against the Presence of the Spirit* (London, England: R. Royston, 1649), 38–42. http://name.umdl.umich.edu/A63653.0001.001.

that they may not allow the pastor to fit his prayer to the needs of his congregation—is limited to public worship. It is clear from the prayers he includes in almost every chapter of his devotional and pastoral works that he considers private prayer a more than appropriate setting for extemporaneous and newly-written prayers. His pastoral insight continues to shine through here: in public prayers (such as in the Eucharist), the human heart needs formation and feeding with an authorized and time-tested form; in private, the individual needs to address individual affections, but written prayers are still a helpful lattice on which to hang one's intentions—hence Taylor's inclusion of his own compositions in so many works. Deference to the prescribed liturgies of the Church always colors his own compositions; his view of the set forms established in history would match a common view of classic hymns which says, "We do not love the 'good old songs' because they're old, but because they're good."

This attitude towards the "good" and "old" is present in an aspect of Taylor's writing which shines through all his works: the patrimony of the ancient Church is near his heart and on his mind in all circumstances. Indeed, Taylor embodied the *ad fontes* spirit of the Reformation, for in all his writings, particularly in those places where he defended High Churchmanship against either Roman or Puritan criticism, he appealed reflexively to Scripture and the church fathers. His instinct applied not only to theological matters, but also to matters of practice. For Taylor, the question of what the ancient church did was no less important than what the ancient church believed. Once again, contemporary Christians will learn much from his example. How many classics of the patristic age go unread or unmarked by the modern churchgoer, and yet how sweet the meditations which St. Ignatius and St. Athanasius bring! How many Anglicans feel uncomfortable or unconfident in their liturgy and practice, out-of-joint and against the grain with contemporary Western culture, not knowing or trusting that they stand in a stream flowing from Christ himself through the Apostolic tradition to the present? May Taylor's understanding of these matters hearten the reader to seek out the treasures of history and stand firm on the grounded Apostolic Church.

Given Taylor's immersion in patristic writers and his lifelong defense of the public worship of the Church, it should not be surprising that many of his theological treatises centered on the sacrament of Holy Communion. The polemic against the doctrine of transubstantiation, which he wrote in 1654, as well as his later writings on the same subject, would seem to indicate a devotion to the Sacrament that engendered suspicion of Roman leanings, and yet his writings consistently highlight the need not only for faith but faithfulness in the spiritual eating and drinking that takes place in the Eucharist. In his later treatise on the subject, *The Worthy Communicant*, he defied both the Puritan mind and the Roman inclination that had infiltrated the Church; he would have no truck with those who said the only benefit is mental exercise and an opportunity to be obedient to Christ's command, yet neither would he allow one to say the Sacrament is received beneficially as the Body and Blood of Christ regardless of the attitude of the communicant.

Besides Puritanism and Romanism, Taylor identified a third pitfall which might be identified: the mystic. This person, somewhat separate from the Reformation debates about the nature or mechanism of the Sacrament, focused too much on the effect the Sacrament had and the affections it aroused, but would therefore be driven to distraction and doubt. Experience, Taylor explained, is an imprecise and fickle measure of the nature of anything. He seemed to have more sympathy for this group, but cautioned readers to avoid enumerating titles or attributes to the Sacrament which are not present in Scripture.[5]

In the remainder of *The Worthy Communicant*, he describes the attitudes which the communicant should pursue: faith, charity, and repentance. In each chapter he closes with prayers to help the communicant ask earnestly for these things and finally closes the book with a reverent explanation of each moment of celebration and reception as it pertains to the sign and inward affections of the communicant. Consider the charge he gives as the communicant receives:

> As soon as ever you have taken the holy elements into your mouth, and stomach; remember that you have taken Christ into you, after a manner indeed which you do not understand, but to all purposes of blessing and holiness, if you have taken Him at all. And now consider, that He who hath given you His son, with Him will give you all things else; therefore represent to God through Jesus Christ all your needs and the needs of your relatives; signify to Him the condition of your soul; complain of your infirmities; pray for help against your enemies; tell Him of your griefs; represent your fears, your hopes and your desires.[6]

Such words speak both to Taylor's pastoral sensitivity in desiring his reader to receive all that the Lord is willing and to his deep reservoir of personal experience in receiving the sacrament. Contemporary Christians, buffeted by the storms of the world, fighting the spiritual battles of the day, would do well to emulate Taylor's focus on the Sacrament of Holy Communion. There they will find true food and drink, spiritual nurture for the soul as they work out their salvation with fear and trembling.

St. Paul's closing remarks to the Philippians help frame Taylor's own attitude to his life circumstances: "for I have learned in whatever situation I am to be content. I know how to be brought low, and I know how to abound. In any and every circumstance, I have learned the secret of facing plenty and hunger, abundance and need. I can do all things through him who strengthens me" (Phil 4:11–13, ESV). Taylor had his share of abundance early on—he was a rising star who caught the attention of the two most powerful men in England—and yet his fall with them and the plunge into his status as *persona non grata* did not break him. Though the fall of King Charles I and Archbishop Laud coincided with his first son's death, and though in subsequent years he would see his first wife and all seven of his sons pass away, he kept a disciplined thankfulness in all his writings. Indeed, it was not until the end of his life and his conflict-filled episcopacy that he seemed to indulge in true sullenness.[7]

Taylor did not shun the low places to which he was consigned as a result of his conviction. Indeed, he dared the dangers of Cromwell's London to preach when allowed, and conducted Eucharistic services according to the prayerbook in homes in order to serve those who were faithful to the tradition which the Puritans rejected. Though his

---

[5] Taylor, *The Worthy Communicant*, ed. Reginald Heber and Charles Page Eden (Galesburg, IL: Seminary Street, 2022), 3–5.

[6] Ibid., 258.

[7] Carroll, "Introduction," 36.

service as a bishop in Ireland was not a happy one, he nevertheless devoted much of his personal funds into renovating the churches within his diocese and requested burial at the Dromore cathedral where he served.

Anglicans, particularly in the West, have been blessed with abundance—high status in society, respect from intellectuals and rulers, influence and power to build such institutions as schools, hospitals, orphanages, and more. As with Taylor in Puritan England, however, the socio-political situation of the West is forcing Anglicans worldwide to choose as he did: stay in position but lose one's soul, or face exile by staying true to one's convictions and practicing what is found in Scripture and the ancient Church. Let those who worship in a storefront, cafeteria, or home take heart, for while such lowliness may feel foreign to Anglicans in the West, disjointed from the surrounding material prosperity, it is churches such as these that God used to seed the renewal of his kingdom in England. Therefore, let our priests not shun these small congregations.

Whether he preached in the great churches in London or to private gatherings in homes, Taylor was assured that he stood in the stream of the Great Tradition, which both preceded and would outlast the debates and conflicts of his own day. The Lord does not care whether worship takes place in a living room or in a cathedral, outside or in a chapel; the Holy Scriptures and the tradition of prayer that he has given to the Church will endure the conflicts which rage through the culture. The topics or ideas may shift, but the battleground between the Kingdom of Heaven and the kingdom of this world remains the same: the human heart is fickle, prone to wander, concupiscent. The contemporary Christian must grasp the lifeline Christ has thrown us in the stability of his Word and the traditions of the ancient Church.

In high places and in low, today's Christians should recommit themselves to prayer. Taylor's life shows a strong and fruitful vine—much-pruned—that hung on a sturdy lattice of the prayers of God's people. The Scriptures, the prayers of the Church given to us through the *Book of Common Prayer*, and the spiritual classics are gifts that God the Holy Spirit has provided for his people to speak with him and seek his grace in their everyday lives. If the clergy or laity are discouraged at the disuse into which these gifts have fallen, if the movements of the Offices feel rote or empty, if comparison with the flash and numbers of culture-shaped worship is a temptation, read Taylor's manuals for *Holy Living* and *Holy Dying*. There and in his other writings may be found, presented in beautiful and soaring prose, the spiritual realities of prayer and obedience.

Few Christians in the West have known the desolations that Jeremy Taylor endured: the death of his wife and seven of his sons, exile, imprisonment, and an episcopacy marked by conflict during his final years. Yet he knew consolation in the Lord's Supper. Here the contemporary Christian ought to meditate, hunger, and pursue God's grace and nourishment for the journey to eternity. Some from other traditions may scoffingly label the communicant as "Catholic," shadowboxing against some half-understood Roman straw man, but Christ's commands to eat and drink are clear. Following Taylor's guidance for preparation before the sacrament, grasp the faith with both hands, and see how the Lord strengthens and blesses all who come in faithfulness to his Table.

Chapter 24

A Kingdom Not of This World:
The Witness of the Nonjurors

The Rev. Daniel H. Logan

Near the end of AD 371, the Arian emperor Valens, "eager to impose his creed on his subjects,"[1] sent one of his prefects, Modestus, to confront the archbishop of Cappadocian Caesarea, St Basil the Great, known for his commitment to orthodoxy. Flanked by a troop of Arian bishops, Modestus summoned Basil for an interview. St Gregory of Nazianzus recounts the interchange in his funeral oration for Basil:

> Modestus "claimed submission in the name of the emperor," but "Basil refused it in the name of God."

> "...you do not honor the religion of your sovereign," Modestus protested, "when all others have given way and submitted."

> "I do not," Basil retorted, "for this is not the will of my true Sovereign..."

> Modestus trotted out a litany of punishments for resistance: "Confiscation, exile, torture, death."

> "...none of these you mentioned can affect me," the archbishop replied.

> "How can that be true?" Modestus asked.

> "Because the man who possesses nothing is not liable to confiscation..." Basil maintained.

> "No one," the prefect said, "up to this day has ever spoken in such a manner and with such boldness to me."

> "Perhaps you have never met a bishop," St Basil replied.[2]

King James II encountered seven bishops on May 18, 1688. The Archbishop of Canterbury, William Sancroft, and six of his brother bishops had affixed their names to a petition, respectfully, yet forcefully, informing His Majesty: "We find in ourselves great averseness to the distributing and publishing in all our churches your Majesty's late

---

[1] Philip Schaff and Henry Wace, eds. *Nicene and Post-Nicene Fathers*, (Peabody, MA: Hendrickson, 1995) 8:xxiii–xxiv.

[2] *Funeral Orations by Saint Gregory Nazianzen and Saint Ambrose*, trans. Leo P. McCauley (Washington, DC: Catholic University of America Press: 2004), 67–69.

declaration for Liberty of Conscience."[3] In April of the year prior, the king had issued a *Declaration of Indulgence* in England, eliminating penalties for those who did not conform to the established Church. While many Protestant Dissenters rejoiced at this windfall of royal magnanimity, others[4] suspected James, an unapologetic Roman Catholic who had made overtures to the pope regarding the reunion of England and Rome, of attempting to lay the groundwork for the restoration of Popery.[5]

Nevertheless, it seems public gratitude outweighed suspicion at the time, and, if James had not insisted on overplaying his hand, the house of Stuart might have held the throne for generations. Almost a century later, James' grandson, the "Bonnie Prince" Charles Edward would bitterly remark from exile in Rome as he observed a liturgical procession, "Oh that our family should deprive themselves of three kingdoms for such nonsense."[6] And yet deprive themselves they did. James reissued his declaration in April 1688 with a caveat: the bishops must now have their clergy read the declaration in church during divine service within a few weeks' time. Even "passive obedience," that great nonjuring tenet, had its limits. Whatever inertia the post-Restoration bishops might have experienced, being naturally inclined to support both the throne and the Stuarts, James woke them from their slumber. The septuagenarian archbishop summoned the prelates to Lambeth Palace, and the Petition was drawn up.

James did not expect this rebuff from his bishops. In 1685, when the crown passed from his brother's licentious hands into his own, James had assured the Privy Council of his intention to support and defend the Church of England, regardless of his own religious persuasion, for "[the established church] was always in favour of the monarchy."[7] And indeed, there had been a natural inclination in England towards close cooperation between the monarchy and the episcopacy, initiated most signally in the reformed Church of England by the (admittedly at times testy) relationship between Henry VIII and Thomas Cranmer. Bishop Lake of Chichester could even remark that he understood "non-resistance and passive obedience" towards the monarch to be "the distinguishing character of the Church of England."[8] In the mid-seventeenth century, this alliance between the throne and the episcopate seemed to be sealed in blood by the executions of Charles I, the Royal Martyr, and his Archbishop, William Laud, by the parliamentarians. At the "Glorious Restoration" of the monarchy in 1660, state services were drafted for the revised prayer book to commemorate the death of Charles I and the

---

[3] Herbert Mortimer Luckock, *The Bishops in the Tower: A Record of Stirring Events Affecting the Church and Nonconformists from the Restoration to the Revolution* (New York: Thomas Whittaker, 1887), 163.

[4] Including Richard Baxter, John Howe, and John Bunyan.

[5] The king's private chapel actually housed the consecration of a Roman bishop at Jesuit hands in only the second year of his reign, on Christmas day 1686 (Luckock, *Bishops*, 121). John Evelyn, the famous diarist, remarked at the sight of the "sumptuously habited" altar party and their "divers cringes" and censing before the altar, "I could not have believed I should ever have seen such things in the King of England's palace, after it had pleased God to enlighten this nation…"

[6] Thomas Lathbury, *A History of the Nonjurors: Their Controveries and Writings; with Remarks on Some of the Rubrics in the Book of Common Prayer* (London: William Pickering, 1845), 410.

[7] Luckock, *Bishops*, 117.

[8] John Henry Overton, *The Nonjurors: Their Lives, Principles, and Writings* (London: Smith, Elder, & Co., 1902), 81.

enthronement of Charles II. These cultural and sociopolitical factors would have strongly predisposed the bishops against challenging the sovereign. As oblivious and misguided as he was, James' reaction to the bishop's petition is therefore predictable: "These are strange words," he said to the six bishops[9] at the late hour of their visitation, "It is a standard of rebellion."[10] While making many assurances of their loyalty (which they would famously have greater opportunity to demonstrate later), the bishops also made it clear to their king that, in the end, they must obey God rather than men.

London was soon abuzz with the news of the bishops' stand against their Romanizing king. Against the advice of wiser councilors, James moved forward with a prosecution of the prelates for "false, malicious, and seditious libel against the King."[11] Only three weeks after the petition, the bishops presented themselves at Whitehall and were promptly ferried to the Tower. It is difficult to conceive of a strategy that would have been more damaging to the king's interests than the one he adopted. Seemingly overnight, Sancroft and the other bishops—ever after known as "the Immortal Seven"—became national heroes. The guards at the Tower fell on their knees at the arrival of the bishops, begging for a blessing, and would later drink their health at table. At the trial on June 29, even the king's stacked jury could not secure the desired judgment, and the bishops were acquitted, to the rapturous delight of the people. The sequence of events (compounded by the birth of James' first male heir in the midst of everything else) occasioned the invitation by several of the nobility[12] to James' Dutch, firmly Protestant son-in-law, William of Orange, to "free the nation from a despotic absolutism and the threatening danger of Papal tyranny."[13] The prince landed on British shores on the significant date of November 5. James lit the fuse to his own gunpowder plot, accomplishing the ruin of the house of Stuart.

Before the end of the year, James had fled the kingdom, plunking the great seal into the Thames as he made his exit.[14] Lacking the authority to summon Parliament, William called a Convention in January 1689, which moved speedily to declare James' flight an abdication, and by a vote of fifty-one to forty-nine in the House of Lords, elected to have a new King rather than simply a Regent, a distinction that would later prove to be of incredible import for the nonjurors' consciences. The Whig battle cry, "*Salus populi est suprema lex*,"[15] carried the day, and William and Mary were coronated in Westminster Hall on April 11, 1689.

New monarchs, especially those of such creative legal standing, needed new oaths from their subjects. "I, *A.B.*, do sincerely promise and swear to bear true allegiance to

---

[9] Sancroft was in poor health and could not attend. The six were William Lloyd of St. Asaph (not to be confused with the nonjuring bishop of Norwich of the same name), Francis Turner of Ely, John Lake of Chichester, Thomas Ken of Bath and Wells, Thomas White of Peterborough, and Jonathan Trelawney of Bristol.

[10] Luckock, *Bishops*, 152.

[11] Ibid., 155.

[12] And one bishop: Compton of London.

[13] Luckock, *Bishops*, 169.

[14] J. W. C. Wand, *The High Church Schism: Four Lectures on the Nonjurors* (London: Faith Press, 1951), 7.

[15] The welfare of the people shall be the supreme law.

Their Majesties, King William and Queen Mary." These were the eighteen words that cost the nonjurors (that is, non-swearers) their earthly livelihoods and worldly standing. In a turn of events almost elegant in its irony, nearly all the bishops who had made the stand that, in effect, cost James his throne, now refused to transfer their allegiance to his replacement. Five of the imprisoned seven, Archbishop William Sancroft, Thomas Ken of Bath and Wells, Francis Turner of Ely, John Lake of Chichester, and Thomas White of Peterborough, would not ascribe to the sovereigns *de facto* what they had already pledged to the sovereign *de jure*.[16] They were joined by 400 of the English clergy, all the Scottish bishops and clergy, and one Irish bishop, William Sheridan of Kilmore. To retrieve the phrase often found in the histories of the nonjurors, those who opposed James in his prosperity would not now desert him in his adversity.

With the solemn penning of consecutive legal fictions, William, that "little ambitious Dutch savior," as Samuel Grascome called him,[17] returned the Convention's favor of being declared King by declaring the Convention a Parliament, and this Parliament, without even the pretense of an appeal to Convocation or any other ecclesiastical body, prepared to declare vacant sees in Christ's one, holy, catholic, and apostolic Church. Those bishops who refused the oaths were given until February 1, 1690. Whigs who would countenance toleration of all manner of dissenter and nonconformist would not extend the same courtesy to the consciences of their duly ordained fathers in God. The nonjuring divines were not impressed by this exercise in nominalism; the princes of the Church would not render to Caesar the episcopal thrones that belonged to God. This crisis of the Church's independence prompted by the vacancy of the bishops' sees was sealed when the government assigned their replacements. With these new bishops, "altar was set up against altar," and the schism was complete.

Here we find the crux of the nonjuring witness. Whether James threatened them with the Tower or William with despoilment, here we find *episkopoi* resolved to keep "without spot, unrebukable, until the appearing of our Lord Jesus Christ" the commandment to "fight the good fight of faith, lay hold on eternal life, whereunto thou art also called, and hast professed a good profession before many witnesses" (1 Tim 6:12, 14).[18] Their conduct remained congruent with the vow made at their ordination to "banish and drive away all erroneous and strange Doctrine, contrary to Gods Word," (whether papist or plebist), "and both privately and openly to call upon, and encourage others to the same."[19] The Deprived Fathers continued the tradition of the prophet Daniel, who was able to offer unfeigned fealty to multiple generations of foreign kings while remaining unmoved on what was nonnegotiable in his fealty to God.

When Rome fell to the Visigoths in 410 A.D., the subsequent crisis produced one of the greatest fruits of Western Christianity in *The City of God* by St. Augustine of Hippo.

---

[16] William Lloyd of St Asaph and Jonathan Trelawney of Bristol took the oaths, but the number seven was rescued by the addition of William Lloyd of Norwich and Robert Frampton of Gloucester. Thomas Cartwright of Chester, the duplicitous arch-Jacobite, was never counted among the nonjurors, though he also refused the oath.

[17] Overton, *Nonjurors*, 210.

[18] Unless otherwise noted, all Scripture quotations are from the King James Version.

[19] *The Book of Common Prayer: The Texts of 1549, 1559, and 1662*, ed. Brian Cummings (Oxford: Oxford University Press, 2011), 648.

"It is recorded of Cain that he built a city," he writes, "while Abel, as though he were merely a pilgrim on earth, built none. For, the true City of the saints is in heaven, though here on earth it produces citizens in whom it wanders as on a pilgrimage through time looking for the Kingdom of eternity."[20] Though the earth be removed, and though the mountains be carried into the midst of the sea, Augustine knew he need not fear, for his heart was set on the city which hath foundations, whose builder and maker is God. However one's opinion might fall on the matter of the oaths, the nonjurors' commitment to the independence of the heavenly city in the teeth of the encroachment of the earthly city is the pure gold of their inheritance, the gift laid at the feet of Christ and His Church at the end of their buffeted, ragged careers during that most torturous of Anglican centuries. Much attention has been drawn to the coziness in England between her Church and her State, but the Nonjuring Fathers continue the legacy of St. Thomas Becket by placing their own wellbeing between the king's might and the Church's altar. As J. H. Overton observes, "[The nonjurors] realized far more vividly than most of their contemporaries the existence of the Church as a distinct spiritual society with laws of its own, whose connection with the State, however beneficial, was purely accidental; and, as a consequence, they insisted on the independency of the Church of any power on earth in the exercise of her purely spiritual power and authority."[21] It was belief in the Church, not in the State, that was confessed in the creeds. In attacking the Church, William's government attacked the Faith.

The implications of the tectonic shift that had been accomplished with the ejection of so many conscientious, devout clergy and their replacement with men burdened with fewer qualms was soon apparent.[22] "Revolution" bishops like Henry Compton, John Tillotson, Edward Stillingfleet, and (supremely) Gilbert Burnet predictably defended the new regime, making a theological compromise that drew them inexorably into latitudinarianism. In effect, those who believed in the rights of the Church were siphoned off from positions of influence, and preferments were heaped upon those willing to champion Erastianism and downplay the Church as an independent, divine Body. Barred from their pulpits, many nonjuring clergy employed their pens in the defense of the Church in which they still understood themselves to be the rightful ministers and pastors. Oceans of ink were spilled in the conflict that followed, perhaps best typified by the skirmishes directed against the latitudinarian Benjamin Hoadly, involving, among others, the nonjuror and author of *A Serious Call to a Devout and Holy Life*, William Law.[23] In 1717, Hoadly, lately made bishop of Bangor by George I, preached

---

[20] Saint Augustine, *The City of God: An abridged Version from the Translation*, trans. Gerald G. Walsh, Demetrius B. Zema, Grace Monahan, and Daniel J. Honan, ed. Vernon J. Bourke (New York: Doubleday, 1958), 325.

[21] Overton, *Nonjurors*, 7.

[22] Though it must be acknowledged that many with nonjuring sympathies were among those who took the oaths (especially in Oxford), and a variety of motives and factors must have contributed to each individual's decision. It is only before our own Master that each of us stands or falls. I do not mean to suggest that broad judgments can be levied on such complex questions.

[23] While not especially pertinent to our subject, it may be of interest to some readers to consider the claim made of Law by the Rt Rev'd William Warburton, that "William Law begat Methodism," (Overton, *Nonjurors*, 387) with *A Serious Call* (1729). Indeed, John Wesley at one point found Law's moral ideals to be too lofty for his own taste!

before the king a sermon on "The Nature of the Kingdom or Church of Christ."[24] In this sermon, clearly crafted in response to the lofty Church claims of certain nonjurors like George Hickes, Hoadly plummets to the depths of a "snake-belly low" ecclesiology: such a low understanding of the Church, in fact, it could hardly be said to exist at all in his estimation. In some ways anticipating the works of Schopenhauer, Hoadly argued that the Church was "purely spiritual," built upon "the sole ground of sincerity," that "Christ's authority is directed immediately to the individual soul," and that "Jesus left behind no visible, human authority; no vice-gerents, no interpreters upon whom absolutely His subjects are to depend; no judges on the consciences or religion of His people." The Rt Rev'd Hoadly subsisted off the fruit of a branch that he was vigorously sawing off with all his might.

While the latitudinarians passionately argued against the ground of their own existence, many of the later nonjurors of the eighteenth century quietly explored the treasures of devotion, worship, and liturgy to be found in the ancient Church. Untethered from the obligations of the State and her Erastian religion, the nonjuring remnant felt free to revisit the established liturgy; unable to avail themselves of worldly preferments, their gaze drifted heavenwards, adopting the Cranmerian perspective *ad fontes* in elevating the pure gospel of the ancient fathers in the common prayers of the Church. This gave rise within the nonjuring community of what became known as the "Usages" controversy. The usages in question consisted of (1) prayers for the faithful departed, (2) the mixed chalice, (3) the epiclesis (invocation of the Holy Spirit on the eucharistic elements), and (4) the Prayer of Oblation (offering the elements to the Father). Accordingly, proponents of the usages (known as "Usagers," and, when they became insistent, "Essentialists") preferred the 1549 prayer book, which preserved each of these. Nonjuring leaders like Jeremy Collier, Thomas Brett, the young Thomas Deacon, and the Scottish bishop Archibald Campbell championed the revival of these usages, and, while the characteristic nonjuring refusal to countenance compromise initially precipitated a split within the small (and ever shrinking) communion with those who did not wish to present yet another obstacle to reunion with the Established Church, the passage of time eventually brought consensus. By 1733, the internecine schism was overcome with most of the nonjuring party adopting a modified 1549 Communion Office, and, it should be noted, when Samuel Seabury was consecrated the first bishop of the Protestant Episcopal Church of the United States in 1784, it was at the hands of Scottish nonjuring bishops who sent him back with a liturgy owing much to the 1549 and ever after shaping the American prayer book tradition.

Given these liturgical proclivities and their Jacobite sympathies, the nonjurors are often associated with the "high church" tradition, if not outright papistry. And there is an argument to be made that the nonjuring schism is what accomplished, more than anything else, the perception of a "low church" party and a "high church" party within the Church of England.[25] Accordingly, they are often wielded in partisan debates as

---

[24] Wand, *High Church Schism*, 51.

[25] "…until quite the close of the seventeenth century these terms [of 'high' and 'low' Church people] were hardly known. Before then, Church people were simply Church people, without any

continued

bludgeons to make a case for which churchmanship represents "true" Anglicanism, though of course this is the wrong question. It is not England with which we will have to do at the judgment, but the Lord Jesus Christ, and so we are not as concerned with true Anglicanism as with true Christianity. Far from placing their faith in the right party, the nonjurors understood themselves as Protestant (that is, Confessing) Christians of the Catholic Faith, and any careful student of their works will find they produced some of the most thoroughgoing Protestant works in opposition to Romanism that one could hope to find around the turn of and into the eighteenth century. Witnesses to the Protestantism of the nonjurors abound in J. H. Overton's towering work, *The Nonjurors*, including the letter of one (necessarily anonymous) nonjuring layman in response to the accusation of being a papist:

> If you will needs have me to be a papist, and there is no help for it, I must tell you that I am such a papist as disowns the Pope's supremacy over the Catholick Church, such a papist as disbelieves his infallibility both in and out of a general Council, such a papist as disbelieves the corporall presence of Christ in the Sacrament, such a papist as cannot worship images, such a papist as abhorres divine service in a tongue unknown to the congregation....I declare that I am...as much as a protestant as ever, as much a Church of England man as ever.[26]

Similar sentiments can be found in the *Dialogue* likely written by "one of the most eminent of the later nonjurors," John Lindsay.[27] The dialogue is between a "country gentleman" and his nonjuring neighbor. At one point in the conversation, the country gentleman comments, "I do not remember to have ever seen you at our Parish Church, which has made many of us conclude you are not a member of the established Church of England," to which the neighbor gives his reply:

> I assure you, Sir, it is far otherwise. I really am, and trust in God to enable me steadfastly to continue a member of the Established Church of England, as it was happily reformed from the errors of Popery, and distinguished in Doctrine by her 39 Articles and Homilies, in Discipline by her Canons, and in worship according to her Liturgy or Common Prayer, maturely settled by Church Representation in Convocation in 1661, and enforced by the temporal Sanction of the Laws of the Land in the Act of Uniformity.[28]

The Deprived Fathers had no interest in perpetuating competing churchmanships, much less in giving even an inch to Rome. Rather, they insisted on the rights of the

---

epithet..." (Overton, *Nonjurors*, 171) Accordingly, this "Old High Church" tradition should not be confused with the Oxford Movement, the ritualist party it produced, and modern Anglo-Catholicism: cf. Peter B. Nockles, *The Oxford Movement in Context: Anglican High Churchmanship, 1760–1857* (Cambridge: Cambridge University Press, 1994).

[26] Overton, *Nonjurors*, 277.

[27] Full title: *The Grand and Important Question about the Church and Parochial Communion, Fairly and Friendly debated in a Dialogue between a worthy Country Gentleman and his Neighbour newly returned from London* (Overton, *Nonjurors*, 222, 284–285).

[28] Ibid.

Christian Church in what may be called her Anglican "recension,"[29] in the Church of England's divine witness to what Peter Toon often referred to as "reformed Catholicity,"[30] in what might be beneficially understood as the Anglican *ressourcement* of the universal Church. They understood, with John Jewel, that "God's holy gospel, the ancient bishops, and the primitive church do make on our side, and that we have not without just cause left these men, and rather have returned to the apostles and old catholic fathers."[31] And perhaps the strongest argument for their cause can be found in the "broad church" wave that swept across England in their absence. The latitudinarians hawked a milquetoast brand of "mere Christianity" with its affection for the lowest common denominator that survives in the United Kingdom today as "dual integrity," that most insidious of theological accommodations. "Every kingdom divided against itself is brought to desolation," our Lord told us (Matt 12:25). "MENE, MENE, TEKEL, UPHARSIN," were the words scratched into Belshazzar's wall by the Lord's finger, "God hath numbered thy kingdom, and finished it" (Dan 5:25-28). "Ye adulterers and adulteresses," St. James asks, "know ye not that the friendship of the world is enmity with God?" (Jas 4:4) Sancroft and his brethren resigned themselves to penury and obscurity before changing "the truth of God into a lie" (Rom 1:25), before crowning and blessing what *is not* as if it *is*.

The bishops' modern descendants, however, have discovered in "walking together" the many benefits of a broad way, of worshiping and serving "the creature more than the Creator" (Rom 1:25). On February 9, 2023, barely five months after the death of Elizabeth II, the Defender of the Faith, Her Majesty, the Queen, the General Synod of the Church of England, in the throes of "deep listening" and receiving votes in the affirmative from 36 of her bishops, agreed to "welcome the decision of the House of Bishops to replace Issues in Human Sexuality with new pastoral guidance," namely, the blessing of same-sex couples. The Archbishops of York and Canterbury remarked, "For the first time, the Church of England will publicly, unreservedly and joyfully welcome same-sex couples in church." The Bishop of London called it "a moment of hope."[32]

On May 18, 1688, England's sovereign encountered an Archbishop who led his brother bishops in holding the ancient course as they were flung from their episcopal palaces, in the vein of Daniel, Basil, Augustine, and Thomas Becket. These bishops, living in the love that cannot be separated from the faith that was "once delivered unto the saints" (Jude 3), refused to usher their nation to empty cisterns, to Egypt's poisonous meatpots, to Gehenna's undying flame. They knew it was not in the nature of integrity to be dual or that a double-minded man should expect to receive anything from the Lord except to be spewed from His mouth. These Immortal Fathers, deprived in the eyes of the world, would not accept deliverance; they endeavored to obtain a better resurrection. Bishops

---

[29] Credit for this phrasing is due to the Rev. Dr. Nathaniel Kidd, vicar of Reconciliation Anglican Church in Bellingham, WA.

[30] Peter Toon, *The Anglican Way: Evangelical and Catholic* (Wilton, CT: Morehouse-Barlow, 1983), 69.

[31] John Jewel, *An Apology of the Church of England*, ed. Robin Harris and Andre Gazal (Landrum, SC: Davenant Institute, 2020), 14.

[32] "Prayers for God's blessing for same-sex couples take step forward after Synod debate," September 2, 2023. www.churchofengland.org/media-and-news/press-releases/prayers-gods-blessing-same-sex-couples-take-step-forward-after-synod.

who knew how to die well, the dead tombstones of those in their communion proclaim the gospel better than some of their living heirs: "*Christo qui vivit, morte perire nequit. Resurgam,*"[33] we read atop the remains of the Rev'd John Blackbourne.[34] When Bishop John Lake, who died in 1689, was told his persistence in refusing the oaths would win him his suspension on August 1 and his deprivation on February 1, he is said to have responded that the "day of *death* and of *judgment* are as certain as the 1st of *August* and the 1st of *February*."[35] And the Blessed Archbishop Sancroft, who passed from this life in 1693, had the following words inscribed on his tomb:

> William Sancroft, borne in this parish, afterwards by the same Providence of God, Archbishop of Canterbury, and at last deprived of all that he could not keep with a good conscience, returned hither to end his life where he began it, and professeth here at the foot of his tomb that as he naked came forth, so he naked must return. The Lord giveth and the Lord taketh away, blessed be the Name of the Lord.[36]

Those of whom the world was not worthy, the Deprived Fathers, did the work of bishops in an otherworldly kingdom. Three centuries later, something a bit more terrestrial seems to have captivated the attention of those who hold, or perhaps we should say haunt, those venerable chairs today. May God raise up a new generation of overseers less infatuated with that which passeth away; may the bishops of His Church hold first to the will of God, which abideth forever.

---

[33] Christ who lives cannot perish by death. I will rise again.
[34] Lathbury, *History*, 395.
[35] Overton, *Nonjurors*, 80.
[36] Ibid., 37.

Chapter 25

The Old Made New: John Keble (1792–1866) and the Revival of Reformed Catholicism

The Rev. Dr. Charles Erlandson

Introduction

John Keble lived at a decisive time in English Church history when the relationship of the Church to the State was in flux and the Catholic essence of Anglicanism was waning. Although Keble was a humble and unassuming man, his influence as priest, pastor, prophet, poet, and professor helped launch and nourish the revival of the Catholic face of the Church of England. Keble accomplished this great work of revival by envisioning a comprehensive return to the Reformed Catholicism manifested especially by the Book of Common Prayer and the Prayer Book rule of life. Remembering how God used his ministry as an instrument of renewal in the nineteenth century can teach us much about the possibility of a revival of Reformed Catholicism in North America in the twenty-first century.

In Keble's day, the catholic side of Anglican Reformed Catholicism was not entirely effaced, but it had been impoverished through a kind of collective amnesia. The word *catholic* was seldom used in reference to Anglicanism, and many parts of the prayer book rule of life had been greatly diminished. Unlike the dynamic and unstable John Henry Newman, Keble was a hereditary High Churchman, and his mission was not to innovate but to restore what had been lost. In other words, Anglicanism needed to be reformed: the old had to be made new in the nineteenth century.

J. C. Shairp, one of the many contemporary non-Anglicans who highly valued Keble's contributions to the Church, wrote:

> Out of that great past he brought some of the sterner stuff of which the martyrs were made, and introduced it like iron into the blood of modern religious feeling. A poet who received all these influences into himself and vitalized them, *could not but make the old new*. For not till the authoritative had been inwardly transfused into the moral and spiritual did it for the most part find vent in his poetry. There are exceptions to this which form what we regard as the shortcomings of *The Christian Year*. But in all its finer, more vital poems, the catholic faith has become personal, rests frankly on intuition and experience, as frankly as the vaguer more impersonal meditations of greater poets.[1] (Emphasis added)

I want, therefore, to discuss John Keble's legacy and what it has to teach us today in the three-fold movement described below: Anglican identity re-evaluated, Anglican identity re-established, and Anglican identity renewed.

Anglican Identity Re-evaluated

At the heart of the Oxford Movement was a re-evaluation of Anglican identity. While many forces caused concern among the Tractarians, such as the growing religious

---

[1] J. C. Shairp, "Keble and 'The Christian Year,'" *Little's Living Age* 91 (1866): 210.

liberalism, it was, in particular, a political issue that necessitated this re-evaluation. In 1833, Parliament sought to suppress ten Irish bishoprics at a time when Roman Catholics had recently obtained the right to vote. This provoked Keble's Assize Sermon on "National Apostasy,"[2] delivered on July 14, 1832, as well as the realization by the leaders of the Oxford Movement that it was time to re-establish the Church of England on a different theological basis other than Erastianism.[3]

Keble's Assize Sermon must have seemed innocuous enough at the time and was largely unnoticed, but John Henry Newman claimed, "I have ever considered and kept the day as the start of the religious movement of 1833.[4] In Keble's sermon we can find the seeds of the turn from the Erastian paradigm to an apostolic paradigm on which to base the Church of England.

One of the questions Keble posed was: "What are the particular duties of sincere Christians whose lot is cast by divine providence in a time of such dire calamity?" His answers do not represent the kind of response one commonly finds to the ecclesiastical problems of our day, for they represent a humility and reserve that are rare in a culture consumed by social media and reality shows. His answers do, however, suggest a proper attitude towards the crises of Anglicanism we face in the twenty-first century.

Keble's first answer is to be constant in intercession, for this will secure all else that is necessary. Undoubtedly, many traditional Anglicans frequently pray for the current state of the Church, yet there remains a fair amount of anxiety, suggesting a certain prayerlessness. Keble's second answer is this: "The constant sense of God's presence and consequent certainty of final success, which can be kept up in no other way, would also prove an effectual bar against the more silent but hardly less malevolent feeling of disgust, almost amounting to misanthropy, which is apt to lay hold on sensitive minds when they see oppression and wrong triumphant on a large scale." Again, we would do well in our own time to follow Keble in seeking God's presence as the antidote to anxiety in times of crisis.

We might be more inclined to follow Keble in his third response: "Remonstrance calm, distinct, and persevering, in public and private, direct and indirect, by word, look, and demeanour, is the unequivocal duty of every Christian, according to his opportunities, when the Church landmarks are being broken down." Notice how remonstrance, or protest and complaint, comes only after prayer and seeking God's presence.

Remonstrance is also followed by resignation, Keble's next response:

> After all, the surest way to uphold or restore our endangered Church, will be for each of her anxious children, in his own place and station, to resign himself more thoroughly to his God and Saviour in those duties, public and private, which are not immediately affected by the emergencies of the moment: the daily and hourly duties, I mean, of piety, purity, charity, justice.

---

[2] The Assize Sermon is readily available online, for example, at anglicanhistory.org/keble/keble1.html.

[3] Around 1834, Keble actually favored disestablishment but backed off of the idea after a year or so. Thus, by 1835, one might say that Keble's position was one of "antidisestablishmentarianism."

[4] John Henry Newman, *Apologia Pro Vita Sua* (Toronto: J.M. Dent, 1921), 56.

Keble continues:

> As to those who, either by station or temper, feel themselves most deeply interested, they cannot be too careful in reminding themselves, that one chief danger, in times of change and excitement, arises from their tendency to engross the whole mind. Public concerns, ecclesiastical or civil, will prove indeed ruinous to those, who permit them to occupy all their care and thoughts, neglecting or undervaluing ordinary duties, more especially those of a devotional kind.

Lost among all the chatter and noise of contemporary discussions is Keble's advice that we not obsess over the current state of the Church or culture. Keble closes the Assize Sermon with a stirring, prophetic call to devote ourselves to the Church and take a more eschatological view of things:

> These cautions being duly observed, I do not see how any person can devote himself too entirely to the cause of the Apostolical Church in these realms. There may be, as far as he knows, but a very few to sympathize with him. He may have to wait long, and very likely pass out of this world before he see any abatement in the triumph of disorder and irreligion. But, if he be consistent, he possesses, to the utmost, the personal consolations of a good Christian: and as a true Churchman, he has that encouragement, which no other cause in the world can impart in the same degree:—he is calmly, soberly, demonstrably, SURE, that, sooner or later, HIS WILL BE THE WINNING SIDE, and that the victory will be complete, universal, eternal.

Such words still have the power both to reassure and to encourage Anglicans today.

The Oxford Movement also re-assessed the identity of the Church of England in terms of its lack of catholicity and is aptly named "The Catholic Revival."[5] According to Chadwick, the Oxford Movement met the greatest theological need of the day: "a revival or reconsideration of the corporate authority of the Church."[6] The Oxford Movement represented a restoration of the concept of the Church as a divine institution, and Keble himself promoted the idea that the Church was the extension of the Incarnation.

The Catholic turn of the Tractarians is also represented by the Tractarian emphasis on the church fathers. Many of the *Tracts for the Times* consist of catenae of quotations from the church fathers in support of various theological and historical points. This appreciation for patristics resulted in the publication of *The Library of the Fathers* and other endeavors, leading to a resurgence of interest in patristic literature.

Tradition was of great importance to the Tractarians. In his 1836 sermon "Primitive Tradition Recognized in Holy Scripture," Keble argues that there are three distinct fields of Christian knowledge that cannot be advanced satisfactorily without an appeal to tradition: "the system and arrangement of fundamental articles," "the interpretation of Scripture," and "discipline, formularies, and rites."[7] In spite of the great emphasis placed on tradition, no one maintained a clearer sense of the authority of the Bible than the

---

[5] The Catholic Revival had been preceded by the Evangelical Revival of the eighteenth century.

[6] Owen Chadwick, *The Mind of the Oxford Movement* (Stanford: Stanford University Press, 1967), 37.

[7] Available at anglicanhistory.org/keble/primitive.html.

Tractarians, and they were among the first to realize the dangers of the incipient theological liberalism of the early nineteenth century.

The essential Anglican character of the catholicity of the Oxford Movement is demonstrated by the allegiance they had to both the prayer book and the *Articles*. The *Tracts for the Times* frequently appeal to the prayer book, and an entire *Tract* (No. 86 by Isaac Williams) was dedicated to a discussion of "a superintending Providence in the preservation of the Prayer-book."

Many authors have written about the great influence for good the Oxford Movement had on the nineteenth-century English Church, including a revival of the catholicity of that Church. Stephen Neill summarized the effects of the Oxford Movement this way: "greater frequency of the celebration of the Holy Communion, liturgical experiment, more ornate ceremonial, the practice of 'sacramental confession,' the founding of theological colleges, the renewal of the monastic life, a stronger sense of continuity with the past ..."[8]

Other effects of the movement included effects on literature, hymns, and hymnals; works of scholarship that revived interest in the catholicism of the early Church; and a revival and interest in architecture and other arts.[9] In addition, a restoration of the daily nature of the Daily Office, more frequent pastoral visits, and greater observance of the Prayer Book Calendar and fast days were also the fruits of the Oxford Movement.

This re-assessment of the catholic nature of Anglicanism was mediated by the prayer book, through which an Anglican understanding of such standards was commonly filtered. For the Tractarians, the prayer book was the Anglican rule of life through which worship, theology, and spirituality were organically integrated.

Anglican identity today is in need of another re-evaluation. Keble's method was to reassert the essential Reformed Catholic character of Anglicanism through a return to the prayer book rule of life. While entities such as the ACNA represent a kind of reform and renewal movement in North American Anglicanism, reform and renewal can only take place when a relatively clear religious identity exists. A return to the catholic and apostolic roots of Anglicanism, as well as a vigorous reassertion of the Prayer Book rule of life, should be part of the much-needed re-evaluation of Anglican identity in our own time.

Anglican Identity Re-established

After identity is re-evaluated and even as the work of re-evaluation is in process, identity must be re-established. That is, we must live out the principles by which we are constituted and defined. John Keble helped to re-establish Anglican identity through his worship, holy living, pastoral dedication, and scholarship.

Keble and Worship

Martin Thornton believed that the "basis of both the Prayer Book and the *Regula* [the Rule of St. Benedict] is the fundamental, and biblical, threefold Rule of the Catholic Church:

---

[8] Stephen Neill, *Anglicanism*, 4th ed. (London: Mowbray, 1977), 258.
[9] S. L. Ollard, *A Short History of the Oxford Movement* (London: A. R. Mowbray, 1915), 145–188.

Office-Eucharist-personal devotion."[10] This threefold Rule is crucial to Thornton's life project of establishing an Anglican ascetical system founded upon traditional Anglican spirituality derived from Benedict and Augustine and compatible with the spirit of the twentieth century.

What was the state of the Christian religion in nineteenth-century England? Wickham Legg comments that weekly or even monthly communion was often not possible due to the apathy of the laity and that the minimum frequency expected was three times a year.[11] On Easter Day, 1800, there were only six communicants in St. Paul's Cathedral.[12]

Wickham Legg's assessment of the Daily Office was not a flattering one, either. "In 1824, the daily services had fallen almost as low as they could without being extinct. Only nine parish churches in London and Westminster had preserved them."[13]

Keble embodied Thornton's three-fold rule at his rural parish of Hursley. He regarded the Eucharist as an extension of the Incarnation: "Why or how should it be otherwise in respect of that which divines have truly called 'the extension of the Incarnation,'—the participation of the Incarnate One by His true members, in and through the spiritual eating and drinking of His present Body and Blood?"[14] As a result of his high view of the sacraments, Keble restored weekly Holy Communion to Hursley, which became a model for other parishes.

Keble and his brother, Thomas, were among the first to restore the Daily Office as well. J. T. Coleridge, Keble's first biographer, recorded that "The Daily Services he prized much for others; for himself they were refreshment and delight, never palling; he never failed to attend when at home unless absolutely prevented, and if he could only be at part of the service he went to that."[15] Coleridge later explains that Keble "thought that much knowledge of the Bible was acquired by attendance at Daily Service, and once when it was proposed to keep the school-children from church on week-days in order that they might have more time for preparation before an examination, he said that their time in church might be made a great means of preparing them for examination in Holy Scripture."[16]

It's clear from a study of Keble's life that he not only devoted himself to the Holy Communion and Daily Office but also to much private devotion. His love of the Bible came through in all that he did, including the publication of a translation of the Psalter into English verse and his poetic meditations on the Bible found in *The Christian Year*.

The world has moved on past Keble, and yet the three-fold Rule remains essential to Anglican worship and piety. Largely as a result of the Oxford Movement, weekly

---

[10] Martin Thornton, *English Spirituality* (London: SPCK, 1963), 258.

[11] J. Wickham Legg, *English Church Life from the Restoration to the Tractarian Movement* (London: Longmans, Green, and Co., 1914), 21–37.

[12] Horton Davies, *Worship and Theology in England: From Watts and Wesley to Maurice, 1690–1850* (Grand Rapids, MI: Eerdmans, 1961), 58, quoting the Hibbert Journal.

[13] Legg, *English Church Life*, 90.

[14] John Keble, *Eucharistical Adoration*, Chapter 1, Section 8, accessed March 9, 2023, anglicanhistory.org/keble/adoration/chapter1.html.

[15] J. T. Coleridge, *A Memoir of the Rev. John Keble*, 3rd ed. (Oxford: Parker, 1870), 578.

[16] Coleridge, *Memoir*, 604–605.

communion has become the norm in North American Anglicanism. The Daily Office, however, is still woefully neglected. Private devotions exist among Anglicans, but these are not always seen as bearing much relationship to the prayer book and its three-fold Rule.

Keble's Holiness

Holiness is a much-neglected virtue among contemporary Christians, but it was one of the keynotes of Keble's life and, consequently, the Oxford Movement. As for Keble himself, the holiness of his character was axiomatic to almost all. Typical of the many nineteenth-century praises of Keble is this entry in a biographical dictionary: "Keble was one of the most saintly and unselfish men who ever adorned the Church of England and, though personally shy and retiring, exercised a vast spiritual influence upon his generation."[17] It was Keble who coined the word *ethos* in the modern sense: the thought that holiness and being moral were more important than natural gifts and that holiness led to the right use of reason.

Keble's Pastoral Dedication

Once again, we discover that John Keble is a wonderful model of pastoral dedication. One area where Keble's diligence was inspirational was in the religious education of his parish. He diligently catechized his parish's children, both in Sunday school and in the local boys' school. When he had finished catechizing, he lectured from the pulpit on what had been the subject of his questioning. "He made a point at all times of the children having their Bibles in church, and following the Lessons; and for some years it was his *daily* custom to call up some of them after the service, and question them for a few minutes in the two chapters which had been read. No wonder the Hursley children had more than the usual knowledge of the Scriptures."[18]

Keble spent a year preparing his confirmands. "The knowledge of the Bible possessed by his village children long before their preparation for Confirmation began, and the way in which it was interwoven in their minds with the Creeds and Catechism, was something very uncommon indeed."[19] Keble's test of the success at which a good educator should aim was this: "Make a few saints."[20] His concept was always to consider "tuition as a species of pastoral care."[21]

Keble set aside every morning at 9:00 to remember those who had been brought into spiritual relation to himself. He also believed that confession was very important in dealing with the spiritual health of parishioners. Although he was not as strict as Pusey or Froude when it came to confession, he felt that as Communion became more frequent, the discipline of confession was more necessary. Likewise, Keble showed a firm but moderate view of fasting compared to others of the Tractarians.

---

[17] John W. Cousin, "John Keble," in *A Short Biographical Dictionary of English Literature* (London: Dent, 1910), 220.

[18] Coleridge, *Memoir*, 573.

[19] Ibid., 609.

[20] John Keble, "The Strength of Christ's Little Ones: A Sermon Preached at Coggeshall, on September 6, 1849," Project Canterbury, anglicanhistory.org/keble/coggeshall1849.html.

[21] Coleridge, *Memoir*, 73.

It would be hard to find a more faithful shepherd of the soul when it came to pastoral visitation. His motto was "Ourselves your servants for Jesus' sake," and "he seemed to realize so vividly that each of his parishioners was his own special charge, that no duties elsewhere, or public affairs, were allowed to interfere with a watchful and anxious care for them, only to be compared to that which a father feels for his children."[22] Keble's fellow Tractarian, Pusey, provides another window into Keble's pastoral heart: "What a picture it gives one to see dear Keble finding his way with a lantern through the snow to his little church at 5:30 on a winter morning to say the Litany for the Church 'in its present distress'; or again, as an American saw him, sweeping the snow off the path in the churchyard for his parishioners, that they might come with dry feet to the early Communion."[23]

Keble loved administering the Holy Communion: "After giving Bread, he used to become so absorbed in prayer for the sick person, that more than once, when no one was present who would remind him, he entirely forgot to give the Chalice, and after long prayer went on with the rest of the service."[24] He exhorted those he counseled and taught "to take all from our Lord as personally present. 'Christ is all and in all,' would best sum up his teaching both in public and in private.'"[25]

Keble's pastor's heart was revealed especially in the Sacrament of Baptism.

> [O]f all of his pastoral duties the one which seems to have given him the greatest joy and satisfaction was the administration of baptism.... No one seems to have thought to describe Keble in the act of celebrating Holy Communion but almost everyone who has left any account of him talks of him in connection with baptism, 'his loving care and intense earnestness,' 'the kiss of peace' which he always gave the child before handing it back to the godparent, the way in which, when the actual baptism was over 'he seemed loath to part with the child and there was a pause of a minute or two.[26]

Battiscombe's summary is typical of the praise others gave Keble for his pastoral fidelity and his humility and reserve regarding his labors: "During the next thirty years, he was to work and pray and teach and visit so effectively that in the end, Hursley came to be regarded as a model parish by everyone except its Vicar, who continued to agonise over its shortcomings until the very end of his life."[27]

Keble's Scholarship

Keble's scholarship is the fourth and final way he helped to re-establish the Catholic identity of Anglicanism in the nineteenth-century Church of England. The Oxford Movement was, of course, a scholarly endeavor, although not merely an academic one. Some of the topics covered by the *Tracts for the Times* included the Catholic Church,

---

[22] Coleridge, *Memoir*, 602.

[23] J. O. Johnson and W. C. E. Newbolt, eds., *Spiritual Letters of Edward Bouverie Pusey* (London: Longmans, Green, and Co., 1989), 288–289.

[24] Coleridge, *Memoir*, 608.

[25] Ibid., 610.

[26] Georgina Battiscombe, *John Keble: A Study in Limitations* (London: Constable, 1963), 292.

[27] Ibid., 174.

alterations in the liturgy, the ancient liturgies, apostolic succession, episcopacy, primitive practice, and reprints of Anglican Divines.

Keble's scholarship extended well beyond his founding role in the *Tracts*. Largely on the basis of the enormous success of *The Christian Year*, he served as Professor of Poetry at Oxford from 1831–1841. He had a role in the patristic scholarship of the Oxford Movement, which included the Library of the Fathers, a series promoting knowledge of the Church Fathers, and the Anglo-Catholic Library, a series promoting Anglican divines such as Andrewes, Beveridge, Bull, Laud, Pearson, and others. Keble's 1836 edition of Hooker's *Laws* is still the standard edition, almost two hundred years after its first publication.

One of the necessary components of a catholic revival of Anglicanism in our day will be encouraging scholars who are also fervent churchmen. A relatively large number of traditional Anglicans are pursuing an intellectual revival of classic Anglicanism. We must do all we can to support such pursuits, especially if they are done under the auspices of the Church.

One of the secrets of the Oxford Movement was the power that emanated from the close personal ties of the Oxford men, many of whom were close personal friends in close geographical proximity. A certain divine synergy ensued from the common, focused labors of these men. While such geographical proximity is not possible in the contemporary world, technological developments in communication make a close network of like-minded scholars and churchmen possible again.

Lost in modern calculations of efficiency and our lust for numbers is the godly effect of a truly holy priest.

Anglican Identity Renewed

After Anglican identity has been re-evaluated and re-established, it must also be renewed. When the Tractarians determined that the Church of England needed to be established upon a more catholic and apostolic basis, they had to find or develop resources to renew that catholic and apostolic identity that lay fallow to some degree within Anglicanism. While the Oxford Movement found many vehicles for renewing Anglican identity, few had a greater effect in producing a catholic revival in the Church of England and reinvigorating her than Keble's book of poetry, *The Christian Year*. This would not have been news to nineteenth-century Englishmen, but it is likely to meet with surprise or resistance from contemporary students of Anglicanism.

The Christian Year is the cornerstone of Keble's legacy, the unexpected source for much of the Oxford Movement and its influence, and a seminal devotional work that powerfully brought together many factors conducive to a religious revival in nineteenth-century England. The work's full title, which Keble published in 1827, is *The Christian Year: Thoughts in Verse for the Sundays and Holydays throughout the Year*. The volume begins with a "Morning" and "Evening" hymn, corresponding to Morning and Evening Prayer services, followed by a poem for every week in the Church year. These are followed by poems for the various saints' days, Holy Communion, Holy Baptism, and the occasional services. In 1828 poems for the state services were added as well.

When Keble published the work in 1827, he added to it his Advertisement,[28] in which he admirably sets out his aims: "The object of the present publication will be attained, if any person find assistance from it in bringing his own thoughts and feelings into more entire unison with those recommended and exemplified in the Prayer Book." Keble makes clear that his goal in publishing his poetry was to have his readers use *The Christian Year* as a companion to the prayer book. Keble also expected that his poetry, along with the prayer book, would provide "a sober standard of feeling in matters of practical religion." The liturgy, he believed, disciplined the tempers which needed disciplining in such an age of excitement.

There is, therefore, a dual origin and dual purpose of *The Christian Year*. The original poetic impulse for the poetry came from Keble's desire to express himself as an individual soul addressing His God, often out of a need for comfort. This original source for the poetry was then fitted for use as an Anglican devotional manual which had specific reference to the prayer book. This dual origin and purpose of the poetry are highly significant for explaining the astounding success of the poetry in the nineteenth century and its continuing value.

A work of High Church devotional poetry was not expected to succeed at a time when interest in poetry was beginning to wane, and yet as many as one million copies of *The Christian Year* were sold in the nineteenth century.[29]

Christians from many different denominations read *The Christian Year*, and one writer said that the spiritual life and feeling of Keble's poetry "exist in Christian hearts, whether reared under Episcopalian, Presbyterian, or Nonconformist influences."[30] A great number of major figures in the nineteenth century had read *The Christian Year*, and many people had virtually memorized it. Thomas Carlyle, Florence Nightingale (who sent a trunk-load of the volume to the Crimean War), Christina Rossetti, Oscar Wilde, Thomas Hardy, William Gladstone, and many others have left testimony to having read it.

Many have also left a testimony to the spiritual effect of *The Christian Year*, both on the Church as a whole and on individuals. One of many such testimonies reads:

> Without being in any way didactic and dogmatic, these hymns none the less furthered High Church ideas more effectively than many sermons and controversies. Inspired by the author's doctrines with regard to the dignity and authority of the Church, the seriousness of matters of belief, the mysteries of Faith, the sanctity of worship, the grace of the Sacraments, and the Communion of Saints, they awakened a piety which implied these doctrines or led up to them; they created, almost without their readers suspecting it, and, as a consequence, without rousing their distrust, a state of mind which paved the way for a return to a less incomplete and more living Christianity. The sadness with which the state of religion was often deplored in the hymns tended to make people feel the necessity

---

[28] Available at ccel.org/ccel/keble/year/year.ii.html.

[29] This is my own estimate, based on a variety of sources.

[30] J. S. Rowntree, "Notes on the Christian Year," *Friends' Quarterly Examiner* 17/46 (1883): 292.

of such a transformation, and throughout one caught glimpses of the ideal, too long forgotten, to which the poet so ardently desired to see his Church return.[31]

In 1869, just three years after Keble's death, A. P. Stanley concluded that *The Christian Year* had become nothing less than a formulary of the Church of England. He continued by saying,

> The "Christian Year" has taken its place—certainly for this generation—next to the Authorised Version and the Prayer-Book, far above the Homilies and the Articles. For one who would enforce an argument or defend a text by quoting the Eleventh Article or the Homily on Charity, there are a hundred who would appeal to the "Christian Year."[32]

The organization of the poetry, based on the Church year, lent itself to being read week by week along with the propers for the week from the prayer book. Many read it before church on Sunday, and many others read it in their time of family worship, which was much more common in the nineteenth century. It brought family devotions under the prayer book system, united the objective and subjective sides of religion, and was shared widely by the church community.

But just how did *The Christian Year* go about "making the old new"? The first means by which Keble's poetry made the old new was through its symbiotic relationship with prayer book spirituality, for the *Book of Common Prayer* is essentially the rule of life for Anglicans that yields the fruit of a common life and community and a common reading and meditations. Price was convinced that *The Christian Year* produced an extraordinary effect on the nineteenth-century Church by relying on the prayer book and its sacramental system:

> It was not by teaching a new truth, but by the poet's own art of revealing that Keble helped people to recognize the Church as a peculiar and special means of grace. For two and a half centuries the Church had used the same formularies of prayer, worship, and instruction, and they ... were bound to produce a special and distinct type of life and feeling.... The type, then, was possessed, but people knew not whence it came. What Keble did was to account to us what we were.[33]

The Christian Year also helped make the old new by preparing the way for the catholic revival. According to *The Weekly Register and Catholic Standard* in 1866, "There was probably no work which did so much in preparing the way for the Oxford movement.... 'The Christian Year' was freely admitted into every Church of England family, and had irrevocably formed numerous minds, before any one began to be afraid of the name of its author."[34] Those affected by the Oxford Movement as a whole were confined mainly to the parochial clergy and those more academically minded: by contrast, *The Christian Year* seemed to appeal to virtually every segment of the literate population.

---

[31] Paul Thureau-Dangin, *The English Catholic Revival in the Nineteenth Century* (London: Simpkin, Marshall, Hamilton, Kent, 1914), 1:14.

[32] Arthur Penrhyn Stanley, *Essay Chiefly on Questions of Church and State* (London: John Murray, 1870), 594.

[33] Clement Price, *Leading Ideas of Keble's Christian Year* (Young, 1890; London: SPCK, 1900), 34.k[

[34] *The Weekly Register and Catholic Standard* (7 April 1866): 219.

Rogers's testimony is one of the most forceful: "The 'Christian Year' did more to diffuse the spirit of the Puseyite movement than all the elaborate subtleties of the *Tracts*. It affected men unconsciously to themselves, and created a sentiment more powerful than any mere logical conviction."[35] Temple, writing in 1875 at a time close to the height of Keble's influence, is certain about the influence *The Christian Year* had on reviving Prayer Book religion and how he did it:

> But it was Keble's peculiar fortune to be the first to rescue the *Prayer Book* and the Church's Services from the charge of Formalism under which they lay, to prove their powers of adaptation to modern wants, to bring to light the undercurrent of devotion and sympathetic helpfulness which pervades them—so that we, coming a little later in the day, have entered upon a new era in Church life. And this result, under God, is mainly due to the little volume we are considering.[36]

Thus, for many, *The Christian Year* pointed to the prayer book as a complete system of religion and life in the Church, and one that led to a deeper or renewed Christian life.

Temple continues by saying, "This was to be Keble's achievement: to blend High Anglicanism and romantic sentiment in a piety reserved and restrained, yet the more intense for being half-repressed."[37] He also adds: "the old dry forms of the Prayer Book were to be invested with the new romantic sense of awe, and mystery and wonder, with an exalted moral sentiment and love of nature, and with a half-hidden ardour in which the wildness of naked feeling was refined and chastened and subdued."[38]

A list of ways in which the Oxford Movement, and *The Christian Year* in particular, made the Church of England new again as it revitalized the Catholic aspect of Anglicanism would have to include the following:

1. promoted a higher view of the Church
2. restored catholic principles
3. inspired the external glory of the Church
4. promoted a higher view of worship and church services
5. promoted the church year
6. offered a complete spirituality based on the Prayer Book as a rule of life
7. demonstrated that the Prayer Book Anglicanism was adaptable to changes in culture
8. revived a sacramental worldview
9. had a unifying effect (The Christian Year, but not the Oxford Movement)

Making the Old New Today

What can Keble teach us about how to make the old new today? This is always a pressing question for Anglicans since the nature of Anglicanism as Reformed Catholicism

---

[35] J. Guinness Rogers, *The Church Systems of England in the Nineteenth Century* (London: Hodder & Stoughton, 1881), 203.

[36] William Temple, *John Keble: A Memoir*, preface to *The Christian Year* (New York: H.M. Caldwell, n.d.), xxix.

[37] Ibid., xvi.

[38] Ibid.

strongly suggests that there is a fundamental essence (the noun *Catholic*) that must periodically be renewed (the adjective *Reformed*).

A good starting point would be to examine what resources Keble tapped into through *The Christian Year* that enabled him to facilitate the catholic revival. These resources included the prayer book spirituality that was ebbing in Keble's day but which remained the backbone of Anglican life; the latent catholic ideas expressed by the prayer book and implicit in Anglican identity; dissatisfaction with the Church; a crisis point in society; the flourishing of Romantic poetry and feeling and the existence of a poetic culture; a desire for mystery, awe, and reverence; the English love of nature; and, finally, people's knowledge of the Bible.

Some of these resources are not necessarily abundant in our context. While the prayer book and its spirituality are still the bedrock of Anglican life, it must be taught, expressed, and lived more intentionally and even creatively. We do not enjoy the geographical proximity of Keble's day, nor the relatively unified culture he inhabited, and we are most certainly not a poetic age and culture!

Difficult as it may be to believe, there is still a love of the Bible among many people in the United States. Anglicans have an opportunity to reach our culture if they recover their historic ability to interpret narrative, comprehend poetic and sacramental language, and find the Christological import of each Bible passage. Dissatisfaction with the Church is still widespread, and there is a feeling that we have reached a crisis point in society. Many are discovering that, in the wake of a shallow fundamentalism and Evangelicalism, a desire for mystery, awe, and reverence is re-emerging in this post-modern world. The possibility of understanding the world as sacrament has also re-emerged, even if it is often expressed in rather pagan ways. Finally, in a world whose situation is primarily one of broken relationships, homelessness, and meaninglessness, a desire for genuine community lies deep in many.

All of this suggests aspects of a strategy for promoting a catholic revival in our day. We traditional Anglicans often are not very creative folk, and a simple return to the polemics of the *Tracts for the Times* or the poetry of *The Christian Year* is not possible. The importance of a close-knit group of like-minded scholars and pastors should not be underestimated, and, as in Keble's day, there is a great need for visionary writers and thinkers. We can and must, however, use the mass media and technologies today, which are our equivalent of both the *Tracts* and the geographical proximity that were central to the success of the Oxford Movement. We must inspire, train, and captivate the younger generation. Chadwick reminds us that "Keble collected round him pupils—Isaac Williams, Robert Wilberforce, Hurrell Froude—and won their allegiance by personal stature.... In this way, Keble helped form the moral ideal of the movement, more by his person than by his thought."[39]

Finally, we must tap into the great interest in "spirituality" at the very time the Church appears unable to feed this spiritual hunger. We need a rule of life for the twenty-first century. For Anglicans, this should necessarily be established upon the prayer book, and yet it must be applied thoughtfully and creatively as we understand the times. There is no Church of England to unite and enforce such a Rule. We have lost our way, and we

---

[39] Chadwick, *The Mind of the Oxford Movement*, 34.

must consider that we are in a deregulated religious economy (in the language of the sociology of religion). Yet we must set our hearts and hands to this work.

Cranmer adapted the monastic offices and Roman Catholic system for sixteenth-century England in the state-sponsored Church of England. We need to build upon this but also find a way to inculturate it into American life in the twenty-first century.

As Keble discovered, it was not so much that Anglicanism was broken but that, discerning its Catholic heritage, it needed to be reformed and revitalized. Your job and mine, therefore, is "to make the old new," as Keble did in his day.

Chapter 26

"Because we would be penitents": Edward Bouverie Pusey (1800–1882) and the Patristic Doctrine of Repentance

The Rev. Ben Jefferies

Edward Bouverie Pusey published an enormous quantity of writing during the course of his lifetime. He had a published work in print and for sale during nearly every year between 1830 and his death in 1882. His published works include almost every genre of theological writing: sermons (given in the university and in parishes), translations, letters, disputes, histories, and commentaries; all running into several editions.[1] Throughout this great body of work, there is a theme that recurs again and again—a theme that everywhere courses through subjects, prefaces, concluding words—a leitmotif of his entire oeuvre. It is not that which he is chiefly remembered for as being the namesake of the Oxford Movement after Newman's succession—viz., a high and devout view of the Sacraments (though that occurs with great frequency as well). Nor is it a mystical vision of our real union with Christ Jesus, although that breaks through plenty. No, the dominant practical theme that holds all of Pusey's work together as a received whole is *repentance*.[2]

I shall demonstrate that this is the case through significant examples, showing along the way the central features of Pusey's doctrine of repentance, and gathering them up in synopsis at the end, as well as making a few suggestions about his sources for this doctrine along the way.

Examples of the Central Role of Repentance in Pusey's Writings

In 1828, the year when he had become professor of Hebrew at Oriel (Oxford) and had also been ordained priest, Pusey published his first book-length work. It contained his analysis of the causes of the lamentable state of German theology. It was a meaningful

---

[1] It is worth remembering that Pusey personally reviewed the printer's proofs for corrections, and often edited and added new prefatory material to later editions. He was integrally involved in a lifetime of publishing. A full bibliography of his published work occurs as an appendix to volume 4 of Liddon's biography: Heny Parry Liddon, *Life of Edward Bouverie Pusey*, 4 vols. (London: Longmans, 1894).

[2] I am aware that I appear to be opposing a preeminent living Pusey scholar, Dr. Toby Karlowicz, in this assertion. Karlowicz writes, "The heart of Pusey's theology is not in his denunciations of sin ... the true heart of Pusey's theology is the exceeding depth of God's love for humanity": *The Sacramental Vision of Edward Pusey* (Edinburgh: T&T Clark, 2021), 117. I happily grant that at the level of logical priority, this is true. Pusey's doctrine of the love of God is *logically* prior to the Christian practice of repentance. But Pusey does not always speak of God's love, and when he *does* in the same breath he always speaks of the need of repentance. Pusey is always practical, and repentance is the practical exhortation by which the sinner might get to experience the love of God. My intention is to meet Dr. Karlowicz's analysis of the logical structure of Pusey's thought with an analysis of what occupies his attention and exhortation with the greatest frequency.

but minor academic publication, generating little interest outside of specialist circles.[3] Six years later, in January 1834, having found his feet as a husband, father, professor, and also as a theologian, Pusey published his first practical theological work, a tract entitled, "Thoughts on the Benefits of the System of Fasting Enjoined by Our Church" as the 18th issue of the lately-launched *Tracts for the Times*.[4] Pusey attached his initials to the tract (which was not customary for the first 17) in order to distinguish himself as *not* party to the 'Authors of the Tracts'[5] It is a delightful irony that the giving of his initials gave a personal name to the otherwise anonymous authors, and at once the movement got dubbed 'Puseyite'. Tract 18 is a bracing and sobering vision of the fundamental and necessary role of fasting in the life of the Christian. The animating argument is summed up in the concluding paragraph,

> Regular and stated Fasts formed a part of the Discipline by which, during almost the whole period since the Christian Church has been founded, all her real sons, in every climate, nation, and language, have subdued the flesh to the spirit, and brought both body and mind into a willing obedience to the Law of GOD.[6] They thought this Discipline necessary *as an expression and instrument of repentance*, as a memorial of their SAVIOUR, to "refrain their souls and keep them low," to teach them to "trust in the LORD," and seek communion with Him.[7]

Thus the life-theme of Repentance is introduced. Tract 18 was such strong brew that it caused quite a stir and a number of letters in the *British Magazine*, etc., to which Pusey replied with a doubling-down in the form of Tract 66 which was titled as a supplement to Tract 18.[8] It was the next set of tracts, however, that would reveal the full scope of Pusey's understanding of repentance, and would catapult Pusey into infamy within the Church of England. Across the country he was recognized as an intellectual giant; a giant that many felt they needed to oppose.[9]

---

[3] And a debate of letters between himself and the Rev. H. J. Rose on where exactly the tail of the donkey should be pinned.

[4] Begun in September 1833.

[5] "'Oh, no,' said Pusey, 'I will not be one of you!' This was said in a playful manner; and before we parted Newman said, 'Suppose you let us have that letter of yours which you intend writing, and attach your name or signature to it. You would then not be mixed up with us, nor in any way responsible for the Tracts!' 'Well,' Pusey said at last,' if you will let me do that, I will.'" Recorded in Isaac Williams's *Autobiography*, quoted in Liddon, *Life*, 1:275–297 (ch. 12).

[6] The capitalizing of the name(s) of God was a typographical gesture of reverence utilized by all the Tractarians.

[7] Tract 18, written Dec 21, 1833; published in early 1834 (emphasis mine), anglicanhistory.org/tracts/tract18.html.

[8] Published in April 1835.

[9] Recalling Newman's assessment in his *Apologia pro Vita Sua*, "I had known [Pusey] well since 1827–1828, and had felt for him an enthusiastic admiration. I used to call him ὁ μέγας. His great learning, his immense diligence, his scholar-like mind, his simple devotion to the cause of religion, overcame me; and great of course was my joy, when in the last days of 1833 he showed a disposition to make common cause with us. His Tract on Fasting appeared as one of the series with the date of December 21. He was not, however, I think, fully associated in the Movement till 1835 and 1836, when he published his Tract on Baptism."

Tracts 67, 68, and 69 were all written by Pusey in the fall of 1835, and their publication launched a major theological furor in the Church of England. They each are titled "Scriptural Views of Holy Baptism," a work divided into Three Parts. Part One (Tract 67) asserts the teaching of Baptismal regeneration, as laid out in the Scriptures, Parts Two and Three attend down-stream to connected doctrine and practice.[10] It was Part Two (Tract 68) in particular which agitated so many, as it dealt with the deduction: If all actual sins are washed away in Baptism, what about actual sins committed willfully after Baptism? Pusey synthesizes the teaching of the church fathers by saying that there is no "second baptism" and that forgiveness for any grave sin after baptism may only be obtained by a deep and lengthy penitence, indeed, one that lasts for the rest of one's life. Such an answer shocked vast swaths of the clergy who believed it to be *prima facie* incompatible with the teaching of the Church of England. As Liddon summarizes, "The tract on Baptism at once ... placed Pusey before the world as a leader of the Oxford Movement, and ... occasioned some characteristic expressions of hostile opinion."[11]

In his preface to a second printing of the *Tracts*, Pusey offers an *apologia* for Tract 68. It is worth quoting at length, as it surveys the whole terrain of the doctrine which Pusey would spend the rest of his life articulating in different ways.

> On one point, I fear that the doctrines of the ancient Church are so distinct from modern ultra-Protestant theology on the one hand, (as also) from the Romanist on the other, that the view, which I have exhibited, of the character of grievous sin after Baptism may cause perplexity.

Note, the authoritative appeal to antiquity.

> It cannot be otherwise; and I pray only that it may be healthful. For our modern system, founded as it is on the virtual rejection of Baptism as a Sacrament, confounds the distinction of grievous sin before and after Baptism, and applies to repentance, after falling from Baptismal grace, all the promises which, in Scripture, are pledged, not as the fruit of repentance simply, but as God's free gift in Baptism.

Note the comment that, while still 15 years antecedent to Gorham, the sixteenth century Anglican view of Baptism "as a sacrament" was in deep decay:

> Yet our reformers thought differently; for had their theology been like ours, there had been no occasion for an article on "Sin after Baptism" (Art. 16), or for denying that "every such sin is sin against the Holy Ghost, and unpardonable." It had been[12] a matter of course. The possibility or efficacy of such repentance I have not denied; God forbid: but that such repentance is likely, especially after a relapse, or that men, who have fallen, can be as assured of the adequacy of their repentance, as they might have been of God's free grace in Baptism, daily experience, as well as the probable meaning of Scripture, forbid us to hope.

---

[10] In 1839 Pusey revised Tract 67 into a second edition. It went from a 49-page tract to a 400-page monograph. This second, enlarged edition entirely assumed the title of *Scriptural Views of Holy Baptism* and Tracts 68 and 69, as written artefacts, faded away into history. The text of them is not to be found even on such comprehensive online collections as that of anglicanhistory.org.

[11] Liddon, *Life*, 1:343–358 (ch. 15).

[12] i.e., "would have been."

To antiquity Pusey adds the testimony of experience:

> Had repentance been so easy a thing, as men would persuade themselves, how is it that there are so very many hardened sinners, who never apparently repent; so many, of whose repentance one can hardly hope that it is real; so many half penitents? Again, the pardon in Baptism is free, full, instantaneous, universal, without any service on our part: the pardon on repentance for those who have forfeited their Baptismal pardon is slow, partial, gradual, as is the repentance itself, to be humbly waited for, and to be wrought out through that penitence: were the repentance at once perfect, so, doubtless, would the pardon be; but it is part of the disease, entailed by grievous sin, that men can but slowly repent; they have disabled themselves from applying completely their only cure: the anguish of repentance, in its early stages, is often the sharpest; it is generally long afterwards that it is in any real degree purified and deepened; and therefore the ancient Church diligently noted out of the Old Testament the means whereby repentance might be heightened and secured, as humiliation, voluntary affliction, prayer, self-denying bountifulness, and the like.

In this outrageously long sentence (characteristic of Pusey's early work, prior to the mid-1840s), we note a couple of things: The framing of the work of repentance as a long one, toward which the earnest Christian strives. Penitence is an aspiration. Additionally, for the buttresses of his case he points to the *Old Testament* which is non-coincidentally his area of study. Though, note, not as interpreted by the ascendant higher-critical school of his day, but as "the ancient Church diligently noted out."

> Again, the penitent must regard himself, not merely as a novice, but as a very weak one: he has already cast away the armour wherewith he was clad; he is beginning an irksome, distasteful course, and having already failed, it becomes him not to be impatient of suspense, or too confident in his new steadfastness, but to be content to wear "doubt's galling chain",[13] until God shall see it healthful for him gradually to be relieved. The fears, and anxiety, whereof he ignorantly complains, and would rid himself by the one or the other system of theology, is a most important, perhaps an essential condition of his cure, otherwise God would not have sent troubles, often so intolerable.

Here we see an interpretation of the misery-causing troubles of life, as an assistance in growing in lowly penitence, and an honest admission that it is an "irksome" task to come from post-baptismal sin to post-baptismal repentance.

> Man desires to have, under any circumstances, certainty of salvation through Christ: to those who have fallen, God holds out only a "light in a dark place," sufficient for them to see their path, but not bright or cheering as they would have it: and so, in different ways, man would forestall the sentence of his Judge; the Romanist by the *Sacrament* of penance: a modern class of divines by the appropriation of the merits and righteousness of our Blessed Redeemer: the Methodists by sensible experience.

---

[13] A quotation from Keble's *Christian Year.*

This is a deft and dazzling interpretation of the theological milieu into which Pusey recognizes he is speaking. He sees man's fleshly anxiety for "certainty of salvation" as the common motivator for the creation of all alternate theological systems, including the Roman Catholic. The Continental Protestant tradition locates assurance of forgiveness in the self-knowledge that one has saving faith.[14] The Methodists rely either on the experience of having been forgiven as the ground of their assurance, or on simply the belief that they *are* saved.[15] The Roman Catholic tradition has hyperbolized the efficacy of the Keys in Absolution, rendering it comparable to a "second baptism" and an adjudicated clean slate.

> Our own [Anglican Church] with the ancient Church, preserves a reverent silence, not cutting off hope, and yet not nurturing an untimely confidence, or a presumptuous security ... in proportion to his sin, must be his repentance. Only of this he may be sure, that man always undervalues his sin, and overvalues his repentance; and on this account also, theories, which smooth or shorten the path of repentance, are so peculiarly dangerous.[16]

And thus, the challenge is leveled: That Anglicans must have—in light of the Biblical and Formulary teaching of Baptismal Regeneration—a patristic view of repentance, that comports neither with Roman Catholicism or the various other forms of Protestantism.

The next major theological work that Pusey produced was his translation of St. Augustine's *Confessions*, a work concerning penitence if there ever was one. And the following year (1839) amidst his grief over the death of his wife Maria, he preached one of his heaviest sermons "The Day of Judgment" which, like Tract 68, described in no uncertain terms the necessity of lifelong repentance:

> And for us, the larger portion of whose account is already there, labour we the more, that what is already there against us, may be at the last blotted out; what yet remains, may be more according to His will. For all which yet remains, be diligent; for all the past, repent; for all you must be brought to judgment, for *all repent*. Watch over *all* your acts, thoughts, deeds, as having to give account for *all*; repent day by day of "*all* the sins, negligences, and ignorances" of *all* your past lives; bring them all before Him, at least when you repeat His Son's own words, "Forgive us our

---

[14] Pusey explains his meaning here more carefully in his theologically ultra-precise sermon, "Justification" given in 1853: "Again, such propositions as 'no one is truly justified save he who believes that he is justified'... are only Lutheran statements which the framers of our Articles carefully excluded." He gives in a footnote the following comment: "This definition of justifying faith occurs six times in the Confession of Augsburg. Art. 4, on Justification, 'They teach, that men cannot be justified before God by their own strength, merits or works, but that they are justified freely for the sake of (propter) Christ by faith, *when they believe that they are received into grace* ... [etc.]'"

[15] Which Pusey does not demur to call a "heresy"; a claim he would later defend and more definitely articulate in published notes ("Note F") to his sermon *Patience and Confidence the Strength of the Church*" (1838) describing the Methodist view of repentance by citing their own words, "Believe that you will be saved, and you will be saved," and with the addition that the Methodists generally urge and teach that to continue to feel or be penitent actually *undermines* the claim of real salvation.

[16] Preface, *Tracts for the Times no. 67, 68, 69: Scriptural Views of Holy Baptism* (London: Gilbert & Rivington, 1836), xiv.

trespasses;" pray Him for His Son's sake to forgive them all, to blot out all; do "works meet for repentance;" acts of restitution; acts of humiliation; acts of penitence, acts especially of self-denying charity, whereby Scripture saith, "iniquity is purged away:" and though you must see your sins once again read out of that book at the judgment-day, they will not be your condemnation.[17]

The quality of this repentance in order to be effective unto forgiveness is described in the gravest of terms, e.g.:

Of what use then will it be, my brethren, what we have persuaded ourselves in this life; what, to have counted that all will be well with us, to the very hour of death, when after death, there is yet the judgment? Rather how far better to have endured all the heaviness of doubt and fear and dread of hell up to the very moment of death, if God should in any case even until then send no full relief, and thereby to deepen our repentance and cries for mercy, than with the rich man to awake in hell in torments![18]

Pusey had become sufficiently aware at this point of how difficult his teaching was in the ears of most of his colleagues, and additionally some who had heard the sermon "live" were already spreading misinformation about its content. It was therefore published with an explanatory preface in which Pusey reveals the discernment and motivation for his sermon. Unlike his preface to his Tracts, Pusey makes an effort to show the precedent for similar teaching as his own from within the Anglican fold. He quotes from Jeremy Taylor, Dean Jackson, Lancelot Andrewes, and Bishop Wilson. He particularly highlights Andrewes, citing at length the most-sobering sentiments from the *Preces Privatae*[19] that in Pusey's eyes exemplify the true and necessary penitence that all Christians who have sinned in any way seriously since their baptisms should have.

How fearful is Thy Judgment, Lord! When the thrones are set, the Angels stand by, men are brought in, the books are opened, deeds sifted, the thoughts, the secret things of darkness, brought to light! What judgment will be passed upon me! Who shall extinguish my flame? unless Thou pitiest me. Lord, as Thou art merciful to man, grant me tears, grant me great streams of tears, grant them me to-day. For then will the Judge be without appeal, the Judgment-seat terrible, excuse unavailing, proofs unanswerable, punishment inexorable, hell unending, the Angels unpitying, the pit opening its mouth, the stream of fire sweeping away, fire unquenchable, the prison-house dark, the darkness without light, the beds of hot coal, the worm unsleeping, the chains indissoluble, the abyss interminable, the wall impassable, the wailing uncompassionated. None to stand by, to plead, to deliver! But I repent, Lord, I repent; help Thou my unrepentance; and, more and yet more, prick, rend, break my heart. Behold! Lord, that I myself have indignation against myself, for the senselessness, unprofitableness, injuriousness, dangerousness, of

---

[17] Pusey, *The Day of Judgment: A Sermon Preached on the Twentieth Sunday after Trinity, 1839, in S. Peter's Church, Brighton*, 3rd ed. (Oxford: J. H. Parker, 1839), emphasis original, 43–44, archive.org/details/a605527300puseuoft.

[18] Ibid., 20–21.

[19] Incidentally the *Private Devotions* of Lancelot Andrewes were re-published by Newman in his own translation the very next year (1840) as Tract 88.

my desire; that I abhor myself for its madness, vileness, deformity, worthlessness, shame, reproach; that my confusion is before me all day long, and the shame of my face hath covered me. Alas! Woe! Woe! Woe is me! How long? Behold, Lord, that I myself adjudge myself worthy of eternal punishment, yea, and of all the troubles of this world. Behold me, Lord, self-condemned: behold, Lord, and enter not into judgment with Thy servant. And now, Lord, I humble myself beneath Thy strong hand; I bow my knees to Thee, Lord; I fall upon the earth, upon my face. Let this cup pass from me. I stretch out my hands unto Thee; I smite upon my breast, upon my thigh. (Jer 36:19) Out of the depths my soul crieth unto Thee, as a thirsty land unto Thee; and all my bones, and all that is within me! Lord, hear my voice.[20]

Pusey connects these sentiments as in accord with patristic doctrine: "So well did these holy men accord with the maxim of the Ancient Church"[21] and goes on to cite St. Hilary of Poitiers to the same end. Pusey then rhetorically invites the reader who is put off by the intensity of such sentiments to consider, "If any would not readily use the like [prayers], let him think whether that holy man [Andrewes] were too penitent, or himself too little."[22]

Following the brouhaha subsequent to Newman's publication of Tract 90, and Pusey's explanations to various Bishops (Oxford and Canterbury), in which Pusey vigorously demonstrates how the teaching of the *Tracts* is to be sharply distinguished from Roman Catholic doctrine, Pusey then picks up the theme of repentance again, although from another angle. In his (in)famous sermon of 1843, which got him banned from preaching in Oxford for two years (purportedly on grounds of false teaching), Pusey presents a realist view of the Presence of Christ in the Sacrament, confining himself to verbiage that is found either in church fathers or Anglican formularies.[23] Everyone remembers this aspect of the sermon, but what is forgotten is the *reason* Pusey was inspired to preach: Because such a view of the Eucharist is a comfort to *penitents*. Indeed, the title of the Sermon is *"The Holy Eucharist: A Comfort to the Penitent"*! Placing this sermon side by side with the emphasis on repentance between 1836–1839, we see Pusey appending teaching to his prior severity, though not as a negation but as a corollary. Pusey explains it thus in his preface to the published sermon:

> Nothing, throughout the whole Sermon, was further from my thoughts than controversy. I had, on such occasions as my office afforded, commenced a course of Sermons on the comforts provided by the Gospel for the penitent amid the consciousness of sin, with the view to meet the charge of sternness, involved by the exhibition of one side of Catholic truth; in this course, the sacred subject of the Holy Eucharist, of necessity, came in its order; and it was my wish (however I may have been hindered by sudden indisposition from developing my meaning as I wished)

---

[20] The midnight devotion of Lancelot Andrewes, occurring in the *Preces Privatae*, cited in Pusey's Preface to *Day of Judgment*.

[21] Pusey, Preface to *Day of Judgment*, 12.

[22] Ibid.

[23] The Regius professorship of Hebrew had a canonry in Christ Church Cathedral annexed to it. Therefore Pusey, as canon, was among the regular scheduled preacher at the Cathedral services, at which large portions of the Oxford faculty and student-body were generally in attendance.

to point out its comforting character to the penitent in two ways; 1ˢᵗ) indirectly, because it is the Body and Blood of his Lord, and is the channel of His Blessed Presence to the soul, 2ⁿᵈ) because in Holy Scripture the mention of remission of sins is connected with it.[24]

During his two years out of the pulpit, Pusey translated and adapted a powerful penitential work by the French Roman Catholic Jean-Baptiste Avrillon (1652–1729). In his preface Pusey expresses the groundswell of desire to grow in penitence, found in his own heart and lately stoked in others by his sobering example, "In the present time there is a craving after a higher life; stricter and more abiding penitence."[25]

He goes on in a crucial sentence for our purposes,

Penitence is a great gift, persevering penitence a greater and rarer. The narrow way of life is narrower and straiter [sic] to him who has deeply fallen. Pardon is his, but it hangs suspended on the continuance of his penitence.[26]

Going on,

The very thought of what the Fathers speak of, "a deep and lengthened process of healing for great wounds"; "great amends for great wickedness"; "toil and tribulation in penitence"; "continual weeping"; "severity proportioned to the sin"; "to judge ourselves that we be not judged of the Lord", would to most seem like a dream, an intolerable and impossible service, a legal bondage. because we have lost together the very conception of the magnitude of sin and of the value of "revenge" [2 Cor 7:11] as a part of penitence.[27]

The force of this argument builds for pages, and just when the reader feels lost in hopelessness as to the insincerity of their present penitence, Pusey pivots and speaks to the reader as a shepherd of souls, "We must not be ambitious, even in penitence." And going on, we are furnished with what I see to be the center of Pusey's doctrine:

We must be patient even in penitence, or the more, *because we would be penitents*.[28] In vehement penitence there is often impatience, as though we would at once obtain relief, or cast off our slough, or burn out our corruptions, instead of waiting God's time to cleanse our souls with the fire of the Holy Spirit.[29]

Pusey goes on to speak about keeping the Lenten fast, and how of necessity we cannot do what the Ancients did, at least not at first, and that all such austerities should be started slowly, and humbly, with an eye to developing the habit. "Let everyone do what he can, and commit the rest humbly to God."

We see this same sentiment expressed in a letter written the same year,

---

[24] Pusey, *The Holy Eucharist: A Comfort to the Penitent*, (Oxford: J. H. Parker, 1843), iii–iv.

[25] Pusey, ed., "Preface," to Jean-Baptiste-Élie Avrillon, *A Guide to Passing Lent Holily* (London: James Burns, 1844), v.

[26] Ibid., xxv.

[27] Ibid., xxvi.

[28] "Would" in the sense of "desire" in nineteenth century English parlance. I.e., "Because we *desire* to be penitents."

[29] Ibid., xxxv (emphasis mine).

There may be a secret impatience or irritation that you cannot at once be what you would, which is not true penitence or humility. We are what we have made ourselves; and we must pray God to unmake and remake us.[30]

In his preface to Avrillon's *Lent*, he gives very practical examples of what this penitence might look like in daily life, clarifying that these are just ideas for "beginners." In this list we see that Pusey is very far from suggesting hairshirts and horse-whips (although he himself did wear a hairshirt underneath his clothes for the last several decades of his life).

The wandering of our eyes we might restrain, and fix them on the ground, as unworthy to lift them up ... visit the poor and sick, as our superiors in God's sight and His friends ... give way to all ... take, everywhere that we can, the lowest and last and worst place, or thing, simply as our desert; do any irksome secular occupation which may come before us, as most suiting persons so unspiritual as we ... fill up our broken intervals of time with words of the penitential Psalms ... be thankful for pain, or reproach, or ill esteem, as our fittest portion ... take our food as unworthy of it, through our abuse of God's creatures; drink (if so be) a cup of cold water with a secret confession that we deserve to be in hell where the rich man longed in vain that his tongue should be cooled with one drop from the finger of Lazarus ... lie down to rest as deserving only to lie down where there is no rest, yet trusting through His mercy to lie down in the Everlasting Arms.[31]

Such were Pusey's own personal penitential disciplines, and much besides, which he codified into a Rule of Life approved by his spiritual director, Keble,[32] in 1846. Liddon summarizes the larger portions of the Rule in Volume 3 of his biography:

Pusey did nothing by halves; and he resolved to bring his devotions and his ministerial work under the domain of penitential rule. The sense of penitence was to colour all the departments of prayer and even praise. He would join in Intercessions, "as unfit to be heard for any one"; in the Gloria Patri and Pater noster, as "unworthy to take on my lips the Name I have so dishonoured"; in professions of duty in the Psalms, as "what I would do, but the contrary of what I have done"; in Thanksgiving, "to thank God that I am not in hell, and for my absolution, and that the devil did not enter into me altogether, as he did into Judas"; in the responses after the Commandments, so as to "pray for the conversion of the worst sinners—myself chief." ... Other resolves about devotions were ... "To repeat the Penitential Psalms or verses of them when walking alone, or in Chapter ... To pray for some grace at every Communion, and be watchful to treasure it, and now, at first, at least, humble penitential love. To pray God daily for any trouble which may be good for my soul, and not injure the Church. To pray God daily, if it be good for me, to give me sharp bodily pain before I die, and His Grace in it." ... The same spirit was

---

[30] Pusey, "Letter XIV, Feelings," in *Spiritual Letters of Edward Bouverie Pusey*, ed. J. O. Johnston and W. E. C. Newbolt (London: Longmans, Green, and Co.), 26, archive.org/details/a605473000puseuoft.

[31] Pusey, "Preface" to *Guide to Passing Lent Holily*, xl–xli.

[32] Although they both disapproved of the title "Spiritual Director."

carried into his ministerial work; he was to do everything in the spirit of a penitent. He would "aim at commencing every ministerial act with inward confession," that he was "so very unfit to be a minister of God." ... "Never, if I can, to look at beauty of nature, without inward confession of unworthiness.[33]

The list goes on. In that same year Pusey planted a church in the industrial city of Leeds—St. Savior's. He funded its construction almost entirely out of his own pocket, under the donor name "Penitent."[34] The church opened with a week of special services every day, and the sermons were gathered into a collection entitled, "A Course of Sermons on Solemn Subjects chiefly bearing on Repentance and Amendment of Life."

The next year (1846) Pusey dug deep into the reality of ministerial Absolution (that is, in the setting of auricular confession). It must be remembered that at this point auricular confession had been all but unheard of in the Church of England since at least the sixteenth century, the idea being buried as it was in a rubric in the Visitation of the Sick. Pusey's applying himself to Absolution took two forms. First, upon being permitted to preach again at the cathedral, he took up the same series that had been broken off by his prohibition in 1844: "Comforts to the Penitent," although instead of continuing to explicate Holy Communion, he switched his sights to Absolution. On Epiphany IV he preached "Entire Absolution of the Penitent," and, just like the sermon two years prior, drew a lot of ire from his low-church colleagues.[35] He met this ire with a "Part II' of the sermon at the end of the same year (Advent Sunday), which doubled down on his thesis.

Significant for the theme I am tracing is the fact that the efficacy of Absolution by a minister after auricular confession is directly proportional to the depth of penitence, not only before but also after the Absolution. He quotes St. Ambrose to this effect (again revealing the patristic origin of his thought), "whoso hath heaped up sin, let him heap up penitence; for greater sins are washed away with greater tears."[36] And St. Cyprian, touching the proleptic quality of Absolution *vis-à-vis* the Great Day of Judgment, says, "We do not ... anticipate the judgment of the Lord Who will come to judge, but that, if He shall find a sinner's penitence full and entire, He will then ratify what has been determined by us."[37] And, continuing to develop the thoughts of Tract 68, distinguishing the grace of Baptism from the grace of Absolution, Pusey says:

> In Baptism, a man becomes a new self, and being another man, has no more to do with his former sins, than if they had been committed by another, except to love and thank God Who had freed him from them; by Absolution, pardon is given, life is renewed, but *the penitent is the same as the sinner.* In Baptism, sins are suddenly and painlessly blotted out through grace; deep sins after Baptism are forgiven, but upon deep contrition which God giveth; and deep contrition is, for the most part, slowly and gradually worked into the soul, deepening with deepening grace, sorrowing

---

[33] Liddon, *Life*, 3:94–111 (ch. 4).

[34] Construction had begun in 1842 and was completed in 1845. See Liddon, *Life*, 2:466–514 (ch. 34).

[35] Which, at this point, the year after Newman's secession, was most all of his colleagues.

[36] St. Ambrose, *On Repentance* I, quoted in Pusey, *The Entire Absolution of the Penitent, Part I* (Oxford: J. H. Parker, 1846), 37, archive.org/details/a605616200puseuoft.

[37] St. Cyprian, Epistle 55, quoted in ibid., 46.

still more, as, by God's grace, it more deeply loves; grieved the more, the more it knows Him Whom it once grieved, and through that grief and love inwrought in it by God, the more forgiven.[38]

This exploration of Absolution became existential for Pusey when he made his own first auricular confession to Keble on December 1.[39] The effect on Pusey was tremendous, and yet, perhaps not quite what one would have expected, based on the (accidentally) Romish views of absolution we generally harbor today when it comes to understanding Absolution. In a letter written to Keble a week after, Pusey relays:

> I cannot doubt but that through your ministry and the power of the keys, I have received the grace of God, as I know not that I ever did before. I can no more doubt of His mercy vouchsafed to me thus far, than of my own past misery. All indeed is very bad.... However, things seem with me other than they ever were before; at least, I seem to hate myself more thoroughly, and, bad as my prayers are, still to have a love and hope I never knew before.

This doubling-down on penitence subsequent to Absolution shines a very practical light on Pusey's doctrine of repentance. Indeed, it is the aspect that first grabbed this writer by the lapels. It is a thought that Pusey elaborates deftly two decades later in a fragment captured in the *Spiritual Letters* volume:

> A holy man wondered much why souls are so stunted? Why there is not a more vigorous growth? He thought of all sorts of things: "Is it the want of asceticism? Is it the want of love? or prayer?" At last he discovered that it arises from "want of sorrow for forgiven sin."[40]

For a couple more years after 1846 Pusey continued to translate and edit some of the choicest penitential gems from the Roman Catholic continent: Surin's *Spiritual Life*, Scupoli's *Spiritual Combat*, the *Paradise of the Christian Soul*, as well as additional works of Avrillon.

In 1848 his first collection of Parochial Sermons was published, in which we see that Pusey has found his groove in speaking beyond the walls of the University; translating the depths of his conviction into a vernacular that common Christians could hear and understand.[41] His parochial sermons would be published and republished throughout the rest of his life, and were one of the chief means by which actual 'Puseyism' got an earnest hearing, in England and America.

---

[38] Pusey, *Entire Absolution, Part I*, 25.

[39] In the decades that followed, Pusey would hear more confessions than any other Church of England priest at the time, and single-handedly normalized the practice for the subsequent generation of the Oxford Movement.

[40] Pusey, "Fragments of Conversation and Letters," in *Spiritual Letters*, 295. I think the "Holy Man" was Keble, since this is how Pusey often veils Keble's identity in other places. Keble died in 1866, and the two other occurrences of this phrase ("sorrow for forgiven sin") are in his Lenten Sermon "David in His Sin and in His Penitence" preached in 1864 ("The deepest of David's psalms of penitence express the sorrow for forgiven sin.") It occurs once more in Pusey's *Eleven Addresses during a Retreat of the Companions of the Love of Jesus* (1868), where he commends "a loving sorrow for forgiven sin."

[41] His sentences, for instance, are much shorter than in his earlier works.

The great theme that courses through the sermons? Penitence. Even when he is preaching in Easter season, he is led to speak on the theme. One of the startling Easter sermons is titled "Our Risen Lord's Love for Penitents" in which Pusey unpacks the significance that the very first person to whom Jesus reveals himself in his resurrected state is Mary Magdalene, the chief of penitents.

Throughout the mid-1850s, Pusey is drawn into various theological (especially Eucharistic) controversies and creates some of his most thorough writing on the Real Presence of Christ in the Eucharist, but he never leaves penitence apart. In 1857 he publishes a sermon, "Repentance, from Love of God, Life-long," in which he puts his doctrine in the plainest terms possible:

> It has been assigned to me to speak to you of that mark of true loving repentance, that is, *life-long*. In other words, true sorrow for sin, out of love for Jesus, does not pass away. The more we hope that we are the objects of the love of Jesus, the more we hope that He has forgiven our sins and renewed us by His Spirit and loves us, the more we must sorrow, if we love, that we ever sinned against His Infinite Love.[42]

And further in the sermon he draws out two additional clarifying points: (1) The fact that all post-baptismal sin is considered forgiven "in hope" in this life, that is, in a promissory, proleptic way. But the actual sentence of "forgiven" is not meted out until Judgment Day, and (2) The way in which the quality of penitence changes before and after the reception of the gospel-knowledge of promised forgiveness—true Christian penitence is characterized by love for God. Speaking of St. Peter after the cock crowed,

> He wept bitterly and yet he knew himself forgiven. This is another mark of true repentance. He sorrowed for forgiven sin. Repentance cannot be real unless it remove from occasions of sin; it cannot be deep, unless it continue when its sin is (*as it hopes*) forgiven. This is the characteristic difference between true and surface repentance. True repentance is life-long. So far from ending with forgiveness, one might rather say that it then begins. While the soul fears that it is unforgiven, its penitence is a penitence of fear. It dreads Hell; it dreads the wrath of God, and at best, it dreads being shut out for ever from His Presence. Its object is chiefly itself. The penitence of forgiven sin is a penitence *of love*.[43]

And then in a most memorable image, instantiating this abstract doctrine in flesh and blood, "Morning after morning, cock crowing after cock crowing, St Peter wept his fall."

In 1860 he published his long-worked-on *Commentary on the Minor Prophets*, and his comments naturally often recur to themes of penitence, since this is so often the call of the prophets.

By the 1860s, the general reception of the catholic-revival movement of which Pusey had accidentally been the leader had gained not only acceptance but momentum toward ascendency. What was scorned in the 1840s was now, in the main, at least respected (in most quarters). This led to a diffusion of Pusey's intellectual powers into all manner of topics: terms of reunion with Rome (in the form of his *Eirenica* written to Newman),

---

[42] Pusey, "Repentance, from Love of God, Life-long," in *Sermons for the Church's Seasons: From Advent to Trinity*, (London: Kegan Paul, Trench & Co., 1883), 209 (emphasis mine).

[43] Ibid.

university issues, attacking the influx of unbelieving Biblical criticism, etc., but throughout all of this work the central matter of lifelong penitence is never forgotten, either in his life or in his writing.

In 1874 a collection of the various Lenten sermons he had given over the years was gathered and published under the title "Lenten Sermons"—a more sobering and sorrow-making collection of sermons there has not been in the English language since the days of Jeremy Taylor.

In 1878, Pusey lent his hand once again to the work of translation. He produced his adaptation of Gaume's *Manual for Confessors* in which he seeks to anchor the next generation of zealous confession-hearing clergy in the true principles of penitence and absolution, while defending the practice in Anglican formularies and luminaries in a preface that runs over 180 pages. In it, he settles once and for all the rightful place of auricular confession in the life of the Anglican church.

In the very last years of his life (1880–1882), though an octogenarian, he engaged full tilt with the heresy of Universalism[44] that had been propounded by Canon Farrar in 1877 in a series of sermons given in Westminster Abbey.[45] Pusey answered with his *What is of Faith as to Everlasting Punishment?* (1880). As well as giving a definitive take-down of supposed inter-testamental and patristic data that would support a Universalist reading of the Scriptures, Pusey lands where (by now) we might expect him to land: the necessity of repentance *in this life*, because there will be no such opportunity on the other side of death. Quoting Cyprian, for instance: "Then [After death] there will be pain of punishment, *without the profitableness of penitence*.... Once gone forth from hence, there is no more place for repentance; no satisfaction can be accomplished; it is here that life is either lost or saved."[46]

And then, on September 16, 1882, Pusey himself died, as a penitent.

What Is Pusey's Doctrine of Repentance?

Having surveyed the whole of Pusey's life for his development of his practical doctrine, let me gather up what I can into a synopsis, as a sequence of theses, so we can try and take it in whole:

- Repentance is a lifelong action.
- True, earnest, sorrowful Repentance is to be distinguished from temporary, partial, shallow repentance.
- True repentance is a gift from God.
- True repentance is therefore to be asked for, from God.
- The goal of the Christian is to become a true penitent. It is something to aspire toward.

---

[44] By today's taxonomy, we might call it a "Balthasarian Universalism."

[45] The series was published under the title "Eternal Hope" (1877) and was partly occasioned by Pusey's widely published sermon "What is of Faith as to Everlasting Punishment" of a few years prior.

[46] St. Cyprian, quoted in Pusey, *What is of Faith as to Everlasting Punishment*, (Oxford: Devonport Society, 1880), 195 (emphasis mine), archive.org/details/whatisoffaithastoopuse.

- Repentance can be deepened by outward actions of penitence.
- Sins before baptism are forgiven by God entirely in the act of baptism.
- Sins after baptism are forgiven by God if we *continue* in *true* repentance.
- In repenting, we can be *hopeful* of forgiveness, but the actual forgiveness will not be meted out until Judgment Day when Christ raises us from the dead.
- When a priest declares Absolution, this is a proleptic advance of the Judgment Day verdict. (And, theoretically, it could be reversed by the Lord).[47]
- True Christian penitence is characterized by love for God, who shows us his mercy in the face of Christ Jesus.
- It should therefore deepen lifelong, even after any Absolution and whatever other Gospel comforts the Lord provides.
- A sorrowful, sober comportment should therefore be normal for all Christians who have sinned seriously after their baptism.

If Pusey is right about all this, (and I think he is), then it is plain that we Anglicans seem to have imbibed doctrines that miss it on either side. Either an Evangelical view of "If you believe you are forgiven, you are, so don't worry about it" (in effect) or a Roman Catholic view that would equate clerical Absolution as a final verdict akin to a second baptism. In both cases, true, ever-deepening sorrow is displaced, to our eternal spiritual loss.

Some Concluding Thoughts on Sources for Pusey's Doctrine of Repentance

Pusey's doctrine of repentance can be traced to one major source, and two secondary tributaries. The tributaries are: (1) The church fathers, and (2) The penitential devotional books of the counter-reformation that Pusey translated in the mid-1840s. But the major stream—and this is very significant—is none other than the doctrine embedded in the *Book of Common Prayer*.

This is Pusey's own assessment of his sources in retrospect (writing in 1851):

> It was out of Holy Scripture and the Formularies of the Church that Tractarianism arose. It was cherished by our English Divines. It was deepened by the Fathers. It was ripened while most of the writers knew scarcely a Roman book, and only controversially. Tractarianism was entirely the birth of the English Church. Its life must be co existent with the formularies in which it is embodied.[48]

And in many places, on the practical doctrine of repentance, Pusey takes pains to show that everything he is urging is "right there on the page" of the *Book of Common Prayer*. For instance, in the Commination, in the sober language of the Confession in the Daily Office, and in the pleas of the Great Litany. Pusey is simply saying "I really mean that"

---

[47] This is nothing more than the teaching of the parable of the ungrateful debtor.

[48] Pusey, *A Letter to the Right Hon. and Right Rev. the Lord Bishop of London: in explanation of some statements contained in a letter by the Rev. W. Dodsworth* (Oxford: J. H. Parker, 1851), 258, archive.org/details/a605301300puseuoft.

about the prayers in the prayer book. One point he makes to this effect concerns all the times the prayer book adds a modifier to the word "repentance" (or "penitent"). In his "Entire Absolution of the Penitent (Part II)" he writes,

> And therefore the Church of England wherever, in her Liturgy, she speaks of repentance, is careful to speak also of "true," "earnest," "unfeigned," "faithful," "hearty," "worthy," repentance, nor ever names it without some word to express its reality; well knowing how easily and how fatally we might mistake for it a false repentance, itself to be repented for, everlastingly, but hopelessly. David said, "I have sinned," and the Prophet said, "Therefore hath the Lord put away thy sin." Saul said, "I have sinned," but the Prophet answered, "Thou hast rejected the word of the Lord, and the Lord hath rejected thee from being king over Israel." Judas said, "I have sinned," and went and hanged himself. All confessed alike; but Saul had no humility, Judas no hope.[49]

Pusey shows in a footnote from where he extracted those modifiers:

- "*true* repentance"—twice in the daily Absolution, thrice in the Visitation of the Sick
- "add seriousness to his repentance"; "*unfeigned* repentance"—Visitation of the Sick
- "*earnest* and *true* repentance"; "*faithful* repentance with *all* contrition"—Commination Service
- "if with a *true* penitent heart"; "repent you *truly*"; "ye that do *truly and earnestly* repent you";
- "who with *hearty* repentance"; "all that *truly* turn to Him," —Holy Communion
- "worthily lamenting our sins,"—Collect for Ash Wednesday [50]

May God grant us this true repentance. Worthily lamenting our sins, or at least, in the meantime, desiring to worthily lament our sins. I offer to you that only if we, like Pusey, desire to be penitents, will Re-formed Catholicism avail for our spiritual well-being.

---

[49] Pusey, *The Entire Absolution of the Penitent, Sermon II* (Oxford: J. H. Parker, 1846), 16–17, archive.org/details/a6056177rs00puseuoft/a6056177rs00puseuoft.

[50] Ibid., 16.

Chapter 27

John Henry Newman (1801–1890): *Sic et Non*

The Rev. Dr. Gerald McDermott

John Henry Newman (1801–1890) is one of the most famous Anglican minds. For a good part of his ministry, he was a brilliant Anglican theologian and pastor. His *Parochial and Plain Sermons* fill a handsome volume of 1700 pages, full of deep spiritual and biblical insight grounded in an Anglo-Catholic perspective that saw Anglicanism as the *via media* (middle way) between Reformed Protestantism on the left and Roman Catholicism on the right.[1] From these sermons and other works in his Anglican period, we Anglicans can learn much. For before his swim across the Tiber in 1845 he had been an evangelical and then a liberal. He knew both worlds and shows in these hundreds of Anglican sermons how catholic Anglicanism is a more biblical and faithful way than either evangelicalism, liberalism, or Roman Catholicism. There is much in Newman we can say Yes (*sic*) to, and other parts to which we must say No (*non*).

Sic: Faith and Reason

Does faith have anything to do with reason? Is it a blind leap? Just a feeling? Can it be rationally proved?

For thousands of years Jews and Christians have struggled with these questions. Newman thought long and hard about them and came up with answers that made his *Essay in Aid of a Grammar of Assent* a bestseller and have helped believers ever since.[2] He said the popular view of faith and reason is obviously wrong. It tells us that all good reason is based on sensory experience and logic. But what about the most important things in life like love? Sensory experience, Newman argued, does not get us very far in discriminating the difference between true and false love.

The popular view also disguises the fact that even so-called scientific reason is based on presumptions that cannot be proven by either sensory experience or logic. Take the presumption of the uniformity of nature. We cannot know if nature has behaved in the same ways over the last thousands or millions of years. Newman's skepticism on this point has been vindicated by modern physicists whose work in quantum mechanics has proven that nature behaves differently when it is observed, especially at the sub-atomic level. Nature behaves in different ways when observed, and we cannot prove uniformity. So even hard science is built on assumptions which it takes on faith.

All reasoning, Newman argued, proceeds on the basis of *antecedent probability*. This means that in everyday life we—and all scientists, by the way—make decisions based on what we believe (and do not know for sure) to be true. Our beliefs are based not on 100% proof but the *probability* that what we have considered reliable in the past can be trusted ahead of time (thus "antecedent") so that we can proceed today and tomorrow. Let's say our friend George told us that based on his experience a certain country is safe to explore

---

[1] John Henry Newman, *Parochial and Plain Sermons* (San Francisco: Ignatius, 1997).

[2] Newman, *An Essay in Aid of a Grammar of Assent* (Garden City, NY: Image, 1955).

even though we have heard reports otherwise. Since George's reports have been vindicated in the past, we trust him on this one.

Faith is therefore neither blind nor merely emotional. It is based on reports from eyewitness observers whose testimony can be trusted in Christian faith, for example, because they died for the truth of their testimony. We cannot say with 100% certainty that we know they are right, but we can say we trust that their accounts are *probably* true. Enough to stake *our* lives on it. Reasoning in the rest of life is very similar.

Since all reasoning involves some faith—based on principles that cannot be proven such as the truth of what we have been taught by fallible professors—the line between faith and reason is blurred. All reasoning involves some faith. And faith—certainly orthodox Christian faith—uses reason to develop its own principles. It accepts the resurrection of Jesus, for example, because of the testimony of eyewitnesses and then uses reason to see the implications of that miracle for the rest of faith and life.[3]

Sic: Conscience

I wrote earlier that Newman started as an evangelical in the Church of England and then became a liberal. Years later he looked back and realized his liberalism came in part because of the evangelical method (*sola scriptura*) that makes us our own interpreters of the Bible and therefore God. Part of his return to orthodoxy came from his recognition that God speaks through the conscience to every human being (see Paul's reference to conscience in Romans 2:14–15 and numerous mentions in Paul's letters), and that deep down inside of us is where God reveals himself if we would but listen. That was the beginning of his return to orthodoxy: "If I am asked why I believe in a God, I answer that it is because I believe in myself, for I feel it impossible to believe in my own existence ... without believing also in the existence of Him who lives as a ... being in my conscience."[4]

Newman said that the surest way for us grow in knowledge of God is to obey our conscience, even if on a matter it is off kilter a bit. "Obedience even to an erring conscience was the way to gain light.... [I]t mattered not where a man began, so [long as] he began on what came to hand, and in faith."[5]

Since the conscience is the location of moral guidance, especially when submitted to God's Word, Newman taught that the right moral disposition is necessary to have faith and grow in it. A mere intellectual acceptance of the notion that Jesus died for my sins is useless if I do not have the moral determination to change my life in whatever way God wants. Similarly, I will never grow in faith if I am morally resistant to obeying God in the area of my favorite sin. In that sense, then, faith has a moral component. Newman taught that the moral component is necessary both to gain faith and grow in it.

Sic: Preaching

Newman knew there were two kinds of preaching, the prophetic and the priestly. The prophetic afflicts the comfortable while the priestly comforts the afflicted. Because easy believism—the notion that as long as you believe in your head that Jesus died for your

---

[3] Newman, *An Essay in Aid of a Grammar of Assent*.

[4] Newman, *Apologia Pro Vita Sua* (Boston: Houghton Mifflin, 1956), 193.

[5] Ibid., 199.

sins, then you are protected from God's wrath—was common then as it is now, Newman asserted that it was more important for preachers to be prophetic than to be priestly. For the purpose of life is holiness, not happiness. Besides, he wrote, too much assurance corrupts. "Comfort is a cordial, but no one drinks cordials from morning to night."[6]

We might be surprised to learn that people did not listen well in Newman's day, just like ours. Hence, Newman believed, repetition in preaching—at least over the course of a year—is actually a good thing. For the same reason, each sermon should have only one major point, even if it has been said on previous Sundays. If it is a theme that is opposed to contemporary culture, "People need the same thing being said a hundred times over in order to hear it."[7]

Preachers and their listeners need to be reassured that crises in the Church are nothing new. Newman often pointed out that this is not the first era in which church attendance has declined, morals have been abandoned, and church leaders have scandalized the public. During the seventy years of the Arian crisis, *after* the Council of Nicaea when we thought the Arian heresy was defeated, the majority of the bishops continued to embrace variations of the Arian heresy. Newman reminds us that while leaders compromised, most of the laity held fast to the full divinity of the God-man Jesus. And corruption in the church, Newman, goes back to the Twelve apostles. Think of Judas, he reminded his hearers. Church corruption is "almost a dogma."[8]

Sic: Disciplina Arcana

Newman has a word of wisdom for evangelicals and Anglicans who think they need to dump all gospel truths on whatever seeker who starts asking questions. He pointed to the *disciplina arcana* or "discipline of secrecy" which started in the centuries of persecution and continued after Nicaea when Christianity became legal. This was the practice of priests and other Christians who would keep the great Christian doctrines hidden from inquirers. They quoted Jesus' order to his disciples not to throw pearls before swine. They believed that most inquirers then had brains incapable of understanding the deeper gospel truths and so unloading the mysteries on them would do more harm than good. Not unlike researchers today who say that porn changes the brain and makes it incapable of faith, they believed that the sex-saturated Roman society made even seekers incapable of understanding true gospel truth.

Newman pointed out that ever since "the Creator clothed Adam, concealment is in some sense the necessity of our fall."[9] This was why Paul never said a word about justification or God's love to the philosophers on Mars Hill, telling them only about the coming judgment and the Judge who had risen from the dead. It's why Paul spoke only of the Law and resurrection to Agrippa—and not a word about grace. It explains why the early Church kept hidden the mysteries of justification, Eucharist, the Trinity, and the atonement from seekers, and told them to live by the Ten Commandments—especially the sixth on sexual purity—for at least six months before coming back with further

---

[6] Cited in Ian Ker, *John Henry Newman: A Biography* (Oxford: Oxford University Press, 1988), 21.

[7] Ibid., 92, 113, 170.

[8] Ibid., 482, 485, 586.

[9] Newman, *The Via Media*, cited by Ker, *John Henry Newman*, 705.

questions. Only after they did that were they ready to understand more and perhaps be admitted to catechesis, during which time they were ordered to leave the Mass before the liturgy of the altar. They were admitted there only after at least a year of catechesis, and to communion itself after another year or two of teaching and testing.

Sic: Development of Doctrine

Newman is famous for his doctrine of development of doctrine, articulated in book-length form in his *Essay on the Development of Christian Doctrine* (1845).[10] He argued that the idea of doctrinal development can be seen in the Bible, and that most Christians have accepted it in one form or another.

First, we see doctrinal development in the Bible. Even in the Pentateuch this can be seen. The chapters in Exodus 21 and following show how the Ten Commandments of Exodus 20 are developed when applied to concrete situations. God told Abraham in Genesis 12 that he was calling him to be the father of the Jews who would be a blessing to all the families of the earth, the historical books show how David and Solomon illustrated that blessing by radiating the light of biblical truth to many nations in the Ancient Near East when the nations encountered the height of the Israelite empire, and the prophets then talked about Israel being a light to the nations. Jesus the Messiah did not abolish the Law or the Prophets but fulfilled them and taught them in a way that the apostles took to the Gentile nations. This was development of the early Mosaic revelation.

Take the concept of sacrifice. God showed the Jews that it is central to worship but that it is not only giving what is valuable to us, like a very costly animal, but also that our hearts should be given to God. Even Leviticus and Deuteronomy talk about the need for the circumcision of the heart that should accompany animal sacrifices (Lev 26:41: Deut 10:16; 30:6). The prophets developed this further, saying over and over that sacrifices without circumcised hearts are worthless. In Hosea God said, "I desire mercy and not sacrifice" (Hos 6:6). As many scholars have observed, this did not mean one to the exclusion of the other. It was a Semitic way of saying that one is better than the other. The point was to accompany outward sacrifice with inner mercy. Then in the New Testament Jesus quotes Hosea but also says that his perfect sacrifice on the cross (another live victim killed) was the perfect sacrifice and was to be joined by his followers with *anamnesis*, the Jewish remembrance or *zikkaron* that joins the sacrifice and re-presents it to God. Again, we see the development of doctrine.

Newman says doctrine develops in the history of the Church. At Nicaea the bishops ratified the doctrine of Jesus as *homoousios* (of the same being) with the Father. This was not stated by the Bible but is a clear development from the Bible. Neither the word *Trinity* nor its doctrine—one divine Being in three divine Persons—is anywhere stated in the Bible. But all orthodox Christians have accepted the word and the doctrine as proper developments of doctrine from the biblical story.

Newman told evangelicals and Anglicans that they have accepted a long list of doctrines and practices which are not explicitly mentioned in the Bible but are widely regarded as legitimate developments of biblical truth. Consider the following: the

---

[10] Newman, *An Essay on the Development of Doctrine* (Notre Dame: University of Notre Dame Press, 1989).

doctrine of original sin, the lawfulness of bearing arms, the substitution of the first for the seventh day as the Christian sabbath, holy days and seasons, using a ring in marriage, venerated images, singing the *Kyrie Eleison*, and reciting the creeds.

Newman was not blessing all development as good development. Liberals have claimed, for example, that gay marriage is a proper development from Christian teaching about biblical marriage. Newman would disagree, saying it violates "continuity of principle," one of his seven marks of faithful development. For two indispensable principles of biblical marriage are union of difference—in which two opposite sexes become one—and the potential for procreation.[11] Gay marriage is the joining (not union) of sameness which cannot produce children without using other bodies, which the Church has condemned.

Newman's other six marks of faithful development are that they correspond to their rudiments, assimilate and absorb what comes before rather than starting something markedly new and different, are a logical result of original teaching, can be seen in earlier anticipations, conserve orthodox teaching from the past, and show energy and permanence.[12]

Newman's theory of development of doctrine can help us understand our liturgy and sacraments. We speak of Real Presence when that phrase is not in the Bible explicitly. But Jesus told the apostles (and by extension, to their successors the bishops) that he would send the Spirit to tell them things they could not receive at the time (John 16:12). He also told them, "This is my Body," and "This is my Blood." The phrase Real Presence, though not in the Bible explicitly, is a faithful development from what Jesus told his apostles about what would happen when they celebrated his *anamnesis*, the Jewish "remembrance" which brings the past into the present.[13]

Sic: Universal Revelation

What about the world religions? Do they have any truth? Or are they wholly demonic realms of satanic darkness? Do converts from Islam and Buddhism need to forget everything they have ever known and start from scratch?

If you know any of these converts, you know that they often say that Christian faith is different, but not *wholly* unlike what they formerly believed and practiced. Don't get me wrong: there is no other Creator than the God of Israel, and no other Redeemer than Jesus of Nazareth. Allah is a false God, and the Buddha is a false redeemer. He didn't even promise anything close to what we know to be salvation from sin, death, and the devil. Nevertheless, Islam's moral teachings are similar to the Bible's, and the Buddha taught rightly that this material world is not ultimate reality.

Newman's doctrine of "universal revelation" helps us understand why there are some similarities in other religions to the orthodox Christian faith. Basically, he develops what Paul says in Romans 1 and 2 that all human beings can see God's deity and power through

---

[11] Infertile couples are the exception that proves the rule, which is set by Scripture in its first command to the first couple, "Be fruitful and multiply" (Gen 1:28).

[12] Newman, *An Essay on the Development of Doctrine*, 170–206.

[13] For more on anamnesis, see McDermott, *Deep Anglicanism: A Brief Guide* (Nashotah, WI: Nashotah House Press, 2024), chaps.15–17; and McDermott, *A New History of Redemption: The Work of Jesus the Messiah Through the Millennia* (Grand Rapids: Baker Academic, 2024), 181–82.

creation in the world (1:20) and can know his moral law from what he has put on their conscience (2:14–15). Since God gives these revelations of himself through nature *out there* and nature *in here* (the conscience), it is no wonder that world religions contain a bit of truth. Thus there is universal revelation, which means God's revelation has gone out through all the world outside the Jewish and Christian worlds. It is what Paul told the people at Lystra about God never leaving himself without a witness (Acts 14:17) but that in every nation, as Peter taught, he accepts those who fear and obey him (Acts 10:34). It helps explain the partial truths we find in nearly every religion.

Newman also pointed to the world's poetry, art, and music. Perhaps even more in those domains, there are whispers of universal truths that cohere with Christian revelation. Newman reminded his readers that God seems to have used pagan truths to help form some of his greatest leaders. Moses was "instructed in all the wisdom of the Egyptians" (Acts 7:22) and was perhaps influenced by what was true there. Paul quoted Epimenides the Cretan philosopher and Aratus the Greek poet to suggest they had religious truth (Acts 17:28). He probably was not influenced by them much if at all but implied they knew something about God.

Newman did not speculate about the salvation of pagans. Nor did he suggest they could be saved by pagan religions. He believed that no man comes to the Father but by the Son. But he did affirm that when other religionists come to see the beauty of the Triune God, they look back and realize that they were being led by the Spirit all along, and that God used partial truths in other religions and cultures to bring them to the one who is Truth itself.

Non: Rome

The first and most important *difference* that we re-formed catholic Anglicans have with Newman is over his departure to Rome. In his early book *Via Media*, Newman warned that Rome had adopted doctrines about Mary and salvation that could not be supported by Scripture or the fathers in the undivided Church. We agree, and wish he had not ignored those red flags and yielded to Roman fear-mongers who threatened his damnation if he did not join Rome. Those red flags are still there, as we shall see in a moment, and Rome has more recently assured faithful Anglicans that they are saved and need not go to Rome to avoid damnation.

> For the Spirit of Christ has not refrained from using [separated Churches] as means of salvation which derive their efficacy from the very fullness of grace and truth entrusted to the Church.... Among those in which Catholic traditions and institutions in part continue to exist, the Anglican Communion occupies a special place.[14]

---

[14] *Decree on Ecumenism* 3, 13: www.vatican.va/archive/hist_councils/ii_vatican_council/ documents/vat-ii_decree_19641121_unitatis-redintegratio_en.html.

See also *Lumen Gentium* 15–16: "For there are many who honor Sacred Scripture, taking it as a norm of belief and a pattern of life, and who show a sincere zeal. They lovingly believe in God the Father Almighty and in Christ, the Son of God and Savior. They are consecrated by baptism, in which they are united with Christ. They also recognize and accept other sacraments within their own

continued

Newman should have stuck with his earlier convictions that the faith of the fathers was the rule of the early Church and of the undivided Church for the first millennium. He doubted the later Marian devotion that came after the first millennium and then the new doctrine of papal infallibility. On those two and other grounds he believed there was no good reason to abandon Canterbury for Rome. He realized what the Eastern Orthodox declared in a letter to Pope Leo XIII, that Rome was the "Church of Innovations."[15] Only his mistaken fear for his own soul caused him to change his mind.[16]

Non: Mary

Newman was right to question later Marian devotion in Rome that could not be traced back to either the Bible or the Fathers. In 1854 Pope Pius IX declared that Mary had been conceived without original sin. This became the doctrine of original sin that Pius pronounced "necessary to salvation," which means (we need to realize) we will be damned if we do not hold to it.[17] Yet it contradicts the statements of important Fathers. Anselm wrote that Mary was conceived and born in sin. Bernard believed she was conceived in sin but sanctified before birth. Both Aquinas and Bonaventura, principal theologians for today's Roman Church, agreed with Bernard.[18] Scripture teaches the universality of birth in sin: "Behold, I was brought forth in iniquity, and in sin did my

---

Churches or ecclesiastical communities. Many of them rejoice in the episcopate, celebrate the Holy Eucharist and cultivate devotion toward the Virgin Mother of God. They also share with us in prayer and other spiritual benefits. Likewise we can say that in some real way they are joined with us in the Holy Spirit, for to them too He gives His gifts and graces whereby He is operative among them with His sanctifying power." www.vatican.va/archive/hist_councils/ii_vatican_council/documents/vat-ii_const_19641121_lumen-gentium_en.html.

We should also note these statements from the *Decree on Ecumenism* 3: "Even in the beginnings of this one and only Church of God there arose certain rifts, (19) which the Apostle strongly condemned. But in subsequent centuries much more serious dissensions made their appearance and quite large communities came to be separated from full communion with the Catholic Church—for which, often enough, men of both sides were to blame. The children who are born into these Communities and who grow up believing in Christ cannot be accused of the sin involved in the separation, and the Catholic Church embraces upon them as brothers, with respect and affection. For men who believe in Christ and have been truly baptized are in communion with the Catholic Church even though this communion is imperfect. The differences that exist in varying degrees between them and the Catholic Church—whether in doctrine and sometimes in discipline, or concerning the structure of the Church—do indeed create many obstacles, sometimes serious ones, to full ecclesiastical communion. The ecumenical movement is striving to overcome these obstacles. But even in spite of them it remains true that all who have been justified by faith in Baptism are members of Christ's body, and have a right to be called Christian, and so are correctly accepted as brothers by the children of the Catholic Church. Moreover, some and even very many of the significant elements and endowments which together go to build up and give life to the Church itself, can exist outside the visible boundaries of the Catholic Church: the written word of God; the life of grace; faith, hope and charity, with the other interior gifts of the Holy Spirit, and visible elements too. All of these, which come from Christ and lead back to Christ, belong by right to the one Church of Christ."

[15] J. L. C. Dart, *The Old Religion: An Examination into the Facts of the English Reformation* (Eugene, OR: Wipf & Stock, 2016 [orig. 1956]), 145.

[16] See McDermott, *The Great Theologians* (Downers Grove, IL: InterVarsity, 2010), 153.

[17] Obviously this contradicts the statements from Vatican II that we quoted above.

[18] Dart, *The Old Religion*, 161.

mother conceive me" (Ps 51:5); "Sin came into the world through one man, and death through sin, and so death spread to all men because all sinned" (Rom 5:12).

The Anglican Newman would have also rejected the Roman innovation teaching as dogma the assumption of Mary's *body* into heaven. This was declared by Pope Pius XII in 1950. Newman would have been skeptical in his Anglican days on Anglican grounds, that it is neither hinted in the Bible or the Fathers before the sixth century.

More recently Vatican II (*Lumen Gentium* 62) and Pope John Paul II (*Redemptoris Mater*) have declared Mary to be Redemptrix, subordinate to Christ the Redeemer, they say, but dangerously threatening, we Anglicans would say, the biblical and patristic singularity of Jesus Messiah as our sole Redeemer.

Non: Papacy

Newman's surrender on papal infallibility is another dangerous precedent. This too is neither biblical nor patristic, both of which are required for Anglican doctrine. Even after Newman became Roman Catholic he doubted this doctrine and worried that it would undermine the authority of the Church and encourage future popes in various errata. He was prescient on this latter fear, as we have seen in the present Pope Francis who has rejected biblical and patristic teachings on the eternality of hell, the need for repentance before absolution, and the justice of the atonement.[19]

There are many problems with this Roman innovation. Newman himself reminded his earlier readers that St. Peter, whom Catholics call the first pope, was not infallible at Antioch when St. Paul disagreed with him. Nor was Liberius, the bishop of Rome, when he excommunicated Athanasius. Nor Pope Damasus when he exonerated Pelagius from the charge of heresy.

There is also the problem of popes claiming not just primacy—which many Anglicans can accept in the same way they accept Peter as the first apostle among equals and an Anglican Archbishop as the first bishop among equals—but juridical authority. This means the legal authority (in canon law) to rule other bishops and their flocks. That is, Peter is regarded by Rome as not just leader of the Twelve but their lord. As Anglican theologian Eric Mascall argued in the last century, this mistakes an accident for an essential.[20] The Nicene Creed treats the unity of the Church (as in "One, Holy, Catholic, and Apostolic") as essential to the nature of the Church. And just as the Church is the sacrament through which we receive salvation and communion with Jesus and heaven, so too every office and means of grace is sacramental to a point. But the papacy is a bureaucratically elected office, not a sacrament. Even Roman Catholics would agree with that distinction, though of course they insist that this particular election is guided by the Spirit. The point is that Church essentials are sacramental, and the papacy is not among them. Newman agreed with this, even for a time after he decamped to Rome.

---

[19] See, for example, McDermott, "Is Pope Francis a Liberal Protestant?" *First Things* (Nov 15, 2017), www.firstthings.com/web-exclusives/2017/11/is-pope-francis-a-liberal-protestant, and Fr. Thomas Weinandy, "Repentance for Sin and Sacramental Absolution," *The Catholic Thing* (Jan 25, 2023), www.thecatholicthing.org/2023/01/25/repentance-for-sin-and-sacramental-absolution.

[20] E. L. Mascall, *The Recovery of Unity* (London: Longmans, 1958), 215–233.

Non: Development of Doctrine

This is why we Anglicans must say that while there is truth in Newman's thesis of development of doctrine, it has been often abused, not only by liberal Protestants and Anglicans who co-opted it to support their sexual heresies but also by recent Romans to support the innovations of the last two centuries on Mary and the papacy. When Roman Catholics have done this, they have also violated Newman's own "notes" or criteria for faithful development. For neither the Marian nor papal innovations had precedents in Scripture or the fathers. These were the precedents which Newman characterized as continuity of principle, correspondence to the rudiments, and logical results of original teaching.

These Roman divergences which Catholics have accepted by misusing Newman's theory of development have also missed the Church's repeated insistence on conciliarism—the final authority of world councils of bishops over the authority of any one bishop. This was particularly demonstrated during the Great Schism of the fourteenth and fifteenth centuries when there were two and three rival popes. Only a later council of bishops, the Council of Constance (1414–1418), was able to resolve the dispute and settle on one bishop of Rome.

Let all this be a reminder that Roman Catholics and even Anglicans can misuse Newman's theory and story to seek an authority in Rome that is unnecessary and problematic. Far better to find and support re-formed catholic Anglicanism where the Messiah's "little flock" can enjoy the riches of grace and truth.

Chapter 28

Transitory Controversies and Immutable Truths: A.P. Forbes (1817–1875), Doctrinal Development, and the Rule of Faith

Mr. Clinton P. Collister

Can Christian doctrine change? For many, the question brings to mind the words of John Henry Newman (1801–1890), one-time member of the Catholic Revival in the Church of England, convert to Roman Catholicism, and canonized saint, that "In a higher world it is otherwise, but here below to live is to change, and to be perfect is to have changed often."[1] The adage could describe Newman's personal journey from Evangelical, to Anglo-Catholic, to Roman Catholic. In this argument, Newman examines the nature of doctrinal development and argues that a philosophy or belief necessarily changes as it faces new circumstances.

Since the time of its publication, Newman's *An Essay on the Development of Christian Doctrine* has remained a touchstone in debates surrounding what it means to keep the faith in changing times. Roman Catholics, such as Aidan Nichols in *From Newman to Congar: Idea of Doctrinal Development* or Matthew Levering in *Newman on Doctrinal Corruption*, commend Newman's approach.[2] In contrast, Anglican Rowan Williams, in *Arius: Heresy and Tradition*, and Eastern Orthodox David Bentley Hart, in *Tradition and Apocalypse*, contradict Newman's claim that genuine developments occur within a continuous tradition, and, instead, contend that doctrinal development entails rupture and redirection.[3] Alexander Forbes, a leading systematic theologian in the Catholic revival in the Church of England, argues against Newman's theory of development and insists that true development occurs in continuity with the Apostolic deposit and according to the Evangelical Catholic rule of faith.

Newman wrote *An Essay on the Development of Christian Doctrine* to work through his own beliefs about the sources of Christian knowledge. In the nineteenth century, developments in the natural sciences, modern philosophy, and Biblical criticism challenged settled Anglican beliefs about the inspiration of Scripture, authority of the church, and nature of Jesus Christ. All of these forces, along with liberalizing and secularizing movements in politics, combined to make questions of Christian truth pressing for Newman and the other members of the Oxford Movement. As liberal theology and politics threatened to overthrow the norms and convictions maintained in British institutions, Newman asked where Christians should turn to find authoritative

---

[1] J. H. Newman, *An Essay on the Development of Christian Doctrine* (London: Pickering, 1878; 1st ed. James Toovey, 1845), 40.

[2] See Aidan Nichols, *From Newman to Congar: The Idea of Doctrinal Development from the Victorians to the Second Vatican Council* (London: T&T Clark, 1990), and Matthew Levering, *Newman on Doctrinal Corruption* (Washington, DC: Word on Fire Academic, 2022).

[3] See David Bentley Hart, *Tradition and Apocalypse: An Essay on the Future of Christian Belief* (Grand Rapids: Baker Academic, 2022), and Rowan Williams, *Arius: Heresy and Tradition* (Grand Rapids: Eerdmans, 2002).

teaching and eternal truth. Initially, he turned to Anglican Divines such as George Bull and Lancelot Andrewes for answers:

> If I must specify what I mean by 'Anglican principles,' I should say, e.g. taking Antiquity, not the existing Church, as the oracle of truth; and holding that the Apostolical Succession is a sufficient guarantee of Sacramental Grace, without union with the Christian Church throughout the world. I think these still the firmest, strongest ground against Rome—that is, if they can be held" [as truths or facts]. "They have been held by many, and are far more difficult to refute in the Roman controversy, than those of any other religious body.[4]

Reflecting on his earlier "Anglican principles," Newman admits the firmness and strength of a rule of faith that looks to the first Christians when searching for the truth. These Anglican principles, therefore, remain an important alternative for Newman as he feels his way to his new Roman Catholic convictions about tradition and authority.

Christ explains to his disciples that he is "the way, the truth, and the life, and no one comes to the Father" apart from him (John 14:6). But the question remains where the truth revealed in Christ is to be found. Before his Crucifixion, Resurrection, and Ascension, Christ also promises that when the Spirit of truth comes, he will guide the Apostles "into all truth" (John 16:13). After Pentecost, after God fills the first Christians with the Spirit, the Apostles spread out across the known world preaching the gospel and establishing congregations of Catholic Christians. The Apostles teach the first Christians to stand firm in one mind (Phil 1:27) and contend for the faith once for all delivered to the saints (Jude 1:3). Newman searches for a way to reconcile Christ's promise to guide the Church with the Apostles' insistence that they taught eternal and unchanging truths.

Catholicity and Doctrinal Development

In Newman's *An Essay on the Development of Christian Doctrine*, he takes the Anglican approach to the rule of faith, the method of discerning between orthodoxy and heterodoxy, and the Anglican approach to doctrinal development as a counterpoint to his own argument. The battle cry of the Christian humanists of the Reformation, both inside and outside the Roman Communion, was "back to the sources." As Newman grants, "It is indeed sometimes said that the stream is clearest near the spring."[5] Christ said that he is the living water (John 4:14) and the Apostles teach through Christ (1 Thess 4:2). Their teaching participates in Christ and can be said to pour forth Christ, to pour forth truth. Newman recognizes this way of thinking and demarcates the limits of the analogy: "Whatever use may fairly be made of this image, it does not apply to the history of a philosophy or belief, which on the contrary is more equable, and purer, and stronger, when its bed has become deep, and broad, and full."[6] Are the Christian waters of truth clearer near the source or after the bed has deepened? Newman challenges the assumptions of Christians who believe Catholic truths are clearest in the teaching of Christ, the Apostles, or the church fathers. Christian theology, as is the case with other

---

[4] J. H. Newman, *Apologia Pro Vita Sua* (Garden City, NJ: Dover, 2005), 120.

[5] Newman, *Development*, 38.

[6] Ibid.

beliefs and philosophies, grows in sophistication and fullness of truth as it addresses more problems and questions over time.

Confronting the challenges posed by modern skepticism, Newman concedes "to the opponents of historical Christianity, that there are to be found, during the 1800 years through which it has lasted, certain apparent inconsistencies and alterations in its doctrine and its worship, such as irresistibly attract the attention of all who inquire into it."[7] Christians claim God has once and for all delivered the true faith to the saints, and the assertion that their worship and doctrines have changed challenges this foundational belief. These inconsistencies "are not sufficient to interfere with the general character and course of the religion," Newman remarks, and still, they raise questions about the reality of Christian beliefs and the meaning of these seeming contradictions.[8]

Noticing different responses to alterations in Christian faith and practice, Newman sees Christians proposing a few different theories to vindicate their religion. There are, first, those who insist "that Christianity has even changed from the first and ever accommodates itself to the circumstances of times and seasons."[9] The notion that Christian claims about the nature of reality, morality, and God's relationship with mankind perpetually change strikes Newman as untenable: "it is difficult to understand how such a view is compatible with the special idea of revealed truth, and in fact its advocates more or less abandon, or tend to abandon the supernatural claims of Christianity."[10] Whether they abandoned the claims of the creeds or commandments, Newman's contention captures the experience of Christians who are tossed around by every wind of doctrine (Eph 4:14) and submit to the spirit of the age (Eph 6:12).

Anglican Divines offer the second explanation for apparent changes, Newman observes, and err in the opposite direction "by cutting off and casting away as corruptions all usages, ways, opinions, and tenets, which have not the sanction of primitive times."[11] Such primitivists mistakenly assume that what is old is more true than what is new: "They maintain that history first presents to us a pure Christianity in East and West, and then a corrupt; and then of course their duty is to draw the line between what is corrupt and what is pure."[12] Exponents of this hypothesis have found justification for their belief that Christian truth consists in the original beliefs and practices of the first Christians in the maxim articulated by St. Vincent of Lérins, "revealed and Apostolic doctrine is '*quod semper, quod ubique, quod ab omnibus*,'[13] a principle infallibly separating, on the whole field of history, authoritative doctrine from opinion."[14] Newman argues that this commitment to antiquity turns out to be unworkable when new doctrinal controversies confront the Church.

---

[7] Newman, *Development*, 9.

[8] Ibid.

[9] Ibid., 10.

[10] Ibid.

[11] Ibid.

[12] Ibid.

[13] Revealed and Apostolic doctrine is that doctrine received always, everywhere, and from all.

[14] Newman, *Development*, 10.

Only by affirming the truth and goodness of doctrinal development and ongoing revelation in the Christian religion, Newman concludes, can Christians answer modern historical critiques of doctrinal inconsistencies around the world and across the generations:

> From the nature of the human mind, time is necessary for the full comprehension and perfection of great ideas; and that the highest and most wonderful truths, though communicated to the world once for all by inspired teachers, could not be comprehended all at once by the recipients, but, as being received and transmitted by minds not inspired and through media which were human, have required only the longer time and deeper thought for their full elucidation. This may be called the *Theory of Development of Doctrine*[15]

Newman argues that this third theory of development offers a better explanation for doctrinal changes than either the relativistic hypothesis that doctrines have and will always change to fit their surroundings, or the belief that true and false doctrinal changes can be determined by reforming faith and practice according to the standard of what has been believed everywhere, always, and by all.

The "increase and expansion of the Christian creed and ritual," Newman asserts, requires the Church to discern between development and corruption. To this end, he identifies a test of Catholic development. Each doctrinal development must demonstrate identity of type, continuity of principle, assimilative power, logical coherence, fecundity, conservation, and vitality. These criteria, argue Newman, are necessary but not sufficient to determine the veracity of a development. The test also "implies a present informant and guide, and that an infallible one; not a mere abstract declaration of Truths unknown before to man."[16] The Reformation led Christians to look to the Bible as a guide when new controversies and questions test the Church. Protestants rejected the living voice of ongoing revelation found in the papacy and the Roman magisterium and looked to Scripture for answers. But Newman argues "that the inspired Volume is not adapted or intended to subserve that purpose."[17] Thus Christians are "forced to revert to that living and present Guide, who, at the era of our rejection of her, had been so long recognized as the dispenser of Scripture, according to times and circumstances, and the arbiter of all true doctrine and holy practice to her children.[18]

The wreck of faith caused by divisions and sectarian innovations acts demonstrates enough to justify a return to submission to Roman jurisdiction. Newman implies that the failure of Scripture as a living authority appears all around the reader, and the need for an alternative is clear. The "present and infallible" guide to navigating the storms of controversies, he insists, is the Catholic Church, and he equates catholicity with communion with the Papacy and submission to the Roman magisterium.[19] The final and

---

[15] Newman, *Development*, 21.

[16] Ibid., 87.

[17] Ibid.

[18] Ibid.

[19] For a more comprehensive account of Newman's understanding of the relationship between the See of Rome, Catholicity, and the Papacy, see Aidan Nichols, *From Newman to Conger: The Idea of Doctrinal Development from the Victorians to the Second Vatican Council*, "Newman in Rome."

sufficient determinative factor, in Newman's third explanation of how Christians seek to explain changes in Christian faith and practice means that the Roman Catholic Church, or the bishops in communion with the Bishop of Rome (the contemporary occupant of the papal office and the guardian of unity of the Church) has the power of right judgment about the contents of the Apostolic deposit and development of doctrine.

Considering alternative explanations, Newman rejects the liberal hypothesis that revelation is mutable and progressive, rejects the Anglican conviction that the original revelation and interpretation, as understood within the consensus of the Church, provides a standard of doctrinal truth and falsehood, and champions the Roman Catholic theory that development occurs organically as the papacy and Catholic magisterium discern between developments and corruptions.

On Development and Exaggeration

The decisive response to Newman's theory came from E. B. Pusey in his sermon, *The Rule of Faith, as Maintained by the Church Fathers and the Church of England*.[20] Pusey doubles down on the Anglican conviction that the Scriptures contain all things necessary for salvation and argues that the Church, where she maintains Apostolic succession of teaching and laying on of hands, holds the authority to teach doctrine and apply the rule of faith to answer controversies. This means that the Anglican and Eastern parts of the Church retain the authority to apply the rule of faith to interpret Scripture and teach Catholic Christian doctrine.

Whereas Pusey's response to Newman's theory of development centers on returning to the Scriptural and patristic sources that comment on the nature of the rule of faith, J. B. Mozley, in *The Theory of Development*, sets out to answer Newman's theological and philosophical argument in defense of his Roman Catholic theory of development.[21] Contra Newman's presentation of Anglican principles as a form of primitivism that eschews the possibility of a more expansive and considered understanding of Christian truth, Mozley agrees that "there can be no doubt that Christianity was intended to develop itself. It was intended to do so on the same general law on which great principles and institutions, we may say all things, great or small, do."[22] People change when they enter into a room with other people, and beliefs inform new thoughts and practices. As a convert to Christianity develops as he enters more deeply into union with Christ, "people who became Christians would have to act upon, and to think of, what Christianity imparted to them. The peculiar Christian temper, in the first place, would be brought out more prominently, as different relations, religious or secular, social or civil, had to be sustained and responded to."[23] When the Church responds to new intellectual, moral, social, and technological challenges, she, in certain cases, develops in her understanding and articulation of doctrine.

---

[20] See E. B. Pusey, *The Rule of Faith, as Maintained by the Church Fathers and the Church of England* (London: J. H. Parker, 1851).

[21] See J. B. Mozley, *The Theory of Development* (New York: B.P. Dutton, 1871).

[22] Mozley, *Theory*, 19.

[23] Ibid.

Protestantism leads to division and liberalism, Newman accuses, and Mozley admits the threat of such distortions through subtraction:

> The tendency of Protestantism is to decay: it diminishes, dilutes, speculates away Christian truth: it dislikes mystery, distrusts awe; and therefore the Christian religion, as an essentially mysterious and essentially devotional one, would gradually lose its fundamental characteristics and original type under the sway of unchecked Protestantism.[24]

The Christian Humanists and Reformers rightly called to return to the sources of the faith in Scripture and the fathers. Returning to this earlier form entails the cutting back of false growths. In excess, Protestants unmoored from tradition over-prune and cut off true continuities and expansions in belief and practice continuous with the original deposit.

Roman Catholics, Mozley contends, suffer from the opposite vice. Instead of over-pruning, they cultivate excessive growth of convictions and devotional practices that twist and disease the original branches of faith. They distort through addition:

> Keeping the original type, it has introduced an exaggerative corruption of it. The care for the dead, the veneration of saints, the peculiar reverence to the mother of God, the acknowledgment of the change in the Eucharist, the sense of punishment due to sin, are all Christian feelings and doctrines, and they all exist in the Roman system; but they are asserted to exist in an immoderate and disproportionate way.[25]

Mozley argues that Newman's theory of development, and its criteria of true development, fails because it lacks a guard against corruptions born of exaggeration: "[Newman] excludes the idea of excess, because he has limited the idea of corruption so as to exclude it. But surely this is no legitimate reason, for the question is easily asked, why did he so limit his idea of corruption?"[26] Newman has set out to prove that new Roman Catholic dogmas represent orthodox developments of the Christian faith, and yet he fails to engage with the problem of errors of excess. "He does not relieve himself of this task by saying that he does not admit this particular wrong thing into his definition of corruption," Mozley declares: "it exists all the same whether admitted into that definition or not, and whether outside or inside of the meaning of that word; and, existing, has to be disproved."[27] Continuities of logical sequence, typological resemblance, and movement in a single direction fail to anticipate the problems caused by mistakenly teaching opinions and speculations as if they are essential parts of the Christian faith.

Mozley questions the ability of Newman's test of logical relation between an idea contained in the Apostolic deposit and later developments to guard against errors of excess: "On every kind of question in religion has human logic from the first imposed imperially its own conclusions; and encountered equally imperial counter ones."[28]

---

[24] Mozley, *Theory*, 30–31.
[25] Ibid.
[26] Ibid., 38.
[27] Ibid.
[28] Ibid., 82.

Certain later doctrinal developments in the Roman tradition take a universal and imperialistic approach to truth, such that they preclude the beliefs of earlier Catholic Christians. The Apostles maintained that the Scriptures offer an infallible guide to discerning doctrinal truth. Single individuals, Mozley contends, lack the authority to speak as infallible logicians: "Whenever such infallibility speaks to us, if ancient proved tradition be such, or if the contemporary voice of the universal Church be such, we are bound to obey; but the mere apparent consecutiveness itself, which carries on an idea from one stage to another, is no sort of guarantee, except to the mind of the individual thinker himself.[29]

Anglican principles, according to Mozley, privilege Scripture and ancient tradition when discerning between true and false doctrine. Newman admits as much, and he rejects this approach as a form of sectarian primitivism. But Mozley also affirms the living voice of the Church when she speaks as a whole in ecumenical council to put down heresy and explain orthodoxy.

Thus, Newman's claim that Anglican principles foreclose the possibility of doctrinal development fails to square with history. While his critique of Anglican isolation from other parts of the Church Catholic remains a fair one in different times and places, the separated state of the Eastern Orthodox and Roman Catholic parts of Christ's Church remains a scandal and tragedy. Christ calls each part of the whole to pray and labor for the healing of his visible Body.

Mozley demonstrates that Newman builds his theory on sand. He argues that Scripture, tradition, and reason testify that Catholic Christianity entails doctrinal development, and such development requires authority in the Church. Anglicans, from this perspective, depart from the Catholic faith by rejecting the theory of doctrinal development and remaining out of communion with the other parts of the Church Catholic. Mozley, admitting these challenges to Anglican principles, demonstrates that Anglicans hold to a more Scriptural and traditional theory of development. Their principles call them to pursue reunion with those parts of the Church that uphold the teaching of Scripture and the decisions of Ecumenical Councils as determining the essentials of Catholic orthodoxy. The conflict between Mozley and Newman really lies in the authority of the papacy and the Roman see:

> We enter on another and a further field of argument, and perceive that, in distinction to taking any representation, however large, ingenious, and exuberant of the simple notion of development, any explanation, however full, of its naturalness, probability, commonness in ordinary life, and the career of nations and schools, as a single step towards settling the question of the rightness or wrongness, the justness or immoderateness of any given development, we are referred, as the ultimate point on which the whole argument turns, to the asserted existence of an infallible guide, who is able to, and does in each case, decide the question by that simple gift of infallibility; and pronounces with certainty the fact of a development being right or wrong. The doctrine of the Papal Infallibility comes

---

[29] Mozley, *Theory*, 43.

out as the keystone of Mr. Newman's whole argument, and according as he proves, or fails to prove, that doctrine, that argument stands or falls.[30]

Newman fails, Mozley contends, to demonstrate the catholicity of the doctrine of papal infallibility, the doctrine on which his theory of development stands or falls. Mozley concedes that Catholic Christians need to develop their understanding of doctrine in changing circumstances, and he agrees that parts of the Church must look to Catholic authority when discerning between truth and error. Unlike Newman, though, he believes that the consensus of the Body of Christ represents the mind of Christ to the Church. The Vincentian Canon, calling Christians to look to what has been believed everywhere, always, and by all, still holds as a guide to reforming the Church and turning away from false teaching. Newman's theory of development fails to check against errors of exaggeration, and it fails to make a persuasive case for the papal system as a more orthodox or catholic authority than the conciliarism of the approach of the undivided Church of East and West.

Evangelical Catholicism and Anglican Dogmatic Theology

The Catholic Revival in the Church of England responded to changing cultural circumstances by calling men to return to the fullness of the Christian faith. Pusey, an Old Testament scholar at the University of Oxford and disciple of the Anglican Divines and church fathers, marshaled reams of evidence from the Anglican tradition and early church to reawaken contemporaries to the Apostolic authority of the Church Catholic. As part of this mission, he defended the authority of the Church of England, the inspiration of Scripture, and Christ's saving grace given in the regeneration of Baptism and the real presence of Communion. As a writer, pastor, and professor, he inspired many to give their lives to the cause of the Oxford Movement, dedicating themselves to the service of Christ and his Church. Alexander Penrose Forbes (1817–1875), the first Tractarian bishop in the United Kingdom, was one such student. In the introduction to *An Explanation of the 39 Articles*, he thanks Pusey in the most reverential terms:

> You have devoted your time and your talents, and the varied gifts which God has bestowed upon you, to adorn the Church of England; by bringing forward in her service your varied stores of patristic learning; by the evolution of a more accurate theology; by the publication of heart-stirring and thoughtful sermons; by placing within the reach of her members adapted editions of the devout works of spiritual authors in other communions; by supplying to the student of Holy Scripture the beginning of a deep, affective, and exhaustive commentary on the Word of God; by the development of the dogmatic element in the Church's teaching as the strongest bulwark against rationalism and infidelity; by defending the authenticity and inspiration of that Prophet whose work has been the battle-ground of modern criticism.[31]

As Pusey's protégé, Forbes shared his spiritual father's desire to contribute to the "evolution of a more accurate theology" and "development of the dogmatic element in

---

[30] Mozley, *Theory*, 43.
[31] A. P. Forbes, *An Explanation of the 39 Articles* (Oxford: J.H. Parker, 1871), 13.

the Church's teaching."[32] To this end, he wrote *A Short Explanation of the Nicene Creed* for students of theology in the Church of England.

"Amid the great revival of the last twenty years,"Forbes recounts, "as deeper views of God's truth have by His mercy been accorded to our aching hearts, a desire of a more systematic theology has almost of necessity been engendered."[33] The Catholic Revival persuaded many that "an exact theology is at once the most reverent and the most satisfactory" and "the only sure guarantee for orthodoxy of faith."[34] Forbes believes that "the faith of our own Church, on the subjects that were left as open questions, has shriveled and withered away," and it is this conviction that underlies his work as a theologian.[35]

Through his commentaries on the Creed and the *Articles*, Forbes expounds a systematic theology for Evangelical Catholics. This dogmatic theology holds to the evangelical conviction that the inspired Word of God contains all things necessary for salvation, and the catholic conviction that God is guiding the whole Church into all truth. "Our Lord has promised, 'I am with you always, even to the end of the world,' "but He has not promised to be always present in the same degree or the same way."[36] And we can only come to understand the relationship between doctrinal development and the rule of faith when we see how God relates to his people in different ways in different times and places. By distinguishing between the ways that the Holy Spirit has guided the Church throughout her history, he clarifies the relationship between Scripture and the great tradition in his explanation of how God uniquely acted through the Apostles: "They spake as 'moved by the Holy Ghost,' so that what they spake were the words of God, and have been, ever since, a fountain of truth to the Church of Christ, such as no words, since spoken through men, are or can be. This does not mean that Christ abandoned his Church, or the Holy Spirit ceased to lead her into all truth. Instead, Forbes observes that "He has been with the Church, in different degrees, since, according to her faithfulness."[37]

Forbes turns to the Vincentian Canon to determine what beliefs are essential to the Catholic Christian faith. Considering the faith and practice of the original Christians, as this faith and worship spread among Christians around the world and across the ages, demands careful study of the Bible and church history. In his commentary on the Articles, he contrasts Newman's theory of development with the posture of Roman Catholics and Protestants writing at the outset of the Reformation:

> The theory of development had not yet been used as the master-key to explain all existing phenomena. It had been propounded in Lerins in the fifth century, and in a very modified manner taught by St. Thomas Aquinas: but neither had Catholics used it to account for the dissidences between primitive practice and the actual

---

[32] Forbes, *Explanation of the 39 Articles*, 13.
[33] Forbes, *A Short Explanation of the Nicene Creed* (Oxford: J.H. Parker, 1852), Preface.
[34] Ibid.
[35] Ibid., Preface.
[36] Ibid., 289.
[37] Ibid.

state of things; nor did the Protestants use it to justify their novelties. Both parties appealed to antiquity.[38]

Contrasting the Roman Catholic theory of development and Anglican principles, Newman argues that St. Vincent's claim that what has always been believed is impracticable as part of the rule of faith because so much remained unclear and undecided among the first Christians. Forbes shows that historically both Romans and Protestants claimed to hold a faith in harmony with that of the early church, and both claimed to appeal to a catholic biblical faith: "The Roman Church to Scripture and coordinate tradition, as expounded by the living Church, especially by the successor of St. Peter; the Anglican to Scripture, witnessed to and expounded by the tradition of the Church."[39] Forbes sees parallels between the historic approaches of Romans and Anglicans absent in Newman's method.

The *Articles of Religion*, according to Forbes, address early modern debates in a manner that assumes the faith of the Bible, as represented and explained in the Church's tradition. His purpose in commenting on the *Articles* is to display how they can be turned from "the transitory controversies of the sixteenth century to those immutable truths which have been taught in the Church, and by the Church, in all ages."[40] As Newman sought to explain apparent inconsistencies encountered when Christians faced different kinds of cultural conflicts and contexts, Forbes seeks to show that it's possible to develop doctrine in such a way as to address new challenges while holding fast to unchanging truths. Both theologians sought to guide faithful Christians as they strive to stay on the straight and narrow despite the controversies obscuring the way.

Forbes casts light on what might be called the Evangelical Catholic rule of faith in his explanations of the Articles focusing on the doctrines of Scripture and the Church. First, he looks at the sufficiency of Scripture described in Article VI: "Holy Scripture containeth all things necessary to salvation: so that whatsoever is not read therein, nor may be proved thereby, is not to be required of any man, that it should be believed as an article of the Faith, or be thought requisite or necessary to salvation." The Article delineates the parameters of the Church's teaching office in a limited manner: "It defines the sense in which it means that Holy Scripture contains all things necessary to salvation, by the most important qualifications. It leaves the amplest room for the deductions which tradition or even individual doctors may gather from it."[41] The scope of this article maintains the Church's traditional role as "guardian and the expounder" of the Scriptures.[42]

God once and for all reveals himself in the person of Christ and the Scriptures, Forbes maintains, and Christianity should not be confused with progressive sciences. Doctrinal development occurs in response to heresies in order to more clearly enunciate or definitely define the truths handed down in the Apostolic deposit. It also occurs when

---

[38] Forbes, *Articles*, 45.

[39] Ibid.

[40] Forbes, *Short Explanation of the Nicene Creed*, 12.

[41] Ibid., 98.

[42] Ibid.

saints meditate on the mysteries of the faith, and by the grace of God, the Holy Spirit guides them into a more vivid description of those mysteries.[43]

Second, Article XX further clarifies the relationship between Church and Scripture: the Church has "authority in Controversies of Faith: And yet it is not lawful for the Church to ordain any thing that is contrary to God's Word written, neither may it so expound one place of Scripture, that it be repugnant to another." Forbes sees the Church "expounding" Scripture in such a way as to authoritatively decide "controversies in matters of faith." These matters of faith, particularly of what beliefs are necessary for salvation, arise out of the matter of Scripture. In the Church's teaching office, she explains which beliefs are essential parts of the catholic faith and how Christians should interpret the passages that speak to such doctrines when adjudicating between contradictory and mutually exclusive interpretations. Forbes looks to Christ's promise that the Father has sent him into the world, so he analogously sends the disciples. He commissions them to do the sort of thing that he did and assures them that he will always be with them (John 20:21). According to Christ's commission, Forbes concludes, "When He ascended, He left His mystical Body a society which in its turn should be the living expositor of the truth and represent Him."[44] Jesus Christ provides true interpretations of the Old Testament and answers passing controversies with immutable truths. He commissions the Apostles, as overseers and representative members of the Church, to do the same.

The Church, therefore, represents Christ across time and space: "The Church is the Body of the Lord; it is in its universality His visible form, His permanent ever renovated Humanity, His eternal revelation. He dwells in the community. All His promises and gifts are bequeathed to it, but to no individual, as such, since the days of the Apostles."[45] Forbes' final point in this description of the Church raises a question. If the teaching office of the Church, the reliable voice of Christ, does not rest in, say, the bishop of Rome or the bishop of Canterbury, where can the faithful look to reliably find Christian truth?

"Christian Tradition' includes," Forbes contends, "the concurrent testimony of antiquity, universality, and consent."[46] St. Vincent saw that "A doctrine which the Church has received and taught in every age, in every country, and concurrently by all, must be, as agreeable with the Divine Scripture, infallibly true." And Forbes recovers this canon to contest Newman's theory of development.[47] In doing so, he offers a rejoinder to Newman's argument against the Vincentian Canon on the basis of the absence of certain terms integral to the doctrine of God among the first Christians: "inasmuch as the Church is indwelt by God the Holy Ghost, it is no mere concocter of formularies after a mechanical and lifeless fashion; it has been guided to express wisely and rightly the form of faith, and therefore has availed itself of new terms, such as 'the consubstantial,' rejecting it in the wrong sense, accepting it in the right."[48] The Church develops terms

---

[43] Forbes, *A Primary Charge Given to the Clergy of His Diocese* [Eucharistic Sacrifice and Real Presence] (London: Joseph Masters, 1858), 7.

[44] Forbes, *Articles*, 270.

[45] Ibid., 280.

[46] Ibid.

[47] Ibid., 281.

[48] Ibid.

and explanations to refute heresy and clarify orthodoxy, and she does so with infallibility in certain cases.

The Church stamps the decisions of Ecumenical Councils as infallible interpretations of Scripture and developments of Christian doctrine. Forbes discovers the origins of faith in the correspondence of unity and truth in the teaching of St. Paul (Eph 4), more scientifically defined in St. Cyprian's *The Unity of the Church*, and a key to understanding the organ of the Church's teaching office in the Body of Christ: "So long as the Church was undivided, the organ was in perfection and did its work. The decisions of the ecumenical Church are the voice of the Holy Ghost; nothing can exaggerate the veneration or submission with which they ought to be received."[49] Disunity appears as an illness that impairs the healthy action of this organ. After the great schism of East and West, the Church's teaching office is more or less "limited to the authorization, inculcation, and application of truths already infallibly defined, or to the declaration of truth which had not yet that test of infallibility, the reception by the whole Church of Christ."[50]

The Articles on the authority of Scripture and the Church explain where Christians should look as they search for the truth. They can find Christ revealed in the inspired Scriptures, and guiding the faithful in the correct interpretation of this revelation through the tradition of the whole Church, especially in the creeds and decisions of Ecumenical Councils.

Forbes contrasts the catholic decisions of the Church marked as infallible by the conclusions of ecumenical councils received by the whole Body of Christ with peculiar Roman innovations:

> It is another thing, that a new growth of doctrine should spring up beside the Catholic Faith, that anthropomorphic tendencies should be gathered into the Church under a licensed image-worship, that the sympathetic nature of woman should be canonized in "the delegated omnipotency" of Mary, and that the dread of the next world and the shrinking of the natural instinct from the idea of eternal punishment for temporal sin should have shaped itself into such a theory of indulgences and purgatory as, practically speaking, in the case of those who die in the Church tends to obscure the notion of hell.[51]

Forbes proposes a test for Anglicans to apply when determining whether doctrinal developments measure up to the Evangelical Catholic rule of faith. This test should inform all legitimate decisions of the Church of England: "No decision is morally binding which is founded on one of these sources to the prejudice of the rest. Direct depravation of an article or contradiction of the Prayer Book, or of Holy Scripture, or of the concurrent voice of catholic antiquity."[52]

---

[49] See Forbes, *Articles*, 286 and also Cyprian, *The Lapsed: Unity of the Church*, trans. Maurice Bevenot (Westminster, MD: Newman Press, 1957) for what Forbes considers the first scientific treatise on the subject.

[50] Forbes, *Articles*, 286.

[51] Forbes, *Real Presence*, 7.

[52] Ibid., 8.

Applications of the Rule of Faith

As the first Tractarian bishop in the United Kingdom, Alexander Forbes applied his not inconsiderable gifts as a dogmatic theologian to his ministry as overseer of the clergy of Brechin. He sought to spark a catholic revival in the Scottish Episcopal Church comparable to the Oxford Movement, and his charges to his clergy often speak to the same sacramental and ecclesiastical themes present in Pusey's work.

In the 1857 Primary Charge to the clergy of his diocese, Forbes champions the doctrine of the real presence of Christ in the Holy Eucharist. This charge answers one of the "passing controversies" of the day with an appeal to the "immutable truths" revealed in Scripture and explicated in the theology of the formularies and reflections of English divines informing Anglican Orthodoxy.

Surveying the spiritual confusion around him, Forbes remarks on the effects of higher criticism that "new errors rise year by year. The inspiration of Holy Scripture is attacked by self-sufficient and fearless criticism; its very canonicity is doubted, and men in despair ask, 'What is the Scripture?'"[53] Rising skepticism coincides with rising credulousness: "Mormonism among the poor, and Irvingism among the upper classes, as we said before, are alike appealing to some supposed fresh outpouring of the Spirit."[54] The skepticism engendered by certain forms of historical critical scholarship and the heretical sects claiming to add to the Christian faith revealed in Scripture represent two departures from the Evangelical Catholic rule of faith propounded by Forbes. Such additions and subtractions from the faith of the Church catholic open the door to theologians questioning the hard teachings, for instance, those on death, judgement, heaven, and hell: "the eternity of the future state of woe is being extensively denied."[55] Presumption appears to inform the eschatology as well as the ontology of the *avant garde*: "a vague spiritualism and religion of sensations is taking the place of the old orthodox Christianity [and] a beautiful but most dangerous Pantheism is the foundation of much of the mental philosophy of the day."[56] Forbes insists that the renewal of Christian faith rests on an "appeal to the universal tradition and consent of the Christian Church, the Bride of her Lord, to whom was given the promise of the Comforter."[57] The softening of the heart, the sanctifying of the intellect, and the reorientation of the will are requisite to resist the spirit of such an age.

Christ's Eucharistic sacrifice and real presence in Holy Communion, Forbes argues, offer an antidote to the ills plaguing society:

> If there be one blessing and privilege peculiar to the true faith, it is the Ever-Living Presence of Jesus Christ in the Mysteries of the New Law. If there be one doctrine more than another that touches the heart, and subdues the intellect, and influences the will, it is that blessed one, that the Eternal Son of God, not content with taking upon Himself our nature in the Mystery of the Incarnation, has, by an extension of the same, found out a way whereby to communicate Himself to us, saying to us, "He

---

[53] Forbes, *Real Presence*, 9.
[54] Ibid., 10.
[55] Ibid.
[56] Ibid.
[57] Ibid., 58.

that eateth My Flesh and drinketh My Blood dwelleth in Me and I in him." What a difference does the realization or rejection of this most overwhelming and august doctrine make upon the soul? What a tender delight, mixed with reverence and holy fear, does this truth infuse into Christian hearts, transported by gratitude and joy! To feel and to know that Jesus is set forth as a Propitiation, not only for the universal redemption, but for our individual salvation—that the Objective Atonement made for us by the Life and Death of our dear Redeemer, is here made Subjective—that all He did and suffered for the human race is here made over to us and sealed to us by an everlasting Sacrament—that the ties which sin had broken and mortality had loosened are here again united, and we are in Christ, and Christ in us—all this surely surpasses the language of man to describe.[58]

Forbes retrieves a vast array of evidence from Anglican Divines and Scripture to support his high Eucharistic theology and hopes for the renewal of his contemporaries through the grace of the Sacrament. The lack of faith in Christ's sacrifice and presence, Forbes indicates, explains much of the confusion plaguing modern Anglicans: "Alas that men should so seek to stunt and cripple the Gospel, as to deprive it of this its highest manifestation, and after nineteen hundred years of the holy experience of the saints, should still demand, in doubt and coldness of heart, 'How can this Man give us His Flesh to eat?'"[59] Forbes applies the Evangelical Catholic rule of faith to the doctrine of the real presence and discerns its immutable truth, first revealed in Scripture, buttressed by the Church's tradition, received in the Anglican formularies, and confirmed by her most faithful divines.

Members of the Scottish Episcopal Church, persuaded that Forbes' defense of the real presence constituted a capitulation to the Roman Catholic theory of transubstantiation and violation of the Anglican formularies, brought Forbes up on heresy charges for his Primary Charge. Adherence to Evangelical Catholic principles, though, ensured that Forbes remained within the pale of Anglican Orthodoxy, and a court found him innocent.[60]

A second application of the rule of faith further demonstrates Forbes' commitment to the catholicity of the whole Church, as received in the Church of England, rather than Roman Catholicism. In the lead-up to the first Vatican Council, Pusey and Forbes sought to establish a basis in the consensus of the undivided Church of East and West on which to hold a genuinely ecumenical council. They hoped to see Anglican, Eastern, and Roman bishops represented and the Church's teaching office restored to address modern controversies facing the Church. Their hopes for a true council of the whole Church catholic failed to manifest, and Roman dogmatic declarations regarding the Papacy and Mary undermined efforts to restore catholic unity on a conciliar basis.[61]

---

[58] Forbes, *Real Presence*, 10.

[59] Ibid.

[60] For more details about the Eucharistic controversy and trial, see Rowan Strong, *Alexander Forbes of Brechin: the First Tractarian Bishop* (Oxford: Oxford University Press, 1995) "Controversy and Trial."

[61] See Mark D. Chapman, *The Fantasy of Reunion: Anglicans, Catholics, and Ecumenism, 1833–1882* (Oxford: Oxford University Press, 2014), "An Ecumenical Front Against Liberalism."

Pastor aeternus, the dogmatic constitution issued by the First Vatican Council, promulgates the dogma of papal infallibility and consolidates the dogmatic basis of universal papal jurisdiction. Forbes, dedicated to the cause of reunion among Orthodox Christians in Apostolic Succession, considered both dogmatic declarations violations of the rule of faith grounded on a misunderstanding of the nature of doctrinal development: "Henceforth Christianity must stand on a new dogmatic basis," he laments.[62] Commitment to papal infallibility uniquely imperils the ability of the church to return to the sources of her faith and implement conciliar reforms: "The appeal to history is now heresy. The consent of the peoples is nothing, all depends on the will of one man, whose opinion, apart from the opinion of the whole body of Christ, is in itself irreformable."[63] In consequence, "The bishops have ceased to be judges of doctrine, and are now the Pope's vicars. Their jurisdiction as ordinaries is infringed by the authority of Rome" and "the *quod semper, quod ubique, quod ab omnibus* is discredited forever. There is one living oracle of God, from whose lips all men are to receive the truth."[64] Roman Catholic faith in the true development of papal infallibility on the basis of the Petrine claims and the primacy of the bishop of Rome in the early church leads to the Roman Church's exaggerated claims of supremacy and infallibility. Forbes believes that these changes to Christian doctrine will lead Roman Catholics to abandon the rule of faith, and it will stand in the way of reforming corruptions and exaggerations.

Scottish Episcopalians and other Anglicans, Forbes suspects, will question why they should care about changes to Roman Catholic doctrine. But Forbes argues that this new doctrine calls Christians to contemplate the nature of revelation and the reality of immutable truths—"the question presents itself to us as Christians and as members of the English branch of the Church Catholic, Is this, in its present manifestation, the faith once delivered to the Saints?"[65] Challenging his clergy to discern between development and error, he points out the discrepancies between the biblical and early Church understandings of Peter and the see of Rome and the claims of Vatican I:

> Is this the real and true interpretation of the passages in Scripture which refer to St. Peter? If it is of faith, it must have been part of the original revelation. Did the Apostles know anything of this? Did St. Peter himself realize his high destiny? There is not a trace in the Holy Scriptures of St. Peter being the one living oracle of divine truth. That our Lord gave him a certain primacy or pre-eminence; that he took the lead in the infant community, as is clear from the first chapters of the Acts; that he wrote from Rome, the mystic Babylon, and there, according to a most ancient tradition, sealed his testimony with his blood, we concede; but this is not the question at issue. In no exclusive or precise sense was St. Peter the pastor and doctor of all Christians, and his successor cannot claim from the divine assistance promised to him (*per assistentiam divinam ei in Beato Petro promissam*) to be what he was not.[66]

---

[62] Forbes, *The Church of England and the Doctrine of Papal Infallibility* (Oxford: J. H. Parker, 1871), 15.
[63] Ibid.
[64] Ibid.
[65] Ibid., 16.
[66] Ibid.

The Church should measure claims of development according to the Scriptures, Fathers, and consensus of the Church catholic. Forbes reminds his clergy that their province is a "branch of the Church Catholic" and asks them to question the claims of Vatican I on the basis of Scripture and the witness of the conciliar Church. Forbes' belief in the teaching office of the Church and the infallibility of ecumenical councils filled him with a longing for the reunion of the parts of the Church in Apostolic succession.[67] His critique of infallibility in no way arises from Protestant triumphalism or satisfaction with the divisions in the Church. In contrast, he applies the rule of faith to form Evangelical Catholic clergymen and laymen, conforming to the authority of the Scripture, sitting at the feet of the fathers, and seeking to represent the mind of Christ in their faith and practice.

---

[67] For an explanation of Forbes' commitment to unity, see Forbes, *The Notes of Unity and Sanctity in Reference to Modern Scepticism, a Charge* (Linfield: Joseph Masters & Son, 1864).

Chapter 29

The *Ressourcement* of Liturgical Music by John Mason Neale (1818–1866)

Dr. Joel W. West

For the past century, the Anglican church has been known for the music that it incorporates into its worship, both that which is sung by the congregation and that which is performed by the choir. Yet little of this existed in the Church of England (CofE) or its affiliated national churches before the great English Choral Revival in the second half of the nineteenth century. Unlike the nonconformists, the CofE lacked hymnals or its own hymns, congregational singing had largely disappeared, and the great cathedral and chapel choirs had declined precipitously since the Elizabethan era.[1]

Of course, the initial thrust for the nineteenth-century *ressourcement* within the CofE—a return to the undivided church of the first millennium and often to the ancient patristic church—came from the Oxford Movement, both the Tractarians of 1833–1845 and their successors. For example, beginning with Edward Bouverie Pusey's translation of Augustine's *Confessions*, the 48-volume *Library of Fathers of the Holy Catholic Church* (1838–1885) made accessible patristic writing "anterior to the division of the East and West" by Ambrose, Athanasius, Augustine, Chrysostom, Cyprian, Cyril, Gregory and Irenaeus. This Anglo-Catholic milestone also had an indirect effect, spurring a flurry of other Victorian translations of first millennium theologians, such as the *Select Library of the Nicene and Post-Nicene Fathers of the Christian Church* (1886–1900).

While the Oxford men had pushed a renewed interest in patristic writings and apostolic succession with *The Tracts of These Times*, it is widely recognized that their focus on doctrine meant that little thought was given to worship, including matters of aesthetics, liturgy, and ceremony. Instead, it was their High Church allies from Cambridge who built upon these earlier Tractarian efforts to transform the practice of worship. As Nicholas Temperly wrote:

> [The] Tractarians ... enhanced enormously the beauty and impressiveness of worship, so that even their most inveterate enemies were ultimately shamed into putting some of their ideas into practice.... The details of Tractarian worship were worked out primarily by the Cambridge Camden Society.[2]

From 1839 onward, the Cambridge Camden Society (later the Ecclesiological Society) led the push for reform of church architecture, art, and music within the CofE. These men and their allies were responsible for both restoring sacred music to the ordinary parish church and helping raise the standards of both choral and congregational singing.

The best known of these Cambridge ecclesiologists was John Mason Neale (1818–1866), a student at Trinity College Cambridge from 1836 to 1840. Not only was he a leader and a key author in the Society's early years, but through his prodigious research he

---

[1] The decline of English congregation and choral singing from 1550–1850 is documented by Peter Le Huray's *Music and the Reformation in England 1549–1660* (1978) and Nicholas Temperley's *The Music of the English Parish Church* (1979), both from Cambridge University Press.

[2] Temperly, 250–251.

played a leading role in the nineteenth-century *ressourcement* of ancient liturgies and hymn texts.

Neale's main contribution to the Anglican Choral Revival was as the pre-eminent English hymn translator of the nineteenth century, both in quality and quantity. Neale accounted for 63 of the 643 hymn texts in the 5ᵗʰ edition of *Hymns Ancient & Modern* in 1904—more than Isaac Watts, Charles Wesley, and Catherine Winkworth combined. He had a similar impact upon English language hymnody throughout the twentieth century—with 41 of 600 hymns in *The Hymnal 1940*—and is credited with 25 of the 639 hymns in *The Book of Common Praise 2017*, the first Anglican hymnal of the twenty-first century.

Neale's lasting impact on Anglican sacred music comprised four major areas. First, with his Cambridge colleagues, he restored and adapted an aesthetic of beauty for Anglican liturgy and worship. Second, he recovered and translated theologically sound pre-Reformation hymn texts, both from medieval Catholic worship and from the undivided church of the first millennium. Third, his process for *ressourcement* of these ancient and medieval texts set a model and stimulated further *ressourcement* of lost texts throughout the nineteenth and twentieth century. Finally, Neale and the Society stimulated a parallel effort for liturgical music, with the emphasis on aesthetics, recovery of lost tunes, and congregational participation.

About John Mason Neale

For his *ressourcement* of ancient texts, John Mason Neale (1818–1866) was known as "that greatest of all translators" of Anglican hymns. The son of a strict Evangelical CofE churchman who died in early 1823, he later became a leader in the High Church party, and a forerunner of the late nineteenth-century Ritualists and twentieth-century Anglo-Catholics.[3]

The seminal period in Neale's professional development came with his years at Trinity College Cambridge. At Trinity, Neale distinguished himself throughout his skills in classical languages, failing to earn first class honors only due to his limited math skills. An author of original poetry and hymn texts, on 11 occasions from 1845–1863 he won the Seaton Prize, the annual award given for the best sacred poetry by a Cambridge graduate.

Neale graduated from Trinity College in 1840. In 1842, he married Sarah Norman Webster, daughter of a Cambridge parish priest, and sister of the wife of Neale's fellow ecclesiologist E. J. Boyce. John and Sarah Neale had five children: Agnes (1844), Cornelius (1846), Mary (1848), Katherine (1850), and Margaret (1853).

In 1842, he was ordained a priest and for two months worked as the vicar of a parish in Sussex—but he never again served as a parish priest. Some biographers attribute the latter to his frail health, while others point to restrictions by diocesan bishops suspicious of the catholic reform efforts of the Cambridge Ecclesiologists, of which Neale was the most visible symbol.

---

[3] In addition to Eleanor Towle's biography and the letters edited by Neale's daughter Mary Lawson, key biographical data are provided by the *Guardian's* August 15, 1866, obituary (available at books.google.com/books?id=dMpVAAAAcAAJ) and the introduction to Leon Litvack's *John Mason Neale and the Quest for Sobornost* (Oxford: Oxford University Press, 1994).

In his last 20 years, he held two positions in East Grinstead, a village in West Sussex (midway between Brighton and London and nine miles east of modern-day Gatwick airport). In 1846, he obtained a preferment as warden of Sackville College, an almshouse for the poor established in 1608. During Neale's tenure, he and Sackville College were supported by the latter's patron, the Earl De La Warr. As warden, starting in 1849, he chanted a fivefold liturgy of the hours: Prime, Morning Prayer, Nones, Vespers and Compline.

In 1855, he founded the Society of St. Margaret, a religious nursing order that trained nuns to minister to the poor, which later expanded to Scotland and Boston. In 1856, it relocated to East Grinstead and had Neale as chaplain until his death. His daughter Katherine later became a nun and eventually mother superior of the order. He died in 1866, four months after Tractarian John Keble, but decades before E. B. Pusey and John Henry Newman.

Restoring a Transcendental Aesthetic to Sacred Worship

While at Cambridge, it was Neale's role in forming the Society that shaped the remainder of his career. In May 1839, Neale met and discussed church architecture with first year student Benjamin Webb, and three days later, the two joined with fellow Trinity student Edward Jacob Boyce to form the Cambridge Camden Society. Their initial sponsor was the Ven. Thomas Thorp, fellow and tutor of Trinity College, and they moved quickly to enlist a wide range of prominent patrons as well as hundreds of other members.

Their first task was to launch a revival of the Gothic architectural style prominent in Britain from the twelfth through fifteenth centuries. Through both its research and zealous self-promotion, the Society and its leaders developed a national reputation that soon eclipsed a similar church architecture group founded earlier the same year in Oxford. In 1841, the Society launched its journal *The Ecclesiologist*. The inaugural issue proclaimed its scope to include not only church architecture, but also "Church Musick and all the Decorative Arts which can be made subservient to Religion."

Also in 1841, the Society published *A Few Words to Church Builders*, a 40-page booklet that listed among its patrons the archbishop of Canterbury and 15 other bishops, including prelates from Scotland, Ireland, Canada, the United Staes, and New Zealand. In it, the 23-year-old Neale offered clear (and opinionated) guidelines for English church architecture, cautioning that "care must be taken that the beauty of the building be not sacrificed to the accommodation of worshippers." On the next page, he argued that

> THERE ARE TWO PARTS, AND ONLY TWO PARTS WHICH ARE ABSOLUTELY ESSENTIAL TO A CHURCH—CHANCEL AND Nave. If it have not the latter, it is at best only a chapel; if it have not the former, it is little better than a meeting-house. The twelve thousand ancient churches in this land, in whatever else they may differ, agree in this, that every one has or had a well-defined Chancel.[4]

Neale's arguments for architectural revival were not merely aesthetic, but also sought to recapture underlying theological principles of Christian symbolism manifested by the

---

[4] Cambridge Camden Society, *A Few Words to Church Builders* (Cambridge: Cambridge University Press, 1841), 4–5.

earlier architectural style. In 1843, the Society published its first edition of *The Symbolism of Churches and Church Ornaments*, Neale and Webb's translation of a thirteenth-century treatise on that topic. In their 130-page preface, they concluded that "we are assured that, if there is any truth ... in what has ever been proposed by any who have appreciated the genius of Pointed Architecture, ... no other period can be chosen at which all conditions of beauty, of detail, of general effect, of truthfulness, of reality are so fully answered as in this."[5]

Together, these and other Society efforts sparked a century-long Gothic revival in Anglican church architecture, one carefully chronicled by James White.[6] By 1870, their once controversial architectural principles had set the pattern not only for the Church of England, but also for thousands of churches throughout the world.

However, the Society soon got caught up in an effort by Evangelical churchmen alleging "popery" in the Oxford, Cambridge, and allied high church efforts at reforming the Church of England. Among other offences, in their church restorations the Ecclesiologists had replaced wooden tables (mandated by the Reformation) with stone altars, and in 1845 lost a notorious Canon Law case that concluded that such a "Romish church" altar must be removed. In 1846, the Cambridge Camden Society relocated to London (where most of its leaders now lived) and renamed itself the "Ecclesiological Society"

In addition to the founders, other prominent leaders from Trinity College included Thorp, Alexander James Beresford Hope, Henry L. Jenner and S. S. Greatheed. New members after the relocation to London included Thomas Helmore (who soon led its musical efforts) and William Dyce, the Scottish painter who created the frescoes at All Saints, Margaret Street after earlier publishing English translations of Renaissance and medieval chants.

After its 1846 relocation to London, the Society had an immediate impact on the design of Victorian churches there. Early examples were St. Andrew's, Wells Street (1847)—where Webb was the rector from 1862–1881—St. Barnabas, Pimlico (1850), St. Stephen's, Westminster (1850), and St. Mary Magdalene, Munster Square (1852). The peak of the Society's influence came with its decade-long supervision of the construction of All Saints, Margaret Street (1859), which Adelmann termed "an early flagship for Tractarian worship" that today remains an exemplar of Victorian High Gothic architecture.

Neale's interest in aesthetics and Christian symbolism extended into liturgical practice. As Scott de Hart wrote:

> For Neale, the Holy Sacraments of the Church are proof, in the highest degree, of the principle of symbolism and ritual. The Sacraments are in reality not only signs of things unseen, but channels and instruments of God's grace. The necessity for

---

[5] John Mason Neale and Benjamin Webb, *The Symbolism of Churches and Church Ornaments* (Leeds: T. W. Green, 1843), xxx.

[6] For more details on the influence of the Cambridge Camden Society on architecture, liturgy, music, and Ritualism, see Dale Adelmann, *The Contribution of Cambridge Ecclesiologists to the Revival of Anglican Choral Worship, 1839–62* (New York: Routledge, 2020); James F. White, *The Cambridge Movement: the Ecclesiologists and the Gothic Revival.* (Cambridge: Cambridge University Press, 1962); and John Shelton Reed, *Glorious Battle: The Cultural Politics of Victorian Anglo-Catholicism* (Nashville: Vanderbilt University Press, 1996).

Ritualism in Christian worship finds a convincing attestation in the institution of the Sacraments ordained by the Son of God.[7]

Finally, within these churches, Neale, Helmore, and other Society men applied these sensibilities to liturgical practice. As with architecture, they adopted an anti-anti-Catholic stance in seeking to restore beauty to worship, particularly in the ceremonial. They had to overcome the suspicion of medieval practices held not only by the Evangelical party, but also the Oxford Tractarians. Between the Society, the *Ecclesiologist*, and his own personal research and ministry, Neale led efforts to re-instate these formal practices into Anglican worship—because he was personally frustrated with doctrines that lacked outward expression. Kenneth Hylson-Smith wrote:

It was Cambridge rather than Oxford, and more especially John Mason Neale, who first treated ceremonial seriously, "as an indispensable and important part of worship, instead of something to be apologized for and left to the weaker brethren."[8]

In the 1840s, Pusey and Neale were among those Tractarian priests who secretly heard confessions, so that the penitent would not be pressured or condemned by family or higher church officials. Over initial opposition by Pusey, Neale sought the restoration of liturgical vestments: in 1850, he was one of the first three Anglican clergymen of his era to wear a chasuble. Within three years after Neale launched services at the Society of St. Margaret's interim chapel, the sacrament was reserved on the altar, Stations of the Cross were observed, the altar was stripped for Good Friday and censed for Easter. At the same time, Society clergy such as Benjamin Webb, Thomas Helmore, H. L. Jenner and others worked out the practical implications of their philosophy in more conventional parish ministry.

Neale's Call for Excellence

As a High Churchman, classics scholar, and poet, Neale held strong opinions about the need to bring hymn singing to the Church of England. Much as the Oxford reforms brought a *ressourcement* of older Latin and Greek theological texts, Neale sought to do for the theology taught in older hymns. As the preface to the harmonized *Hymnal Noted* explained:

The translation into English of the really Catholic Hymns, in such wise as to be capable of being sung to the old Catholic tunes, was a work second only in importance to the translation of the Psalter, the Offices, and the Liturgy.[9]

While sharing with his Evangelical contemporaries the goal of strengthening congregational hymn singing, Neale criticized both the theology and aesthetics of the English hymn singing of the previous three centuries, as promoted and controlled by Puritan and other Reformed churchman. Originally led by the Dissenters—notably the

---

[7] Scott D. de Hart, "The Influence of John Mason Neale and the Theology of Symbolism," Project Canterbury, 2002, anglicanhistory.org/essays/dehart1.pdf.

[8] Kenneth Hylson-Smith, *High Churchmanship in the Church of England: From the Sixteenth Century to the Late Twentieth Century* (Edinburgh: T & T Clark, 1993), 213.

[9] Thomas Helmore, ed., *Accompanying Harmonies to Hymnal Noted* (London: Novello, 1852), i.

Congregationalists, Presbyterians, and Methodists—they later were joined by clergy of the Evangelical party within the CofE such as John Newton, who with William Cowper published the *Olney Hymns* (1779).

Neale's 42-page essay "English Hymnology: Its History and Prospects" both detailed his criticism of these earlier efforts, and laid the theoretical groundwork for the *ressourcement* of lost hymn texts for the Church of England. Neale bemoaned not only the loss of these specific texts, but even more so, the loss of a true sung service. He began by saying:

> AMONG the most pressing of the inconveniences consequent on the adoption of the vernacular language in the office-books of the Reformation, must be reckoned the immediate disuse of all the hymns of the Western Church. That treasury, into which the saints of every age and country had poured their contributions, delighting, each in his generation, to express their hopes and fears, their joys and sorrows ... henceforth they became as a sealed book and as a dead letter.....
>
> The Church of England had, then, to wait. She had, as it has been well said, to begin over again. There might arise saints within herself, who, one by one, should enrich her with hymns in her own language; there might arise poets, who should be capable of supplying her office-books with versions of the hymns of earlier times.[10]

He lamented the Puritan influence of the sixteenth and seventeenth centuries, and how their (Genevan-inspired) policies had limited CofE singing to versified psalter and tunes. He attacked the two most popular English compilations of versified psalms, both "the versions, or rather perversions, of the Psalms" provided by Sternhold & Hopkins (1562) and the "still lower abyss of wretchedness" of Tate & Brady (1696).

Much of his essay focused on the theological emphases if not outright heresy of the eighteenth-century hymns created outside the Church of England. For the prolific Congregationalist hymnwriter Isaac Watts, Neale attacked his representation of a wrathful (rather than loving) God and what he said were persistent Apollinarian, Arian, and Sabellian heresies. Overall, "we shall hardly open a page without being shocked by some gross piece of irreverence." In the hymn collections of Charles and John Wesley, he criticized "the mischievous Wesleyan idea of the necessity of faith only, for the forgiveness of sins" and the "dogma of the sinless state of perfection attainable by every Christian."

With these theological objections, he lamented the potential corrupting influence of the Dissenters' hymns upon the catechizing of young Anglican children. Already the father of three (later five) children, Neale held out for specific criticism the impact of Watts' *Divine and Moral Songs*, then used by Evangelicals within the CofE. In contrast, he offered the example of his own three volumes of original children's hymns (1842–1845), which he said was written

> in accordance with the Catechism.... Their recommendation is, that they teach no false doctrine, and that they are written in easy measures; their great fault, that many of them are intolerably prosaic.[11]

---

[10] J. M. Neale, "English Hymnology: Its History and Prospects," *Christian Remembrancer*, October 1849, 301–342 at 303.

[11] Ibid., 337.

Four hymns from these volumes remain in use today: *The Hymnal 1940* includes: "Around the throne of God a band", "O thou, who through this holy week" and "O very God of very God" (from *Hymns for Children*) while *Book of Common Praise 2017* includes "O Lord of hosts, whose glory fills" (from *Hymns for Youth*).

Beyond theology, in anticipation of a much later conflict over hymnody, Neale's other main complaint was against "that individualizing tendency" of "modern hymns" to use the first-person singular that "the ancient scrupulously avoided". He lamented the "intense subjectivity" of Charles Wesley's hymns, which focused on the experience of the individual rather than the believer's "connection with, or acknowledgement of, the Man CHRIST JESUS."

For the best of these first-person hymns, Neale argued for a distinction between hymns for personal devotion versus those for corporate church worship. He praised Augustus Toplady's "Rock of ages" as "undoubtedly the best original hymn in the English language, provided it be taken as a penitential devotion," while William Cowper's "There is a fountain fill'd with blood" "might, perhaps, be admitted as a Lent Hymn." Less qualified praise is given to Watt's "When I survey the wondrous cross" and Wesley's "Jesus, lover of my soul."

Neale's Lasting Impact on Anglican Hymnody

By 1849, Neale had already begun his answer to these objections, the *ressourcement* of ancient hymns and liturgies that would become the focus of the final portion of his life. As part of travels to warmer climates for his health, Neale identified and studied liturgies in the libraries of Continental Europe. From 1849–1859, he published editions of Gallican, German, Spanish, and Portuguese liturgies, as well as the earlier liturgies of St. Mark, St. James, St. Clement, St. Chrysostom, and St. Basil. From 1847–1873, Neale (and later his heirs) published an authoritative five-volume *History of the Holy Eastern Church*.

Neale's efforts to research liturgies of the first millennium produced hymn texts that (through translations by Neale and others) are in regular use for Anglican worship today. While Neale did author his own hymn texts (such as "Good King Wenceslas"), he is best known for his hymn translations from Greek and Latin from the first 1500 years of the Christian Church. Some of these original texts were from hymns or other liturgies, while others were adapted from sacred poetry. During the last 15 years of his life, he published five major compilations of these translations: *Mediæval Hymns and Sequences* (1851), the *Hymnal Noted* (1851–1855), *Carols for Christmas-tide* (1853), *Carols for Easter-tide* (1854), and *Hymns of the Eastern Church* (1862).

The most influential of these was *Hymnal Noted*, a fulfillment of Neale's dream to recover pre-Reformation hymns from the first 1500 years of the church, with Neale as the lead editor of the text and Helmore leading the music efforts. It began in 1850 as an officially sanctioned project of the Ecclesiological Society, with the first volume published in 1851 and the second in 1854. While Neale penned most of the translations, other Society members authored or contributed to translations, of which the best known is "O love, how deep" by Benjamin Webb.

Neale's efforts changed permanently the face of Anglican hymnody and indeed English-language hymnody overall. Although some translations have been altered,

Neale's influence also extended to America: 26 of the hymns from *Hymnal Noted* were published in 24 American Protestant and Catholic hymnals from 1905–1991.[12]

Of these five compilations, the texts for *Carols for Christmas-tide* and *Carols for Easter-tide* were adapted from texts from *Piae Cantiones*, after the British Ambassador to Sweden gave Neale a rare copy of this 1582 Finnish compilation of medieval Latin carols. Meanwhile, the remaining three compilations—*Mediæval Hymns and Sequence* (MHS), *Hymnal Noted* (HN) and *Hymns of the Eastern Church* (HEC)—all included translations of texts from the first millennium.

To find a list of such hymns used in American Anglican hymnody, I reviewed all hymns listed in the *Hymnal 1940 Hymnal Companion* as dating before 1000 A.D.—dropping one that more recent sources suggested dates from the eleventh century. The remaining hymns most probably date from the second through tenth centuries, although the exact dates of some will never be known.

This resulted in 52 hymn texts (some with multiple tunes) from the first millennium in *The Hymnal 1940* (H40), of which 40 are also published in *The Hymnal 1982* and 33 in *The Book of Common Praise 2017*. The 1982 is now used by almost all Episcopal churches in the U.S., while U.S. Anglican churches today employ all three hymnals.

Of the first millennium texts found in these three hymnals, 28/52, 21/40 and 15/33 were respectively based (to a greater or lesser degree) on translations by Neale, drawing from Latin and Greek sources from the third through ninth century. Table 1 shows these Neale texts in chronological order.

Table 1. Neale Latin and Greek Translations in Chronological Order

Source	Text†	Author§	H40	H82	B17
HN	The eternal gifts of Christ the King	St. Ambrose, 340–397	132	234	
HN	Of the Father's love begotten	Prudentius, 348–413	20	82	462
HN	That Easter Day with joy was bright	Latin, 5th C	98	193	134
HN	Now that the daylight fills the sky	Latin, 6th C	159	4	229
HN	Come, Holy Ghost, with God the Son	attributed to Ambrose but 6th C†	160	19	
HN	O God of truth, O Lord of might	attributed to Ambrose but 6th C†	161	22	
HN	O God, creation's secret force	attributed to Ambrose but 6th C†	162	15	
HN	O blest Creator of the light	Latin, 6th C	163	27	240
HN	O Trinity of blessed light	Latin, c. 6th C	171	30	238

---

[12] Joel W. West, "Neale's *Hymnal Noted* and its Impact on Twentieth-Century American Hymnody," *The Hymn* 69, no. 3 (Summer 2018): 14–24.

Source	Text†	Author§	H40	H82	B17
MHS	Draw nigh and take the Body of the Lord	possibly 6th C†	202	328	
HN	The royal banners forward go	Fortunatus, 569	63	162	
MHS	Sing, my tongue, the glorious battle	Fortunatus, 569	66	166	113
HN	To thee before the close of day	Latin, 7th C	164	44	
MHS	Blessed city, heav'nly Salem	Latin, c. 7th C	383	519	634
MHS	Christ is made the sure foundation	Latin, c. 7th C	384	518	498
HEC	A great and mighty wonder	St. Germanus, 634–734	18		
HEC	Thou hallowed chosen morn of praise	St. John of Damascus, 8th C	93		
HEC	Come, ye faithful, raise the strain	St. John of Damascus, 8th C	94	200	138
HEC	The day of resurrection!	St. John of Damascus, 8th C	96	210	123
HEC	The day is past and over	6th or 7th C†	184		
HEC	Christian, dost thou see them	St. Andrew of Crete, 660–732	556		100
HEC	Those eternal bowers	St. John of Damascus, 8th C	581		
HN	Thou art the King of Israel	Theodulph, c. 820	62	154	
HN	O come, O come, Emmanuel	Latin, 9th C	2	56	7
HN	Creator of the stars of night	Latin, 9th C	6	60	18
HEC	Stars of the morning, so gloriously bright	St. Joseph the Hymnographer, 9th C	121		
HEC	Let us now our voices raise	St. Joseph the Hymnographer, 9th C	136	237	198
HEC	Jesus, Name all names above	St. Theoctistus, c. 890	342		427

§ as reported by *Hymnal 1940 Hymnal Companion*
†as reported by later sources

Hymnal Noted accounted for half of these 28 texts. The most popular in American hymnody have been "All glory, laud and honor," "O come, O come Emmanuel," "Christ is made the sure foundation," "Of the Father's love begotten," and "O sons and daughters, let us sing." Neale's four other Latin translations were from *Medieval Hymns & Sequences*. Finally, 10 translations from Greek originals are taken from *Hymns of the Eastern Church*, all dated to the seventh, eighth, or ninth century.

As with other Victorian translations, the greatest impact of Neale's works came when they were included in the most popular nineteenth-century English hymnal, *Hymns Ancient & Modern*, which has been published in various editions since 1861. As the original hymnal editor, Henry Williams Baker both selected earlier texts and modified many of them—changes that remain in use today. These updates included "All glory, laud and honour" (Neale wrote "Glory and laud and honour"), "O come, O come, Emmanuel" ("Draw nigh, draw nigh, Emmanuel") and "Of the Father's love begotten" ("Of the Father sole begotten"). The most popular were later included in *The English Hymnal* (1906), the most influential Anglican hymnal of the twentieth century.

Baker was the first, but not the last to change (and sometimes improve) Neale's original works. However, the impact of Neale was not limited to his original or modified translations, but also included an approach that was adopted by others over the next 150 years.

Continuing *Ressourcement* in Anglican Hymnody

The patristic translations of Pusey, early Tractarians, and other allies spawned an interest in reclaiming the long-forgotten theological writings of the first millennium, a process of *ressourcement* that shows no sign of abating. Neale similarly sparked a *ressourcement* of hymn texts from this era that also continues to this day.

Neale was not the only one to contribute to this recovery of ancient texts within Anglican hymnody. Of the aforementioned texts from the first millennium in the 1940, 1982 and 2017 hymnals, 24/19/18 of the texts (respectively) were by other translators.

Beyond Neale, the most prominent translator of Latin and Greek texts in the mid-nineteenth century was Edwin Caswall (1814–1878). Like Neale, Caswell was a classics student (at Oxford) and the son of an Anglican priest who was ordained in the CofE; unlike Neale, he became Roman Catholic. In his 1849 article, Neale praised Caswall as a translator but slighted him as a poet.

In 1849, Caswall published a compilation of his own translations, *Lyra Catholica*. The latter brought two familiar texts, "Earth Has Many A Noble City" and "Hark a Thrilling Voice is Sounding." Like Neale's translations, these texts benefitted from both the visibility and translation modifications that came from being included in *Hymns Ancient and Modern*.

In the early twentieth century, Percy Dearmer (1867–1936) contributed 12 translations and 7 original texts as text editor of *The English Hymnal* (1906), updating some of these as editor of *Songs of Praise* (1925). Of the first millennium texts, four by Dearmer are found in all three hymnals (1940, 1982, 2017)—"Hail thee festival day" for Easter, Ascension and Pentecost—as well as "Father, we praise thee, now the night is over".

Of the hymns from the first millennium, about one fourth (13/52, 12/40, 9/33) were from the ancient church of the first five centuries. In addition to Neale's "Of the Father's love begotten" and Caswall's "Earth has many a noble city," the best known of these early hymns include "Let all mortal flesh" translated by Gerard Moultrie (1815–1885) and St. Patrick's Breastplate ("I bind unto myself today") by Dublin-born Cecil Frances Alexander (1818–1895).

Spawning the Anglican Choral Revival[13]

A classics scholar and poet, Neale focused on the texts and was a man of limited musical abilities. Instead, the Anglican Choral Revival of the mid-nineteenth century required the efforts of the more musically talented among the Ecclesiological Society and its allies to both recover historic melodies, and help revive congregational singing. As Helmore wrote in *The Ecclesiologist*:

> The fitness or unfitness of any musical mode of expression, as applied to the Offices of the Church, can only be judged of by the Church musician; not by the ritualist who is no musician, nor by the musician who is no ritualist; far less by the common-sense view of those who are notoriously neither.[14]

Such men restored older tunes and particularly chants to Anglican worship, and helped lead the nineteenth-century Anglican choral revival. They did so by building on the work of Neale and others, who had laid down the principles for aesthetics in architecture and ceremonial, as well as the recovery of sacred texts for congregational singing. But while many such texts were available from the first millennium, few ancient tunes survived due to the absence of a consistent notation process until the emergence of neumes in the Eastern and Western chant of the ninth century, so nearly all of the recovered tunes came from the undivided Western (i.e., Catholic) church of the Middle Ages.

Of the original Cambridge men, those with the most musical abilities were Benjamin Webb, H. L. Jenner and S. S. Greatheed. Their ranks grew with later members, particularly John Hullah (1843), William Dyce (1845), Thomas Helmore (1849), Robert Druitt (1853), and John Jebb (1860). Early allies in these efforts included Druitt and his Society for the Promotion of Church Music (with its journal *Parish Choir*) as well as the Tractarian newspaper *English Churchman*, at least from 1843–1884. These musically talented Ecclesiological Society leaders recovered ancient and medieval melodies, as well as improving choral and congregational singing.

Beginning in 1840, Dyce and others reprinted and translated Latin anthems by English (Tallis, Byrd, Gibbons, Purcell) and Continental (Palestrina, Victoria and Lassus) composers. Dyce also published an 1843 prayer book annotated with plainchant responses and canticles. Meanwhile, in the second half of the nineteenth century, various editions, commentaries, and translations were published of the Sarum Rite text and music, including one by F. H. Dickenson (with help from Webb, Neale, and other fellow Society members) and later contributions by Walter Frere.

---

[13] In addition to Adlemann's *Contribution of Cambridge Ecclesiologists*, see Joel W. West, "The Contribution of Cambridge Ecclesiologists to the Revival of Anglican Choral Worship, 1839–62," book review, *Journal of Anglican Studies* 21, no. 1 (May 2023): 161–163; Bernarr Rainbow, "Thomas Helmore and the Anglican Plainsong Revival," in *Bernarr Rainbow on Music: Memoirs and Selected Writings* (Woodbridge, UK: Boydell & Brewer, 2010), 319–324; Rainbow, "John Jebb (1805–1886) and the Choral Service," in *Bernarr Rainbow on Music*, 345–355; Rainbow, "Thomas Helmore and the Revival of Carol Singing," *The Musical Times* 100, no. 1402 (Dec 1959): 683–683; and Nicholas Temperley, "The Anglican Choral Revival," *The Musical Times* 112, no. 1535 (Jan 1971): 73–75.

[14] Thomas Helmore, "The Cantus Collectarum," *The Ecclesiologist*, June 1850, 104–110 at 109.

But the most musically influential member was Thomas Helmore (1811–1890), credited with leading the Victorian revival of Gregorian chant. In 1849, Helmore published *Psalter Noted*, with the Coverdale psalter set to historic Gregorian chants, and the next year published the first edition of the *Manual of Plainsong*, updated by John Stainer in 1902.

Helmore's skills in adapting and arranging plainsong were essential to completing Neale's efforts to recover ancient hymns, providing many of the melodies that today are credited as the tune "always used with this." At Dyce's urging, Helmore adapted Sarum Rite chants for the music of *Hymnal Noted*. In other cases, he used medieval tunes, as when he used the tune for "Divinum Mysterium" from *Piae Cantiones* to set the text for what became "Of the Father's love begotten."

In the various hymnals since *Hymnal Noted*, the tendency of the music editors has been either to include more recent compositions or add their own. For example, the 1906 tune SALVE FESTA DIES—paired by *The English Hymnal* with Neale's "Hail thee, festival day"—was written by music editor Ralph Vaughan Williams for that purpose. A rare exception was the work of Charles Winifred Douglas, who as editor of *The Hymnal 1940* incorporated mass settings from his 1915 *Missa Marialis*, which was adapted from twelfth to fifteenth century settings of the Latin *Kyrie*, *Agnus Dei*, *Sanctus*, and *Gloria*—and a Lord's Prayer which he asserted was of "ancient" origin.

Restoring Excellence to Choral Singing

In addition to recovering these choral works and applying tunes to recovered texts, the musical talents of the Ecclesiological Society were applied to the more difficult (and perhaps longer lasting) task of restoring liturgical singing. The aesthetic principles that Society men had applied to architecture, ceremonial, and poetry were extended to singing by Helmore in his first contribution to *The Ecclesiologist*, a November 1849 article entitled "Ecclesiastical Music":

> And the revival of Church music may now, under God's blessing, be again a means of re-uniting some scattered sheep within the true fold. The object of devoting art to the purposes of religion is first to glorify God with the *best* of His gifts, whether material or intellectual; and secondly, to stir up our own affections and those of our fellow-worshippers to a more lively participation of the sentiment or feeling to be expressed. And music eminently fulfils both these objects: by it the language of praise is clothed with its richest beauty, and there is no method in existence for influencing the human mind comparable to it.

The principle of glorifying God applied to both the choral and congregational singing. However, the two differed markedly in terms of the beauty of performance and also the degree of participation.

At the same time, improving the quality of Sunday worship music was long overdue. Since the Reformation, the approaches (and standards) of English choral music had been bifurcated between the ordinary parish, and a "cathedral" system that survived in diminished form after the expropriation of church resources under Henry VIII. However, despite their lingering status and resources, the choral musical performance standards of the cathedrals (along with that of university and royal chapels) endured several centuries of decline until the nineteenth century.

In the 1840s—before either became Society members—Jebb and Druitt were among those mounting vociferous calls for improvement to the cathedral and chapel choral worship. They both made moral arguments for raising standards of sung performance by choirs and demonstrated such singing in their own choirs. Jebb (joined by Frederick Ouseley) also sought to promote a completely sung service, not only in cathedrals but in everyday parish churches. Related efforts were made by composer, cathedral organist, and former chorister Samuel Sebastian Wesley—who was more interested in improving the elite choirs than ordinary singing, and never became a Society member because he vehemently opposed its efforts to promote the use of plainsong.

Jebb quickly rose to national prominence in his reform efforts with his 1843 manifesto, *The Choral Service of the United Church of England and Ireland*. The 549-page study provided a stark picture of the mediocrity (if not collapse) of the choral performance standards for the three once-elite bastions of choral worship: cathedrals (both old and new), collegiate churches, and the royal chapels. His 79 chapters examined both the different types of choirs and choral organizations, and the different sung elements of the principal sung services—Morning Prayer and the Communion Service.

The problems were so severe that to improve worship at cathedrals in England and Wales, in 1852 Queen Victoria appointed a 13-member commission that included the archbishops of Canterbury and York, and the bishops of London and Oxford. They investigated 13 "old foundation" cathedrals, 13 newer cathedrals established under Henry VIII, other cathedrals and chapels, and Westminster Abbey, the former Benedictine monastery. In three reports from 1854–1855, they summarized governance, resources, and staffing at the cathedrals, which in most cases had a choir (primary) school for younger boys and a grammar (secondary) school to prepare them for universities and often priestly vocations. Among other things, they recommended better pay for the men ("lay clerk") of the choirs, and better education and supervision of the choristers.

Improvements in the cathedral and chapel worship occurred over the last six decades of the nineteenth century, including efforts by Society members as parish clergy. Benjamin Webb established choirs in Brasted and Sheen, and then from 1862–1885 won acclaim at St Andrew's, Wells Street in London. In addition to Webb, Adelmann detailed the success of other Society members in creating and improving choral worship in their parishes, including H. L. Jenner, William Hodge Mill, and Thomas Tharp.

Introduced to the Society in 1837 by his friend Webb, A. J. B. Hope played an active role in Society leadership, becoming president in 1859. A member of parliament for more than 30 years—his last 19 years representing Cambridge—his main influence was using his inherited wealth to support parishes that modelled the Society's architectural and choral ideals. His patronage included the establishment of St. Augustine's Missionary College, Canterbury; All Saints, Margaret Street, and St. Matthias, Stoke Newington, as well as funding Webb's curacy at Sheen.

Outside the Society, a close ally was Frederick Ouseley, a regular guest at the home of Thomas Helmore, older brother of his Oxford classmate Frederick Helmore. A chaired professor of music at Oxford, Ouseley used his inherited wealth to found and endow a model choral school, St. Michael's Tenbury, whose chapel celebrated daily choral service for more than a century. At the chapel's 1856 consecration, the dedication ceremony choir included 14-year-old treble Arthur Sullivan, and the next year its first organist was a 16-year-old John Stainer. Ouseley also accumulated a library of rare manuscripts—including the score Handel used to conduct the Dublin premiere of the *Messiah*—that later became part of the Oxford library collection.

But the greatest influence on congregational and choral singing came from Helmore, who introduced the topic of Ecclesiastical Music to readers of *The Ecclesiologist* in November 1849. A follow-up article three months later by (another) Society official advocated the use of Gregorian chant both for choral and congregational singing—while calling for the use of vocal harmony for the latter.

Beyond his role spawning the Gregorian chant, Helmore had numerous opportunities to put these reforms in practice and set national standards for choral performance. The first was at St. Mark's College, Chelsea, where he was appointed the founding vice-principal (and later precentor) for this nationally known teacher training program. Until his 1877 retirement, at St. Mark's he prepared future teachers to teach singing in their school, their parish church, and their local village.

Perhaps the most prestigious post was at the Chapel Royal of St. James—the post-Reformation bastion of sung service during the Elizabethan era—where he served as choirmaster from 1846–1886. In 1854, the newest choirboy was Arthur Sullivan, who successfully auditioned less than five weeks shy of his twelfth birthday. Sullivan sang with Helmore for two years, until winning a scholarship to attend the Royal Academy of Music and Leipzig Conservatory—and remained a family friend for the remainder of his life.

Helmore also led the Motett Choir—partly staffed by Chapel choirboys—after the Society restarted it in 1852 until it was spun off again as an independent organization in 1862. The choir continued both its missions, publishing and translating long-lost Renaissance music, and modelling performance standards for such music.

Finally, no discussion of improved choral performance would be complete without considering late nineteenth-century reforms in the English collegiate choirs that created what today is considered the "traditional" English choral sound. Current listeners might assume that these elite and historic boy choirs have maintained high standards of selection and performance since their beginnings, which for King's College Choir would have been its founding in 1441 by Henry VI.

However, as noted, the collegiate choirs had suffered from the same problems that plagued cathedral choirs—first the drastic budget cuts of Henry VIII, and then centuries of neglect and decline that went unremarked until John Jebb, and later the Cathedral Commissioners, highlighted these problems. In the mid-nineteenth century, choral standards were raised by Webb at the Chapel Royal and at the great cathedral choirs by fervent reformers such as Jebb and S. S. Wesley.

Ironically, while the reform efforts began in the colleges, it took decades for such reforms to reach the collegiate choirs. Early on, the Cambridgemen and their Oxford counterparts brought student-led awareness, while faculty such as Frederick Ouseley (Oxford) and later C. V. Stanford (Cambridge) continued reform efforts and trained the next generation of musicians and clergy.

High expectations were instituted by John Stainer, organist and choirmaster at Magdalene College Oxford from 1860 until he left in 1872 to become organist of St. Paul's

Cathedral. However, the enduring (and long-overdue) reforms to the recruiting, training, and performance expectations of the college boy choirs came with the 1876 appointment of a new organist for the King's College Choir: Alfred Mann, former Norwich Cathedral chorister and Oxford undergrad.[15] In less than a decade, he dramatically raised the standards of the choristers, attracting greater attention and attendance to these services.

Also, to improve the quality of the men's voices, in 1880 the great-nephews of Jane Austen funded two choral scholarships to attract qualified Cambridge undergraduates to sing as lay clerks in the King's College Choir. The program was so successful that fifty years later, the scholarships had risen to 12 (where they remain today) and were imitated by other collegiate choirs. Some of the choristers returned as choral scholars, and later applied their musical talents as clergymen and schoolmasters.

Today, Mann is best known for his role in instituting Kings College Choir's signature accomplishment: the sung Festival of Lessons and Carols, the chapel's annual Christmas Eve service. Mann led the choir for its first service in 1918—instituted by the college's new dean, Rev. Eric Milner Milner-White, recently returned from chaplaincy with the British Army. Mann also led the musical service for its first BBC broadcast in 1928, an annual tradition that spread the choir's performance standards and reputation nationally, and later worldwide.

Improving Congregation Singing and Participation

The Society had its most direct impact by setting the standard for improved music performance for almost three decades, providing both examples and practical solutions for future clergy to lead a choral revival in their own parishes. In addition to (re)establishing and improving choral worship, as parish clergy, Society leaders worked out the practicalities of reforming church music, notably including congregational singing.

Such reforms came in four parts. First, as much as allowed by local and episcopal expectations, they employed plainsong and other musical works consistent with the Society's understanding of the historic sung liturgy. Second, many chanted the sung liturgy on Sunday and even daily services. Third, they selected and trained choirs that would lead congregational worship.

Finally, they sought to increase both the quality and frequency of congregational singing in their churches: at a minimum, singing hymns, but in many cases chanting psalms, canticles, or responses. They often cited the successful congregational singing by Dissenter churches as a club to shame their CofE opponents into cooperation.

They built upon a national movement to improve adult singing launched in 1841 by John Hullah. With his novel method for training adult singers, Hullah's workshops trained as many as 50,000 participants in its first two years. Improved congregational singing was also taught by the Cambridge Church Music Society, formed in 1853 with Thomas Helmore as its music director, which with its earlier Oxford counterpart, trained dozens if not hundreds of future CofE clergy. Meanwhile, improved singing proficiency allowed Webb's St. Andrews' parishioners to sing psalms (to Anglican chant) at every Sunday mass.

---

[15] Timothy Day, *I Saw Eternity the Other Night: King's College, Cambridge, and an English Singing Style* (London: Penguin UK, 2018).

Meanwhile, the success of congregational singing fueled (and was reinforced) by the 1861 publication of the most influential Anglican hymnal of the nineteenth century (if not all time): *Hymns Ancient & Modern*, which combined earlier hymn translations by Neale, Caswall, Winkworth, and others with earlier nonconformist and contemporary Victorian hymns.

The overall editor was William Henry Baker, who graduated Trinity College Cambridge four years after Neale, who (unlike Neale) worked as a parish priest, the last 26 years in one parish near Leominster. A retrospective on the hymnal described Williams as heavily influenced by Neale and other Society leaders, with his 1865 parish architecture and liturgy demonstrating "high churchman", "Ecclesiologist," and "ritualist" tendencies.[16] Conversely, Baker had very little influence on the Society: he was listed as a member on all available rosters from 1846–1864, but was not mentioned in the *Ecclesiologist* or Society histories, with one only passing mention of Baker in Towle's 1907 Neale biography about an undated letter to Neale regarding *Hymns A&M*.

Assessment

Neale was a man of many limitations. He was organizationally challenged: while he wrote for the Society as his health permitted, the Society depended on others to keep the effort moving forward, notably Thomas Helmore, Benjamin Webb, William Dyce, and A. J. B. Hope. Untempered by ordinary parish ministry, Neale had the most extreme Ritualist tendencies of the Society leaders. His parochial impact was thus limited by his health, his inflexibility—and his bishop's resulting opposition.

Still, the nature of what and how we Anglicans sing in the twenty-first century was permanently transformed by his vision of *ressourcement* of long-lost hymn texts. This included the specific texts that he reclaimed from the undivided church of the first millennium, and the liturgy of the Latin rite medieval English church. It also included the interest and process for such reclamation that continued with others through the nineteenth century and into the twentieth.

Because he died on the Feast of the Transfiguration in 1866, Neale is today remembered every year on the following day, August 7. The date is observed by the Church of England, the Episcopal Church, and the ACNA (which, in its 2019 prayer book, refers to Neale as "Priest and Reformer of the Church").[17]

With or without a formal observance, Neale's legacy endures today. During the last 27 years of his life, Neale permanently transformed the nature of Anglican church music—with his aesthetic eye, his hymn text translations, and his process for recovering lost ancient and medieval texts. Meanwhile, the Cambridge movement that he launched attracted a range of musically proficient clergy who extended these reforms to the composition, choral, and congregational performance of Anglican liturgical music.

---

[16] John Harper, "Towards *Hymns Ancient & Modern:* Anglican Parish Worship and music in the mid-nineteenth century," in *Hymns Ancient & Modern and Henry Williams Baker* (Leominster, UK: Leominster Historical Society, 2013), 8–26.

[17] Ironically, guided by their Anglican Missal, Anglo-Catholics in England (1921 edition) and the U.S. (1942, 1959, 1995 editions) ignore Keble, Neale, and Pusey but include Ignatius (leader of the Counter-Reformation) as well as more obscure post-Reformation Catholic saints such as St. Joseph of Cupertino.

Chapter 30

Teaching Anglo-Catholicism:
The Catechism of Vernon Staley (1852–1933)

The Rev. Calvin Robinson

Throughout the Oxford Movement in the nineteenth century, Tractarians were often referred to as Newmanites and later Puseyites, after the two most prominent leaders of the movement. St. John Henry Newman and Edward Pusey catalysed the Oxford Movement. The next generation of Tractarians, however, often remain somewhat less celebrated. Vernon Staley is a prime example: here is a man who continued that momentum with his works in the early twentieth century, with significant contributions including *The Catholic Religion: A Manual of Instruction for Members of the Anglican Communion* (1893), *The Practical Religion* (1897), *The Ceremonial of the English Church* (1900), and *Liturgical Studies* (1907).

With *The Catholic Religion*, Vernon Staley produced an Anglo-Catholic catechism. Where the likes of Newman and his contemporaries were intellectuals, with *Tracts* making for interesting academic reading, Staley was the everyman's theologian. *The Catholic Religion* is an accessible approach to working through the Anglican Formularies from a catholic persuasion, offering a broad perspective of Anglicanism as the English expression of the catholic faith.

This is not a purely instrumental catechism. Staley begins with the foundation of the Church and the outpouring of the Holy Ghost at Pentecost forming the Catholic religion. In the early chapters he explores Christ founding his Church, intentionally using first person pronouns, "I will build my Church" when he speaks to St. Peter, whose *faith* he builds the Church upon, not the person. This view of Staley's is in line with the teaching of early church fathers, despite the best assertions of our Roman friends.

Where Staley originally piqued my interest, though, is in his chapters on "The Conversion of England" and "the Church in England." Here we learn that the Church has nearly always existed in England. There are myths of St. Paul journeying West to preach the Gospel in England. There is the tale of King Lucius begging Eleutherus—the bishop of Rome—to send Christian teachers to England. In addition, of course, there is the ancient legend of Joseph of Arimathea—the man who buried our Lord—going to England as the first missionary. Some even talk of him taking a young Christ along with him at an earlier date, although Staley does not mention that. The most probable start to Christianity in England, however, is via immigrants from Gaul—now France—as early as the second century. We know of a Roman who was martyred for his faith in Christ in the fourth century, St. Alban, and we know from historical records that British bishops attended the council of Arles in 314 and the council of Ariminum in 359. Thus, Christianity was present in England from the very beginning of the faith.[1]

Of course, the most notable story of the faith arriving in England is the one of St. Gregory the Great, before he was bishop of Rome, who caught wind of a number of Saxon

---

[1] Something I take a little pride in as an Englishman, when people try to claim we were nothing but pagans until the Roman mission showed up.

slave boys for sale at a market. As the story goes, he noticed their fair complexion and asked where they were from. A Jew answered, "From Britain: the people there have these fair complexions," to which Gregory asked, "Are they heathens or Christians?" Gregory continued: "'Alas! that such bright faces should be in the power of the prince of darkness—that with outward forms so lovely, the mind within should be sick and empty of grace! How do you call their nation?"

"Angles," said the Jew.

Gregory replied, "'Tis well, they have Angels' faces; it were meet they should be fellow heirs with Angels in heaven."[2]

To cut the story short, he took a fancy to the men from England, and this is why when he later became Pope, he sent a band of forty monks in 597 to convert the fair-faced heathens. Among these monks was a priest named Augustine, St. Augustine, of course, became the first Archbishop of Canterbury. The common assumption is that this is when Christianity arrived in England, but we know that by this point there were many Celtic Christians. One of Augustine's first battles was bringing the Christians who had established themselves in Wales and Cornwall under his authority. They joined forces to preach the Gospel to the Saxons. Bear in mind, this is a time before there was a properly formed England, never mind a United Kingdom. Eventually, they were joined by the Scottish Christians in Iona and those from the North in Lindisfarne, whom we know managed to retain their distinct flavour, thanks to the writings of St. Bede, the father of English history.

Thus, the Anglican Church has always been quite disparate and diverse. We had influences from Wales, Scotland, England, France, and Rome, combining to form what became the Church of England. It was not until AD 664 that we fell under the authority of the bishop of Rome, and even then it was only a matter of adopting Roman customs rather than Papal Supremacy—for instance, bishops were still selected locally. Until that point, there had been conflicting liturgical calendars and customs between the Roman and the Celtic Christians. The King of Northumbria called a council at Whitby Abbey to settle the matter. The battle started over when they should keep Easter, but quickly became about who should be arbiter in such matters, which is a problem we never really solved, it seems. There is something about the English—a trait we share with Americans evidently—which makes it impossible for us to be governed by a foreign power.

A thousand years later the issue reared its head again in the Reformation. Staley explores Peter's Pence, essentially a foreign tax, along with annates and papal bulls, which were to be paid for by Englishmen to Rome. There is a symmetry here with the American call for independence over "no taxation without representation." One could say the Reformation was the first Brexit—England gaining her sovereignty back from a European superstate.

Staley delves into the grievances that were building up prior to the Reformation, around political allegiances, taxation, and the infamous indulgences used to fund St. Peter's Basilica. All of this is in stark contrast to the Protestant Reformation happening on the continent, which was far more theological than our own. There are a number of

---

[2] Staley, *The Catholic Religion*, 13th ed. (London: Mowbray, 1904), 72.

revisionists who would like to paint the English Reformation as an overly Protestant movement that was Calvinist in nature, but I think that is a twisting of the truth.

We only have to look at the documents coming out of the English Church following the break from Papal authority to know that to be untrue. Henry VIII was more Catholic than most Roman Catholics I know today. When England split from Rome, we had 35 years of incredible soundness. I would describe those years as peak Anglo-Catholicism: Catholicity without the Pope.

Prior to the *Thirty-Nine Articles*, the Ten Articles and, for the most part, the Six Articles (that were published in what were known as the Bishop's Book and the King's Book) outline a very Anglican understanding of the Catholic faith. Take for example the Ten Articles, from 1536.

Articles related to doctrines:

1. That Holy Scriptures and the three Creeds are the basis and summary of a true Christian faith.
2. That baptism conveys remission of sins and the regenerating grace of the Holy Spirit, and is absolutely necessary as well for children as adults.
3. That penance consists of contrition, confession, and reformation, and is necessary to salvation.
4. That the body and blood of Christ are really present in the elements of the eucharist.
5. That justification is remission of sin and reconciliation to God by the merits of Christ; but good works are necessary.

Articles related to ceremonies:

1. That images are useful as remembrances, but are not objects of worship.
2. That saints are to be honoured as examples of life, and as furthering our prayers.
3. That saints may be invoked as intercessors, and their holydays observed.
4. That ceremonies are to be observed for the sake of their mystical signification, and as conducive to devotion.
5. That prayers for the dead are good and useful, but the efficacy of papal pardon, and of soul-masses offered at certain localities, is negatived.[3]

These sound very Anglo-Catholic. It is only after Henry VIII's death that Cranmer managed to push through his Protestant agenda due to the extremely young age of King Edward VI, who was nine when he came to the throne.

Of course, England returned to Rome under Mary I, but then under Elizabeth I we had the re-settlement and the compromise of the *Thirty-Nine Articles*, and with them the birth of the Anglican *via media*.

What strikes me as interesting is the fact that we had such theological conviction during those times. The existence of the 10 articles, 6 articles, 42 articles, 39 articles indicates that we had strong theological debate and pushback. We fought to define what

---

[3] www.henryviiithereign.co.uk/1536-ten-articles.html.

we believed in. There was positive movement and readjustment with the Caroline Divines, but for many years since then, we seem to have stagnated. That is, until the Oxford Movement, when people like Newman provided more Catholic interpretations of the *Articles*.

This brings me to Vernon Staley's take on *The Thirty-Nine Articles*. He begins with the outline that the *Thirty-Nine Articles* are not articles of faith like the Creeds, and they are not imposed on members of the Anglican Church as necessary terms of communion. The clergy only subscribe to them, and the sense in which the subscription is understood, has been stated by Archbishop Bramhall as follows:

> We do not hold our Thirty-Nine Articles to be such necessary truths, "without which there is no salvation"; nor enjoin ecclesiastical persons to swear unto them, but only to subscribe them, as theological truths, for the preservation of unity among us. Some of them are the very same as that are contained in the Creed; some others of them are practical truths, which come not within the proper list of points or articles to be believed; lastly, some of them are pious opinions or inferior truths which are proposed by the Church of England as not to be opposed; not as essentials of Faith necessary to be believed.[4]

Staley makes the point that the *Thirty-Nine Articles* are Articles of peace and preservation, not religious tests, and not even articles of faith. And most importantly, he says they are to be interpreted and understood in accordance with the general rule of Catholic tradition.

An example of how this might be applied is in the interpretation of the *Book of Common Prayer* teaching on sacraments. Staley prefaces his remarks by reminding the reader that to the early church, the term *sacrament* was used in a wider sense than that which we now attach to it. St. Augustine defines a sacrament to be "a sacred sign," and speaks of "the sacrament of the Creed, which they ought to believe; the sacrament of the Lord's Prayer, how they ought to ask."[5]

Today we define a sacrament as an outward sign of an inward grace. Staley reminds us that these "effectual signs of grace" would previously have been defined as:

> Any holy thing of which it could be said, This possesses a hidden power or meaning.... But in later times, and by degrees, the term *sacrament* came to be restricted to seven ordinances. Some of these owe their existence to our Lord's direct institution, as recorded in the Gospels; others to the apostles acting, we may believe, under unrecorded commands of Christ (see Acts i. 3).[6]

There are, of course, the two greater Sacraments of Baptism and the holy Eucharist, and the five lesser sacraments of confirmation, penance, holy order, holy matrimony and unction. Staley insists our Lord's authority can be traced directly or indirectly for the institution of them all.[7] In his words,

---

[4] Staley, *The Catholic Religion*, 385.

[5] Ibid., 257.

[6] Ibid.

[7] Ibid., 258.

The Church of England does not teach that there are two Sacraments only; but that there are "two only, as generally (or universally) necessary to salvation." The five lesser Sacraments she also acknowledges, but not as generally necessary to salvation. The lesser Sacraments are not on this account to be set aside as of no importance; for they are, in their degree, visible signs of invisible grace, and form part of the divine plan for our safety and perfection, according to our needs or conditions of life.[8]

Staley's catechism then provides a thorough examination of each Sacrament. For example, for Baptism he talks of the threefold effect of Baptism, to remove all sin, original and actual; to bestow sanctifying grace, and endue the soul with the heavenly virtues of faith, hope and charity; and to make the recipient a member of Christ, the child of God, and an inheritor of the kingdom. He explains the baptismal vows as being to renounce the devil and all his works; to believe in God; and to serve him.[9] This is a very solid and sound catechism which could still be used today.

On touchy subjects such as the Communion of Saints, Staley provides helpful insight.[10] Communion is often translated as "fellowship," and in that sense, the Communion of Saints is a fellowship of saints grounded on the truth that all saints living and departed are united to Jesus Christ and form his mystical body. The term *saints* or "holy ones" in the New Testament tended to be applied to all baptised peoples living on earth who have not forfeited their baptismal grace, baptised persons being sanctified by baptism and called to lead a holy life. In later use it has become custom to use the term "saint" when applied to Christians who have departed from this life. It is a term we use to honour the Blessed Virgin Mary, the apostles, the martyrs, and other great leaders in the army of the faithful, "the spirits of just men made perfect" (Heb 12:13 KJV). Staley reminds us of St. Chrysostom saying, "Let us not then be weary on giving aid to the departed, and of offering prayers for them."[11] On the topic of Article XXII, the Church condemns "'the Romish doctrine concerning invocation of saints,' that is to say, that system of prayer to the saints which led to their regarded otherwise than exalted suppliants."[12] In other words, we are to avoid the superstition that saints had any godly power due to their own merits, or were kinder or had greater sympathy to sinners than Christ our Saviour. Staley says, "Modern Roman books of devotion speak of the blessed Virgin Mary especially, in a manner which we believe to be quite inconsistent with the honour due to our Lord."[13]

As a man with a particular devotion to Our Lady, this Roman teaching on Mary is something I am often weary of. I ask for her prayers, and I seek her intercession with her Son, who interceded for us with the Father, but I do not believe titles like "Mediatrix of all Graces" to be helpful. I understand where they are coming from, in that she bore Christ and all grace comes through him, but it is a clumsy analogy which could easily be

---

[8] Staley, *The Catholic Religion*, 259.
[9] Ibid., 260–263.
[10] Ibid., 220–226.
[11] Ibid., 224.
[12] Ibid., 223.
[13] Ibid.

interpreted as Mary replacing Christ as our mediator. These are some of the issues which stoked the Reformation, so I think it is very good that Staley addresses them head on.

Recently, I have experienced a rise in Nestorianism as a direct result of this misinterpretation of Marian devotion. Some of my more Protestant friends have denied the title *Theotokos*, denied Mary as the Mother of God, and denigrated her to nothing more than another earthly creature. The argument is, "she was just a woman who had a son, and she is not the mother of God, just the mother of Christ the man." The problem is obvious, because it denies the divinity of Christ. The term *Theotokos*, "God-bearer," mother of God, puts this straight and defends the doctrine of Christ being fully man and fully God. I had thought the Third Ecumenical Council had settled this, but the problem with many Puritanical Protestants is that they often forget everything prior to the Reformation.

The Reformers were intent upon re-forming the Church, re-centring our faith on Christ, by re-learning the theology of the apostles, the early church fathers. It was not about creating a new religion, or even a new denomination: it was about ridding the Catholic Church of superstition and corruption. I think that is the strength of the Anglo-Catholics: we remember that we are part of the Church Catholic. We regard apostolic succession as important, we adhere to the Creeds and Councils, and we are not afraid to call ourselves catholic. Reformed catholic, if you will, but even that terminology has a double meaning, for some intend it to mean Calvinist.

We have a duty to bring our more Protestant or Calvinist brethren along with us. We should remind them that Martin Luther, John Calvin, Thomas Cranmer, et al., had a lot to offer, but they were working on reminding us of the church fathers, not on replacing them. They were part of the Church Universal, not creating new churches. They were reforming, not reinventing. There is over a millennium of church history and teaching that comes before them, and we must remember this. Otherwise, we do Christ's body on earth a disservice.

It could be argued that before Vernon Staley, before Newman, Pusey, and the Tractarians, the Catholic Revival began with the Caroline Divines. We are now living in a post-Oxford Movement era, in need of revival, and we find ourselves—coincidentally—living in a new Caroline era. It is time for a new generation of Caroline Divines. We may be that revival: we are the continuation of the Oxford Movement. It is our job to bring the catholic faith to new ears. In a time where the established or official Anglican bodies are dying out due to liberalism in America, Canada, Australia, New Zealand, and unfortunately the United Kingdom, it is an opportunity for us to reclaim what it means to be Anglican. With a renewed emphasis on the Anglican formularies interpreted through a catholic lens, we can pick up where the Reformation left off, not in a protest of Rome, but in re-forming Western Christianity.

Orthodox Anglicanism is not anti-catholic: it is the exact opposite, for we profess to be part of the holy catholic and apostolic church. We pray that, as we recite the Creeds every day. Let us hold ourselves accountable to the words of the Church Fathers.

Vive la Reformation!

Chapter 31

Percy Dearmer (1867–1936) and the English Use of the Prayer Book: Loyalty to the Aesthetical and Ascetical Theology of the English Liturgy

The Rev. Michael Templin

Loyalty is not something many take seriously in the age of church shopping, undisciplined Christianity, and the current instant gratification culture. Alliances shift quickly for whatever best supports the theology of "me." Loyalty and the sacrifice of the will and wants, for many, is no longer a virtue or obligation; it is, rather, the seeking of what's best in the moment. We are hardly surprised when men leave ordained ministry in one communion and go to another. We are becoming less surprised when they leave the ministry—or, even the faith—altogether. We have been desensitized to the weight of duty and loyalty which our forefathers held to so tightly.

Percy Dearmer was cut from the old cloth of our fathers. When men were leaving the priesthood in droves from Anglicanism to convert to Roman Catholicism, he remained faithful to his mother church in the post-Newman era. When ministers were replacing the *Book of Common Prayer* from the holy table with unauthorized and illegal missals, he was advocating that the *Book of Common Prayer*[1] did not need to be replaced: it needed to be properly used. The Rev. Percy Dearmer was what we call today a "Prayer Book Catholic." He was serious about the formularies, worship, and discipline of the Church of England. He is most often associated with a movement called the "English Use," along with other members of the Alcuin Club: The Rev. Vernon Staley, The Rt. Rev. Walter Howard Frere, Dr. E. G. Cuthbert F. Atchley, Sir William Henry St John Hope, The Rev. Colin Dunlop, and others. The Alcuin Club was dedicated to preserving, restoring, and teaching *exact* rubrical conformity to the *Book of Common Prayer*, based on English liturgical and ceremonial history, and not that of the Roman Counter-Reformation.

Percival "Percy" Dearmer was born in Kilburn, Middlesex, United Kingdom on February 27, 1867. Art was an integral part of his life, as his father Thomas Dearmer was an artist. Dearmer studied at the Westminster School and Christ Church, Oxford (B.A. 1890, M.A. 1896). He was ordained to the diaconate and priesthood at Rochester Cathedral in 1891 and 1892 respectively. He served a long tenure (1901 to 1915) as the Vicar of Saint Mary's Primrose Hill, London, was professor of ecclesiastical art at King's College, London in 1919, and in 1931 he became a canon of Westminster Abbey, where he served until his death in 1936.

In his *Parson's Handbook*, first published in 1899, we observe careful liturgical scholarship that treated the *Book of Common Prayer* as the *regula*, or rule, of the Anglican

---

[1] When the *Book of Common Prayer* (BCP) is mentioned in this paper, it is assumed to be the 2004 printing from Cambridge University Press of the 1662 prayer book (unless otherwise specified). This edition has been used in subsequent reprints; thus, the page numbers are more readily accessible for reference. The author has certified that the content referenced is the same as The Rev. Percy Dearmer would have been utilizing during his ministry.

Church. Though Dearmer most certainly was a part of the liturgical movement (or Ritualist movement) in the Church of England, he always maintained that he was a legalist to the rubrics[2] and a loyalist to the prayer book, not a revisionist. For this reason, he dedicated much of his time to understanding the "Ornament Rubric" in the 1559 and 1662 prayer book.[3] This rubric prescribed all the vestments, ornaments, altar arrangements, etc., that were legal in the Church of England by examining the ornaments in Use of Sarum[4] in 1557–1559. The Use of Sarum was made the national liturgy under Henry VIII when he suppressed other local "uses" and it continued through the first two years of Edward VI until the first *Book of Common Prayer* became the only legal liturgy on Whitsunday June 9, 1549 for the Church of England. The 1549 *Book of Common Prayer* ordered the same ornaments and vestments that were legal in the second year of Edward VI, i.e., those in the Use of Sarum:

> Upon the day and at the time appointed for the ministration of the holy Communion, the Priest that shall execute the holy ministry, shall put upon him the vesture appointed for that ministration, that is to say: a white Albe plain, with a vestment [English word for Chasuble] or Cope. And where there be many Priests, or Deacons, there so many shall be ready to help the Priest, in the ministration, as shall be requisite: And shall have upon them likewise the vestures appointed for their ministry, that is to say, Albes with tunacles. Then shall the Clerks sing in English for the office, or Introite, (as they call it,) a Psalm appointed for that day.[5]

Therefore, any ecclesiastical ornamentation of the church, vestments for the minister, and any ceremonial advocated by Dearmer, was only permissible in the Sarum Use, yet not *illegal* rubrically in the 1662 prayer book – the legal liturgy during his life. We see this quite evidently in his many works including *The Parson's Handbook* (1899), *Loyalty to the Prayer Book* (1904), *The Prayer Book: What It Is and How We Should Use It* (1907), and *Some English Altars* (1928). Moreover, Dearmer was also responsible for helping the Church of England restore and implement Church music and hymnody into her services. Dearmer was an editor of the classic *The English Hymnal* (1906), with the illustrious Ralph Vaughan Williams.

---

[2] Percy Dearmer, *The Parson's Handbook* (London: Richards, 1899); Project Canterbury. anglicanhistory.org/dearmer/handbook/1899/intro.html. In the Introduction of the *Parson's Handbook* (1–39), he explains his methodology for approaching the liturgy—especially from a legal standpoint.

[3] The 1559 and 1662 Ornaments Rubric (found at the beginning of Morning Prayer in both books) directs: "The Morning and Evening Prayer shall be used in the accustomed Place of the Church, Chapel, or Chancel; except it shall be otherwise determined by the Ordinary of the Place. And the Chancels shalt remain as they have done in times past. And here is to be noted, that such Ornaments of the Church, and of the Ministers thereof, at all Times of their Ministration, shall be retained, and be in use, as were in this Church of England, by the Authority of Parliament, in the Second Year of the Reign of King Edward the Sixth."

[4] The Use of Sarum was the liturgy of medieval Salisbury Cathedral's local adaptation of the Roman Mass. Prior to the publication of the Missal of Pius V (1570), local adaptations of the Gregorian mass, monastic uses, and regional rites like the Ambrosian and Mozarabic were common all over Europe.

[5] The fourth rubric before Holy Communion in the 1549 prayer book.

When one reads Dearmer, it sometimes seems as if he is "picky" and annoyed with traditions that are not his own. But we must work to understand how he felt within his own context: the Church of England was catholic, the prayer book was catholic, and he was a catholic priest. Why should he look to contemporary Rome for vestments, liturgical ceremonial and manual acts, color sequences, altar ornaments, etc., when many of the things done in the post-Tridentine ritual books of Rome were never practiced in pre-Reformation Catholic England, let alone in the reformed Catholic Church of England? These were later innovations that had no historical authority in the English rites and ceremonies. Moreover, the Roman authorities had abolished the English liturgy under the reign of Mary Tudor (1553–1558) and denied the legitimacy of Anglican Holy Orders.[6] On the other hand, *legal* vestments and ornaments prescribed by the Ornaments Rubric were frowned upon, because the Church of England had so long disobeyed the prayer book due to various religio-political factions within Great Britain.[7]

What Dearmer advocated was not much different from what the original Tractarians, nor the Non-Jurors and the Caroline Divines before them, had desired: celebrate Holy Communion when the prayer book directs it (each Sunday and Holy Day when propers are provided), pray the Daily Offices *every day* in the church as required in the prayer book[8], make special confession when needed as directed in the Exhortation[9] and Visitation of the Sick,[10] fast when the church fasts,[11] catechize the children[12] all while using proper ornaments for the minister, the church, and the Holy Table. He was a loyal advocate for what the Church had given to him, England, and the Anglican Church throughout the world: a comprehensive rule of faith, prayer, and Christian life in the *Book of Common Prayer*. He convincingly stresses this in his *Loyalty to the Prayer Book*:

> One of the shallowest objections to this claim for loyalty is that it is "insular," the idea being, apparently, that to be really Catholic one must pick and choose on one's own authority as the fancy takes one. I need hardly remind you that if loyalty to the prescript order be insular, then insularity is the key-note of the Roman and Eastern Churches. If English Priests had stuck to their formularies as Romans and Easterns have to theirs, then the English Church would to-day be as marked as the Roman or the Eastern Churches are by such practices as frequent Services, fasting, the supremacy of the Eucharist, and the use of distinctive vestments for the Sacraments. Those who still fancy that obedience is insular would do well to consider seriously what alternative they have to propose. They will find that the only alternative is anarchy, under which each parson may set up his own ideas of Church order and worship; and these ideas have persistently differed, not in details only, but in essentials, from the principles of the Church Catholic. By this system, or

---

[6] A good example is *Apostolicae curae* the papal bull issued in 1896 by Pope Leo XIII, that declared all Anglican ordinations to be "absolutely null and utterly void."

[7] Massey Shepherd, *The Oxford American Prayer Book Commentary* (New York: Oxford University Press, 1950), 67.

[8] 1662 BCP, X, 1 and 16.

[9] Ibid., 247.

[10] Ibid., 317.

[11] Ibid., lvi.

[12] Canons 1604, LIX, and 1662 BCP, 296.

want of system, you may have a pseudo-Romanism in one parish, a pseudo-Puritanism in another, and a decorated worldliness in another, but in few will you have Catholic worship and order. Nor will you gain the respect or trust of the rest of the Church or of the world at large. The man of the world will accuse you, as he does, of doing one thing when you have undertaken to do another: the Papist will say, as he does, that your Church is no Church because it can only attain a mock Catholicism by flaunting the plumes which you have borrowed from him: the Puritan will use the law-breakers on his own side to claim that the English Church is but an unjustly privileged sect; and the law-breakers on the other side, will give him, as they have given him, the opportunity of stirring up the narrowest and bitterest prejudices in the country. But loyalty to the Prayer Book disarms the enemies of the Church, at the same time as it restores the effectiveness of her friends. And if we set – as we should – the fortunes of the Church Universal above those of our own communion, we shall still do well to remember that the weakening of Anglicanism would remove the greatest agency which God in His providence has left in the world for the reunion of Christendom.[13]

Thus, Percy Dearmer, though routinely acclaimed as an *aesthetical* historian/theologian, was actually an *ascetical* theologian. Vestments and ornaments were not a means to an end, but a way to further remain faithfully loyal to his *regula fide* in the prayer book system. This is why he prioritized the availability of the Daily Offices each day as a comprehensive system of prayer, the learning of the Bible, the observation of Holy Communion with frequency, devotion, and beauty to feed Christ's flock spiritually, and the catechetical life of the church to be rich and disciplined, so that Christians would grow mature in the faith. He said of "Common Prayer" in *The Prayer Book* (1907):

> But prayer is difficult. Yes: like all things that are worth doing it cannot be done without taking trouble. And the first thing is to acquire the habit of following the service, of really joining in all the prayers and praises with our minds and hearts. It is a great help in this if we make a point of saying or singing our part of the service heartily: to join in the singing stirs our hearts, and we should not let our praises be sung for us by others...It is not, indeed, difficult to make our Father's house a House of Prayer if we come joyfully—not once a week as a matter of form; but as often as we are able—and if we come with the deliberate intention of praying when we get there—praying, and praising, and giving thanks, and making intercession also for those who are still outside the fellowship of Common Prayer. For a devout congregation is one of God's magnets. It is always drawing into its fellowship fresh servants of Christ.[14]

Thus, we must ask ourselves the same question Dearmer asked his contemporaries: are we loyal? Archbishop Thomas Cranmer, the architect of the *Book of Common Prayer*, gave Anglican Christians a "reformed catholic" rule of faith and worship. First, he

---

[13] Dearmer, *Loyalty to the Prayer Book* (Oxford: Mowbray, 1904), 28–29; Project Canterbury, anglicanhistory.org/dearmer/loyalty1904.html.

[14] Dearmer, *The Prayer Book: What It Is and How We Should Use It* (London: Mowbray, 1907); Project Canterbury, anglicanhistory.org/dearmer/prayer_book1907.html.

changed the language from Latin to English so that public prayer would be in the common tongue. Second, he simplified the Daily Offices to be two-fold, which predated the seven-fold office, so Mattins and Evensong would be prayed daily in every parish, cathedral, chapel, and collegiate church in England, and therefore accessible to all people. Third, he simplified the Holy Communion service from the older missals so that it was less medieval and more biblical, while maintaining the integral parts of the earliest eucharistic liturgies of the Church. He also made preaching obligatory at the Communion and restored reception of Holy Communion in "both kinds." Fourth, he provided forms for all the major Christian events in life: Holy Baptism, Confirmation, Ordination, Matrimony, Churching of Women, Visitation of the Sick, and the Burial of the Dead.

Dearmer's simple mission was to do Common Prayer, and to do it properly with loyalty to the aesthetic and ascetic. In contemporary Anglicanism, there seems to be the same resistance to using Common Prayer as it is written—we must constantly tamper with the language, the lectionary, and even the liturgy (i.e., the infinitude of local usages). We have a vast number of occasional service books, missals, contemporary translations, but we rarely have churches that celebrate Common Prayer precisely to the intention of our Anglican fathers and to exact obedience to the rubrics therein. The issue is not ignorance of what is prescribed; it is that many do not see Common Prayer as "good" and we believe ourselves above *the rule* to which we should have submitted. When you survey many local parish calendars you immediately see how few offer the Daily Offices, while even fewer offer them every single day. In Dearmer's day, there were several churches that had ample communicants, but priests were unwilling to regularly celebrate the Holy Communion on Sundays and Holy Days when directed. Another thrice weekly service (Sunday, Wednesday, and Friday), the English Litany, is almost extinct. This was the first official English service (1544), ordered after Morning Prayer or before the Holy Communion in every official English *Book of Common Prayer*, although it is rarely used today.

Moreover, in regard to the traditional, legal vestments and ornaments that Percy Dearmer researched, recommended, and even had tailored (i.e., the Warham Guild),[15] many outright rejected them. Rather, we find short cottas instead of full surplices, lace instead of apparels, fiddlebacks instead of gothic chasubles, and even the priests celebrating the Divine Services in no vestments at all! How few holy tables have full frontals ordered by canon law?[16] How many altars with six candles instead of the two that were universally legal prior to and after the reformation?[17] How rarely do we see

---

[15] Dearmer was instrumental in founding and leading the Warham Guild in 1912 to make vestments according to the standard of the Ornaments Rubric as understood by him and his associates. The Warham Guild's patterns have been owned by J. Wippell & Co. since 1969.

[16] Canons 1604, LXXXII.

[17] In the injunction of King Edward VI, put forward in 1547, it is ordered, "that all Deans, Archdeacons, Parsons, Vicars, and other ecclesiastical persons, shall ... suffer from henceforth— no Torches nor Candles, Tapers, or Images of wax to be set before any image or picture, but only two lights upon the High Altar, before the Sacrament, which, for the signification that Christ is the very true light of the world, they shall suffer to remain still": *Hierurgia Anglicana* (London:

continued

unbleached linen during Lent? How many churches do ablutions before the Post-Communion prayers and *Gloria*, but not after the benediction as directed in the rubrics?[18] This is not meant to be an indictment, rather a suggestion for us to consider if our loyalty is still with the prayer book given to us by our forefathers. And if we have departed from the path, how can we return to better practice obedience to our own beautiful tradition? Do we look to Geneva or to Canterbury? Do we look to Rome or to York? Do we look to Constantinople or to Salisbury? Do we look to Costa Mesa or to Durham?

One of the foremost areas in which Dearmer proved his loyalty to the prayer book, and more importantly to the people under his cure, was in his frequent catechizing ordered by the *Book of Common Prayer*. The prayer book directs that "the Curate of every Parish shall diligently upon Sundays and Holy-days, after the second Lesson at Evening Prayer, openly in the Church instruct and examine so many Children of his Parish sent unto him, as he shall think convenient, in some Part of this Catechism."[19] Dearmer's strict loyalty to the prayer book ensured that 1) Evening Prayer would be prayed on all Sundays; 2) Evening Prayer, along with Mattins and Holy Communion, would be offered on all Holy Days; 3) the curate would fulfill his duty to catechize the youth in his cure, at *all* the prescribed times. Frequent catechism in the common tongue was a reformation principle amongst the Lutherans, continental Reformed, and the Anglicans. This was one of those reformation principles that was a recovery of the ancient catholic practice, and was frequently promoted by Dearmer. In his *The Prayer Book* (1907) he writes of catechizing:

> The Church Catechism holds a very special place, for one of its rubrics says that it is to be the text-book of instruction at Evensong on Sundays and Holy-days. The Catechism, then, contains the doctrine which we Church folk have to understand and believe. Not the Thirty-nine Articles, as some people imagine,—you are not obliged to understand them, though they are very good and useful, for no one can understand them without a good deal of knowledge and study. But the Catechism everyone can understand; and that is the religion which, according to the Prayer Book, you must thoroughly know and believe. God grant that it may be understood, and believed, and practiced more and more![20]

Thus, the Reformed Catholic Church has her Articles of Religion, the Ecumenical Creeds, and a catholic liturgy, calendar, catechism, and ordinal found in the *Book of Common Prayer*. She has her own formularies grounded in Holy Scripture and the ancient Church. The Elizabethan Canons of 1571 made this clear:

> But chiefly they shall take heed, that they teach nothing in their preaching, which they would have the people religiously to observe, and believe, but that which is

---

Rivington; Oxford: Parker, 1848), 1. Queen Elizabeth I who first ordered the Ornaments Rubric in 1559, had a crucifix and two candles that stood on her altar: *Hierurgia Anglicana*, 2–6.

[18] 1662 BCP, 257, and 262.

[19] 1662 BCP, 296.

[20] Dearmer, *The Prayer Book*.

agreeable to the doctrine of the old Testament, and the new, and that which the catholic fathers, and ancient Bishops have gathered out of that doctrine. (Canon 6)[21]

We must view our formularies and prayer book as consistent with the Holy Scriptures and catholic fathers, and therefore strive to understand, keep, and teach them consistently in the light of the wealth of information that we have at our disposal. Indeed, we should be encouraged that many have taken up the duty of understanding the English Church by reading John Jewel against the Romanists (*Apology of the Church of England*) and Richard Hooker's defense against the Puritans (*Of the Laws of Ecclesiastical Polity*), or the writings of Thomas Cranmer on the Lord's Supper and John Cosin's notes on the *Book of Common Prayer* (*The Durham Book*). There is a current movement to go back to the sources of the English Reformation, just as our English Divines went back to the sources of the Holy Scripture and the earliest fathers during the time of the Reformation. This *ad fontes* ("to the sources") methodology is a chief distinction of what it means to be a Reformed Catholic—holding dearly and clearly to that which is truly catholic, provable by the witness of Scripture, and the earliest fathers. In this manner, Bishop John Cosin succinctly defined Anglicanism as "Protestant and Reformed according to the principles of the ancient Catholic Church"[22] and how Dearmer lived out his vocation to Christ and His bride.

In conclusion, we should view this *ad fontes* approach to the faith that was so widely practiced by our reformers and by traditional "reformed catholics" even today, as *the* guiding principle of Dr. Dearmer. His life's work was dedicated not only to serving the church in the priesthood, but by spending much of his time also researching the rubrics of the *Book of Common Prayer* and mining the history, application, and intent of them. His goal was to make the wealth of his research available to the common member of the Church of England, and the simple parish priest, so that Common Prayer, as it is written and intended by his fathers, would be put into practice for the benefit and devotion of the people. He did all this so that they could worship Christ in the beauty of holiness and consume the Holy Bible while doing it. He said in *The Prayer Book*:

> For the men of our race, two books stand out above all others. The Bible has, of course, a place by itself; it is the sacred-library of the Christian revelation, and first among the books of the world. But next to it England would place the Book of Common Prayer.[23]

We, as Reformed Catholic Anglicans today, must once again strive for what Dearmer was striving for: the primacy of Holy Scripture and next to it, common prayer. It goes back to the Apostolic principle in Acts 2:42 that Dearmer so often referenced: "And they continued steadfastly in the apostles' doctrine and fellowship, and in breaking of bread, and in prayers" (KJV). Dearmer died in 1936, after a complete life in service of the church and the academy, fulfilling Jesus' first Great Commandment to "love the Lord God with

---

[21] Henry Gee and William John Hardy, ed., *Documents Illustrative of English Church History* (London: MacMillan, 1914), 476–477; Hanover Historical Texts Project, history.hanover.edu/texts/engref/er82.html.

[22] John Cosin, *The History of Popish Transubstantiation*, new ed. (Oxford: Parker, 1840), ch. 1; Project Canterbury, anglicanhistory.org/tracts/tract27.html.

[23] Dearmer, *The Prayer Book*, ch. 1.

all his heart, soul, and mind" (Matt 22:37), and by running a canteen for the unemployed at Westminster Abbey, fulfilling the second Great Commandment, "to love [his] neighbor as [him]self" (Matt 22:39). Percy Dearmer was a man of loyalty to Christ and Christ's Church.

Chapter 32

The Rev. Roland Allen's (1868–1947) Theology of Spirit & Order: A Framework for Anglican Missionary Ecclesiology

The Rev. Dr. Steven Richard Rutt

Roland Allen's Missionary Ecclesiology

In this chapter I will attempt to disclose the central planks of the apostolic principles which shaped Roland Allen's missionary ecclesiology of "Spirit and Order." Some years ago while doing doctoral research on Roland Allen's published and unpublished archives in Oxford, England, I endeavored to develop an intellectual biography that disclosed how this prescient Anglican missionary and missiologist clearly influenced the thinking and practice of missionaries and missionary societies within the Anglican Communion, established Protestant denominations, the Roman Catholic and Orthodox Communions, as well as the independent branches of the Western and non-Western Church, especially throughout the Majority World of Africa, Asia, and Latin America.

On the one hand, many of these branches of Christ's Church were quite successful with obeying the Great Commission (Matt 28:18–20) as they planted churches throughout the world. On the other hand, when some missionary societies began to replace their original focus of gospel evangelism, discipleship, and indigenous church planting with the development of *mission station* schools and hospitals, Roland Allen believed that the missionary societies diverted from the primary calling to plant churches and to make disciples in these foreign nations. He also believed that by developing schools and hospitals, instead of planting churches, the missionaries created a continual dependency on foreign financial support. Allen argued that this dependency upon foreign support was *not* St. Paul's missionary methods and practice. Allen observed how the indigenous inhabitants understood the *mission stations* as foreign businesses—held in trust by Europeans—where the missionaries financially organized and permanently managed these properties. For Allen, the *mission station system* lacked apostolic precedent. His solution to the problem was basically: *What Would St. Paul Do?* Allen conformed to and argued for the essence of St. Paul's missionary methods and practices to address the problem.

His writings were shaped more and more by St. Paul's missionary practice, and it was this understanding that motivated Allen to proactively argue for implementing a *Gospel method* for Church growth. St. Paul's example of investing his time and energy in mentoring and appointing indigenous leadership, Allen argued, was indicative of why he was so successful with church planting in Galatia, Macedonia, Achaia, and Asia between the years AD 47–57. This significantly influenced Allen's thought, especially because of how St. Paul proactively applied these principles to promote self-extending churches that were not dependent on him to be their resident leader. His understanding of what St. Paul did cannot be understood from an autocratic practice—operating in isolation—Allen argued, but from a selfless practice of his apostolic ministry which sought the wellbeing of the indigenous church and the church's ability to be self-governing. So to set the parameters for his missionary ecclesiology and unpack the apostolic principles which encompass his missionary theology, he carefully designed principles and practices that were more in line with St. Paul's three missionary journeys. Allen disclosed his belief in the transcendence of the Holy Spirit's work in the life of the Church and argued for a return to the proper apostolic emphasis—*Spirit and Order*. His integrated pneumatology and ecclesiology formed the basis for his church planting missionary theology which he was convinced encompassed true historic apostolicity and catholicity.

Allen's Missionary Theology: Spirit (pneumatology) and Order (ecclesiology)

Apostolic Method: Spirit *before* Order

Roland Allen's apostolic method of Spirit *before* Order advanced a theology of mission that sent missionary clergy with some of the disciples that they had mentored with them to do missionary work (i.e., on-the-job training). These missional clergy and disciples were to serve as "explorers" within the kingdom of God's harvest field, and their commission was to essentially scout out the land for church planting opportunities.

- Church-planting by birthing new churches from new Christians.
- Make disciples.
- Witness to salvation in King Jesus.

Apostolic Principle: Spirit *with* Order

Allen's missionary ecclesiology also argued for the apostolic principle of Spirit *with* Order. This apostolic principle "did not argue that episcopal ordination was of no importance" but rather that it was a "divine order [that] is for building up, [and] not for destruction: it is to maintain the sacraments of Christ not to annul them: it is to establish the Church not to hinder its establishment."[1] That said, Allen's ecclesiological argument affirmed the *normal* Order of Anglican clergy (ordained by bishops) presiding over the Lord's Table. His defense for sacramental ministry in the newly formed churches actually created a context for a *well-ordered* ecclesiology to eventually emerge, that being, Spirit *with* Order.

Apostolic Order: Spirit *empowered* Order

As an Anglican churchman and missionary, Allen had reverence for apostolic order that advances a *Spirit empowered Order*. He, also in his writings, clearly distinguished between itinerate *apostolic order* (i.e., apostles, prophets, evangelists, teachers) and the resident local ministry (i.e., bishops, priests, deacons) from what he believed was primarily inspired within the Bible, and, secondarily, outlined within the early Church's application of apostolic instruction as revealed in the *Didache*. It is important to disclose that Roland Allen's missiology actually proposes a Spirit-*inspired* ecclesiology, that being,

---

[1] Formerly an unpublished work by Roland Allen, "The Ministry of Expansion: the Priesthood of the Laity" (1930), USPG X622, Box 3, Number 27, Oxford, Bodleian Library. In 2017, this work was published as: *The Ministry of Expansion by Roland Allen: the Priesthood of the Laity*, ed. J. D. Payne (Pasadena, CA: William Carey Library, 2017).

a Spirit *empowered* Order, designed to accommodate the *charismatic* dynamic in order to equip, commission, send, and expand the Church throughout the world.

Roland Allen's Missionary Experience in China (1895–1903)

Allen's articulation of his missionary experiences in China and how these informed his missionary ecclesiology is made clear in his letters both during and after his ministry in China,[2] his chronicle of the Boxer Rebellion entitled *The Siege of the Peking Legations* (1901),[3] papers he presented, and subsequent articles he wrote concerning China. All of these sources disclose the experiences of cross-cultural mission in China and how this influenced his thought and practice. In fact, it was during his ministry there that his vision and mission for developing indigenous churches began to take shape. Before analyzing his missionary experiences in China from 1895–1903, it is helpful to take note of a summary statement he made at the conclusion of his ministry time in China:

> The Chinese are apt to compare the antiquity of their religion with the modern character of ours.... If Christianity is to be presented acceptably to the Chinese, surely it ought to be through Chinese teachers who have remained Chinese in thought and education, but whose Chinese thought is permeated with Christian doctrine and belief. So one might find an Apostle.[4]

This demonstrates how Allen began to formulate a missiology which anticipated the emergence of an indigenous Christianity, which incorporated the apostolic doctrine and belief and which would eventually influence the thinking of Chinese Christians concerning the development of their own churches, local leaders, theologians, and those who will do the apostolic ministry of Church expansion. For Allen, foreign missionaries had the opportunities to evangelize and plant churches, ordain, and equip indigenous leadership, and then immediately retire from that region to establish churches in newer areas. He believed that once these new Christians embraced the Christian faith—not necessarily the forms and customs of the foreign missionaries—then a truly Chinese Christianity would develop. He would view that as mission accomplished! And yet, when he first arrived in China in 1895, he did not naturally think this way. What, then, were the contributing factors which can be attributed to this change?

First, Allen argued for an indigenous "how to" methodology that focused on "how to win Native Converts ... how to organize village churches ... how to educate Coreans [*sic*] to understand and use intelligently any Prayer Book at all ... [and] how to adapt a native hut for worship."[5] Lamin Sanneh correctly interprets Allen's argument here when he suggests that he was challenging "the Western cultural captivity of the gospel," which was, in effect, "strangling the gospel."[6] He called this a misrepresentation of Christianity, "slavery to a Foreign system" which was "not their own" and, consequently, the

---

[2] Deposited papers: Allen, USPG X622, Boxes 1–8, Oxford, Bodleian Library.

[3] Allen, *The Siege of the Peking Legations* (London: Smith, Elder, 1901).

[4] Allen, "Chinese Character and Missionary Methods," 317–329, USPG X622, Box 2, File J: 35, Oxford, Bodleian Library.

[5] Allen, "The Work of the Missionary," Box 2, File J: 4, 8, Oxford, Bodleian Library.

[6] Lamin Sanneh, *Disciples of All Nations: Pillars of World Christianity* (Oxford: Oxford University Press, 2008), 224–225.

imposition of a "foreigner's Church."[7] As far as Allen was concerned, this was a betrayal of St. Paul's missiology, which opposed slavery to a "foreign system," as clearly demonstrated when he defended the freedom of the Galatian churches to reject the Judaizing system which they attempted to impose upon the churches (Epistle to the Galatians).

Second, he believed the only way for the missionaries to reverse what Robert Young has referred to as the "long-lasting political hegemony"[8] toward independence would be to apply the following three principles as part of the training process:

> (1) to teach the native converts to recognize their responsibility as members of the Church; (2) to avoid the introduction of any foreign element unless it is absolutely essential; (3) to be always retiring from the people to prepare the way for final retirement.[9]

These three apostolic principles began to shape his thinking as he was attempting to train catechists in China. He recognized that the Anglican conventional methodology for leadership training limited any possibility to expand beyond his context. He quickly figured out that unless the local converts took responsibility immediately to disciple, train, and lead their own churches, then any idea of expansion would be slow. He reflects upon what he did in China:

> I called the people together, told them it was high time that they were doing something for the spread of the Gospel, and asked them what they meant to do. I observe that people in England sometimes view such conduct with surprise. If they treated their people at home in the same way, I believe they would feel less surprised that it succeeded in China.[10]

Allen argued that his successful experiences in China shaped his missionary thinking to undergo reform by embracing a different methodology. This reform was shaped more through practice than theory. He began to flesh out his missiology by analyzing every aspect of missionary societies' practices. This led him to develop as a methods analyst concerning the *whys* and *wherefores* of missionary methods.

Third, he warned against missionaries forcing foreign laws and customs rather than allowing the converts to adopt familiar local customs with "principles which they valued" as part of the contextualization process for local church development. He emphasized that missionaries needed to be more self-critical concerning their tendency to force conformity to a foreign system that would likely be abandoned once either independence came through a devolved process, or, if the indigenous churches' frustrations with paternalism would eventually "lead to rebellion."[11]

Fourth, he applied the principles of self-government and self-support to the Chinese catechists so that they would take ownership with what they learned. He told the delegates how his reformed methodology in China worked in bringing independence to

---

[7] Allen, "The Work of the Missionary," Box 2, File J: 4, 12.

[8] Robert Young, *Postcolonialism: An Historical Introduction* (Oxford: Blackwell, 2001), 334.

[9] Allen, "The Work of the Missionary," Box 2, File J: 4, 9.

[10] Ibid., 4, 11.

[11] Ibid., 4, 12.

the churches but that it was contingent on the locals taking ownership of their worship services and daily responsibilities within these churches. He said that the missionaries who expected quick results by imposing a cast-iron system generally failed. In contrast, he told the delegates that the *apostolic principle* he applied was to build slowly and that "we had better at first give them only so much as they can easily assimilate."[12]

Finally, Allen comments on the extent to which the *three principles* had been adopted: the first principle (i.e., converts recognizing their responsibility) was "practised in different shapes very widely;" the second principle (i.e., restraint from imposing foreign elements unless it's necessary) was less widely practiced; and the third (i.e., missionaries retiring from their converts) was "scarcely recognized at all."[13]

Hence, he concluded that the "problem of independent native churches is the great problem of the day" and that the western Church's missionaries needed to come to terms with: (1) understanding the native mind; (2) feeling "sympathy for the natives in their early efforts;" (3) watching slow growth with patience and hope; (4) realizing "that western Christianity is not the whole of Christianity;" and (5) watching how "the Holy Spirit transforms strange forms of life into Christian forms of life unlike our own" by uniting multiethnic Christians as a "complement of our own needs."[14] His developing ecclesiology presupposed an application of *apostolic principles* which reinforced independent native churches to emerge slowly and which were led by the indigenous people. Allen's insistence that all members take responsibility for their own development and maturity is an argument against a *Peter Pan* philosophy of mission station paternalism.

His belief was that if the mission societies released control giving the works over to the indigenous converts, the latter could rely on the Holy Spirit's ability to govern, sustain, and propagate the Church's growth apart from foreign influence. The centrality of his pneumatology was influenced by Paul's epistles and Luke's historical account of the Acts of the Apostles, which he called "missionary history."[15] Consider the following influence of St. Paul's practice upon his mission theology:

> St. Paul was a preacher of a Gospel, not of a law.... This is the most distinctive mark of Pauline Christianity. This is what separates his doctrine from all other systems of religion.... He did not establish a constitution, he inculcated principles. He did not introduce any practice to be received on his own or any human authority, he strove to make his converts realize and understand its relation to Christ.... He never sought to enforce their obedience by decree; he always strove to win their heartfelt approval and their intelligent co-operation. He never proceeded by command, but always by persuasion. He never did things for them; he always left them to do things for themselves. He set them an example according to the mind of Christ, and he

---

[12] Allen, "The Work of the Missionary,". Box 2, File J:4, 13.

[13] Ibid., 4, 15.

[14] Ibid., 4, 14–15.

[15] David Paton, *The Ministry of the Spirit* (Grand Rapids: Eerdmans, 1970; World Dominion, 1960), 15.

was persuaded that the Spirit of Christ in them would teach them to approve that example and inspire them to follow it.[16]

In terms of St. Paul's theology, Allen believed that the Apostle's practice of church planting was permeated with a dependency on the Holy Spirit's ability to lead the Church into all truth, as revealed in John 16:13. That said, he believed that the Church's global expansion was based upon foundational *apostolic principles* organically energized through a realized pneumatology, empowered ecclesiology, and an applied mission theology he believed stemmed from Pauline practice. For Allen, the apostolic principles (not systems) are the centrality of his missionary ecclesiology. Arguably these key missionary principles are generated by the charismatic dynamic within Christianity which produces self-supporting, self-governing, self-propagating indigenous churches that find their rootedness in the Bible, a basic creed, trans-local and domestic ministers, and an ongoing sacramental life.

The key *apostolic principles* Roland Allen emphasized are: (1) belief that the one holy catholic and apostolic Church is ordered by the Scriptures, a basic creed, holy orders, and sacraments; (2) apostolic evangelists were called and sent to plant and equip indigenous churches; (3) church-planters were to organize, train, and retire from young church-plants as soon as possible;[17] (4) indigenous churches then were to maintain self-support, self-government, and self-propagation;[18] (5) self-supporting churches spontaneously produce home-grown leadership from the inception (non-devolution); (6) ordination of indigenous voluntary clergy who are authorized to administer the sacraments frequently;[19] (7) trust in the ministry of the Holy Spirit to empower the spontaneous expansion of the Church;[20] (8) a belief that all Christians are missionaries – and that the Church is a missionary body;[21] (9) emphasize the priesthood of the laity, by which he referred to the empowerment of the church community;[22] and (10) an ordered ministry in apostolic succession through a proactive missionary ecclesiology.[23] Having identified these apostolic principles, I now want to unpack them.

---

[16] Allen, *Missionary Methods* (Grand Rapids: Eerdmans, 1962 [1912]), 148–149.

[17] Allen, *Missionary Methods*, 81–83, 95–107; Allen (Chaplain to the Bishop of North China), "The Work of the Missionary in Preparing the Way for Independent Native Churches," a paper read before the Federation of Junior Clergy Missionary Associations in connection with the SPG, Resume of Proceedings at the 19th Conference of Delegates, John Rylands Library, Manchester, November 11–12, 1903, USPG X622, Oxford, Bodleian Library.

[18] Allen, a paper read at the *Church Missionary Society Conference of Missionaries*, High Leigh, 1927, Box 2, Number 23; Allen, "The Establishment of Indigenous Churches," typed manuscript refused by the *International Review of Missions*, 1927: 17, USPG X622, Box 3, Oxford, Bodleian Library.

[19] Allen, *Voluntary Clergy* (London: SPCK, 1923). Also, Allen, *The Case for Voluntary Clergy* (1930).

[20] H. R. Boer, "Roland Allen—Voice in the Wilderness," *World Dominion Press*, xxxii/4 (July/Aug. 1954): 224–231. Cf. Allen, *Missionary Methods*, 48.

[21] Paton, *Ministry of the Spirit*, 40, 61, 67, 75, 77–80, 165. Also, Allen, "The Work of the Missionary in Preparing the Way for Independent Native Churches" (1903), USPG X622, Oxford, Bodleian Library.

[22] Allen, "The Priesthood of the Church," *Church Quarterly Review*, IV (1933): 234–244, USPG X622, Oxford, Bodleian Library.

[23] Allen, "The Ministry of Expansion," Preface 3–4.

A cursory and selective study of Roland Allen's writings has caused some to misrepresent his missiology. One must come to terms with what he meant by words such as: *Church, Spirit, mission, apostolic, catholic, apostolic succession, indigenous, expansion, sacraments, orders,* and *principles.* First, he defined these words from what he believed was Pauline missionary principles and practices. Second, as a High Churchman this presupposed a framework of belief that embraced historic Christianity—the faith once delivered to the saints (Jude 3)—that being, *apostolic* and *catholic.* And, when reading him carefully, one will find a catholic understanding of the Christian faith, especially articulated through the first five centuries of the *undivided* Church. That said, an understanding of his mission theology will contribute significantly to contemporary missiology.

Roland Allen's Contribution towards Missiology: A Contemporary Perspective

By *charismatic ministry* I mean here a ministry which is exercised by a man who is moved to perform it by an inward, internal, impulse of that Holy Spirit who desires and strives after the salvation of men in Christ. I do not deny that men receive a charisma, a gift of grace, for their ministry in ordination: but I use the word *charismatic* to express the ministry which is exercised in virtue of that direct internal impulse of the Spirit, as distinguished from the ministry which is exercised by those who have been ecclesiastically ordained or commissioned.[24]

Allen's vision for the Church encased a combination of *Spirit* and *Order*—that is, pneumatology and ecclesiology. He believed that the Holy Spirit empowers Christians to apply *apostolic principles* in any given situation. His contribution to missiology stemmed from St. Paul's understanding of an indigenously-led Church that was, therefore, "fully equipped" with ministry to function as a permanent Church. He proposed the restoration of an apostolic order to enhance evangelism, particularly through the laity, by reaching out to pioneer regions where the Church had no current witness. His ongoing contribution to *missiology* advances (1) the historical significance for what he believed were universal *apostolic principles* and (2) how these principles provide flexibility within a framework of Spirit-driven Church growth to deal with a changing missionary environment.[25]

When missionaries discuss Allen's writings, they typically refer to either *Missionary Methods: St. Paul's or Ours?* (1912) or *The Spontaneous Expansion of the Church* (1927). While, arguably, these two books are his most famous published works, it is important to realize that he wrote extensively for over fifty years—books, pamphlets, journal contributions, articles, ecclesiastical letters, speeches, sermons, and various unpublished works.[26] Indeed, his grandson and biographer, Hubert Allen, categorically states that his

---

[24] Allen, "The Ministry of Expansion: the Priesthood of the Laity" (1930).

[25] Steven Rutt, "An Analysis of Roland Allen's Missionary Ecclesiology," *Transformation* 29/3 (July 2012): 201.

[26] Deposited papers: Allen, USPG X622, Boxes 1–8, Oxford, Bodleian Library.

grandfather's booklet entitled *Pentecost and the World*[27] (1917) was his most characteristic work then and still "can speak to us today as cogently as when it was written."[28] "My grandmother once remarked to me," recalled Hubert Allen, "that Roland himself believed his best piece of writing to have been his brief *Pentecost and the World*,"[29] and that "on his death, for this reason, Grannie gave bound copies to each of us, his three grandchildren."[30]

Allen's main thesis in *Pentecost and the World* can be summarized by stating that the Pentecost story is the fulfilled promise of the Holy Spirit's coming in supremacy to baptize, fill, indwell, lead, inspire, and empower the missionary Church as a witness to all nations. He argued that the main emphasis in Acts is that Pentecost marked the turning point in the Church's emergent juncture in "that they were the recipients of a gift of the Holy Spirit sent upon them by Christ, and that all the labours and successes of their lives were due to the influence of that Spirit."[31] A missionary within the Reformed Church, Harry Boer, agreed and was convinced that Allen was the preeminent "missionary thinker of the Spirit" and that "except by Roland Allen, a missionary theology centering around Pentecost and its continuing meaning for the Church has not been developed."[32] Things have progressed since 1961, when Boer made that remark. Today, many books now stress a missionary theology that engages the charismatic dynamic of Pentecost within the Church's mission, as can be seen in the growth of Christianity (and in particular the Anglican Communion) in the Majority world of Africa, Asia, and Latin America. That said, we might ask whether Allen's writings have influenced past and current trends in mainstream missionary theology. There can only be one answer. Yes.[33]

A century ago, Roland Allen envisaged a global Church emerging from indigenous Christianity that was free of the trappings of the *mission station* system. Allen said "A mission station is indeed a contradiction in terms: mission implies movement, station implies stopping."[34] He argued that Pauline missiology was a better way to do mission, (1) by transferring missionary churches to indigenous converts without going through a devolutionary process; (2) by ordaining local ministers—stipendiary and voluntary—to direct, manage and administer the Sacraments for their own churches by means of an indigenous episcopate; and (3) by trusting the Holy Spirit to direct these churches without foreign control. Today, these are considered mainstream practices, but this was not the case a century ago.

---

[27] Allen, *Pentecost and the World: the Revelation of the Holy Spirit in the Acts of the Apostles* (London: Oxford University Press, 1917). Reprinted in Paton, Ministry of the Spirit, 1–61.

[28] Hubert Allen, *Roland Allen: Pioneer, Priest, and Prophet* (Grand Rapids: Eerdmans, 1995), 104.

[29] Email correspondence from Hubert Allen (19 May 2011).

[30] Hubert Allen, *Roland Allen*, 104.

[31] Hubert Allen, *Roland Allen*, 3.

[32] Harry R. Boer, *Pentecost and Missions* (Grand Rapids: Eerdmans, 1961; Reprint, 1964), 63.

[33] See Hendrik Kraemer, *A Theology of the Laity* (London: Lutterworth, 1960), 20; Donald A. McGavran, *Church Growth and Christian Mission* (New York: Harper & Row, 1965), 43, 54; Eckhard J. Schnabel, *Paul the Missionary* (Downers Grove, IL: IVP Academic, 2008), 11–14, 21.

[34] Roland Allen, *Spontaneous Expansion*, 105.

The Contribution towards Missiology in India

In 1910 Roland and his wife visited "Delhi, Calcutta and Madras" upon an invitation to preach within the Diocese of Dornakal.[35] He met with Vedanayagam Samuel Azariah and probably saw Henry Whitehead, Bishop of Madras. This visit initiated an ongoing friendship with both men over the years, especially with Azariah who, in 1912, was consecrated as bishop of the Dornakal Diocese. In 1927 Allen was invited back to minister for Bishop Azariah.[36] Bishop Azariah's familiarity with Allen's writings in general, and his *apostolic principles*, in particular, contributed to an environment for Church growth expansion. Azariah and Allen saw that Church expansion was certain since the bishop was willing to ordain the existing teachers and catechists as fully equipped priests and to distinguish from among the pastors those who were gifted as trans-local evangelists. Azariah embraced his principles wholeheartedly and sought ways to administer diocesan adjustments wherever necessary. The time was right for Church renewal and transformation because Azariah had already "proved to be such a competent leader and administrator."[37] Therefore, Allen's teachings reinforced the clergy troops to prepare for planting more missionary churches. According to Susan Harper, some years later, the facts reveal that

> under the leadership of Bishop Vedanayagam Samuel Azariah (1874–1945), Dornakal became the fastest growing Anglican diocese in South Asia. The total Anglican Christian population in the Dornakal diocese increased from 56,681 in 1912 to 225,080 in 1941, a number that exceeded the total number of Anglican converts for all of Japan, Korea, and China combined. In 1936 the Dornakal Church baptized over 200 converts each week, and a total of 11,400 converts that year, and sustained this general level of accession throughout the decade.[38]

The Dornakal diocese was enriched by the teaching ministry of Roland Allen during his missionary journey in 1927–1928. It was the application of these apostolic principles which shaped Allen's proactive missionary theology for China, India, and his ministry later in Africa, that can still significantly contribute to missiology for the situation of the changing structures within World Christianity today.

Roland Allen's Missiology of the Holy Spirit

Allen's missiology of the Holy Spirit is systematically articulated in *Missionary Principles—and Practice*[39] (1913) and *Pentecost and the World: the Revelation of the Holy Spirit in the Acts of the*

---

[35] Hubert Allen, *Roland Allen*, 86.

[36] Roland Allen, "Diary of a Visit in South India" (unpublished), USPG X622, Box 7, File N, Oxford, Bodleian Library.

[37] Susan Harper, *In the Shadow of the Mahatma: Bishop V.S. Azariah and the Travails of Christianity in British India*, Studies in the History of Christian Missions (Grand Rapids: Eerdmans, 2000), 132.

[38] Susan Harper, "The Dornakal Church on the Cultural Frontier" in *Christians, Cultural Interactions, and India's Religious Traditions*, ed. J. M. Brown and R. E. Frykenberg (Grand Rapids: Eerdmans, 2002), 185.

[39] Roland Allen, *Foundation Principles of Foreign Missions* (Bungay, Suffolk: Richard Clay & Sons, 1910; reprint, entitled *Essential Missionary Principles*, Cambridge: Lutterworth Press, 1913; Reprint, *Missionary Principles—and Practice*, 2006).

Apostles[40] (1917). Subsequently, this broadly pneumatological understanding is interspersed throughout his sermons, teaching notes, articles, and correspondence. His emphasis on pneumatology and ecclesiology—Spirit and Order—stem from his devotion to Pauline thought, especially with his instruction on spiritual gifts (I Cor 12–14),[41] which the apostle's concluding emphasis underscores: "Let all things be done decently and in order" (I Cor 14:40).

Additional disclosure of his pneumatology is located within an unpublished work entitled "The Doctrine of the Holy Spirit"[42] which incorporates a symphonic blend — pneumatology, ecclesiology, and missiology—that shaped his overall missionary ecclesiology. For Allen, the missionary Spirit creates, nourishes, fills, and empowers "the native apostles"[43] to plant the Church and provide sacramental spiritual food. His missiology of Spirit and Order incorporates a central fostering of the faith through the sacramental means of grace. This argument for native clergy presupposes the necessity of the sacramental life of the Church and demonstrates how his theology embraced the frequency of its administration. The organic nature of Church growth stems from people who have embraced the faith, he believed, and subsequently desire to share what they have received.[44] This is natural. Allen compares this with how Muslim missionaries—traders, soldiers, teachers—that is, common people who have embraced Islam, share their faith with people and eventually see that "a mosque springs up, a school is established, a Moslem community arises."[45] He critiqued his fellow Anglicans' reluctance to share their faith in the way that Muslims did and concluded that much of the hesitancy in "our fellow churchmen who go abroad" is due to a past reliance upon *professional clergymen* to provide for them all the ministerial services, especially the sacraments.[46] This comparison serves as his charge for them to exercise faith in the missionary Spirit's creativity. He cites how the layman Frumentius (AD 300–380)—referred to as the "Apostle of the Abyssinians"—evangelized Alexandria and was later consecrated bishop of Axum (Northern Ethiopia) by Athanasius.[47] "I suppose," Allen said, that "most of our Bishops would deny that they had ever met a Frumentius. So rare a thing is it for a layman to think that as a Christian he has the right [and] duty to propagate his religion and instruct the ignorant in his faith."[48]

The basis for Allen's ecclesiology originates in his interpretation of the way the universal common priesthood of Christians functions through the presence, direction,

---

[40] Allen, *Pentecost and the World*, 1–61.

[41] Roland Allen, "The Ministry of Expansion: the Priesthood of the Laity," USPG X622, Box 3, Number 27, chapter 7: 4, (1930).

[42] Roland Allen, "The Doctrine of the Holy Spirit," USPG X622, Box 3, 13: Introduction, 1–16, Oxford, Bodleian Library.

[43] Ibid., 12.

[44] Allen, "The Doctrine of the Holy Spirit," 3.

[45] Ibid. Allen's engagement with Muslims intensified later in life.

[46] Ibid.

[47] F. L. Cross and E. A. Livingstone, *Dictionary of the Christian Church* (Peabody: Hendrickson, 1997), 644.

[48] Allen, "The Doctrine of the Holy Spirit," 4.

and ministry of "the missionary Spirit."[49] This pneumatology shaped Allen's church planting methodology, in that it served both to advocate the oversight by missionary bishops[50] for the ordaining of a specialized ministry and to support the administration of the Sacraments by the "priesthood of the body"[51] whenever they were outside the range of the organized church due to the absence of ordained clergy. Again, his argument was always that "the universal priesthood cannot be annulled by an absent specialized priesthood."[52] Does Roland Allen's missionary ecclesiology remain influential today?

Allen's Impact and Contemporary Relevance

It is rather ironic that Allen's influence today encompasses an ecclesiastical sphere far beyond the Anglican Communion which he faithfully served. On the one hand, my analysis has identified his significant contribution to Anglican missiology in India through his friendship with and influence of Bishop Azariah's ministry within the Dornakal churches and their expansive missionary undertakings outside of their diocesan borders. The archival research disclosed two letters (1912) from Bishop Henry Whitehead[53] (Madras) thanking Allen for supporting Azariah's consecration as the *first indigenous bishop* in India. Ongoing correspondence between Azariah and Allen disclosed how Azariah not only thanked him for writing *Voluntary Clergy* (1923)[54] but also assured him that the episcopacy was "in favour of an order of permanent Deacons and Voluntary Permanent Deacons."[55]

After Roland Allen's death in 1947, it was Hendrik Kraemer, in his *A Theology of the Laity* (1958) who cited from Roland Allen's *The Spontaneous Expansion of the Church, and the Causes which Hinder It*,[56] to disclose how the significant growth of the Church during the first centuries was accomplished through the laity's witness. Allen's contribution to Kraemer's missiology is the first example where he had an influence on a major ecumenical theologian a decade after his death. Shortly after Kraemer's book was published two other noteworthy missiologists—Sir Kenneth Grubb and Lesslie Newbigin—men who already had been reading Allen's works, each contributed to writing the *Foreword* in 1962 for both republished books: *Missionary Methods: St. Paul's or Ours?* (1912) and *The Spontaneous Expansion of the Church* (1927). And again, the Reformed missionary in Nigeria, Harry Boer, in 1948 wrote an article for the missionary journal—*World Dominion*—in appreciation of Allen's work. And, in his *Pentecost and Missions* (1961) he engaged with Allen's missiology throughout the book.[57] Unlike many later

---

[49] Allen, "The Ministry of Expansion: the Priesthood of the Laity," Box 3, Number 27, 1930, chapter 6:7.

[50] Allen, "The Doctrine of the Holy Spirit," 14.

[51] Allen, "The Ministry of Expansion: the Priesthood of the Laity," 6:7.

[52] Ibid., 7:3.

[53] Letters from Whitehead to Allen (7 June 1912 and 11 June 1912), USPG X622, Box 1, File A, Oxford, Bodleian Library.

[54] Letter from Azariah to Allen (29 December 1923), USPG X622, Box 1, File A: 12, Oxford, Bodleian Library.

[55] Ibid.

[56] Kraemer, *Theology of the Laity*, 20; cf. Allen, *Spontaneous Expansion*, 143–146.

[57] Boer, *Pentecost and Missions*, 48, 61, 63–64, 99, 136, 163 and 210ff.

missiologists who generally quote only from Allen's two most published books,[58] Boer purposefully quoted from some of Allen's articles[59] and other books[60] that later missiologists tend to neglect. Hubert Allen pointed out to me that it was Boer who best understood his grandfather's thinking on how the Holy Spirit's power effects mission expansion.[61]

Grubb's honest analysis and Boer's advocacy of Allen's works incited a substantial interest in Allen's works. And it was Grubb's influence with World Dominion Press to then republish these works, including *The Ministry of the Spirit: Selected Writings of Roland Allen*, edited by David Paton (1960), which caused the missiological thought of Allen to spread. Then, it was the Anglican—Canon David Paton—who carried Allen's missiological baton within ecumenism after the dismantling of colonialism. Paton's contribution to Allen's legacy is commendable. Another voice within Christianity who advocated Allen's works was Bishop Lesslie Newbigin, who believed that "Allen was right"[62] and that it was his emphasis on an *apostolic ministry* which relied upon the *pneumatological dynamic* and also placed *the sacraments* as central to the community's life, contributed much to mission studies.[63] In 1962 Newbigin argued that Allen's impact had affected the "assumptions of churches and missions, and slowly but steadily the number of those who found themselves compelled to listen has increased."[64]

In 2006 the contemporary missiologist Brian Stanley argued that Allen's missional pneumatology can be summarized as: "if the Holy Spirit is given, a missionary Spirit is given."[65] Stanley went on to say that "Allen thus foreshadows also the prominence which (in marked contrast to his own day) is now given to the Holy Spirit in Christian theology and in the churches of the majority world, so many of which are pentecostal in emphasis."[66] It was Francis Anekwe Oborji, the Nigerian-born Roman Catholic professor of missiology (Pontifical Urban University, Rome), when highlighting the success of Pauline mission said that "Allen suggests [that it] was due to the fact that he trusted both the Lord and the people to whom he had gone."[67] Oborji agreed that "Allen alerted his readers [*Missionary Methods*] to the glaring difference between Paul's missionary methods and those of contemporary mission agencies."[68]

---

[58] *Missionary Methods* (1912) and *Spontaneous Expansion* (1927).

[59] Roland Allen, "The Revelation of the Holy Spirit in the Acts of the Apostles," *International Review of Missions* VII (April 1918): 162; Allen, *Mission Activities Considered in Relation to the Manifestation of the Spirit*, 2nd edition (London: World Dominion, 1930): 32.

[60] Allen, *Pentecost and the World*, 39–41, 42–43, 85, 87; Allen, Educational Principles and Missionary Methods, 41–42; and Allen and Sydney James Wells Clark, *A Vision of Foreign Missions* (London, 1937), 132.

[61] Interview with Hubert Allen on 4 February 2011. Hubert told me that his father (John Allen) thought Harry Boer understood Roland's thinking better than any other missionary author.

[62] Lesslie Newbigin, *The Gospel in a Pluralist Society*, (London: SPCK, 1989), 146–147.

[63] Ibid., 147.

[64] Newbigin in Allen, *Missionary Methods*, Foreword i.

[65] Stanley in Allen, *Missionary Principles* (2006), Foreword VI.

[66] Ibid.

[67] Francis Anekwe Oborji, *Concepts of Mission: The Evolution of Contemporary Missiology* (Maryknoll: Orbis, 2006), 92.

[68] Ibid.

The aforementioned African missiologists and missionaries who engaged with Allen's works are indicative of various leaders from within the 2008 Global Anglican Future Conference (GAFCON) who were influenced by him: Michael Nazir-Ali (former bishop of Rochester), Roger Beckwith, Vinay Samuel, and Chris Sugden. GAFCON's confessional statement—*The Jerusalem Declaration*—basically echoes Allen's Anglican apologia in terms of a clear 'Gospel' emphasis, primacy of Scripture, creedal fidelity (1–5); clerical orders and sacramental practice (6–8); and missional ecclesiology that is dependent on the pneumatological dynamic (9–14).[69] As my research has disclosed, two archbishops—Nicholas Okoh (Nigeria) and Eliud Wabukala (Kenya)—argued that the current crisis in Anglicanism is due to the fact that "the Church of England [ought to] go back to the basic principles and develop new structures while remaining firmly within the Anglican Communion" and further that "its leadership should be focused not on one person or one Church, however hallowed its history, but on the one historic faith we confess."[70] These statements from the younger churches of Anglicanism reflect Roland Allen's *apostolic methods* for church planting (Spirit *before* Order), the *apostolic principles* that served as the central planks for his theology of mission (Spirit *with* Order), and the *apostolic order* that has clearly advanced St. Paul's missionary ecclesiology (Spirit *empowered* Order) within the One, Holy, Catholic, and Apostolic Church.

---

[69] Nicholas Okoh, Vinay Samuel, and Chris Sugden, eds., *Being Faithful: The Shape of Historic Anglicanism Today, a Commentary on the Jerusalem Declaration* (London: Latimer Trust, 2009), 6–7.

[70] E. Thornton, "We should elect our chair, say Primates," *Church Times* (April 2012): 5.

Chapter 33

Lay Guide to a Complete Spiritual Life: Evelyn Underhill (1875–1941)

The Very Rev. Cn. Lawrence Bausch

From an early age, it was apparent to the parents of Evelyn Underhill (1875–1941) that she had keen intelligence and serious curiosity. An only child, she was raised in London and educated at home until attending a boarding school as a teenager. She was baptized and confirmed in an Anglican Church, but neither she nor her parents were regular church goers. She earned a degree from London's King's College for Women. At 23, she went to Italy with her parents for the first time, where she was deeply attracted to Catholic culture and theology. She returned to Italy annually with her mother for the next 15 years. As she wrote to a friend after her first visit, "This place has taught me more than I can tell you; it's a sort of gradual unconscious growing into an understanding of things."[1]

Between 1902 and 1908, she published a book of poems and 3 novels. In 1907, she married childhood friend Hubert Stuart Moore. It was also in 1907 that she acknowledged what she described as the truth of the Catholic Religion. She did not become a Roman Catholic, however. This decision was made partly because of resistance from her husband, but also because of concerns she had regarding their use of authority, which she found antithetical to her intellectual approach to religious experience. In 1907 she began work on what would become one of two major books she would write, *Mysticism*, which was published in 1911. Also in 1911, she began a friendship with Baron Von Hugel, a well-known Roman Catholic author and layman.

During the following decade she published several more books, most of which followed up on the themes raised in *Mysticism*. By the end of these years, she began spiritual direction with Von Hugel. Under his direction, she came to realize that her intellectual assent to the Catholic faith was inadequate, especially given her conviction that the direct experience of God was available to every Christian. This belief needed to be lived out as an active participant in the Body of Christ. She became a practicing Anglican in 1921. Some years later, in a letter she wrote to a Roman Catholic Priest and friend, "I ... solidly believe in the Catholic status of the Anglican Church, as to orders and sacraments."[2] This commitment significantly changed her approach to how God communicated himself to people. In addition to the individual experience one might have, the Sacraments were dominical means of grace which assured his Presence. The Eucharist became the center of her devotional life. In addition to becoming a regular Communicant, she also would spend time of Adoration before the Reserved Sacrament, and particularly enjoyed attending Benediction. What she had admired in attending Roman Catholic churches, especially in Italy, had now become direct Communion with our Lord, and she both participated in and commended this practice regularly.

---

[1] Charles Williams, ed., *The Letters of Evelyn Underhill* (London: Longmans, 1956), 8, archive.org/details/lettersofevelynuoooowill.

[2] Ibid., 25.

From 1922 on, Evelyn devoted her attention to leading retreats, providing spiritual direction, and engaged in weekly service to poor people she came to know. Most of her writings from this point on, apart from her second masterwork, *Worship* (1936), were either retreat notes or lectures and talks she had delivered. During this time, she became the first woman lecturer on the list for Oxford University, the first woman Fellow of King's College, London, and one of few women to be awarded a D.D. from the University of Aberdeen.

For the remainder of this paper, we will look at some of the wisdom she imparted in these mature works, with special focus on things which offer spiritual guidance for contemporary Anglicans. We will do this under three headings: Personal Direction, Corporate Life, and Anglican Christianity.

Personal Direction

From the beginning of her study and writing about mysticism, she believed that the direct experience of God, the 'mystical experience', was available to every Christian. In *Mysticism*, she showed that God could be experienced in the context of daily life and in any part of creation. She wrote later, "The experience of God may come in many ways and under many symbolic disguises. It may be steady or fleeting, dim or intense. But in so far as it is direct and intuitive, it is always a mystical experience."[3] In her later writings, she usually wrote of saints rather than mystics, while continuing to stress that any Christian could experience intimacy with God. She continued to teach that the spiritual life was intrinsically connected with ordinary life. In an early retreat address, she wrote, "I always have my doubts about the real sanctity of saints who let the pot boil over or forget to sweep the floor. Practical life is for most of us our own school of divine service and we are required to bend our whole minds, steadily and quietly, on each thing given us to do."[4]

An extension of her conviction about the spiritual possibilities of ordinary Christians, coupled with her experience under spiritual direction and her demonstrated ability to communicate her faith in her writings, led her to spend most of her energies for the remainder of her life in offering spiritual direction, addressing religious gatherings, and leading retreats. She understood that each person was unique, and that spiritual direction needed to address one's particular circumstances as well as its corporate context. She wrote, "We take as our first principle the humble and diligent use of the degree of prayer natural to a soul at any particular stage in its course, and not the anxious straining towards some other degree yet beyond it."[5] The goal of the spiritual life was union with God, and the way to live toward that goal began with the concrete life of the individual. The rhythm Underhill assumed in providing direction was that God is the one who initiates and calls, and the person is the one who receives and is obedient to what God initiates. We need to learn to listen, to attend to his Presence in all

---

[3] Lucy Menzies, ed., *The Collected Papers of Evelyn Underhill* (London: Longmans, 1946), 109, archive.org/details/collectedpapersooooounde_m2j6.

[4] Evelyn Underhill, *The Mount of Purification* (London: Longmans, 1949), 78.

[5] Cropper, Margaret, *The Life of Evelyn Underhill* (New York: Harper, 1958), 104, archive.org/details/lifeofevelynundeooocrop.

circumstances, and to act upon what he communicates to us: If he did everything, we would not be able to love him; if we succeeded by our own efforts, we would not need a Savior.

From the time Evelyn Underhill began to receive spiritual direction in 1921, she received it for the remainder of her life (following Von Hugel's death in 1925, she received direction from two Anglican Clergymen). As she herself became a director, she accepted a variety of individuals, including several Anglican Priests. She was frequently invited to offer guidance to Priests, both in public addresses and private counsel. Four passages in particular reveal her perception and wisdom in serving them. I believe these may be helpful: 1) for priests or those who may be called to this ministry, 2) for parishioners' prayers for their priests, and 3) for each believer, recognizing that what the priest is in the Church, the Church is in the world. Underhill understood the "priesthood of all believers" not as describing a priesthood of each believer in a sacramental sense but of all believers corporately in their mission to the world.

In a letter to a young priest, she wrote,

> It has been a crucial week for you, hasn't it? When you had to make the choice, which will color all your life, whether you will be (a) a real priest, offered to God, standing before His altar as a sacrifice to Him to be used for His people's needs, or (b) a thoroughly nice young clergyman. How splendid that He pressed you to choose (a). Having done so, you can feel quite sure that although there will be very dark and dreary bits to get through, in all real necessities He will provide the support and light you need.[6]

This passage underscores her teaching that the role of a priest is that of a double servant: first, of God, to whom his life is consecrated and submitted, and second, to those whom he has been called to serve; his authority is contingent on being a servant-leader. He is neither the "hired help" of the Institution and its leaders, nor the "boss" who treats his congregants as employees who are to follow his orders. This understanding provides the context for her teaching about the spiritual life of a priest.

In 1926, she delivered an Address to a Diocesan Clergy Conference. In her emphasis on the priest in the Eucharist, her particular insight was evident, and was reported to have startled some of those present:

> You do far more for your congregation for helping them to understand what prayer really is, and to practice it; for quickening their religious sensitiveness, by your unselfconscious absorption in God during services, than you can hope to do by any amount of sermons.... These congregations are probably far too shy to come and tell you what it is that helps them most in the things you do; but there is no doubt at all that your recollectedness, your devotional temper, will be one of the things that do help them most.[7]

This counsel expresses her conviction that Eucharistic worship embodies the same pattern of life which we noted—Divine initiative and human response. The behavior she

---

[6] Quoted in *Life*, 219.
[7] *Life*, 145.

describes for the priest, however poorly imitated today, remains sound if our worship is going to fulfill its function in strengthening the spiritual lives of the people.

In another Diocesan Clergy Conference a decade later, she described the function of the parish priest more generally:

> He is meant to be one of the channels by and through which the Eternal God, manifested in time, acts within the human world; reaches out, seeks, touches and transforms human souls. His real position in the parish is that of a dedicated agent of the Divine Love. The Spirit of Christ, indwelling His Church, is to act through him.[8]

She wanted priests to understand that their behavior in worship was the template for all aspects of parish ministry.

One final passage addressed to priests speaks to the question of evangelism, an important theme for today's Church, involving clergy and laity alike: "Evangelism is useless unless it is the work of one devoted to God, willing and glad to suffer all things for God, penetrated by the attractiveness of God."[9] In a Christian's response to God, our love for him is to be foundation for receiving his love for others and expressing it to them.

As her development continued after becoming an active Anglican, and her focus shifted from mystical experience to worship, she began addressing individual spiritual development in the context of life in the Church. Regarding prayer, she wrote,

> Any study of it which conceives it mainly, so to speak, as the action of discrete spiritual individuals, surely misses its central truth; namely, the solidarity of that total and supernatural action which is brought into existence by the Divine energy and exerted by God through and in the corporate activity of all praying souls.[10]

This necessarily involves institutional structures. She described the relationship between these in a Biblical reflection:

> When Peter and John—types of the institutional and mystical elements of Christianity—ran together to the Holy Sepulchre, John the seer reached the mystery first; but it was Peter, the Church, who went in first. So, the intuition of the spiritual realist may arrive first, but his fullest lights and convictions came to him when he followed where the Church has first trod. Then he exercises his true function within the Mystical Body ... to enter into and explain ever more fully the wonder and significance of the revealed.[11]

We will now look at her insights pertaining to the relationship of the individual to the church.

Corporate Life

When Evelyn Underhill acknowledged the essential truth of the Catholic religion, she was 32. As we have seen, she believed that the riches of the spiritual life were to be incarnated in the lives of believers. She became a practicing Anglican when 46. She had

---

[8] *Papers*, 123.

[9] Ibid., 125.

[10] Ibid., 82.

[11] Underhill, *Mixed Pasture: Twelve Essays and Addresses* (London: Methuen, 1933), 142–143.

come to see that the incarnated spiritual life needed to be embedded in corporate worship and life. Together, these expressed the fullness of the mutual indwelling: He in us and we in Him: "Human beings have developed through acting together; and unless they do so, a part of their nature fails to expand."[12] This insight underscores an additional reason for evangelism: to the extent that there are still people outside the Church, we are unable to fulfill our Lord's desire that all people be saved (1 Timothy 2:4). She wrote, "Real, fully corporate worship, genuine institutional religion, rests on the solidarity of the whole Christian family—the blessed company of all faithful people past and present, living and dead, from St. Peter and Paul to the last baptized baby."[13] Given this perspective, it is no surprise that she was a strong advocate for prayers for the departed.

Her emphasis on incarnating the spiritual life in daily life led her to describe the importance of including the whole self in our worship and life: "Further, because men are creatures of sense as well as spirit, of body as well as soul, we must bring our senses and our bodies in, and let them play their part in the worshipping act."[14] (It is noteworthy for Anglicans that the Summary of the Law in our Liturgy is taken from Matthew 22:37. In his rendering of Deuteronomy 6:5, we are commanded to love God with all our "heart, soul, and mind"; when this is referenced in Mark 12:30 and Luke 10:27, the word "strength" is added, which brings out the importance of the body in response to God's commandment explicitly.)

The dynamic relationship between worshipping individuals and corporate, liturgical worship was addressed significantly in her teaching. We have considered her challenge to priests in celebrating; she was equally challenging to lay people: "The force, depth, and realness of the common worship depends largely on the sincerity and devotedness of the individuals taking part in it."[15] Each worshipper is to do his or her part in devotion; it is also true that the liturgy itself both challenges and assist them in this effort. She wrote,

> Perhaps the greatest of the things which the discipline of corporate worship does for those who submit to its influence is that it delivers them from that cramping tendency to self-occupation by which nearly all human beings—and especially pious human beings—are beset: my soul, my spiritual life, my sins, my problems, my communion with God. All true and important facts, no doubt; but facts that get on best, like many hardy annuals, if well thinned out in the first instance and then left to themselves.[16]

Our worship is designed to open us up to our Lord and to one another, and the liturgy invites each worshipper to receive these benefits. She wrote,

> Here the individual must lose his life to find it; the longing for personal expression, personal experience, safety, joy, must more and more be swallowed up in Charity. For the goal alike of Christian sanctification and Christian worship is the ceaseless

---

[12] *Papers*, 67.
[13] Ibid., 74.
[14] Ibid., 67.
[15] Ibid., 77.
[16] Ibid., 78.

self-offering of the Church, in and with Christ her head, to the increase of the glory of God.[17]

Underhill described the liturgy as having two essential points, which are dealt with in great detail in *Worship* and in several of her retreat addresses; indeed, of her twelve retreats (she gave each multiple times and in varied places), five had themes connected with either parts of or the whole of the Eucharist. She described these succinctly in a lecture: "If the first point of worship is the creature's adoration of God, the second is that same little creature's total self-offering—total willing capitulation to that God; the essential notes of the worship man is called and privileged to pay."[18] Apart from some seasonal variations, the Eucharist in the Anglican Church in North America (ACNA) Book of Common Prayer begins with "Blessed be God: the Father, the Son, and the Holy Spirit" and ends with "Go in peace to love and serve the Lord": adoration and service.[19]

In a lecture she gave in the year following the publication of *Worship*, Evelyn Underhill wrote that the Eucharist is not merely given to help us in our devotion and service, but to lead ever deeper into the reality of the Divine Presence. As we conclude this section with a passage from this lecture, I am reminded of something a priest friend often said— God loves us so much that He accepts us where we are; but he has no intention of leaving us there!

> The Spirit of Worship is the very spirit of Exploration. It has never finished discovering and adoring the ever new perfections of that which it loves. 'My beloved is like strange islands!' said St. John of the Cross, in one of his great poems. Islands in an unchartered ocean, found by the intrepid navigators after a long and difficult voyage, which has made great demands on faith, courage, and perseverance; islands that reveal beauties that we never dreamed of and a life of independent loveliness, to which our dim everyday existence gives no clue; yet never reveal everything, always have some unanswered questions, keep their ultimate secret still.[20]

She reminded us that the destination towards which we are being led by God is not reached finally in this life; we participate in the risen life of our Lord now, but this participation will not complete until we ascend in him to the place where he is "seated at the right hand of the Father."

Anglican Christianity

As noted above, Evelyn Underhill became a practicing Anglican, believing in the validity of its Orders and Sacraments in terms of their catholicity. Although she frequently expressed displeasure with some Anglo-Catholic clergy and congregations, nevertheless she described herself as an Anglican Catholic, *Catholic* being the noun and *Anglican* the adjective. It is not surprising that she gave much positive attention to the Oxford or Tractarian Movement and its legacy for Anglicans. Prior to this, many in the Church of

---

[17] Evelyn Underhill, *Worship* (New York: Harper, 1937), 82.

[18] *Papers*, 80.

[19] *2019 Book of Common Prayer* (Huntington, CA: Anglican Liturgy, 2019), 105/123, 122/138.

[20] *Life*, 215.

England could easily believe that the Church was either of English or sixteenth-century origin. In "Worship," she wrote,

> The new life which entered the Church of England with the Tractarian movement has now penetrated and transformed in various ways and degrees the whole temper of her worship, and brought it back into harmony with Catholic tradition. This achievement has won its greatest triumph at the centre … in an ordered worship which is faithful to the spirit of the BCP. That worship, at once biblical and sacramental, carries through all that is best in the spirit of the past, yet preserves the flexible and synthetic character of Anglicanism.[21]

In a paper written in celebration of the 100th anniversary of the Movement (1933), she described the restoration of Anglicanism to its inherent catholicity as a deepening of the Evangelical spirit, which had been helpfully re-introduced in the eighteenth century:

> The Evangelical mind tends to present spiritual expression as a duet. For the Catholic mind it is, or should be, a symphony; and now English Christians heard once more the mighty orchestration of the Saints. The bringing back of this concept of the social nature of Christian spirituality into the field of practical religion has profound effects upon the soul. It is, for one thing, completely incompatible with an attenuated, comfortable, this-world Christianity. The standard of the Saints, in love, in suffering, and in service, becomes the standard of the Church.[22]

For us to benefit in this way, we cannot be content merely with matters of language and ritual; that was the sort of Anglo-Catholic she was critical of. For her, catholic worship was far more substance than style. In the same article, she reviewed the Movement in this spirit: "But the final test of a religious movement is not to be sought in the realms of doctrine and practice, but in the souls that it forms. The promotion of holiness—this alone can guarantee any institution's spiritual worth."[23] In this regard, she pointed out the revival of Religious Orders and the sacrificial lives of many priests which came about as a consequence of the Movement.

The appeal made to Anglicans to avail themselves of the rich resources in our catholicity was not in any way intended to denigrate Christians of other Communions. Indeed, she was invited to give talks and retreats to ecumenical groups, including clergy. Her catholicity was deep enough to exclude any trace of sectarianism. In an address given on the occasion of the 100th anniversary of Evelyn Underhill's birth, Anglican priest and scholar, A. M. Allchin, wrote the following about the significance of her work:

> One of the reasons why Evelyn Underhill became so convinced an Anglican was because she saw Anglicanism not as complete in itself, but as part of a greater whole, "a respectable suburb in the city of God", to quote her own words. She found here a way of living an inclusive and comprehensive Catholicism, and thus became a great pioneer of spiritual ecumenism. Her book, *Worship*, gives a sympathetic

---

[21] *Life*, 209.
[22] *Mixed Pastures*, 128.
[23] Ibid., 138.

account of all the major traditions of Christian worship, Protestant as well as Catholic and Orthodox, as though she had been able to get inside them all.[24]

In this way, she is a fine model for us today—we are grateful for God's dispensation to us but are always ready to acknowledge with gratitude the gifts he has given others.

Conclusion

When the centenary of her birth was celebrated in 1975, Evelyn Underhill's works were seldom being read, and a revival of interest in her was only just beginning. Since that time, most of her earlier works have come back into print, as well as several previously uncollected writings and anthologies. She is now included in the Church Calendar of several Anglican jurisdictions, including the Anglican Church in North America. As I hope to have shown in this paper, she is well worth our attention today, and through her writings continues to be an excellent spiritual guide. Her implicit catholicity is especially welcome at a time when many churches, including some Anglican, seem to be content to wander away from this organic identity in the Body of Christ. The more we follow her spiritual guidance, the more likely we will be to grow in God's love and service.

We will close with a memory of one of her friends who visited her when she was recovering from a serious illness (during the last few years of her life, her health limited her significantly):

> As I entered, she got up and turned round, looking as fragile as though "a puff of wind might blow her away" might be literally true in her case, but light simply streamed from her face, illuminated with a radiant smile.... One could not but feel consciously there and then (not on subsequent recognition or reflection) that one was in the presence of the extension of the Mystery of our Lord's Transfiguration in one of the members of His Mystical Body. I myself never saw it repeated in any later meeting.... It told one not only of herself, but more of God and of the Mystical Body than all her works put together.[25]

In closing, here is the collect for the Feast Day of Evelyn Underhill, June 15:

> O God, Origin, Sustainer, and End of all creatures: Grant that thy Church, taught by thy servant Evelyn Underhill, guarded ever more by thy power, and guided by thy Spirit into the light of truth, may continually offer to thee all glory and thanksgiving, and attain with thy saints to the blessed hope of everlasting life, which thou hast promised us by our Savior Jesus Christ; who with thee and the same Holy Spirit liveth and reigneth, one God, now and forever. *Amen.*[26]

---

[24] A. M. Allchin and Michael Ramsey, *Evelyn Underhill: Two Centenary Essays* (Oxford: SLG, 1977), 7.
[25] *Letters*, 37.
[26] *Lesser Feasts and Fasts*, 4th ed. (New York: Church Publishing, 1988), 261.

Chapter 34

The Theology of Charles Williams (1886–1945)

The Very Rev. Cn. Lawrence Bausch

Introduction

Charles Williams (1886–1945) was neither a professional theologian nor an academic. He spent most of his adult life working in the editorial department of Oxford University Press, serving in their London Office from 1908 until being moved to Oxford during WWII. He was a life-long Anglican and practicing Anglo-Catholic, married in 1917, and had one son, born in 1922. His first books to be published were poetry, and his first novel to be published was in 1930. The first of his few theological works was published in 1938. As his friend C. S. Lewis wrote about him, "The belief that the most serious and ecstatic experiences either of human love or of imaginative literature have theological implications, and they can be healthy and fruitful only if the implications are diligently thought out and severely lived, is the root principle of all his work."[1]

While he did not write often about his Anglicanism, Williams was nevertheless quite influential among other prominent Anglicans. T. S. Eliot expressed enthusiasm for his work in his Introduction to William's final novel, *All Hallows Eve*. Dorothy Sayers was so moved by Williams' understanding and insight that, following his advice, she spent the years following his death translating Dante's *Divine Comedy*. Williams was also selected to write the lengthy and insightful introduction to the *Letters of Evelyn Underhill*.

Typical of Anglo-Catholics, Williams was not sectarian but believed that the Anglican Church was but a part of the One, Holy, Catholic, and Apostolic Church of the ancient Creeds. His book, *Descent of the Dove*, is subtitled "A Short History of the Holy Spirit in the Church," and includes a generous appraisal of various movements throughout Christian fellowships. In May 1995, I spoke with British Orthodox Bishop Kallistos Ware about both Lewis and Williams, and he said that Lewis was the most effective apologist of the Christian Tradition in English in the twentieth century, and that Williams actually *contributed* to the Tradition. I suggest that it was at least in part because of his Anglo-Catholicism that he was able to have such a broad appeal and value.

Williams' theology was present in all of his writings; indeed, it seems to have been present in every aspect of his life. For several years, he wrote plays centering on his office life and those he worked with, ennobling each with deep and joyful significance. His first published novel, *War in Heaven*, involved the Anglican archdeacon of a small parish in which the Holy Grail, the vessel used in the Last Supper and subsequently brought to England according to the Arthurian myth, was found to be. The priest believed that it ought to be protected due to its value but acknowledged that a drop of the precious Blood of Christ was of infinitely more value. His two volumes of Arthurian poems, regarded by many to be his greatest work, center on the quest for the Grail, the centrality of the Eucharist, and the Church. In his novel *The Greater Trumps*, one key scene takes place at an Anglican Church on Christmas where the liturgy is reflected upon.

---

[1] C. S. Lewis, ed., *Essays Presented to Charles Williams* (Oxford: Oxford University Press, 1947), vi.

While Williams was not a systematic theologian, I will be using traditional theological categories to explore what his contribution to the tradition might entail. For the purposes of this chapter, the references will be mostly restricted to his theological writings.[2]

In this survey, we will see that the word which is at the heart of his theological vision and understanding is *co-inherence*. Things may coinhere that exist in an essential relationship with one another as innate components of the other. For example, St Paul identifies one of the Christian's responsibilities as "speaking the truth in love" (Eph 4:15),[3] and we may say that truth and love coinhere; each is inseparable from the other and is intrinsically in the other. Williams believed co-inherence to be the primary principle of all reality, based on the Divine Life Itself and extending throughout all creation.

The Holy Trinity

Charles Williams accepted unconditionally the *Nicene Creed* and the decisions of the undivided Church in Council. For him the Creed was the starting point for meditation and not merely the structure of Christian faith. He believed that the doctrine of the Holy Trinity not only expresses what the Divine has revealed about himself, but also conveys a divine pattern which is imprinted throughout the entire created order, and of humankind in particular. He referred to this mystery as *co-inherence*, and this becomes for him the central image of all reality. Mary Shideler, quoting him, wrote:

> The three do not cohere, "stick to each other", but they co-inhere, "abide with each other", as the unborn child abides in its mother, the lover in his beloved, spirit in body, the Word in flesh. This is "a union very much beyond our powers to conceive, more than a union, a unity" and a unity so heightened in its perfection that Christianity makes good its claim to monotheism.[4]

Describing an aspect of this, Williams wrote, "For the Son, in his eternal Now desires subordination, and it is his. He wills to be so; he co-inheres obediently and filially in the Father, as the Father authoritatively and paternally co-inheres in him. And the whole Three Persons are co-inherent together—and co-equal."[5] Exploring how dynamic this mystery is, Williams wrote, "Co-inherence depends upon individuality, as much as individuality on co-inherence."[6]

We believe that "God is love" (1 John 4:8), and Williams perceived this as the very life of the Trinity. The co-inherence of the Trinity at its deepest is love. Referring to the Council of Nicaea (325 AD), he wrote, "If there had been no creation, would Love have practiced love? and would Love have had an adequate object to love? Nicaea answered

---

[2] The primary works cited are: *He Came Down from Heaven* and *The Forgiveness of Sins* (combined edition, London: Faber & Faber, 1950; *He Came Down*, originally London: Heinemann, 1938, and *The Forgiveness of Sins*, originally London: G. Bles, 1943); *The Descent of the Dove* (London: Longmans, Green, 1939); *The Figure of Beatrice* (London: Faber & Faber, 1943); *Image of the City and other Essays* (Oxford: Oxford University Press, 1958).

[3] Unless otherwise noted, all Scripture quotations are from the Revised Standard Version.

[4] Mary McDermott Schideler, *The Theology of Romantic Love: A Study in the Writings of Charles Williams* (Eugene, OR: Wipf & Stock, 2005), 80, quoting from *Image*, 76.

[5] *Descent of the Dove*, 39–40.

[6] *The Figure of Beatrice*, 43.

yes.... The Godhead itself was in Co-inherence."7 Because God is in some way present and reveals himself in everything he has created (Ps 19:1, Rom 1:20), the co-inherence of the Trinity is also the principle informing everything that exists.

Creation and Fall

The complete harmony and goodness throughout all creation described in Genesis 1 and 2 showed the world as it was intended to operate. Humans were created in the image of God and given the vocation of stewardship, of caring for our environment. Yet, as we were created *out of* love, so were we created *for* love. If we had allowed God's love to fill and flow through us, the co-inherence of the Trinity would have extended throughout creation.

However, love must be freely chosen and freely given, and this requires that an alternative be available. It is in this context that the serpent was permitted to tempt us. And, as Genesis 3 tells us, in Eve and Adam we fell. Williams described this in a quite particular and significant way: "They knew good; they wished to know good and evil. Since there was not—since there never has been and never will be—anything else than the good to know, they knew good as antagonism. All difference consists in the mode of knowledge."8 As he put it more plainly, "The definition of the Fall is that man determined to know good as evil."9 This view centers the "original sin" neither on the eating of the fruit nor in seeing that it was appealing, but in believing that God's word was "evil," that the serpent's interpretation of what He meant was to be preferred; as St. Paul put it, "They exchanged the truth about God for a lie and worshipped the creature rather than the Creator" (Rom 1:25).

Williams portrayed the consequences of this in a way which disclosed its trajectory apart from God's action: "Unfortunately to be as gods meant, for the Adam, to die, for to know evil, for them, was to know it not by pure intelligence but by experience. It was, precisely, to experience the opposite of good, that is the deprivation of the good, the slow destruction of the good, and of themselves with the good."10 Our human condition today (and in every age) bears witness to this. As in a kind of post-apocalyptic vision, he wrote, "The contradiction in the nature of man is thus completely established. He knows good, and he knows good as evil. These two capacities will always be present in him; his love will always be twisted with anti-love, with anger, with spite, with jealousy, with alien desires. Lucidity and confusion are alike natural and there is no corner into which antagonism to pure joy has not broken."11

Williams's description of our condition and its trajectory is not the end of the story; it simply shows how dire our circumstances are apart from divine intervention.

---

7 *Descent of the Dove*, 52.
8 *He Came Down*, 21.
9 *Image*, 77.
10 *He Came Down*, 20.
11 Ibid., 22.

Christ and Redemption

The orthodox doctrine of the Incarnation proclaims that Jesus is both fully human and fully divine. Williams stressed that the two natures co-inhere in the one person of Jesus Christ: "He himself likewise partook of the same nature" (Heb 2:14). The two natures co-inhered in him. If he had lacked any part of our nature, then it wouldn't have been redeemed; if he was not God, he could not have saved us. He summarized this in the context of 1 Corinthians 15:22:

> "As in Adam all die, even so in Christ shall all be made alive"; co-inherence did not begin with Christianity; all that happened was that co-inherence itself was redeemed and revealed by that very redemption as a supernatural principle as well as a natural. We were made sin in Adam but Christ was made sin for us and we in him were taken out of sin. To refuse the ancient heritage of guilt is to cut ourselves off from mankind as certainly as to refuse the new principle. It is necessary to submit to the one as freely as to the other.[12]

Williams stressed the connection between Jesus' death and rising and placed this in relation to the Fall:

> The Passion and the Resurrection have been necessarily divided in ritual and we think of them as separate events. So certainly they were, and yet not as separate as all that. They are as two operations in one; they are the hour of the coming of the kingdom. A new knowledge arises. Men had determined to know good as evil; there could be but one perfect remedy for that—to know the evil of the past itself as good, and to be free from the necessity of the knowledge of the evil in the future; to find right knowledge and perfect freedom together; to know all things as occasions for love.[13]

Elsewhere he expanded this understanding, connecting Christ's victory on the Cross with human life as we live out redemption:

> By that central substitution, which was the thing added by the Cross to the Incarnation, He became everywhere the centre of, and everywhere He energized and affirmed, all our substitutions and exchanges. He took what remained, after the Fall, of the torn web of humanity in all times and places, and not so much by a miracle of healing as by a growth within it made it whole. Supernaturally He renewed our proper nature.... When He had made hope a virtue He had prevented it from being a natural habit. In all failures of love there is left to us only a trust in His work; that is what we call "faith," a kind of quality of action. It is, however, a trust in what is already done. Not only His act, but all our acts, are finished so. "Thy will be done on earth as it is in heaven" means precisely that at any moment the holy desire is already accomplished—not perhaps in the sense that we desire it, but in the sense that He wills it. It is finished; we too do but play out the necessary ceremony.[14]

---

[12] *Descent*, 69–70.

[13] *He Came Down*, 58.

[14] *Image*, 137–138.

We were not left to live out this 'necessary ceremony' as solitary individuals but with a further extension of co-inherence, also achieved in Christ's redemptive acts.

Church and Sacraments

Jesus prayed to his Father on the night before his death for all of his followers, not merely the 11 who were with him to hear the prayer: "I do not pray for these only, but also for those who believe in me through their word, that they may all be one; even as thou, Father, art I me, and I in thee, that they also may be in us, so that the world may believe that thou hast sent me" (John 17:20–21). Williams wrote:

> Our Lord promised to the members of His Church a particular and intense union with each other through Himself. He defined that union as being of the same nature as that which He had with His Father. The later definitions of the inspired Church went further; they declared not merely that the Father and the Son existed co-equally, but they existed co-inherently—that is, that the Son existed in the Father and that the Father existed in the Son. The exact meaning of the preposition may be obscure. But no other word could satisfy the intellect of the Church. The same preposition was used to define our Lord's relations with His Church: "we in him and he in us". It was in that sense that the Church itself in-lived its children: "we are members one of another."[15]

The "mutual indwelling" between Christ and his Church is established in Baptism, in which one is "born again" or "born from above." The dominical means by which the faithful participate in this "new life" is the Eucharist. Williams wrote, "The great Rite of this (as of much else) within the Christian Church is the Eucharist, where the co-inherence is fully in action: 'He in us and we in Him.'"[16] Also on the Eucharist, he wrote, "There, visibly hidden, perfect under either species, were the subtlety, the glory, the agility, the impassibility. They were there for sacrifice and communion. The True Priest (hidden in wafer and in wine) offered them and generously permitted the Church and City a participation in His Act."[17]

As the communicant receives Christ in the Eucharist, this enrichment of the co-inherence involves participating in the forgiveness which is central to the new life. Considering the petition for forgiveness in the Lord's Prayer, Williams wrote:

> The condition of forgiving then is to be forgiven; the condition of being forgiven is to forgive. The two conditions are coexistent; they are indeed the very point of coexistence, the root of the new union, the beginning of the recovery of the co-inherence in which all creation had begun. Out of that point of double submission the City of God was to rise.[18]

Further,

> If our Lord was indeed the very Person of forgiveness, then certainly it is the very passion of forgiveness which is communicated in the Eucharist; it is a mutuality

---

[15] *Image*, 149.

[16] Ibid., 154.

[17] C. S. Lewis, ed., *Arthurian Torso* (Oxford: Oxford University Press, 1948), 204.

[18] "The Forgiveness of Sins" in *He Came Down*, 152.

between God and man which is also expressed between man and man. To feed on that with a grudge or a resentment present in the brain, or still lingering in the blood below the brain, is to reject the divine Food that is swallowed; it is not only to set schism between the body and the soul but literally in the body itself.[19]

The willingness to forgive and to be forgiven is the proper spirit in which to receive the Sacrament. Williams sees this as also central to the portion of the *Apostles' Creed* which centers on the Holy Spirit:

> "The Communion of Saints, the Forgiveness of Sins, the Resurrection of the Body and the Life Everlasting"... are but four titles for the same co-inherence of relationship. The Communion of Saints involves the resurrection of all the past, and therefore the forgiveness of sins. The resurrection involves forgiveness and communion. But the forgiveness is the necessity of all.[20]

Williams wrote extensively on how we embody this essential calling under the direction and empowerment of the divine grace.

Life in the Spirit

Two aspects of living the Christian life were given special attention in Charles Williams' writings. First, he frequently contrasted two different primary vocations a Christian might have; second, he stressed a fundamental activity common to both vocations as they respond to the Holy Spirit.

The Two Ways

In writing about the two *ways* or vocations, he frequently used a phrase, the source of which he never cited: "This also is thou; neither is this thou." The first phrase declares that everything that exists bears the mark of the Creator; the second phrase clarifies that no created thing is equivalent to the Creator. Together, these phrases describe the complementary vocations and the dynamic tension their connection entails. Before going further, it should be acknowledged that many if not most Christians do not consider their lives as a vocation, and if some do, it would not likely conform to either of these alternatives. However, we do lean in one of these directions or the other. Most of us, especially in our relatively affluent culture, tend towards enjoying the good things of creation and practice self-denial in special areas only, whereas a smaller number of us tend towards simplicity of life and avoid much indulgence in worldly goods.[21] Nevertheless, we can each benefit from considering Williams' characterizations, using them as a means by which to think about how we connect our relationship with God in our daily lives.

---

[19] "The Forgiveness of Sins" in *He Came Down*, 182.

[20] Ibid., 189.

[21] Williams paid much attention to the aspect of affirmation in the phenomenon of romantic love and believed we needed to come to think theologically about romance rather than be romantic about theology.

He wrote,

> The one Way was to affirm all things orderly until the universe throbbed with vitality; the other to reject all things until there was nothing anywhere but He. The Way of Affirmation was to develop great art and romantic love and marriage and philosophy and social justice; the Way of Rejection was to break out continually in the profound mystical documents of the soul, the records of the great psychological masters of Christendom.[22]

He cited two medieval works "in which the imagination of Christendom at the time expresses itself. The first is the *Cloud of Unknowing*; the second is the works of Dante. The Way of the Rejection of Images and the Way of Affirmation had hardly been better expressed before, nor perhaps since."[23] Williams was clear that the two *ways* are complementary, albeit that their connection involves a dynamic tension.

He also believed that they each need the other: "The essentials of the one Way are the accidents of the other.... We call it the Way and the other Way, but each is included in the other!"[24] Williams detailed the relationship between the ways clearly:

> Neither of these two Ways indeed is, or can be, exclusive. The most vigorous ascetic, being forbidden formally to hasten his death, is bound to attend to the actualities of food, drink, and sleep, which are also images, however brief his attention may be. The most indulgent of Christians is yet bound to hold his most cherished images—of food, drink, sleep, or anything else—negligible beside the final Image of God. And both are compelled to hold their particular Images of God negligible beside the universal Image of God which belongs to the Church, and even that less than the unimaged reality.[25]

Williams showed that Jesus himself embodied, and thus endorsed, both ways:

> Our sacred Lord, in his earthly existence, deigned to use both methods. The miracle at Cana and all the miracles of healing are works of the affirmation of images; the counsel to pluck out the eye is a counsel of the rejection of images. It is said that he so rejected them for himself that he had nowhere to lay his head, and that he so affirmed them by his conduct that was called a glutton and a wine-bibber. He commanded his disciples to abandon all images but himself and promised them, in terms of the same images, a hundred times what they had abandoned. The Crucifixion and Death are rejections and affirmations at once, for they affirm death only to reject death; the intensity of that death is the opportunity of its own dissolution; and beyond the physical rejection of earth lies the re-affirmation of earth which is called the Resurrection.[26]

As with everything else, "we have this treasure in earthen vessels, to show that the transcendent power belongs to God and not to us" (2 Cor 4:7). St Paul described the challenge faced by every Christian in responding to God's grace, "So I find it to be a law

---

[22] *Descent*, 50.
[23] *Descent*, 129.
[24] *Letter*, quoted in *Image*, XL.
[25] *Figure*, 9–10.
[26] Ibid., 10.

that when I want to do right, evil lies close at hand. For I delight in the law of God, in my inmost self, but I see in my members another law at war with the law of my mind and making me captive to the law of sin which dwells in my members" (Rom 7:21–23). Because of this "law of sin," we are subject to the perversion of images, whether they are affirmed or rejected. We may so prefer the good things of creation that we reject or ignore the Creator (a form of materialism); we may pursue worldly things as if this world is all there is (a form of pantheism); we may reject the physical world as irrelevant, that only spiritual things matter (a form of dualism). Whatever else we may do, we will be tempted to consider the good of the self above all others, including God and neighbor.

Substitution and Exchange

God is the source of our vocations, and only by his redeeming and sanctifying grace can we fulfill them. As St. Paul wrote shortly after the passage cited above, "There is therefore now no condemnation for those who are in Christ Jesus. For the law of the Spirit of life in Christ Jesus has set me free from the law of sin and death" (Rom 8:1–2). The only adequate remedy for the incoherence of our Fallen nature is co-inherence. Williams uses the terms "substitution" and "exchange" to describe how we are to live in the Spirit.

In his meditation on Galatians 6:2 ("Bear one another's burdens, and so fulfill the law of Christ"), Williams saw both an expression of the co-inherence for which we were made and a description of how to live it. He believed that this encompassed every aspect of life, from the physical to the social and the spiritual. As we saw earlier, Williams said that we were created *out of* love *for* love; we were made *from* others; we are to live *for* others. Williams saw that exchange occurs at the most fundamental level in our humanity:

> There is one great natural fact—a fact at the very root of all human facts—which involves a relation very much of the nature of exchange, or of something more than exchange. It is the fact of childbirth.... By the substitution of the woman for the man the seed fructifies. New life (literally) exists. It exists by the common operation of the woman and the man, and that operation involves something of the nature of substitution.[27]

The bearing of one another's burdens can occur at any and every level of our lives. Williams believed that

> if the principle of exchange, substitution, and co-inherence (inhering in each other) is at all true, then it is true of the whole nature of man. If it is true, then we depend on it altogether—not as a lessening of individuality or moral duty but as the very fundamental principle of all individuality and of all moral duty.[28]

One does not need an extraordinary sensitivity or set of gifts in order to live out this principle: "The mere attention of the mind to such a life of substitution will itself provide instances and opportunities. What is needed is precisely that attention. And, of course, common sense. There are as many dangers in that life as in any."[29] Addressing particularly intercessory prayer, he wrote that, "It is with the intention of substituted

---

[27] *Image*, 150.
[28] Ibid., 150–151.
[29] Ibid., 152.

love that all intercessory prayer must be charged, and with care that there is no intention of emotional bullying."[30]

Williams did not believe that this extension of a simpler interpretation of helping one another detracted from its pragmatic grounding. He wrote:

> So great a business of exchange and substitution fills the phrase "bear ye one another's burdens" with a much fuller meaning than is generally ascribed to it. But that fuller meaning is no less practical than the usual meanings of being sympathetic and doing exterior acts "of kindness and of love". It is very proper that they should be done. But that is because we ought to be "members one of another"—*membra*—limbs, not members of a club.[31]

For Williams, substitution and exchange constitute the fundamental fabric of life in the Spirit, directed by God through our unique vocation. "Since it is impossible to escape this Life, all that remains to us is to deepen it. In this sense to consider how we live *from* others may be even more profitable at times than to consider how we should live *for* others. Both are necessary to the perfect exchange."[32]

There was no such thing as a sovereign, self-contained individual; each person is porous, subject to external influences over which one has little control, and is interconnected in countless ways to God, to others, and Creation. To live out a commitment to exchange and substitution under God is to fill the place for which we were made in the web of co-inherence. Williams wrote,

> We are to love each other *as* he (Christ) loved us, laying down our lives *as* he did, that this love may be perfected. We are to love each other, that is, by acts of substitution. We are to be substituted and to bear substitution. All life is to be vicarious—at least, all life in the kingdom of heaven is to be vicarious. The difference between life in the kingdom and life outside the kingdom is to be this.[33]

Consummation

Charles Williams approached the Kingdom of God as the fulfillment of co-inherence. He described John's vision of the Heavenly City in Revelation:

> The centre is everywhere and the circumference nowhere; that is, it is hierarchic and republican at once, as all good states, even on this present earth, are known to be, where everything and everyone is unique and is the subject of due adoration so, and yet all being unique, 'none is afore or after other, none is greater or less than another.[34]

Throughout his novels, poetry, and plays, he describes this either in its rejection or in its fulfillment. When it is embodied on earth, it is a foretaste of the Kingdom. Concerning the "hierarchic and republican" characteristic of the City, he wrote, "existence is equal,

---

[30] *He Came Down*, 92.
[31] *Image*, 151.
[32] Ibid., 107.
[33] *He Came Down*, 86.
[34] Ibid., 98.

function hierarchical", and, "at every moment the hierarchy alters, and the functions re-ladder themselves upward."[35]

Since the Holy Spirit was sent to "guide [us] into all truth" (John 16:13), Williams stressed that nothing will remain hidden. "It is this which has distinguished the doctrines of Christendom; nothing is to be lost or forgotten; all things are to be known. They can be known as good, however evil, for they can be known as occasions of love. But known they must and shall be: 'the Lord God giveth them light'."[36] Indeed, Williams wrote, "Men had determined to know good as evil; there could but be one remedy for that—to know the evil of the past as good, and to be free from the necessity of the knowledge of the evil in the future; to find right knowledge and perfect freedom together; to know all things as occasions of love."[37] In *The Divine Comedy*, Dante envisioned this healing culminating in souls bathing in two rivers before entering Paradise: in Lethe, they are purged from the knowledge of their sin as sin; they "forget"; in Eunoe, they are enabled to see what God was doing at every moment of their lives, seeing from God's perspective. This is an effective way of describing God's redeeming and sanctifying of our knowledge as described by Williams.

Williams believed the human condition after the Fall was infected with antagonism and fracture. In the Kingdom, our healing will be complete: "The principle of that City, and the gates of it, are the nature of Christ as the Holy Ghost exhibits it and inducts us into it; it is the doctrine that no man lives to himself or indeed from himself. This is the doctrine common to nature and grace."[38] The co-inherence will be complete at every level: "When all things are subjected to him, then the Son himself will also be subjected to him who put all things in subjection under him, that God may be all in all" (1 Cor 15:28).

Conclusion

The theology of Charles Williams is grounded in the orthodoxy of the undivided Church, its Creeds and Councils. In *Descent of the Dove*, he displayed an ecumenical openness, including the freedom to be critical of church actions while affirming goodness in movements which come from vastly differing communions. He maintained throughout his conviction of the one Church, under "the Presidency of the Holy Spirit" and his dedication was "For the Companions of the Co-inherence."[39] Regarding Bishop Ware's conviction that Williams contributed to the Tradition, I believe this was primarily in the way he understood the Trinity, not simply in creedal terms but relationally. The co-inherence he saw in the mystery of God was thereby the pattern and purpose of everything, and it was in considering how this was revealed throughout creation and particularly in humankind, that his contribution was especially manifest. His understanding is well summarized in the following lengthy passage:

> The doctrine of the Christian Church has declared that the mystery of the Christian religion is a doctrine of co-inherence and substitution. The Divine Word co-inheres

---

[35] *Figure*, 197.
[36] *He Came Down*, 98.
[37] Ibid., 58.
[38] *Image*, 104.
[39] *Descent*, vii.

in God the Father (as the Father in Him and the Spirit in Both), but also He has substituted His Manhood for ours in the secret of the Incarnation and Atonement. The principle of the Passion is that He gave His life "for"—that is, instead of and in behalf of—ours. In that sense He lives in us and we in Him, and we co-inhere. "I live; yet not I but Christ liveth in me" said St. Paul, and defined the web of universal power towards substitution. To love God and to love one's neighbour are but two movements of the same principle, and so are nature and grace; and the principle is the Word by whom all things were made and who gave Himself for the redemption of all things. It was precisely the breach in that original nature which the new Nature entered to fulfill. But either way it is our nature that is concerned. Our natural life begins by being borne in another; our mothers have to carry us. This is not (so far as we know) by our own will. The Christian Church demands that we shall carry out that principle everywhere by our will—with our friends and with our neighbours, whether we like our neighbours or not. Such a labour has, almost immediately, two results. In the first place, it encourages a state of mind which may perhaps be called humility—but not so much as a virtue as a mere fact. Humility, said the author of the "Cloud of Unknowing", consists in seeing things as they are. If our lives are so carried by others and so depend upon others, it becomes impossible to think very highly of them. In the second place there arises within one a first faint sense of what might be called "loving from within". One no longer merely loves an object; one has a sense of loving precisely from the great web in which the object and we are both combined. There is, if only transitorily, a flicker of living within the beloved. Such sensations are, or are not; they are, in themselves, of no importance. But they may do for a moment encourage us, and they may assist us to consider still more intensely the great co-inherence of all life.[40]

Since I first read a novel by Charles Williams in the autumn of 1971, God has allowed him to be for me a constant companion and guide through his works, especially following my ordination as a priest in the Anglican Church in 1975. While my embodiment of his vision as described in this paper has been manifestly imperfect, his vision of the ultimate co-inherence of all things in the co-inherent Trinity has continued to illuminate the path before me, and his counsel regarding substitution and exchange stands as a challenge for daily living. One fundamental way in which he continues to inspire me is to do my best to discover and offer to God what I believe to be his will and then let it go to serve in whatever way serves his purposes. He wrote, "Usually the way must be made ready for heaven, and then it will come down by some other; the sacrifice must be made ready, and the fire will strike on another altar."[41] This produces in me, when I am faithful, a high sense of the need to pray for discernment, serve in obedience, let go in humility, and ground all in gratitude for the privilege in participating in his life and mission.

To conclude this introduction to the theology of Charles Williams, I will quote some words he wrote which connect the historic prayer book's post-Communion prayer to the Christian life as he understood it:

---

[40] *Image*, 152–153.
[41] *He Came Down from Heaven*, 25.

The "good works which thou hast prepared for us to walk in" are those belonging to "that holy fellowship"; they are therefore those peculiarly of exchange and substitution. They are prepared and they are there; we have only to walk in them. A little carrying of the burden, a little allowing our burden to be carried; a work as slow, as quiet, even as dull as by agreement to take up or give up a worry or a pain— a compact of substitution between friends—this is the beginning of the practice. The doctrine will grow in us of itself.[42]

---

[42] *Image*, 154.

Chapter 35

A Hand from a Hidden Country: C. S. Lewis (1898–1963) and the Anglican Way in the Modern World

The Rev. Tyler Kerley

"If you're thirsty, you may drink." For a second [Jill] stared here and there, wondering who had spoken. Then the voice said again, "If you are thirsty, come and drink," and of course [Jill] remembered what [Eustace] Scrubb had said about animals talking in that other world, and realized that it was the lion speaking.... "Are you not thirsty?" said the Lion. "I'm dying of thirst," said Jill. "Then drink," said the Lion.... "Will you promise not to—do anything to me, if I do come?" said Jill. "I make no promise," said the Lion. Jill was so thirsty now that, without noticing it, she had come a step nearer. "Do you eat girls?" she said. "I have swallowed up girls and boys, women and men, kings and emperors, cities and realms," said the Lion. It didn't say this as if it were boasting, nor as if it were sorry, nor as if it were angry. It just said it. "I daren't come and drink," said Jill. "Then you will die of thirst," said the Lion. "Oh dear!" said Jill, coming another step nearer. "I suppose I must go and look for another stream then." "There is no other stream," said the Lion. It never occurred to Jill to disbelieve the Lion—no one who had seen his stern face could do that—and her mind suddenly made itself up. It was the worst thing she had ever had to do, but she went forward to the stream, knelt down, and began scooping up water in her hand. It was the coldest, most refreshing water she had ever tasted. You didn't need to drink much of it, for it quenched your thirst at once.[1]

The pleasure of reading Clive Staples Lewis is like drinking water on a hot day. Marked by both a simplicity of style and a depth of thought, Lewis's works appeal to the deepest longings of both a child and an academic. Lewis helps us to feel like a child again, and we cannot help but identify with characters like Jill: hesitant, reluctant, and yet longing for something more.

My own first experience with Lewis coincided with my first experience in an Anglican church. I was beginning seminary, and my Rector was a historian and C. S. Lewis scholar named Lyle Dorsett. I felt comfortable entering this strange new world of liturgy and sacraments because although Father Lyle was an Anglican priest, he preached like a Baptist. Lyle did not fit my image of an Anglican priest, but his Anglicanism intrigued me and made me long for something more.

I wonder if many lovers of Lewis do not have a similar experience when they discover that Lewis was a member of the Anglican tradition. Lewis's own Roman Catholic friend J.R.R Tolkien was perplexed by Lewis's spirituality, describing it as exhibiting some anti-

---

[1] C. S. Lewis, *The Silver Chair* (New York: HarperCollins, 1953), 21–23.

Catholic prejudices while "he reveres the Blessed Sacrament and admires nuns."[2] Although many of Lewis's books like *The Chronicles of Narnia*, *Mere Christianity*, and *The Screwtape Letters* have shaped the imaginations of many readers, is Lewis's Anglicanism something which has to be excused or a tradition by which Lewis was deeply influenced?

Father Lyle began my love for C. S. Lewis. Every Christmas, he and his wife Mary would gift our church's interns with one of Lewis's books, and Lyle would often quote Lewis in his sermons, including the phrase, "A hand from a hidden country." The title of this paper is "A Hand from a Hidden Country" because C. S. Lewis can be a spiritual director for the Anglican church today in how to reach a modern world that has lost its way but that, like Jill, is longing for something more.

The Modern World

Lewis warns that the modern, progressive worldview will leave us dissatisfied. According to Lewis, the false progress of the modern world leads not only to a totalitarian state and the corruption of the Church, but it also inevitably leads to the destruction of humanity.

Chronological Snobbery

Lewis described the modern worldview as "chronological snobbery": the belief that newer is better, older generations were primitive, and humankind is improving with each generation.[3] It is a progressive, materialistic outlook which Lewis elsewhere describes as "Men Without Chests,"[4] who "make a clean sweep of traditional values and start with a new set."[5]

Lewis himself once held this skeptical view. Although raised in a Christian family in Belfast, Ireland, Lewis abandoned the Christian faith after his mother died of cancer when he was only nine. Fighting in World War I did not help Lewis's atheism. Lewis describes his early worldview in the introduction to *The Problem of Pain*: "When I was an atheist, if anyone had asked me, 'Why do you not believe in God?' my reply would have run something like this: 'Look at the universe we live in. By far the greatest part of it consists of empty space, completely dark and unimaginably cold."[6]

The character Mr. Enlightenment from Lewis's allegory *The Pilgrim's Regress* expresses the spirit of chronological snobbery:

> The Landlord is an invention of those Stewards. All made up to keep the rest of us under their thumb.... They have no knowledge of modern science and they would believe anything they're told.... Your people in Puritania believe in the Landlord because they have not had the benefits of a scientific training.... This is called the inductive method. Hypothesis ... establishes itself by a cumulative process: or, to

---

[2] Quoted in Lyle W. Dorsett, *Seeking the Secret Place: The Spiritual Formation of C. S. Lewis* (Grand Rapids: Brazos, 2004), 84.

[3] Lewis, *Surprised by Joy: The Shape of My Early Life* (New York: Harper Collins, 1954), 254.

[4] Lewis, *The Abolition of Man* (New York: Harper Collins, 1944), 1–26, esp. 25.

[5] Ibid., 12.

[6] Lewis, *The Problem of Pain* (New York: Harper Collins, 1940), 1–3.

us popular language, if you make the same guess often enough it ceases to be a guess and becomes a Scientific Fact.[7]

As Mr. Enlightenment suggests, key to chronological snobbery is the belief that nature is something which must be manipulated and mastered. Like Mr. Enlightenment, the diabolical character Weston from Lewis's *Space Trilogy* is another great example of what Lewis means by chronological snobbery. In the first volume of the series, *Out of the Silent Planet*, Weston attempts to describe his worldview to the native aliens on their home planet Malacandra:

> To you I may seem a vulgar robber, but I bear on my shoulders the destiny of the human race. Your tribal life with its stone-age weapons and bee-hive huts, its primitive oracles and elementary social structure, has nothing to compare with our civilization—with our science, medicine and law, our armies, our architecture, our commerce, and our transport system which is rapidly annihilating space and time. Our right to supersede you is the right of the higher over the lower.

The protagonist, Ransom, translates Weston's monologue for the aliens who do not understand him. "He says we know much. There is a thing happens in our world when the body of a living creature feels pains and becomes weak, and he says we sometimes know how to stop it. He says we have many bent people and we kill them or shut them in huts.... Because of all this, he says it would not be the act of a bent [being] if our people killed your people."[8]

The modern spirit of chronological snobbery fashions itself as scientific and objective, but Lewis points out that the modern worldview and magic are ironically strange bedfellows. "There was very little magic in the Middle Ages," Lewis claims. "The sixteenth and seventeenth centuries are the high noon of magic." Magic and science "were born of the same impulse."[9] Whereas for pre-modern society, "the cardinal problem had been how to conform the soul to reality, and the solution had been knowledge, self-discipline, and virtue," for the modernists like Weston or Mr. Enlightenment, "the problem is how to subdue reality to the wishes of men."[10] In other words, reality is something that conforms to me, not something to which I conform.

The "Materialist Magician" from Lewis's *Screwtape Letters* is perhaps his best example of humanity bending reality to its wishes.[11] The Materialist Magician is like Weston with just one exception: he is not a pure materialist. He denies the existence of spirits on the one hand and yet worships vague forces, such as sex or life, on the other. As a child of both Marxist socialism and Freudian psychoanalysis, the Materialist Magician is the senior demon Screwtape's ideal patient.

It is interesting that over eighty years after the publication of *Screwtape*, the Materialist Magician is a perfect description of Western culture today. Many people

---

[7] Lewis, *The Pilgrim's Regress: An Allegorical Apology for Christianity, Reason, and Romanticism* (Grand Rapids: Eerdmans, 1933), 23–28.

[8] Lewis, *Out of the Silent Planet* (New York: Scribner, 1938), 134–136.

[9] Lewis, *Abolition of Man*, 76.

[10] Ibid., 77.

[11] Lewis, *The Screwtape Letters* (New York: Harper Collins, 1942), 31–32.

today describe themselves as "spiritual, but not religious." New Age spirituality, witchcraft, and meditation are growing in popularity. It is common for people to believe that there is a God or Being who exists, but who is impersonal. Somewhat prophetically, Lewis had the foresight to see where the premises that were starting in England in the 1940s would naturally lead.

Social Justice: The Modernizing of the State

For Lewis, chronological snobbery could have especially dangerous effects on the state and the church. In a way, Lewis was not interested in politics. In 1951, Lewis was offered the honorary title "Commander of the Order of the British Empire" by conservative Prime Minister Winston Churchill, but Lewis declined the offer so that he did not come across as merely anti-leftist. Lewis also did not believe that the Church could enforce its own sexual ethic on non-Christians in secular law. Unbelievers will live like unbelievers, and they should not be coerced into Christian morals.[12]

If anything, Lewis feared the modern world was growing too political. For example, in *The Problem of Pain*, which was written during World War II, Lewis warns against an overemphasis on what he calls a "social consciousness," which overemphasizes "corporate guilt" at the expense of "personal guilt."[13] Screwtape also writes about how effective a device it is for demons to tempt Christians with putting a political party or a social cause above their Christian faith.

> Let him begin by treating ... Patriotism or ... Pacifism as a part of his religion. Then let him, under the influence of partisan spirit, come to regard it as the most important part.... Once you have made the World an end, and faith a means, you have almost won your man.... Provided that meetings, pamphlets, policies, movements, causes, and crusades, matter more to him than prayers and sacraments and charity, he is ours.... [W]e want very much to make men treat Christianity as a means; preferably, of course, as a means to their own advancement, but, failing that, as a means to anything—even to social justice. The thing to do is to get a man at first to value social justice as a thing which the Enemy demands, and then work him on to the stage at which he values Christianity because it may produce social justice.[14]

The Nazis were a living example of how "chronological snobbery" inevitably leads to abusing individuals for the execution of a political agenda. For Lewis, the Nazis were the reality Weston and the Materialistic Magician were meant to represent, and England needed to stand up to them.

Since much of his writing occurred during World War II, Lewis was also very concerned with inspiring patriotism in his English audience. As someone who was injured fighting in World War I and who lost friends in battle, Lewis knew firsthand how horrible war is, yet he also understood that war was sometimes a sad necessity. World War II was one of those times. During this time, Lewis delivered a paper titled "Why I Am not a Pacifist" to a pacifist society. Although many today might associate the image

---

[12] Lewis, *Mere Christianity* (New York: Harper Collins, 1952), 112.

[13] Lewis, *Problem of Pain*, 54.

[14] Lewis, *Screwtape*, 34–35, 126–127.

of a knight with religious oppression like the crusades, Lewis—a professor of Medieval and Renaissance Literature—felt very differently:

> The idea of the knight—the Christian in arms for the defence of a good cause—is one of the great Christian ideas. War is a dreadful thing, and I can respect an honest pacifist, though I think he is entirely mistaken. What I cannot understand is this semi-pacifism you get nowadays which gives people the idea that though you have to fight, you ought to do it with a long face and as if you were ashamed of it.[15]

Patriotism, or a love for one's country, is for Lewis somewhat like my love for the Atlanta Braves. I live in the Atlanta area. I have many friends who also love the Braves, and I respect the Braves organization. But the St. Louis Cardinals are my favorite team, because the St. Louis area is my real home. Since the Braves are my second favorite team, I root for the Braves in every game—except for when they play the Cardinals. My love for Atlanta lasts until it conflicts with my higher love for St. Louis. What Lewis is saying is that our love for our country is similar. We are loyal to our country until the kingdom of our country conflicts with our real home, the Kingdom of God. When we truly love our country, we will seek to reform it, not revolt against it. As Lewis writes later in *The Four Loves*, "'No man,' said one of the Greeks, 'loves his city because it is great, but because it is his.' A man who loves his country will love her in her ruin and degeneration."[16]

Lewis feared that English citizens—with their growing attachment to a "social consciousness"—were actually not all that different from the Nazis. Both the Nazis and British citizens were buying in to the modern lie that this world is all there is. The only difference between the two was that, whereas the Nazis loved their country too much, the English loved their country too little. Reforming legislation is important, but we have more control over and impact in how we treat our neighbor. Lewis closes his classic sermon *The Weight of Glory* with this important reminder:

> It is a serious thing to live in a society of possible gods and goddesses, to remember that the dullest and most uninteresting person you talk to may one day be a creature which, if you saw it now, you would be strongly tempted to worship, or else a horror and a corruption such as you now meet, if at all, only in a nightmare.... All day long we are, in some degree, helping each other to one or other of these destinations.... There are no ordinary people. You have never talked to a mere mortal.... It is immortals whom we joke with, work with, marry, snub, and exploit—immortal horrors or everlasting splendours.... Next to the Blessed Sacrament itself, your neighbor is the holiest object presented to your senses. If he is your Christian neighbour, he is holy in almost the same way, for in him also Christ—the glorifier and the glorified, Glory Himself—is truly hidden.[17]

---

[15] Lewis, *Mere Christianity*, 119.

[16] Lewis, *The Four Loves* (New York: Harper Collins, 1960), 35.

[17] Lewis, *The Weight of Glory* (Grand Rapids: Eerdmans, 1949), 14–15.

Progressive Christianity: Modernizing the Church

There was in the England of Lewis's day not only a modernizing of politics, but also a modernizing of the Church. In *The Four Loves*, Lewis recounts encountering two clergymen at a conference, who were obviously friends. The clergymen started to discuss "uncreated energies" other than God. Lewis asked how uncreated energies could be consistent with the Creed's statement that God is the Maker "of all things, visible and invisible?" "Their reply," according to Lewis, "was to glance at one another and laugh."[18] In the words of my friends from Alabama, their laugh was saying, "Bless your heart."

That scoffing "chronological snobbery" has been characteristic of the Church of England since Lewis's day. In a similar scene from *The Great Divorce*, the anonymous main character meets a demythologizing bishop in the afterlife. This "Episcopal Ghost" has a paper he is presenting to the "Theological Society," in which he is reminding people that Christ was a young man when he died. Jesus' views did not have the opportunity to mature. "What a different Christianity we might have had," the bishop concludes, "if only the Founder had reached his full stature!"[19]

The caricature Mr. Broad from *The Pilgrim's Regress* puts words to this spirit of liberal Christianity:

> As I grow older I am inclined to set less and less store by mere orthodoxy. So often the orthodox view means the lifeless view, the barren formula. I am coming to look more and more at the language of the heart.... That has been the great error of my profession in past ages. We have tried to enclose everything in formulae, to turn poetry into logic, and metaphor into dogma; and now that we are beginning to realize our mistake we find ourselves shackled by the formulae of dead men. I don't say that they were not adequate once: but they have ceased to be adequate for us with our wider knowledge.... These great truths need re-interpretation in every age.[20]

The name Mr. Broad is shorthand for the term "broad church," which is the designation used for clergy in the Anglican church who have liberalizing tendencies.

The Episcopal Ghost and Mr. Broad personify the innovations that were happening within the Church of England hierarchy in Lewis's lifetime. Two innovations Lewis observed particularly troubled him. The first was the "historical Jesus," the view that Jesus was a great moral teacher, but not God. As Screwtape writes, "In the last generation, we promoted the construction of such a 'historical Jesus' on liberal and humanitarian lines; we are now putting forward a new 'historical Jesus' on Marxian, catastrophic, and revolutionary lines." The historical Jesus "tends to direct men's devotion to something which does not exist, for each 'historical Jesus' is unhistorical.[21] But Lewis did not have any patience for this view.

> A man who was merely a man and said the sort of things Jesus said would not be a great moral teacher. He would either be a lunatic—on a level with the man who says

---

[18] Lewis, *Four Loves*, 106.

[19] Lewis, *The Great Divorce* (New York: Harper Collins, 1946), 43–44.

[20] Lewis, *Pilgrim's Regress*, 128–129.

[21] Lewis, *Screwtape*, 124.

he is a poached egg—or else he would be the Devil of Hell. You must make your choice. Either this man was, and is, the Son of God: or else a madman or something worse. You can shut Him up for a fool, you can spit at Him and kill Him as a demon; or you can fall at His feet and call Him Lord and God. But let us not come with any patronizing nonsense about His being a great human teacher. He has not left that open to us. He did not intend to.[22]

The second innovation was the role of women. While Lewis preferred to stay out of controversy and to focus instead on "Mere Christianity," when the ordination of women became a serious debate in the Church of England in the 1950s, Lewis felt strongly enough about the issue that he wrote an essay titled "Priestesses in the Church?"[23] Christ was a man and should be represented by men, Lewis reasoned. Ten years before this essay, Lewis published his novel *That Hideous Strength*, whose character Jane Studdock was like many young women today. Jane, a newlywed, is torn between her career on the one hand and her husband and the prospect of having children on the other. By the book's end, Jane embraces the joys of family life. Lewis was not opposed to women being educated and driven—he was married to Joy Davidman, after all—but for Lewis, for women to be ordained or to put their careers above being a wife and mother was just another innovation of chronological snobbery: it is an attempt to manipulate nature. It assumes that we know better than the generations which preceded us.

The Anglican Way

Lewis, however, does not simply rail against the sins of the world. Rather, like a skilled guide, Lewis points the way back to the right path by telling the Christian story. "We all want progress," Lewis counseled in *Mere Christianity*. "But progress means getting nearer to the place where you want to be. And if you have taken a wrong turning, then to go forward does not get you any nearer. If you are on the wrong road, progress means doing an about turn and walking back to the right road; and in that case the man who turns back soonest is the most progressive man."[24]

The Way: Longing of Mythology

Lewis made this "about turn" from chronological snobbery to what he called "the Way." Unlike chronological snobbery, the Way is not original but ancient. The Way is a term Lewis borrows from Eastern religions.[25] In the Eastern worldview, "the Tao" or the Way designates a path or a way of life. Whereas chronological snobbery throws off traditional values in the false pursuit of pure reason, the Way is the universal moral code that has been generally accepted throughout history, and it indicates a deep longing within all of humanity for something more. The Way for Lewis is similar to that familiar quote from *Mere Christianity*, where Lewis says, "If I find in myself a desire which no experience in

---

[22] Lewis, *Mere Christianity*, 52.

[23] Lewis, "Priestesses in the Church," in *God in the Dock: Essays on Theology and Ethics*, ed. Walter Hooper (Grand Rapids, MI: Eerdmans, 1970), 234–239.

[24] Lewis, *Mere Christianity*, 28.

[25] Lewis, *Abolition of Man*, 27–51.

this world can satisfy, the most probable explanation is that I was made for another world."[26]

Emeth—a character from the last book of the Narnia series, *The Last Battle*—is a great illustration of this universal longing for another world. Emeth, whose name means "truth" in Hebrew, thought he was fighting for the kingdom of Calormen and serving Calormen's foreign god Tash all his life. So Emeth is surprised to awake in Aslan's eternal kingdom. What Lewis says through Aslan may surprise us as much as it did Emeth: "Because [Tash] and I are opposites, I take to me the services which thou hast done to him. For I and he are of such different kinds that no service which is vile can be done to me, and none which is not vile can be done to him.... Beloved ... unless thy desire had been for me thou wouldst not have sought so long and so truly. For all find what they truly seek."[27]

In his *Reflections on the Psalms*, Lewis similarly imagines the Greek philosopher Plato, the Roman poet Virgil, and a fourteenth-century Egyptian Pharaoh saying to Christ in heaven, "I see ... so that was what I was really talking about.... That is what my words really meant, and I never knew it."[28] Emeth and these pagan writers illustrate some advice Lewis offers in *Mere Christianity*, "If you are a Christian, you do not have to believe that all the other religions are simply wrong all through.... There are people in other religions who are being led by God's secret influence to concentrate on those parts of their religion which are in agreement with Christianity, and who thus belong to Christ without knowing it."[29]

Like these pagans, mythology had prepared Lewis for Christianity. Lewis once described himself in contrast to the modern Western world as "a converted pagan living among apostate Puritans." In the allegorical story of Lewis's own conversion, *The Pilgrim's Regress*, the main character, John, leaves home to pursue a beautiful Island of which he had only a momentary vision. Like the vision that awakened in John a longing for that Island, the ancient myths stirred in Lewis a longing for something more. It was Lewis's friend, J. R. R. Tolkien, who helped Lewis to make this connection between "the Way" of pagan myths and the story of Christ. "Why do you love all these myths?" Tolkien asked Lewis. Christianity is just like all the myths with just one difference: in Christ, "myth became fact."[30] Christ is the reality to which the longings of all the myth writers pointed. As Lewis puts it in his essay *Is Theology Poetry*, "I believe in Christianity as I believe that the sun has risen, not only because I see it, but because by it I see everything else."[31]

What Lewis helpfully points out is that this longing for ultimate truth, beauty, and morality is not unique to any one culture. By choosing the Way—an Eastern, not distinctively Christian term—Lewis underscores that truth, beauty, and morality are universal, objective values which God has written on every human heart, not socially constructed tools that are the sole property of any one culture. It is ironically modern Western culture that, because of its denial of natural law as oppressive and outdated, is

---

[26] Lewis, *Mere Christianity*, 136–137.

[27] Lewis, *The Last Battle* (New York: Harper Collins, 1956), 189.

[28] Lewis, *Reflections on the Psalms* (New York: Harper Collins, 1958), 125.

[29] Lewis, *Mere Christianity*, 35 and 209.

[30] Alister McGrath, *C. S. Lewis: A Life* (Carol Stream, Ill: Tyndale, 2013), 149.

[31] Lewis, "Is Theology Poetry?" in *The Weight of Glory* (New York: HarperCollins, 1949), 116–140.

intolerant and suffers from cultural superiority due to its own "chronological snobbery." Objective values have undergirded every human society until quite recently.

At the same time, Lewis teaches us here not to belittle even the smallest amount of spiritual searching in anyone. Lewis did not argue with the world on the world's terms. Like Tolkien pointing out Lewis's love for mythology, or Aslan drawing Jill to the water by appealing to her thirst, a large part of Lewis's effectiveness as an apologist is that he appealed to these deep longings within every person, Christian and non-Christian. Lewis showed them how the modern world is failing to meet those longings, and then he re-directed them to their ultimate fulfillment in Christ. For example, if Lewis encountered someone today who was outraged by injustice, Lewis would ask that person, why are you outraged? "A man does not call a line crooked unless he has some idea of a straight line."[32] Lewis understood that it takes more than logic to win people to Christ. For Lewis, as I once heard Alister McGrath put it, "The truth may persuade, but it is beauty that attracts."

Mere Christianity: The Anglican Way

For Lewis, chronological snobbery despises history, but at the heart of the Christian faith is history. Again, borrowing a term—this time from the Puritan Richard Baxter—Lewis described the Christian Way as "Mere Christianity." Although Lewis personally held certain High Church beliefs like purgatory and prayers to the saints,[33] his catholicity went deeper than denominational distinctives. Mere Christianity, in Lewis's own words, is "a standard of plain, central Christianity, which puts the controversies of the moment into proper perspective."[34] Lewis compared Mere Christianity to a hall. A hall is a place everyone shares in common with other members of a house. A hall is not where we lay down to sleep or start a cozy fire, but the hall is a place we leave our own room to converse with others who live with us in our home.[35]

Mere Christianity had taught Lewis the importance of learning from the Church. The Church, in Lewis's view, is like a spiritual director. When he was seventeen, Lewis went to live with a tutor named William Kirkpatrick—or "The Old Knock" as Lewis calls him in *Surprised by Joy*. Like Lewis, the Pevensie children from Narnia go to live with a professor named Digory "Kirk." There also appears in *The Pilgrim's Regress* a wise old lady named "Mother Kirk," whose character represents the Church and who at the end of the book is crowned and holds a scepter as a queen. It is possible that the name "Kirk" in these books is Lewis's way of paying his respects to his old tutor. Probably Lewis was thinking that the Church serves as a spiritual director for Christians as William Kirkpatrick tutored him in the classics of learning. Like the Deacon Philip guiding the Ethiopian Eunuch in Acts 8, church history helps us to properly interpret Scripture.

Mere Christianity is opposed to chronological snobbery in that Christians are to learn from those who have gone before us. Lewis was careful to caution against us holding our own version of chronological snobbery that distrusts any kind of authority.

---

[32] Lewis, *Mere Christianity*, 38.

[33] Lewis, *Letters to Malcolm: Chiefly on Prayer* (New York: Harper Collins, 1963), 18–19 and 145.

[34] Lewis, "Preface," in *On the Incarnation by St. Athanasius*, trans. John Behr (New York: St. Vladimir's, 2011), 9–15, esp. 10.

[35] Lewis, *Mere Christianity*, xv–xvi.

"Do not be scared of the word authority," Lewis helpfully reminds us.[36] Ninety-nine percent of the things we believe, Lewis claims, we take on authority. For example, I have never been to London, but I believe London exists on the testimony of the many people who have been to London. I have not personally seen an atom or a black hole, but I believe they exist on the authority of experts who know science better than I do.

Unlike chronological snobbery, Mere Christianity is not skeptical of authority, and Lewis felt that we should at times rely upon the direction of the "experts" in the faith. Lewis's own writing was greatly informed by reading spiritual guides like Dante, John Milton, George Herbert, George MacDonald, and G.K. Chesterton. In his personal practice, Lewis received spiritual direction from an Anglo-Catholic monk named Father Walter Adams, and he carried on an extensive correspondence with a nun named Sister Penelope and an Italian Roman Catholic priest named Don Giovanni Calabria.[37] Trusting a spiritual director is similar to trusting a pilot. I would much rather have a trained pilot in uniform fly my plane than have a fellow passenger dress up and try to fly it.

At the same time, however, Lewis was not overly clerical. Many of Lewis's own experiences with the Church of England clergy were not positive, and it is important to remember that as a lay-person Lewis's writings have taught countless clergy. Additionally, Lewis received spiritual direction not only from clergy like Walter Adams or writers like MacDonald, but also from his tight-knit circle of academic friends at Oxford, The Inklings, a group composed of lay men and women. Thus speaking about the importance of friendship from personal experience, Lewis concludes that the early Christians survived because "they cared exclusively for the love of the brethren."[38]

In a modern world that is growing more like the hostile world in which the early Christians lived, maybe Lewis's own example of Mere Christianity can be our guide in the Anglican Communion. Lewis reminds us of the importance of spiritual direction, lay ministry, and friendship in the Christian life. Just as Lewis is perhaps better known outside of Anglicanism than within it, the Anglican Way in the spirit of Mere Christianity shows us that Anglicanism is at its best when it is in service to the broader church. Maybe we can learn something from a man who enjoyed reading both a High Churchman like Richard Hooker and a Puritan like Richard Baxter.

A Hand from a Hidden Country: Spiritual Formation in the Anglican Way

In addition to its different attitude from chronological snobbery regarding history, Mere Christianity also has a more positive stance toward tradition. If history is at the heart of the Christian faith, then not only has Christian theology been handed down but also Christian worship. While the modern world seeks to throw off tradition, Mere Christianity embraces the sacredness of tradition.

As a professor of the Middle Ages, Lewis admired ritual and tradition. With respect to tradition, Lewis contrasts the individualistic rationalism of the modern world with the ritualistic community of ancient cultures:

---

[36] Lewis, *Mere Christianity*, 62.
[37] Dorsett, *Seeking the Secret Place*, 109–130 and 149–150.
[38] Lewis, *Four Loves*, 101.

The state of affairs in which ordinary people can discover the Supernatural only by abstruse reasoning is recent and, by historical standards, abnormal. All over the world, until quite modern times, the direct insight of the mystics and the reasonings of the philosophers percolated to the mass of the people by authority and tradition; they could be received by those who were no great reasoners themselves in the concrete form of myth and ritual and the whole pattern of life. In the conditions produced by a century or so of Naturalism, plain men are being forced to bear burdens which plain men were never expected to bear before.[39]

Until the advent of chronological snobbery, people were universally formed through ritual. Discovery of the supernatural is received not only through reason, but through a "whole pattern of life" for "plain men." Formation in the Christian Tradition, too, happens primarily through practice in its rituals—walking along the Way—not first through understanding or through feelings.

In Lewis's view, ritual was crucial for corporate worship. While some may believe that being creative or "mixing it up" helps keep worship fresh and exciting, Lewis instead stressed the importance of familiarity.[40] Novelty may be entertaining, but novelty hinders worship, because novelty draws our attention to the service itself, rather than to God. We do not gather for worship to be entertained; we gather to worship God.

Familiarity, on the other hand, draws us into worship because we do not have to think about what we are doing. Corporate worship is like a dance, Lewis claims. When we dance, "as long as we are counting the steps, we are not yet dancing, but merely learning how to dance."[41] As a dancer rehearses a piece of choreography, the movements become more personal, not less. For Lewis, the ritual of corporate worship works in a similar way. Worship is not like a high school prom, in which many individuals are gathered in a large dark room, and who, while they are dancing to the same music, are merely expressing how the music makes them feel. Worship is, rather, more like a ballet, in which an entire company coordinates their movements and conforms its corporate life to a script. For Lewis, worship—like dancing—is primarily about corporate formation, not self-expression. Like a ballet company, the Church is harmonizing voices and conforming her corporate life to the Word of God. The perfect worship service, Lewis believed, is one of which we were entirely unaware. We would be so familiar with the service that our attention is lifted from ourselves and onto God.

Also, with Holy Communion, Lewis emphasized the practice of receiving Communion over the understanding of it. For Lewis, Communion was a mystery, and its purpose is to unite believers. As Lewis points out, Jesus said, "Take, eat; not take, understand."[42] Trying to analyze the elements of bread and wine outside of the Eucharistic celebration is like taking a coal out of a fire: it loses the very source of its power.[43] Food has a special way of bringing people together, and it troubled Lewis that

---

[39] Lewis, *Miracles* (New York: Harper Collins, 1947), 66–67.
[40] Lewis, *Letters to Malcolm*, 2.
[41] Ibid.
[42] Lewis, *Letters to Malcolm*, 141.
[43] Ibid.

this sacred family meal that Christ mean to unite Christians so often divided them based on their particular understanding.

Yet, for Lewis, Holy Communion was not just like any other meal. Lewis's understanding of Communion is similar to when my wife and I dated long distance before we married. Distance did indeed make the heart grow fonder. We texted and talked on the phone; we even watched a show on Netflix together over FaceTime. But no amount of communicating with each other through a screen could replace those moments when we could sit on the couch together and watch a show, or take a walk and hold one another's hand. Communion, in Lewis's view, is the act by which Christ closes the distance in a long-distance relationship; it is where a virtual and verbal relationship becomes a visible and physical relationship; Christ reaches out and touches His bride. In Communion, Lewis writes, "a hand from the hidden country touches not only my soul but my body."[44]

Prayer was likewise central to Lewis's spiritual formation. When we do not feel like praying, we can be tempted to feel like we are being inauthentic or to think that we are not "getting something out of it," but Lewis believed our understanding and our feelings will conform to our practice. When we pray the "Our Father," for example, it is like an actor wearing a mask, who, while pretending to be someone else in the beginning, is surprised when he later removes the mask to discover he actually resembles the role he was playing. Lewis concludes that prayer may begin in acting but over time conforms us to the image of God's Son.[45] Since he prayed through the Psalms once a month as well as daily prayed the Prayer Book's Daily Offices, which include the Lord's Prayer, Lewis may have been speaking from personal experience According to Screwtape, one of the best temptations against prayer is to "teach [people] to estimate the value of each prayer by their success in producing the desired feeling; and never let them suspect how much success or failure of that kind depends on whether they are well or ill, fresh or tired, at the moment."[46] Often it is when we least feel like praying that we need to pray the most. Like a father who takes a few steps away from his toddler and says, "Come to me," God sometimes withholds feelings in order to teach us to walk on our own.

Further Up and Further In: The Hope of Heaven

Whereas chronological snobbery is a materialistic worldview whose end is social progress, the Way of Mere Christianity is a supernatural journey whose end is universal hope. Every day, Lewis writes, we all are becoming either more a creature of heaven or a creature of hell.[47]

That is, hope is not progress. Lewis admitted that if there were one doctrine he could throw out, it would be the doctrine of hell, but according to Lewis, neither Scripture nor the Christian tradition allow one to do so. There were many people in Lewis's day who wanted to throw out the doctrine of hell. One of Lewis's own favorite writers, the nineteenth-century author George MacDonald, believed in universal salvation. The poet

---

[44] Lewis, *Letters to Malcolm*,, 138.
[45] Lewis, *Mere Christianity*, 187–194.
[46] Lewis, *Screwtape*, 17.
[47] Lewis, *Mere Christianity*, 92.

William Blake, too, wrote about the great marriage between heaven and hell. Against such views, Lewis wrote a fantasy titled, *The Great Divorce*, in which a bus makes daily trips from hell to heaven. Even when presented with this opportunity, the citizens of hell still choose to remain in hell rather than to move to heaven. As Lewis puts it elsewhere, "The doors of hell are locked from the inside."[48] Hell is not a punishment that God inflicts on innocent people against their will; hell is a place some people *want* to be. In the end, there are only two kinds of people in the world, Lewis says. Those who say to God, "Thy will be done," and those to whom God says, "Thy will be done."[49]

Hope is not, however, a retreat from the world. Rather, hope changes how we live in this world. Those who did the most for the present world, Lewis points out, were precisely those who thought most of the next: the apostles who conquered the Roman Empire, the great men and women of the Middle Ages who gave us civilization, and the English Evangelicals who abolished the slave trade.[50] Hell is like a grey, colorless town, whose inhabitants are shadows living thousands of miles apart from each other, whereas heaven is like a colorful place bursting with beauty, whose citizens are solid and dwell in close community one another. "Aim at Heaven and you will get earth 'thrown in': aim at earth and you will get neither."[51] All of life, to borrow Lewis's phrase from *The Last Battle*, is a journey "further up and further in" to God's Kingdom.

Hope, finally, reminds us what is ultimately important in this life. In one joyful scene from *The Great Divorce*, the nameless main character sees a great procession going on in heaven, and so he asks his guide what great person this procession is honoring. His guide tells him that it is probably someone he never met on earth, a woman by the common name Sarah Smith. Although she was not celebrated on earth, Sarah has such a large procession of people because in her life "every young man or boy that met her became her son.... Every girl that met her was her daughter.... Her motherhood was of a different kind. Those on whom it fell went back to their natural parents loving them more."[52] As Lewis puts it in *Letters to Malcolm*, "Joy is the serious business of heaven."[53]

C. S. Lewis and the *Via Media* in the Modern World

So, how does Lewis provide a model for the Anglican Communion today to reach a modern world that is longing for something more?

Anglicanism has often been described as a *via media*, or a middle way. Our middle way is sometimes seen as Tolkien saw Lewis's spirituality: anti-Catholic, while it continues to revere nuns and the Blessed Sacrament. But the Way for Lewis is much closer to Lesslie Newbigin's description of the Church as the "pilgrim people of God."[54] For Lewis, we as Christians are those who have started the journey, and we believe we are on the right path—but we still have a long way to go.

---

[48] Lewis, *Problem of Pain*, 130.
[49] Lewis, *Great Divorce*, 75.
[50] Lewis, *Mere Christianity*, 134.
[51] Ibid.
[52] Lewis, *Great Divorce*, 119.
[53] Lewis, *Letters to Malcolm*, 125.
[54] Lesslie Newbigin, *The Household of God: Lectures on the Nature of the Church* (Eugene, OR: Wipf & Stock, 1953), 25.

For Anglican Christians, C. S. Lewis is a great ambassador of the Anglican *via media* in the modern world. Lewis foresaw the dangers that lie ahead for the modern Western world, but he also points us towards a better world for which every person longs. Lewis cautions us as Christians against a chronological snobbery towards both historic Christian theology and historic Christian liturgy. The sacredness of myth, authority, tradition, and ritual are not shackles to be despised, but gifts to be retrieved. In the largely post-Christian West, Lewis can show Christians of all denominations how we can be faithful to the Great Tradition of historic Christianity, while also engaging a post-Christendom world. Like "a hand from a hidden country," Lewis is our spiritual guide along the Way to a hidden country, whose voice still speaks today, "If you're thirsty, you may drink."

Chapter 36

An Anglican Teacher of Catholic Truth:
E. L. Mascall (1905–1993)

The Rev. Blake Johnson

On the dedication page of his history of Anglicanism, *The Panther and the Hind*, Aidan Nichols, O.P., writes: "To Eric Lionel Mascall, *magistro Catholicae veritatis*" (teacher of Catholic truth).[1] For a Roman Catholic scholar and priest to dedicate a book to an Anglican scholar, priest, and friend would not necessarily be unusual. But Nichols names his Anglican brother a "teacher of *Catholic* truth." Obviously, Nichols does not mean to say (nor would Mascall claim) that Mascall teaches *Roman* Catholic truth, but that his works are characterized by the truth of the Catholic tradition.[2] Mascall would and certainly did defend that validity of the Anglican Church, but we find in Mascall more of an interest in defending the Catholic Faith. The opening of the *Athanasian Creed* proclaims, "Whosoever will be saved, before all things it is necessary that he hold the Catholic Faith." Throughout his writings Mascall speaks of the "Catholic" faith and tradition, which he sees as belonging as much to Anglicans as to other traditions. Mascall is not so much an Anglican apologist as he is a Catholic theologian. We might say that Mascall is first a Catholic, zealous to present the Great Tradition of the Faith in its fullness, and then an Anglican, grateful for the unique ways his own Anglican tradition has received and contributed to the Catholic faith.

E. L. Mascall's theological output was impressive both in its volume and range. He was grounded in the classical theological tradition of St. Thomas Aquinas (i.e., he was a Thomist) and drank deeply from the well of the fathers of the early church. He was also conversant with the best contemporary theologians across the traditions—Roman, Eastern, and Protestant. In the preface to his first published book, for example, *He Who Is: A Study in Traditional Theism*, he acknowledges his indebtedness to the French-speaking Roman Catholic theologians of his day and submits that "Anglicans have as least as much to learn from them as from the more widely publicized Protestant thinkers of Germany."[3] Mascall felt it necessary to draw from outside of the mainstream Anglican and Protestant theology of his day and look to the best of Rome and the East because "Anglican Theology in recent years has itself departed from its own tradition."[4] That tradition that is too often left behind is the Catholic tradition and worth recovering because it is true and better. The ascendent liberal theology of Mascall's day was far from satisfying and could only be corrected by a strong dose of the Catholic faith.

Mascall covers major topics of theology in his works, always aiming at a clear restatement of the Catholic faith in his Anglican voice. His most comprehensive work is *Christ, the Christian, and the Church: A Study of the Incarnation and Its Consequences*. Mascall

---

[1] Aidan Nichols, *The Panther and the Hind* (Edinburgh: T&T Clark, 1993).
[2] Following Mascall, I will capitalize the "C" in Catholic. I will make it clear when referring to Roman Catholics.
[3] E. L. Mascall, *He Who Is: A Study in Traditional Theism* (Longmans: London, 1943), x.
[4] Ibid.

elegantly and clearly shows how the Incarnation is the foundation for understanding our incorporation into him (salvation), and our participation in Christ's mystical body, the Church. In this chapter, we will consider Mascall's contribution to each of these areas (Christ, the Christian, and the Church) and consider how his project provides a promising theological and ecclesial path forward for present day Anglicans.

North American Anglicans may be familiar with the phrase "the future of the Church is ancient." Mascall would have heartily agreed. And he gives us Anglicans theological substance to that claim, while modeling a Catholic sensibility and way of doing theology that is not trapped by the debates *du jour*. Catholic, of course, means "according to the whole," and the term has a historical and global dimension. Mascall engages "the whole," inviting us into a more Catholic way of being an Anglican.

Incarnation: The Permanence of the Manhood of Christ

C. S. Lewis called the Incarnation "The Grand Miracle," the central miracle on which every other miracle in the Christian tradition refers.[5] Mascall likewise sees the Incarnation as central to Christian theology. The Incarnation is "the foundation and unifying principle of the life and thought of both the individual Christian and the Church of which he is a member."[6] For Mascall, to understand salvation (soteriology), the Church (ecclesiology), and the Sacraments requires first a proper understanding of the Incarnation.

Mascall is keen to emphasize "the doctrine of the permanence of the manhood of the glorified and ascended Christ" as not just central to the Incarnation but a principle that helps us get past either-or theological contrasts like "imputation and impartation," "realized and futurist eschatology," "the Church as "ark of salvation and the universality of grace," the "Eucharist as a representation of Calvary and as participation in the worship of heaven," and "personal and corporate devotion in the liturgical and corporate life in the Church, faith and mysticism, rational theology and revelation."[7] Mascall is not trying to artificially resolve tensions, but to show the "architectonic and synthetic power of the central truth of the Christian Faith," the Incarnation. Get the Incarnation right, then other things will fall into place.

Mascall refreshingly calls us back to first principles of the Catholic faith. Reading his exploration of the Incarnation is a reminder to us that those classical Christian doctrines age well. Mascall is not seeking to be novel or subtle in his theology, though he is certainly nuanced and precise; he is re-presenting classic Christology, defined by the Church at Chalcedon (AD 451). Mascall may at times sound repetitive, but he is intent to restate the classical formulations settled by the Church. If he is cutting edge, it is because he is insistent on the Catholic faith amidst theological trends that break with the tradition.

Mascall is also a Catholic theologian in the best of the Anglican spirit, showing how a Catholic understanding of the Incarnation leads us to a satisfying acceptance of many theological tensions. The Incarnation itself is a tension because it presents seemingly

---

[5] C. S. Lewis, *Miracles: A Preliminary Study* (New York: Harper-Collins, 1947, revised 1960).

[6] Mascall, *Christ, the Christian and the Church: A Study of the Incarnation and Its Consequences* (London: Longmans, 1946), xvii.

[7] Ibid., xix.

incompatible but nonetheless essential truths: "The Word was made flesh" (John 1:14 KJV). The Incarnation is a synthesis, to use an imprecise term, of Word and flesh. But this union of Word and flesh is the heart of the Catholic faith. We may think of Word and flesh as representing the Divine and the human natures respectively. So, as Mascall recounts the early Church councils, the first Ecumenical Council at Nicaea dealt primarily with the divinity of the Word. The next three councils at Constantinople, Ephesus, and Chalcedon took up "the flesh." For Mascall, these early councils give us all the material we need to flesh out our Christology.

Importantly, the Incarnation does not produce a new person. There never was a time when the Son was not; the Person of the Divine Word is the eternal Son of the Father. The Incarnation, however, is "the assumption of human nature by a previously existing divine Person" in the womb of the Blessed Virgin.[8] In the Virgin's Womb, God the Son unites himself to a human nature with a body and soul in the man Jesus. Because a new Person is not created in the womb of Mary, the doctrine of the virginal conception necessarily follows. The Son has no human generation but is conceived in Mary's womb, as Mascall puts it elegantly, "in which the divine overshadowing and the human fiat are most wonderfully blended."[9] What is new in the Incarnation is the union of the Divine Word with real flesh.

Mascall dwells on what the Incarnation means for human nature. He refers to the collect for the Second Sunday of Christmas, that God has "wonderfully created, and yet more wonderfully restored, the dignity of human nature." He shows that the Incarnation means nothing less than the re-creation of humanity. God has created humanity in the first Adam, but he has more wonderfully recreated humanity in the second Adam. This re-creation begins at the Incarnation when the Divine Word unites with humanity.

Mascall emphasizes that something happens to humanity itself in the Incarnation. We tend to think about the Incarnation as primarily something happening to God. The Word does become flesh, but Mascall wants us to see the Incarnation from a different angle. He continually refers us to the line from the *Athanasian Creed* which states that the Incarnation is "not by conversion of the Godhead into flesh, but by taking of the Manhood into God." The proper starting point when reflecting on the Incarnation is not to ask what change must happen to the Divine Word if he takes on flesh (this would lead to theological problems!), but rather what happens to human nature when the Divine Word is united to it. The risk of not starting in the right place, Mascall cautions, is that we might degrade the Divine Person but also miss the exaltation of human nature made possible by the Incarnation.

God is first the creator of humanity in his special creation of Adam, but now by becoming man, God is the re-creator of humanity. Taking up humanity into the Godhead, however, does not mean that God changes. Here Mascall maintains the impassibility of God (God cannot suffer). Theologians of his day believed that divine impassibility was at odds with God's compassion. But Mascall answers that divine impassibility would be at odds with compassion only for a finite being. Yet God is

---

[8] Mascall, *Christ, the Christian and the Church*, 3.
[9] Ibid.

infinite, and so can both sympathize with humanity and enjoy perfect fullness in his divine life, which can neither be supplemented nor diminished by his creation.

Along these lines, Mascall has an important insight into how Creation and Incarnation relate. Creation, as it relates to God, is not in time because the Creator is outside of time. Yet the creation as it relates to creatures is bound by time. Creation involves change, but the Creator does not change. In the same way, argues Mascall, the Person of the Word is not in time "but in relation to Christ's human nature and to us he is in time, for Christ's human life is lived in time and so is ours."[10] In Christ's human nature he experiences change and suffering. Here Mascall tracks with St. Cyril who maintained that "[Christ] suffers in his own flesh, and not in the nature of the Godhead."[11] Mascall also echoes the Definition of Chalcedon when he writes: "In the incarnate Lord, then, two natures, a divine and a human are inseparably and unconfusedly united in one divine Person."[12] The two natures, however, relate to the Divine Person differently. The Person of the Word has the divine nature from eternity. He takes up human nature, however, at a point in time. Put simply, "He *became man*; he never 'became God.'"[13]

Mascall critiques modern Christologies that rely on psychological categories by reasserting the language of the tradition. Theology, Mascall contends, "should quite fearlessly move within the conceptions which are proper to it and resist the temptation to transfer itself into the modes of thought of other sciences."[14] We should not shy away from theological categories or even tedious scholastic language (he is a Thomist after all!). For Mascall, retaining the proper categories of theology is critical for "explaining the Father to the contemporary world in a language it can understand."[15] This might seem implausible at first (*Aren't scholastic categories unfriendly and inaccessible?*), but Mascall's own work shows how freshly restating the tradition may actually bring greater clarity than does the current theology (often obtuse) which he engages and critiques. But as is his custom, after surveying theological trends he sees as unmoored from the tradition, Mascall summarizes his project:

> I need only reaffirm...[my] purpose has been simply to expound the traditional Catholic doctrine of the Incarnation under the guidance of the Holy Spirit, the Church was led to formulate it against the Christological heresies of the first centuries, in order that we may have a sure foundation on which to base our subsequent discussion of the nature and implications of the Christian life.[16]

We turn now to some of the implications of the Incarnation Mascall explores.

---

[10] Mascall, *Christ, the Christian and the Church*, 17.

[11] St Cyril of Alexandria, *On the Unity of Christ*, ed. John Behr, trans. John Anthony McGuckin, Popular Patristics Series 13 (Crestwood, NY: St Vladimir's Seminary Press, 1995), 130.

[12] Mascall, *Christ, the Christian and the Church*, 20.

[13] Ibid.

[14] Ibid., 9.

[15] Ibid.

[16] Ibid., 67.

Salvation: The Re-creation of Humanity

The Incarnation is when the re-creation of humanity begins. The beginning of the re-creation project anticipates the Passion. Mascall uses the scholastic distinction between first and second act to show the relationship between Incarnation and Cross. The first act of a being refers to *existence*; the second act refers to the *purpose* of the being's existence. The second act brings the first act to full perfection. The Incarnation is the first act, but the Incarnation exists for the sake of man's salvation, which leads to the second act, our Lord's Passion. When the Divine Word takes on human nature, he takes up the very human nature all humanity shares. Yet this does not mean that human nature is perfected by the Incarnation alone (the first act). The recreation of humanity in the Word must be communicated to *sinners*.

The problem of sin is not just the barrier between God and man. Sin is the impediment to human nature realizing its potential. The divine Word-made-flesh must not just take up human nature for sinners; he must also deal with their sin. The two main atonement theories in the Catholic tradition are both necessary: the tradition articulated by St. Anselm, in which the penalty of sin must be paid, and the *Christus Victor* tradition, in which Christ overcomes the forces of evil in death. As Mascall puts it:

> For only God can pay the debt which man owes, and yet it must be paid in the person of man. And only God can overcome man's ancient enemy, while the battle must nonetheless be fought in human nature, since its fruits are to be communicated to man.[17]

The Incarnation thus atones by recreating humanity in the Word-made-flesh: "If it was necessary for manhood to be assumed, it was no less necessary for it to be sacrificed."[18] Recreation happens through the divine Word's assumption of human nature and his sacrifice of that nature. This recreation is for and communicated to sinners. Christ recreated humanity on the cross by paying our debt *and* destroying our enemies in his human nature.

The communication of the life and benefits of the Incarnation and Cross comes to sinners by being incorporated into the human nature of Christ. By this incorporation, our human nature becomes recreated in His human nature. Mascall reminds us of two principles of "sound theology" from the Great Tradition. First, God's act precedes man's: "What a being *is* precedes what it *does*; our actions are a consequence of what we are."[19] Second, "Being a Christian is an ontological fact, resulting from an act of God."[20]

This is a key point to understanding Mascall's theology. He insists with the Catholic tradition on an ontological framework of salvation. Salvation is God's act that creates a new being in the Christian. The Christian is truly a "new creation." A new creation produces new actions. Ontology means "being"; it refers to what something really is. Being a Christian is nothing less than the transformation of our human nature—our true being—into the human nature of Christ. To put it into Pauline language, we are

---

[17] Mascall, *Christ, the Christian and the Church*, 75.
[18] Ibid., 76.
[19] Ibid., 77.
[20] Ibid.

being transformed (truly and really) into the image of Christ (cf. Rom 8:29; 2 Cor 3:17–18). As the branch is grafted to the life of the vine, so is redeemed man incorporated into the life of Jesus Christ. Salvation is an ontological reality: "The Christian is a man to whom something has happened, something moreover which is irreversible, and which penetrates to the very roots of his being; he is a man who has been re-created in, and into, Christ."[21]

We have seen that the Incarnation and Cross are necessary for this full recreation. The benefits gained by the Cross are realized in the resurrection and ascension of the glorified manhood of Christ to the right hand of the Father. So then how are these benefits communicated to the sinner? How is the sinner actually incorporated into the humanity of Christ? The Catholic tradition and the Anglican formularies point to the sacrament of Baptism. Mascall shows that in the Anglican tradition, citing the *Articles of Religion* and the *Book of Common Prayer*, Baptism is the instrument by which we are truly grafted into Christ and made regenerate.[22]

For Mascall, Baptism and justification involve the same ontological reality. He explains in a passage that serves as summary of his theology of salvation:

> The point is this: that the work by which God accepts us in Christ is not a merely external, legal or "logical" fiction, but a supernatural rebirth which brings about an ontological change in us; that in baptism we are brought into a real relation with the glorified manhood of the Redeemer, that in baptism there is a real supernaturalization of our human nature in its essence, which can result, if we co-operate with the grace of God, in a progressive supernaturalization of its operations and the manifestation of supernatural virtues.[23]

Baptism bestows a grace on human nature that does not destroy it but "heals it and strengthens it and brings it to perfection."[24] We can hear the language of the Thomistic tradition: grace does not destroy nature but perfects it. Baptism and justification introduce man into the supernatural life.

Mascall critiques the Protestant tendency to deny that grace can "produce a real supernaturalization of the soul."[25] If this is the case, if something is not really happening to our *being*, then it will affect how we see our *actions*. Mascall argues, however, that the Catholic tradition sees man as able to cooperate with God's grace in his actions. While God is the first cause of redeemed man's good works, man is the second cause and a true subject of his actions. Mascall holds together the imputation (a Protestant point) and impartation (a Catholic emphasis) by claiming "God is the creator; he cannot impute without imparting."[26] He gives the illustration of God's first act of creation: "God said let there be light, and there was light." Just as God's creative declaration brings about a new reality, so his redemptive declarations do the same. Mascall cites Richard Hooker, the great Anglican theologian of the sixteenth century, who writes that we participate in

---

[21] Mascall, *Christ, the Christian and the Church*, 75.
[22] Ibid., 78–79.
[23] Ibid., 82.
[24] Ibid., 80.
[25] Ibid.
[26] Ibid., 82.

Christ by imputation and "by habitual and real infusion, as when grace is inwardly bestowed [on us]."[27] Imputation and impartation, then, are not at odds.

Mascall locates the origins of a major problem for theology in the late-medieval philosophy of nominalism. Nominalism, as Mascall shows in *The Recovery of Unity*, affected both Roman Catholic and Protestant theology, but Protestants have had the most difficulty breaking free from the late-medieval corruption. Nominalism denies the idea of universals and focuses rather on the particulars of a thing. A thing exists in "name only" (nominalism comes from the Latin *nomen*, which means "name"). A table is a table because we call it that, not because a particular table shares in some universal form of table. If we use the same name (*nomen*) for lots of different things, what does this mean? Nominalists see *table* as simply a name that we use for convenience. There is no real "tableness," only particular tables that we happen to call "table" by convention. Nominalism says that reality is only what is observable. Following St. Thomas, Mascall pushes back against nominalism with a "moderate realism," which holds that "the universal had a real existence, but that, except for its existence as an exemplar in the mind of God, it existed only in the particular."[28] That is to say a particular thing really participates in the universal reality.

If one operates with nominalist principles, then justifying grace cannot *really* affect a change in man's being: "For on nominalist principles there is nothing beneath the observable level to transform." Nominalism rejects ontological change. In this view, justification is something that remains outside of us. Imputation, being treated as if we were sinless, works in the nominalist framework. Justification as impartation of grace in man's being, producing a real change, does not. But with a moderate realist framework, which Mascall would argue is the Catholic tradition, one is not just justified by declaration, but one is really justified by impartation, that is, ontologically.

Clearing the ground of nominalism, we can see our incorporation into Christ as a real participation in the life of God. Mascall refers to three unities: our adoptive union with Christ, the hypostatic union of the divine and human natures in the divine Person of the Word, and the Son's union with the Father. Adopted into Christ through Baptism, we become sons and share in everything the Son has. Mascall movingly writes that "through our union with Christ we are caught up into the activity whereby he eternally adores the heavenly Father. We are made, in the New Testament phrase, 'partakers of the divine nature.'"[29] The implication of this reality is that the ordinary Christian along with the mystic lives with the "life of God."[30] God is present to all his creation, but he is most intimately present to the soul of a Christian, such that the Christian "enjoys an intimacy with God that exceeds all that a creature could dream of. He is admitted into the very life of the triune God."[31]

---

[27] Mascall, *Christ, the Christian and the Church*, 83.

[28] Mascall, *The Recovery of Unity: A Theological Approach* (London: Longmans, 1958), 24.

[29] Mascall, *Christ, the Christian and the Church*, 96.

[30] Ibid., 99.

[31] Ibid.

The Church: The Mystical Body

We have explored Mascall's Christology as the foundation for the Christian's recreation in Christ and incorporation into him. Just as salvation, the recreation of humanity, is a consequence of the Incarnation, so is the Church, the body of Christ into which the Christian is incorporated by Baptism and faith. Mascall summarizes the Christian faith: "We can sum up the essence of Christian gospel in the assertion that God the Son united human nature to himself in order to create a new human race."[32] Here we see the interrelated themes of the person of Christ, the Christian, and the Church. We are born into a fallen humanity of Adam; but we are reborn into the redeemed humanity of the Second Adam. Jesus, the Second Adam, is head of a new humanity. For Mascall, this new humanity is the Catholic church.[33]

But what is the nature of this Church? Mascall takes the Pauline metaphor of the body of Christ as a starting point.[34] Individual Christians are members of Christ's body. That might seem straightforward enough, but such an organic metaphor cannot mean a merely external relation between Christ and the Christian, and between the Christian and other Christians. But if our relation to Christ (e.g., justification) is only extrinsic and nominal, then our relationship to his body and others will be as well. Yet for Mascall, the Pauline metaphor of the body of Christ must be taken ontologically: just as the Christian has a real ontological union with Christ so he does with members of his body, and members of his body have such a union with one another.

Mascall once again relies on the Anglican Divine Richard Hooker, who draws a connection between justification and the Church. Just as justification is not just a forensic but an ontological reality, so also the Church is a supernatural organism, the "mystical body of Christ."[35] The justified are incorporated into this mystical body. As the Father is in the Son and the Son in the Father, so Hooker writes, "His Church and every member thereof is in him by original derivation, and he personally in them by way of mystical association wrought by the gift of the Holy Ghost"[36] The Holy Spirit, who forms this union between a Christian and Christ—and Christian and Christian—is the principle of unity in the mystical body.

It is this principle of the Spirit's uniting and life-giving character that makes the Church a dynamic organism, a truly *mystical* body. At this point one might wonder if Mascall is contending that the Church is, in the end, invisible. The Church's inner reality is constituted by the life of Spirit, but the Church is a sacramental reality and thus must have a visible form. We may find this outward "organ of unity" in the Apostolate, ordained by Christ and continued in the historical Episcopate. For the Fathers, bishops were the link between the local congregation and universal church, a visible sign of the sacramental reality of the Church.[37] For much of Protestant theology, however, the Church is entirely invisible: its membership is only known to God, and it is not

---

[32] Mascall, *Corpus Christi: Essays on the Church and the Eucharist* (London: Longmans, 1953), 38.

[33] Ibid., 39.

[34] Mascall, *Corpus Christi*, 39.

[35] Ibid.

[36] Mascall, *Christ, the Christian and the Church*, 116.

[37] Mascall, *Corpus Christi*, 13.

constituted by outward signs. For the Roman Catholic, on the other hand, the Church is exclusively visible and easy to locate; it is where Christians who are in visible communion with the Pope. But Mascall contends that the true Catholic view holds together the invisible and visible aspects of the Church by highlighting its sacramental nature: "The Church is a visible and tangible society, but it is a sacramental one, and the organ of its unity will be a sacramental organ."[38] The apostolic Episcopate is a suitable organ of unity for the sacramental church because "the episcopal character is conferred by a sacramental act" (i.e., the laying on of hands).

Here it is worth considering Mascall's critique of the Papacy. Given Mascall's thoroughly Catholic theology and his sympathetic engagement with his contemporary Roman interlocutors, it is reasonable to ask what kept him from being *Roman* Catholic. Mascall challenges the *way* in which the visibility of the Church has evolved in Rome:

> I think the Roman Church is right in insisting that the Church is a visible and not an invisible body, but I think it has gone wrong in treating the Church's visibility as an organizational rather than as a sacramental one, and so in locating that unity in the organizational organ of the Papacy rather than in the sacramental organ of the Episcopate; and the consequence has been ... that the Papacy has infringed upon the Episcopate and, in the Papal Communion, has all but absorbed it.[39]

Mascall believes a case could be made for the primacy of the Roman See and believes the Pope would almost certainly have a central role in a reunion of Christendom. But he balks at the modern development of the Papacy in which "absolute supremacy in governing and teaching the Church" rests solely in the Bishop of Rome.[40] He is direct: "Modern Papalism is thus not simply something more than true Catholicism; it is also something less."[41] Mascall is too Catholic to be *Roman* Catholic.

Mascall has historical objections to the Papacy. He is not persuaded that the doctrine of development can satisfactorily account for the ways the papacy has absorbed the historic episcopate. For example, modern papal theory maintains that the Pope has immediate, universal, and episcopal jurisdiction over the entire church, and every Christian soul. The Pope is essentially the bishop of every diocese; he can appoint and remove bishops at will, and he can make infallible pronouncements that are irreformable and uncontestable. Further, obedience to the Roman See is materially necessary to salvation. It is difficult to claim St. Peter, or his earliest successors, had anything like this power. The problem, Mascall maintains, is that modern papal practice is unlike anything found in the undivided Church of early Christianity, even if considered in embryonic form. But more important to his argument, Papal supremacy is a development not of the *sacramental* nature of the Church but of its organizational and juridical needs.[42] For Mascall, the Catholic Church is a sacramental reality, not an administrative one, and so its organ of unity must be sacramental, not administrative: "And this is why it seems impossible to locate the organ of the Church's unity in the Papacy, for the papal character

---

[38] Mascall, *Corpus Christi*, 17.
[39] Ibid., 19.
[40] Mascall, *Recovery of Unity*, 197.
[41] Ibid., 231.
[42] Mascall, *Christ, the Christian and the Church*, 153.

is not conferred by a sacramental act at all, but by the purely administrative and organizational process of election," at the end of which, unlike an election of a bishop, there is no sacramental consecration.[43] If the Protestant error is making the church almost exclusively invisible, then the Roman error is making the church essentially institutional, in which the institution of the Papacy has become the essence of the Church. Against both of these errors, Mascall asserts what he sees as the Catholic nature of the Church: a sacramental Church.

For Mascall, the sacramental reality of the Church is expressed most vividly in the Eucharist: "In the Eucharist the true organic nature of the Church is manifest."[44] Following Augustine and his contemporary Henri De Lubac, Mascall affirms the triform Body of Christ.[45] The historical Body of Christ was born of a Virgin, died on a cross, rose and ascended in his glorified humanity. The mystical body of Christ is the Church we join by baptism. Then there is the sacramental body, which we partake in the Eucharist. These are not three different bodies, but one body. The sacramental body of Christ renews and even *makes* the Church.

Mascall's Eucharistic theology starts in heaven where the glorified Christ in his humanity is presenting his perfect and eternal offering to the Father. I note here that while Mascall is not prone to constantly cite chapter and verse to justify all his theological arguments, it is clear his theology is growing out of the rich soil of his own biblical reflections as filtered through the interpretive tradition of the Church. For example, the depictions of heavenly worship in Revelation where Jesus the Messiah is the slain Lamb before the Father, along with the Book of Hebrews' theology of Christ's eternal sacrifice, inform Mascall's Eucharistic theology at every step.

Mascall draws an important analogy between the Eucharist and Incarnation. In the Incarnation it appears that God comes down from heaven, but, as Mascall reiterates, in the Incarnation Christ is taking *up* humanity into the Godhead.[46] In a similar way, in the consecration at the Eucharist, while it appears the ascended Christ is coming down to the altar, there is a taking up of the bread and wine to be identified with the glorified body in heaven. Because the Eucharist starts in heaven, at each Eucharist there is an entry into heaven where we are joined with the one eternal sacrifice of Christ.

The Eucharist is not a repetition of Christ's sacrifice or a mere memorial of Calvary; it is, however, "identical" with Christ's one sacrifice which is ongoing in heaven.[47] The natural, glorified body is in heaven offering his perfect sacrifice. In the Eucharist, the Church, the mystical body, participates in the glorified body by means of the Eucharistic body on the altar. We may say that the Eucharistic body on the altar connects heaven and earth, the perfect glorified body in heaven and the being-made-perfect mystical body on earth. The Eucharist then allows a still sinful Church to join in a perfect worship and sacrifice. Christ unites our human nature to his "so that we may be able to offer his offering or, rather, that he may be able to offer it through and in us."[48]

[43] Mascall, *Corpus Christi*, 17.
[44] Ibid., 122.
[45] Mascall, *Christ, the Christian and the Church*, 161–162.
[46] Ibid., 162.
[47] Ibid.
[48] Ibid., 161.

In the Eucharist, our human bodies are joined to the glorified body of Christ such that our bodies are being offered "as living sacrifice." And yet in the Eucharist, we offer the one sacrifice of Christ. Who is being offered in the Eucharist? If we understand the union of Christ with his body, then we can say with Augustine that "the Whole Christ offers the Whole Christ."[49] The whole Christ is always Christ and his Church.

The Church lives and draws its life from the Eucharist. In the Eucharist, we who have been torn apart by sin are put back together again: the Eucharist is the restoration of unity, uniting us to the glorified humanity of Christ, which restores us to ourselves, one another, and God. The Eucharist is not just a picture of unity, it is its very cause: the Eucharist makes the Church.

In his work, Mascall counters two errors related to Eucharistic sacrifice. Both Catholic and Protestant theology inherited an understanding of sacrifice post-Reformation that focused exclusively on the death of a victim. So, when it came to an understanding of the relationship between the Eucharist and Calvary, Protestants insisted that the Lord's Supper is a *commemoration* of the one sacrifice of Christ. Catholics tended to see the Eucharist as a "non-literal" repetition of Calvary. But what is needed for both, Mascall shows, is a fuller understanding of sacrifice, which is not just the death of the victim. Christ's whole human life from Incarnation to Ascension is lived as an offering. Paul states in Romans 5:10 that we will be saved by his life.

Mascall uses the categories of offering, acceptance, and transformation. Christ's death was the "offering of his life and not its destruction, and in the Resurrection that offering was accepted by the Father and transformed into a condition of perpetual efficacity. Christ ever-liveth to make intercession for us."[50] The ascension is a critical component of Mascall's understanding of Eucharistic sacrifice. The ascended Christ's eternal offering is being presented to the Father in his glorified humanity: "It is the ascended Christ, Christ as he is now, that we receive in Holy Communion, and we receive him under sacramental signs" of bread and wine.[51] It is this offering, of the crucified, glorified, and ascended Lamb that we partake in the Eucharist. The mystical Body does not partake of a dead victim or simply remember the death of a victim; the mystical Body partakes of a sacrificial victim who is living, risen, and glorified.

In his Eucharistic theology Mascall is an Anglican teacher of Catholic faith. He draws from the fathers in relating the eucharist to the Church. He critiques both Protestants and Catholics for falling into traps created by late medieval theology. Yet drawing from both his contemporary Roman Catholic and Protestant theologians, he sees a growing *reproachment* in an understanding of Christ's one sacrifice and its implications for the Eucharist. He is also willing to critique his own Anglican tradition in pursuit of a more Catholic Eucharistic theology. For example, Cranmer, in over-reacting against late medieval notions of sacrifice, depicted the Eucharist as the Church's "sacrifice of praise and thanksgiving."[52] Yet Mascall makes a keen exegetical observation. The sacrifice of praise and thanksgiving in Hebrews refers to the Levitical peace offering, which was a

---

[49] Mascall, *Christ, the Christian and the Church*, 183.
[50] Mascall, *Corpus Christi*, 102.
[51] Ibid., 210.
[52] Ibid., 184.

sacrifice and meal that the worshiper enjoyed with God. "What Hebrews, then, is telling Christians to offer up with their lips is not their own praises but the sacrifice of the peace-offering, the one sacrifice which would continue in the Messianic kingdom; and this is in its Christian context is nothing other than the sacrifice of Christ, who is 'our peace.'"[53] Mascall shows us that as Anglicans our Eucharistic theology should not rely exclusively on a few decades in the sixteenth century but draw from the breadth of the Catholic tradition.

Conclusion

E. L. Mascall gives orthodox Anglicans a fresh voice for Catholic truth in our own time. For his lucidity and theological output, it is surprising that Mascall is not better known. But Mascall's theological project represents a hopeful way forward for Anglicans who are searching for anchors of identity. In Mascall we have a compelling and refreshing vision for Anglicanism that is Catholic, and because it is Catholic—deeply rooted in the Great Tradition—it can be confident. Given the perpetual crisis state of Anglicanism, one may wonder if a confident and Catholic-minded Anglicanism is a mirage. Mascall was well aware of the ways theological liberalism had shaken up the Anglican Communion. But it seems that Mascall was so Catholic in his theology and thinking he was able to operate with a sort of Catholic patience, playing the long game and learning to live with the tensions present in Anglicanism.

In the foreword to *Corpus Christi*, we get a glimpse of what animates this Anglican Catholic teacher of truth:

> Appealing as it does to Scripture and the Fathers, [Anglicanism] is peculiarly fitted to grasp the opportunities of a situation in which the most vigorous movements in theology are in the realms of Biblical exegesis and patristic study. Free, as the dogmatic Protestant is not, to see the Bible steadily and see it whole, and free, as the modern Roman Catholic is not, to see the Fathers as they are and not as recast in the mold of the Council of Trent, the Anglican theologian today is uniquely favored for the task of recovering the lost unity of an integrally Catholic theology.

The renewal of orthodox Anglicanism surely must be a deep re-engagement with Scripture and the tradition; reading Scripture with the fathers. It will reckon not just with the last few decades of the Church, nor be caught in the dead ends of liberal Protestantism or the rootlessness of evangelicalism; it will embrace the *Catholic* truth—the whole of the Church.

Mascall invites us Anglicans to see ourselves as a Church *in via* not *in patria*.[54] That is, to see ourselves as part of a Catholic yet very imperfect Church that is *on the road* not yet already arrived at its destination. He cautions against falling for visions of an over-realized ecclesiology even as we work for a true recovery of Catholicity in a broken communion. The effect of his work is to encourage Anglicans seeking a better ecclesial country or a more perfect communion: "If he [the anxious Anglican] tries faithfully to live as a loyal member of the Church, receiving sanctifying grace through prayer and the

---

[53] Mascall, *Corpus Christi*, 190.
[54] Mascall, *Recovery of Unity*, 230.

sacraments, he does not find the task impossible."[55] The Anglican does not have to pretend the Church militant is perfect or infallible. But longing for the recovery of a Catholic unity, which comes by embracing the Catholic truth, puts the Anglican in a unique place that Mascall describes as "exacting and invigorating."[56] Mascall invites us into Catholic truth in an Anglican way which is at once exacting and invigorating.

---

[55] Mascall, *Recovery of Unity*, 230.
[56] Ibid.

Chapter 37

Teach Us to Pray:
Martin Thornton (1915–1986)
and the Church's Life of Prayer

The Rev. Ben Williams

Introduction

One of the hardest things to do in ministry is to teach others how to pray. The agonizing moments when someone is invited to pray aloud for the first time are not even the most difficult. It is when I experience the same agony when praying with seasoned Christians that is most troubling. But this is understandable in certain settings because prayer is often reduced to extemporaneous petitions, usually of an intercessory nature. But what if our imagination of what prayer is could be expanded? What if, in addition to brief discursive intercessions, we could understand the entirety of our life and experience in terms of prayer? What if the life and ministry of the Church were wholly dependent on God's relationship with his people in prayer? This was the great concern of the twentieth-century English priest and spiritual director Martin Thornton.

Thornton (1915–1986) was a farmer-turned-theologian and spent the second half of his life as an Anglican priest and author.[1] He graduated from King's College London in 1946 and received an M.A. from Christ College, Cambridge, in 1955. That same year he joined the Oratory of the Good Shepherd, a non-residential order within the Anglican Communion governed by a strict rule that required daily Eucharist, praying the Daily Office, and spending much time in private prayer. Later, he taught theology at General Seminary in New York as well as Philadelphia Divinity School in the United States. His final years were spent in Truro, England as Canon Chancellor at the cathedral where he developed a four-year course in spiritual direction. Throughout his career, Thornton published thirteen books, many of which are out of print. It may be an understatement to say that the corpus of his writing and the burden of his ministry was to inspire, teach, and train others to pray.

What follows is an introduction to key themes in Thornton's thought on prayer and its centrality in the life and ministry of the Church. It will be divided into two parts, the first of which will focus on Thornton's Remnant Hypothesis. Here we will find in fresh form the old idea of the parish as a vicarious organism at prayer. It is because of the atoning death and victorious resurrection of Christ that the Church can be said to be a unified Body. In this sense, the Church's faithful Remnant prays *for* the entire parish. The Remnant at prayer, then, formulates the second half in which we will unpack Thornton's three-fold Church Rule. It is only by praying the Daily Office, attending Holy Communion, and engaging in private prayer that the Remnant can truly adore her Lord.

---

[1] Biographical information on Martin Thornton is scarce. I am greatly indebted to Matthew Dallman who has compiled a concise biography at akensidepress.com/thornton/about. For more information on Thornton, access to some of his articles and lectures, and an annotated bibliography, visit akensidepress.com/thornton/.

These themes are the subject of his book, *Pastoral Theology: A Reorientation*, and rather than providing a novel approach to life and ministry, Thornton presents a timeless framework for Anglicans in the twenty-first century. I intend to convince the reader a re-formed Catholic Anglicanism cannot occur without it.

The Remnant Hypothesis

Prayer and Religion: Locating a Local Ascetical Theology

There is a crisis in North American Christianity. We have too often reduced "the faith" to dogmatic propositions, separable from any response those propositions might elicit from the believer. We highly value our orthodoxy (right doctrine), but seldom think about our orthopraxy (right practice). This is not a new phenomenon, and Martin Thornton recognized it in his day. He begins his book *Pastoral Theology* by saying that our religion—the relation between human souls and God[2]—is inseparable from our orthodoxy. That is, we cannot simply assent to theological propositions and call it a day. The particular theological propositions that we accept and believe require a response from us. This response is what he defines as prayer.

To be sure, this is a very broad approach to prayer, but it is essential to understanding its place in the center of the Church's life and ministry. Just as a study of mathematics is useless unless the mathematician knows how to apply theorems in the real world, so too is our belief in the Incarnation, Atonement, Resurrection, and return of Christ useless unless we apply these beliefs through the activity of prayer. In Thornton's parlance, pure theology (our orthodoxy) is a science, and applied theology or prayer (our orthopraxy) is an art. Ascetical theology is the name given to this art throughout *Pastoral Theology*, but this does not get us out of the woods of misconceptions.

This could easily lead us to another problem that plagues the North American Church. Through Evangelical Revivalism and pietistic movements over the last century or two, one's spiritual progress is often understood in terms of how we might *feel* about our relationship to God. One difficulty many Protestants face when trekking the Canterbury Trail is that Anglicanism's rites, practices, and services are prescribed and are often thought to encourage Anglicans to "go through the motions." But this is not how we should measure our progress in the faith. Instead, the cumulative effect of ascetical practice should be measured by moral theology. The question is not, "Do my ascetical practices make me feel closer to God?" but "Are my ascetical practices leading me to live more like Jesus?" This is an apt antidote to our culture's elevation of individualism over the corporate nature of the Church's life and ministry. As such, the individual's ascetical practice should not be divorced from the Christian community but take part from within it. I do not grow closer to Jesus without also growing closer to my fellow Christians. Ascetical theology is profoundly local.

---

[2] Martin Thornton, *Pastoral Theology: A Reorientation* (London: SPCK, 1956; Eugene, OR: Wipf & Stock, 2010), 4.

God's Athletes: Spiritual Direction

How does a Christian community develop a shared ascetical theology? Thornton's answer is that it is accomplished through spiritual direction. To understand this, we must first understand what the word *ascetical* means. The Greek word *askesis* is an athletic term, which can be translated into English as exercise. A simple sports analogy helps us understand ascetical theology and practice.

It is one of the greatest mysteries of my life that I grew up in the southeast United States and managed to reach adulthood with no knowledge (or interest) in American football.[3] It was not until I got married in my late twenties that I finally learned the basics of the game. Sunday lunch at my in-laws' home always ended with watching a few quarters of an NFL game; my wife had to instruct me on the rules. To this day, the extent of my knowledge goes no further than understanding the down system. I learned this by being verbally instructed by my wife. Not once did she pull out a football and take me to a field to demonstrate how to play the game; she merely explained the rules to me—the science of football. With my pathetically limited understanding, I was no more ready to play the game myself than I would have been the day before she explained it. For that, I would need to join a team, receive coaching, and attend many practices—the art of football. This is the value of *askesis*. Ascetical practice is the difference between learning the facts about God, the Bible, or even prayer, and receiving Baptism, consulting with my spiritual director, and praying the Daily Office. And no one scores a touchdown without both. We must understand the cognitive truths of the faith *and* regularly participate in *askesis*, or spiritual exercise. But it is difficult to imagine a successful football team without a good coach, which is where spiritual direction comes in.

One of Anglicanism's strengths is its retention of the practice of spiritual direction. Thornton defines spiritual direction as "coaching in prayer."[4] Notice he did not say teaching in prayer, but coaching. The difference is subtle but important. We see the difference in the life of Jesus. The Lord taught much in his earthly ministry, but he also directed his disciples to do certain things: have faith, fast, pray, etc. It is one thing for me to throw a football to another player, it is another thing to have a coach tell me what to do to improve my strength, accuracy, and agility. Spiritual direction, which Thornton says is at the heart of pastoral practice, is meeting someone where they are and guiding them to greater intimacy with and likeness to the Lord. Direction is not what we think of as therapy or counseling, which is another important distinction here. While Thornton is keen on the psychology of his day, he is quick to point out that the spiritual director is concerned with something much different than the psychologist. The spiritual director does not seek to solve mental problems, nor is he equipped to. Likewise, the director is not out to improve the moral lives of those he directs. A well-directed individual will surely see moral progress, but his director will aim to guide him

---

[3] Thornton's analogy involves the sport of cricket. Because my knowledge of cricket is even less than my knowledge of football, and because of its popularity in the US, I have opted for the latter rather than the former.

[4] *Pastoral Theology*, 8.

at a much deeper level. In Thornton's words, "[moral direction] aims at the eradication of bad fruit, [spiritual direction] at the creation of the good tree."[5]

This will certainly require that most parishioners adopt a considerable amount of humility. In the spiritual milieu of our cultural context, granting expertise and authority to our clergy is a challenge. We are more apt to consider our mechanic an expert in his trade than we are our priests. While this might be warranted in some cases, it is to the detriment of our spiritual health. The question we must always ask is whether we are willing to be coached or if we think we'll be better off on our own. The latter is no option for those seeking to advance in their walk with Christ.

The Parish Is Not a Monastery

If our ascetical practices—our life of prayer—are taking place within the local community under the direction of a spiritual director, how are we to understand our individual participation in the broader context of our neighborhoods and cities? To answer this, we must first consider the parish. For the author of *Pastoral Theology*, the concept of the parish was second nature. Unless we have spent time in Louisiana, an American state that still refers to its geographical counties as parishes, this word might mean little to us in North America. If we are familiar with it, we understand it to refer to our local Anglican church. "I belong to St. John's parish," we might say. But to understand Thornton's concept of "parochial theology"[6] we need to understand that our local churches are part of geographical boundaries called parishes. St. John's is my parish only because it is the church that exists within the broader parish. For us to appropriate Thornton's parochial theology, we need to simply understand that our parish churches are firmly planted within a certain neighborhood inhabited by particular people in a particular town or city in a particular state in a particular region. This has two important implications.

First, ascetical practice will take on a particular character depending on the particular parish where it is taking place. For example, I live in a city that is heavily influenced by Southern Baptist churches. The ascetical practices of my parish will be, to some extent, informed by this fact. Furthermore, I am a church planter, which means most of the men, women, and children in our parish church are unfamiliar with the church calendar, infant baptism, and contemplative prayer. This will be significantly different from a parish church in the American northeast where there are many Anglican churches or in Cleveland, Ohio where there are a great many Catholic churches.

The second implication of the particularity of each parish is that any ascetical system we might adopt was also borne out of a particular context. This means that not all ascetical systems are translatable into our particular parish contexts. This seems to be an overlooked reality in a consumer culture such as our own. I can order any book on St. Ignatius' Spiritual Exercises or St. Benedict's Rule and get to work. As long as we are isolating particular practices, there does not seem to be much of a problem. Anyone can add fasting to their rule of life. But imagine discovering the Rule of St. Benedict for the first time. What is stopping you from adopting the rule for your own devotional practice?

---

[5] *Pastoral Theology*, 10.
[6] Ibid., 7.

Well, a quick scan through the table of contents will answer this question. Most of the Rule prescribes times and manners for praying the hours. Give it a shot and you'll realize that you'll need to join a monastery to do this for any length of time. I remember a friend complaining to me after reading Benedict's *Rule* that it seemed quite draconian. Public beatings and requiring brothers who show up late for prayers to lie prostrate in the doorway until everyone else steps over his body does seem a bit harsh for our day. None of this is to say that the *Rule* cannot be of great benefit to us, but only that it must be adapted to our particular and local parochial situation. The local parish, it turns out, is not a monastery.

So what is the local parish? For Thornton, it is a cure (or care) of souls. This antiquated term refers to those for whom a parish priest is responsible. So for whom *is* a parish priest responsible? Is he responsible for every soul within his geographical boundary or just the souls who attend his parish services? This question eventually plagues every clergy member and if we answer one over the other, we make a royal mess of things. To suppose the priest's responsibility is to care for the entire parish. This is what Thornton labels the "multitudinist" approach. [7] In modern parlance, this is the seeker-sensitive megachurch trying to draw as many people as possible for maximum kingdom impact. For Anglicans, this is a problem, because, for reasons explained below, no parish can be said to be present at the Mass[8] unless every single member of the neighborhood or city is present. Not only would this exhaust the parish priest, but it also is not likely to ever happen. On the other hand, were we to suppose that the parish priest is merely responsible for those who attend his church's services, we make the mistake of forming what Thornton calls "a nice little nucleus."[9] This is the small neighborhood church that declines in membership but insists on maintaining the status quo. It remains an insulated nucleus detached from the broader parish in which it is situated. Nor is it wise to aim for a balance between the two. Parochial theology, then, seeks a broader framework that avoids these two extremes, a framework rooted in the incarnation of Christ.

It might be helpful to recall the distinction between pure and applied theology. Theological propositions remain abstract until they are lived out and applied to real life. The crucifixion of Jesus remains an abstract concept until I am faced with the opportunity to demonstrate the same selflessness to my wife. Likewise, the Word who was with God in the beginning remains an abstract concept in my mind until the Word became flesh and dwelt among us. Similarly, the "cure of souls" remains an abstract concept until we acknowledge that souls are real, enfleshed human beings with jobs, dreams, and various personality types. Of the various souls within a particular parish and their various personality types, some are fit to play football and some are not. So too are some fit for the rigors of ascetical practice and others are not. And herein is the dilemma to which Thornton has led us. How can the Church remain faithful to her call to make disciples of all nations (the multitudes) while remaining a faithful few hard at

---

[7] *Pastoral Theology*, 15.
[8] Thornton refers to Holy Communion or the Eucharist as the Mass throughout his writing.
[9] *Pastoral Theology*, 25.

prayer (a nice little nucleus)? How does a "parochial theology" avoid one or the other, or confuse them both in a messy balance? Two related concepts form an answer.

It's (Not) About the Numbers

I have heard it my entire life: "It's not about the numbers." This is uttered by every pastor, music minister, Sunday school teacher, and parishioner I've ever known. It is uttered by men and women of large megachurches down to declining rural chapels. We all know that faithfulness is not concerned with how many people show up to our services, and yet this sentence usually follows a statement of how many people showed up for a particular service or event. Church planters may be the worst offenders. We know that the numbers do not indicate God's faithfulness or even our own, yet every Sunday is a reminder that we need more people to get this thing up and running. So, which is it? Is it about the numbers or not?

Parochial theology as a framework does not have to answer the question because if the particular parish church is made up of particular souls with particular personality types who work in particular jobs and live in particular homes, then we have a unified whole to consider. No longer must we talk about the total of individual people, but a unified body. St. John's parish (singular) is a single organism. This is a subtle but vitally important point. When Jesus prays in John 17 that the Church would be unified in a single body, he was not thinking in abstract concepts. As Anglicans, we believe that our Eucharistic celebration is partaking in the One and Real Body of Christ and that by participating in this celebration "we are made one body with him, that he may dwell in us and we in him" as our liturgy states. This unity can be referred to as a *recapitulation*, a gathering of many into a single body with Christ as our Head. Recapitulation is how Christians understand our relationship to Christ. St. Paul tells us that we have been "baptized into Christ" and therefore, "into his death," which results in our being raised with him and united to him (Rom 6:3–5 ESV). This is the Father's answer to his Son's prayer in John 17. It is a real uniting into one body, Christ's body! In this way, we are recapitulated into Christ.

Similarly, we can now understand our local parish in terms of a *microcosm*. The parish is the Catholic[10] Church in microcosm.[11] It is worth quoting Thornton at length on this point:

> This Church, moreover, is threefold. The holy concourse in paradise and in heaven does not split itself up into insular parties of patrons-per-parish. If the whole Body is complete at every altar, the whole communion of saints are in attendance at every altar.... When parochialism is organic and when ye are the Body of Christ, it is the antithesis of narrow because it is, in place, the Catholic Church. There is but one Bread, so each altar is microcosmic of the Throne of the Lamb in heaven. There is one Church and one Body, so that the work of each server, each organist, each verger, each good lady who arranges the flowers is of Catholic significance because it is truly parochial. This is why the Church's Office, said by two souls in the village

---

[10] Understood as universal. As an Anglo-Catholic, Thornton almost always refers to the Church as "the Catholic Church."

[11] *Pastoral Theology*, 20.

church on Monday night is an infinitely tremendous thing; the "special" service with its teeming congregation is trivial by comparison.[12]

By the twin concepts of recapitulation and microcosm, it is possible to avoid multitudinism and the "nice little nucleus" because any concern for numbers is preceded by the reality that we are not talking about the parish as the total of individuals, but as a unified organism. At the center of this organism, its heart is the Church. Thus, the entire parochial organism can be thought of in three concentric circles: the faithful few (including clergy), the occasional churchgoer, and everyone else. And it is the faithful few that form Thornton's Remnant Hypothesis.[13]

The Remnant: a Vicarious Few

The concept of the faithful remnant is replete throughout the Hebrew Scriptures. The story of Israel is a constant tension between those who stray from the Lord and those who remain faithful. God's interaction with Elijah in 1 Kings 19 comes to mind, where the Lord tells the prophet that he has reserved 7,000 men who have not bowed the knee to Baal. To Elijah's surprise, he was not the only remnant. Thornton finds four marks of the faithful remnant in the book of Isaiah, which are 1) monotheism, 2) Israel as the "chosen race," 3) the world's salvation depends on Israel's faith, and 4) the vicarious principle.[14] These are important because the term *remnant* can connote an isolated elite or an amputated member of the whole of Israel. This will not do if we are to consider the "faithful few" in the parish as part of the parish itself rather than cut off from it.

Returning to the football analogy, we may think of the faithful remnant within the parish as the players, the regular churchgoers as the spectators, and the rest of the occasional attendees as the bandwagon fans. The team may be really good or really bad. The local enthusiasm will have some correlation with how well the team plays. If they land in the Super Bowl, you can expect the fanbase to be more faithful and at least a few disinterested citizens to pay a little more attention. If they are not good and lose most of their games, the fanbase would likely weaken and contribute to the disinterested population. But what will remain constant in both situations is the remnant; there will still be a team whether anyone shows up to watch them or not. Attend any family function or sports bar and you will hear the discussions. "*We* made it to the playoffs!" or "*We* can't win a game to save our lives." Far from being an amputated member, the faithful remnant—the players—still belong to the whole. This, Thornton insists, is also the case with the parish. If the faithful remnant continues to be faithful in her *askesis*, that is, if she keeps showing up for practice— receiving the Eucharist, praying the Daily Office, and pursuing ceaseless prayer—then the parish "becomes a virile organism pervaded by the power of the Remnant's Prayer."[15] And this is the seed for Anglican missiology. It is only by the active prayer life of the faithful that the faith becomes contagious. As we have already said, the spiritual progress of the faithful is not measured by the faithful's feelings, but by their morals. That is not to say that morals are the end

---

[12] *Pastoral Theology*, 20.

[13] Ibid., 21.

[14] Ibid., 22–23.

[15] Ibid., 24.

goal, they are just the measuring rod, and the resulting holiness of the Church at prayer is a contagion that transforms the entire parochial organism.

The Remnant at Prayer

If it is true that prayer is the religious person's response to God, and that Christians pray at their best when they are coached through spiritual direction and if it is true that the well-directed Christian is bound to a particular time and place—the parish—and if it is the case that the life of the parish church is best understood as a microcosm of the whole Body of Christ so that the faithful few vicariously pray for the entire parish (as a football team plays for the city or college), then what shape does the local parish church's life of prayer take? Thornton answers this question with the three-fold Church Rule of Daily Office, weekly Eucharist, and private prayers (or devotions). How the three interrelate can be understood by the analogy of building a fence.[16] Evenly placed fence posts represent the weekly Mass or Eucharist. This is to be taken by the faithful Remnant weekly as well as on special feast days (Red-Letter Days). Interspersed between the fence posts are support stakes, which represent the Daily Office. Finally, horizontal trusses connecting stakes and posts provide greater support, which represents private devotion. Without all three, there is no fence. We will look at the value of each of these elements in Thornton's order, beginning with the Daily Office.

The Daily Office

Anglicans love the Daily Office, or at least they say they do. One of Thomas Cranmer's brilliant contributions to Church history is his insistence that the laity can and should participate in the monastic observance of set daily prayers. However, instead of the seven offices throughout the day (and night) typical in the monastery, he reduced them to Morning and Evening Prayer as the primary hours to be kept by laity and clergy alike. All clergy are expected to pray Morning and Evening prayer, but for Thornton, our fence falls apart without all Christians keeping this discipline. New Anglicans may find the Daily Office a breath of fresh air for a season, but sooner or later, such a steady and constant discipline becomes difficult and even burdensome. This is both necessary and unfortunate.

Thornton sees the three-fold Rule in a trinitarian scheme where the Eucharist focuses primarily on the Son, while private devotions are primarily interacting with the Holy Spirit.[17] The Daily Office, then, is objective prayer offered to the Father. The word *objective* is important and helps to clarify why so many Anglicans—especially new Anglicans—may find keeping the Daily Office difficult. At the most basic level of Christian *askesis*, the Christian speaks to God as a friend. This is a subjective understanding of prayer because we pray as subjects to God, who is the recipient of our prayer. Every human being begins his or her prayer life, his or her religious life, as a subject. All prayers, then, are generated from the subjects: us. Not only this, but our

---

[16] *Pastoral Theology*, 206.

[17] In no way does Thornton imply that all three persons of the Godhead are inactive in any of the three elements of this Rule. He merely sees an emphasis on each person of the Trinity in each of the elements.

prayers tend to be initiated by us as well, often without regard to God or what he may be seeking from us at any given time. When we pray the Daily Office or any "set prayers," we are praying something that does not generate from our hearts, nor is it initiated by us. Someone else wrote it and we are told to pray it. In this way, praying the Daily Office is objective. Thornton likens this to a little girl wishing to give her father a gift.[18] Her father is a mystery to her because she does not quite understand who he is. She knows of his love and affection for her but is not quite sure what sort of gift he would like, so she asks her mother for suggestions. In Thornton's analogy, the mother suggests some nice pipe tobacco, which is disgusting to the little girl. However, because the mother knows the father well, she knows what would please him, so the little girl offers her father the tobacco, much to his delight. The Daily Office is the incomprehensible gift (tobacco) given to God the Father (the girl's dad). Unsure what to offer the Father, Christians seek the counsel of the Church (the mother), who answers, "The Daily Office." This might sound strange, but a few times through Morning Prayer should shed some light on its logic. From Morning Prayer's opening acclamation, the Office is full of praise to the Father. Consider the *Venite* (Psalm 95) and other canticles. We offer our confession of sin and pray the psalter, returning God's words to him in praise and thanksgiving. We submit ourselves to the reading of Holy Scripture and recite the dogma of our faith (the *Apostle's Creed*). We pray as the Lord taught us (the Lord's Prayer) and join our voices in the Collects with saints who have gone before us. We offer our thanksgivings and intercessions and close with the General Thanksgiving. We offer all of this because the Father loves it just as the little girl's father loves tobacco. It pleases him. The Daily Office, then, is an objective offering given to the Father *for His sake*. This is not to imply that we do not benefit from it; in fact, we benefit from it in at least two ways.

First, it is training. Like football players running drills, running plays, or just running, we offer the Daily Office to learn how to pray. It is difficult to offer the General Confession every day for a few years and not know how to confess our sins to God when we do not have a prayer book handy. We have a language. We understand that our sins are not only in our thoughts but also in our words and deeds. The Psalter teaches us to praise the Lord wholeheartedly, but also how to lament and admit frustration with the Lord. All of the language we find in the Daily Office keeps us in shape, ready for gameday, and trains our hearts for our private devotional life.

Secondly, we benefit from praying the Daily Office because it leads us to contemplative prayer, and here is where Thornton is really helpful when we find the Daily Office a burden. The most basic interaction with the Daily Office is what might be called *attention*.[19] There are a lot of words in the liturgy, and we pay attention to them to varying degrees. After praying these prayers over any extended amount of time, certain words and phrases stand out in our minds. We may still be thinking about living a "godly, righteous, and sober life" by the time we hit the antiphon before the *Venite*. In this way, we are thinking about the words. But before long, we begin to recite these prayers "by rote" and this is the antithesis of what many newcomers to Anglicanism have been taught. We must "mean" what we pray. But this "going through the motions," says

---

[18] *Pastoral Theology*, 213–214.
[19] Ibid., 209.

Thornton, is the goal.[20] The familiarity of the Daily Office should be welcomed and not feared, because when the liturgy itself becomes second nature, we are poised to move beyond mere attention to *affection*.[21] This is simply receiving what the Father is pleased to give as we are praying the Office. In other words, we do not pray Morning Prayer to "get something out of it" any more than a daughter gives her father tobacco "to get something out of it." However, her father's pleasure in receiving the gift results in the delight of the daughter. She benefits from the offering, but she does not offer it *for* the benefits. This reciprocal, mutual benefit between subject and object, Christian and Father, if achieved, can lead to contemplative adoration, wherein we maintain attention to the words of the liturgy while "raising within [ourselves] an efficacious affection to God."[22] If we are patient and attend football practice long enough, there is great gain in the season ahead.

It must be remembered that praying the Daily Office is one of three elements of a whole. It cannot be mistaken for the whole itself. It will go no further than "going through the motions" if weekly Communion and private prayer are neglected. It must also be remembered that the Daily Office is a team sport; it is a common prayer that we are after, which is why it is important to pray with the faithful Remnant. But as rigorous and objective as this element of the three-fold Church Rule is, and as difficult as it can be to maintain, it finds a center in the much easier and glorious discipline of partaking of the Eucharist, to which we now turn.

The Eucharist

While the Daily Office is primarily focused on offering prayer to the Father, the Eucharist's central focus is on the Son. According to Thornton, the Eucharist is much easier than the discipline of praying the Daily Office. The reason for this is that there is less rigidity. This may sound strange at first. The priest is always careful to say the correct thing at the correct time. Everyone seems to be in sync when bowing or genuflecting. There are still rubrics to follow, customs to adopt, and Alleluias to avoid during Lent. How is this easier than praying the Office? The answer is twofold. First, "doctrinally, metaphysically, and psychologically it is a glorious and finally incomprehensible mystery."[23] The Eucharist will ever call us into contemplation and meditation on the incarnate Christ. Secondly, it is more complex, which allows for a variety of ways to interact with it, unlike the Office. Every man, woman, and child of every stripe and background can participate in the Eucharist and appreciate any aspect of it that appeals to their particular temperaments. Everything from the liturgical colors, vestments, and vessels to liturgical language, theological significance, and metaphysics is available to point anyone who attends to Christ. One's intellectual capacity has nothing to do with participation in the Eucharist. A rudimentary understanding of the gospel is required of the faithful, but what occurs at the altar does not need to be dissected into theological categories to benefit communicants. Excepting the obvious limits of Baptism and

---

[20] *Pastoral Theology*, 212.

[21] Ibid., 211.

[22] Ibid.

[23] Ibid., 218.

minimal catechesis, the Eucharist has been democratized in that all the faithful can and should participate in it weekly, and this is significantly easier than praying Morning and Evening Prayer every day.

But we must keep our parochial theology in mind. The Eucharist is open to "all baptized followers of Christ," as many Anglican priests say as they fence the table, but that does not mean it is too common for the Remnant to bother with. Rather, according to Thornton, the Eucharist is the "focus or fulcrum of balance" when it comes to the three-fold Church Rule.[24] Another analogy is given to illustrate its central location. Imagine a cyclist riding a bicycle along a high wire. A long pole is required for him to keep his balance. The Eucharist is the center of balance, countered by the Daily Office and Private Prayer on either end. That is how vital the Mass is to the Rule, and when we consider its emphasis on the Cross, it is easy to see why.

The Cross of Christ is central to the Mass in that the crucifixion of Christ required the Incarnation. Not only this, but his sacrificial and atoning death on the cross is what makes our salvation possible. It is the Incarnation of Christ in which the Church participates during Holy Communion. "Indeed," said Thornton, "this is the God who became Incarnate and still becomes Incarnate on the altar."[25] What the Incarnation and Cross do is offer both aid (succor) and demand, which can be seen in the traditional way the Eucharistic liturgy is split.

The liturgy for Holy Communion is often said to be split between the Liturgy of the Word and the Liturgy of the Table. In the Liturgy of the Word is offered succor. This word, rarely used in modern English, but replete throughout older forms of the Prayer Book and Psalter, simply means "aid." God is certainly our primary aid or helper, and this is evident throughout the reading of Holy Scripture, the Collects, and preaching, which all make up the first half of the Eucharistic liturgy. Here, we are not only reminded of our need for redemption but hear the proclamation that such redemption has objectively occurred in Christ. This is true succor indeed and it leads us to what Thornton says is the cost of our redemption, which is the Cross.[26] In the Liturgy of the Table, we encounter the Cross and the demand that it makes of us. From the Offertory to the Ministration of the elements, the entirety of our lives is demanded. "If anyone would come after me," said Jesus, "let him deny himself and take up his cross and follow me" (Matt 16:24 ESV). Each Sunday the Christian is faced with the surrender of his or her entire being to the Lord, but in the great Eucharistic mystery, the giving of ourselves, the emptying of ourselves, is immediately—even simultaneously—met with a filling or being filled with God himself! The Eucharist ends with thanksgiving and adoration, of course, which is the proper response to this mystery. Thanksgiving and adoration, said Thornton, meld into love and joy: "Holy Communion is our loving embrace with and in Christ, for in communion we are both giving and receiving all in an identical moment."[27] Here, in opposition to what Thornton has said about the objectivity of the Daily Office is a very subjective and joyful part of the three-fold Rule. It still requires objectivity—dogmatic

---

[24] *Pastoral Theology*, 222.
[25] Ibid., 224.
[26] Ibid., 220.
[27] Ibid.

and intellectual content as well as objective offering of the self—but it yields great subjective benefits, which are the most natural expectations of any efforts in prayer or "religious activity." No wonder it is a much easier discipline than praying the Daily Office! All of this is the case for every Christian who shows up for weekly Eucharist, but it is especially the case for the Remnant.

Prayer, then, can be said to begin with the daily *askesis*, or exercise, of the Daily Office and continually participated in at Holy Communion each week. These have varying degrees of subjectivity and thus varying degrees of personal benefits or feelings. But these alone will bring us crashing down from the high wire if we are not balanced by the horizontal cross beams of our fence, which is private prayer. This will make up the final element of Thornton's three-fold Church Rule.

Private Prayer

For Thornton, private prayer covers a vast landscape of ascetical practice which includes mental prayer, colloquy (petition, self-examination, confession, intercession, thanksgiving, adoration), and recollection. Each of these terms has specific applications in the life of the Christian, which are the subject of his book *Christian Proficiency*. It is not necessary to expound on each of them except to say that habitual recollection serves as a sort of end goal in all private prayer—and perhaps the end goal of the three-fold Church Rule. Recollection is defined as "momentary acts of prayer throughout the working day; a simple, periodic 'practice of the Presence of God.'"[28] This is the "gameday" for which the Rule prepares us, for it is habitual communion with God. Here, we are not objectively offering praise to the Father, nor are we partaking in the incarnate Son's body and blood at Holy Communion, but are moved, inspired, and comforted by the Holy Spirit. This could be through discursive petitions as well as contemplative, wordless meditation. This is St. Paul's ceaseless prayer (1 Thess 5:17). I do not think that it is overstating the case to say that this "habitual recollection" is the prayer life all Christians long for, but rarely achieve. The reason for this is that the *askesis* of praying the Daily Office is usually neglected because it is so difficult to maintain. The result is a somewhat anemic parish that may faithfully attend Holy Communion but because they do not pray the Daily Office, their spiritual muscles cannot maintain *attention* long enough to sustain their *affection* in private prayer. Thus, private prayer will always suffer unless it is part of the three-fold Church Rule. Private prayer, then, is the normal prayer life of the Christian, and especially the Remnant, but unlike the Mass or the Daily Office, it varies greatly from person to person.

Private prayer is the most subjective part of the Church Rule, for it necessarily includes our feelings as well as all other faculties (thoughts, emotions, volitions, interests, etc.). In private prayer, we pray as the psalmists pray. We pray as ourselves, and this brings us back to the importance of spiritual direction. The skilled director knows how to point the directee in encountering God *as he or she has been created by him*. In contemporary language, we often speak of how we are "wired," meaning what Thornton calls *attrait*.[29] This French word refers to our natural attractions or proclivities. "I am an

---

[28] Thornton, *Christian Proficiency* (London: SPCK, 1959; Eugene, OR: Wipf & Stock, 1988), 21.
[29] *Pastoral Theology*, 230.

introvert," implies that a person is likely to encounter God through practices of solitude and contemplation. A spiritual director will know how to coach such a person according to the way God has made them. A director will also be familiar with various schools of prayer.[30] Depending on one's *attrait,* he or she might be more helped by the subjective Spanish Carmelites and modern Trappists or the objective early Cistercian emphasis on the Humanity of Jesus. None of this is to suggest that the subjective emphasis of a particular school should or could be adopted to the neglect of the objective emphasis of another. It is only to say that every individual is unique and must be directed with this in mind. This, for Thornton, is more of an art than a science. As it turns out, ascetical theology is profoundly local, and direction must occur within the context of the local parish.

It is important to remind ourselves, once again, that Thornton's concern is for the Remnant. To imagine an entire parish gathering to keep the three-fold Church Rule and submit itself to individual spiritual direction is not only unrealistic, but it also brings us back to the multitudinist approach to parish ministry. In reality, there will be only a few who can submit themselves to the three-fold Church Rule and thus develop in private prayer to achieve the highest level of habitual recollection. Parochial theology and the Remnant hypothesis are, by definition, not for everyone. But, at the same time, it is *for* everyone in a vicarious sense. Once again, when our team wins, so does the entire school, city, or state. The entire parish is a united organism, remember, and it makes little sense for the foot to say, "because I am not a hand, I am not of the body" (1 Cor 12:15 ESV). In other words, there is no need or room for any member of the parish to bemoan their part in the parish-in-microcosm. The Remnant is no more elite, or a nice little nucleus, than the nervous system; it is not to exclude the occasional churchgoer or disinterested parish member any more than Israel was to exclude the nations. So, the purpose and point of the Church at prayer are for the sake of the entire parish; the Remnant is to make disciples of all. This is another way of saying that every occasional churchgoer or disinterested parish member is a potential Remnant member. The Daily Office is always available to and can be prayed by those willing to sacrifice the short time it takes to keep it. Holy Communion is open to all baptized believers each Sunday. And private prayer, habitually recollected or occasionally offered, is limitless to those who give it the slightest amount of attention. But again, the sacrifice must be made. The offer to take up one's cross and follow Christ is never retracted. The well-directed Remnant member, by virtue of his or her life at prayer maintained through the three-fold Church Rule, will necessarily grow and develop into such Christlikeness that the entire parish benefits. This is not only because the Church is to be a blessing to all, but because the leaven of holiness leavens the whole lump.

---

[30] This is a significant theme in Thornton's work and is the primary focus of his book, *English Spirituality* (London: SPCK, 1963; Eugene, OR: Wipf & Stock, 2012), in which he argues for a particular school of prayer and spirituality that is distinctive to the English people. This, he argues, is significantly Benedictine as well as Celtic, which distinguishes it from much of Roman spirituality.

Conclusion

Through his parochial theology, Martin Thornton has not given us a new and novel model for the Church's life and ministry. Instead, he has preserved for us a classic and Catholic understanding of how the Church at prayer relates to the life of its local context. For Anglicans old and new, the Remnant hypothesis and the three-fold Church Rule will be vital if a reformed Catholic witness is to leaven the lump of North American Christianity. As important as our various doctrines are, until they are lived out in the world by the faithful Remnant, they will remain abstract dogma. Great orthodoxy is pointless without its corresponding orthopraxy.

There is no shortage of theories, hypotheses, methods, techniques, systems, and solutions on offer to combat the darkening of Western culture. It is always the easiest solution that gets our attention, which means an old and difficult Rule will often be overlooked. It is my hope in sharing this overview of Thornton's three-fold Church Rule that a reformed Catholic delight and love of prayer as Thornton describes—with all its difficulty, antiquity, and simplicity—would so capture the hearts of Anglicans that each parish Remnant would swell beyond its boundaries and show forth the glory of our God. But rather than give you five easy steps to implement Thornton's parochial theology in your parish, I will leave you with these few simple steps to join the Remnant: find a spiritual director, pray the Daily Office, pray without ceasing, and go to Mass. It is worth the sacrifice.